VALLEY OF DECISION

VALLEY OF DECISION

The Siege of Khe Sanh

John Prados and Ray W. Stubbe

A Marc Jaffe Book

HOUGHTON MIFFLIN COMPANY

Boston · New York · London · 1991

For information about permission to reproduce selections from
this book, write to Permissions, Houghton Mifflin Company,
2 Park Street, Boston, Massachusetts 02108.

Library of Congress Cataloging-in-Publication Data

Prados, John.
Valley of decision : the siege of Khe Sanh / John Prados and Ray
W. Stubbe.
p.   cm.
"A Marc Jaffe book."
Includes bibliographical references and index.
ISBN 0-395-55003-3
1. Khe Sanh, Battle of, 1968.   I. Stubbe, Ray W. II. Title.
DS557.8.K5P72   1991   91-25531
959.704'34—dc20   CIP

Maps by Kevin Zucker

Printed in the United States of America

AGM 10 9 8 7 6 5 4 3 2 1

To the Lives That Have Been Touched by Khe Sanh

"Multitudes, multitudes, in the valley of decision"

JOEL 3:14

Contents

6 · To Some a Fortress (Summer–Fall 1967)

7 · Boxing in Darkness (1967–1968)

8 · Contact

9 · "Khe Sanh Already Shows Signs of Battle"

Maps

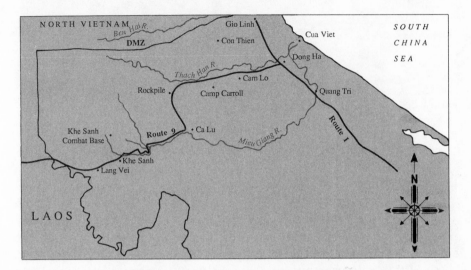

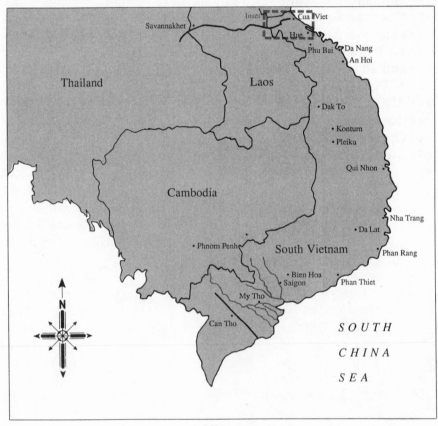

1 · Vietnam

Preface

Ray Stubbe went to Khe Sanh in the summer of 1967. On a plateau in the hill country at the northwest corner of what was then South Vietnam, Khe Sanh became the locus of one of the most clearly definable major battles of America's Vietnam war. Ray saw it all as the Lutheran chaplain of the 1st Battalion, 26th Marines, one of the first American military units at the Khe Sanh combat base. Intimately involved with the Marines whose experiences he shared, Stubbe visited all their positions, went along on patrols and other missions, stayed overnight with the young men manning the hills of Khe Sanh. Stubbe stayed on through the fall and into the winter. When Khe Sanh became a battlefield he was there. When the combat base came under siege he shared its fate.

Elsewhere Ray Stubbe has been called a kind of Samuel Pepys for Khe Sanh, an individual attuned to all that passed who recorded every report and rumor. Stubbe kept a diary and in it he did indeed record every kind of fact and rumor. The Stubbe diary has long been open to researchers at the Marine Corps History and Museums Division. But Stubbe, like many of us who lived through the war, both in "the Nam" and in "the World," as the veterans like to say, has remained restless, driven by the demons of Vietnam, by what is and what could have been, by who remains and who is gone and what happened to them.

Ray took it upon himself to find out. The Stubbe diary became merely the first step in a long quest, the result of which you have before you. Trying to identify those who had not come back, to assemble a sort of verbal equivalent for Khe Sanh of the famous Wall of the Vietnam Veterans Memorial in Washington, D.C., Stubbe went on to research a list of the men who had died at the battle, by name, unit, date of death, and location of the fatal action. He relied on hospital unit admission records and chaplain memorial service records, on Marine casualty files, and so forth. The more Ray researched, the more he wondered about the larger outlines of the battle in which he had participated. Stubbe broadened his research to encompass more of the Khe Sanh siege. Now he used Marine records, award citation files, official debriefings, and a certain amount of material obtained under the Freedom of Information Act. Stubbe also began to interview Khe Sanh survivors wherever he could find them. Eventually he turned all of his researches into a manuscript.

My role in this book began with a telephone call. My agent had a manuscript and wanted an opinion as to whether its substance was interesting in its detail and, as far as I could tell, accurate. I was happy to oblige. The result was the appearance quickly thereafter of an enormous manuscript by Ray W. Stubbe. It did not take me long to decide that Stubbe's account of Khe Sanh definitely merited publication — I am a professional historian and analyst of international security affairs and I was familiar with the literature on Khe Sanh. It was clear that the wealth of detail and description in the Stubbe manuscript surpassed anything available to readers. It was the real story of Khe Sanh.

This conclusion I reached with some trepidation, for I myself had been collecting material on Khe Sanh for some time and had intended to write on the subject in due course. I did not flinch from advising publication, however. Subsequently I was honored with an offer to collaborate with Stubbe, I accepted, and the result is *Valley of Decision*.

Despite the selection of material I have had to make and the considerable shortening of the manuscript, and despite abandoning my own thoughts of a Khe Sanh history, I am mightily pleased because I believe this book is greater than either of us could have produced alone. Ray Stubbe's account flowed from his research and reflected his sources. He was primarily interested in the stories of the men of Khe Sanh. His history actually seemed weak on the larger operational and strategic context in which the siege of Khe Sanh occurred. My own predilection runs to macro-history, and I had specifically focused my research on precisely those facets of the campaign. This turned out to be an ideal combination. I had knowledge that plugged critical gaps in Stubbe's account and he had answers to questions about which I had always wondered.

Our division of labor has been conditioned by the way in which this project originated. I wrote the narrative, selecting material from Stubbe's work, correcting such errors as I could detect, contracting and supervising the artwork and book production, and adding material which I had but Stubbe did not. Tireless in his own efforts, Ray continued collecting Khe Sanh stories, wrote a second draft of his basic manuscript, and cheerfully responded to all my requests for clarification or amplifying material. We have shared research materials. In what follows Stubbe is the basic source for the Khe Sanh battle narrative while I am primarily responsible for material on the North Vietnamese, the conduct of the campaign in Washington and Saigon, and certain particular battle scenes.

Each of us brought special skills to the project. While Ray interviewed his comrades, I got certain materials declassified or documentary collections opened for research. These included segments of William Westmoreland's historical notes (which are essentially a diary) and backup materials, documents in the accompanying history backup files, a small amount of the heretofore top secret back-channel cable traffic that passed between Generals Westmoreland and Earle Wheeler, then chairman of the Joint Chiefs of Staff, and summaries and translations of captured North Vietnamese documents. The latter enable us to make a start at least toward providing an account of the other side of this campaign.

The discovery of which I am most fond in researching *Valley of Decision* is our uncovering a set of summary memoranda that record details of many of General Westmoreland's telephone conversations, especially with subordinates. It turns out there is an entire series of these, beginning during the Khe Sanh period and extending forward through Westmoreland's years as Army chief of staff. These telephone calls were carefully logged and listed by Army staff assistants, but in twenty years no one had ever found them.

My search began while reading Westmoreland's daily schedules for the period of Khe Sanh and Tet 1968, where I found a handwritten notation that recording of telephone calls had begun. When I attempted to find out what had happened to these recordings I was referred to the Army Center for Military History, which had had custody of the Westmoreland papers until they recently were given to the National Archives and Records Administration's Lyndon B. Johnson Library. Four different distinguished historians, all authors on the Army's Vietnam official history project, knew nothing of any telephone records. Some of them advised me that I was wasting my time looking. Later, however, senior national security archivist David C. Humphrey at the Johnson Library looked through unboxed Westmoreland papers in the vault and found the entire series. Apparently the records were never found because the telephone or "*Phone*" memoranda were filed under "*Fone*." Such are the wiles of military staff work.

Despite all efforts, I am obliged to report, some material germane to the Khe Sanh battle remains classified. Nevertheless Stubbe and I have brought to bear an unparalleled array of research sources, in which documents and interviews are probably the two most important. We believe *Valley of Decision* advances our knowledge of every single facet of the Khe Sanh campaign from the activities of the elusive MACVSOG, to the concerns in the White House, to the planning of operation PEGASUS and the fighting at Khe Sanh after the siege was over. Nothing in print today even comes close.

Unlike previous accounts of Khe Sanh this book makes an effort to tell the whole history of the place, not merely that of the 1968 siege. This includes battles the previous year, the evolution of the Special Forces camp, the place of Khe Sanh in the high command's strategic vision, and also the village and the indigenous Bru. We feel the space thus devoted sets the proper context for the siege, and we aimed from the beginning to get as close as we could to a definitive account of the campaign. Of course this has limited the space we could devote to the men of Khe Sanh, so we start with a special apology to all those individuals whose stories form part of the Khe Sanh epic but could not be told here. We hope they will find it equally valuable to learn the hidden history of Khe Sanh.

We have also tried throughout to provide space for the North Vietnamese side, at least to analyze motives and standard procedures where specific narrative detail remains unavailable. We can only hope the new Vietnam sees fit to release new information and improve our knowledge of the adversary at Khe Sanh. Except where such terms appear in quotations, we have deliberately avoided using various pejorative phrases often used at the time to refer to North Vietnamese, all Vietnamese, or Viet Cong specifically.

At the same time, however, we have taken care to use quotations fairly and accurately. In the style of oral history, also, we want quotations to convey the atmosphere of Khe Sanh, down to the styles of our witnesses. We have therefore not rewritten quotations, cluttered them with scholarly impedimenta (such as *sic*) that trumpet obvious faults in the grammatical construction of men speaking colloquially, or played other tricks with them. In the style of narrative history we do not presume that quotation can tell the whole story.

From the outset we have been concerned that Khe Sanh receive fresh cartographic treatment. The use and repeated reuse of a few official maps, convenient because they were in the public domain, have gone beyond the point of informing in a great number of the available accounts. Now the hackneyed old maps just make the books seem the same. Moreover, many important features do not even appear on the existing maps. We have compiled a completely fresh set of maps, some in astonishing detail, most never before seen. Many more maps were possible but we have included as many as are practical. Artist Kevin Zucker did a fine job on the maps and contributed significantly to the presentation of *Valley of Decision*. Incidentally, we have taken a similar attitude toward photographs and have selected a variety of fresh images of Khe Sanh along with some very traditional ones.

Although we acknowledge below the many persons who contributed to this work, Russell Galen deserves a special word here. A fine individual and very competent agent, Galen not only initiated what became *Valley of Decision* but supported it along the way, as did the Scott Meredith Literary Agency of which Russ forms part. Special thanks to both.

Finally a word about narrative voice. Since Ray Stubbe participated in the events recorded here as both actor and chronicler and now is participating as coauthor of a reflective history, the choice of a proper voice for Stubbe has been difficult. To prevent the text from having to shift voices, therefore, we have adopted the expedient of the historian's narrative voice. Thus where Stubbe appears in the story he becomes a character like all the other men of Khe Sanh, he is quoted like them, and he performs certain actions that he did, historically, accomplish.

Author Stubbe wishes to acknowledge all those who gave of their time and themselves in interviews, along with Joyce Bonnett, Joyce Conyers, Corporal Walters, and Corporal Henry of the Marine Corps Archives; Dan Crawford, Robert Aquilina, Ann Ferrante, and Lena Kaljot of the Reference Section of the same; Evelyn Englander and Pat Morgan of the Marine Corps Historical Center Library; Ben Frank, Colonel Miller, Colonel Hart, and Colonel Greenwood of the Historical Center professional section; TSgt. Roger A. Jernigan and Mrs. Lynn O. Gamma of the Air Force Historical Archives; Stephen M. Eldridge, Wanda R. Radcliffe, W. A. Anderson, and William A. Walker the U.S. Army Archives; Larry R. Strawderman, Carl

Rohrer, and John H. Wright of the Central Intelligence Agency; and Robert A. Hardzog plus Robert DeStatte of the Defense Intelligence Agency.

Author Prados wishes to acknowledge the invaluable assistance of the staffs of the Library of Congress, the Martin Luther King, Jr., Library, and the Wheaton Regional Library, all in or just outside Washington, D.C. Vital aid came from the staff of the Lyndon B. Johnson Library in Austin, Texas, most important from David C. Humphrey, Regina Greenwell, and E. Philip Scott. Individuals who were an important help include April Powers, James Dingeman and Richard Jupa, Jane Warner, D. Gareth Porter, Mark Perry, Bill and Abbott Kominers, and Jill Gay.

Though many persons helped make the fine qualities of this book, the authors are exclusively responsible for any errors of omission or commission.

John Prados
Washington, D.C.
October 1990

Acronyms and Abbreviations

AK	Assault rifle (Soviet designation)
AM	Air matting
AO	Area of operations
AP	Associated Press
AR	Assault rifle
ARVN	Army of the Republic of Vietnam
ASRAT	Air Support Radar Team
BAR	Browning Automatic Rifle
BV	*Bataillon volontaire* (Laotian Army unit)
CAC	Combined Action Company
CAP	Combined Action Platoon
CIA	Central Intelligence Agency
CIDG	Civilian Irregular Defense Group
CINCPAC	Commander-in-Chief Pacific
CJCS	Chairman, Joint Chiefs of Staff
COC	Combat Operations Center
COFRAM	Controlled fragmentation
COMUSMACV	Commander, U.S. Military Assistance Command Vietnam
CP	Command post
CPO	Chief Petty Officer
CRP	Combat Reconnaissance Platoon
CS	A type of nauseating gas agent
CSM	Chairman (JCS) staff memorandum
DIA	Defense Intelligence Agency
DMZ	Demilitarized zone
DRV	Democratic Republic of Vietnam
DZ	Drop zone
FAC	Forward Air Controller
FBI	Federal Bureau of Investigation
FO	Forward Observer
FOB	Forward Operating Base

FM	Frequency modulation
FROG	Free rocket over ground (Soviet missile)
FSCC	Fire Support Coordination Center
GPES	Ground Proximity Extraction System
GVN	Government of Vietnam
GySgt.	Gunnery Sergeant
HALO	High-altitude, low opening (parachute technique)
HHM	Marine Heavy Helicopter Squadron
HMM	Marine Medium Helicopter Squadron
JCS	Joint Chiefs of Staff
JCSM	Joint Chiefs of Staff memorandum
JGS	Joint General Staff (ARVN high command)
JTAD	Joint Technical Advisory Detachment
KIA	Killed in action
kilo	Kilometer
KSCB	Khe Sanh combat base
LAPES	Low-altitude parachute extraction system
LAW	Light antitank weapon
LCpl.	Lance Corporal
LLDB	Luong Luc Duc Bac (ARVN airborne special forces)
LSU	Logistics Support Unit
LZ	Landing zone
MACV	Military Assistance Command Vietnam
MACVSOG	MACV Studies and Observation Group
MAF	Marine Amphibious Force
MAG	Marine Air Group
MAW	Marine Air Wing
MCB	Mobile Construction Battalion
medevac	Medical evacuation
MIA	Missing in action
MIKE	Mobile Strike Force
mm	Millimeter
MSgt.	Master Sergeant
NCO	Noncommissioned Officer
NPIC	National Photographic Interpretation Center
NSC	National Security Council
NVA	North Vietnamese Army
PAVN	People's Army of Vietnam
PF	Popular Forces

POW	Prisoner of war
PSP	Pierced steel plating
RF	Regional Forces
RLG	Royal Laotian Government
RPG	Rocket-propelled grenade
RR	Recoilless rifle
RVN	Republic of Vietnam
SAM	Surface-to-air missile
SEAL	Sea-air-land soldier (Navy Special Forces)
SEATO	Southeast Asia Treaty Organization
SESU	Signal Engineering Survey Unit
SLAM	Seek, locate, annihilate, and monitor
SLAR	Side-looking airborne radar
SOG	Studies and Observation Group
SOP	Standard operating procedure
Sp.	Specialist (rank with grades 4 and 5)
SSgt.	Staff Sergeant
TOC	Tactical Operations Center
TSgt.	Technical Sergeant
USARPAC	U.S. Army Pacific
USMC	U.S. Marine Corps
USSF	U.S. Special Forces
V	Naval aviation squadron designator (denotes heavier-than-air craft as opposed to lighter-than-air craft, such as balloons)
VC	Viet Cong
VMA	Marine Attack Squadron
VMFA	Marine Fighter-Attack Squadron
VMO	Marine Observation Squadron
VPA	Vietnam People's Army
WPA	Work Projects Administration
WIA	Wounded in action
3/26	3rd Battalion, 26th Marine Regiment

VALLEY OF
DECISION

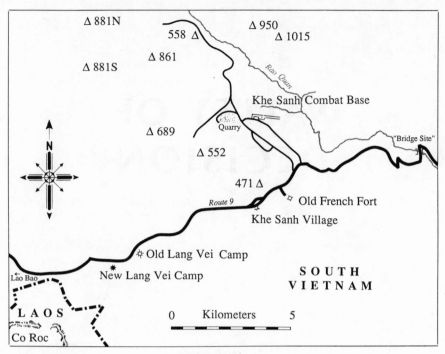

2 · Khe Sanh Area

1

The Encounter

"THE DISTANCE COVERED TODAY is comparatively long," Tran Quyen recorded in his diary. "I feel pain in my legs." Quyen remained far from his destination, indeed was still deep inside North Vietnam. A soldier in the North Vietnamese Army (NVA), properly the Vietnam People's Army, Quyen numbered among the replacement troops Hanoi sent south in January 1968. Between eight and thirteen thousand NVA soldiers entered South Vietnam, along with Quyen, that February. The way was hard. On January 21, as compatriots began the decisive battle to which he would be sent, Quyen noted, "The road is winding and so slippery that one has the impression of walking on grease." Vietnamese peasants asked him to pay for the firewood Quyen used to cook his lunch.

A staff assistant for operations and training, Quyen noticed the birthplace of Ho Chi Minh when he entered Nghe An province. Nam Dan district, Ho's ancestral home, gave the passing troops a warm welcome on January 30. The NVA typically moved its people in three- or five-man cells as part of so-called infiltration groups (doan), except when they moved as full combat units, and Quyen belonged to Doan 926. The group had to change its route when crossing Ha Tinh province. Quyen noted, "Generally speaking, none of the former groups could pass this area without being attacked and shedding blood." On February 16: "How intense the anti-aircraft activities were on the first night we spent here."

For days the group hiked uphill to cross the Annamite chain. Sometimes the slopes got as steep as eighty-five degrees; a forty-five-degree angle seemed nothing special, and "the route [was] cut through masses of stone." One segment proved so tough that, for three days, the doan returned to the same rest station at the end of its march. Only on February 23 did the unit finally enter Laos on the Ho Chi Minh Trail.

As the doan progressed southward the American presence became palpable. Quyen found the people of Kham Noi village rejoicing at having downed an aircraft. But the planes were over all the routes — L-19 spotters, helicopters, fighter-bombers. "They are continuously flying overhead both day and night," Quyen wrote toward the end of February. "I long to smoke but the present circumstances do not allow me."

Doan 926 had been sent to replace NVA soldiers lost in the fighting at Khe Sanh. The aerial firepower committed against them would be formidable, in particular the awesome power of B-52 strategic bombers, greatly feared by the North Vietnamese. Before Doan 926 reached Khe Sanh, some three hundred of its men deserted rather than face the B-52s. Quyen did not. He was assigned to the North Vietnamese 304th Division. That act sealed his fate.

Trinh Khao Lieu was another 304th Division man, from the 9th regiment of that unit. He transited much the same route on the way south, successively through the provinces of Thanh Hoa, Nghe An, Ha Tinh, and Quang Binh and then through Laos on the Ho Chi Minh Trail. Lieu was on hand from the beginning of the big fireworks at Khe Sanh, his unit having reached its position, three kilometers from American defenders, on January 23, 1968. He would fight on throughout the campaign.

The very essence of the American presence at Khe Sanh, the man wore boots caked full of mud, so red it blended with the stains of the blood shed by his comrades, mud that seemed to reach through the skin to the very soul, mud that weeks of showers seemingly could not remove. He stood, hungry but a little uncertain, in the officers' mess at the hospital of the Naval Support Activity, Da Nang. Amid the silver and white tablecloths and real glass goblets, amid the polished boots or patent leather shoes of the rear area crowd, it was those muddy boots that shone the brightest. It was as though he were from a different land, even a different world, a world of mud soaked red, from centuries of the blood of centurions.

As the man, a chaplain, walked through the civilized rubble that was Da Nang, he thought of his arrival in "the Nam," only six months before. It had been in this same town, after landing at the large Da Nang airstrip, that he had encountered Harper Bohr, future intelligence officer of Khe Sanh. There had been many others, far more men than planes could transport, and all was confusion at the field. Seizing an opportunity, they boarded a C-130 Hercules transport. It was near midnight as they flew out.

Moments later the stillness at Da Nang was rent by the shock of blasts and noise of explosions as, from two different directions, the air base suffered an estimated fifty hits from 120mm and 140mm rockets. When silence returned, three of the big C-130s were smoking ruins and a dozen Americans lay dead. By then the chaplain was already approaching Khe Sanh, for an encounter that would change him, and everyone else who experienced it. Like the North Vietnamese soldiers, he would be thrown into a maelstrom, a violent shadow war in a setting of dark, dank jungle, precipitous cliffs, and tortuously twisted gorges. The incident at Da Nang had been just a harbinger of what lay ahead.

The Dreamscape

Reality, in the Vietnam experience, is often the opposite of first images — peace and serenity contrasting with the absolute terror, horror, and fear of battle. Observing Khe Sanh from a distance left an impression of beauty: rolling hills with green velvetlike cover, an occasional stream visible among the thick vegetation, some majestic cliffs on the slopes of the higher hills. Near where the Americans eventually located their airfield and built a combat base, there was even a waterfall. "There were some powerful, almost spiritual ties to the place we were in," recalls Marine Lieutenant Ernest Spencer. "I thought I was in a magical kingdom."

The cool air was striking, so different from most of South Vietnam, and the silence could be unnerving. Often the only noise was the loud drone of the insects in the jungle, a sound that over time became soothing. There were wild boar and deer, elephants that could be used for transportation, a tiger that could be met in the jungle. Khe Sanh seemed beautiful and innocent, like the Americans who came there and saw that beauty.

Americans learned that evil is dressed in awesome beauty. Life fed on life, the luxuriant vegetation grew in inexorable competition, a fight of tree against tree, bushes clinging to slopes that were not rolling and gentle at all, but steep forty to sixty percent grades and often sheer cliffs. On maps the triple-canopy rain forest was shaded a simple green. On the ground the forest was a chaos of vegetation, the rolling hills a hell of elephant grass, taller than a man, with razor-sharp edges that cut into the skin of hands and arms and was loaded with bacteria that quickly festered into ugly and persistent sores. Movement was a strenuous exercise in controlled falling followed by pulling oneself up mud-slicked hillsides. The streams that looked like strips of tinsel from the air were raging, violent rapids full of cube-shaped boulders five or six feet across. Often there were no banks at all, only slippery rocks or muck that oozed over the tops of boots. The daily patrols devoured one's strength.

There are several significant hills in the area. To the north across the Rao Quan (*rao* means "stream") looms Dong Tri mountain, which Marines referred to as Hill 1015 for its height, in meters, above sea level. All the hills had numbers. About a kilometer to the west of Dong Tri lay Hill 950, the end of a mountain range Americans always suspected to be infested with North Vietnamese observers gazing down upon every move in the valley below. From Hill 950 one could look directly into the valley, to the Special Forces camp that marked the beginning of the American presence and that would become the combat base, near Ta Cong village.

Eventually the Americans came to use Hill 950 themselves, for an observation post and a radio relay station. The frequency-modulated radios U.S. troops carried, principally the PRC-25, had relatively short range and broadcast in line of sight. Humping up the hills and valleys all around the Khe Sanh quickly cut off direct communications. The relay station atop Hill 950 solved that problem.

Most of the inhabitants of the area were mountain tribespeople, "montagnards," after the French term for mountaineer. The major montagnard tribe in this area was the Bru. It was the Bru, along with American reconnaissance patrols, who had the most encounters with the fauna of the area. One Sunday morning in 1958 five Bru women were working their rice paddy, pulling out the weeds, when a tiger came out of nowhere, reared up at one of the women, and slashed her neck. The others screamed loudly and tried to save the woman, pulling at her legs as the tiger pulled at her head. Finally the tiger departed, leaving the Bru woman grievously hurt. That year twelve other people fell victim to the tiger, which terrorized the villagers. Megarde, a Vietnamese military hunter, managed to kill the tiger in 1959. On another occasion concerned plantation owners organized a tiger hunt and the planters killed forty-seven of the animals.

Marines had their encounters too. During one reconnaissance patrol the team reached its extraction point, a landing zone (LZ) along a riverbed in a valley with sharply sloped walls. The Marines had to stand on boulders awaiting the helicopters. Three men, "Junior" Reather, Kevin Macaulay, and Lionel Guerra stood together in silence until they suddenly heard a tremendous roar.

"It must be a water buffalo," Guerra said. Everyone laughed. No water buffalo ever made a sound like that.

Moments later the bushes rustled and out stepped an enormous Bengal tiger, about eight and a half feet long, not more than six or eight feet away. Luckily the Marines were downwind and the tiger did not immediately sense them. It strode to the stream and began to drink.

Reather quietly opened his pack, extracted a Kodak Instamatic camera, and snapped a picture of the tiger. At the sound of the shutter it turned and faced them, beautiful and terrible, its markings a brilliant orange. The tiger looked at the Marines and crouched to jump. Guerra then took a deep breath and hollered "AAAH-OOGH!" like a submarine diving alarm. Startled, the tiger growled, turned away, and walked off.

On another patrol Marines had settled in for the night in the middle of a thicket of thorn bushes. Such inaccessible "harbor" sites were chosen in the expectation that anyone following would make plenty of noise and alert the Marines. Imagine the surprise around midnight when booming noises awakened them. Kevin Macaulay awoke to look straight up into the eyes of an elephant. Its trunk hung down between Macaulay's left leg and the right leg of teammate Terry Young, who had just joined the squad.

Young, a black Marine who had joked earlier in the evening that he needed no camouflage paint, was now exclaiming "O! My God! O! My God!" in a sort of chant. At the strange sounds the elephant turned to look. Macaulay recalled its breath as being like an open cesspool. Then the elephant made a complete turn, trumpeted, and took off running. Fifteen minutes later Young was still chanting. From their harbor site the reconnaissance patrol could hear the elephant for miles.

Then there was "Doc" Bugema's story. Bugema was a Navy corpsman assigned to the Marine recon company. He stood about six foot two, had broad shoulders and very narrow hips, and seemed the perfect embodiment of the devil after a few days in the bush, with the stubble growing like a goatee on his chin.

On one patrol it was Bugema who carried the team's M-60 machine gun. After crossing a small stream the others suddenly heard the M-60 open up. Everyone dove to the ground, assuming they were under attack, except Doc Bugema, who stood blasting away at the ground in front of him.

The patrol leader turned around and asked incredulously, "Doc, what the hell are you doing?"

"Come back and look!" Bugema exclaimed.

It was a fifteen- or twenty-foot-long snake, at least a half foot in diameter, with a huge mouth. Despite forty or fifty rounds pumped into it, the snake slithered away into the jungle. Inevitably, after that Doc Bugema was known as "Snake Charmer."

Another night, another patrol, the stillness was broken by a slapping sound, followed by "O my God! O my God! They're on us! They're on us!"

But it was not the NVA at all. Instead a little spider monkey had dropped out of a tree onto the patrol leader, Jim "Thunder Legs" Hutton, and was slapping him in the face. While Thunder Legs went crazy, the rest of the men laughed their heads off.

"It's not funny, it could have been NVA," sneered Hutton.

"Nah," replied a teammate, "the NVA are a little bit bigger than that."

What everyone at Khe Sanh remembers most are the rats. These were not ordinary rats — nothing seemed ordinary in this magical and mysterious land. These rats were immense, and they were everywhere. It was not unusual to hear them at night inside bunkers, rattling cans, chewing on anything with food particles on it, even the paper labels on jars. One gunnery sergeant (typically called a "gunny") on one of the hilltop outposts became so incensed at a rat that kept visiting his bunker that one night he pulled out his .45-caliber pistol and shot the thing as it scurried above a poncho the gunny had hung across the ceiling. He killed the rat, but the hole in the poncho became a drain for rainwater — and in the monsoon season, that was plenty!

The rats were bad enough, but worse was that many of them

carried fleas infected with plague virus. The official word was always to drown rats after killing them to get the fleas. So, after killing the rat in a trap, the men drowned it and then burned it. Everyone had advice on a favored method or bait — many said the peanut butter from the C-rations was irresistible to the rats. The animals couldn't be poisoned; local Bru children who helped fill sandbags and cleaned out the garbage dumps collected the rats, broke their legs, and put them in their pockets to take home. Later they would be eaten. To horrified Marines the Bru children simply said, "Numba one chop chop!"

Setting the Stage

Why anyone would want to fight a battle for Khe Sanh is virtually inexplicable. True, Khe Sanh village stood astride Route 9, the northernmost transverse road in South Vietnam, a road that gave access to Laos and the legendary Ho Chi Minh Trail. But the road was not a highway to anywhere, for it had not been maintained, and security along its length, at least once it ascended from the coastal plains, was virtually nil. A simple macadam road, sometimes poorer than that, a single lane in places, built through valleys where the going had been a little easier, Route 9 was incapable of sustaining a major logistics flow. Hills towered over the road for much of its course through the uplands, so every convoy entailed significant military risk. Khe Sanh was not worth holding for the mere purpose of keeping open Route 9; quite the opposite: for some time the only reason vehicles transited the road was that Americans held Khe Sanh.

General William C. Westmoreland was Commander, United States Military Assistance Command Vietnam (MACV), the top boss for all Vietnam operations. Westmoreland believes there *was* a geographical reason to hold Khe Sanh: to bar access to the coastal plains to an enemy coming across the mountains. At least that is one of the rationales he expressed in public. But in fact, until the battle that is the major focus of this book, Khe Sanh was never held in strength sufficient to keep the North Vietnamese from moving to the east of it. Khe Sanh was held in force only once it became clear that there would be such a battle.

The Vietnam war was supposed to be about winning the hearts and minds of the people, about gaining the loyalties of citizens for their government. In this respect, without prejudice to the heroic efforts of combined action company (CAC) Oscar, Khe Sanh was small change. The South Vietnamese government cared little for its montagnard minorities, and the Bru numbered only forty or fifty thousand among a population of eighteen million. The Bru were dispersed anyway, some in North Vietnam, some in Laos, and some in the southern provinces of Quang Tri and Thua Thien. Huong Hoa district in Quang Tri, the location of Khe Sanh, contained only a fraction of a tribal minority.

North Vietnamese generals in particular could anticipate little from operations at Khe Sanh. The Americans had long worked with the Bru, so there was little reason to expect the tribe to rally to the NVA. As for access to the lowlands, the North Vietnamese had other routes and more valued objectives than Quang Tri — they could move down the A Shau valley to the old imperial capital of Hue and the American base at Da Nang, further south across the mountains to Binh Dinh province, or into the more populous montagnard regions of the Central Highlands.

Another argument General Westmoreland used in his exchanges with Washington was that the NVA intended, by capturing Khe Sanh, to outflank the defenses below the demilitarized zone (DMZ) which separated North from South Vietnam. As will be seen, those defenses did not require a deep strategic move to neutralize them.

General Westmoreland insists that the decision to fight a battle at Khe Sanh was one taken in Hanoi, a decision to make that battle the centerpiece of NVA plans for a decisive military campaign. Some observers and historians accept that view, others do not. Until Vietnam opens its own archives, the only evidence available is less than authoritative, consisting of U.S. intelligence data on NVA troop movements, captured documents, and personal statements by individuals. Troop movements speak to capability, not intentions; the captured documents do not include NVA plans for Khe Sanh; personal statements, like General Westmoreland's opinion, are not authoritative.

A few individual statements are worth citing. The most explicit is that of General Tran Cong Man, editor of the newspaper *Quan Doi Nhan Dan*, official organ of the Vietnamese military. General Man told Marine veteran and American journalist William Broyles in 1984 that "Westmoreland thought Khe Sanh was Dien Bien Phu. But Dien

Bien Phu was the strategic battle for us. We mobilized everything for it. At last we had a chance to have a favorable balance of forces. . . . We never had that at Khe Sanh; the situation would not allow it. Our true aim was to lure your forces away from the cities, to decoy them to the frontiers, to prepare for our great Tet Offensive." Man's comment was in 1984. In 1989 another Vietnamese general, Cao Pha of the NVA historical office, made certain comments regarding Khe Sanh at a conference of American and Vietnamese historians, but he was silent about the basic dimensions of Hanoi's decision and how it was made.

The contemporary account of North Vietnamese writer Nguyen Van Ba generally follows the opinion General Man expressed. In a piece published in December 1968 Ba argued that "Westmoreland had adopted the view that the northernmost provinces, especially the defense line along Highway 9, were the main front." Thus, "from a purely military standpoint, Khe Sanh was drawing the attention of the American strategists."

Was the decision Hanoi's? Some of the overriding reasons for holding Khe Sanh were American ones. The place was a useful observation post, a platform for launching special operations forays and the so-called road watch teams the United States used to monitor NVA activities in Laos. Moreover, Westmoreland cherished the notion of invading Laos himself and would have used Khe Sanh as his starting point. It would have greatly compounded the difficulties of that project to have to retake Khe Sanh prior to launching an invasion. This is a subject to which we shall return, a rationale with rather more substance than the reasons imputed to Hanoi.

It may be that the reason the North Vietnamese were interested in Khe Sanh was simply that the Americans were there and that Khe Sanh, as Nguyen Van Ba wrote, would draw the attention of American strategists. There was *a* decision made in Hanoi, but it was not necessarily one to have a battle at Khe Sanh; it may have been a decision to try to distract MACV from preparations for the great countryside offensive that has become known as Tet, to lure the Americans, as General Man put it. Though the North Vietnamese claims may be self-serving, this perception is not entirely after the fact. The possibility was known and commented on as events unfolded in 1968. In notes prepared for a press briefing at the height of the battle, Westmoreland himself admitted as much. Though he did not believe that Hanoi's intention had been to distract the Americans, Westmoreland noted, he admitted that "it is conceivable that the enemy's build-up around Khe Sanh is a feint."

Westmoreland and others have preferred to think that Khe Sanh was supposed to be Hanoi's bid for victory, as Dien Bien Phu had been in 1954, the all-out, decisive battle of the war. What was Khe Sanh? Decisive battle? Lure to trap the Americans? Just a match where the contenders punched at shadows? The answer matters to the Marines who served there. As a key series of events that occurred at a decisive moment of the Vietnam war, the battle of Khe Sanh and what really happened there are important to our full understanding of the entire conflict. The stage may have been set at the very beginning.

So close to the Laotian border, inhabited by a tribe whose settlements straddled that border, Khe Sanh would always be affected by what happened in Laos. In May 1959 North Vietnamese generals received orders to organize a route through Laos to send supplies and cadres to the guerrillas in the south. That route, which became known as the Ho Chi Minh Trail, permitted an NVA buildup in southern Laos that always threatened the security of Route 9 and the Khe Sanh area.

As early as November 1959, Route 9 was considered too insecure to be included in a request for U.S. funds for a South Vietnamese road improvement program. A year later State Department intelligence authorities in Washington were reporting NVA troops massed along the border and were fearing the possibility of "a major terrorist-guerrilla campaign throughout South Vietnam and/or a military offensive across the North Vietnam or the Laos frontier." Thus the situation in 1960 seemed virtually identical to what it would be toward the end of 1967.

The problem seen by the general then at the head of the U.S. military advisory group was to take effective steps to "plug up [the] porous border." The officer, Lieutenant General Lionel C. McGarr, amplified this view a year later to Secretary of Defense Robert S. McNamara. "The sparsely settled and rugged jungle terrain along the [Vietnam]-Lao border," McGarr wrote in October 1961, "make it exceedingly difficult to stop or materially slow down Communist infiltration from North Vietnam through Laos." McGarr believed that the antigovernment rebels, called Viet Cong (VC), were capable of selective large-scale operations and that "this capability is significantly increased by Communist control of the terrain along the Lao-[South Vietnam] border." McGarr suggested creation of a *cordon sanitaire* along the border, but the project never got off the ground.

Another idea of the military advisory group was the "border control" strategy. Major studies of the idea were completed at Saigon headquarters and sent to Washington and the Honolulu offices of the U.S. Commander-in-Chief Pacific (CINCPAC). This strategy led to initiation of certain CIA programs such as mountain scouts and trail-watchers and later to participation by the U.S. military in the form of Green Berets — Army Special Forces. The Special Forces were drawn in as trainers and then as advisers to a CIA village defense program that sought to enlist the montagnard tribesmen.

Despite these CIA initiatives the agency was never confident that southern borders could be sealed. In 1961, after John F. Kennedy became president, the White House ordered formation of a Washington special group on Vietnam policy headed by Roswell Gilpatric, Robert McNamara's deputy at the Pentagon. At a May 1961 meeting of the Gilpatric committee, William E. Colby, representing the CIA, told the group he doubted that the border could be effectively sealed. General Charles M. Bonesteel concurred in the name of the Joint Chiefs of Staff (JCS), adding that a serious U.S. commitment to South Vietnam might mean a sizable requirement for U.S. forces. Kenneth R. Young, ambassador designate to Thailand, then observed that this "raised the question as to why we should pour hundreds of millions into Vietnam if we can't choke off the problem."

A most ambitious idea for sealing the border was to physically block passage along the Ho Chi Minh Trail by implanting a military force across both the southern edge of the demilitarized zone and the Laotian panhandle. This idea was first explored in late 1961 as a joint international effort by nations of the Southeast Asia Treaty Organization (SEATO). A McNamara assistant told the Joint Chiefs, however, that "the proposal to put forces along the border was made for political reasons." The JCS accepted the concept only on condition that any forces committed *not* be deployed along the borders. Its official view, set forth in JCSM-716-61 of October 9, 1961, was that placement of SEATO forces along South Vietnamese borders as envisaged under SEATO Plan 5/61 was not feasible and that deployment solely along the DMZ line, running generally across the 17th Parallel, was militarily unsound. Nevertheless one JCS member, the chief of naval operations, believed that the North Vietnamese had had "free access to the Vietnam border" by a "secure and well concealed route" since the fall of the Laotian provincial capital Tchepone in the summer of 1961. In spite of Admiral George W. Anderson's information that few supplies were moving by sea, but rather were coming south through Laos, Anderson proved unwilling to go along with SEATO Plan 5.

To test new concepts and familiarize national contingents with other members' operating practices, SEATO held major exercises every other year. These had featured such concepts as pathfinder troops and long-range force-level reconnaissance in exercises STRONG-BACK (1958) and BLUE STAR (1960). The 1962 exercise was called TULUNGUN, a colloquial Filipino word for "mutual assistance," and was held in the Philippines between March 2 and April 12. It tested the SEATO plan, using an area on the western coast of Mindoro as the objective for a hypothetical nation called Manvos, which represented South Vietnam in this exercise.

The TULUNGUN scenario was played out with friendly forces against a notional enemy, the so-called Aggressor, at that time used as the enemy in all U.S. maneuvers and exercises. The scenario specified that Aggressor had used the Ho Chi Minh Trail and Route 9 network "to infiltrate large numbers of guerrilla elements into northern Republic of Vietnam." By February 1962 in the game, "direct attacks" on military posts of the Army of the Republic of Vietnam (ARVN), plus subversion and terrorization, created a situation in which "Aggressor was able to seize control of the area . . . without overt commitment of military units." The game opened at that point, with a request by South Vietnam for SEATO support of ARVN efforts.

When the Joint Chiefs heard that the motivation for SEATO Plan 5 was political, they were getting the straight poop. Some of the high-level interest in the scheme came from inside the White House, where deputy national security adviser Walt W. Rostow was a strong supporter. The military made their objections stick, however, while Rostow, toward the end of 1961, moved over to the State Department to take up a job he wanted more than his National Security Council (NSC) post, that of director of State's policy planning council. Rostow's last major task for the NSC was to make an evaluation visit to Vietnam in conjunction with General Maxwell D. Taylor, the president's special military representative.

The Taylor-Rostow mission marked a milepost on the U.S. road to war in Vietnam. It produced a long list of recommendations intended to improve the situation for the Saigon regime, officially termed the

Government of Vietnam (GVN). Among the recommendations was one directly relevant to the question of border control. The Taylor-Rostow mission suggested the formation of a special command it called the Northwest Frontier Force, about thirty-three hundred ARVN rangers in twenty-three companies who would operate in all five provinces of South Vietnam that bordered Laos. The force would have been matched with a special pacification organization that included a unit to operate in Quang Tri. It was intended that the pacification units would be made up primarily of montagnard minorities. Since the Bru of Hoang Hoa district, containing the Sanh and Ta Cong villages, constituted the largest population along the western border of Quang Tri, they would have been a natural focus for the project.

This frontier force initiative never came to fruition. Nevertheless, something still had to be done about security in western Quang Tri. The Taylor-Rostow study group itself had reported intelligence indicating that two NVA divisions, the 304th and 324th, were deployed in the vicinity of Route 9 while another, the 325th, lay just north of the DMZ. Eventually the response was dictated by the CIA and its montagnard village defense program. This initiative began in the Central Highlands in early 1962 and involved mobilizing montagnards in defense militias and strike units. The units were trained and advised by U.S. Army Special Forces detachments and commanded by their ARVN counterparts, the Luong Luc Duc Bac (LLDB), or airborne special forces.

It was not very long before village defense came to Khe Sanh. In July 1962 the first Special Forces A detachment arrived at Khe Sanh. They drove up from Da Nang, across Route 9, in a World War II–vintage GMC 2½ ton truck. Led by Captain Weaver, the team was on a six-month rotation and had already spent most of it at Da Nang training Bru tribesmen. Two of the Green Berets, George Grooms and Frank Quinn, had actually been captured by Viet Cong near Da Nang. So innocent was the war then that the VC turned them loose to return to their buddies.

Captain Weaver's detachment first occupied abandoned French installations near Khe Sanh village just off Route 9. The site, which became known as the Old French Fort, had been a new concrete structure just a decade before. The effects of climate and jungle were so corrosive that when the Special Forces arrived they found but one small, partly caved in bunker. They called it The Alamo. The team got a new leader, Jacques Standing. His executive officer was Lieutenant

Hancock; Sergeants Jerry Howland and Westbrook were medics; Grooms, Quinn, and Hugh Sheron were the weapons specialists. A CIA case officer supervised them. "We were told when we went in there to stay away from everybody," Standing recalls. "We were told: just build your camp, protect yourself, and we'll give you orders down the line. . . . Every time we would try to do something, we would meet with objection. They would say: 'You stay within your close proximity to necessary security patrols, and that's it; don't wander the area.' "

Only one exception was made. That was for medic Howland, who was permitted to make calls in the villages, providing medical services in the name of civic action. The Green Berets still managed to get in at least a little action, as Howland tells it. "Any kind of security patrol or listening or anything, we listed it as a 'tiger hunt,' and we went, just me and [a] Frenchman, alone." Life was extremely tenuous at Khe Sanh. No relief force was available in case of attack, and support was practically nonexistent, limited to flights of small C-7 Caribou transport that came in from Thailand, landing at a small airstrip next to a prison at Lao Bao on the Laotian border. "Neither the Vietnamese nor the Laotians knew where the border was and they didn't care," Howland says. Once the Caribou landed too fast and skidded off the strip into a river. Suddenly thirty or forty Laotian troops appeared, brandishing weapons and dressed in camouflage utilities. But they only wanted to help pull the plane out. The C-7 nonetheless remained for several days. "We'd sit down there at night guarding the stupid thing," remarks Howland. "The Bru would leave us if the tigers came. That was every night. They didn't believe you could kill a tiger, so they wouldn't mess with them. They attributed a lot of religious power to a tiger." Team leader Jacques Standing recalls, "The whole situation up there was just crazy."

Food runs by vehicle to Quang Tri meant uncertain trips along hazardous Route 9, with its cliffs, bends and bridges, and a thousand places ideal for an ambush. Only two Americans were allowed on the runs, and they had standing orders to pick up any Bru encountered along the road to reduce the possibility of ambush. The team eventually was able to complete a team house for the Special Forces detachment that would follow, but no one ever used it — a typhoon blew it away. On the plus side, the typhoon also knocked down the camp's sixteen-foot radio aerial — right into the barbed wire — and communications with Saigon, which had always been spotty, were suddenly loud and clear. The typhoon had changed atmospheric conditions while giving communications specialists a greatly enhanced antenna system in the barbed wire.

The French Fort position was itself a source of apprehension. Special Forces learned that Viet Minh — forerunners of the VC — had dug a tunnel under the camp ending in the well. The tunnel had collapsed at the place where the Americans had filled it in. Villagers said the tunnel went across a field and out the back slope near the jungle. Jacques Standing worried that the VC would not even need to attack; they could just pack the tunnel with explosives and blow up the Special Forces camp. "That was a very uncomfortable feeling. But the more people you talked to," Standing recalls, "you didn't know whether it was an old wives' tale."

Around September 1962 came the first Special Forces detachment to spend an entire six-month tour at Khe Sanh. That was team A-131 led by Captain Chuck Korchek. It was at this time that a Vietnamese engineer unit built the first Khe Sanh airstrip, leveling the ground and covering it with honeycombed metal strips. As with his predecessors, the CIA case officer prohibited distant operations, telling A-131 troopers they could not go to Lao Bao and even confiscating a .50-caliber machine gun from the team weapons specialist, Frank Fowler. Intelligence came from the local French priest.

The reason the CIA took the machine gun, the officer told Fowler, was that there was too much chance of its falling into the hands of the VC or NVA if they overran the camp, and the CIA did not want to do anything to endanger aircraft flying over the area. "It really makes you feel good," Fowler acidly commented.

The characteristics of life at Khe Sanh were as they would remain: isolation; hands tied by higher authority; lack of supplies. And there were always the rats. "One time we went into the village," Frank Fowler recalls, "and bought some metal rat traps because it was so bad. We were using mosquito nets on our bunks to keep the rats off. I remember one night there was a big metal rat trap with teeth on it. And I remember the first rat we got. When [the trap] snapped it woke me up. And then the rat started dragging the thing off!"

Exercise TULUNGUN, mounted by the SEATO allies, also served as cover for the introduction of Marine helicopters into South Vietnam. These supported operations in the Khe Sanh area by Special Forces and by the ARVN I Corps ("Eye" Corps). Available records reflect hardly any operations into the site that would become Khe Sanh combat base. Almost all landings occurred at the French Fort, also called Fort Dix, at Huong Hoa district headquarters in the Khe Sanh village; at the Lao Bao site; or at a fortified position in the Rao Quan valley about three and a half kilometers west of Hill 950.

Captain Edward J. Hughes, Jr., a 3rd Marine Division officer on temporary duty with the helicopter units, recalled during the later Khe Sanh battle that he had once landed at the site with Captain Gillesby of A-131 for a field reconnaissance prior to a scheduled landing of several ARVN companies. The day after their mission they found the LZ covered with sharpened wooden stakes. They had the obstructions removed but the ARVN landing was canceled. Later Hughes learned that the NVA 304th Division had done the deed.

Marine helicopters conducted operations at a significant tempo in late 1962 and the new year. On December 13 a dozen ships of squadron HMM-163 made ninety-two sorties (a sortie is one flight by one aircraft) transporting 304 troops of the ARVN 1st Division from Hiep Khanh airstrip to an LZ that would eventually become the second site of the Lang Vei Special Forces camp. On March 31, 1963, seventy ARVN paratroopers jumped from H-34D choppers into the French Fort area. A week later six UH-34Ds lifted 130 ARVN soldiers to a point at the extreme northwest corner of South Vietnam, just over two kilometers from the Laotian border, where they explored a trail network at the foot of Hill 743. Marine helicopters also conducted numerous medical evacuations or lifts of prisoners or dead.

Not often encountered, the NVA and VC were still a constant presence, apt to turn up at the most awkward moments. On April 11, 1963, two O-1B light observation planes came under small arms fire northwest of Khe Sanh village. The engagement occurred in the valley between hills 861 and 881 South, points that would become infamous to another generation of Marines.

In a later incident, in March 1964 an O-1 "Bird Dog" was shot down. The pilot, Captain Richard Whitesides, was reportedly killed in the crash. Flying with him, Captain Floyd Thompson, who commanded Special Forces detachment A-728 at Khe Sanh at the time, broke his back and was captured. He regained consciousness just as one of his captors began trying to cut off a finger to get at a ruby ring Thompson wore. The captain became the longest-held POW of the Vietnam war.

Thrown into disarray by the disappearance of the team captain,

Special Forces reacted with some urgency. At Fort Bragg, Special Forces headquarters, the 7th Group commander called in Captain Allan B. Imes, a friend of Thompson's, and detailed him to take over A-728 and find out what had happened to the missing American.

"Every time we sent a patrol out and we encountered montagnard tribesmen out in the hills and villages and so forth, we would interrogate them and ask what they knew about it," Imes recollects. "We found a lot of montagnard tribesmen who remembered the plane going down.

"When I finished my tour there in November '64, we had gathered enough evidence from montagnard tribesmen that we sincerely thought Floyd Thompson was dead."

By then the Green Berets at French Fort were housed in wood and thatch huts. Imes turned one cement block building into a combined operations and communications center and mess hall, while the medical dispensary was established down the hill toward the village to facilitate contact with the Bru. Captain Imes had his own A team plus an attached Australian captain and two sergeants major and thirty-five or forty Nung tribesmen, very popular as CIA mercenary troops, who acted as a personal guard for the Americans and Aussies. The Nungs occupied an inner perimeter at the Special Forces camp; Vietnamese and Bru manned the outer perimeter.

The Australian captain, Reginald Pollard, happened to be senior to Imes and was in fact the son of the chief of staff of the Australian army. One of the sergeants, George Chinn, also was senior sergeant major of the Australian army. It was a high-powered contingent, but the Aussies were excited to be part of the Vietnam adventure and subordinated themselves to Imes gladly.

A typical patrol operation might include two or three Green Berets or Australians, a similar number of Vietnamese special forces, a core squad of seven to twelve Nungs, and a platoon to a company (thirty or forty or up to a hundred) of Bru, organized into a Civilian Irregular Defense Group (CIDG) unit. The CIDG troopers, colloquially called "strikers," distinguishing CIDG strike force units from village defense militias, would continue to be the mainstay of the tribal war in Vietnam. The patrol would sweep up along the Laotian border, sometimes crossing it though not penetrating too deeply into Laos. The usual duration would be two or three days; long patrols could be out five or six. "Those are hillacious mountains!" Imes recalls. "I have gone all day up the side of a mountain and didn't go three hundred yards!"

The other major source of information on the North Vietnamese and Viet Cong was the Royal Laotian Army, which had a *Bataillon volontaire* (BV-33) just inside the border at Ban Houei Sane. The BV-33 commander would give briefings periodically, every month or two, and Captain Imes would travel to Tchepone to hear them. The Laotian battalion commander sometimes came east into Vietnam with his family, and Khe Sanh soldiers escorted him along Route 9 when he was in their area. In 1964 one BV-33 commander was killed when his vehicle struck a landmine on Route 9 east of Khe Sanh.

An Army adviser to ARVN saw the Laotians in 1964 and thought they "looked like a gypsy band." The officer, Captain Francis X. Harrison, senior adviser to the 3rd Battalion, 1st Regiment, ARVN 1st Division, observed that the Laotian troops "had their families with them. They had kids. They had supplies all over the place. I mean the whole area was just one big ammo dump. There were open boxes of grenades, open boxes of mortar shells, and machine gun ammunition. They must have kept pulling their ammunition with them as they withdrew."

In truth there was some friction between the Marines and Special Forces at Khe Sanh. Captain Imes's patrols found evidence of VC or NVA presence south of his camp — structures optimized for hospitals, for barracks to rest, bleachers to listen to training lectures, vines with bells to warn of an enemy approach — the stuff of base camps. But Imes could get no help from the Marines. "They would not participate in any way. I tried and I became very frustrated with the Marine Corps. They had the choppers; we had the evidence there was something [out there]. . . . We felt that if we could get further south and come back north we could catch them. We planned a heliborne operation and then the Marines backed out on us."

Later, in October 1964, Khe Sanh strikers made what Imes believes was the first confirmed, positive-proof contact with North Vietnamese Army units inside South Vietnam. This occurred during a patrol commanded by the Australians Captain Pollard and Sergeant Major Chinn. Across the Laotian border the patrol came upon an estimated NVA company in bivouac, surrounded them, and then shot them to pieces. The patrol brought back plenty of confirmatory information such as ID cards and NVA-type equipment. Though the incident might have shown that, contrary to Hanoi's expressions, NVA troops were beginning to enter the south, the United States was denying equally vehemently that any activities were being carried on in Laos. Such is covert warfare — a duel of dissimulation.

Intelligence was indeed the primary *raison d'être* for Khe Sanh at that stage of the Vietnam war. Its proximity to Laos and North Vietnam meant that teams from Khe Sanh could cross the border to monitor traffic on the Ho Chi Minh Trail or attempt to infiltrate North Vietnam, bypassing the DMZ. If there were to be a major NVA attack into South Vietnam it would of necessity fall first upon Khe Sanh, providing a modicum of warning for I Corps, ARVN, Saigon, and the U.S. command, which had been reconstituted in early 1964 as Military Assistance Command Vietnam (MACV). There is a word in French military terminology, *sonnette* (literally "doorbell"), that describes precisely this use of Khe Sanh.

The doorbell metaphor seems quite apt applied to the Khe Sanh area's function as a site for communications intelligence listening posts. The very high mountain peaks together with the very peculiar radio propagation effects of the area provided excellent opportunities for radio monitoring of the NVA and even mainland China, a prime U.S. intelligence target. As early as 1961 South Vietnamese sources told William J. Jorden, then of the State Department's policy planning council, that although VC and NVA regional commands made extensive use of radio in their communications with higher command, radio direction finding indicated that the communications net operated over too extensive an area to be subjected to crippling military strikes. If the point was to exploit this source, the logical corollary was to monitor the traffic for its intelligence value.

The Marine Corps responded to this perceived need by activating a specialized unit, the Signal Engineering Survey Unit (SESU). Created in April 1964, SESU consisted of five officers and 152 enlisted men, including a detachment (three officers and 27 enlisted Marines) from the 1st Radio Company, Fleet Marine Force Pacific; an infantry element from Company G of the 2nd Battalion, 3rd Marines; and a section of 81mm mortars. The unit was commanded by Major Alfred M. Gray, Jr., and achieved the distinction of becoming the first U.S. Marine ground unit to conduct independent operations in South Vietnam. That was at Khe Sanh.

Initially Major Gray went in to conduct a preliminary reconnaissance. It happened that, at the same time, General Westmoreland was making the rounds on an inspection prior to assuming the MACV command. At Khe Sanh Westmoreland lent Gray his UH-1 helicopter while taking the C-7 Caribou in which Gray had arrived. Both had close calls. Westy in the Caribou was over the A Shau valley when a round hit his plane and he was wounded. Accompanied by a small group of South Vietnamese, Major Gray almost crashed in the helicopter when it flew up to insert him on Tiger Tooth mountain (Hill 1739), also known as Dong Voi Mep, almost 5,500 feet above sea level. Gray's helicopter lost power as it approached and had to land on the wrong side of the mountain.

Once in place, Major Gray stumbled from one difficulty to another. The monsoon began too soon and good weather for his group's extraction never came. Gray made initial arrangements but then could not get out. His party subsisted on reduced rations of a half canteen cup of rice per day. They finally had to walk out. Gray tells the story well:

> When we came out, we had a big argument about which way to go, of course. We were up there damn near a month, and as we came off the mountain and through the heavy savannah grass there north of Miet Xa, which was eleven, twelve kilometers north of — the ARVN had an outpost there. The South Vietnamese had a small unit there and they had two 105[mm] howitzers.
>
> Well, we got within seven or eight kilometers of Miet Xa. We stumbled into a Viet Cong command post. We had a big fire fight and we killed some Viet Cong. They were on both sides of this little river, and we called in artillery fire and broke up the ambush. It was sort of a mutual surprise.
>
> But the important thing is, we killed the commander there and captured all the papers. They had their plans for the whole region, which included the key Viet Cong people in each of the forty-three villages in that whole complex, a real intelligence windfall. It had all their orders, you know — build so many punji stakes, do so much of this, so much of that, etc., etc. So that really kinda cleansed things out for a good period to come.
>
> And then that night we got into Miet Xa, and I got something to eat. I remember I had a terrible sore throat. We had all been out of halizone tablets [to purify water for drinking], and I had drunk some of that water. I had a terrible sore throat, I couldn't even eat.
>
> The next morning we moved into Khe Sanh and went down to Da Nang. I remember going to bed for twenty-four hours. And then I went to Saigon to report what we found out and what we were going to do.

Gray spent a day at MACV and then returned to Khe Sanh, where his SESU unit was now arriving. Personnel came mostly by Air Force C-123, equipment by road convoy over Route 9. It was the end of May 1964.

Emplacement of this radio intelligence unit was a major operation. Two officers and five enlisted men remained behind at Da Nang for liaison and logistics. Another four-man team went to Phu Bai, where the Army Security Agency had an intelligence facility supporting I Corps. At Khe Sanh the unit used the cover designation Advisory Team One and initially concentrated on building a logistics base. Landing zones were established on both the crest and slopes of Tiger Tooth; one was called "mountain," the other "hill." On May 9 choppers of HMM-364 delivered a dozen water cans and then two days later fifteen men and a thousand pounds of equipment. On May 13 an advance party of ARVN troops were lifted from Miet Xa to Tiger Tooth hill, from which they climbed to the crest and hacked out a mountain LZ. A month later, on June 13, Major Gray, nine enlisted Marines, and several thousand pounds of equipment went into the mountain LZ. Violent wind eddies and reverse down currents made the LZ really dangerous. Despite maximum power, one H-34D was forced into the trees, rolled over onto its back, and crashed. For a week bad weather made further lifts impossible. Then on June 22, emplacement was completed with the lift of another 10,200 pounds of cargo, sixty-three more Marines, and additional ARVN troops. Ultimately there would be one hundred ARVN troops on the mountain together with seventy-three Marines. Eighty-one Leathernecks remained at French Fort and provided a personnel pool from which, weather permitting, Tiger Tooth was replenished every two weeks.

Horrible weather made resupply of food and water a special problem. Starting with thirty days of rations, the Marines on Tiger Tooth were restricted to two canteens of water per man per day (about *four times* the ration allowed during the 1968 Khe Sanh siege). A severe storm in mid-July blew away antennas and tents, and on July 17 an enemy force probed the Marine sector of the perimeter. Though there were no casualties and no enemy dead were found the next morning, Tiger Tooth had been compromised. Major Gray's orders to make no patrols or take any other action that might reveal SESU's presence had been vitiated. "The threat got really bad up there," recalls Gray, "and there were a lot of indications they were going to come after us big time." Between July 16 and 19 the SESU detachment withdrew from the mountain and was redeployed to Da Nang.

Meanwhile, a by-product of the operation was to furnish at least a modicum of evidence to Special Forces that the Marines were in fact cooperating with the Army. During this time the Corps stationed a couple of helicopters forward at French Fort for search and rescue plus support of Tiger Tooth or missions in Laos. The presence of the security detachment of SESU at Khe Sanh also became a welcome addition to the CIDG strikers. Captain Imes recalls, "I'm convinced that because I had that platoon in my camp we did not get attacked. We had all kinds of signs of intelligence that we were going to be attacked at Khe Sanh, but I had that Marine platoon in my camp and that gave us a lot of additional firepower."

Americans, ARVN troops, Nungs, and Bru garrisoned Khe Sanh; the North Vietnamese posed a threat everywhere. "Everything got real edgy," says Captain Imes. "All of a sudden I got a message one day that General John K. Waters was coming to Khe Sanh. Waters was the USARPAC [U.S. Army Pacific] commander, a four star general and Patton's son-in-law. I didn't know why he was coming."

At the CIDG camp General Waters got the usual tour, inspection, and briefing. "Finally he said, 'OK, now it's my turn,' and he told us there were fifteen thousand North Vietnamese soldiers massed on the DMZ and that the American command fully expected the North Vietnamese to attack across the DMZ, try to take I Corps, cut it off and declare it a neutral country; then Russia, Red China, and North Vietnam would recognize it. He said that when that happened, the mission of my Special Forces was to go underground and become the guerrillas against them. It scared me to death! Our mission from the mouth of the USARPAC commander was to let the Vietnamese and montagnards fend for themselves, take our Nungs and the scout platoon [an elite Bru unit the A team had trained], and become our own guerrilla force."

It was in 1964 that Special Forces decided to abandon French Fort and establish a base at the airstrip. This decision resulted from an agreement among Major Nantz, commanding the B detachment at Da Nang, his executive officer, and Captain Imes. The real mover in the project was Major David Watts (later to become a general), who engineered the whole thing and even hired montagnards to make bricks for the new post. The camp moved because from French Fort it was impossible to secure the airfield and because the airfield position stood on fairly level ground with good fields of fire in every direction. The scheme was supposed to make Khe Sanh more defensible.

It was a new Special Forces team that made the actual move to the airstrip, one from the 1st Group on Okinawa, not the 7th at Fort Bragg. Captain Charles A. Allen's detachment arrived in November 1964, overlapping briefly with the Imes team, who discovered their replacements had a whole different way of doing things. Allen's team spent six months building a central command bunker, four corner bunkers, and about fifteen buildings for the new CIDG camp. The team once waited seventeen days before the weather opened to let a supply plane land at the strip.

Chuck Allen, from Fort Lee, New Jersey, stuck it out, setting up a civilian council to promote a Bru civic action program. Allen also established various agent nets for intelligence gathering and continued liaison with the Laotian army. Though Special Forces in Vietnam generally anticipated that about a third of the CIDGs in a camp might be enemy agents, at Khe Sanh the Green Berets depended on their Nungs. Master Sergeant Thomas Barrett of Brooklyn, New York, explained to a visiting reporter: "If we didn't trust them the whole team would be awake, nervous and on guard, with weapons in their hands twenty-three hours a day. We have to trust them."

But a handful of Nungs, Bru scouts, and CIDG strikers were not going to hold back the North Vietnamese Army or block the Ho Chi Minh Trail. Among the options available to do that, SEATO Plan 5 remained the leading candidate. After he became Army chief of staff in the summer of 1964, General Harold K. Johnson resurrected the plan, proposing that a force of four divisions be emplaced along the 17th Parallel from the South China Sea to the Mekong River on the Laotian-Thai border. Johnson wanted it to be an international force under SEATO but would have settled for an all-U.S. force. Lyndon Baines Johnson, now president, raised the blocking force concept with General Westmoreland in December 1964. Westmoreland pronounced himself enthusiastic but cited the many difficulties involved in the creation of such a SEATO force. When, in the spring of 1965, he and diplomat U. Alexis Johnson articulated a modified version of the concept, they found Washington cold to the idea. President Johnson was already preoccupied with his decision to commit American ground troops to combat in Vietnam. Perhaps experiences in the

Dominican Republic also soured LBJ on the subject of multinational military forces. In any case, Westmoreland notes: "After a first flurry of interest in an international anti-infiltration force in late 1964, officials in Washington never evidenced any more enthusiasm for it." At that point the only alternative became an invasion of Laos, an operation that would necessarily have to be supplied across Route 9 and mounted from Khe Sanh.

The Anthropology of Death

KHE SANH VILLAGE EXISTED as a result of the presence of French coffee planters. It began with Eugène Poilane, a son of peasants, born at Saint-Sauveur de Landemont, France, on March 16, 1888. Poilane, by profession an "artillery worker," arrived in South Vietnam, then the French protectorate of Cochinchina, in 1909. He worked at the naval arsenal for some years, until he chanced to meet naturalist Auguste Chevalier, who after the First World War appointed Poilane as a prospector for the Botanical Institute. In 1922 Poilane became an agent of the Forest Service of Indochina.

Eugène Poilane first passed through what became Khe Sanh village in 1918, when it consisted of only one house, that of the engineer supervising construction of Colonial Route 9, the first metaled road to Laos. Like the Americans who followed, he was captivated by the lush vegetation and thought the red soil as fine as anything in Tuscany. He returned in 1926 to start a coffee plantation, importing chiari coffee trees and tending them for the ten years they need to become productive. His plantation extended throughout the area subsequently occupied by Khe Sanh combat base. In fact, the access road from the base airfield to Route 9 was Poilane's private thoroughfare. His motorcar was the first vehicle in the region.

Not only did Poilane establish the first plantation, he fulfilled his avocation of botanist with aplomb, traveling throughout Indochina, even to the borders of China and Burma, in behalf of the Forestry Service. Poilane collected specimens that he sent to the museum at Saigon. Until 1947 his submissions numbered between fifteen hundred and five thousand every year, for a total of more than thirty-six thousand, and he was credited with having discovered twenty-one species of plants and producing the second known specimens of nineteen others. The genuses *Poilania* and *Poilaniella* will forever give homage to this venturesome man. Poilane began an experimental orchard, attempting to introduce numerous types of fruit trees native to tropical and even temperate climates. He imported grafts from France, Japan, and other countries.

As the trees grew, so did the Poilane family. Madame Bordeauducq, Eugène's formidable first wife, who bore him five children, kept her maiden name to show her independence. Indeed, when Poilane divorced her, Bordeauducq merely moved a kilometer down the road and started a plantation of her own. Poilane then married a Nung woman and sired five more children.

Soon more planters came to Khe Sanh. One was M. Simard, whose house was the last one at the western edge of the village (Map 3). His plantation included a vegetable garden near Lang Bu. Simard married an Eastern European woman, who lived a long time in Vietnam but departed toward the end of 1967. Another planter was M. Rome, whose land lay east of the village along Route 9. His wife and gardener, both Japanese, reportedly lived pretty high during the Japanese occupation of Indochina in World War II. According to Madeleine Poilane, the wife of Poilane's son Felix, the three spied on French positions for the Japanese and the Viet Minh and were later killed, "some say by the VC, others say by the French."

The Rome plantation then went to a renter, M. Llinarès, who lived in Tonkin but had lost almost everything at the end of the Franco-Vietnamese war, when he abandoned his property in what became North Vietnam. Llinarès had no love for the North Vietnamese, but his Vietnamese wife was said to have had contacts with the Viet Cong, and a VC network was discovered in a village at the edge of the Llinarès plantation. After that, Bru tribesmen inhabiting that village were resettled and any who had pro-VC sympathies left. Nevertheless, two workers were murdered in the Llinarès house, after which the wife left Khe Sanh to demand protection from the Quang Tri province chief. She never returned.

Llinarès has been quoted as telling visitors to the village that he wanted only one thing of God: "I ask to die at Khe Sanh." On April 30, 1964, Llinarès was a passenger in Eugène Poilane's well-known yellow Citroën when the two were ambushed by the Viet Cong. Llinarès survived, Poilane died.

Mme. Bordeauducq by then was in retirement, with her son Felix

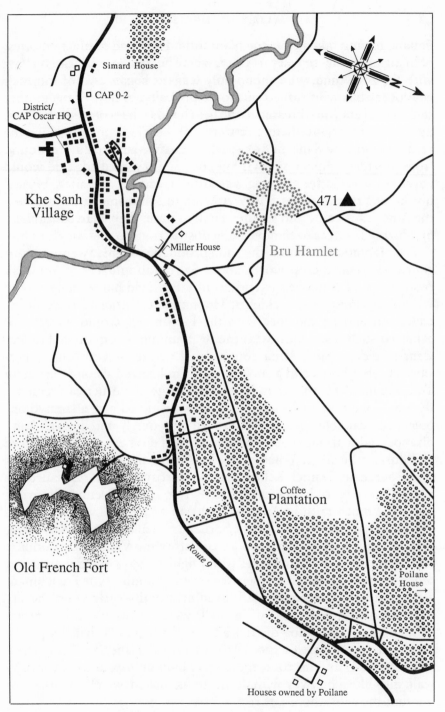

Simard House

CAP 0-2

District/
CAP Oscar HQ

Khe Sanh
Village

Miller House

471 ▲

Bru Hamlet

Old French Fort

Coffee
Plantation

Route 9

Poilane
House
→

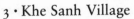

Houses owned by Poilane

3 · Khe Sanh Village

Poilane having taken over the plantation. Felix had many memories: of living in Hue from 1945 to 1947, where he had been educated along with the Bru Anha, who supposedly was the son of two of Eugène's employees but who turned out to be his half-brother; of his mother shooting tigers who threatened the field hands (she reportedly had run up a tally of forty-five before retiring); of the Viet Minh attacking the area around Khe Sanh in 1954, when Eugène suffered a leg wound from mortar shrapnel and M. Simard's wife was killed. Life would never be easy. Coffee growing was arduous enough. Japanese burned his father's trees in 1945 and Viet Minh did the same in 1953; when the Americans came and set up a combat base, they were continually bulldozing his trees to remove these obstructions to their fields of fire.

The plantations around Khe Sanh produced roughly twenty tons of coffee per year, a crop worth about $250,000 in a virtual noncash economy, and employed twenty to fifty Bru field hands daily.

Anha became deputy chief of Huong Hoa district because of his education and prominence with the French. He would never have achieved such distinction with the Bru, among whom official offices went to elders. Still, Anha commanded respect — with highly polished combat boots and a spotless uniform he lived among the Bru in Ta Cong hamlet rather than Khe Sanh village. An American sergeant who worked with Anha liked him but considered him a shrewd opportunist, capable of intrigue though not overly intelligent. Anha disappeared without explanation for several days at a time just before and during the siege. When asked by Americans about the assistant chief, Sergeant Daniel Kelley painted a rosy picture "because we needed every bit of help we could get." But upon reflection, "I myself don't put much faith in Anha as an idealist."

Lao Bao, tucked just inside the border a few miles west of Khe Sanh, was an old French prison abandoned before the Vietnamese conflict. At the time of the French–Viet Minh fight in 1954 the Poilanes and other residents took refuge there for several months. One Frenchman, a tall, red-haired mechanic, still lived nearby. By early 1967 the site was in ruins, though some of its walls were twenty feet thick. James Whitenack, Huong Hoa district adviser then, recalls that the prison "had cells in one area exposed to the weather and the elements — concrete walls and no roof; there were bars on top. And you would walk into like a hallway with doors going into these cells . . . open to the sun, the rain, the weather."

In March 1964 Father Poncet of the Fathers of Foreign Missions in

Paris came to Khe Sanh as rector. He sat on a civilian board, with Madeleine Poilane and others, that helped Special Forces orient its civic action work. Poncet also passed on snippets of intelligence to the Green Berets. Later, Marines saw him frequently pedaling by on his bicycle, usually wearing blue trousers. In Hue on February 13, 1968, at the height of the Tet offensive, Viet Cong gunned down Father Poncet in the middle of a street. At Khe Sanh, Marine chaplain Walt Driscoll took over Poncet's familiar bicycle.

Then there were John and Carolyn Miller of the Wycliffe Bible Translators, who arrived in January 1962 and first settled in Lang Bu, a hamlet beside Route 9 between Khe Sanh and Lang Vei. They listened to the Bru language to develop a written form, not only translating the Bible for the montagnards but teaching them to read and write at the same time. Their work was amazing, and a genuineness of goodness and truth radiated in their presence, a surfeit of goodness one finds perhaps once in a lifetime. Harper Bohr, Jr., regimental intelligence officer for the 26th Marines in late 1967, once remarked, "If Jesus Christ were to be walking on earth today, I could see him as John Miller." Marines were often to be found visiting the Miller home.

The Millers got their basic supplies, such as rice, flour, and oil, up Route 9 from Dong Ha and Hue. Vegetables and, once or twice a week, meat could be had from the small market at Khe Sanh. John Miller built an outhouse behind their home, to the great amusement of the Bru, who regarded it as a dirty method of elimination. For bathing there was the river at the foot of the hill. Language was not an insuperable difficulty — the Millers and a few of the Bru all spoke Vietnamese. Pastor Bui Tan Loc, a Vietnamese missionary, also sent a young fellow around to help teach the Millers Bru, but he lasted only a week or so — the VC sent word threatening his family if he continued. Once when the Millers were away, the VC came by and emptied their house, warning the Bru against them. The tribesmen convinced the VC not to burn the belongings, though, as the bonfire would have been set in the middle of their hamlet of thatched huts. When the guerrillas left, the Bru moved everything back inside. The village chief had been sleeping in different houses every night as a security precaution. Drunk, the chief one night blurted out that he was no longer afraid — the VC were after John Miller!

At that point the Huong Hoa district chief asked the Millers to stay in Khe Sanh village. Later they departed for six months in Saigon, where Carolyn gave birth to a son, Gordon. When they returned, the district chief assigned about a dozen young men to train with the Millers to become village teachers. Carolyn was preparing for the daily session one afternoon when a jeep drove up from the American Special Forces camp. Bombers were striking North Vietnam, the Hue consulate wanted the Millers out for their safety, and they had *one hour* to pack and to get to the airstrip for evacuation.

For the Millers that started a peripatetic existence — living at Hue, Saigon, traveling out of country, and finally returning. The Miller family rented the former home of Felix Poilane's aunt at the eastern end of town, just a ruin really, with no roof, doors, or woodwork, but walls three feet thick. By then Khe Sanh had become the site of an operating base for the MACV Studies and Observation Group (SOG), a very secretive special mission force, and SOG unit commander Major Fred Patton undertook to help refurbish the place. More help came from Marines when they moved into the sector. Chaplain David Meschke of the 1st Battalion, 26th Marines conducted a fundraising drive to pay for the work, which was completed during April and May 1967. John and Carolyn Miller moved into their new home in mid-May. By then Khe Sanh was a pretty active hub of pacification and special operations, with a CIDG camp at Lang Vei, the SOG base, a Marine combined action company, and a Marine combat base at the airstrip, replacing the old Special Forces camp. All this was for the purpose of conducting modern warfare among the primitive Bru.

Tribal Villagers and Lowland Vietnamese

In the beginning was Yuang Sorsi. This god created a man and a woman, who lived together in warmth and happiness, hunting wild animals and looking for fruit in the forest. So begins the Bru creation tale, which continues like a metaphor for teeming Asia. Man and Woman lived long and prospered, troubled only because they had no children. One day they met Yuang Sorsi in the woods and He promised them what they wanted.

Woman was soon with child. In fact, she gave birth to eight sons at once. Rather than achieving contentment, the parents became more troubled than before — the children gave them no peace and, as they grew, ate so much that Man and Woman were unable to support them. It was in desperation and sorrow, but with determination, that the parents took their eight sons to the high mountains and abandoned them. A hard life of misery faced the boys, but one of them finally found a beautiful and precious sword that had remarkable powers: when it was grasped securely by the handle, rain would fall; if it was held by its blade, the sun shone brightly.

The son took his sword to look for food. By the bank of a river he found a fig tree, surrounded by delicious figs being eaten by a ferocious civet cat. Starving, the boy asked the civet for food, but the cat told him he had to become a civet if he wanted to eat figs. The cat handed the boy a skin to put on, and he became a civet, sleeping in the shade of the tree.

One day a beautiful maiden came paddling along the stream in a boat, saw the civet-boy, and took him home for a pet. The girl was the daughter of Anha, the chief of the area, who shortly encountered Yuang Sorsi in the forest. God warned Anha of a coming flood and commanded him to make a boat. The chief tried to hire workers to help him, but no one believed in the flood. Anha worked alone. When the boat was finished, Anha took his family aboard — his wife, two sons, and four daughters. The youngest daughter brought her civet cat.

Yuang Sorsi commanded the civet to take his sword by the handle, not once but several times. It rained for eight days and eight nights. The water rose up to the heavens, destroying everything on earth. The fish nibbled at the stars. As the flood receded, Anha's daughter realized that her civet was really a man and fell in love with him. Her father gave permission for them to marry. At the wedding ceremony, while a buffalo roasted on the barbecue, the civet removed his disguise and threw the skins into the fire. In his place stood the handsome young man, from whom the Bru tribe would grow.

The Bru were muscular and stocky, of Malayo-Polynesian stock, their language of the Mon-Khmer group. They practiced slash and burn agriculture and, until 1965, when the Saigon government forced many to resettle in villages within a zone extending three miles on either side of Route 9, most Bru lived in isolated settlements near pure water sources.

Of the estimated forty to fifty thousand Bru, between eight and twenty thousand lived in Huong Hoa district, and another eight thousand in the vicinity of Lao Bao. An additional ten thousand or so lived farther to the east along Route 9, centered at Cam Phu. The tribe has also been known by the names Brou, Ca-Lo, Galler, Leu, Leung, Van

Kieu, and Muong Kong. An assessment by social scientists hired by the U.S. Army concluded that the Bru were "capable" fighters, defending themselves vigorously, although "the inclination of the Bru to fight aggressively is one that must be deployed and supported with modern weapons and training."

Except, perhaps, for the Green Berets, it was always a surprise to newly arriving Americans that the local people at Khe Sanh were not Vietnamese. "You mean they're different people?" one Marine lance corporal exclaimed. "I always thought they were just Vietnamese who lived in the hills, in the boonies, backwoods; I never realized they were different!"

What impressed American troops so much was the honesty of the Bru: they would say exactly what they felt. This was very different from the Vietnamese, who would not express emotions or would try to appear outwardly according to what they thought others wanted to see or hear, even among themselves. The Bru were very straightforward. Bru folklore has it that Vietnamese possess two gallbladders, one for what they really felt, the other for the face they presented to the world (for the Bru the gallbladder was the seat of emotion and thought).

The Bru believed that breaking the law upset the harmony of the world by disturbing the spirits. Indeed, the Bru lived in constant fear of spirits — of the deceased, of animals, even of places and things. They were animists by religious persuasion, as is typical of small societies. Large portions of the meager food a Bru might have would end up strewn across fields or in homes to feed, placate, or otherwise appease spirits. This practice left the Bru themselves half-starved and all the more susceptible to the myriad ravages of insects, bacteria, and microbes that infested the jungles of Khe Sanh. In the 1960s, on average, seven of ten infants died. All their physical hardships, the Bru believed, were due to their not having fed the spirits enough, or having fed the wrong ones, and the cycle would repeat itself anew.

The Bru always had a smile. Those fortunate enough to know them were invited to participate in their rituals, ceremonies, and meals. They possessed remarkable powers of observation. Colonel David Lownds, Marine commander during the siege, once marveled at the accuracy and detail of the carving of a helicopter made by a Bru boy just from seeing the craft pass overhead.

The Vietnamese who lived in this upland valley were merchants, bureaucrats, mostly people claiming to provide services to the Bru population. There were about twelve hundred lowland Vietnamese in Huong Hoa district, centered in Khe Sanh village, when the district town was abandoned in the early 1960s. They looked down on the Bru as uncultured and often became offended when they heard Americans address Bru as equals. In turn, Americans would comment that if they had to die for anyone in this forsaken land, it should be for the Bru, certainly not the Vietnamese. The Bru had no obvious cultural accomplishments, but they were friendly, hospitable, honest, kind, loyal, cheerful, resilient in adversity, and to weather, disease, and terrain; they did not steal. In Americans' memories they were a great people.

Spooks in a Spooky Place
(1965–1966)

Khe Sanh became the playground of the intelligence services as well as the locale for mobilizing the Bru montagnards into the Vietnam war. Independent agent nets were run by the district chief, the police chief, the Special Forces, and the Central Intelligence Agency. The airstrip was used for airborne reconnaissance, which involved simple spotter planes as well as craft equipped with such exotic paraphernalia as infrared detectors and side-looking airborne radar. (The latter sensed targets either by the heat they gave off or by their movement against a stationary background.) Khe Sanh also became a staging base for ground missions west and north run by such entities as the Marine 3rd Force Reconnaissance Company, the Special Forces Project DELTA, CIA's Joint Technical Advisory Detachment, and MACV's Studies and Observation Group (SOG). All these activities had different interests and responded to different chains of command. Some involved themselves in local intrigue, some in detecting signs of NVA and VC activity in the northwest, and others in monitoring the far-off Ho Chi Minh Trail.

At Fort Bragg between October 1964 and March 1965 the Special Forces provided pre-mission training for a new A detachment that then deployed to Khe Sanh. Captain Bostick was detachment commander, Master Sergeant Peter Morakon was team sergeant, and intelligence sergeant was Claude Ruhl, later replaced by Charlie Biddle. The radio men were Staff Sergeant McFadden and Sergeant Louis

Wells, the medics Sergeants O'Leary and Cobb, the weapons sergeants Higgins, Charles Black, and Al Keating. When they arrived, the new Special Forces camp was still under construction by Charlie Allen's team. Concrete bunkers and a team house (see Map 4) were going up but were not completed. In just a couple of years this Special Forces camp, on the site later to become Khe Sanh combat base, lived its full life cycle. Contrary to the beliefs of the Marines of 1967 and 1968, the ruins of bunkers on their base dated not from French colonial times but merely from their Green Beret predecessors of two years before.

The Special Forces camp consisted of corner bunkers, concrete structures on which the weapons specialists rigged makeshift rocket launchers to fire 2.75-inch rockets, many of which had been left behind by the Marine helicopters that had worked in the sector. The rockets made a great deal of noise when fired. General Lew Walt, commander of the III Marine Amphibious force (MAF), the command that corresponded to ARVN I Corps, saw the launchers during one of his inspection visits and thought they were some outlandish Army secret weapon until they were explained to him. Walt decided that the launchers were a grand idea. Following their tours, visitors like General Walt could be entertained at the camp team house, which boasted a large stone fireplace and could house pilots overnight.

The Khe Sanh airstrip was large enough to take a C-130, the four-engine transport that was the workhorse of Air Force airlift in Vietnam. Oriented roughly east to west, the strip had a slight uphill slope. The big "Herky Birds" would land at the eastern end and use the slope to help them brake, making a racket as the metal plating on the runway undulated before and behind the heavy planes as if the land were the sea. Final approach to the strip was also tricky, since immediately beyond the eastern end of the runway the land dropped off about eight hundred feet into a ravine through which flowed the Rao Quan. Into this trough the prevailing winds pushed warm moist air, which, at the edge of the strip, met the cooler air coming off the Annamites. The Air Force called it a "fog factory." Locals often asked the Americans why the strip had been located there, since the spot was frequently shrouded in clouds while other places nearby stayed clear and bright.

The mission of the Special Forces and their CIDGs at Khe Sanh was to interdict North Vietnamese resupply across the Laotian–South

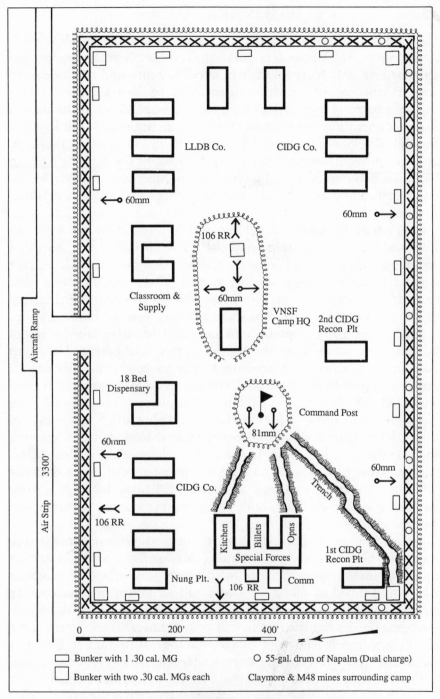

4 · Khe Sanh Special Forces Camp, 1965

Vietnamese border, provide early warning intelligence of NVA movement, and protect the local population. The camp's area of operations
stretched roughly forty kilometers north to south and twenty east to
west. Patrols would vary from three to fifteen days. Once or twice a
month a patrol would cross into Laos and visit BV-33 at Ban Houei
Sane. Cooperation was such that the Laotians organized their logistics
through Khe Sanh, frequently landing a C-47 transport at the strip,
and then moving the supplies overland across the border. The Laotian
battalion had two or three hundred troops, and Sergeant Pete Morakon recalls that they still had "their families, chickens, and everything
else" with them.

Other friendly forces in Huong Hoa in 1965 included a unit of
Regional Forces (RF), colloquially called "Ruff-Puffs" for their usual
grouping with Popular Forces (PF), descended from the CIA village
defense forces and Saigon's civil guards. The Ruff-Puffs were controlled by the district chief. There was also an ARVN artillery battery
at Lang Vei that had two American advisers, one a Marine captain.

In October 1965 Captain John D. Waghelstein replaced Captain
Bostick as commander of the Special Forces detachment. The camp
contained a platoon of thirty Nungs (Khe Sanh was the only Special
Forces camp in I Corps to have Nungs), two CIDG companies, and
an LLDB detachment of Vietnamese. Suspicions were mutual. The
Nungs worked directly for Special Forces, but the Vietnamese, in
their official capacity as camp commanders, were constantly trying
to give them orders. The LLDBs also mistreated the Bru CIDG
strikers. Americans suspected the Vietnamese special forces of being
infiltrated by the Viet Cong. At least the Bru and Nungs got on
guardedly with each other, both being oppressed minorities in South
Vietnam.

Meanwhile recon patrols reported suspicious movements in the
area. The Green Berets were running at least five agent nets at that
time and these produced more intelligence. One was of Bru agents
who could travel up along the DMZ and across the border, another
an internal net within the CIDG force in the camp, the third surrounding the district chief (who was considered a reliable source), the
fourth penetrating Khe Sanh village, and the last running to BV-33 in
Laos. Bru reported seeing the enemy near Khe Sanh. Nancy Costello,
a Wycliffe Bible translator staying at Pastor Loc's guest house, thought
the situation quite tense. Captain Waghelstein, glancing out his win-
dow the very day of his arrival, saw one of the Nungs sighting a
machine gun on the LLDB team house.

Team sergeant Pete Morakon voiced what everyone felt: "We knew it would only be a matter of time and we would get hit because we started to be a thorn in their side. We were hitting them on the trail networks."

During November, reports indicated that NVA units were no longer just passing by on their way south; the North Vietnamese had halted and had begun stockpiling supplies. In early December there was a report that four NVA battalions had entered South Vietnam about eighteen kilometers northwest of the CIDG camp. Khe Sanh was just drying out after the monsoon, which had broken at the beginning of December after socking in the camp for twenty-eight consecutive days. Captain Waghelstein doubled his patrols. Agents now indicated that two full regiments of North Vietnamese were across the border.

The better part of a North Vietnamese regiment became lost in the monsoon fog, taking the wrong fork as they crossed the border, Waghelstein surmised, because their subsequent actions seemed completely atypical. The NVA blundered into Ruff-Puffs guarding a small village, overran them, and then constructed antiaircraft positions in the surrounding hills. The positions were spotted the next day when the fog temporarily lifted, and they were immediately hit by fixed-wing air strikes. Waghelstein then sent a sixty-five-man patrol to skirt the border and attempt to locate the North Vietnamese. The patrol heard Chinese voice transmissions on their radio, but fog restricted visibility to less than forty meters and they saw nothing.

On December 23 a local told Waghelstein that a VC propaganda team was holding a meeting at one of the coffee plantations, so an eight-man squad was sent to investigate. They heard muffled shots and the sound of a man running toward the CIDG camp but could see nothing in the fog. Soon after, a Bru striker came back to report enemy soldiers in gray uniforms on the plantation. Waghelstein diverted his big patrol north of the camp and used it and the CIDG squad as arms of a pincer to snare the adversary. Just then the fog began to dissipate, and within thirty minutes the patrol had made contact. In a battle almost two hours long, forward air controllers were able to direct artillery and air strikes with some success.

Strikers found thirty-two enemy dead, one of them thought to be a Chinese adviser. The North Vietnamese had seemed as green as grass, and it turned out that all the bodies sported fresh haircuts. Their abandoned equipment was brand new, much of it still packed in Cosmoline.

Though the NVA fled, apparent victory did not end the matter.

Captain Waghelstein soon received reports that the North Vietnamese were returning to the area with 120mm mortars carried by elephants. On Christmas Day Nancy Costello had been invited to dinner at the Poilanes'. Instead, that morning she was summoned to the CIDG camp for her own protection. At a higher command level, III MAF decided to send a Marine engineer platoon to Khe Sanh to help improve the camp defenses.

Khe Sanh very soon received reinforcements. On January 3, 1966, another company of Nungs came to augment the garrison. Shortly thereafter arrived two Air Force O-1 Bird Dog observation planes, which were supposed to initiate local activity for Project TIGER-HOUND, an air reconnaissance effort General Westmoreland intended to aggressively smell out the North Vietnamese. The Bird Dogs would observe enemy movements up to twelve miles inside Laos and call in Air Force, Marine, or Navy fighter-bombers. If a fixed target was considered sufficiently lucrative and William Sullivan, U.S. ambassador to Laos, concurred, Westmoreland could send in B-52 strikes as well.

The Vietnamese special forces commander of Khe Sanh camp held formation in the evening, typically delivering a harangue just before supper. During formation the strikers, their American advisers, and the LLDB team would be concentrated in a small part of the camp. The Vietnamese commander persisted in doing this at the same time of day. Just at dusk on January 3 the LLDB officer was dismissing the formation when three 120mm mortar shells exploded on the parade ground. It was the heaviest ordnance the North Vietnamese had yet used in the war.

Counterbattery fire proved impossible. The NVA had put their mortars just outside the range of Khe Sanh's 81mm mortars. Moreover, though the calculated enemy site was within range of the ARVN 105mm howitzers at Lang Vei, those guns could not actually be used at that range because they lacked recoil pits that would allow them high angle fire. The defenders could do little more than scramble for cover in their bunkers.

After hitting the formation, the North Vietnamese shifted fire in an effort to hit the bunkers. Soon they struck the big team house where, because it was the coldest part of the year, a fire was always burning. A mortar shell blew out the fireplace and set the entire structure ablaze, thereafter providing all the illumination the NVA could have desired. Communications specialist McFadden kept up contact with the outside until pulled from the burning rubble and sent to the medical center.

The medical center was in a large underground bunker once used for ammunition storage (and destined to become combat operations center for Khe Sanh during the 1968 siege). By now there were thirteen killed and fifty or sixty wounded, some of whom had lost limbs. Team senior medic, Sergeant Cobb, happened to be in Da Nang that day, leaving Sergeant Robinson plus missionaries Nancy Costello and Eugenia Johnson to face the emergency. Four young Bru women also served as nurses. Their work was well done: of twelve or fourteen wounded who were evacuated by helicopter from the camp, only one died. The Marine medevac helicopters, called "Ridgerunners," began to land about midnight inside the camp, with no assistance other than the light from the burning team house.

The shelling eventually died out and the NVA made off. Morning brought clear skies, continuation of air strikes, and another Nung company, the I Corps Mobile Strike (MIKE) Force. The LLDB camp commander then had two companies of CIDG strikers and two of Nungs, plus the platoon of Nungs regularly assigned to Khe Sanh.

Riposte for the shelling and the other operations around Khe Sanh that December and January did not come cheap for the North Vietnamese either. On January 17 the Defense Intelligence Agency reported that an NVA unit had had to move two hundred wounded from a point six miles south of the DMZ to a tunnel complex containing a hospital about six miles west of it.

Meanwhile Project TIGERHOUND, using four pilots and two planes, began operations out of Khe Sanh and received credit for locating numerous North Vietnamese units. Its first major loss occurred on March 15, 1966, when detachment commander Lieutenant Colonel David H. Holmes was lost inside Laos. Special Forces prepared a rescue operation, but it was canceled by higher headquarters. Holmes was later presumed dead.

Of the local planters, the Poilanes were considered trustworthy but Llinarès was believed to have questionable motives, at least by Minh, Captain Waghelstein's intelligence agent handler. One night, during an operation from Khe Sanh, Llinarès was seen on the road alone at about two in the morning. Shortly afterward a patrol of VC or NVA were reported in the same area. Nothing could be done, however, and Llinarès professed to hold no love for the North Vietnamese. Eventually, before the siege, he left the area voluntarily.

After the cleanup and rebuilding from the mortar attack, life at Khe

Sanh regained a semblance of normality. Two of the Green Berets were usually in Da Nang acquiring supplies and delivering paperwork that had to be hand carried. Coming from the uplands made acquiring supplies by barter easier: the Special Forces men were always careful to take with them crossbows, spears, and baskets made by the Bru at Khe Sanh, and they might also have exotic weapons inherited by the CIDG while working for "somebody else" (CIA). There were always rear-echelon people willing to trade broken lots of beer or soda for such items. The camp commander returned to Khe Sanh from one trip with an ambulance full of fresh food, a variation for Khe Sanh strikers who depended on the local economy.

Despite its remoteness, a trickle of prominent visitors could always be found at the Khe Sanh camp. During this period, besides Generals Lew Walt and William Westmoreland, visitors included journalist Joe Alsop, actors Hugh O'Brien, who played Wyatt Earp on television, and Raymond Burr, who portrayed Perry Mason, plus Father Stroud, the chaplain of the 5th Special Forces Group, who liked to accompany his men on operations.

There were basically five valley or plateau approaches to the Special Forces camp or, seen another way, five sally ports for the CIDG strikers leading into the North Vietnamese hinterland. That every approach crossed twisted and tortuous terrain was a measure of this inhospitable land (see Map 2). One avenue followed a stream valley, a tributary of the Rao Quan, that entered South Vietnam about eighteen kilometers northwest of the camp; a trail that paralleled this route led onto the plateau north of Ta Cong and the CIDG camp. A second approach followed the ridge line through the valley between Hills 881 North and South; here too was a convenient trail. The most obvious approach was almost due west along Route 9 itself. One could also approach from the north and east, following the Khe Xa Bai river valley to a point just north of Hill 558. Finally, from the southwest, one could follow the Da Krong valley past Lang Vei to its intersection with Route 9. Patrols and other maneuvers on both sides used all these approaches at one time or another, and this lay of the land would exert a marked influence on MACV dispositions in the Khe Sanh sector at the time of the siege.

Meanwhile, the traces of past conflict seemed ever present. Like an archeology of death, digging a trench or bunker occasionally yielded a human skull. Excavation for a bunker on one of the hills uncovered a mass grave site, in which perhaps hundreds of the enemy had been entombed in their cave shelter by an air strike. On other occasions patrols encountered plane or helicopter wreckage, pieces of bomb assemblies, footprints, pieces of plastic. There was the occasional North Vietnamese bunker or antiaircraft position, sometimes a canister with odd Chinese markings, once an old French minefield near Lang Vei. Always there was a sense of presence. One became aware that others had been here, perhaps recently. But who, and how many, remained a mystery.

Virginia (1966)

The first large-scale American infantry operation in the Khe Sanh sector was a Marine Corps sweep code-named VIRGINIA. Carried out between April 17 and May 1, 1966, VIRGINIA was a search and destroy movement essentially covering the northeast approach to Khe Sanh, from Hill 558 north, with Dong Tri mountain looming on the right flank. The operation occurred at the instigation of General Westmoreland who, more than III MAF commanders, suspected the North Vietnamese of massing for attacks in the northwest corner of South Vietnam.

Intelligence painted very different pictures at Saigon, MACV headquarters, and Da Nang, headquarters of the Marine Amphibious Force. Experts at MACV postulated a significant and growing threat to the entire DMZ: the NVA 324-B Division moving from the Ha Tinh region of North Vietnam to positions just above the zone, creating a new Tri-Thien-Hue Military Region, its name taken from Quang Tri and Thua Thien provinces, which included Hue, the former imperial capital. According to MACV, the region contained three NVA regiments and possibly a fourth. North Vietnamese infiltration was running high: 7,000 a month average from January to March 1966. Those represented only the "confirmed" movement. If the "probable" and "possible" categories were added, the monthly average stood closer to 12,500.

The picture from Da Nang looked different. North Vietnamese troops estimated in the two northern provinces were thought to consist of only two regiments; a third, the 6th NVA, was added to the order of battle holdings by intelligence (G-2) only in mid-April. In contrast to the high infiltration rates estimated at Saigon, Da Nang could point to an extremely low number for April — only 1,772 for all categories combined. The Marine command felt the arrival of the 4th Marines at Phu Bai in late March had turned the balance of forces far in its favor and attributed the sparse contact with the VC and NVA to this factor.

Then, in March, the CIDG camp at A Shau was smashed in a stiff battle with the 95th NVA Regiment. Westmoreland feared that the North Vietnamese might try to repeat that accomplishment at Khe Sanh. Saigon urged Lew Walt to conduct a battalion-size operation at Khe Sanh; III MAF at Da Nang planned such an effort, but other activities forced its postponement. Meeting with Walt at Chu Lai on March 24, Westmoreland continued to emphasize the threat in the DMZ region. Walt issued the necessary orders, and on March 27 the commander of the 3rd Marine Division, Major General Wood B. Kyle, directed the 4th Marines to deploy a battalion supported by a battery of 105mm howitzers and one of mortars to the Khe Sanh area.

Selected for the operation was the 1st Battalion, 1st Marines, with a new commanding officer, Lieutenant Colonel Van D. Bell, Jr. Bell flew up to the CIDG camp and met Captain Waghelstein. He thought the strikers looked very nervous and heard that the Americans were not patrolling but were leaving that function to the Nungs and the Vietnamese LLDB. The Marine official history quotes Bell:

> Surprisingly, the Special Forces commander believed their reports. . . .
> During the [intelligence] briefing, I was shown the enemy contact pro-
> file and it appeared they had the Special Forces camp surrounded.

This is fantasy, according to Waghelstein, who reports that he informed the advance party of the 1st Battalion that if they really wanted to find the NVA they should operate to the south of Route 9, since CIDG patrols had scoured the valleys to the north during February and March, destroying the resupply points and way stations they had found. Patrols had also covered areas east, northeast, north, northwest, and west of Khe Sanh, according to Waghelstein, who notes that operation VIRGINIA was "based on someone's intel[ligence], not mine!"

As for Americans patrolling, Waghelstein and others insist the standard procedure was to have at least two Special Forces men with each patrol. This was indeed Special Forces practice throughout Vietnam; it is doubtful that the standard would have been ignored at Khe Sanh or that Special Forces would have depended on ARVN patrol leaders for their information.

In any case, Colonel Bell's order on April 5 provided for a sweep north of Khe Sanh, within range of the 105mm howitzers. His advance guard, consisting of one rifle company, logistics personnel, and the battalion executive officer, arrived on April 4. Then followed more than a week's delay as bad weather and a South Vietnamese political crisis made operations impossible. Deployment resumed on April 17, only to be halted again by weather when about half the Marines had arrived. The lift was completed the following day.

Bell had the cooperation of an ARVN battalion that blocked off the southeast quadrant, while his own troops carried out a three-phase effort. He planned for the 1st Battalion to probe the northeast first, then the northwest, then finally the southwest. But after searching to the northwest, the second phase of VIRGINIA was canceled and the third was never carried out; they were supplanted by the idea that the battalion should *march* out of Khe Sanh, *east* along Route 9 to the lowlands. "It was territory hitherto untouched by the war," wrote the 3rd Marine Division intelligence officer, while III MAF's operations staff officer, Colonel John R. Chaisson, thought the move was a touch of "bravado" so that Bell could do things "a little differently from anyone else up there."

Bell, whose inevitable sobriquet was "Ding Dong," prepared for the walk out by setting up a fire base at Ca Lu with three 105mm howitzers and a security force. The only trouble arose with a recalcitrant ARVN company attached to the force. In all of operation VIRGINIA only one shot was fired at the Marines.

The walk out said little about the North Vietnamese but a good deal about Route 9, reflected vividly in the report of chaplain John J. Scanlon:

> We started our hike at midnight and really, it was so dark (no moon) that you couldn't see your hand in front of you . . . when the column stopped, usually we ran into one another. We sweated profusely and we drank water and ate salt profusely. It had been anticipated that we would reach our first checkpoint by dawn and pick up rations flown. The territory proved tougher than expected and by mid-afternoon we were still heading for the checkpoint. . . . The path we had been following had been a road large enough for cars some twenty years earlier and we did see traffic signs which looked rather ludicrous since they were now practically in the middle of the jungle. Bridges over scenic

chasms gave mute evidence of past hostility since some of them had
been blown by charges and were just hanging on by a few inches of steel
over concrete bases. This was the first time an allied force had been
through here since the defeat of the French many years ago.

Before it was over Scanlon had gone nearly hysterical from heat ex-
haustion. One of the lieutenants later told him that one of the Rao
Quan crossings (Route 9 crosses this stream several times) so scared
him that it was his worst moment in Vietnam.

Lack of contact with the NVA was interpreted as their absence.
Reporting that they had found no trails, the Marines felt that no major
enemy units had been in the area for months. Radar indications were
now evaluated as elephants in the jungle, while infrared emissions
were interpreted as Bru engaged in burning off the jungle for farmland
with fires that continued at night.

It is tempting to suspect that the Marine higher command did not
want to find North Vietnamese at Khe Sanh. There are other possibilities as well, none of them auguring very well for American chances
in the war. The VIRGINIA fiasco could simply reflect such antago-
nisms as existed between Marines and Special Forces. Alternatively, it
might be that the plans had already been made for the operation with
little room for flexibility or that there was little trust in the word of
local commanders who supposedly did not have the big picture. A
further possibility is that the plans for VIRGINIA exhibited the dis-
dain shown by operations staffs for the intelligence function. In Vietnam arrangements for operations often represented what G-3 (operations) staffs wanted to do, regardless of what the intelligence was.
Discussion would be stifled because, in addition to everything else,
operations staff officers frequently outranked their counterparts in
intelligence.

Whatever the explanation, operation VIRGINIA miscarried. The
North Vietnamese were out there, in numbers, though no one knew
what they were doing or where they might appear next. The fear of
what the North Vietnamese *might* do, the desire to find out what they
were doing, and the wish to obstruct their activities drove a great
many MACV and Marine actions over the succeeding two years.

CHAPTER 3

"One of the Busiest Places Around" (1966–1967)

RECONNAISSANCE MISSIONS IN THE ENVIRONS of Khe Sanh increased as the Americans perceived the growing threat to the CIDG camp there. On September 26, 1966, a MACV intelligence report, pinpointing an NVA troop concentration and base camp fourteen kilometers northeast of Khe Sanh, crystallized a debate between Saigon and Da Nang over the defense of this mountain plateau of twelve square kilometers.

It was in 1966 that Marines came to the DMZ region in a big way. Their plans centered on the lowlands, however, where they fought big battles south of the DMZ and established strong points near Dong Ha and in the Annamite foothills at a place they called the Rockpile. Fighting for the coastal plain made sense to III MAF. That was where the population was, where hearts and minds stood to be gained. Relatively sophisticated in their approach to pacification, the Marines put great emphasis on population control and pioneered the use of American-Vietnamese combined units for village security. These units, called combined action companies (CACs), featured small groups of Marines who provided leadership to village units that otherwise might have been lackluster Ruff-Puffs. General Walt accepted that Vietnam was a "strange war" and was prepared to adopt a "strange strategy" to pursue it. He stood foursquare behind the CAC program. The basic concept was that the large Marine units and the ARVN of I Corps would provide a screen behind which the combined action companies could take root.

A large unit war in western Quang Tri province would have vitiated much of this strategy, drawing Marines away from the population they regarded as the primary objective. A finding that North Vietnamese were around Khe Sanh in strength could have led to such a diversion. These factors structured III MAF perceptions at the time of VIRGINIA and continued to form the basis for Lew Walt's debate with MACV.

"When you're at Khe Sanh, you're not really anywhere," said Brigadier General Lowell E. English on one occasion. Assistant commander of the 3rd Marine Division, English at least could not be accused of not having the big picture. "It's far away from everything," English said of Khe Sanh. "You could lose it and you really haven't lost a damn thing."

William C. Westmoreland saw things differently. For him Khe Sanh was the base for the TIGERHOUND reconnaissance planes and many of the SOG missions into Laos. Moreover, as Westmoreland puts it, "I still hoped some day to get approval for a major drive into Laos to cut the Ho Chi Minh Trail, in which case I would need Khe Sanh as the base for the operation." Thus the MACV commander believed in an absolute requirement to hold Khe Sanh, while the III MAF leaders believed that defense of that sector depended on developments on the coastal plains.

As the days wore on, intelligence accumulated that the North Vietnamese too had an active interest in the area. One prisoner interrogation yielded information that NVA authorities were creating a bicycle trail through the Laotian panhandle. The prisoner maintained that since June 1966 seventy to a hundred bicycles a day were being pushed along this route, underneath overhead camouflage. For its part Khe Sanh Special Forces camp reported the presence of the NVA 312th Division fifteen kilometers to the north and the 320th Division to the east between Khe Sanh and the Rockpile. According to this report, each NVA formation had a hundred Chinese advisers. Marine headquarters at Da Nang considered the latter improbable. The Defense Intelligence Agency reported on September 22 that "possible" elements of the NVA 324-B Division or other unidentified units had been reorganizing near Khe Sanh about a week before.

The 3rd Marine Division had direct responsibility for reinforcing Khe Sanh if it came under attack, and on September 14 it issued Operations Plan 415-66 to cover relief of the Special Forces camp. The plan anticipated that the isolation of Khe Sanh would permit the VC or NVA to prepare detailed attack plans and marshal substantial forces over a relatively long period of time and to ambush relief forces and interdict helicopter landing zones. The plan also stated that "attacks are most likely to occur during periods of low visibility when our air support capabilities are restricted" and that "survival of the camps is dependent upon early detection of a threat, or the speed with which artillery, air, and/or ground support can be rendered." At the time there were exactly four (ARVN) 105mm howitzers in the Khe Sanh area, two of them temporarily at the airstrip and two at Lang Vei with an ARVN rifle battalion.

Reconnaissance was to be the first line of defense. If so, that source had already turned up some disturbing indications. The Marines employed four combined CIA–Vietnamese teams of the Joint Technical Advisory Detachment. These groups fed material to teams of an officer and two enlisted men, with liaison assigned to both 1st and 3rd Marine Divisions.

Agent reports repeatedly mentioned sightings in the northwest, just below the DMZ, to the extent that III MAF requested a heavy strike by B-52 bombers. Also in this area, a Marine fighter-bomber pilot of VMFA-323 saw an obviously well traveled road with a trench line and numerous gun positions adjacent to it. Bomb craters had been converted into gun emplacements. Although rating its information and source relatively poorly, Quang Tri district passed along a report that a full division of Viet Cong was in the area. Other estimates raised the bidding as high as *two* VC divisions; but these reports were judged very poor as to both source and content. The CIDG camp itself reported a regiment of the NVA 324-B Division at one of the supposed VC locations, raising further suspicions regarding the adversary.

The intelligence led to crystallization of differences between Generals Westmoreland and Walt. Fearing that the North Vietnamese intended to mount a major offensive in the northern I Corps area, Westmoreland directed the Marines to war game the possibility. He came to Da Nang in September to review the results. In their simulation, III MAF had retracted outlying positions such as Khe Sanh and then held a front in the Annamite foothills around the Rockpile.

According to John Chaisson, then III MAF operations officer, Westmoreland observed, "I notice you haven't made any comment about putting a force in Khe Sanh. What's your reason for this?"

"We think it would be too isolated," Marine officers replied. "We think it would be too hard to support." The NVA could easily sever Route 9 while the weather shut down operations to a great extent during the October through February monsoons.

"Nevertheless," the MACV commander shot back, "I think we ought to have a larger force out there." Westmoreland proposed at least one battalion at Khe Sanh.

Operations officer Chaisson notes that Walt and his staff remained doubtful: Khe Sanh was just too remote. "We didn't want a force isolated out there, not a force that size . . . because you had to hold those outlying hills with something. Then you wouldn't have that much back in the valley. . . . Our only previous experience with that type of an attack was in the A Shau valley, when they had hit the A Shau camp. . . . It didn't stand much of a chance. They ran over it pretty easily. We didn't think that a battalion was a large enough force to hold Khe Sanh, and we thought that the force might be too large for us to sustain out there with anything but a very, very serious effort."

Of his frequent visits to Marine headquarters at Da Nang, Westmoreland himself notes, "I gained the impression that the Marines in their supreme self-confidence, however admirable that might be, were underestimating the enemy's capabilities."

Almost simultaneously, on September 27, came another sighting report that probably dotted the *i* for MACV. A SOG patrol found a North Vietnamese base camp *inside* the DMZ almost due north of the CIDG camp. Recon men saw a company or so of NVA eating under jungle canopy. The troops wore dark green uniforms with packs, cartridge belts, canteens — full field equipment — and they were armed with Soviet-bloc AK-47 assault rifles and old French MAS-36 bolt action rifles.

Westmoreland concluded that there was going to be a massive offensive in the northern provinces, and he told Lew Walt that Khe Sanh was the likely target of a North Vietnamese attempt to repeat Dien Bien Phu, their climactic victory over the French that had ended the first Indochinese war. Westmoreland directed III MAF to improve the Khe Sanh airstrip so it could handle C-130s in all weather conditions and to restudy North Vietnamese capabilities. He might have gone further but lightened up once General Walt agreed, after all, to post a battalion to Khe Sanh.

The MACV commander also argued his case with Walt's Marine boss, Lieutenant General Victor Krulak, chief of the Fleet Marine

Force Pacific, and with the overall Pacific commander, West-moreland's boss, Admiral U. S. Grant Sharp, the Commander-in-Chief Pacific. To "Oley" Sharp on September 29 Westmoreland sent a cable claiming that "unprecedented rapid buildup of enemy forces in areas along entire length of DMZ presages initiation of coordinated massive attacks." Concluding, he argued that "it appears that a unique opportunity exists to break the back of the [NVA] 324B and 341 Divisions by application of massive combat power if attack occurs."

Although he acquiesced to a superior's desire to send a Marine detachment to Khe Sanh, the fifty-three-year-old Lewis William Walt was by no means convinced by Westmoreland's insistence. A native Kansan who had been a football star at Colorado State, had won two Navy Crosses and a Silver Star in the Pacific in World War II, and had gone on to Korea, Lew Walt was no stranger to tight situations. He had been through the worst of Guadalcanal, New Britain, Peleliu, and the endless hill war in Korea. As Walt looked at the amount of pa-trolling his III MAF Marines were doing and at the sparse contacts with the NVA and VC, he read the reports of North Vietnamese around Khe Sanh as a routine enemy measure. As late as December 1966 Walt argued in a top secret letter to another general that "far too much emphasis" was being placed on the importance of the infiltration threat and that "with few exceptions" infiltration came from north of the DMZ, not from Laos, so that "we should not fall into the trap of expending troops unduly seeking to prevent the entry of individuals and units who pose the lesser threat to our ultimate objective."

For Lew Walt, "my conviction [is] that our primary enemy here remains the guerrilla." The North Vietnamese Army was not native to the area, could not submerge among the people, and so "cannot qualify as a full fledged guerrilla." The III MAF commander insisted that "we beat these [NVA regular] units handily each time we en-counter them."

Lew Walt thought he understood something about Asia and the war in Vietnam. He had first witnessed combat as a platoon leader in the 4th Marines, guarding the International Settlement in Shanghai at the height of the Sino-Japanese war. That conflict, which the Japanese styled an "incident" in their effort to pretend it was not a war, had much in common with Vietnam. The masses of China, not to say the eleven siblings in his family, had taught Walt something about politics, about the contest for hearts and minds that became so important in Vietnam. Westmoreland talked about pacification, but his heart was really in the big unit war.

Though the generals' differences remained, Westmoreland had one thing Walt lacked: four stars. Westmoreland's desires became strategy, and Lew Walt sent a battalion to Khe Sanh. Walt also asked Krulak to accelerate arrival of the 3rd Force Reconnaissance Company and planned for more SOG patrols and, beginning October 15, for six teams from Special Forces Project DELTA. Meanwhile, additional support would become available around the end of September when four 175mm guns of Battery C, 6th Battalion, 27th Artillery were scheduled to move into position at Camp Carroll south of the DMZ, the first significant Army unit to serve in combat in northern I Corps, hitherto a Marine preserve. Finally, Da Nang took the various North Vietnamese sighting reports and plotted eighteen ARC LIGHT contingency strikes, bombings to be carried out by huge B-52 aircraft from very high altitude.

Perhaps the point on which Walt and Westmoreland most agreed was what to do about Laos. Lew Walt used to say that he begged and pleaded for permission to invade that country, and we have already seen Westmoreland's interest in that very project. It was at this time that MACV began detailed planning for such an invasion, asking III MAF in late September 1966 for critical information: the status of Route 9 from Dong Ha to the Laotian border, with trafficability stated in maximum vehicle size for each section, specific segments passable for nonmotorized vehicles and foot traffic, flooding information, and map coordinates of road cuts and downed bridges that could impede traffic. The key tipoff that Laos was under consideration came when MACV requested material on the Xe Pone river, which formed part of the border itself and then ran south of Route 9 toward Tchepone.

Meanwhile III MAF headquarters, as instructed, did its comparison of Khe Sanh and Dien Bien Phu. The resulting area report noted many similarities and no substantial differences, save perhaps that Khe Sanh had good drainage whereas much of Dien Bien Phu had become flooded during the rainy season. A significant difference *not* noted was that at Dien Bien Phu, for all their tactical disadvantages, the French had had a stream running through the middle of their camp and water purifiers to exploit that source. At Khe Sanh, American water parties had to visit the Rao Quan in its deep ravine to bring water up to the rest of the troops.

Marines Come to Khe Sanh
(1966)

General Westmoreland evinced great concern for the speed with which Khe Sanh could be prepared for the mass offensive he expected. As he recounts it, "I . . . ordered the U.S. Navy's Seabees to begin a crash program to upgrade the air strip at Khe Sanh . . . a project I saw as a race against time, both because of approaching *crachin* weather and of possible enemy attack." This assignment went to Chief Petty Officer Shannon G. McMillen and sixty-five teammates of Naval Mobile Construction Battalion 10, who arrived from Da Nang on September 10.

Theirs was not an easy task. It amounted to replacing all 3,300 feet of the World War II–vintage heavy steel matting, substituting newer, lighter aluminum plating called AM-2. In addition they were supposed to extend the strip by three hundred feet at each end, building from scratch, and add an airfield parking apron. The large C-130s bringing in bundles of the AM-2 plating repeatedly damaged plates already laid, though the Herky Birds also were not quite big enough for some of the equipment the Seabees needed for the task. Thus heavy earthmoving equipment was so scarce that when Seabees Kenny Schiwart and Thomas "Shorty" Stuart learned that, for some six months, a bulldozer had lain abandoned about thirty kilometers from Khe Sanh, they wanted to mount a mission to rescue the machine. Special Forces sent a patrol of two Americans plus a dozen CIDG strikers to accompany the Seabees. All helicoptered into the area, which was considered infested with Viet Cong. The Seabees patched a bullet hole in the fuel tank, made other repairs, and had the dozer purring within a half hour. The patrol drove it back to Khe Sanh, fording the Rao Quan three times on the way.

"You can't let a beautiful hunk of equipment like that just sit and rot out there," said Shorty Stuart. After scratching the stubble on his chin Stuart continued, "Can you imagine how much more work we can get done now that we have that thing here!"

The task remained an immense one to accomplish in the twenty-two days allotted under the schedule. The job just couldn't be done with McMillen's original Seabee force. On September 24 Navy Lieutenant Donald Woodford flew in to become officer-in-charge, bringing nineteen more construction men. Another thirty-two Seabees ar-

rived on the last day of September. Work was delayed several days by
deployment of the long-awaited Marine battalion, and then on October 4 Khe Sanh received the last of 1,385 bundles of AM-2 matting.
Seabees closed the airstrip all the next day and installed it. The last of
the work was done in cold driving rain.

Mobile Construction Battalion 10 rightfully believed its personnel
"gave every last bit of their strength, ingenuity, and resourcefulness to
surmount obstacles to do a job." General Westmoreland added an
official accolade in an October 18 message to the Vietnam naval
commander:

> I have been impressed with the rapid and highly professional job done
> by the MCB 10 in designing and constructing the all-weather C-130
> capable airfield at Khe Sanh. There is no more important airfield in
> Vietnam from a tactical standpoint than Khe Sanh. MCB 10 has
> performed a timely and important service to the fighting troops in
> Vietnam. The airfield was constructed under the most difficult circum-
> stances since the weather was marginal and the threat of enemy attack
> ever present.

Twenty-two Seabees stayed to build personnel facilities. Another
twenty-two-man detachment from MCB-7 also came in October to
construct six concrete bunkers for the defenders of Lang Vei.

"I later wondered," Westmoreland wrote in his memoir, "why the
North Vietnamese made no effort to interfere with that construction
and could only deduce that they wanted to let it proceed in the hope
that eventually they could use the air strip themselves." The notion
that the North Vietnamese, with a minuscule air force, would be able
to use the field in the face of the literally thousands of aircraft and
gunships in the U.S. and South Vietnamese forces is ridiculous on the
face of it. The more likely conclusion is that the NVA lacked either the
intention or the capability to mount the mass offensive MACV feared.

In any case, the mission of the first Marine unit to deploy to Khe
Sanh was directly linked to the airfield. Platoon and company commanders were told that "we were going up there to be the protective
cordon around the Special Forces camp. We were to protect the vital
intelligence-gathering activities and protect the airfield complex during its repair." The unit was Lieutenant Colonel Peter A. Wickwire's
1st Battalion, 3rd Marines. It got only twelve hours' notice for the
move. Short-timers openly wept, and sick call was suddenly very
crowded. "I am confident the walls of Jericho collapsed amid less
confusion," chaplain George R. Witt recalled, "but we made it."

After their short flight from the coast, the Marines reached Khe Sanh in the late afternoon of September 29. It was difficult to tell whether the Marines or the Green Berets were the more dejected. The Marines had to clear campsites for themselves, in an area covered with tall elephant grass. Much of their work had to be done that very night, when it became so dark each man had to put his hands on the man in front of him to keep oriented. The area that D Company cleared, just west of the CIDG camp, was called "the Ponderosa," a name that remained in use through the 1968 siege.

The battalion began to patrol within a circle of 10,000 meters' radius of the CIDG camp, essentially the range of a 105mm howitzer. In fact, four Marine guns of that type arrived during the first week of October. This support was augmented by a detachment of two 155mm guns and later, in November, by a detachment of two 4.2-inch mortars. Once the 155mm guns arrived, patrols were expanded to their range of 15,000 meters' radius.

Contact with the North Vietnamese was light but real. Company A, manning an outlying position about a kilometer northwest of the CIDG camp, reported contacts or received a few rounds of small arms fire or grenades daily from October 7 to 9. Colonel Wickwire's headquarters and support company, manning part of the battalion perimeter, was the target of three grenades on October 14. "We never worked much outside the artillery fan," George O'Dell recalls. "They stayed pretty much outside that. On some other patrols, we discovered hospitals . . . you knew they were out there."

The Marines' misery began with the onset of the monsoon on October 17. Chaplain Witt later reported: "I believe that along with combat pay, there should be 'monsoon pay.' Even Noah would complain. Everyone gained about twenty pounds due to wet utilities [field uniforms] and muddy boots. Sure, those utilities dry out fast — in the Canal Zone maybe but not at Khe Sanh." The rain even drove the rats inside. Colonel Thomas M. Horne, formerly intelligence officer for the 3rd Marine Division, came to Khe Sanh as commander of the Marine task force there with the title Senior Officer Present, Khe Sanh/III MAF Representative, and the radio handle "Franchise Rep." While the Vietnamese coastal plain sweltered, Horne found average temperatures of forty degrees Fahrenheit at Khe Sanh. During December and January, he estimates, there were only six days when the weather was good enough for air support.

Under the circumstances Air Force transports did pretty well, delivering more than 75 tons of cargo to Khe Sanh during December.

Marine transport aircraft brought in 637 tons plus a thousand passengers. *Crachin*, the soupy mixture of cloud and fog that covered hills and jammed the valleys every morning, created problems too. During the first weeks of January the winds were a constant 20–25 mph with gusts to 40–45 mph, and high cross winds closed Khe Sanh to aircraft even on days otherwise flyable.

The logistics people were never able to attain their goal of a fifteen-day stockpile of all types of supplies. Instead stocks of food and fuel occasionally fell to less than one day's consumption.

Poor supply and bad weather meant misery. Clothing rotted. Web gear rotted. The wet soil became unstable and dugouts collapsed. Roads became impassable to trucks — a major problem given the need to descend to the Rao Quan for water. Luckily the Marines of the 3rd Motor Transport Battalion brought tracked M-76 "Otters" to Khe Sanh and these found the going better. Hauling tank trailers up and down with the precious fluid, the Otters soon became known as "water buffaloes." Unfortunately there was a limited supply of spare parts for the Otters and, as the rains continued, even they found the ravine slopes impossible to negotiate. The solution was a pump and pipe system capable of drawing water from the stream and pushing it up ninety feet over eight hundred feet distance.

Meanwhile Colonel Horne presided over a constant program of emplacement of what became the Khe Sanh combat base (KSCB). During November Marines built a double apron barbed wire fence, laying 134,000 feet of regular wire and another 22,000 feet of concertina. That was something Colonel Horne had seen a good deal of, from the opposite side, as a tank officer in the 4th Marine Division during the assaults on Kwajalein, Saipan, Tinian, and Iwo Jima in World War II.

Tom Horne had been a Texas oilman by trade, working for Humble Oil before and after the war. Pressed for officers at the height of the Korean war, when Horne was a reserve captain running an oil rig off the Louisiana shore, the Marine Corps had offered him a commission as a regular major. Horne had spent a year in Korea, several more at Marine Corps headquarters, and then a year at language school learning Russian. In 1960 Major Horne had been sent to Moscow as assistant naval attaché. He returned in 1963 to senior officers school at Quantico, and then commanded the tank battalion at Camp Lejeune until he made colonel. In June 1966 he went to South Vietnam. Khe Sanh was Colonel Horne's most vital Vietnam field assignment. "My memory of that place," he recalls, "is waking up with fifteen or twenty rats on the bed with me!"

As senior officer at Khe Sanh, Horne was responsible for coordination of CIDG patrols, the reconnaissance program, and the nascent pacification effort, featuring three combined action platoons the Marines soon sent to Khe Sanh. Relations with Special Forces Detachment A-101 were especially difficult. The Marines tended to view the Green Berets as an undisciplined rabble, while Special Forces saw the Jar Heads as a collection of clumsy, overarmed, overheavy units who would never be able to cope with the VC and NVA. Mistakes were inevitable. On one occasion a CIDG patrol came under Marine fire by mistake. Another time the Marines held their fire, assuming that a group of about twenty Vietnamese who were passing them were strikers. It turned out that Special Forces had had no one in the area at the time.

Special Forces also felt their own operations were especially classified and therefore did not always inform Horne of them. At this time the Green Berets' attention was increasingly being diverted toward the west, to what was happening along the border and with the Laotian 33rd Volunteer Battalion. Bill Steptoe, team sergeant of A-101 at the time, says of BV-33: "They were playing both sides of the fence — I know for a fact." Special Forces spotted what they thought were Russians and Chinese in addition to NVA right around the Laotian army checkpoint. Once a CIDG patrol was ambushed at this location. Detachment executive officer Lieutenant Stallings called in fire from a 4.2-inch mortar, smashing a village thought to have given information to the North Vietnamese.

Reacting to their failure to fire at an enemy mistaken for CIDG strikers, the Marines told Special Forces they would shoot at anything that moved near the Khe Sanh combat base. For their part, Special Forces felt itself at a disadvantage trying to cover the border from Khe Sanh airstrip. Colonel Horne and the Special Forces finally agreed on a general redeployment. The CIDG camp moved to Lang Vei during the week just before Christmas.

From that moment the post at French Fort served as headquarters for the South Vietnamese 3rd Battalion, 2nd Infantry. Soon after Special Forces moved the CIDG camp, I Corps commander Major General Hoang Xuan Lam took the opportunity to bring his ARVN battalion back down to the coastal plain. In effect, Westmoreland's posting of a Marine battalion to Khe Sanh simply enabled ARVN to withdraw its equivalent force. Evidently the South Vietnamese did not believe in MACV's thesis of an impending enemy offensive.

The combat base absorbed the Khe Sanh CIDG camp. Facilities acquired included underground concrete living quarters, mortar pits, a mess hall, a combined intelligence center, a communications bunker, quarters for TIGERHOUND personnel, and a medical dispensary. There were also three underground timber barracks for the CIDGs, an aboveground cookhouse, and a supply building with a partial concrete floor. Some of these structures were just a few months old. The Marines were asked to preserve the permanent structures in case future movement of the 1st Battalion, 3rd Marines required the CIDG camp to move back to the airfield.

Patrols in the Wilderness

Though Lew Walt acquiesced in the dispatch of Marines to Khe Sanh, his intention remained to protect the sector through timely reconnaissance and countervailing firepower rather than deployment of a large garrison. To this end recon operations continued and were even stepped up; they would lead to some of the first American ground force combat deaths in this sector.

Da Nang hoped for and expected much from Project DELTA, scheduled to conduct its operation 13-66 from mid-October. Project DELTA was a unit formed in May 1964 with a combination of a U.S. Special Forces B detachment (B-52) and ARVN Airborne Ranger personnel. Americans trained and commanded a number of recon and "Roadrunner" teams that could find the adversary and try to maintain contact while larger reaction forces deployed to engage in combat. DELTA included its own reaction force, comprising six companies of the 81st Airborne Ranger Battalion, four of which would usually deploy in support of a DELTA operation. The concept was to discover the enemy by saturation patrolling around some central point, in this case Khe Sanh. DELTA fielded a dozen recon teams, each composed of four Green Berets and six Vietnamese special forces, and a dozen so-called Roadrunner teams, each consisting of five CIDG strikers dressed and armed to resemble Viet Cong. Attached helicopters could lift in one or more of the 128-man Ranger companies if significant contacts developed.

Major Charlie Beckwith led the Project DELTA forces that arrived at Khe Sanh on October 15, 1966. Their area of operations was to be the northwest corner of South Vietnam, from a line of four or five kilometers north of Hill 950 right up to the DMZ and from east of Khe Sanh clear to the Laotian border. After almost two weeks of familiarization and preparations, DELTA was ordered into action on October 27.

Signs of North Vietnamese presence were detected almost immediately. Roadrunner Team 102 reported finding an old bunker with an underground tunnel leading from it, plus a meter-wide trail. Members of another patrol recounted that they had evidently been detected, for their progress through the jungle was marked by unseen hands sounding bells and bullhorns from the hills to their front. When Team 104 got into a tight spot on October 30, Major Beckwith requested that III MAF hold an infantry battalion plus helicopters on standby to intervene if necessary. Da Nang responded that more precise information was required before it could take such action.

During the second phase of the DELTA operation, extending through November into December, teams discovered a large North Vietnamese supply dump. Subsequent air strikes touched off secondary explosions. On the morning of December 2, at map grid coordinates that would place the action in Laos, a UH-1D helicopter was shot down while attempting to extract recon team 1, of six men, who reported they were surrounded by a sizable enemy force with automatic weapons. This DELTA patrol met destruction: team leader Sergeant First Class Willie E. Stark was wounded and Staff Sergeant Russell B. Bott last seen giving him aid, while Sergeant Irby Dyer III was killed outright. Only LLDB team members escaped; they were spotted that afternoon about four kilometers to the southeast and were rescued by American helicopters.

The area of the contact then became the target of an ARC LIGHT strike, and a tactical air strike in this area on December 18 triggered secondary explosions.

Message traffic pertaining to the fatal DELTA patrol has apparently been removed from III MAF combat operations center records.

During the two months it operated around Khe Sanh, Project DELTA fielded an average of only one recon team daily, for patrols of four days to two weeks duration. Colonel Horne remained unhappy with this pace of activity and finally asked III MAF to deploy a detachment of the 3rd Force Reconnaissance Company, recently arrived in South Vietnam.

The Project DELTA casualties were not the first troops struck down on reconnaissance missions. That sad distinction probably belongs to MACVSOG, whose teams incurred losses during the weeks before DELTA's arrival. One team had been inserted atop Co Roc massif, across the Laotian border southwest of Khe Sanh, on July 29. Ambushed, the recon men never even had the chance to communicate, though they were in an ideal position for FM radio transmission to their launch officer at the airstrip, and an airborne command plane out of Thailand was monitoring their frequency.

Master Sergeant "Crash" Whalen led the Co Roc patrol. The sobriquet came from his propensity to fall on his head after bouts of heavy drinking at the SOG club in Da Nang, a so-called Forward Operating Base. Buddies there had built a seat belt for Whalen so he would not injure himself. At Co Roc, at least, Whalen did not need his seat belt, as he evaded the ambush, scaled a cliff, forded the Xe Pone river at a raging rapid, and made it back to Khe Sanh by himself. Teammates Sergeant First Class Delmer L. Laws and Specialist-4 Don R. Sain were not so lucky. A recovery team the next day under Master Sergeant Billie Waugh found the ambush site, Sain's body, and a leg identified as belonging to Laws.

During another patrol action on September 28 Staff Sergeant Danny Gene Taylor died just below the DMZ. On October 3 came a further disaster: a team gone missing within *fifteen minutes* of insertion. Again the action occurred just below the DMZ. The team radioed the prearranged code Blue-6, which signified they had landed and were moving away from the LZ. It was the last anyone heard from them. Billie Waugh, again the SOG launch officer at Khe Sanh, went with a "Hatchet" reaction force on a search for the three men, without success. They are still carried as Missing in Action.

Before very long Force Reconnaissance Marines were added to the reconnaissance assets operating out of Khe Sanh. It was not the first time Marine recon men had visited the place — there had been a subunit of the 1st Force Reconnaissance Company with the Green Berets in May 1965, while the 5th Platoon of that company had participated in VIRGINIA. It is tempting to speculate on the effects of permanent employment of Force Recon at Khe Sanh to obtain long-range intelligence for III MAF in accord with their recon doctrine and Marine Corps official mission. Such a course might have furnished earlier warning of NVA moves and promoted unity of command at Khe Sanh. Instead, scouting was an on-again, off-again activity by a hodgepodge of MACV, Special Forces, and Marine units that usually did not stay long enough to develop real familiarity with the area.

In any case, the 3rd Force Reconnaissance Company had been formed on June 4, 1965, at Camp Lejeune, North Carolina, from elements of the 2nd Company. A detachment of the unit arrived at Okinawa on May 25, 1966, and went to Vietnam under operational control of the 3rd Marine Division's reconnaissance battalion. Unlike that unit, which had a tactical function, Force Recon was supposed to provide strategic reconnaissance to meet III MAF requirements. Given the dispute between III MAF and MACV over the possibility of a North Vietnamese offensive at the DMZ, Khe Sanh seemed a good prospect for Force Recon operations.

When Force Recon arrived, they called the Marines of 1/3 the "orange men" for the skin tint imparted by the clay soil. Force Recon proceeded to forge much better relations with the Green Berets, now at Lang Vei, than had their Marine brothers. Kenneth D. Jordan recounts:

> As a matter of fact, we were getting Air America supplies; we'd get bourbon and cold beer and stuff like that, and they had a Vietnamese baker up there that could make jelly donuts and stuff like that that were real good, and we used to trade our stuff for his baked goods. We'd give him a bottle of bourbon for a dozen jelly donuts. There was a humorous twist on one occasion. He saw us with some yellow mustard. We had got a little can of mustard that was pretty yellow. They don't use mustard. He made some jelly donuts with mustard in them because it looked nice. It looked pretty. When we took a bite of it, it was just grotesque. He disappeared for two hours because he saw us spitting the stuff out.

East of Khe Sanh, shortly after noon on January 16, 1967, team 5-2 of the 3rd Force Recon moved out by truck to look for trails and other evidence of the adversary. After about four hours the recon team heard voices and a shot. The Marines went into a defensive formation but the noises moved away to the south. Without further incident the Marines completed their patrol on January 19; the men were picked up by helicopter. They had found Dong Chio mountain not suitable as an observation post because of the heavy foliage blanketing it.

That patrol had worked pretty well, but luck would not always be with the Marines. Sergeant Tom Willson's simultaneous patrol led to tragedy — the first Marine battle death at Khe Sanh. Willson led a seven-man team that went in on the night of January 17. Just a few hundred meters from the insertion point, as they were choosing a harbor site for the night, they heard shooting and chopping sounds. After first light the patrol searched for a place from which to survey the area. Instead, shortly after noon an NVA force of thirty or forty troops blundered into them.

At first Willson estimated that the North Vietnamese might pass them by, and he posted two men to provide security on the left flank. The NVA did pass Willson, but they saw Corporal Michael J. Scanlon, one of the flankers, and opened a brisk fire. Scanlon shouted a warning, allowing Willson to deploy the recon team for combat, and then the corporal charged, killing two NVA immediately and, after reloading, two more. At that moment, however, a fresh force of perhaps twenty North Vietnamese joined the fray, trying to envelop the American patrol. Scanlon was trapped in front of his buddies and went to the ground less than fifteen meters from the enemy. Wounded in the leg and shoulder, he continued to fire.

Corporal Clayton H. Ernst, the other Marine flanker, now tried to move up and rescue Scanlon. He threw a grenade to cover his advance but it proved to be a dud. Shot in the right forearm, Ernst had to fire his M-79 grenade launcher left-handed. He found Scanlon on his back, his chest covered with blood, dead. Trying to bring back the body, Ernst was wounded again, this time in his left arm.

Willson and others believed that Scanlon had jumped on one grenade they heard go off with a peculiar muffled roar. That may have been what killed him. When Ernst was forced to return to the Marine perimeter without Scanlon's body, team communications man Leonard S. Bessent braved heavy fire to retrieve it. Bessent and Willson, both wounded themselves, then carried Scanlon's body until they were met that afternoon by a platoon-size reaction force from 1st Battalion, 3rd Marines. Even in death, Marines try never to leave their buddies behind.

Mike Scanlon's death shocked the men of Force Recon. In life Mike had enjoyed shocking people, who were amazed that this very short (only about four feet tall) Marine could be such a tower of energy despite his mild manner. The red-haired Scanlon had been a wrestling champion in high school; in the Marines he had volunteered for diving school, wearing scuba tanks that just about dwarfed his body. In 3rd

Force Recon, Scanlon had been the butt of many practical jokes. Now he was dead. Tom Willson worried that one of his grenades had been the one that killed Scanlon. Other patrol members remain convinced it was an enemy grenade. A few years afterward Willson himself died in an aircraft accident at Camp Lejeune. Scanlon won a posthumous Silver Star, and Willson, Ernst, and Bassent were recommended for Bronze Stars.

"He cut my hair. He was my driver. I loved that little kid, I'll tell you," said Lieutenant James Capers of Scanlon. "He was just a tremendous young man. And so when he was killed I think all of us — the war came home to us."

Numerous reports, including agent reports, TIGERHOUND sightings, and side-looking airborne radar (SLAR) readouts, suggested North Vietnamese movements along the Laotian border northwest of Khe Sanh, the area of the northernmost of the approaches to the combat base. The latest of these had been SLAR indications dated January 24/25. Force Recon reacted by inserting patrol 5-2 on January 26, consisting of six men and a dog under Gunnery Sergeant Charles Homer Hopkins. Their insertion point was right on the border, about twenty kilometers northwest of the base. From there "Mad Dog" Hopkins led his patrol almost due north.

About eight hours into the mission the recon team spotted ten enemy armed with AK-47 assault rifles just fifteen meters away. The patrol waited until all the North Vietnamese bunched up nearby and then opened fire, killing all ten. That turned out to be like kicking a hornet's nest, however, for the team immediately received heavy automatic weapons fire. An estimated thirty-five or forty NVA snared the patrol in a real donnybrook. Something had also gone wrong with their navigation. As Ken Jordan notes, "I can tell you we were outside the border. At the time it was very politically sensitive, and we weren't supposed to go outside. . . . We were out there and there was a lot of high-level discussion about how to — hoping that no one would read a map."

Within twenty minutes team 5-2 knew they were in trouble, scattered in an area perhaps a hundred meters long and fifteen wide and surrounded by a growing NVA force, now estimated at 150 men. Well beyond friendly artillery support, they were at least atop a 2,300-foot-high hill and could hope for copters and fixed-wing air support. Hopkins lost no time requesting a reaction force and air cover. Two

H-34 helicopters of squadron HMM-163 launched from Khe Sanh, escorted by two UH-1E gunships of VMO-2.

Arriving over the battle area at about 6:12 P.M., only seven minutes after launch, the helicopters found the recon team completely surrounded. The escort leader asked 5-2 to mark their position with yellow smoke and the closest NVA with red. The smoke showed the enemy at only thirty meters. Told they would be picked up, the recon team replied that copters would not be able to get in, that they needed reinforcements. One chopper tried to land but was driven off by the fire.

Then the recon radio man came up on the circuit. "You're not going to leave us," he asked, "you're going to come and get us, aren't you partner?"

"Roger," the pilot replied, "we'll get you."

The helicopter came around and made an approach from the west. Again the NVA fired from three sides of the quadrant. Inside the cockpit, one .50-caliber round went between the pilot's legs and sheared the lines to the gas and hydraulic pressure gauges, spewing gasoline and hydraulic fluid over the pilot and copilot. The crew could not see the patrol, and they had lost radio contact too. The pilot, Lieutenant Robert J. Hein, Jr., lifted out of the killing zone and made a quick transit to Khe Sanh, where he executed a fine emergency landing. The copter had taken nineteen hits.

Back over the recon team the two gunships orbited, making gun and rocket runs despite the return fire. At 6:45 P.M. two more helicopters arrived, CH-46 transports of HMM-265. The lead ship was empty to attempt an extraction, the second carried a reaction force. Weather was deteriorating rapidly and, with darkness coming, it was decided to send back the reaction force. That left Captain Joseph G. Roman's bird, which made its approach following instructions of the gunships. Again yellow smoke marked the LZ.

The big CH-46 came down to the right of the recon team. Already it was taking hits. Corporal W. B. Motter, crew chief, kept firing though wounded. Both of the copter's hydraulic lines were shot out. When the Marines did not attempt to reach the ship and Captain Roman tried to lift out, it proved impossible, even with his strength combined with that of copilot Captain Jimmie E. Cook. Seconds later Roman saw the aft section of the aircraft in flames. Corporal Rolon, the gunner, grabbed the fire extinguisher and doused the fire with foam. Cook shut down the engines and engaged the rotor brake.

Roman emptied his .38-caliber revolver at four NVA who were in a fierce exchange with the recon team at thirteen to eighteen meters range and then took an AR-15 assault rifle in one hand and dragged Motter with the other to the Marine perimeter.

The Americans were not too well off. One Marine had a leg wound but lay on his belly firing. The radio man had been hit in the calf. A critically wounded recon man, hit three times, lay in the center of the perimeter. Then there was the helicopter crew chief, whose ankle had been shattered. Only seven men were capable of fighting. Captain Roman took over the radio and talked with the circling helicopters, confirming that they could not easily move and that they would need the reaction force plus a medical corpsman. Extraction seemed impossible. Flare ships, fixed-wing air support, and an airborne controller would be necessary if they were to survive.

Captain Harold J. Campbell, Jr., Roman's erstwhile wingman, returned to Khe Sanh and got permission to reembark part of the thirty-man reaction force that had been sent home. He calmly approached the LZ in the face of increasing fire, only to lose power in the last seconds of flight, managing a safe crash landing just a few yards from the recon party. Campbell salvaged two .50-caliber machine guns from the burning ship and moved uphill with his crew and the seventeen Marines of the ground element. Luckily only his crew chief, Sergeant J. D. Bunker, had been hurt in the crash.

Now a hopeless situation began to appear salvageable. The Americans expanded their perimeter, posting point men and three machine guns to cover the approaches. Fixed-wing aircraft arrived and made the first air strikes in the vicinity. Roman directed them on one radio while Campbell kept watch with another.

After dark, at about 8:30 P.M., another CH-46 came with fifteen more Marines. The pilot, Major Watson of HMM-164, was directed to land at his own discretion. Unfortunately they were unable to reach the trapped Marines. Instead, in the darkness the rotor blades hit a tree, causing this helicopter to crash land in a valley about five hundred meters to the north. Watson and his group abandoned the craft successfully, their party established radio contact with the recon party, and the North Vietnamese paid no attention to them. They were evacuated the following day.

Far to the east, the Army artillery at Camp Carroll reacted to the emergency in Laos by moving two of their big 175mm guns to Thon Son Lam, the Rockpile. With the 3rd Battalion, 3rd Marines providing ground security, they were set up to fire shortly after midnight.

On the hill the bright moonlight was supplemented by the flares from C-47 Dragonships, commonly called "Spooky" or "Puff the Magic Dragon," which also carried rotating barrel machine guns, so-called miniguns, enough to put out six thousand rounds per minute, a deadly wall of lead. The situation was complicated by a fog bank that rolled in before midnight and covered the area for approximately three hours. Captain Michael H. Clemens of VMO-2 remained overhead in his UH-1E airborne command post except for short intervals to refuel and rearm. Clemens directed at least twenty-five fixed-wing sorties that night. Aircraft participating included A-4, F-4, and F-4B fighter-bombers from squadrons VMA-211, VMFA-542, and VMFA-314 flying from Chu Lai. Roman found it impossible to estimate the number of air strikes flown during the fourteen hours he was on the ground in Laos, except that it seemed to be the entire branch of Marine Corps aviation.

Coordinating the effort from Khe Sanh was Brigadier General Michael P. Ryan, assistant commander of the 3rd Marine Division, who at the time led a task force of Marine forces in the DMZ area. It was at Khe Sanh combat base that night that a CH-46 bringing ammunition up from Dong Ha collided with a UH-1 parked off the side of the runway. Fortunately there were no casualties, although both helicopters were destroyed.

A forward air controller (FAC) came on station at 3:30 A.M. In a C-117 he was able to circle until dawn. When Roman heard whistles to the northeast at about 5:15, the FAC helped switch air strikes to that sector. The whistling persisted even after a half hour of rocket and strafing runs. After dawn the C-117 was replaced by Captain John D. Holt of squadron H&MS-16 flying an O-1 Bird Dog.

The North Vietnamese made their move at 6:15 A.M., massing for an attack from the south. Private First Class Steve A. Srsen, a reaction force Marine from the 1st Platoon of A Company, 1st Battalion, 3rd Marines, stood up and shouted a grenade warning, enabling three other Marines to take cover. Three grenades exploded, causing four casualties, including Srsen, struck by fragments in his right side and right leg. After treatment, however, Srsen returned to his position in the line.

Captain Roman, in conjunction with the FAC, now shifted air strikes to the south, but this did not prevent a second attack only five minutes after the first. Again it began with a barrage of grenades and small arms fire. One grenade landed just a few feet from Roman, wounding him in the head, Captain Campbell in the thigh, and two other Marines. Another grenade landed near Lance Corporal Gregan, who was near Srsen and was changing position. Srsen jumped up again, pushed the other Marine to the ground, and took the full force of the blast, which killed him. A counterattack halted the NVA assault. Campbell and Roman switched roles and together called air strikes only fifty meters from their own positions. Fighter-bombers rolling in on a northerly heading helped suppress the adversary. Mad Dog Hopkins and his assistant patrol leader, Staff Sergeant David A. Woodward, took some grenades, worked their way across the crest to a point twenty meters from the perimeter, and bombarded the enemy as the air strikes continued.

At 8:15 A.M. the Americans were told that three CH-46s would be coming in to get them. They quickly divided into three groups for the extraction. Recon Marines, their dog, and four wounded formed the first group; the air crewmen were second; and a rear guard of eight reaction force men with Captain Campbell in charge formed the last. Remaining ammunition and grenades were pooled and given to Campbell's group.

The first two ships got out without difficulty. By the time the third came down (and switched position and sat on the ground a few minutes), the NVA had completed their envelopment and were again massing for an attack. Campbell and the other men emptied their weapons and threw their grenades as they made for the CH-46. As the last ship got off, the area was taken under fire by 175mm guns and hit by saturation air strikes. Gunships delivered twenty-eight rockets and five thousand rounds of 7.62mm ammunition.

Part of this firepower was intended to destroy the evidence of American presence in Laos. Kenneth D. Jordan, who retired a Marine colonel, notes that "there were two helicopters down there that we eventually had to blow in place because the NVA were all around them. We blew them up with fixed-wing airplanes, and they left the debris of the burnt helicopter carcasses there, and that was indelible evidence that we were outside the country."

The 3rd Marine Division recommended Private Srsen for a posthumous Medal of Honor. This was downgraded by III MAF to a Navy Cross. Some Marines believe this action was taken to avoid calling attention to the fact that the patrol had been in Laos. There had been heroism galore in the action, with other awards including two Silver Stars, three Bronze Stars, and no less than nine Distinguished Flying Crosses. The 1st Marine Air Wing alone wrote up fifty-one individual award recommendations for this particular action.

Gunnery Sergeant Mad Dog Hopkins, having received fragmentation wounds in his right hand and burns on his face, died on February 5, 1968, at Washoe Medical Center, Reno, Nevada, cause of death a coronary occlusion.

To be in Laos was to not exist, a peculiar state of being for organizations in which collecting and specifying details is a way of life. Whether the mission was for the Studies and Observation Group (SOG), for its systematic reconnaissance programs SHINING BRASS and PRAIRIE FIRE, for Force Reconnaissance, or for the CIA, life could be a little strange. On the one hand heroism like that of Private Srsen could go unrecognized. On the other, life in a classified state of being could have light moments too.

Fred Locke was a pilot from squadron HMM-265 who flew SOG missions in Laos in 1966. One day he was scheduled for a mission to Tchepone. The briefing seemed unreal. "I was sitting there," Locke says, "we were ready to go on this mission, and it was the initial stroke of the military telling us that smoking was dangerous to our health. So they get us in this briefing, and here I am ready to go on this mission, and they're worried about smoking cigarettes!"

Things got even more unreal after that. The briefer, in a studied, casual way, warned the pilots to be careful not to call in any air strikes on friendly elephants.

"I'm beginning to wonder if this is Disneyland," Locke recalls.

He thought it had to be some kind of a setup, but he was supposed to be lead pilot and finally he bit, asking how one might tell a "friendly" elephant from an enemy one. The ready room broke up with laughter.

The briefers explained that elephants that had moved down the Ho Chi Minh Trail would have their bellies tinged red from the clay soil farther to the north.

Locke flew his mission. "I'll be dog-gone if we didn't see a whole bunch of elephants, and they did [have red bellies]. We're talking *Lost Weekend*, I know — the 'pink elephants.' But there they were, right in front of me!"

*   *   *

On January 28, 1967, the day after the big Laotian patrol battle ended, 3rd Marine Division commander General Wood B. Kyle took up the matter of Khe Sanh patrols with Da Nang. Kyle recommended that future patrols be limited to the effective range of Khe Sanh's 105mm howitzers, roughly 11,000 meters. Da Nang was not buying, however. On February 1 came the III MAF reply, stating that though one might agree in principle in most circumstances, the critical nature of the area was such that it was essential for reconnaissance and combat patrols to operate outside artillery range. General Kyle turned around, in his operation order 6-67 of February 8, and prescribed that infantry patrols of at least squad size, plus specialized reconnaissance teams, could operate within the 11,000-meter radius, while only assigned recon elements should work outside that range.

Reconnaissance units were to focus on the sector north and west of Khe Sanh, up to the DMZ and west to Laos. Their mission was "to slow the enemy down," recalls James Capers. "We'd go out there and set ambushes, call in artillery strikes, monitor the well-traveled trails, call in interdiction fire, to give Khe Sanh some breathing room."

Under the leadership of Captain Kenneth D. Jordan, the detachment of 3rd Force Reconnaissance Company at Khe Sanh had a very busy February 1967. James Capers says, "Believe me, we were making contact! There was a battle going on every day. [Khe Sanh] was one of the busiest places around that I know of. We were running patrols daily, normally five or six patrols out. We even had Doc Burwell as a patrol leader for a while."

Lowell E. Burwell was no ordinary Navy corpsman. Marines called him "Mr. Everything." Burwell was a parachutist and a demolitions expert, had qualified in both scuba and deep-sea diving, and had graduated from mountain training, jungle training, and escape and evasion school. In the first seven months in-country of 3rd Force Recon, Burwell's team made thirty patrols. Doc went on every one. The Marines failed to sight the enemy only once, and they made positive contact on twenty-five occasions. Doc Burwell never lost a patient. His chance to lead came on two patrols conducted in the ten-day period during which his patrol leader, Staff Sergeant Librado L. Flores, spent on his back with mild malaria.

On February 8 the 3rd Platoon of 3rd Force Recon arrived at Khe Sanh to augment existing reconnaissance capabilities. Over the remainder of the month the platoon conducted twenty-five patrols averaging two and a half days, with mean strength of five and a half

Marines. The patrols made five contacts and seventeen sightings, tallying ninety-one enemy and forty-eight VC suspects. Such raw numbers hardly convey the exhilaration and terror of combat or the sweat and tedium of the constant patrols. Doc Burwell's thirty patrols were only typical. Lance Corporal Henry J. Stanton, for another example, went on eighteen recon patrols from Khe Sanh between January 18 and April 7 and actively engaged the adversary on eleven of them. On one patrol, almost capturing a wounded NVA soldier, Stanton won the Bronze Star.

The reconnaissance units' access to remote areas away from the base was almost wholly dependent on helicopters. A detachment or "package" of ships was being sent to Khe Sanh combat base daily to support its activities. In January the daily package was usually two CH-46s, two UH-34s, and two UH-1Es ("Hueys"). Later the packages were reduced to three UH-34s. Bad weather that delayed helicopter insertions could be especially scary if rescue or reinforcement was being postponed. A patrol from the newly arrived 3rd Platoon learned this the hard way during a mission that began February 12. At first things went quite smoothly, but on the 14th the patrol encountered perhaps forty enemy and called for a reaction force. Though Franchise Rep (Horne, the senior officer present and III MAF representative) and the 3rd Division both approved the reaction force, weather prevented its insertion. The recon team had to withdraw on foot, under cover of white phosphorus and CS tear gas grenades, until they could be picked up the next day.

Then again, the aircraft could help things go quite well indeed. The flexibility that the slicks and gunships permitted played in favor of Force Recon team 5-2 in its mission of February 21. The team was compromised immediately as it alighted north of Dong Tri mountain (Hill 1015). One Marine saw movement to the northwest, and before the men had moved twenty meters the scout dog was alerting in all directions. Clearly the patrol was not going to get anywhere; they returned to the LZ and called for air support and extraction. The 3rd Division combat operations center approved a platoon-size "Sparrowhawk" reaction force, which was alerted for action, but the slicks successfully extracted the patrol at about 1:40 P.M. Huey gunships firing on observed enemy positions touched off a secondary explosion.

Even patrols that made no contact could be anxiety-provoking. One returning patrol, out four or five days, was coming down a hill when the point man ran into a python. The patrol took a look and decided it was the biggest snake anybody had ever seen, but they realized that no one would believe them without evidence.

Nine Marines, already abnormally heavy because they had expected a firefight and had brought extra supplies, jumped on the snake, overpowered it, tied it up, and began to carry the thing on a poncho. Reaching a river they had to cross, the patrol discovered that recent rains had made the river barely passable. The snake was too heavy to carry across safely. Finally the Marines left it on the bank and swam across.

Sure enough, no one at Khe Sanh believed them. Despite the jeers and ridicule, one helicopter pilot allowed the recon men to convince him to ferry them out to retrieve the snake and put down the disbelievers. They laid out the snake to the wonder of all. Then someone brought a duck for the snake to eat, tied it by one leg, and put it in with the snake. The next day the duck was still alive; the snake was dead.

When the helicopter pilots came around to see the snake again, the Marines told them the duck had killed the snake by pecking at it. The airmen played along, taking photographs of the amazing duck that had killed the monster snake. Later recon Marines took the snake to the local montagnards, who promptly skinned it and ate it. When Force Recon rotated out of Khe Sanh they took the snakeskin with them to Phu Bai. We have failed to discover where that skin may be today.

Action on Hill 861

There were plenty of patrol contacts during the first two months of 1967. No question about it — the North Vietnamese were out there. Yet it was at this very moment that III MAF *withdrew* its Marine battalion from Khe Sanh, replacing it with a single reinforced company. Franchise Rep, until then Colonel Horne, also left Khe Sanh, to be followed by Lieutenant Colonel McGee, a former Marine Corps champion handball player.

Colonel Wickwire's 1st Battalion, 3rd Marines departed for Da Nang on February 1, 1967. A week later the battalion left for Okinawa, where it had a period of rest and retraining before duty as a seaborne landing force off the Vietnamese coast. One company stayed behind a few days to cover for the new defenders of Khe Sanh combat base, Bravo Company of the 1st Battalion, 9th Marines under Captain Michael W. Sayers. The company was augmented by a forty-five-man security detachment from the 3rd Marine Division headquarters battalion that had no officers and no one who had ever experienced combat. There were also a section of 106mm recoilless rifles, one of 81mm mortars, additional M-60 machine guns, and one extra 3.5-inch rocket launcher. Bravo Company may have been reinforced with extra elements, but it was not a battalion. There was no way Sayers's company could defend the same perimeter as had Wickwire's men.

Sayers's company had previously participated in the DECKHOUSE V amphibious operation far to the south in the Mekong Delta. Right afterward the company had been detached from its battalion and moved to Khe Sanh. Sayers's men arrived at the combat base on February 6. It would be an eventful deployment.

Patrol activities began immediately. The typical daily effort was four thirteen-man patrols and four four-man listening or observation posts. At night the effort would average four ambushes and four listening posts. Force Recon usually had three or four additional patrols in the field at all times. Helicopters remained essential, but bad weather was frequent. Captain Sayers therefore dispatched longer range overnight patrols of two or three days duration sent out every other day. The level of patrol activity meant that Bravo was not really a company defending its perimeter at all. As many as two of its three platoons were involved in the patrols at any given time, leaving only one to defend Khe Sanh. "We had only one company there at the time," says Marine Tom Ryan, point man of 3rd Platoon, "and then we sent two platoons out . . . at all times, so one platoon's all that was there." It was just as well the North Vietnamese never attacked.

One reason the patrol effort stayed so high is that the assigned mission of Captain Sayers's company remained identical to that of Colonel Wickwire's battalion even though the actual force in place declined to a third or a fourth of what it had been. That Generals Walt and Kyle approved the withdrawal of 1st Battalion, 3rd Marines says a good deal about their perceptions of the North Vietnamese threat. That they made no changes in the orders given to units assigned to Khe Sanh says even more. A key indicator, at least of Lew Walt's strategy, is his dispatch of Marine pacification units to Huong Hoa district at this time. With the continuing high levels of contact with the North Vietnamese, Walt clearly must have believed the threat of a mass NVA offensive against Khe Sanh had diminished.

It is also noteworthy that the ARVN command made no effort to maintain troop levels in the Khe Sanh sector by returning their own battalion that Wickwire's unit had replaced. Thus ARVN I Corps appears to have shared III MAF's views.

A mystery of the Khe Sanh battle is why William C. Westmoreland permitted the withdrawal. Westmoreland had believed himself in a race against time at Khe Sanh, had pushed for Marine deployment in the first place, and was aware of the results of all the scouting being done around the combat base. It was the official opinion of J-2, MACV's intelligence branch, that in February 1967 "enemy activity increased in the area of Khe Sanh and Lang Vei as enemy units were probably infiltrating through the area toward the Lao corridor." In his memoirs Westmoreland is silent on why he allowed the Khe Sanh drawdown. Reduced threat seems an inadequate explanation in view of J-2's reports. As will be shown shortly, the conflict between Westmoreland and Walt over strategy for Khe Sanh had by no means abated.

For the moment Lew Walt had his way. The Marines completed final arrangements for deployment of their specialized pacification units with the Huong Hoa district chief in late January and February. Two days later fifty-two Marines and Navy corpsmen arrived to constitute three combined action platoons (CAPs) with the Bru. Lieutenant William T. Seamus commanded the umbrella unit, combined action company (CAC) O, or Oscar.

Khe Sanh's CAC Oscar held the distinction of being the only Marine combined action company composed of montagnards. Its command post was in district headquarters at Khe Sanh village (Map 3). Two platoons, CAPs O-1 and O-2, functioned in the eastern and western portions of the village. At Ta Cong village outside the main gate of the combat base was Oscar-3. The CAC Marines conducted numerous patrols in the Bru villages and soon developed strong ties with the tribesmen.

Several of the Bru recruited for the combined action platoons had served previously with the French military. There was one man named Houm, whom the other Bru claimed could not be killed. They called him "the Legend." Houm was a forty-five-year-old fellow with a hard, line-etched face and a bristling black beard. He stood about five foot four wearing his Marine utility cap and carried an old beat-up M-1 Garand rifle. Houm loved rice wine; in fact his consumption of it also seemed legendary — a five-gallon can a week.

"He would ask me where I was going when we went out to jump in the jeep," recalls district adviser Captain Bruce B. G. Clark. "Depending upon . . . where we were going and how dangerous he thought it would be, [Houm] would determine how many PFs would have to ride with us. . . . Also, if he decided that we were really going to someplace bad, there were degrees of bad, and you could always tell based on the type of weapon he carried — whether he carried a Thompson submachine gun, a carbine, or his normal M-1 rifle. You talk about reading 'body language' — here we were reading 'weapon language.' "

Meanwhile Bravo Company continued its own patrols in proximity to the combat base. They had many sightings but, until February 25, no contact with the North Vietnamese. That Saturday, Sergeant Donald E. Harper, Jr., led his squad, the first of the 2nd Platoon, augmented by a two-man machine gun team, on a patrol around the circumference of the combat base perimeter. Harper and his men departed the combat base at about 8:00 A.M. and the patrol went without incident until they began to climb a hill near Ta Cong, about 1,500 meters from the base.

Corporal Wright, leader of the first fire team, spotted a man in a khaki shirt running away through the brush at the bottom of the hill and three persons advancing up the trail in the direction the patrol had been heading. Harper reported the sighting, put two of his fire teams on line, and then advanced. On top of the hill, a familiar place to Harper, who had repeatedly led patrols here and used the place as a lunch spot, the Marines ran into the enemy.

"Unknown to us and also, I believe, unknown to the enemy themselves, we just seemed to walk on top of them," Harper recalls. "They was about three yards in front of us. Three of the VC just like they'd pop their heads up and look at each other."

Corporal Wright opened up with his 12-gauge shotgun, as did the M-60 team. One of the adversaries was killed immediately, the other two wounded. Now the Marines came under fire from a spot fifty yards to the right, with the enemy evidently positioned on the reverse slope. It was more than the patrol could handle. Harper pulled back to the base of the hill and called for mortar support. Captain Sayers asked Harper to go back to the crest and recover bodies plus any identification, papers, and so on. Harper chose to take only one fire team and his radio man. The patrol leader was on top of the hill searching one body when the enemy opened fire again.

Harper withdrew to the base of the hill and once more asked Sayers for mortars. After the barrage he climbed again, taking just the four Marines. There was no fire. The Marines made several trips, retrieving documents and equipment. Harper was climbing the hill on another trip when an enemy machine gun fired on his right flank hitting automatic rifleman Lance Corporal Seal in his lower right arm and knocking the shotgun right out of Corporal Wright's hands. The Marines scrambled through the heavy underbrush and reassembled at the foot of the hill.

Now Sayers sent reinforcements, a squad led by Lieutenant Dave Mellon. The Marines scaled the hill, but about forty meters short of the summit they were suddenly hit by mortars, machine guns, everything the VC had. The mortar barrage killed one Marine and wounded six or seven more. The Americans answered with Huey gunships and fixed-wing air strikes. The VC either were silenced or elected to break contact. Sayers sent another two squads of 2nd Platoon up to help, but by the time they arrived the action had ended. The next day, Sunday, Sayers sent two full platoons back to sweep through the battle area. They found a telephone handset and communications wire leading from the hill in several directions.

Tragedy struck the Bru on the evening of March 2, when two Air Force aircraft, sent to bomb VC occupying Lao Bao, hit Lang Vei village by mistake. Cluster bombs fell within the place, damaging more than 140 buildings, nearly three-quarters of all structures in the village. Of a population of slightly more than 2,000, some 112 were killed and 213 wounded, with four more missing. Villagers walked around in a daze. It would have been even worse except that the planes' napalm landed just outside the settlement.

Khe Sanh combat base immediately sent H-34 and CH-46 helicopters to evacuate the wounded. When the weather closed in, the Marines substituted trucks. Captain John J. Duffy's Green Berets of detachment A-101 were first on the scene, soon assisted by Marine infantry and Force Recon men, the first of whom arrived within twenty minutes.

The operations officer of 1st Marine Air Wing, Lieutenant Colonel Aubrey W. Talbert, asked transportation squadron VMGR-152 to fly out a special unit under Major William F. Morley that existed to cope with such emergencies. Major Richard C. Conway in his KC-130F flew the mission. The weather continued deteriorating, with the ceiling down to two hundred feet and visibility varying between a quarter and a half mile, less than the minimum for a ground-controlled approach. Conway's first approach was unsuccessful; he would have been perfectly justified to abort the mission. Instead he circled and came in again — Conway had been told that numerous civilians required immediate medical attention. The crew brought in their KC-130 nicely, landed the emergency team, and lifted out fifty-three critically wounded men, women, and children. Major Conway won a Distinguished Flying Cross for his action.

That night, as the rest of the Bru wounded awaited evacuation at the combat base, it was subjected to a heavy mortar attack for the first time in more than a year. Approximately seventy-four rounds of 82mm mortars hit the base, resulting in two Marines killed and seventeen wounded, seven of whom required evacuation. As the Marines replied with their own 81mm mortars, one round "cooked" at Corporal Thomas H. Price's emplacement, falling to the ground just a few feet from unfired ammunition. Price quickly ordered his men under cover, returned to escort two who apparently had not gotten the word, and then went back to pick up and disarm the still-hot mortar shell. Price was awarded a Silver Star.

The Marine casualties, the remaining Bru villagers with them, were flown out on March 3. At the same time relief efforts for Lang Vei village began. Marines sent in 250 bags of rice, 1,000 pounds of salt, 250 sets of pots and pans, 1,000 sets of chopsticks, 1,000 bowls, 60 cases of cooking oil, 25 tool kits, 20,000 board feet of two-by-fours, and 40,000 board feet of one-by-sixes. Major Morley supervised dispensing of the supplies and the relief efforts of the Army's 29th Civil Affairs Company. The Bru selected two new hamlet sites, which were quickly cleared. Construction of twenty percent of the buildings planned was completed within three weeks. By the end of March most of the Bru wounded had returned to the relocated village. Marines of the 11th Engineer Battalion under supervision of Lieutenant Richard V. DeGryse began construction of a medical dispensary and a school. For a time the rumor circulated at the combat base that Russian MiGs had caused the slaughter. The Special Forces at the CIDG camp knew better, however, for they had seen the aircraft and tried to raise them on the radio but had been unable to find the right frequency.

A second tragedy followed on March 8 when a village just inside Laos and then the airfield used by the Laotian BV-33 were strafed and bombed. The attacking aircraft were positively identified as U.S. C-123 flareships, and expended ordnance on the ground was recovered and established to be American. Fortunately, although facilities were extensively damaged, there were no casualties.

After the American fighter-bombers hit Lang Vei by mistake, General Walt requested a regular district advisory team for Khe Sanh. Previously the commander of A-101 had doubled as district adviser. Walt now sent in a MACV team, with Army Captain James Whitenack tapped for the job. Whitenack had been with the 7th Army in Germany in 1966 when he suddenly received orders to be in Vietnam in thirty days. He reported just after Christmas and without any language course or other specialized training was sent to Da Nang as headquarters company commander for a MACV forward command post. His Khe Sanh assignment came in the same ad hoc way. Whitenack was given an operations sergeant named Humphrey and two carbines and was put aboard an Air America helicopter.

Captain Whitenack arrived at Khe Sanh in midafternoon with just the clothes on his back. Equipment consisted of a radio and a case of C-rations. It took two months just to complete his advisory team: initially he got an Australian warrant officer as assistant district adviser, finally Captain Bruce B. G. Clark. At least Whitenack had heard of Khe Sanh before he got there, but the association was not a good one — the captain had been a classmate at Officer Candidate School with James Thompson, who had gone missing in 1964 while Whitenack was at Fort Benning. Commander of the Khe Sanh Special Forces detachment, Thompson had never returned from an aerial survey to the northwest of the camp.

Whitenack too would find Khe Sanh a trying place, especially toward the end of 1967. Apparently III MAF sent out orders that the combat base was not to support anyone outside its perimeter. The base commander interpreted this as applying to everyone, not just Vietnamese, and since the base had the water point and the airfield, all of a sudden the district team was left high and dry.

"I got on the radio and I called my people in Quang Tri," Jim Whitenack recalls, "and I said, 'Friday, when the Air America chopper comes in, I'm loading my people up and pulling them out of here!' They said, 'You can't do that!' I said, 'Oh, yes I can.' They said, 'Why?' I said, 'We've been cut off.' That lasted about two days, and all of a sudden the order got lifted real quick like. It was a stupid thing."

Meanwhile the Harper patrol battle and the enemy bombardment of Khe Sanh also led, once again, to reinforcement of the combat base, after division commander General Kyle visited on March 3. Kyle was finishing his Vietnam tour, and though he told theater Marine commanders in Honolulu a few weeks later that the NVA neither needed nor wanted Khe Sanh, the general sent an additional infantry company to the combat base. E (Echo) Company, 2nd Battalion, 9th Marines arrived March 7.

With the dispatch of a second Marine company to Khe Sanh and the presence of supporting units, CIDG units, and the combined action company, friendly forces in Huong Hoa district increased to nearly a thousand men. Da Nang and division headquarters apparently agreed to replace Lieutenant Colonel McGee as senior officer present and III MAF representative. "Franchise Rep," the radio handle, stayed the same, as did the telephone switchboard identification, "Radiance." The new senior officer present would be Colonel James M. Reeder.

Lieutenant Colonel Reeder, one-time executive officer of the 4th Marine Regiment, arrived in South Vietnam fresh from several years on detached duty at Central Intelligence Agency headquarters in Langley, Virginia. There he had worked on summary reports of CIA activities in Vietnam and served in other sensitive capacities. At Khe Sanh he took an active interest in the welfare of the troops. He tried to get the post cleaned up a bit, believing that the Green Berets had left the place in a deplorable state.

Reeder hated dust, and he imposed speed limits and took other measures to try to keep down the dust on the roads. He also got a mess hall opened, created a post exchange stocked with beer, and made the engineers rig up hot showers. "I have always been a great believer in hot showers," Reeder says.

Colonel Reeder's efforts in behalf of the troops would undoubtedly have been much better appreciated had he seemed more receptive to the evidence of enemy activities around Khe Sanh. Reeder appeared not to want to believe. Company commander Mike Sayers recalls attending many recon debriefing sessions with Reeder. "It is my personal belief," Sayers later wrote, "that LtCol. Reeder did not believe the reports of the recon unit and did not release all the message traffic concerning the [enemy] build-up." Sayers used to watch the message board at the combat operations center for information copies of the reports. Not all of them came through. Similarly, Lieutenant James Capers of the Force Recon detachment states that Reeder "was preoccupied with keeping the dust down on the streets and planting flowers." Force Recon patrol leader Lawrence Keen is also bitter about Reeder's apparent refusal to accept patrol reports.

Captain Sayers took his problems up the line to Brigadier General Michael Ryan, commander of the forward elements of the 3rd Marine Division below the DMZ, who was a frequent visitor to Khe Sanh. Sayers had previously worked for Ryan at the stateside Marine base Parris Island. Now Sayers went to Ryan with a shopping list of assets he thought were needed to ensure the defense of Khe Sanh combat base. Ryan did in fact send up more firepower.

What Marine subordinates never knew was the degree to which Colonel Reeder's hands were tied by the conflict between Lew Walt and William Westmoreland. Reeder maintains that he did believe the reports of NVA activity and wanted to pass them up the chain of command but that there was "quite a continuing battle between Westmoreland and Walt." The conflict over Khe Sanh strategy had not disappeared at all.

"I happen[ed] to know Lew Walt rather well at the time," Reeder remembers. "He was constantly telling me: 'Now, you don't tell Westmoreland this when he comes up.' And Westmoreland would drop in, make a point. Then Walt would be chugging furiously right after him in his helicopter and inevitably say, 'Did you know he was coming?' And I'd say, 'I didn't have the foggiest.' I truly thought at the time that I could have gotten a lot better service and could have gotten a lot better information — intelligence information — if the two of them hadn't been so at odds."

Still, the Force Recon men knew very clearly what was going on. "We found heavily used trails, ambush positions, bunkers, 75mm recoilless rifles," says Gunnery Sergeant Larry Keen. "We found graves; we found a trail that was as wide as your bedroom. We found where they had bunkered down in the weeds, the grass, just laid the stuff down. We found trail markers — banana leaves, tops of grass tied. . . ."

For their patrol efforts the Marines tried not to advertise the insertion of patrols through the use of noisy helicopters. Instead they utilized a technique of "platoon patrol bases," harbor sites defended overnight by relatively large forces from which the patrols might radiate farther the next morning. The patrol bases shifted constantly, relocating every night to avoid presenting a static target.

It was not long before the new unit at the combat base, Captain William E. Terrill's Echo Company of 2/9, had its first encounter with the shadowy adversary. On the evening of March 13 a platoon moving across the tip of Hill 861, approximately four kilometers northwest of Khe Sanh combat base, was suddenly hit by twelve to fifteen rounds of mortar fire. Friendly 60mm mortars shot back but no one had any idea of the result.

"I remember a couple of times we went over 861 and over the mountains toward Laos," says David Rogers, then an eighteen-year-old Marine of the third squad, 3rd Platoon of Echo Company. "We were supposed to look for the Ho Chi Minh Trail, and I remember we could sit on the hillside and see all the fires at night. There was just oodles of them over there."

During all this time Khe Sanh remained entirely dependent on its airstrip. No vehicle had used Route 9, at least that part of Route 9 between Khe Sanh and Camp Carroll, since September 1964. Even on foot, as had been seen in operation VIRGINIA, the going was rough. Vehicles could still travel from Khe Sanh into Laos, though. Coffee planters like Felix Poilane sent their product to Laos, to the market at Savannakhet, although from the border stone it was 245 kilometers to Savannakhet but just 68 kilometers to Dong Ha on the Vietnamese coastal plain, the junction of Route 9 and Highway 1, South Vietnam's main north–south communications route.

Both MACV and III MAF entertained notions of invading Laos, dreams of cutting the Ho Chi Minh Trail. Both Saigon and Da Nang knew very well that those notions would remain pipe dreams so long as Khe Sanh had to depend solely on the airstrip. Americans could, and did, convince Felix Poilane to ship his coffee by air in 1967, but serious offensive military operations were an entirely different matter. Any invasion of Laos would be a matter of divisions and brigades, of hundreds and hundreds of tons of supply flow daily. Khe Sanh airstrip did not have the capacity to handle that kind of traffic and no conceivable set of improvements would endow it with that capability. Quite simply, Route 9 was the key to the dream.

Between Dong Ha and Khe Sanh, Route 9 extended for just sixty-eight kilometers, but they were some of the most vital ones among the thirty-three hundred in I Corps. This stretch crossed forty-nine bridges, twenty-seven of them on the twenty-five-kilometer upland passage from Ca Lu to Khe Sanh. The road was two-lane blacktop or macadam from Dong Ha only to Camp Carroll, really not sufficient for an invasion, but almost the best any road got in South Vietnam.

From Cam Lo, near Camp Carroll, west, Route 9 had been closed because of flood damage and enemy action since 1964. A Marine battalion had walked out during operation VIRGINIA, but that had been a stunt. The road deteriorated to the point of obliteration. A dirt road past Cam Lo, Route 9 could be a dust bowl in dry weather and bottomless mud in the monsoon. It became a one-lane thoroughfare; at best two jeeps might pass each other. After Ca Lu in the mountains there were numerous tight turns and places where the road had been carved into slopes, with sheer cliffs on one side and sharp precipices on the other.

More than a security operation, opening Route 9 became a construction project. The Marines began in late February 1967, when Company A of the 11th Engineer Battalion sent a detachment of forty men and a dozen vehicles to Ca Lu, where the road ascends after bending through deep valleys. To the engineers Route 9 became Project 9024. The platoon would be reinforced to three officers and fifty-six enlisted men, and then a further thirty-four combat engineers and two cooks augmented the detachment in early March. On March 5 repairs began to the first of three bridges between Ca Lu and Khe Sanh. The engineers strengthened existing abutments by pouring concrete and also reinforced the deck slab to take sixty-ton loads. Just in case, they added a bypass.

The second bridge, a kilometer or so to the west, was repaired on March 11 and 12. Several more days passed as bulldozers and graders cleared and smoothed the old roadbed and scooped out bypasses where repair promised to be more difficult. On March 16 construction began on a new approach for one bridge that had to be completely replaced. The project sucked in more of the 11th Battalion — three officers and seventy men of Company D — plus an Army security detachment, and then the 1st Bridge Platoon, which transported and erected a forty-five-foot fixed-span bridge about six kilometers east of the combat base.

Elated, Lew Walt radioed a message to Westmoreland: "Since Khe Sanh has been closed to vehicular traffic for over two years, I consider the restoration of National Route 9 to service to be an event of great tactical, logistical, and economic significance. It is my intention to continue improvements to Route 9 and to run an appropriate number of convoys."

Meanwhile, a start was made on overland traffic with a "Rough Rider" convoy from Dong Ha on March 27. The convoy consisted of eight radio jeeps, three M-38 jeeps, an M-49 tanker truck, two ONTOS armored assault vehicles, three ¾-ton trucks, thirteen dump trucks, fifteen 2½-ton trucks, seventeen five-ton trucks, two tow trucks, and four M-55 tracked carriers. This initial convoy carried 3,500 pounds of rice, 4,320 pounds of diesel fuel, 4,680 pounds of engineering and fortification materials, and 6,640 pounds of ammunition. The Rough Riders reached Khe Sanh without incident after about three and a half hours on the road.

As the engineers struggled to improve Route 9, a short, bloody fire-fight near the combat base led directly to the first battle of Khe Sanh. Locale for this encounter was Hill 861, the same place Sergeant Harper's patrol had run into trouble. Captain Terrill's Echo Company were the principals, on patrol northwest of the combat base. On the night of March 15, Staff Sergeant Spencer F. Olsen was moving his platoon up the slope of 861 when, about thirty meters from the crest, Marines heard movements in the bushes. Olsen's men took cover and sat out the night.

In the morning, as soon as the Marines crossed the crest and moved down the trail on the other slope, they were ambushed and suffered a number of casualties. Olsen faced the dilemma of having no landing zone from which choppers could evacuate his wounded, for the NVA were behind them on the crest of 861 too. He requested an air strike with napalm, thought better of it, but radioed a cancellation too late. Jets rolled in, hit the hill, and their napalm ignited a fierce brushfire that burned toward the Marines trapped in a ravine. Several men stopped fighting to beat out the flames. Afterward Olsen realized that the error had solved his problem by clearing an LZ for helicopters, though when the Marines actually tried some medical evacuations, NVA antiaircraft fire proved too heavy.

A second platoon ordered in to help took until midafternoon to effect a junction. By then even more Marines had become casualties. Finally there were not enough Marines left to both make up litter parties for the wounded and fight their way out. Captain Terrill and his command group plus Echo's 2nd Platoon were then lifted into a new LZ near the base of 861 from which they furnished manpower to move the casualties plus a covering force to protect them. Evacuation went on through a whole night, in the light of flareships kept continuously overhead.

The Marines ultimately concluded that eleven North Vietnamese had been killed in the initial contact. Those were the only confirmed enemy losses. Marine casualties were eighteen dead and fifty-nine wounded. One missing man was found later, dead.

The firefight on Hill 861 thus turned to tragedy. Echo Company of 2/9 was effectively shattered. When Route 9 opened, the company was withdrawn to Dong Ha to rebuild. Captain Sayers's Bravo Company of 1/9 had also suffered losses and was very tired. The enemy had not been seriously hampered. The best aspect of the situation was the newly established road contact, which, if nothing else, meant a supply of rice to pay local Bru personnel of the CIDG, the PF, the district, CAC, and SOG. The road would help tremendously, and sooner than anybody could have realized, for Khe Sanh was about to become the scene of a major battle.

CHAPTER

4
_____

"These Hills Called Khe Sanh" (1967)

DEPENDING ON WHO TELLS THE STORY, the first major battle at Khe Sanh resulted either from Colonel Reeder's determination to produce proof of an enemy presence, proof that Marine headquarters could not ignore, or despite the Franchise Rep's refusal to credit the reports of enemy activities. Colonel Reeder says he had indications of enemy-occupied caves on Hill 861 and thought an investigation might force Da Nang to take Khe Sanh's problems more seriously. Reeder himself seems to have been in earnest this time, for it was no small reconnaissance patrol he sent on the mission but two full platoons from Bravo Company, to converge on Hill 861 from different directions.

Others contend that Colonel Reeder was still refusing to believe the mounting evidence, that the new hill operation occurred more or less mindlessly, despite the string of suggestive reports through March and into April. A Company of the 3rd Reconnaissance Battalion came to supplement the other scouting forces at Khe Sanh, but even with the extra patrols the higher-ups did not seem to pay attention. When Lieutenant Lee Klein arrived to represent division intelligence at the combat base, his predecessor briefed him on the North Vietnamese threat using reports no one had bothered to read. "He had the whole thing doped out," Klein recalls, "with one exception: he had two regiments in Laos and one in the hill country up there on 861 and 881. Actually there were two in-country and one on reserve." An agent told Marines of CAC Oscar that he had seen a full regiment of NVA on a trail close to 881 South.

There were discoveries of bunkers and base camps, sightings, and another heavy mortar barrage directed at a Marine patrol.

TIGERHOUND aircraft saw more fortifications on the hills near the combat base. Reeder's concentric probe toward Hill 861 may have been intended to assert Marine presence in the face of the presumed enemy or to test channels between the combat base and Colonel John P. Lanigan, commander of the 3rd Marines, who assumed operational control as Franchise Rep on April 20. Now moving into the DMZ sector, the 3rd Marines would henceforth be responsible for reinforcing Khe Sanh.

For whatever reason, Colonel Reeder ordered patrols to sweep Hill 861. It was the same place Sergeant Harper's patrol had stumbled into the NVA and Echo Company had fought a pitched battle. This foray led to the same result.

"Why Don't You Use the Tunnel?"

The mission was to check out caves first discovered by the 1st Platoon of Bravo Company on April 23. Tom Ryan, a Bravo point man, recalls that "the colonel on the base had said, 'We'll just send up two platoons, one on each side, and we're going to clean them up once and for all.' It was crazy." Captain Sayers committed his 1st and 3rd Platoons, leaving only the 2nd to defend the combat base. The platoons moved out in the rain early the next morning, two columns about 250 meters apart, following paths used by previous patrols. "The area was pretty open," observes Ryan. "A couple of guys were saying, 'Well, there probably won't be anything there when we get there.' I knew myself that if there was anything there, it wouldn't be anything that [we] wanted."

As the Marines moved toward the caves, a rifleman in 1st Platoon spotted four or five NVA soldiers coming toward them. Since the North Vietnamese were advancing, the platoon leader Lieutenant James D. Carter, Jr., ordered his Marines to take up ambush positions. The enemy saw the Marines, who then opened fire. Carter moved forward with about eight men to see what they could find — one NVA soldier on a stretcher and another scurrying down the hill. Meanwhile much stronger North Vietnamese forces took the Marines under fire. After a number of casualties, the platoon was ordered to move back to rejoin their company commander.

That same morning Second Lieutenant Thomas G. King had moved up to Hill 700, about a kilometer south of 861, to provide fire support for the sweep. King had thirty men of his own 2nd Platoon, a section of 81mm mortars with 120 rounds of ammunition, and Lieutenant Phillip H. Sauer, commander of the ONTOS section at the combat base. King reached his designated position, set up, and began to bombard the cave area; he then sent five men forward to act as observers. The observation post never reached the crest: they were taken under fire in a bamboo thicket some three hundred meters from the top of Hill 861. One man was wounded, another's rifle barrel shattered by an enemy round. The senior observer, Lieutenant Sauer, had only a pistol. Sauer covered as companion Private First Class William Marks ran back to the remaining two Marines; that was the last anyone ever saw of Sauer. Marks and the others tried to make a run for it. Private Marks was the only survivor.

Captain Mike Sayers flew up to Hill 700 aboard a helicopter but barely managed to make it in under intense fire. King asked Sayers for permission to pull back his body recovery detail, which found suspicious silence on the slope of 861. In the meantime Private Marks was given some aspirin and told to lie down and rest. "I kept seeing those poor guys' faces," he recalled.

Though no observation post could be established atop Hill 861, 81mm mortars effectively helped the 1st Platoon, which reported shells landing directly on an NVA company and asked that fire be continued. However, the platoon could not progress in the face of heavy automatic weapons fire. Lieutenant Carter pulled back to an LZ and got a helicopter in to evacuate the several wounded and then had to make for another LZ and repeat the exercise. The second medevac met more enemy fire, and the platoon suffered another man killed and three wounded. Finally Carter ordered his men to dig in for the night where they were. One of the helicopters had been hit thirty-five times.

The 3rd Platoon did no better. The Marines set up a mortar in the open. "We heard a couple of guys get hit and they were screaming and it kinda shook us up," remembers Corporal Michael A. Brown. "We didn't know what the hell happened. Finally, they told us to pull back." The Marines left half their field equipment behind and had trouble with stretchers they had improvised to bear the wounded. The 3rd Platoon looked for a suitable LZ but they escaped nothing. The North Vietnamese tried to shell them with mortars; fortunately the Marines moved quickly enough that the NVA could not adjust the fire effectively. Then the fighter-bombers, American aircraft, screamed in.

"We got bombed by our jets up there. My squad got six people killed," says Tom Ryan. "They were just telling me to move quick — running down there, more or less falling, and the jets bombed us, blew my whole fire team away. I think they thought we were the enemy the way we were coming off that hill." Lance Corporal Donald A. Clark, halfway back in the column, recalls that the Marines lost radio contact with their own platoon leader. The men had to move through the spot where their comrades had been hit by the U.S. planes. Clark saw parts of bodies and various equipment scattered all over the area. Not until five in the afternoon did a medevac helicopter arrive, and then, under fire, it could retrieve only three wounded.

The tragic friendly fire incident on the slopes of Hill 861 epitomized the dangers inherent in the massive firepower the Americans wielded. Those jet pilots, at typical altitudes and air speeds for close support runs, could not have had much more than *one second* to drop their bombs and hit the targets. Any anticipation or delay radically increased the danger of hitting friendly troops. Furthermore, at speed, it was even harder to distinguish friendly from enemy forces. All kinds of measures, ranging from safety zones to radar guidance, from subordination to forward air controllers, tried to reduce the dangers of friendly fire, but it could never be entirely eliminated. What applied to air power, furthermore, was also true of artillery. The battlefield would always be a dangerous place.

The 3rd Platoon on Hill 861, like the 1st, finally had to hunker down for the night, digging in as best it could without benefit of entrenching tools, with just canteen cups and bayonets. The mortar section with the 2nd Platoon had run out of ammunition and Captain Sayers withdrew it to Khe Sanh. Bravo Company's losses that day numbered fourteen dead, eighteen wounded, and two missing. The remaining infantrymen spent an uneasy night as artillery and air pounded the zone around them. Special Forces agents, Marine recon patrols, and a forward air controller filed reports of more North Vietnamese troop movements. As a result Colonel Reeder reported the presence of the 18th Regiment of the NVA 325-C Division in the Khe Sanh sector.

Early Wednesday morning, April 25, point man Tom Ryan of Bravo's 3rd Platoon was preparing to move out when a North Vietnamese soldier walked right up to him. Other Bravo troopers were putting together their gear and checking ammunition when someone shouted, "Look back! Look back! Hey, come here!" Ryan stood up, only to confront Vu Van Tich of the 4th Battalion, 32nd Regiment, NVA 341st Division. Tich declared that he wanted to quit, he just wanted to go home. Tich had left his unit and had begun wandering four days earlier. American intelligence in fact placed the 32nd Regiment on April 22 in the A Shau valley west of Hue.

Corporal Mike Brown remembered the incident well:

> I couldn't believe it; they were actually talking to a Gook! So I wanted to run for my life because I thought we were surrounded. I know there is no way you can talk civilized to these people. So it turned out it was just this young-looking Gook. He looked surprised. He was smiling. And we were more scared than he was, it looked like. He had a cartridge belt, some ammo and demo[lition equipment], but no rifle. We made him take all this off before he came into our perimeter . . . we just kept him covered and away, out of sight. After that, we just sat there and waited and wondered what we wanted to do. And maybe we were spotted; we didn't know. We just sat there.

One helicopter got into the platoon LZ soon after. It brought up Captain Sayers plus all twenty-two Marines of his 2nd Platoon, and took back several wounded plus the NVA prisoner. But fog dominated the day. That ship would be the only helicopter to reach Bravo Company that day. Sayers hardly maneuvered his people. By evening visibility was down to barely five meters, further restricted in the tall elephant grass. With unknown numbers of North Vietnamese out there all around them, Bravo began to get very nervous indeed. That night they dug in again.

Weather similarly hampered the major Marine initiative of April 25. That was the move into Khe Sanh of the command element of Lieutenant Colonel Gary Wilder's 3rd Battalion, 3rd Marines from Thon Son Lam. Wilder brought his K Company under Captain Bayliss L. Spivey, artillery and mortar forward observers, and a battalion scout. Spivey's 2nd Platoon remained in reserve in the action that followed. Spivey had four other officers, five Navy corpsmen, and 128 enlisted Marines. He had commanded the company for only three weeks. Now Colonel Wilder gave him orders to capture Hill 861. Arriving at Khe Sanh combat base after noon, within hours Kilo Company was in the thick of the action.

At precisely 5:05 P.M. (Spivey recalls the exact time very well), the lead elements, three hundred meters from the summit of Hill 861, came under fire from bunkers on the crest and a mortar on the reverse slope. The Marines never got a good look at their adversaries. Within a half hour the 3rd Platoon had been decimated: only ten Marines were left of what that morning had been a thirty-seven-man unit. The losses made disengagement impossible.

Captain Spivey asked Colonel Wilder to release the reserve platoon. The battalion commander had no alternative. The 2nd Platoon added only twenty Marines to Spivey's meager force. As the sun set on April 25 two Marine companies stood beleaguered in the hills around Khe Sanh.

Given the increasingly serious situation near the combat base, the Marine command determined to commit further forces to the sector. In the late afternoon of April 25 at Camp Carroll, K Company, 3rd Battalion, 9th Marines was told to get ready for an emergency move. Soon after, they loaded out for Khe Sanh. "At first nobody knew where we were going," says Lance Corporal Henry Rose, Jr., of the company's weapons platoon. "We knew we were going somewhere because my company was the reactionary [sic] company for anything that came up." By nightfall the company was in Khe Sanh and under Colonel Wilder's operational control.

Battalion's command group was situated just south of Hill 861. Colonel Wilder and his men were shaken from their slumber at 5:00 A.M. on the 27th by NVA 82mm mortar fire. More mortar and re-coilless rifle fire showered on the combat base itself. Captain Sayers and Bravo Company were close enough to the slope of Hill 881 South that they could see and hear the back blast of the recoilless rifles. Sayers called in artillery and silenced the NVA weapons, while a flareship with miniguns delivered additional fire around both 881 South and 861.

Events forced reevaluation of the North Vietnamese presence near the combat base. Where previously the Marines had estimated that a company of the NVA might lie in the triangle formed by Hills 861, 881 South, and 881 North, now it seemed apparent that the adversary on 861 must be at least a company, while a battalion more was probably within the triangle. Contact eventually established the enemy as the NVA 18th Regiment under Lam Thai Quang. Marine intelligence also concluded that the NVA 18th had had orders to capture Khe Sanh within the folds of a larger battle along the DMZ and that Bravo Company had prematurely drawn the North Vietnamese into battle.

As near as the Marines could reconstruct North Vietnamese intentions, the attack at Khe Sanh would have been supported by mortar bombardments of the allied positions at Camp Carroll, Con Thien, Gio Linh, Dong Ha, and Phu Bai. Blown bridges would interdict Route 9 while the bombardments would disrupt Marine artillery support and helicopter activity. In fact, NVA artillery and mortars rained twelve hundred rounds on U.S. positions during April 27 and 28. The ultimate toll would be ten Americans killed and 226 wounded. The big action, however, would take place not at Khe Sanh but at the Lang Vei Special Forces camp, which the enemy had slated for a diversionary attack.

Meanwhile the dawning appreciation of North Vietnamese strength around Khe Sanh led to further reinforcement of the combat base by Lieutenant Colonel Earl R. Delong's 2nd Battalion, 3rd Marines, which had been assigned to the special landing force since April 13. In Marine practice a special landing force is a floating reserve offshore, typically called upon to participate in important amphibious operations along the coast. It was not in the III MAF chain of command but took orders from 9th Marine Amphibious Brigade on Okinawa. Delong's battalion was in fact engaged in operation BEACON STAR against a Viet Cong stronghold on the border of Thua Thien and Quang Tri provinces. Suddenly the battalion moved by air to Khe Sanh at the direction of Major General Bruno A. Hochmuth, commanding the 3rd Marine Division. Lead elements arrived at noon on April 27, Colonel Delong about an hour and a half later. This time the special landing force was being sent far into the interior of Vietnam.

On April 27 Colonel Lanigan of the 3rd Marines rotated Mike Company of the 3rd Battalion, 3rd Marines to Khe Sanh, pulling Kilo Company back to Thon Son Lam, the Rockpile. That afternoon, Mike Company of the 3rd Battalion, 9th Marines arrived to replace the long-suffering Bravo Company, whose remnants fit aboard a single C-130 for the hop to Dong Ha, after which they trucked to Camp Carroll. Measured by its cumulative casualties, Captain Sayers's company had been destroyed since its deployment to Khe Sanh.

On the third day of the assault up Hill 861 an incident occurred that captured the essence of the U.S. failure at pacification in Vietnam, the dysfunction that existed between Westmoreland's strategy of the big unit war and Lew Walt's desire to win hearts and minds. The incident occurred along the plantation road at the edge of Ta Cong where a Marine major with a radio jeep was observing the attack and relaying instructions to the assault troops. It happened that Anya, the Huong Hoa deputy district chief and several other Bru and Vietnamese stood next to the officer, watching the action. It was a clear day, and the American troop movements were quite visible, even several miles away.

Anya turned to the American major and asked, "Why do you continue to attack up the hill into the face of the enemy cannons?"

Startled to be addressed in English, the Marine snapped, "That's where the enemy is, Charlie!"

"Oh I see," Anya replied, "but I don't understand why you don't use the tunnel running through the mountain and attack from the rear."

Too late, the Marine asked about the tunnel, but the hill fight was already in its final stages. "Why didn't you tell us about the tunnel before?" the major reportedly snarled.

"Because you never asked me, Major," Anya snapped back. He turned on his heel and walked away.

A couple of days later at Khe Sanh, Anya saw William R. Corson, the Marine lieutenant colonel who was head of the combined action program. A former tank battalion commander in the 1st Marine Division, Corson had enjoyed phenomenal success at pacification with his unit. In February 1967, at the request of Lew Walt and Victor Krulak, his division commander had asked Corson to take on the combined action assignment. Like Khe Sanh's Franchise Rep, Colonel Reeder, Corson had served on detached duty with the CIA and was sympathetic to the political aims of pacification. He agreed.

Huong Hoa district and Khe Sanh village were still the province of combined action company Oscar. By the time of the hill battles CAC Oscar had been in place for some six weeks and Corson wanted to see how it was getting on.

At Khe Sanh Corson met Anya and asked him for the real story of why he had not told the Marines about the tunnel on Hill 861.

"Colonel," Corson reports Anya as saying, "I have tried to reach you for five days, your sergeants in the CAPs [combined action platoons] have also tried, but the battle was too important."

Anya recounted that the hamlet chief had left a week before, that the Vietnamese guards at the warehouse refused to release the food the United States had given the South Vietnamese government for the locals, even when offered twice the government-established legal price for the rice. The Bru were starving.

"It was my belief that if you were dumb enough to trust the GVN to worry about what happened to the poor Bru people, then why should I bother to tell your people anything?" Anya told Corson.

Colonel Corson took a few of his combined action Marines and liberated the rice from the warehouse. Later they presented it to the Bru. Anya left Corson with food for thought: "With us you will defeat the VC very quickly," he said, "but without us you will never win — remember we are not easily deceived and never ever forget; the peasant despises nothing more than a fool."

Colonel Delong's 2nd Battalion, 3rd Marines made the final assault on Hill 861 on April 28. In contrast to the tough fighting of previous days, the Marines now found little opposition. Perhaps the enemy had recoiled from the two B-52 ARC LIGHT strikes sent against them that day, or perhaps tactical air support had become more effective (delivering 382,700 pounds of ordnance on the 28th), or possibly the North Vietnamese had merely decided to break contact. Marines now began to hope they could reach their second and third objectives, Hills 881 South and 881 North.

The plan was for Delong's 2nd Battalion to secure and thoroughly search its initial objective, Hill 861. In the meantime Colonel Gary Wilder's 3rd Battalion would follow the former's trail and then wheel to the west to take the ground between 861 and 881 South. Wilder was supposed to attack 881 South from the northwest. This new action began on April 29.

Wilder's lead element was Mike Company of the 3rd Battalion, 9th Marines. About noon, in a valley halfway between 861 and its objective, the 1st Platoon ran into an enemy force in a draw. The North Vietnamese were entrenched with small arms and automatic weapons. Corporal Robert L. Allen, a squad leader, had just ordered men into position when heavy fire hit, wounding two Marines. Allen dashed through the fire to get them under cover, carrying the second even after wounded himself. Second Lieutenant Edward J. Kresty saw that the 2nd Platoon, the company's leading unit, had become isolated from the main body. He moved ahead of his own men to an exposed position on higher ground where, by radio, he directed the Marines back to the company position by a different route.

In the meantime Captain Raymond H. Bennett led Mike Company of the 3rd Battalion, 3rd Marines past the left flank of the engaged Marines to gain the battalion's intermediate objective, a lower hillock northeast of 881 South. Bennett's Marines saw North Vietnamese soldiers atop 881 South — a twenty-man force moving west along the crest and two mortar teams setting up their weapons. Bennett saw Captain David G. Rogers, an artillery observer from Battery C of 1st Battalion, 12th Marines, standing about fifteen meters away and motioned him over.

"Look, Dave," Bennett said, pointing. "There's a North Vietnamese up on top of that hill up there. Get some arty up there real fast!"

Bennett complied and called in the map coordinates. "I think that was about the fastest fire mission I ever fired in my life. I think we got rounds up there within a matter of two minutes or less. . . . You could really hear them whistling."

Those NVA mortars got off only four rounds before the Marine fire forced them to move away. Bennett's company had no further enemy contact that night. "We didn't know exactly what was up on top of Hill 881," said Rogers. "It was a real deceiving place to be in. . . . If somebody were to have told me that there was an entire battalion of North Vietnamese up on top of that hill, I think I would have looked at him and told him he was crazy. First of all, you couldn't really see any signs of North Vietnamese up there . . . a battalion-sized unit, up on top of that hill — I just couldn't imagine it."

Rogers saw some bunkers, maybe five. The others were so well camouflaged that most troopers could not detect them unless they walked right up to them. The North Vietnamese had organized both knobs of the hill for defense, each an independent strong point connected by linear defenses between the knolls. There were six mortar pits, linked with the command posts by communications wire. The main command post was located on the western knoll.

Early the next morning Marines spotted four NVA soldiers on the hill and called in artillery, more shells on top of the barrages that had raked over the objective during the night. Lieutenant Billy D. Crews led the forward platoon of Mike Company, 3/3, in the assault. By 10:25 A.M. Crews's platoon was at the western end of the westernmost knoll and began to swing back. The enemy offered only sporadic small arms fire. Just after Crews told Bennett he could handle the resistance, the Marines ran into heavy opposition. Bennett sent in Lieutenant Douglas Houser's 2nd Platoon to assist, but they were unable to maneuver, either to advance or withdraw. In their bunkers the NVA were invisible. Crews was wounded by the mortar fire but still ran back and forth pulling his men to cover and carrying wounded Marines to safety.

When Mike Company encountered trouble, Khe Sanh combat base ran into a problem of its own. The detachment of 155mm howitzers supporting this attack on Hill 881 South consisted of older guns of the towed variety, heavy cannon with long, awkward trails. In the muddy conditions, Major George Golden found, the artillerymen of the 12th Marines needed half an hour to turn the howitzers to the new facing and commence fire.

Mike Company's commander eventually committed his 3rd Platoon along with the others in a bid to secure the eastern face of the hill. That unit suffered heavy casualties, including the platoon leader. Lieutenant Houser of the 2nd Platoon took over, organized the remnants of both units into a fighting force, supervised medevac of casualties, and directed the Marines' continued assault. Tactical command of the 3rd Platoon went to Staff Sergeant Leo Meier, who became separated from his men and was left with a force of only six wounded Marines. Meier covered the wounded until he was able to get them into a bunker for protection, and then he called in artillery and 81mm mortar fire on the NVA.

"The most impressive thing I saw is the actions of the American youngster," Captain Bennett told reporters from Stars & Stripes. "The same long-haired kid that loves rock and roll music . . . comes through with flying colors when the chips are down."

From Colonel Wilder's standpoint at battalion, there was little question that Hill 881 South was too tough and that his men would have to come off so that the hill could be pounded with more air and artillery. Wilder sent in reinforcements to help Bennett disengage and then reinforced again with Kilo Company of the 3rd Battalion, 9th Marines. The crest of the hill was a maelstrom. Lance Corporal Larry W. Umstead recalls, "You couldn't hardly hear yourself think where we were — so much small arms fire and mortar fire going on." Wilder ordered withdrawal at 12:30 P.M. but it required several hours to accomplish. Even then, though the Marines were able to retrieve their wounded, they had to leave behind the bodies of the dead. Casualties amounted to 43 dead and 109 wounded. Bennett's

Mike Company had ceased to exist as an effective fighting force. "I can still remember coming back," recalls David Rogers. "It was getting dark at the time. . . . And there was lines, more or less a line coming like a line of ants . . . down at the foot of 881 and going to the LZ itself."

Colonel Delong's 2nd Battalion, 3rd Marines also had their hands full that day. Delong's battalion moved off Hill 861 to clear Wilder's right flank and reach a suitable position from which to assault 881 North. There ensued some sharp fighting, including one encounter in the same area where, the previous day, Company M of the 9th Marines had had such difficulty. Now Delong committed two rifle companies to sweep to the foot of 881 North. Artillery fired 1,685 rounds in support of the infantry that day, while 118 air sorties delivered 323,750 pounds of bombs and rockets.

Captain Bennett's Mike Company, decimated by its battle losses, withdrew to Khe Sanh and was rotated back to Dong Ha by air, to be replaced by Company E of the 9th Marines. Bennett himself, who had been on a thirty-day indoctrination tour from one of the aircraft carriers in the Gulf of Tonkin and thus held only temporary command, had gotten far more than he'd bargained for.

Unknown to the Marines, the North Vietnamese withdrew from Hill 881 South during the night of April 30/May 1. Thus the big bombardment of May Day fell upon very little: that day 166 air sorties delivered more than 650,000 pounds while artillery fired an additional 1,445 rounds at both 881 South and 881 North. On Tuesday morning, May 2, Wilder's Marines went in again against 881 South with two companies on the line. They found little resistance and secured the hill by midafternoon. Marines discovered that the pounding of their artillery and aircraft had collapsed all but about 50 of the estimated 250 bunkers on the hill position.

The First Lang Vei Attack

North Vietnamese forces around Khe Sanh without doubt were bloodied by the hill fights. Intelligence established that the NVA 18th Regiment broke contact and returned to base camps in Laos at about this time. Its place was taken by another regiment, the 95-C, also organic to the North Vietnamese 325-C Division. Not content to defend passively, the NVA 95-C prepared an attack of its own. According to Marine intelligence, this attack was related to the widespread shellings that occurred along the DMZ in late April and was to spark a major NVA offensive. The target of the 95-C Regiment's attack, which punctuated the Marines' offensive against the three hills, was the Special Forces camp at Lang Vei.

When Green Beret Captain John J. Duffy had moved his detachment A-101 to Lang Vei just before the beginning of the year, there had been no obvious threat. Feeling secure, Duffy had paid Bru from the village to remove the unmarked minefield, perhaps 180 meters wide, which had protected the CIDG camp. "He did it on the orders of somebody who said that the camp was dirty," recalls Sergeant Bill Steptoe. "It sounded like Colonel Reeder." The minefield had been the camp's sole protective device.

By now Duffy had gone, his place taken by Captain William A. Crenshaw. A new arrival, Crenshaw had been in Vietnam for only two weeks and at Lang Vei for just a few days when the North Vietnamese came at him. It is understandable that the fresh detachment commander missed certain signs of impending attack.

Sergeant Steptoe returned to Lang Vei only that day, May 3. He had been out for more than a week leading a thirty-man patrol that ventured north of the DMZ, keeping one step ahead of the North Vietnamese. A couple of times Steptoe's patrol had been cut off, and there had been one terrific firefight in which they were almost trapped. Steptoe brought his men back convinced they had been in a running contact with the leading elements of an NVA force closing in for an attack, but when Steptoe reported to Franchise Rep enemy presence in divisional strength, the Marine command would not believe him. Nor did Captain Crenshaw. Steptoe told the detachment commander he should have Lang Vei stand to and go on the alert, because his patrol had been followed back. According to Steptoe, Crenshaw retorted that Duffy had told him there was no problem and rejected the advice.

"We got hit that night," recalls Steptoe.

The North Vietnamese may have followed Steptoe's patrol back to Lang Vei, but their attack was no hasty encounter. It was a long and carefully prepared assault. Dinh Nhon, a local who had joined the Viet Cong at the beginning of 1967, had apparently been ordered in April to join the CIDG to get information about Lang Vei camp. Nhon created an intelligence network from within, recruiting Sam Boi of the

101st CIDG Company to plot the location of camp bunkers; A Loi, a member of the 103rd Company, to report on the schedules of guard posts; Than Dinh, a 101st CIDG man, to map Lang Vei; and Sang Dinh to report on supply deliveries. This agent network served the NVA well; American intelligence later established that Dinh Nhon had been in contact with superiors at least four times before the attack. On the night of May 4, the VC agents wore no shirts so their comrades could recognize them.

Bill Steptoe, who went on to become a captain before retiring from the Army, gives the best account of the attack:

> I heard the first rounds. . . . They came in at three o'clock. I was . . . asleep on the lower bunk with [A-101 executive officer Franklin D.] Stallings in the team house. I ran down the team house steps, and mortars were coming in and rockets.
>
> As I went down the steps in my underwear, a man jumped up and fired at me and I dodged, and the bullets hit Stallings. He fell, hit in the chest. I shot at this man; I don't know whether I hit him. I kept going. Stallings was sprawled upside down. By that time there were skirmishes going on along the fence line. Our own CIDG were responding . . . sappers had gotten in the camp. Now I went directly to the main bunker to make sure the CO had notified our C detachment and Khe Sanh as to what was going on.
>
> As I hit the main bunker, a mortar [fragment] hit me, blew off a finger, and got me as I dove through the door. And once I was in there I talked to Crenshaw who was standing against the wall. I had my back to the bunker, and I told him that people were in the camp. And at that time a burst from an AK-47 got me in the left arm and shoulder. And the same bullets that got me killed Crenshaw.

The fighting continued for four hours. By 3:30 A.M. on May 4 Khe Sanh began to receive requests for defensive artillery fire from Lang Vei's communications specialist, who asked for counter-mortar fire to the south and west. The Special Forces men at first supposed that the assault had been preceded by a two-hundred-round mortar barrage, but it was later established that the noise had actually been bangalore torpedoes blowing paths through the wire. In any case the communications man at Lang Vei had no map with him and no knowledge of the available array of preplanned fires. He proved unable to supply grid coordinates for effective artillery bombardment.

Khe Sanh began by firing blind, by the map, one grid square to the south and one to the west of Lang Vei. When communications proved unable to correct fire, Khe Sanh switched to the preplanned close-in concentrations, about ten minutes after commencing the bombardment at 3:50. After half an hour Lang Vei asked that the bombardment be terminated.

Meanwhile the entire situation was further complicated by the fact that the Green Beret communications sergeant had the only working radio at Lang Vei. The camp had two patrols still out in the field, and the man had to change radio channels to speak with them. Finally, it turned out that the list of preplanned artillery fires had been destroyed in Lang Vei's command bunker. Then the communications building, which had a straw roof, was set on fire. Nothing came easily that night.

Meanwhile a flareship had diverted to Lang Vei with the initial contact report. It was on station by 3:40, followed by two gunship helicopters that reached the area about 4:25 and a "Spooky" gunship plus other fixed-wing aircraft that began arriving at 5:25. By then Khe Sanh combat base had long since gone on alert while a relief force was en route from Khe Sanh village. The relief, a little ragged, consisted of four men in a jeep under district adviser Captain James Whitenack, followed by a PF force under Lieutenant Nhe, the district chief. Khe Sanh put a Marine rifle company on fifteen-minute alert to move at 4:05 A.M. but never committed them.

Soon after first light, helicopters arrived at Lang Vei to evacuate the wounded, who numbered two Americans plus thirty-nine CIDG strikers. Two Green Berets and twenty more strikers were dead. Known NVA losses were a mere seven killed, while even the estimate of "possible" additional North Vietnamese dead amounted to only five. The Lang Vei action could only be regarded as a North Vietnamese success.

Why did no Marines go to reinforce Lang Vei? Some blame service animosities. Some note that few Marines were available. Others argue that the NVA seemed to be pulling out before Marines could get into motion. Certainly by dawn, when Whitenack's relief force reached the CIDG camp, most of the NVA had already left. By then only demolitions people remained, tossing satchel charges into camp installations. Asked about his policy on sending Marines to Lang Vei, the next Marine commander, Colonel John J. Padley, would say: "We have to be very leery because the enemy know we're going to defend that place, and if they attack, their attack may be for us to come down the road so they can ambush us." Artillery officer Major Golden made another observation: "The NVA would hit Lang Vei. We would turn our howitzer tubes around and attempt to support the Green Berets . . . and at the same time [the NVA] would hit the Marines on Hills 861 and 881."

The senior officer present, Colonel Reeder, also had no operational control over the Special Forces or, for that matter, over MACV's Studies and Observation Group (MACVSOG) and thus no authority to give them orders. Once, looking for a place to hook up a generator for the combat operations center, Reeder had begun to enter an SOG bunker only to confront an AR-15 leveled at him and a warning that he would be shot if he took another step. Reeder was amused by the incident because none of the SOG men knew of the work he had done for the CIA. Still, with other units responding to their own chains of command, Franchise Rep had responsibility without authority, a situation fraught with danger. Reeder would have liked to order the CIDGs to take cover within the combat base but there was no way he could do it. The identical problem would surface in early 1968 when attack on Lang Vei once again impended.

"We Could Sit on Our Chairs and Watch the Jets"

The Lang Vei attack punctuated the hill battles north of Khe Sanh but hardly interrupted them. The final objective north of the combat base remained Hill 881 North. Earl Delong's 2nd Battalion, 3rd Marines had pushed off for that objective on May 4 after spending two days combing Hill 861. Only about three kilometers separated the two hills, connected along a ridge line running back to the northwest. Sweeping that distance turned out to be a lot more difficult than anyone anticipated, however. Originally Echo Company of the 9th Marines was to have made the initial assault on 881 North on May Day. Instead that unit had had to be temporarily assigned to help Wilder's 3rd Battalion, 3rd Marines on 881 South.

Extra neutralization fire flung at 881 North had little appreciable impact. Nevertheless on the morning of May 2 Colonel Delong sent his Marines against the hill. Echo Company attacked from the south and Golf Company from the east. Hotel Company occupied an intermediate support position in battalion reserve. In little more than two weeks at Khe Sanh these two companies had already witnessed more fighting than in their previous months with the Marine Special Landing Force. Additional support was available from three 105mm howitzers of Battery F, 2nd Battalion, 12th Marines, which were moved from the combat base to the crest of Hill 881 South. The guns were a limited asset in the event of heavy fighting, however, because their entire ammunition supply was heliborne, a good deal of it expended in the preparation phase before the initial advance — 1,400 rounds in front of Golf Company alone.

Golf Company advanced along the narrow ridge line. Almost immediately it made contact. Intelligence later estimated that two North Vietnamese companies were deployed in this area, with a battalion (minus detachments) on 881 North itself. Second Lieutenant Andrew B. McFarlane's 1st Platoon, leading the advance, took a series of casualties including four men missing. There were support problems as well, beginning with bad weather that ruled out fixed-wing air strikes. Two helicopter gunships were all Golf could get. At midafternoon the company drew back so artillery could paste the enemy, but difficulties developed between the forward observer and the battery, which did not believe the observer could have seen the things he was calling in and so refused to fire the missions he asked for. With darkness approaching, McFarlane, his platoon sergeant, two squad leaders, the radio man, and eight other Marines tried to make a rush and recover the missing men, two of whom could be seen lying in a grassy clearing, apparent casualties. Sergeant Harry W. Steere recalled later that any movement at all toward the missing men was hazardous because the North Vietnamese had the ground so well covered with fire.

Several days later the bodies of the missing Marines were recovered. One rifleman was found with his brand new M-16 between his legs, cleaning rod in the barrel and a bullet in the chamber. (The hill battles at Khe Sanh were the first major action where Marines used the M-16 assault rifle, replacing their heavier but reliable M-14s. In the early days the lightweight M-16 was notorious for jamming and misfiring. After Khe Sanh the Marine command at Da Nang actually complained about the M-16s, but their objections were dismissed up the line, where the Marines were accused of not adequately instructing their riflemen in the care of the new weapon. Eventually weapons designers conceded the reality of M-16 technical problems and adopted new ammunition and other features to fix this rifle.)

About 4:30 A.M. on May 3, Sergeant Billy Joe Like, a 2nd Platoon squad leader with Echo Company of 2/3, was walking the lines of his perimeter when he heard a noise outside it. "Who's out there?" he yelled. The answer was a burst of automatic weapons fire that wounded Like in the belly. The squad leader nevertheless remained standing and shouted a warning that alerted the company just in time. Sergeant Like won a Bronze Star that night.

The encounter lasted almost seven hours and brought Echo Company to the brink of disaster. The NVA apparently committed a second rifle company to their attack and broke one sector of the perimeter, reaching a tree line inside it. Before the fight ended, the company executive officer, Lieutenant John F. Adinolfi, had to take over for the wounded commander, Captain Alfred E. Lyon, and Echo required the assistance of Hotel Company. Golf Company joined the others during the day of May 3. All three maneuvering companies of Colonel Delong's 2nd Battalion, 3rd Marines spent the night closed up in a hedgehog on the slope of Hill 881 North. They could hear the Lang Vei battle but could not see it.

Marines held their positions through the day after the Lang Vei action, as Khe Sanh maintained readiness to respond to any further North Vietnamese overtures. The Marine command further reinforced Khe Sanh with Charlie Company of the 1st Battalion, 26th Marines. The day passed without untoward incident. Regimental commander Colonel Lanigan, once he had a new rifle company for reserve, sent forward Foxtrot Company of 2/3 to join Delong's battalion. On the morning of Friday, May 5, Foxtrot and Echo Companies led the assault on 881 North. They met only occasional sniper fire and captured the regiment's final objective by 2:45 that afternoon. Marines had the hills.

On the ground, military logic dominated. It seemed that the North Vietnamese were drawing back, so the Marines followed. Aerial reconnaissance saw enemy formations on the trails; recon parties were inserted, and patrols went out to the northwest of the new hill positions. A *chieu hoi* (defector) and prisoners taken in the last days of fighting gave the Marines more information they could exploit.

The pursuit brought the enemy to ground on May 9. Two platoons of Foxtrot Company were moving down a well-used trail on the northern finger of Hill 778, about three kilometers northwest of 881 North, when the point man saw what he at first thought was the point of an NVA squad. An attempt to shoot one enemy carrying a mortar tube quickly boiled over into a full-scale battle. The Marines pulled off the trail onto higher ground. Captain Douglas W. Lemon, battalion operations officer, coordinated the Marines and their support forces. Colonel Delong ordered up Echo Company to reinforce. When the smoke had cleared, the Marines counted thirty-one NVA bodies, and Echo found a site with more than two hundred freshly dug graves. But 2nd Battalion, 3rd Marines had another twenty-four dead and nineteen wounded.

Then there was the ordeal of recon patrol Breaker, team 1-A-2, led by Sergeant James N. Tycz. At twenty-one Tycz was considerably older than most Marines in Vietnam, a thoughtful man who had once attended St. Francis Seminary in Wisconsin and sometimes led prayers before a patrol. The team needed every prayer this time, when they were inserted on the afternoon of May 9 at Hill 665, a good dozen kilometers northwest of 881 North. Tycz had the mission of observing NVA infiltration routes. Less than two hours after landing, the recon team discovered NVA base facilities, and that night North Vietnamese troops found the Marines' harbor site.

Two NVA soldiers walked into the position and began to unsling their rifles. Private First Class Steven D. Lopez, team radio man, shot them first.

All hell erupted. Tycz immediately requested artillery fire, encouraging his men until he himself was felled attempting to throw back an enemy grenade. Lt. Heinz Ahlmeyer, Jr., a 3rd Reconnaissance platoon commander accompanying the patrol, was killed instantly. Within minutes several more Marines were wounded, including Lopez, who took over the job of calling in support. The vicious fight went on throughout the night, with the NVA kept off by gunships, Spooky aircraft, and artillery that Lopez kept calling closer and closer to the Marines' own positions, to the point that artillery officers feared to fire the requested missions.

Lance Corporal Samuel Arthur Sharp, Jr., was one of the recon men. He loved the outdoors, growing up camping, hunting, and fishing in California and Oregon. Sharp dreamed of buying a Chevrolet Malibu when he returned from the Nam and assured his dad they would hunt deer when he got home. On May 7, just before the Breaker patrol, Sharp wrote his parents: "They took 861-881 now and things are beginning to quiet down around here. We could sit on our chairs out in back of the tent and watch the jets and B-52s make the runs on Hill 861." The letter went out with a May 10 postmark. By then Sam Sharp was fighting his last battle.

Two efforts were made to extract the Marines by helicopter during the night of May 9. Hostile fire frustrated both. Two CH-46 helicopters were badly damaged, a pilot killed, another pilot and several crewmen wounded. Two more choppers were damaged in the morning, and the final extraction was carried out by Major Charles A. Reynolds, piloting the UH-1E slick that was the personal command helicopter of division commander General Bruno A. Hochmuth. Meanwhile two gunship helicopters remained on station, except for refueling, for up to twelve hours.

On the ground Private Lopez coordinated, calling support fires, directing the gunships, warning the rescue helicopters, all the while repeating that he was fine, telling no one that in fact he had been wounded several times. When Major Reynolds at last got into the LZ, only Lopez and Lance Corporal R. Carlson could be rescued. By then the wounded were completely exhausted, but the entire area was becoming engulfed by a grass fire. Bodies had to be abandoned. Lopez, Carlson, and Tycz received Silver Stars, the last posthumously. Relatives of the men whose bodies were never recovered still wonder if they might have been alive when the rest of the patrol was forced to leave.

The Breaker patrol action proved to be the final contact of the Khe Sanh hill battles. Marines had turned back the North Vietnamese 325-C Division, breaking up a carefully planned NVA operation intended to capture the combat base. The American troops had also. mauled the NVA 18th Regiment, captured three critical hill positions, and stood off several North Vietnamese probes or counterattacks. However, Lang Vei CIDG camp had almost been lost. Confirmed North Vietnamese casualties for the period April 24 through May 13 totaled 940 dead. Marine losses amounted to 155 killed in action plus 425 wounded. The official Marine history for 1967 remarks drily that "the cost of stopping the Communist effort was not light."

Cost, however, did not appear to be a factor as Marine leaders surveyed the outcome. "The destruction of the base and forces at Khe Sanh probably has been an enemy objective of long standing," opined

Pacific Marine commander General Victor Krulak in a May 7 report. Krulak understood the drawbacks of a Khe Sanh defense position as well as anyone, noting that "enemy determination to destroy Khe Sanh or to attack it as a means of attracting US/ARVN forces into a Dien Bien Phu type situation has been whetted by the fact that Khe Sanh is located in an area that favors the enemy in terms of terrain and weather." For Krulak the "critical nature" of Khe Sanh outweighed these considerations, thus moving him more toward William Westmoreland's orbit without confronting the corollary question of why, if the locale so favored the North Vietnamese, the United States ought to hold Khe Sanh at all. Lew Walt might have picked up that problem but by this time Walt was due to relinquish command of III MAF in just a few weeks, to be succeeded by Lieutenant General Robert E. Cushman.

The end of the hill battles could have served as a time for reassessment, especially since the Lang Vei action had provided graphic evidence of NVA ability to cause mayhem in the sector. Instead the tactical commanders remained preoccupied with pursuit of the North Vietnamese troops withdrawing from the area while higher commanders concerned themselves with other aspects of the war.

Because Colonel Delong's 2nd Battalion, 3rd Marines had been and still was assigned to the Special Landing Force, when it withdrew from Khe Sanh the unit went back aboard amphibious ships off the Vietnamese coast. One squad, veterans of the hill fights, were gathering mail one day when they found a package addressed to a buddy who had been killed on the hills. They remembered that he was a really good guy who used to get packages of cookies from his mother and share them. The Marines put the box on a table in front of them and discussed the matter long and earnestly. Finally they decided that since their buddy had always shared his cookies, they should open the box. They did. The box contained cookies. The Marines broke them out and shared them in silence. Then they wrote their comrade's mother, saying that they had been buddies of her son and that it was an honor to have known him.

The best epitaph on the hill battles is "Home from the Woods," free verse by William Stoss of 2nd Battalion, 3rd Marines:

> As I stood on the hangar deck with its empty spaces
> That could of held 5,000 strong men —

Only a wooden crate stood, full of broken equipment,
    broken dreams, and bloodstained web gear, staring out
    at me.

All that was left of untold numbers of brown haired,
    sandy haired, bright eyed, innocent young —
Oh so young warriors.

I felt compelled to touch, and turn over, and hold
    every piece of metal, every piece of material,
    trying to feel, trying to bring back, trying to
    remember the faces,
The smiles, the names of the men — the boys that only
    a few days before had been
My friends, my comrades, my buddies. My point man,
    my radio man, my tail end charlie.

I tried to remember what had brought me to this hollow
    wooden graveyard so cold
With the sweet smell of death still surrounding it.
I was numb, I was going back,
Almost running into the hills — the hills called Khe Sanh.
Somewhere else called the foothills of Ohio, or Kentucky,
    or Pennsylvania,
But remember, come back, you are not home.
Remember you are in the mountains, the mountains of Khe
    Sanh, of the country of Vietnam, of the province of
    Quang Tri.

This is the season for walking through the woods,
    dog at my side, rifle at the ready.
Keen eyes, alert senses, await the rabbit or
    squirrel soon to cross my path.

Remember — remember, this is the season for walking in the
woods, but these are not the familiar warm
    woods of Ohio, Kentucky, Pennsylvania.
These are the woods and trails of the mountains,
    the mountains called Khe Sanh.

My rifle is at the ready, my senses are keener and sharper
    than they have ever been.
For no squirrel or rabbit will this day grace my game bag.

For today we are after bigger game, game that is wiser and
    knows the ways of these woods, the hills called Khe Sanh.
They live here, they have lived here for untold thousands
    of years.
These are the men of the woods, the woods called Khe Sanh.

We are the intruder, we are the trespasser, we don't belong,
    not in these hills, these hills called Khe Sanh.

The Advent of the 26th Marines (Summer 1967)

GENERAL LEW WALT'S KHE SANH SWAN SONG, the hill battles, ended just as the crusty general prepared to give up the helm at Da Nang. The III MAF commander was not going to allow grass to grow under the feet of his Marines, and as soon as the contacts petered out Walt ordered withdrawals. Two Marine battalions at Khe Sanh would be succeeded by one, with III MAF using the additional force to help clear the area just south of the DMZ, where the United States planned to install a barrier strong point system that might prevent North Vietnamese infiltration.

On the heels of the changes at Khe Sanh Walt came to visit on May 21, to show the site of the recent battle to Pacific theater commander Admiral Ulysses S. Grant Sharp. Along with them came Major General Hochmuth, the divisional commander responsible for both Khe Sanh and the DMZ. Walt and Sharp went over the ground in some detail, starting with briefings at the combat base that day and going on to the tops of Hills 881 South and 861 on Monday, the 22nd. On Thursday they were followed by General Robert E. Cushman, Jr., then serving a two-month stint as deputy commander of III MAF in preparation for assuming the top post. Cushman brought Vice Admiral John J. Hyland, commander of the Seventh Fleet, and Rear Admiral James R. Reedy, an official of the Defense Communications Agency.

The brass came, they saw, they left Khe Sanh to the Marines on the ground. These were Colonel John J. Padley's 26th Marines, the 1st Battalion of which relieved the assorted formations that had been fighting around the base. Padley replaced Colonel John Lanigan as senior officer present at 3:00 P.M. on May 13. Thus his men had about a week to settle in before the brass came calling.

The Marines who fought the hill battles looked like men who had been through a crisis. Bruce Jones, a recent Marine arrival, one of those observing their departure, recalls the scene trenchantly: "I had never seen anybody who had been in combat. They looked — I mean I talk about a thousand-yard stare — I'll never forget that as long as I live. They just looked right past me. As far as I'm concerned I don't think they thought we were on the same planet!"

In fact, Vietnam was a searing experience for all those who went through combat. World War II veterans may have seen battles unfold on a larger scale, but nothing rivaled Vietnam in the constancy of risk, the immediacy of danger. The average World War II Marine spent seventy days a year in combat. A Marine tour in South Vietnam lasted only thirteen months, but in that time an infantryman could expect to be on combat detail for some 270 days. Moreover, combat in Vietnam seemed wholly illogical — veterans of the "big war" proudly recalled the islands they had captured, the objectives seized. Marines in Vietnam spent their days repeatedly sweeping the same terrain, capturing the same hills and hamlets, sometimes falling victim to ambushes in the same places.

The 26th Marine Regiment would learn these lessons at Khe Sanh unforgettably, for indeed the 26th was a product of World War II. Created to help man the 5th Marine Division, which had been activated on Armistice Day in 1943, the 26th Marines were organized at Camp Pendleton, California, in January 1944. Their baptism of fire occurred under Colonel Chester B. Graham at Iwo Jima in February 1945. From February 19 to the end of the campaign on March 16, the regiment participated in some of the toughest fighting of the Pacific war and suffered 650 killed and 2,025 wounded in action.

For all its horror, the Iwo Jima campaign had lasted twenty-six days. At Khe Sanh, which the regiment would leave for Quang Tri only on April 18, 1968, its campaign would continue for almost a year.

In terms of regimental lineage, not a lot separated these two high points of 26th Marines history, because the unit had been disbanded on March 5, 1946. Having restructured itself as a three-division corps for the postwar battles of the budget, the Marine Corps had found no further use for its 26th Regiment until the Vietnam deployments put intolerable strain on existing forces. The Corps reactivated the regiment on March 1, 1966, at Camp Pendleton. This time there would be no long period of preparation before battle. Under Colonel John J. Padley, the regiment's 1st and 2nd Battalions reached Da Nang by August of that year. Within two weeks, as a battalion team of the Special Landing Force, the 26th was making its first Vietnam amphibious landing.

A native of Clifton Heights, Pennsylvania, John Padley had been a Marine longer than the 26th Regiment had existed. Padley joined the Corps in February 1941, won a commission that May, and served throughout World War II in combat in the Pacific. He commanded F Company of the 2nd Battalion, 23rd Marines at Roi-Namur, Saipan, and Tinian and rose to executive officer of the 2nd Battalion, which billet he held during the Iwo Jima operation.

Padley stayed in the service after the war. By 1951 he was a lieutenant colonel commanding the Marine basic training school at Quantico. He served in recruiting and training posts, attended the Marine senior officers' course himself, went to the Far East in the mid-1950s to command the 1st Battalion, 9th Marines on Okinawa, and returned to command the Marine barracks at Mare Island. From 1961 to 1964 he was an amphibious training staff officer. Then he left for Bangkok and a tour as chief of planning for the SEATO alliance. Padley's extensive experience in training billets made him a logical choice to supervise formation and training of the three battalion landing teams of the 26th Marines. In July 1966, as his battalions went into the Vietnam pipeline, Colonel Padley moved regiment headquarters to Okinawa. In fact, when Padley led a forward staff element to Khe Sanh, the 26th Marines' main headquarters was still at Okinawa and would remain there throughout the battle.

Not Hell, but Still a Very Small Place

John Padley's regiment came to a place that was evolving every day. Khe Sanh had contracted when Mike Sayers's Bravo Company replaced the battalion preceding it, and when the subsequent reinforcements came for the hill battles, the place expanded again. Once again some contraction seemed necessary when Padley's 26th Marines replaced the units at the combat base in May 1967. Padley's initial force consisted of Lieutenant Colonel Donald E. Newton's 1st Battalion,

26th Marines. That was half the previous force and a far cry from the thirteen battalions assembled by the French at Dien Bien Phu, everyone's Khe Sanh nightmare. In both instances the friendly forces had deliberately occupied disadvantageous terrain and then counted on air power and better firepower to overmatch the adversary. The book *Hell in a Very Small Place*, a classic history of Dien Bien Phu by historian Bernard B. Fall, had recently been published in paperback and was beginning to appear in Vietnam. That volume and the other well-known tome on the subject, Jules Roy's *The Battle of Dien Bien Phu*, would make the rounds at Khe Sanh. As life follows art, it seemed the closer these books got to Khe Sanh, the more Khe Sanh seemed like Dien Bien Phu.

Like Dien Bien Phu, Khe Sanh was exercising the role of an offensive base. Marines who arrived during the hill battles and in the summer of 1967 found very little in the way of fortifications, even though the combat base had been built around the defenses of a CIDG camp (Map 5). Living quarters and medical facilities were aboveground, usually only partly sandbagged. The artillery was in open pits. There was little protection for the air traffic control facilities. The combat operations center, headquarters of the 26th Regiment and also the fire coordination center for artillery, was in an underground concrete structure, formerly a Special Forces storage bunker, one of the best protected installations at Khe Sanh.

Completely out in the open were the supply facilities, from food and fuel stocks to ammunition dumps. This was not too surprising for an offensive base that had just come through a round of aggressive actions in the hills. The supply requirements for those actions had been considerable, arming and feeding up to three thousand men a day in the field and another thousand at the combat base, the village, and Lang Vei. The number of aircraft landing at the strip on a typical day jumped from ten before the hill battles to thirty-five. Daily supply deliveries rose to an average of a hundred tons, comparable to the average deliveries at Dien Bien Phu for a much larger force. The velocity of war, so to speak, had increased that much since the days of the French.

Handling all the supplies became the job of logistics support unit (LSU) Bravo under Major John Weeks, originally established in December 1966 to support just one battalion. It was an extension of the force logistic support group Alpha at Phu Bai; most Khe Sanh supplies came up by air from Da Nang or by road from Da Nang through Phu

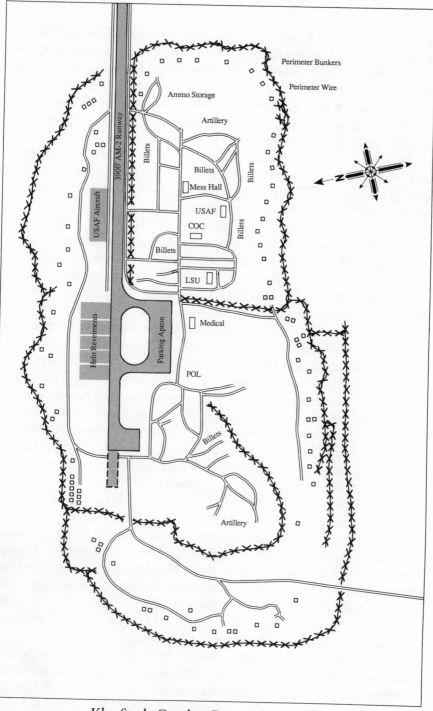

Perimeter Bunkers

Perimeter Wire

Ammo Storage

Artillery

3900' AM-2 Runway

Billets

Billets

Billets

Mess Hall

USAF

COC

Billets

Billets

USAF Aircraft

Billets

LSU

Medical

Helo Revetments

Parking Apron

POL

Billets

Artillery

5 · Khe Sanh Combat Base, May 15, 1967

Bai on the Rough Rider convoys. Supplying the large numbers of troops in the field during the hill battles required numerous helicopter sorties, and that in turn meant extra handling of supplies as they were broken down and reconfigured. A box of cargo could be handled by logistics four or five times before it was passed on to users. This handling was the work of Sergeant James T. Yuspa and two other forklift operators, who worked twenty hours a day.

"Nobody working with the LSU counts the hours or even the days," said Staff Sergeant Louis Hernandez. "We keep the gear moving as long as our guys on the hills need the stuff. If we can't get it done in twenty-four hours, we'll do it in twenty-five!"

The denizens of the combat operations center managed the activities of the rest of Khe Sanh from their underground concrete bunker inherited from Special Forces. It was entered down a semicircular stairway. At the bottom lay an extra-deep step, matched by a drop in the ceiling of the bunker. Marines who forgot to duck going through the entrance often wished they had been wearing their helmets.

Inside the bunker, switchboards lay to the immediate left of the entrance; switchboard Belgrade handled land-line telephones, Intrigue the radio communications. To the right was an empty room that the switchboards had outgrown, followed by a long hall. In the corridor and to the left, a maze of warrens housed the regiment commander, his executive officer, the operations officer, and the air liaison staff. Off the right side opened a large operations room with map displays and banks of telephones or rows of radio operators. Opening off this room to the left was a smaller map room where the operations officer maintained a plot of current activity and where he could have private conferences and briefings for the regiment commander and executive officer.

Adjacent to the plot rooms were rooms housing the artillery and air staffs. Then there was a short set of stairs down to the working space of the intelligence officer. One wall displayed a large-scale map of the surrounding area deep into Laos, another was festooned with maps of the Bru montagnard tribal boundaries and other maps. A room in the center of the intelligence officer's L-shaped space contained an additional array of maps, both French and American ones.

Men of various staff sections emerged from the COC once a day for a regimental briefing attended by about fifty staff members: commanders and senior staff, the officers in charge of the battalions, detachments, and special units that made up the U.S. force. The briefing always occurred in the mess hall in the evening.

At a typical briefing an intelligence staff clerk would bring out a very large 1:50,000 scale map of the entire tactical area, which ranged up to the DMZ, west to Laos, and south and east of Khe Sanh. A similar map set up by the operations people would illustrate the briefing of the S-3, the operations officer. The crowd would gather and mill around until the regimental commander entered, when all would leap to attention. The executive officer, Lieutenant Colonel Louis A. Rann, would start simply by saying "Two!" At that the S-2 (intelligence officer) would begin the proceedings.

The S-2, at first Captain Frank M. Tomeo, and then Captain (later Major) Harper Bohr, would comment on sightings, agent reports, and any other intelligence considered relevant. The S-2 keyed his talk to stickers placed on his display map. He evaluated the reports as he went along, telling what he thought about the reliability of sources and the likely truth of the information. The S-2 would give details of incidents that had taken place: weapons encountered, lights seen, booby traps, and so forth. Then he would summarize important combat actions under way in the sectors of adjacent Marine units such as the 4th and 9th Regiments, comment on the weather, and give the primary and secondary passwords for the night. When the S-2 had finished, the executive officer would say, "Three!"

Major Wayne Wills would array himself in front of the S-3 map, drawing circles with his pointer as he spoke of various actions shown on the map overlay. The acetate overlays had been marked up so many times that the map underneath could hardly be seen. The S-3 would run down the latest data, often reeling off a string of statistics. The reporting system in Vietnam, so reliant on quantification, was often unable to capture the reality of what was happening: the map was forgotten; only the overlays could be seen. It was a perfect metaphor. The Marine patrols would stumble into similar encounters in the same places, again and again.

Supply officer Major Fred McEwan would follow, usually with an exhortation. At the executive officer's call of "Air!" Captain DeVaney would present the day's statistics related to overflights, landings, supply tonnage landed, helicopter inserts, extractions, medevacs, and supporting tactical air sorties. It was sometimes not necessary to say anything in summary; then the artillery staff, supply officer, personnel chief, and others might have comments about their functions. Battalion commanders might make remarks for general edification, and the Seabee construction chief or regimental doctor occasionally had something to say. On a Saturday night the chaplain would announce

Sunday worship schedules and remind everyone to take malaria pills. Finally, Colonels Rann and Lownds would wind up with anything they wished to say. After that the audience would troop out and the clerks would remove the big maps.

By then the entire base was often blanketed in darkness, with no lights that might permit NVA observers to spot and call fire; flashlights were prohibited. Making it safely back to one's bunker could be as difficult as managing the war. Khe Sanh combat base had no paved streets, only one dirt road that could be slippery as ice when wet. And there were holes and obstacles of a hundred different kinds — tent lines and steel stakes, barbed wire barriers, potholes and puddles, even sleeping or sitting men.

All the activity on the base supported troop operations in the field. Nobody thought Khe Sanh a military backwater. Even after the North Vietnamese withdrew from contact following the hill battles the *New York Times* quoted General Westmoreland saying, "I don't think the battle is necessarily over." Of course, Marines continued to differ with Westmoreland. At his end of tour debriefing, the former Franchise Rep Colonel Thomas Horne told interviewers he did not believe the NVA would attack Khe Sanh again in force. Said Horne, "I think the attack on Khe Sanh was of much the same nature, and for the same purpose, as the attack on A Shau in March 1965: Just that they could elicit a bit of propaganda . . . now it's evident that it would cost them more than they can get."

The advent of the 26th Marines and Colonel Padley's succession to command of the base coincided with a new assignment for the base. In operation CROCKETT Marine patrols were to saturate the entire area within artillery range. To do so they were to establish company-size defense positions on Hills 861 and 881 South in addition to holding the radio relay station on Hill 950 and the combat base itself. The North Vietnamese were a shadowy but definite presence: lights seen in the night; tunnels found near 861 and 950; bunkers, trenches, and mortar positions glimpsed from the air. After the inception of CROCKETT, Captain Tomeo remarked, "We've had no rest."

General Hochmuth's 3rd Marine Division staff recognized that the North Vietnamese retained significant capabilities in the Khe Sanh area. With confirmation of the presence of the NVA 95-C Regiment, adversary forces confronting III MAF were estimated to have risen from 18,700 to 20,650. A special intelligence summary by Colonel Philip A. Davis, division G-2, credited the NVA with an ability to deliver heavy rocket and mortar attacks at any time or to launch ground attacks to overrun U.S. forces. The division staff predicted in June, however, that the adversary's most probable course would simply be to continue the buildup.

The intelligence estimates were based on constant reports fed back from air observers, combat units, Special Forces, communications intelligence, and so forth. Typical of the raw material were the agent reports the CIA's Joint Technical Advisory Detachment (JTAD) received from May 13 to May 15. On the 13th an agent reported that Co Roc massif, just inside the Laotian border southwest of Khe Sanh, had long been an NVA bivouac. The report noted caves with two entry holes and three exits and observed that two battalions of NVA 95-C had recently moved through the camp, with six mortars, four anti-aircraft guns, and many light machine guns. On May 14 a report from a casual contact noted that the NVA had used a hundred porters to move one battalion's equipment up to the Laotian border. Another report that covered the 95-C Regiment asserted it had two Russian and three Chinese communications advisers plus a suicide squad that was supposed to attack Huong Hoa district headquarters. Reports like these came from casual encounters with villagers, from regular paid agents, and from locals who passed on information in hopes of being hired as agents.

Air attack could be another effective way to exploit intelligence reports. A good example is a series of strikes on May 27 at targets eight to nine kilometers directly south of Khe Sanh village and Lang Vei. These were set on the basis of agent reports from JTAD and Special Forces. The initial strike triggered a large secondary explosion and five fires from what appeared to be small arms ammunition. Two more fires followed the second strike, which hit a nearby trail, and two more after bombs fell on a supply point. Three waves of strike aircraft dropped bombs and rockets that produced another secondary explosion and seven more fires. The effect was akin to a fireworks display on the Fourth of July.

Some agent reports indicated that the Viet Cong and NVA were more active than previously thought among the local population. For example, a Special Forces agent reported on May 19 that a VC team had visited a Lang Ha 1 hamlet and extracted taxes from the villagers of a kilo of rice and two kilos of salt. On May 26 the same agent further reported a force of three hundred, probably North Vietnamese, visiting Lang Ha 2 and 3. Too heavily armed for Viet Cong, this unit reportedly had three 82mm mortars, four 60mm mortars, two antiaircraft guns, and two machine guns, with the men sporting khaki camouflage uniforms. Then on May 28 JTAD reported a large VC camp about two kilometers northeast of Lao Bao.

As a result of these reports, Special Forces and Marines planned a joint operation to resettle villagers, principally from Sa Tiac and Lang Ta Kut, in the Laotian border area along the Xe Pone river. This operation took place on June 3. As Delta Company of the 1st Battalion, 26th Marines screened the border, CIDG units swept through the villages, gathering 450 refugees and their belongings to be resettled nearer to Lang Vei. Animals that could not be brought out were killed. Once the Bru had their belongings out of their houses, the villages were burned down.

"There was nothing there except old men, old women, and babies," recalls district adviser Captain James Whitenack. "A couple of buildings that we torched blew up even after we searched them. When we searched through the area I found a Russian leather map case and a Russian belt buckle with the hammer and sickle."

Soon after the resettlement, the Laotians, possibly at North Vietnamese instigation, registered an official complaint with the International Control Commission that American troops had fired across the border. The complaint resulted in a visit to the area by U.S. Ambassador Ellsworth Bunker. The United States rejected the Laotian complaint. Actually, as both Laotians and Americans knew perfectly well, the alleged shooting incident, real or not, represented small potatoes in terms of American activities inside Laos. It was far outweighed by the operations of General Westmoreland's shadowy Studies and Observation Group.

Studies and Observation Group

For a long time MACV's ultra-secret special activity unit, the Studies and Observation Group (SOG), had conducted its own reconnaissance missions out of Khe Sanh. The way MACVSOG was organized, until 1967 these missions were in behalf of the forward operating base (FOB-1) at Phu Bai. The FOB commander, Lieutenant Colonel Harry K. Rose, would maintain direct command over all missions, though he might deputize subordinates to act for him at a so-called launch site at the front from which a mission would set out. Khe Sanh was such a launch site.

The senior SOG individual permanently detailed to the Khe Sanh launch site was Master Sergeant William D. Waugh, whose rank was consistent with the status of the site as a satellite. Officers such as Major Jerry Kilburn and Captain Brindell would be sent forward on temporary duty, while Colonel Rose or his deputy, Major Van Sickle, might participate in especially important missions. But Waugh was responsible for day-to-day operations. He acted as controller for more than a hundred operations and participated in many himself.

Two basic types of SOG missions operated from the FOB-1 launch site at Khe Sanh. First were the small reconnaissance teams in project SHINING BRASS. A typical mission would have three Americans who might or might not be accompanied by two or three indigenous personnel. These teams were strictly to seek the adversary, who could then be targeted by other means. Second were the larger "Spike" teams, three Americans and seven to nine natives under project PRAIRIE FIRE. If in danger of discovery the native SOG troops, armed and clothed to look like VC, could pretend to be conducting American prisoners to the rear. For emergencies or especially lucrative targets, platoon-size "Hatchet Force" units could be sent in at a moment's notice. Although earlier accounts use PRAIRIE FIRE as a code name that superseded SHINING BRASS in 1968, describing the same types of operations, it is clear from recently declassified documents that the PRAIRIE FIRE code name referred to activities by larger teams and that it was in use by 1967.

Mission proposals originated in Saigon, where photo interpretation and signals intelligence analysis at MACVSOG headquarters led to ideas for operations. Proposals would be approved at the SOG level by its commander, then Colonel John K. Singlaub, forwarded for endorsement to MACV and CINCPAC, and passed up the line to Washington. The most sensitive targets received consideration by the president of the United States. Approvals came back down the chain of command and were then forwarded by MACVSOG to Colonel Rose at Da Nang. Missions were dispatched from launch sites such as Khe Sanh.

General Westmoreland repeatedly pressed for expansion of his authority for these operations into Laos. In the summer of 1966 he got approval of a five-kilometer-deep operations zone within which teams could be deployed without further reference to Washington. By early

1967 Westmoreland wanted a twenty-kilometer zone and authority to stage multiplatoon forays. That February the MACV commander supported his case with a recent SHINING BRASS mission that had found targets for strikes by 350 fighter-bombers, resulting in 209 observed secondary explosions and numerous fires. Pacific theater commander Oley Sharp concurred with Westmoreland in a January 20 top secret cable. By mid-February President Johnson was aware of these proposals, and late that month he discussed them, probably at one of his very private "Tuesday Lunch" decision-making sessions with close counselors. On February 23 the chairman of the Joint Chiefs of Staff, General Earle G. Wheeler, sent a back-channel cable to both Admiral Sharp and General Westmoreland advising them that they would shortly learn that their recommendations had been approved.

At about this time, possibly in the same round of deliberations in which he approved the expansion of SOG operations into Laos, President Johnson approved a specific target, "Golf-6," a base area on the Laotian side of the border at the head of the A Shau valley. As usual the word went down to FOB-1 and its launch site. For this big mission MACVSOG needed help from the Marines and quickly discovered procedures far different from their own. Waugh tells the story:

> We had a little trouble with the Marines: they didn't want to go in there because they hadn't been told what was going on. When they saw the Laotian border they said, "No way! We've got to get orders from somewhere besides you people." So we had to show them the teletype message from Lyndon Johnson. He wanted that target hit. And they got on the teletype and talked with a Marine general and he said, "Yeah, you got to take them."
> . . . When the team landed there was an NVA running bulldozer, "main digger," trying to square away the road so they could drive faster. He didn't even stop his main digger! We landed all over the place, a hornet's nest, and the weather caved in on us. It was about a two-week deal. We lost two or three units.

In addition to such planned major operations were the fights that developed almost by chance. In one such fight, an SOG team took a prisoner who led the Americans to the site of one of the largest supply caches MACVSOG ever found. It was in Laos about thirty-five kilometers south of Khe Sanh, at a place where a trail crossed a small stream between two mountains.

The bread and butter of MACVSOG operations was gathering intelligence by every possible means. Some of the technical equipment was fairly sophisticated, such as truck counters made up of black boxes plus two long (perhaps thirty-foot) rubber-coated gadgets, similar to the device used by traffic planners. Usually encased wires are strung across a road and connected to the counter, which records data on traffic density and pattern. Since the military could not string wire across roads in enemy territory, photovoltaic or other processes were substituted, and burst radio transmission replaced physical monitoring for data recovery. (An early problem, however, was that the system could not distinguish between vehicles and passing herds of water buffalo.) Other SOG gadgets included the Surveillance System 4-114A Wire Tap Kit for breaking into North Vietnamese telephone land lines. Some of SOG's best work was done by radios at the launch site, simply monitoring NVA radio nets; SOG people often joked that the communications intelligence was so good there was no point going into the field.

In addition to technology and field missions, SOG maintained its own agent networks. For the Khe Sanh sector these extended from the area held by the Laotian 33rd Battalion along the Laotian side of the border to a point some distance above the 17th Parallel. Rhadé montagnards from farther south in the Central Highlands worked for money, and their reports were suspect; Bru were more dependable because their loyalty could be gained, but they were basically ignorant. Agent handlers were well aware of enemy double agents; likewise, some North Vietnamese whom SOG captured had turned against their own side. The best that could be done was to train the agents well in hopes of gaining their real loyalty. At least, the SOG handlers consoled themselves, the double agents led them to plenty of arms caches to demonstrate credibility. Nevertheless the agent net was too strung out and difficult to control for it to be really effective.

Managing SOG could be a problem in its own right. The unit's people were a collection of the toughest hombres and most colorful characters in the U.S. military, men who had signed up when special warfare was by no means a career-enhancing, or even an accepted, assignment. Plenty of people thought they knew exactly what MACV-SOG ought to be doing; bosses did not lack for advice from their subordinates. A typical instance occurred during the summer of 1967, when four Special Forces teams were sent forward from Okinawa to augment SOG at Da Nang/Phu Bai. Captain Lee Dunlap, commanding one of these teams, went to Colonel Rose for assignment. He found the other three captains there already. Rose sent two teams, under John Corley and John McClasky, down to Kontum to join FOB-2. Then Rose told Dunlap that his team would work out of Phu Bai. The last team was Joe Bain's.

"Captain Joe Bain, sir," Dunlap recalls Colonel Rose saying, "you got the lucky draw, and you're going to Khe Sanh with your team!"

Dunlap went back and briefed his Green Berets accordingly. But a couple of hours later Rose called Dunlap back to say that, on second thought, he had decided to keep Bain's A detachment at Phu Bai and send Dunlap's to Khe Sanh.

"Well, sir," Dunlap asked, "would you explain to me the reasoning behind that?"

"Captain Bain has a pretty good argument," Rose replied. "He just graduated from the Defense Language Institute in Chinese and the majority of the recon teams and Hatchet teams and all that at Phu Bai are Chinese — Cholon Chinese . . . and so we feel because of his language ability, he'd be much more . . ."

Dunlap interrupted. "Sir, you know that's a bunch of crap! And I'm telling you that's just a bunch of bull, and he's just trying — and this is not fair!"

"Well, I've made the decision," Rose shot back.

Captain Dunlap had to tell his men it was they who would end up at Khe Sanh after all. He felt their resentment and realized that they feared the incident might show him to be a poor team leader. Fortunately Dunlap soon proved otherwise.

Many MACVSOG troops had known each other for years, so commanders often made allowances for their men. Until one fateful day this was the case with Master Sergeant Skip Minnicks, one of about a hundred Americans with FOB-1 who was seconded to the newly forming FOB-3 at Khe Sanh. Minnicks started having trouble after he damaged a jeep one day and became the subject of dark rumors though the truth was quite funny. As it happened, the jeep needed to be flown out to Da Nang for repairs and thus had to be towed from the Old French Fort to Khe Sanh airstrip. Minnicks was towing the jeep when he saw a Bru village chief on the side of the road hitchhiking. Not thinking of the consequences, Minnicks put the chief in the driver's seat of the jeep with a friend sitting next to him. It quickly became painfully clear that the tribesman knew nothing about driving:

If you can remember in your lifetime the funniest thing that you have ever seen . . . that's what happened to that jeep. . . . Picture the chief, sitting at the wheel. His buddy's sitting beside him. We start off. The slack in the towing chain pays out. Suddenly their necks snap back . . . every turn was an adventure. He didn't know where to turn the wheel. He'd slam into one bank of the road. The chain would come taut again and the jeep snapped sideways. He thought the wheel was merely something to hold. They were scared to death. We never went over ten miles an hour but the jeep smacked into the end of the three-quarter [-ton truck] towing it. The chain would come straight. BANG! He'd crash into one side. BANG! He'd lurch into the bank! And when we got to Khe Sanh, I was sore from laughter. I was hurting. The jeep was destroyed. We hooked the jeep up and sent it out. And when the colonel called, he said, "*What* did you do to that jeep?" I said, "Well it was just scheduled for repair."

Colonel Rose grounded Minnicks for the remainder of his tour.

Then there were SOG's indigenous personnel. The helicopter pilots were Waugh's favorites. "They flew sideways, and they came skimming across the air," he recalls. "They wouldn't tell anybody they were coming or anything else because the first thing they did was to throw all their comm[unications] gear out: they'd lighten their aircraft so they could do tricks with it. But when it came time to fly, they could *fly!* Man, they were good. They were brave, and they all got killed too, see. They all got killed, one by one by one."

One Vietnamese pilot, nicknamed "Moustacio," pulled an incredible feat the day one of the teams had trouble across the border. Moustacio went out on the recovery flight and got hit; the bullet went right through his neck, behind the jugular vein, a shallow wound but one that bled profusely. Instead of seeking treatment, he got rid of half his crew, including the copilot, retaining only the door gunner. Then Moustacio went back for another run, holding his fist into his neck to keep back the blood. He returned with two more recon men. By then Moustacio was so weak he could not even get out of the seat, and a big SOG master sergeant named Scurry lifted the Vietnamese pilot out of the chopper and took him to a Marine medical station. The doctor apparently thought Moustacio was a North Vietnamese and wanted to treat others first. Scurry rasped, "Treat this sonofabitch before I knock you out! He's one of ours!"

Just two weeks later Moustacio was flying again. His eventual end came inside North Vietnam on a clandestine mission. His luck finally ran out and he was captured and killed.

Of course, the ones who had the most trouble with SOG were the North Vietnamese. The territory was so important to them that they had to develop some kind of countermeasure. After a time they did, although no one knows for certain just *what* they did. Sergeant Waugh believes they set up a counterinfiltration screen, perhaps single men, armed and with communications, at intervals of a kilometer or so. When a recon team was inserted, the screen would sound an alarm, permitting larger NVA parties to intervene. The individual screen soldiers would meanwhile drive the Americans into ambushes or toward their confreres merely by firing their weapons, confident that the Americans would seek to evade. Another possibility is that the North Vietnamese somehow had access to SOG's own codes.

In any case a large number of recon teams met the North Vietnamese right on their landing zones at precisely the time of insertion. This was true not only for SOG but for Marine Force Recon, divisional reconnaissance, and other special warfare units. Insertion by helicopter was one giveaway — the sound of the chopper (often accompanied by gunships) or a glimpse of it could furnish warning. An American countertactic was to plot a number of insertion points and fake landings before making a real insertion. Artillery would often be fired at all the prospective LZs to prepare them, another device the enemy could interpret as a giveaway.

The sheer size of teams could make them difficult to conceal. As time went on, SOG began to rely more on parachute drops, both low-level "static line" drops and the high-altitude low opening (HALO) technique. In the latter the team would be dropped at night at heights from 19,000 to 25,000 feet and the men would free-fall to a very low altitude before releasing their parachutes. Because of the difficulty of keeping together in free-fall in the dark, teams using HALO were never bigger than four or five men.

There was no way around the problem of concealing large teams. If big missions were necessary, there had to be enough men for the job. On the scouting missions that were not part of PRAIRIE FIRE, recon teams were smaller. Indeed, the best concealment was to operate as individuals, with the three men of a team moving independently but staying in touch using ultra-high-frequency URC-64 radios. Sergeant Waugh worked that way on some of his missions, which included eleven static line and three HALO insertions. "If you go by helicopter," he observed, "you're dead."

Intelligence was not only the product of SOG operations but their indispensable prerequisite. A clever adversary could not be blamed for failure if a mission was plotted right into NVA strongholds. Missions could be no better than the intelligence on which they were based. A vivid demonstration of this was an operation SOG mounted in conjunction with Navy SEALs (sea-air-land soldiers). The idea was to knock out an apparent underwater bridge the North Vietnamese were using to get vehicles across a stream southwest of Khe Sanh. The joint force reached the objective only to discover that the stream flowed in the opposite direction from what they expected, upsetting the demolition calculations. In places the stream was a mere six inches deep. Destroying the bridge would have made no difference.

By that time the North Vietnamese were closing in on the team. A second SOG team went in to create a diversion while the joint team escaped. The second team managed to capture one NVA soldier who provided interrogators with interesting information — the sole positive result of the adventure.

For all its mishaps, MACVSOG proved effective enough against the NVA that it expanded. When Special Forces moved to Lang Vei they suggested that SOG/Khe Sanh take over the site at Old French Fort. In 1967 this launch site was supplemented by another forward operating base, FOB-3, under Major Fred Patton. As a civic action Patton's men helped John and Carolyn Miller refurbish one of the old Poilane houses in Khe Sanh village and move into it.

Months before the hill battles, SOG told Franchise Rep of finding fighting holes for thousands of NVA in the hinterland. Soon after the hill fights ended, Sergeant Gordon's SOG team saw NVA tanks and artillery pieces, both by night and by day. Who listened now?

Early in June 1967 an ambitious SOG combined operation turned into an unparalleled disaster. This operation, carried out jointly by SOG and the Strategic Air Command, went into an area designated "Oscar-8." Radio traffic analysis showed so many NVA communications emanating from a point about forty kilometers south of Khe Sanh that U.S. intelligence began to suspect not only that it was a headquarters but that it could be the main NVA command for the entire Ho Chi Minh Trail. The point was assigned as a target for an ARC LIGHT strike by B-52 bombers of the Strategic Air Command. SOG's role was to go in right after the strike to assess its effect.

The target was a small valley about 450 meters above sea level, surrounded by hills rising to 900 or 1,200 meters. Studded with cliffs, the terrain was really difficult, ideal for discouraging any American attack. In addition, intelligence estimated that a full NVA regiment guarded the objective.

Bombs fell from the B-52s at altitude as they made their strike on June 2. For reasons that are not yet known, the initial plan to use eighteen B-52s had been scaled back to just four aircraft. Even so, that represented some considerable potential — 240,000 pounds of bombs — and the question became what had they achieved. The entire operation was adversely affected by the weather, high winds, low overcast, and thunderstorms, which forced the planned early morning airlift to be pushed back to late afternoon. Compounding this delay was a mistake in timing: a command helicopter was to enter the target zone immediately after the bombing for an initial check, but the lift choppers followed it so closely that insertion of the SOG team began before the check could be completed. Major Alexander and Sergeant Waugh flew the command chopper and saw secondary explosions, fires, and burning vehicles, but more than a hundred automatic weapons firing tracers at them! By then the SOG landing had already begun.

The air armada consisted of four UH-1E gunships from squadrons VMO-6 and VMO-2, five Marine transport helicopters from HMM-165, and nine Vietnamese H-34 transport helicopters. Together the ships carried an eighty-man SOG Hatchet Force of Americans and Nung tribesmen. The Vietnamese helicopters were first into the landing zone and two of them suffered hits, but by then it had become necessary to land the remainder of the SOG force to give the first elements a fighting chance.

Gunship helicopters furnished what support they could. It was not long before the lead gunship, piloted by Major G. H. Coffin, sustained several critical hits and limped off, only to crash in dense forest about 2,500 meters from the LZ. Major Richard E. Romine, who piloted the lead transport ship for the Marines, disembarked the SOG troopers he was carrying and quickly flew to where another gunship had marked the crash site. Maneuvering along the mountain slope, Romine found the four crew of the downed chopper, discovering that Coffin had a broken back. With no time to wait, Romine tried the rescue himself, hovering at the treetops while lowering his hoist through a gap in the jungle canopy. Romine stabilized his CH-46 in this precarious position for twenty-five minutes, picking up the downed crew and dumping fuel to compensate for the weight as the men were hauled aboard. When the last airman came aboard, Romine's low fuel light had already been glowing for several minutes. He set off for Khe Sanh, warning his own crew they would probably have to crash land along the way. Instead, Romine made it.

At Khe Sanh, crew chief Corporal Michael S. Bradshaw opened the gas tanks to measure the remaining fuel and found not even enough to wet the dipstick.

Back at the landing zone the American and Nung SOG troops organized a perimeter along the rim of one of the craters left by the B-52 bombing. That night the NVA seemed content to keep the Hatchet men under fire, but by morning the pressure was growing worse. At first light the SOG commander requested fixed-wing air support and helicopters to extract his men. Captain Steven W. Pless, who had covered Romine the previous afternoon and had marked the downed chopper for him, was back with a UH-1E gunship. Bad weather kept away the fixed-wing planes, so Pless and his gunships were what stood between the NVA and the embattled SOG troops. Returning to Khe Sanh for fuel and ammunition, Pless would also brief SOG on the latest developments.

The launch site crew did what they could for the beleaguered SOG troops in Laos. Captain James Garvey, who had been a parachute rigger for years as an enlisted man and warrant officer, got a call from Colonel Rose, who told him of the emergency and asked him to get up to Khe Sanh right away to help assemble supply bundles for the troops. At Khe Sanh Garvey joined Sergeant Waugh to put together four bundles of medicine, food, and ammunition. Then they found a pilot willing to fly them to the battle area.

"We were flying along, and I was looking out the windows," Garvey remembers. "We were taking ground fire . . . and these Air Force crew guys — they're just walking around like it wasn't any big deal, and I thought, Geez, they must be really used to this kind of stuff! So if they're not excited, I'm not going to get excited."

The helicopter raised the embattled troops on the radio but could not find them. They dropped one bundle in hopes the ground troops would see it and give them better directions, but that did not happen. Garvey and Waugh returned to Khe Sanh, where Garvey commented to the helicopter crew commander that his men must have seen a lot of fire to be so cool about it. The pilot demurred, and Garvey insisted they had been under fire. The men checked the helicopter to find that it had actually taken seven or eight hits without anyone's realizing it.

Major Romine returned to battle that day. He wanted to help extract the SOG troops before nightfall. Told that contact was light, Romine flew into the LZ, where the worst problem seemed to be that everyone wanted to get on board at once. The SOG force was organized into ten eight-man tactical elements, and the crew chief had instructions to take aboard no more than eight. Corporal Bradshaw had to physically bar the door to Nungs who wanted to escape the battle zone.

Romine's real trouble began when he tried to lift out of the bomb crater landing zone. As his ship climbed through 200 feet it became the target of intense fire; the entire valley seemed to come alive with muzzle flashes and tracers. Suddenly the number two engine quit and the rotor began to lose speed. Romine realized a crash was imminent and turned back to put his ship down in the LZ, broadcasting a Mayday message at the same time. The crash blocked the LZ with fifty-one men, including Major Romine and his newly deposited crew.

Meanwhile Captain Jack H. McCracken, Romine's wingman, was also rushed while his ship was on the ground. He got off with an excessive load of nineteen, but the craft was so tightly packed that three strikers fell from the chopper after it became airborne. McCracken believed he was saved by Steve Pless's gunship, which hovered over him to attract NVA fire.

The third ship in Romine's flight was Captain Stephen P. Hanson's CH-46. He got in and out of the LZ with twelve passengers, including the top Nung commander, Mr. Ky, and three American SOG troopers: Sergeants Ronald J. Dexter, Billy R. Laney, and Charles F. Wilkow. Hanson unknowingly turned into the heaviest concentration of NVA forces as he took off; the helicopter sustained fatal damage, and several passengers and crew chief Sergeant Timothy R. Bodden were wounded. Bodden got up but then suffered a second bullet wound in his belly. The helicopter crashed in an upright attitude, suspended about four and a half feet above the ground by jungle foliage, with a hut not more than two feet from its left side.

Door gunner Lance Corporal Frank E. Cius, Jr., was able to get off a few hundred rounds from his machine gun before the impact but then found himself on his back, which he thought was broken, his body paralyzed. Dexter and Wilkow and a couple of the Nungs were in good enough shape to engage the North Vietnamese. Wilkow followed orders to evacuate the helicopter, saw only one of the pilots, who left to look for a weapon, and escaped. He was rescued, badly wounded and in shock, by a Vietnamese helicopter three days later.

None of the survivors made it back to Major Romine and the SOG perimeter. Instead, Cius, Dexter, and ten Nungs spent the night on a hilltop about 200 meters east of the crash site. After another day and night in the bush they were captured. Cius returned from captivity on March 5, 1973. Sergeants Dexter and Bodden, pilot Hanson, and copilot John G. Gardner are still listed as missing in action.

When the Hanson and Romine ships crashed, Captain Robert W. Byrd took command, requesting fixed-wing air support, which the weather still precluded. Captain Pless stayed with his gunships. Dark forced all the helicopters back to the base, by which time Pless had spent a dozen hours in direct contact with the adversary, not counting the intervals in which he flew back to rearm and refuel. A renewed attempt at extraction would be made the next day. It was clear that that effort would have to succeed or the Hatchet Force remnants would be finished.

Actually, the SOG troops might have been finished already except for Captain Romine and his crew. The crash fortuitously added some extra heavy weapons, ammunition, and a few more men on the ground. Romine himself proved a tower of strength, active everywhere around the perimeter, and when the fixed-wing aircraft finally arrived, the Marine pilot showed himself extraordinarily adept at spotting targets for aircraft and correcting their aim. Through twenty-four straight hours of hell Romine came as close as anyone to being a one-man army. Major Romine won the Navy Cross for this battle. Captain Pless and his entire crew, Captain Byrd, and a number of others were awarded Distinguished Flying Crosses; there were Silver Stars and Bronze Stars galore.

First, though, Romine and the fifty other survivors had to get out of Laos. That happened on June 4, when Major Charles H. Pitman commanded an air armada that included six Marine CH-46s for rescue and recovery, nine Vietnamese H-34s to make the extraction, nine UH-1E gunships for cover, two Vietnamese O-1Es for observation, and two A-1Es for escort. During the final rescue all these aircraft were operating in an airspace of less than two cubic kilometers, in constant danger of midair collision.

Captain Pless set up the gunships so that his division of five operated on the right side of the formation, doing right-hand turns and following an oblong pattern. Another division of four ships took the left side and ran a left-hand pattern. In the center the Vietnamese Air Force H-34s landed and picked up Romine and the others. The third ship into the LZ was shot down as it rose, and another was damaged so badly it could not take any passengers. Two more H-34s diverted to pick up the crew and passengers of the downed craft. When the last of the Vietnamese helicopters had cleared the LZ, there remained a dozen men on the ground awaiting a pickup. Captain Byrd did not hesitate — he dove his CH-46 right in and hovered, two wheels touching the lip of the crater, while the last twelve men climbed aboard.

It had been a near-run thing. A number of SOG personnel were killed or missing and four helicopters were lost, to no good effect. The intelligence that this site was protected by an NVA regiment had probably been right. Sending an eighty-man unit into Oscar-8 had been foolhardy, especially given the weather and reduced ARC LIGHT strike.

Sergeant Wilkow was evacuated on June 10 to the 249th General Hospital at Camp Drake, Yokohama, Japan. Steven Pless finished his Vietnam tour and was transferred to Pensacola, where he died in a motorcycle accident in 1969. Pilot Jack McCracken also died in Pensacola in an accident, a car crash in 1967. After the war Frank Edward Cius returned from captivity in North Vietnam and went home to upstate New York. Only two of the missing have not yet been accounted for.

Attack on the Aerie

If Khe Sanh represented beauty juxtaposed with isolation, uncertainty, and abandonment, then Hill 950 epitomized Khe Sanh. One of the peaks of Dong Tri mountain, across the Rao Quan from the combat base, Hill 950 had originally been occupied as a permanent observation post. Through the twenty-power binoculars atop this hill one could see Laos, the DMZ, such remote Marine positions as the Rockpile, Con Thien, or Gio Linh, even the South China Sea. Surveillance of the immediate Khe Sanh area was child's play.

The war had come to Hill 950 in October 1966, when three Green Berets and thirty CIDG strikers established the observation post. Marines with their FM radios quickly saw the advantages of a radio relay station on the mountain and set one up when they replaced the Special Forces later that year.

Life was Spartan on this aerie. The crest was no more than fifty feet wide and a hundred long, with room for a small landing zone, a few bunkers, and the radio relay tower. There was no water, nothing to do except watch. One could philosophize or one could become bored, and Marines were not too inclined to philosophy. At times the clouds would close in and no helicopters would be able to make the LZ for a week at a time. At those times one couldn't see much either. Hill 950 was the province of eight Marines from the security platoon of the 26th Regiment under Sergeant Richard W. Baskin, six radio operators from the 1st Battalion, and three more from Force Recon.

On the night of June 5–6, 1967, the months of boredom were punctuated by hours of sheer terror. Lance Corporal Charles R. Castillo of Detroit was on watch on the west face of the hill when he saw rockets begin to hit the combat base. His yell awakened Sergeant Baskin just before a grenade exploded in front of Castillo, who called: "Incoming grenades! Everybody get up! We're under attack!"

Moments later a trip flare ignited on the east face of the tiny perimeter, followed by an enemy rocket-propelled grenade, small arms fire, and then grenades. It was just after one in the morning.

Corporal Castillo dashed into Baskin's bunker just as the sergeant got the attention of one of the radio operators, Corporal Wethy, who had been on the other side of the perimeter. Baskin shouted to Wethy to call for artillery on the east face and make sure it was close to the perimeter. Meanwhile four soldiers were seen jumping up and down on top of one of the bunkers. The light of a flare revealed them to be North Vietnamese. It seemed like a victory dance but it was premature. Lance Corporal William C. Balzano shot two down with his machine gun; Private First Class Steven C. Arnold and Lance Corporal Richard Green got the others with rifles.

At almost the same moment the North Vietnamese hurt the Marines with grenades into their machine gun positions. Three Marines were seriously wounded, a major loss for a force of just eighteen men. One Marine covered the withdrawal of his wounded teammates to the main bunker. Baskin saw them coming and wanted to dash out and assist, but then he glimpsed another NVA force coming right up the center of the hill. Baskin and Balzano fired at the new enemy. Baskin estimated that about a reinforced squad of the North Vietnamese had already penetrated his position from the east slope; he could not afford the entry of this new force.

Desperate, Baskin tossed grenade after grenade. Balzano's machine gun froze after firing several hundred rounds. He and Private Arnold stripped it down, trying to find the problem as the enemy assault troops shouted with the excitement of their advance. The NVA reached the Marine snipers' bunker; they blew it up with a shaped charge and shot down the two wounded Marines who staggered out. Now Balzano and Arnold had to share a single rifle. Baskin tried to answer the NVA with a white phosphorus grenade; it struck one North Vietnamese soldier in the chest and also ignited the clothes of another next to him. The next morning Baskin found their bodies, burned to ashes.

At that point Khe Sanh combat base took a hand in the fight. In the base was a detachment of Army troops manning two dual-barrel 40mm cannon, weapons designed as antiaircraft guns that served very well in an antipersonnel role because they provided high-density automatic fire. In Vietnam this kind of 40mm mount was called a "Duster." They must have been assigned to Khe Sanh by someone with Dien Bien Phu in mind, for there the French had turned some quadruple .50-caliber machine guns, the same kind of antiaircraft weapon, to antipersonnel use for the same reasons. At Khe Sanh, as at Dien Bien Phu, these weapons were highly effective.

So it proved this night, even with fog and clouds hanging low over Hill 950. Sergeant Baskin looked up and saw the winking muzzle flashes of the Dusters when they opened fire. "They were like eyes coming out of the fog," Baskin said later. "They were all over the place. It felt good to have this artillery. I felt as though it wouldn't hurt us, because, you know, we were on the same side."

By now the Marine defense consisted of Balzano, Arnold, Corporal J. B. Powell, and Private First Class George Monroe at one position and, ahead of them on the right, Baskin, Castillo, and Green. Several of them were already wounded. Unknown to them, Corporal Wethy remained in a communications bunker and two other groups of Marines were still in action. At the sniper bunker Corporal John R. Burke, though wounded, had shielded buddies with his body, attended to other wounded, and then tried to get back in action. He grabbed a bunch of grenades and charged the North Vietnamese, who cut him down. John Burke won the Navy Cross that night.

The other group of live Marines left on Hill 950 were the radio men in the communications bunker on the north side of the position. They were Corporal David W. Buffalo and two others. When the NVA attack began, the adversary had tried to mask it with mortar fire on Khe Sanh and at the SOG base at Old French Fort. Buffalo had spotted the flashes of mortars hitting the combat base and radioed the information to battalion. Buffalo was wounded about 1:30 A.M. but stayed on the radio to direct artillery fire. His comrades took their rifles to defend the bunker. After an hour or so it seemed to the three communications men that they were the only ones left, since they could see NVA all around them. Buffalo then asked the artillery to fire on their own position.

The artillery at Khe Sanh had come into play earlier, firing preplanned concentrations in the area and then right into the hilltop position. At 2:20 A.M. Marines on 950 asked for a specific fire mission. After 2:30 Colonel James Wilkinson's command post at Khe Sanh could get the relay station not by voice radio but only by pressing the radio handset, which resulted in an audible clicking sound on the receiving set. Informally coded messages could be exchanged by thus "keying" the handset. After 3:00 A.M. it got no response at all.

At 3:10 A.M. the Duster at the east end of Khe Sanh airstrip suffered a misfire that put it out of action and wounded three Army soldiers. Still firing were 106mm recoilless rifles, 4.2-inch mortars, and the 105mm howitzers. At 3:20 recon patrol 2-A-1 took over to correct the fire, assisted by a Spooky gunship.

Marines now believed that Hill 950 had fallen. This was the word Major Ripley at Khe Sanh passed up at 2:30 to the division operations officer, Colonel Edward E. Hammerbeck. Ripley was careful to say that he had only a report indicating the defeat, that the situation was grim, but that the combat base basically did not know the truth. A little later Khe Sanh reported all contact lost with Hill 950.

Colonel Padley planned to dispatch a company-size reaction force to air assault onto the hill at first light. That was the word that reached Dong Ha, where squadron HMM-265 received orders to provide lift for Company D of the 1st Battalion, 26th Marines for a combat assault. Given the available equipment, that boiled down to four CH-46 helicopters led by Major McClellan, with Captain Paul E. Bennett as second section leader. The helicopters were supposed to lift 120 Marines. Also airborne were two helicopters of VMO-3, one a UH-1E gunship, the other a slick carrying General Bruno Hochmuth. When the cloud cover cleared off Hill 950 for a moment at 9:05 A.M., Captain James Korte immediately began a low-altitude pass to look for an LZ and check NVA positions. Korte was so low the North Vietnamese threw hand grenades at him.

On the ground Sergeant Baskin and the other Marines heard the circling choppers. They set off six flares in an effort to get the aircraft to recognize them, but the cloud and fog were so dense that apparently none of the pilots saw anything. Baskin concluded that he would have to capture the communications bunker to regain contact with the outside world. There were three radios in that bunker. North Vietnamese soldiers had set up a machine gun on top.

Corporal Castillo, a trained sniper armed with an AK-47, moved off in one direction trying to outflank the NVA while Baskin crawled up the center. Speaking of the enemy as they parted, Castillo said, "If I see one, Sarge, I'm going to hit him right between the eyes!"

Castillo almost had his head taken off: as he stuck his head around a corner to get a look, someone shot off his helmet.

Baskin threw a red smoke grenade to cover their final assault. The grenade proved to be a dud.

Then Baskin called out to Castillo: "Can you speak French? You've had two and a half years of college at Michigan State."

"Yes," Castillo yelled back.

"Well, maybe those characters understand French. Persuade these guys; use a little psychology," said the sergeant.

"It sounds like a real good idea!" Castillo replied. The lance corporal snapped his fingers and then began hollering something in French. The reply came back: a fierce hail of fire.

The Marines then knew they would have to assault the enemy. Crouching for cover by the sniper bunker, Baskin discovered live Marines inside it and persuaded one to come out. The Marine was in shock but Baskin gave him grenades anyway. He divided up the grenades; there were just six remaining. "Dick, this is it," was all Castillo said.

Baskin shouted, "Move out!" He and Castillo made a dash, throwing their grenades. The North Vietnamese broke and ran down the side of the hill; one was even captured. Castillo the sniper also got his man after all: "Damned if he didn't," Sergeant Baskin said. "He knocked one out of the tree, and that morning we found him: he had a round right between his eyes. And [Castillo] came back shouting, 'I did it! I did it! I got him right between the eyes!' "

Gaining the communications bunker, the Marines once more found wounded comrades inside, in shock to be sure, but communications men who knew how to work radios. This at least simplified things for Baskin, who had been wondering what he could do even if he got to a radio. Now a wounded Marine picked up the microphone and made contact with the combat base. "It was the happiest thing that ever happened to me when I heard him answering questions," Baskin recalled.

Six Marines had been killed. Two Marines had not been hit at all, two were seriously wounded, and everyone else had minor wounds. But the seriously wounded Marines definitely needed a medevac: one man had shrapnel wounds over ninety percent of his body. Yet the fog still blanketed Hill 950 and there seemed no way anyone could get in. Despite this Captain Bennett brought down his chopper under virtual zero visibility and picked up the worst wounded. He flew out on instruments and made Khe Sanh successfully, saving the wounded.

Captain Bennett received a Distinguished Flying Cross. So did Captain James M. Korte. Sergeant Richard Baskin and Lance Corporal Charles Castillo were awarded Silver Stars, radio man David Buffalo a Bronze Star. Artillery fired 3,206 rounds in support of the relay station. When the fog cleared, Company D came in and swept the area, taking a wounded NVA prisoner.

After the battle Delta Company left two platoons at the hilltop station to construct better defenses. Subsequently the standard defense force at Hill 950 was increased to a platoon. The Marines did not abandon the position; they needed it too much.

"Operations There Should Be at Least a Battalion-Size"

The summer of 1967 saw a lot of activity all around Khe Sanh: patrols upon patrols, and more patrols. Some were by reconnaissance teams, some by maneuver units. As always, there were myriad signs of the enemy but relatively few battles. On a number of occasions patrols, usually recon teams, avoided contact successfully.

One of the more significant contacts with the North Vietnamese happened in the course of a patrol off Hill 881 South. Captain James P. B. Connell, Jr., leading Bravo Company of the 1st Battalion, 26th Marines, had been ordered to send a patrol toward Hill 800, about two and a half kilometers to the west. He moved out with two platoons on the morning of Wednesday, June 7. Early in the afternoon a firefight began that lasted several hours and ended with much of Lieutenant Dennis E. McDonald's 2nd Platoon as casualties. The battle petered out about 4:40 P.M. when the North Vietnamese broke contact and retired farther west. Eighteen Marines had been killed and sixteen more wounded, while North Vietnamese losses were put at sixty-three confirmed killed and forty-five more probable.

Over the succeeding days there were more signs of the NVA but no further engagements. Captain Cloud's Charlie Company found a bunker complex with assorted equipment; SOG reported a large company or small battalion between their patrol base and Khe Sanh village; Special Forces supplied several similar reports; and on June 12, recon team 4-A-2 found a company-size harbor site atop Hill 1015 that seemed to have been used one to three days previously. Air observers and Marines at fixed observation posts at the combat base and on the hills added to these reports.

The constant stream of sighting reports generated uncertainty if not concern. Whatever else might be, the irony of the Marine victory in the hill battles of the spring was that it had greatly magnified the defensive problem at Khe Sanh. Where previously only the combat base had had to be defended, plus perhaps the radio relay station on Hill 950 and the CIDG camp, now Marines had to provide defensive perimeters for Hills 861 and 881 South as well. With an increase of the Hill 950 garrison to platoon strength after the battle there and detachment of a company each to 861 and 881 South, coupled with the requirement for at least a company at the combat base, the manpower available for offensive patrolling rapidly disappeared. In June in fact, with a full battalion (the 1st of 26th Marines) at Khe Sanh, the Marines available for operations were typically no more than three platoons, about the same force as had been used when a mere company made up the garrison.

Colonel Padley could not have been satisfied, nor was the Marine command. The result was the dispatch to Khe Sanh on June 13 of the 3rd Battalion, 26th Marines, whose presence might permit saturating the area with aggressive patrols. Though Lieutenant Colonel Kurt L. Hoch's 3/26 was a welcome addition to Padley's available force, it cannot be said that the battalion move was well planned. Quite the contrary, corpsman Paul E. Freese recounted: "Nobody was sure where the hell we were supposed to set up, what we were supposed to do. No arrangements had been made for food; no arrangements had been made for drinking water. In fact there hadn't been any arrangements at all." The battalion brought up enough tents for a sick bay but no one told them where to put them, and much of their equipment stayed at the rear base in Phu Bai.

The next day Kilo Company of the battalion arrived up Route 9, having been kept behind to escort a Rough Rider convoy. The convoy also brought the 26th Regiment's scout sniper platoon and the team's artillery component, Battery C of the 1st Battalion, 13th Marines.

Hill 950 endured another night of hell on June 18–19, but this time the cause was not the NVA. It was quiet but raining hard as the duty radio men recorded perfect reception. Suddenly, at about 10:30 P.M. there was a loud crack followed by explosions. "It was something like falling down a hill at night," remembered Corporal Donald Rogers. "It seemed like ten or fifteen minutes, but it was only a matter of seconds. I felt myself being slammed against the ground, and then being drug along it, raking my face over it, and thrown in the corner. The next thing I remember was the [radio] set being on top of me, sparks flying all over the set, and all out the back and front of it." Two other radio men were also thrown around, one completely out of the bunker. The series of explosions was caused by the hill's entire string of Claymores being more or less simultaneously detonated by the culprit — a bolt of lightning. It had struck the hill's RC-292 antenna, sending an electromagnetic pulse down the guide cables and through the antenna circuits. One guide wire, which ran to the back of a Marine's fighting hole, proved a near-fatal trap: the man's entire back was burnt from the nape of his neck to the tops of his boots and he was paralyzed. Corporal Rogers helped the man to a medevac helicopter and noticed a foot-wide strip corresponding to the burned area where there were no clothes. It was frightening. "There was no clothing at all," Rogers observed. "It wasn't even hanging there. It was just burnt."

A typical lightning bolt carries some 30,000 volts of current, about 25,000 amperes, and can generate up to 50,000 degrees Fahrenheit.

Back at the combat base, the Marines of Lieutenant Colonel Hoch's new battalion went on a sweep southeast of Khe Sanh on June 22, supported by the artillery of Company C of the 1st Battalion, 13th Marines. Helicopters landed a blocking force of Mike Company while Kilo Company plus the battalion command group marched to meet them. The most notable aspect of the excursion turned out to be the fire started by the rockets used to mark the LZ. It threatened to trap the Marines. Hoch considered using demolitions to blast a path along a streambed to escape, but then his men made it to a burnt-out area. While a hastily summoned security force screened them, the remainder of the lead company stripped off their equipment and dashed back to help those still in difficulty.

The new Marines did not get any special warnings about Khe Sanh. While not exactly a rear base, Khe Sanh was generally considered a safe haven among Marines of 3/26. Digging in seemed unnecessary. The new arrivals learned better on June 27. That night, a little after midnight, a barrage of more than fifty rounds of 82mm mortars hit the combat base. The barrage concentrated on the tent area of A Battery, of 1/13, and NVA gunners "walked" their shells from the 3/26 medical aid station to the supply tent, which took a direct hit. For some reason the barrage stopped there, just short of the battalion command post tent. Killed were the ARVN liaison officer, a Navy man, and one Marine who succumbed to his wounds. Others wounded included ten Navy corpsmen and twenty-one Marines. Marine artillery suffered two dead and about thirty wounded.

Old Khe Sanh hands calmed the scared Marines with soothing speculation that there would be no more fire because the NVA would worry about being spotted and targeted for counterfire or air strikes. But at dawn Khe Sanh came under fire once more — about fifty 122mm rockets launched from the base of Hill 1015. Though the launch site was spotted from the radio relay station, the North Vietnamese were not deterred. When the second barrage of the night had ended, the Marine casualty list had grown to nine killed and 125 wounded. After that Hoch's battalion dug in.

In the morning an aerial observer saw what looked like mortar positions at Hill 689 southwest of the combat base. A patrol from combined action platoon Oscar-3 in Ta Cong hamlet investigated. The patrol was ambushed, with three killed, two Marines and one local. In response Colonel Padley dispatched Captain Wayne Coulter's India Company of 3/26. Approaching the crest of Hill 689, India also began receiving fire, including very accurate sniper fire. Khe Sanh decided to air assault a further company into the action. This was Captain Frank Bynum's Lima Company, which lifted into an LZ on the south slope as darkness neared. Both units took mortar fire, but Marine 4.2-inch mortars silenced the North Vietnamese weapons.

Moving on the hill from the east, India Company encountered strong fire pinning the lead elements. Eight Marines were killed and ten wounded. Meanwhile Bynum came up from the south, leading with his 3rd Platoon under Lieutenant Frank H. McCarthy. They reached the crest, but almost immediately McCarthy was seriously wounded by a sniper. Bynum then moved up from his position behind the platoon, but as he reached the top he was shot in the back by the enemy. Lance Corporal Andrew B. Moreno moved through a mined area to rescue Bynum. Moreno put Bynum on his back and then crawled back through the mines, acting as a sort of sled. It was to no avail, however, as Bynum died of his wounds.

As darkness fell, Lima Company held the top of Hill 689 while India occupied an adjacent position that led onto the next hill, 758. Both settled in for an uneasy night in the field. By morning the Marines were growing confident that the North Vietnamese had fled. Colonel Hoch and his 3rd Battalion command group plus Mike Company flew out to exploit the supposed success. That day they found nothing, but toward evening, as battalion held a staff meeting, another few dozen 122mm rockets were launched at them. Most landed outside the perimeter. The Marines of Hoch's group could actually see the rockets being launched, from a site about a kilometer and a half to the southwest.

On the morning of June 29 the battalion moved to the rocket area and found the fire positions together with dud rockets that had been left behind. They discovered several harbor sites, a bunker complex, and some well-used trails, but they had no further contact with the NVA.

Some sweeps never occurred, simply because regiment commanders thought they lacked the troops. One such abortive initiative was a thrust to Hill 918 west of Khe Sanh. John Padley told Marine debriefers, "Operations there should be at least a battalion-size. Whether they're there or not we're never too sure. They've built bunkers. That would have to be a battalion-size to go out there."

As the sequence of patrols and sweeps progressed around Khe Sanh combat base, the 26th Marines were becoming identified with the place. Padley's regiment remained to scour most of the area. The new deployment was a contrast with previous practice, where bits and pieces of many Marine units had been rotated through Khe Sanh in a stream, almost as if staging for some maneuver or other. With the advent of the 26th Marines a major piece took its place for an encounter the fates had arranged, of which no man yet knew.

To Some a Fortress
(Summer–Fall 1967)

A RIDGE LINE RAN OUT toward the Laotian border starting south of Hill 881 South and containing several points that offered excellent observation of Khe Sanh combat base. It was a place that later, during the great siege, some think American reinforcements should have occupied rather than concentrating on low-lying and tactically insignificant features, such as the Rock Quarry. The decision not to occupy the tip of this ridge and defend it was one taken by the Khe Sanh commander. Like so much else, it was a matter of managing the war, and when the moment came the extra troops available seemed to be needed somewhere else.

In any case, an incident in the fall of 1967 offered a harbinger of the gathering forces that would make Khe Sanh the great battlefield it became. The incident was a patrol run by First Lieutenant Ernest E. Spencer, commanding Delta Company of the 1st Battalion, 26th Marines. A Hawaiian boy more comfortable in the jungle than most, Ernie Spencer became the man whom battalion commander Jim Wilkinson most relied on for difficult patrols. In any case, this day Spencer had Delta Company up on that ridge. Just as they forded a stream to commence the climb, the Marines heard a noisemaker halfway up the hill ahead of them. It was the kind of device NVA troops often used to communicate in the field, and the Marines were afraid the sound had been the signal for an ambush. Instead there was no contact.

As the company continued in column, one Marine found a North Vietnamese map on the ground, complete with sketches and notations of features of Khe Sanh. Spencer reported the find to the battalion commander and continued on his way, his Marines increasingly miserable in the rain that had begun to fall. Then, in mid-mission, Delta Company received orders to return immediately; Spencer himself was to come to the combat base and bring the map with him. It did not matter that the men would have to hike into the night; that they would have to ford the stream, now a raging torrent in the rain; or that Delta would have to cross a field ideal for ambush, the very place they had feared contact that morning. Another company commander on patrol recently had been relieved of command precisely for refusing to expose his men on that field. Spencer and his Marines were furious at the risks they were forced to take.

No doubt the North Vietnamese recon map was appreciated by commanders at the Khe Sanh combat operations center. As for Spencer, he was left to deal with his men's ire as best as he could. Regiment felt it needed the intelligence to manage the war.

Practice Nine

The most obvious aspects of war management were the questions of administration and supply, but it was military strategy that underlay all. On the plane of strategy it mattered a good deal just what the tactical approach was going to be. Insofar as the northern sector of South Vietnam was concerned, we have seen already that serious differences existed between General Westmoreland at MACV in Saigon and the Marine III MAF command in Da Nang over the extent of the cross-border threat, which affected places like Khe Sanh. During 1967 it became apparent that those differences replicated themselves when it came to strategy.

Robert Strange McNamara served as the catalyst for this new round of intramilitary conflict. With his particular method of managing the military, the secretary of defense was most at home with numbers. In contrast to some others, he *liked* the intense effort to quantify the Vietnam war. McNamara had come to the Pentagon from business — he had been president of the Ford Motor Company — and numbers were at the heart of profit and loss statements. Though it is important not to overdraw McNamara's fascination with numbers, since he could and did respond to other kinds of arguments, numbers contributed in a special way to the strategic choices made for the III MAF sector. This was due to the old Vietnam problem of isolating the battlefield. Because of numbers, McNamara could take what he believed was a sophisticated approach to the problem: he could avoid the military conundrum of whether isolating the battlefield was possible by focusing on the simpler concept of cost. If the *cost* to Hanoi of moving men and materials into the war zone could be raised, this would reduce the impact and effectiveness of the adversary, even if the battlefield could not be perfectly isolated. This became the rationale for the bombing campaign that began in 1965. By 1967, when McNamara had visibly soured on the efficacy of bombing, the cost rationale still figured in a strategic decision with direct impact on III MAF.

The new issue revolved around what can be called the barrier concept. It was the latest version of the old idea of blocking the "narrow" neck of Indochina to cut off the battlefields in the south, a notion that went back (in the American war) at least as far as SEATO Plan 5. Even in the French Indochina war, generals had fantasized about cutting off the neck to separate the "rotten" north from the less heavily infiltrated south. By the mid-1960s the specific proposals were different but the basic concept was identical to the initiatives of two and five and ten years before.

This iteration of the barrier concept began in Washington in early 1966. That spring McNamara went to the Joint Chiefs of Staff and asked what they thought of a barrier line that would block the DMZ. The Chiefs queried CINCPAC, envisioning a barbed wire barrier from the South China Sea along the DMZ and then across the Laotian panhandle to the Thai border. The line would be cleared and backed with minefields and supported by reaction force troops. Admiral Sharp did not much like the idea, objecting that such a defense system would entail an enormous construction effort and a tremendous logistics burden and then would tie down large numbers of troops, denying MACV the advantage of mobility.

Notions of a barrier would not die, however. That summer a special study was conducted by the JASON Group, a scientific panel run by the Institute for Defense Analysis, a university consortium conducting contract work for the Pentagon, which McNamara also used for detailed studies of the air war. JASON suggested further civil-military study of a barrier concept with two components, one to block foot traffic south of the DMZ, manned by troops, the other to stop vehicular traffic through the Laotian panhandle. McNamara approved implementation without the recommended studies.

The Laotian barrier would essentially be an air operation, employing such new technologies as remote sensors, acoustic, chemical, and others; button bomblets, mines that were designed merely to trip acoustic sensors; and Gravel, air-seeded antipersonnel mines to wound feet and legs. The Gravel mine, which carried the weapon designation XM-41E, actually consisted of a three-inch cloth bag containing powder plus two plastic pellets. The device was undetectable to standard mine detectors, and the pellets were invisible on X-rays. Every wound would have to be treated by exploratory surgery. Large numbers of Gravel mines could be dispensed from each munition casing.

In the barrier system the mines would provide passive defense, the sensors target acquisition. Sensors would be monitored by aircraft that not only would relay the data to a computerized control center in Thailand but could also vector attack aircraft to urgent targets. The air portion of the barrier system was code-named MUSCLE SHOALS, the associated technologies IGLOO WHITE. The cost was not insignificant: $1.6 billion in research and development; a $600 million command center; munitions and aircraft, and so on. But to McNamara these costs were acceptable if they raised the cost for Hanoi to carry on the war in the south.

Combat commanders, most important the theater commander, Admiral U. S. Grant Sharp, distrusted the notion of a technological barrier. In his September 13, 1966, evaluation of the JASON plan, Sharp objected that any barrier could be breached with ease if not tended; an air barrier would not eliminate the need for a ground one. The resources necessary for a ground barrier would be prohibitive. Objections from CINCPAC did not hold back the secretary of defense, however, and two days later McNamara created a joint task force to devise the anti-infiltration barrier system, to be known as Project PRACTICE NINE. The unit was placed under Lieutenant General Alfred D. Starbird, director of the Defense Communications Agency and a former chief of Army research and development.

Westmoreland, who learned of PRACTICE NINE at a mid-September meeting with Starbird, thought it a noble idea but highly theoretical; he shared the CINCPAC view that no barrier could be foolproof without men to cover it. During one of McNamara's periodic visits in October 1966, Westmoreland told the secretary of defense he welcomed the high technology but wanted to employ it in his own fashion. As an alternative, MACV proposed a "strong point obstacle system." Westmoreland put his staff to work on a concrete plan to flesh out the concept. In effect the MACV proposal accepted the aerial barrier, but only for Laos, while placing the strong point system below the DMZ. Force requirements for the plan were put at a division plus an armored cavalry regiment.

The most focused planning was that done by the Marines in support of MACV. Lew Walt still had command of III MAF at the time, but he delegated the task to the 3rd Marine Division, which would be the most directly affected. Walt stipulated, however, that the division's plan should begin with a statement that III MAF disagreed with the whole barrier idea and preferred to use the same forces in mobile operations, as it was already doing. Both the 3rd Marine Division briefing on the barrier plan and General Walt's cover letter submitting the plan to MACV made clear the Marines' dim view of the whole notion.

Saigon took the Marine plan, added a few touches, and sent it to Washington. In its final form the plan called for a linear barrier just south of the DMZ consisting of a swath of cleared ground 600 to 1,000 meters wide containing barbed wire obstacles, minefields, sensors, watchtowers, and the like. The barrier would be backed by a series of strong points, and behind those would be several support bases, from which an armored unit would back up the line. This articulated barrier system would extend about thirty kilometers from the sea to the point where the Annamite mountains begin to rise above the coastal plain. From there to the Laotian border the system would be less extensive, consisting mainly of a selection of twenty or so of the best routes south from the DMZ. Each would be blocked by a "defile barrier" consisting of minefield plus wire obstacles, with manned strong points on hills overlooking the passages. Artillery bases behind the line would also house reaction forces to support the front. Route 9 would be improved to furnish the main lateral communication for the line while, closer to the coast, Highways 1 and 561 would permit north–south movements. Logistics could be improved by expansion of an over-the-beach facility at Cua Viet and construction of a major airfield at Hue.

Secretary McNamara on December 19 ordered General Starbird to prepare a procurement program to provide the material required to have at least part of the system completed by November 1, 1967. Three days of calculations enabled Starbird to propose a schedule of funding and personnel commitments to accomplish the task. Deputy

Secretary of Defense Cyrus R. Vance signed a paper on January 7, 1967, that went to the National Security Council and recommended that PRACTICE NINE be given the highest national priority, a special status for specifically approved programs established by the Defense Production Act of 1950. On January 13, in the name of President Johnson, national security adviser Walt W. Rostow signed National Security Action Memorandum (NSAM) 358 giving PRACTICE NINE the desired priority status.

Meanwhile Westmoreland had ordered up a new requirements plan for PRACTICE NINE to conform with Starbird's Pentagon timetable. The new MACV plan, completed on January 26, estimated troop and logistic requirements for the lowland portion of the line. Additional troop requirements for an effective obstacle system were put at another infantry division plus an armored cavalry regiment. Without this additional force, the study recommended avoiding use of the term "barrier," whose connotations exceeded the capability of the system. Such cautions failed to dissuade Westmoreland, who also remained unimpressed by continued reservations from III MAF and CINCPAC. In a February 6 cable to the Joint Chiefs, CINCPAC agreed the strong point obstacle system (convoluted terminology that avoided "barrier") might be feasible but objected that the level of infiltration across the DMZ was too small to justify diversion of the forces required to construct and man the positions.

In Washington on March 8, McNamara directed Starbird to procure materials necessary for the strong points and support bases plus enough sensors for a ten-kilometer segment of the line. The Pentagon soon let contracts for 200,000 spools of barbed wire (roughly 50,000 miles worth) and more than five million 32-inch and 72-inch steel fence posts. Total cost for the system was soon being put at three to five billion dollars.

Meanwhile Westmoreland gave PRACTICE NINE its official kick-off at a conference at the Da Nang headquarters of III MAF on March 17, 1967. There he presented the plan to ARVN I Corps commander General Hoang Xuan Lam and other South Vietnamese officials. The South Vietnamese not only approved but advised getting an early start to take advantage of weather before the monsoon. Westmoreland ordered Walt and Lam to prepare a joint plan for the actual location and construction of the strong points. Walt in turn directed his PRACTICE NINE plans officer, Lieutenant Colonel Marvin D. Volkert, to meet his ARVN counterpart to begin combined planning. By early

April, though the written plan was yet to be finished, Volkert was able to ensure that plans of Marine units at Con Thien to clear vegetation from a strip of land between there and Gio Linh matched the PRACTICE NINE concept. Walt meanwhile objected to Westmoreland that the PRACTICE NINE assignment was going to tie up his entire 3rd Marine Division.

Published by III MAF on June 18, Operation Plan 11-67 became the actual blueprint for the system. For the western piedmont/mountain area below the DMZ, the PRACTICE NINE plan provided for

> operations . . . conducted from a series of battalion combat operating bases. This plan envisions these bases extending from Camp Carroll westward along Route 9 toward the Laotian border. Logistic support feasibility and weather will probably limit the initial bases to Camp Carroll, Thon Son Lam [the Rockpile], Ca Lu, and Khe Sanh. Subsequent bases would be established in the vicinity of Lang Ru'on [about a kilometer northwest of Hill 881 South] and Lang Vei, with the positioning of an additional battalion at Khe Sanh.

Having originally evolved in January 1967, this concept for the mountain sector was affirmed in Plan 11-67 and again on September 12 in Plan 12-67. Manned to projected levels, the western sector alone would have required almost a full division of combat troops, hardly palatable for a III MAF command already concerned about troop requirements for the system. Thus except for Camp Carroll, the Rockpile, Ca Lu, and Khe Sanh, positions that already existed, *none* of the contemplated western sector combat bases was ever established.

Meanwhile a partial compromise of the code name PRACTICE NINE occurred, though not from III MAF since none of the Marine planning documents used this classified terminology. Saigon renamed the barrier plan DYE MARKER. At about that time McNamara was in South Vietnam and the 3rd Marine Division flew him over sites where DYE MARKER construction was already in progress. Marine briefings maintained that the first phase of construction could be completed by November 1, the date the secretary of defense had set the previous year.

Robert McNamara was impressed enough that, back in Washington on September 7, he gave a press conference announcing the barrier initiative, which, according to the press, troops in Vietnam promptly began calling the "McNamara Line." Westmoreland's Vietnam memoir is misleading on this point, claiming that revelation of the DYE MARKER initiative at the press conference gave the NVA time to move artillery up before construction began. Westmoreland maintains he gave up on the initiative. In fact, 757,520 man-days and 114,519 equipment-hours were devoted to the strong point system by December 31, 1967, and seven of ten positions were complete, with others substantially so. Westmoreland also writes: "To have gone through with constructing the barrier, even in the modified form that I proposed, would have been to invite enormous casualties. Yet I wanted no formal announcement that we had abandoned the project, lest the enemy claim he had forced it." Not only did construction begin long before McNamara ever announced the "line" that eventually bore his name, but, as will become evident, William Westmoreland never abandoned his interest in continuing the strong point obstacle system.

In fact, in mid-October Westy expressed himself as dissatisfied with the pace of work on the system, and on October 22 he specifically told General Robert Cushman, Walt's replacement, that his own observations and staff inspections convinced him that DYE MARKER had not received priority consistent with its operational importance and that quality control was inadequate. As a result, Cushman set up a DYE MARKER special staff under his assistant commander, Major General Raymond L. Murray. Cushman also told subordinate commands that DYE MARKER's priority exceeded everything except emergency combat requirements. This was hardly a project quietly abandoned.

Thus, strategy remained a point in contention. Saigon and Da Nang had different preferences, something that would vitally affect the lives of Marines. A constant tension remained, a tension between those who conceived Khe Sanh as an offensive base in a war of maneuver and those who saw it as the western terminus of the strong point obstacle system, some kind of a fortress.

"Vietnam Really Isn't So Bad"

One man for whom it made a good deal of difference whether Khe Sanh was to be a fortress or a maneuver base was Felix Poilane, who stood to lose many of his valuable coffee trees if the Americans determined to dig in deep and clear large swaths of land for their defense positions. During his time as Franchise Rep Colonel Reeder had grown fond of the expatriate French coffee planter. Poilane clearly tried to help the Bru, felt responsibility for them, even kept their interests as much at heart as his own. Reeder respected that. Poilane was friendly, too. "He was a delightful man in a very difficult situation trying to do the best he could," Reeder remembers.

Poilane had a coffee crop every year. Like any farmer, he had to get it to market, a task greatly complicated by the Vietnam war. It had been Poilane's practice to move his coffee west through Laos to Savannakhet, but this route became impractical as the conflict intensified and North Vietnamese took over the Laotian panhandle, while the Americans busily bombed it. Overland to Dong Ha in the east was not a very practical route either — the Marine Rough Rider convoys had all they could do to carry Marine supplies alone, without concerning themselves with hundred-kilogram sacks of coffee beans. The only alternative for moving the coffee was by air, from the strip at Khe Sanh controlled by the Marines. It is not surprising that Poilane tried hard to maintain good relations with the Americans.

One day in July 1967 a truckload of Marine helicopter pilots made the trip to the plantation along with Lieutenant Hester, who was taking a supply of bread and jam to Bru children at the school the Poilanes ran for their workers. The plantation, which Poilane called "La Petite Fleur," seemed an exotic element of life at Khe Sanh. Felix showed the pilots his pet deer, chatted casually, gave out small bags of his coffee, and served crème de menthe in cold water. It was very pleasant. The yellow concrete buildings contrasted with plentiful red hibiscus and with the coffee beans strewn on concrete slabs in the courtyard. Poilane grew both robusta and chiari beans, one picked in January and February, the other from April through September. Marines gossiped that Poilane must be paying taxes to the Viet Cong. Few of them knew that his father had been assassinated.

Of course the starkest contrast remained that between the peace of the Poilane plantation and the martial milieu of Khe Sanh combat base. There, after the recent mortar and rocket attacks, almost every tent bore numerous shrapnel holes. The view through the roofs at night was like that in a planetarium. Colonel Padley and Lieutenant Colonel Wilkinson were now talking almost continuously about digging in, and Marines were getting serious about building bunkers.

Someone arriving after a seventeen-minute helicopter ride from

Dong Ha would see a hand-lettered sign: WELCOME TO KHE SANH, ELEVATION 1500 FEET. One who made the helicopter ride in late July was John McElroy, Roman Catholic chaplain to the 3rd Battalion, 26th Marines. On the way upcountry he had stopped at Da Nang to visit a senior chaplain, who had air conditioning, maid service, and a swimming pool. They had conversed for some time until the senior chaplain stood up.

"Please excuse me, I have a tennis game to go to," the man remarked. "You know, Vietnam really isn't so bad once you get used to it!"

At Khe Sanh, McElroy lived in a bunker made from a mortar pit, its walls nothing more than red clay, its roof waterproofed by five or six layers of air matting. His first night in the bunker a rat lost its footing on the dirt ledge above, fell on McElroy's chest, and bounced to the floor with a shrill squeal. Da Nang was in a different Vietnam from this.

Showers were prized at Khe Sanh, for which Marines might thank Jim Reeder more than they usually do. The shower was a wooden structure with a fifty-five-gallon steel barrel set above the stall area. It did little good to remove the mud and dirt, since that returned immediately; the real relief was getting rid of the smell and oils. Towels that fell in the mud, as they were wont to do, were permanently dyed red. Sandals and shower clogs stuck in the mud or were frequently lost en route to or from the showers. Alternatively, the tab between the toes could tear out of the clog and a man would step forward to find his bare foot sinking into the mud in front of him.

By late July rain had made the main road on Khe Sanh combat base so soggy it was virtually impassable. The latrines were out in the open, too, uncovered, and when one had to go one simply sat there in the rain. One night a drunk Marine was seen crawling outside the combat operations center of the 1st Battalion, 26th Marines, trying to swim. Corpsmen were summoned but went to regimental headquarters by mistake. At the battalion briefing the next day the operations staff officer joked that it had been raining so much the men were swimming!

The weather and misery played havoc with the Marines' senses and could result in unfortunate incidents. One such occurred on July 29 after NVA snipers fired a few shots at a patrol from Bravo Company of 1/26. The Marines replied with heavy fire, whereupon a reconnaissance team that happened to be nearby assumed they were the targets and answered with fire on the Bravo Marines. Bravo Company replied with mortars, and then the recon team called the combat base to request artillery. Regiment suddenly realized what was happening and ordered everyone to cease fire. Luckily no one was hurt.

At the regimental briefing on July 31 the Navy chief petty officer in charge of the preventive medicine unit told the group that someone had mentioned termites but he did not know who needed help eradicating them.

"Our 1/26 battalion aid station is infested," Wilkinson said.

Intense and serious, the chief asked, "Are they little black bugs?"

"I don't know."

"Well, if they are," the Navy man replied, "they're just wood bores."

"I don't care if they're wood bores or termites," the battalion commander shot back, "they're eating it away!"

By then the audience was convulsed in laughter.

All the rain, however, was a mere prelude to the monsoons. The regimental executive officer McKinney made a point at the daily briefings to remind everyone how many days were left until the monsoon. One chaplain likened it to a fundamentalist stressing the short time left before the Second Coming. The executive officer even had a little red sign outside the regimental operations center that announced the number of days remaining.

As spiritual advisers to the men, chaplains were directly exposed to the erosion of the Marines' élan. "If Jesus were alive today," one Marine asked, "what would He do if He received a draft notice?" Like the other Navy men at Khe Sanh (by custom the Navy provides both chaplains and medical personnel for all Marine units), the chaplains worked hard to stay current with every factor affecting life at Khe Sanh to help themselves deal with the men's doubts. Worship services, celebrations of faith, did not eliminate doubts but helped the men feel that others were with them. Services at one Khe Sanh mess hall had the men standing at chest-high tables, while elsewhere services were held in such places as atop beams at construction sites, in shell craters, and so on. The chaplain for the 1st Battalion, 26th Marines not only stayed overnight at every outlying position, including Lang Vei and Hill 950, but went on combat patrols and experienced numerous misadventures. He tried to understand and found the depth of compassion among Khe Sanh Marines an inspiration.

In early August the regiment suddenly learned there was to be a change of command. Padley would be going home, to be replaced by Colonel David E. Lownds. The 26th Marines arranged a ceremonial parade for the change of command. On August 14 David Lownds took over.

Colonel David Lownds had been special warfare officer on the staff of the Fleet Marine Force Atlantic since the summer of 1965. Previous to that he had earned the Bronze Star while operations officer of the 4th Marine Expeditionary Brigade during the 1965 intervention in the Dominican Republic. Lownds was forty-six, from Holyoke, Massachusetts, and had been commissioned in the Corps at the height of World War II. He had led a platoon in the invasions at Kwajalein, Saipan, and Iwo Jima, suffering wounds in the latter two campaigns. A reserve captain, Lownds was recalled to active duty for the Korean war and became a regular major in 1951. He served in staff positions until the early 1960s, when he returned to troops as commander of the 3rd Battalion, 8th Marines at Camp Lejeune. Later he served as plans officer for the 2nd Marine Division, was promoted to colonel in July 1965, and went to Vietnam in July 1967. Khe Sanh was his first Vietnam duty assignment.

Like his predecessors, Lownds had to learn a good deal about the peculiarities of Vietnam and, among them, the special qualities of Khe Sanh. Though the monsoon was misery, Lownds was perhaps lucky that the reductions in military activities forced by the weather gave him vital time to learn the things he would need to know. Only when the weather got better would the real storm break — a battle for Khe Sanh the likes of which no one imagined.

In the meantime weather was the special cause of one of the first fatalities suffered during Lownds's command. The incident occurred on August 16 at the "Bridge Site," so called because it was the location of the first bridge across the swift-flowing Rao Quan along the stretch of Route 9 to Dong Ha. Franchise Rep typically kept a garrison at the Bridge Site, but that company was withdrawn and the bridge blown at about this time. Private First Class John R. Hinson was helping some Bru montagnards across the Rao Quan at the site when he fell into the river. Hinson was not a swimmer and, swept under, he drowned. Hinson had had little more than a month to go in his Vietnam tour of duty. Lieutenant Epps, platoon commander of Hinson's Company C, though not responsible for Hinson's death, held the incident as one of the reasons he gave up the platoon command a few months later.

Weather, in the form of rain damage, figured directly in one of Colonel Lownds's first command decisions at Khe Sanh. On August 17 Lownds ordered the airstrip closed for maintenance, an action that had been anticipated since July 12, when Ensign Martin J. Kux had brought detail Bravo of Naval Construction Battalion Maintenance Unit 301 to Khe Sanh. Repair required that crushed rock or gravel be laid on the runway five to eight inches thick to form a base under the aluminum plating. Soon the Marines were calling the naval construction men "Rock Crushers."

An outcropping of basalt rock a kilometer west of the combat base, just an eight-minute drive from the perimeter wire, provided the gravel. Ensign Kux deployed heavy equipment to the site, which became known as the "Rock Quarry." The equipment included two rock crushers, earth-moving equipment, and heavy trucks to haul the gravel. Quarrying began on September 2, with a thirty-six-man crew from Naval Support Activity, Da Nang, under Chief Petty Officer Boggess. Rain continued to be the major obstacle to the work, forcing a redesign of the runway to have five slopes instead of one to encourage runoff. The airfield renovation performed by Ensign Kux's Seabees went a good distance toward making Khe Sanh sustainable through the coming siege.

While the airfield remained closed for reconstruction, transports of the Air Force's 315th Air Division used a delivery technique called the low-altitude parachute extraction system (LAPES), in which the planes skimmed a few feet above the ground and cargo on pallets was pulled out of the aircraft by drogue parachutes. General Westmoreland, a paratrooper by specialization, had always been alert for novel methods of supply delivery and had given orders early in the war to prepare and practice air delivery techniques. The first LAPES delivery came on September 6; the practice would become quite valuable during the siege.

Ensign Kux was just one of the 2,849 Americans who experienced this Khe Sanh world during the summer and fall of 1967. They were supported by two 155mm and fifteen 105mm howitzers plus three 4.2-inch mortars. Additional Army and Marine detachments added five M-48A2 "Patton" tanks, ten M-50A1 ONTOS vehicles, and two 40mm dual antiaircraft mounts. Outlying segments of the deployment included the hilltop positions, the CIDG camp at Lang Vei, and CAC Oscar in the villages.

This seemed a reasonably sized force for a combat base, so long as battalion-size operations were not necessary, but it was perhaps less adequate for a fortress. The Khe Sanh deployment became even less satisfactory just a couple of weeks after Dave Lownds's arrival. It was then that the Marine command pulled out the 3rd Battalion, 26th Marines, leaving Khe Sanh once again with a single maneuver battalion.

The Isolation of Khe Sanh

American heavy artillery, specifically Army 175mm guns, supported Khe Sanh from positions at the Rockpile and Camp Carroll. Though it was useful to have this heavy support, the Army artillery was not entirely satisfactory. To reach Khe Sanh, the 175mm guns had to fire at maximum range, using three propellant charges behind each shell. Army planners assumed that gun barrels would wear out after just three hundred rounds. If serious battle required extended support fire for Khe Sanh, that amount of ammunition could be expended quite rapidly. Firing at shorter ranges, the 175mm barrel life could be two or three times longer. In addition, the 175mm gun was not particularly accurate, so at long range it could not be counted on for precise support. Moreover, there were many requests for the fires of the 175mm guns on the coastal plain.

These factors led the Marine command to consider placing additional 175mm guns at Khe Sanh. It cannot have escaped MACV notice that 175mm guns at Khe Sanh would provide U.S. artillery with unprecedented reach into Laos. If there was ever to be an invasion, such heavy artillery would almost surely be a prerequisite. Another likely consideration was the desire to furnish artillery support at less than extended range for the recon teams that ran into trouble in Laos. In the summer of 1967 the U.S. commands agreed to send up the heavy guns.

A Rough Rider convoy organized around the guns on July 21 had more than eighty-five vehicles. As the convoy moved west into the mountains Marine units along its route were to secure the road and provide general cover. These units were a company of Lieutenant Colonel Robert C. Needham's 3rd Battalion, 3rd Marines near Ca Lu, and Wilkinson's 1st Battalion, 26th Marines from the combat base.

Mike Company of 3/3 dispatched its 2nd Platoon on the westward sweep from Ca Lu. The operation went smoothly until the Marine point man encountered a North Vietnamese soldier urinating beside the road. The Marine opened fire, only to be answered by a storm of NVA fire from both the high ground north of the road and a tree line to the south. The Marines quickly engaged the NVA, first estimated to be a platoon and then an entire battalion. The Marines needed help.

It was then that Mike Company moved out to relieve its embattled platoon, supported by a Duster and a truck mounting quad-.50-caliber machine guns, plus two tanks that joined up later. Mike Company returned to Ca Lu, where Needham had ordered the Rough Rider convoy stopped since that was the only place between there and Khe Sanh where the vehicles could turn around.

Meanwhile the 1st Battalion, 26th Marines had been carrying out its own clearing operations eastward from Khe Sanh. The 1st Platoon of Bravo Company was searching along both sides of the road at about 10:35 A.M. when the leading squad stumbled into North Vietnamese, again estimated at platoon strength backed up by a heavy weapons platoon. These Marines received some fifty rounds of 82mm mortar fire plus a few shells from 57mm recoilless rifles, along with the usual rifle and machine gun fire. The initial burst caused several casualties, especially in Corporal Terry G. Henderson's point squad. Henderson calmly directed his men until they gained fire superiority and then led them back to a safer place.

Two Bravo Marines were still pinned down by the North Vietnamese ambush. One was grenadier Lance Corporal Charles V. Richardson, Jr. Spotting a North Vietnamese machine gun position that was devastating his buddies, Richardson used his 40mm grenade launcher until he was almost out of ammunition and then quickly gathered several fragmentation grenades from patrol mates and moved to within throwing distance in spite of the fire. The grenades were still not enough. Richardson got a light antitank weapon (LAW) and moved back toward the NVA machine gun emplacement, finally destroying it and earning himself the Bronze Star.

Soon after initial reports from the patrol, battalion commander Wilkinson moved into action with the remainder of Bravo Company. The patrol meanwhile established that the heaviest enemy fire seemed to be coming from Hill 247, almost midway between Khe Sanh and Ca Lu, about eleven kilometers due east of the former.

The 1st Platoon's situation remained serious through the afternoon. Lieutenant Long, platoon leader, faced an emergency complicated by the fact that the forward observer (FO) group for 81mm mortars that accompanied the patrol were all shot down. Bruce Jones was radio man for the FO group, which consisted of Sergeants Jose Castillo and Gilbert Wall. Castillo had extended his Vietnam tour, had just come back from leave, and was staying on for a few days to teach Wall the ropes before leaving for his next assignment. The FO group was in the middle of the patrol, right behind the command group. When the shooting began, they called for a white phosphorus round to spot the position but could not see it impact. They moved forward to find the smoke and as they rounded a bend in the road all three were hit. Castillo took two bullets in the chest and died instantly. Jones was shot in the throat and later wounded by shrapnel along his right side, in the face, neck, and shoulder. When he got out of the field he was blind in both eyes. Hit by a bullet that entered through his right shoulder and exited his left side, Wall had a collapsed left lung. Both survived with timely medical treatment at Khe Sanh's field hospital "Charlie Med" and hospitals at Da Nang and in Japan.

"Gilbert and I talked about it," Bruce Jones recalls. "We think it might have been a[n] RPG [rocket-propelled grenade] round; it might have been a rifle grenade. It wasn't a rocket or anything because it was too quiet."

These Marines were fighting for their lives. Afterward it would be determined that the North Vietnamese had lain in wait along a two-kilometer-long section of Route 9 to ambush the Rough Rider convoy. The Marine patrols had triggered the ambush prematurely. The NVA had had plenty of heavy weapons and had even set up their own Claymore mines. In a highly unusual development for the adversary, the North Vietnamese bodies that the Marines eventually found bore no identification and had no documents, letters, diaries, or other papers with them.

Soon after the initial reports from Lieutenant Long's patrol, battalion commander Wilkinson moved into action with a relief force including the remainder of Bravo Company. Later he brought up elements of Charlie Company while Needham deployed three companies under 3/3 to conduct an eight-day sweep along Route 9.

That did little for the artillery convoy, however. The Rough Rider convoy reined in at Ca Lu as soon as it received initial reports of the ambush, and the 175mm guns went back to Cam Lo. No further attempt was made to get them to Khe Sanh. On July 22 Lima and

Mike Companies of 3/26 were assigned to provide security and re-action forces for the Rough Rider convoys on thirty minutes' notice. Captain Richard D. Camp's Lima Company flew to Dong Ha on July 25 to guard the remainder of the convoy on its trip to Khe Sanh. Given what had happened to the Marine patrols, Camp made careful prep-arations for an ambush battle. The convoy's passage proved unevent-ful, as did Lima Company's return trip from Khe Sanh on July 28.

Captain Camp took no chances and remained constantly on guard during the Rough Rider convoys. The stretch of Route 9 west of Ca Lu was "real Indian country," he writes:

> All the way, the jungle grows down to the edge of the road. If anything was going to happen, that was the place. Beginning three or four klicks [kilometers] west of Ca Lu, the road verges were covered with spent casings from 40mm rounds fired by Army Dusters . . . and .50-caliber cartridges from Army quad-.50 antiaircraft vehicles. It looked to be the habit of the Army convoy escorts to simply fire randomly into the trees to keep the opposition's heads down. The trail of spent brass was four or five klicks long, really impressive.

Camp learned later that the spent cartridges were the result of the ambush battle rather than random wastage — the Dusters and other weapons had supported Charlie Company's sweep with heavy fire. There could be little doubt that Route 9 was a very dangerous place after the July 21 ambush.

Two large Rough Rider convoys on August 1 and 2 went from Dong Ha directly to Lang Vei with building materials for a new CIDG camp. The heavy-duty construction material, the escort commander recalls, was "great stuff like concrete and milled lumber that the Marine Corps would never think of sending to Khe Sanh." Then on August 3 there was a normal Rough Rider convoy to the combat base. Lima Company had the night off and for once got to sleep in its own tents. The Rough Riders went back down to Dong Ha on Saturday, August 5. Lima Company was then relieved of escort duty and was lifted back into Khe Sanh by helicopter, Camp remembers, in plenty of time for dinner.

That turned out to be the very last Rough Rider convoy. The ex-perience of July 21 and the subsequent Route 9 clearing operation suggested that heavy guards and constant road openings were going to be necessary to continue the Rough Riders. The Marine command

would be under severe pressures of force and space if it was necessary
to use a battalion to move convoys to Khe Sanh in support of just a
battalion or two. In addition, the 3rd Marine Division faced a wors-
ening situation along the DMZ north of Dong Ha and actually felt the
necessity to pull troops *back* from Khe Sanh to that sector. With just
a battalion at the combat base, troops simply were not available to
keep Route 9 open for the Rough Riders.

Heavy equipment that would be necessary for the construction
work at Lang Vei and the repair of Khe Sanh airstrip had to be flown
up in pieces, often by CH-54 "Sky Crane" helicopters, and then assembled on location.

Later, in a diary captured from the adversary, the Marines discovered evidence that the North Vietnamese had established a "Route 9
Front" with the specific mission of closing the road and conducting a
major offensive. The first part of that mission, at least, would be
accomplished. It marked an important milestone along the path to the
isolation of Khe Sanh. Route 9 had been open for just a little over four
months. After that, like Dien Bien Phu, Khe Sanh would be entirely
dependent on aerial resupply. In a fit of irony, Marine communicators
selected SPARROWHAWK as their code word for platoon-size reaction forces. Dien Bien Phu had had a strong point by that very name.

The Marine command daily found itself forced into choices it had no
desire to make. At Da Nang, the III MAF staff saw its role as one of
mounting battalion operations in support of pacification. This was
not simply Lew Walt's hobbyhorse. True, Walt had made the basic
decision for pacification in February 1967, but his successor, General
Robert Cushman, also carried on the pacification program. The program continued to aim at gaining the loyalty and support of the South
Vietnamese by protecting them, meeting basic social and economic
needs through "civic action," and isolating them from contact with
the Viet Cong. As Da Nang attempted to pursue this approach, however, pressure came from Washington to implement the positional
defense system known as the McNamara Line.

Saigon was no help with the strategic dilemma of 1967. MACV
required that the Marines carry forward the planning and engineering
of the defense system. General William Westmoreland may not have
liked Washington's initial concept of the McNamara Line, but he
strongly favored his own version of the vision, DYE MARKER, the
so-called strong point obstacle system.

Marine staff believed that DYE MARKER was fundamentally flawed. According to combined action program chief Bill Corson, the responsible planning officer at III MAF felt there had been no effort to think through the problems of how a barrier system could be developed and used and little attempt at cost-benefit analysis. A real professional, Corson writes, the officer "resented the prostitution of his talents to prepare a plan" under these circumstances.

"They must be smoking hashish," the officer told Corson. "All the barrier will do is cause needless casualties and waste time and money."

General Walt made sure Marine opposition to the barrier plan was noted, but he was in his last months at III MAF and was nearly out the door when construction began. It was up to General Cushman, who took over III MAF on June 1, 1967, to go to the mat with Westmoreland if DYE MARKER was to be stopped. A tough, highly decorated combat Marine, Cushman nevertheless had little enthusiasm for fighting it out with MACV. This was unfortunate because Cushman, like Walt, agreed with the pacification strategy. Cushman discovered that DYE MARKER made increasing demands on his forces and actually decreased support for combined action. Cushman complained, leading Westmoreland to augment Task Force Oregon, an Army component of III MAF, but DYE MARKER sucked additional forces up to the DMZ in exact proportion to the reinforcements Westmoreland sent north.

Perhaps Cushman refused to take on Westmoreland because of an ingrained practice of concealing his intentions and views. He would become known to the press as someone they saw on sufferance, a man extremely cautious in his comments. Cushman's career had brought him into contact with some of the most cautious characters around. He had been detached to the CIA from 1949 to 1951 during an abortive CIA covert paramilitary effort in Albania. He had shared an office with E. Howard Hunt, one of the CIA's Albania program managers. For four years, from February 1957 to January 1961, Cushman had been national security adviser for Vice President Richard M. Nixon. It is said that he played an important role as intermediary between the CIA and Nixon on preparations for another CIA paramilitary operation — the Bay of Pigs. During that period Cushman shared an office with FBI official L. Patrick Gray, who would briefly head the agency under President Nixon years later. Both Hunt and Gray, not to mention Nixon himself, would become major figures in the Watergate scandal, primarily because of their attitudes toward information and its denial. As for Cushman, he went on to become chief of intelligence at Marine Corps headquarters, certainly a position requiring utmost discretion. After Vietnam he would become deputy director of the CIA.

Still, Robert Everton Cushman, Jr., had fought his share of Pentagon battles, both as Marine intelligence chief and as assistant chief of staff for plans, operations, and training. The fifty-three-year-old Minnesotan also had a solid record of command stretching back to World War II: he had commanded Camp Pendleton; the 3rd Marine Division when it was still on Okinawa; the 2nd Battalion, 9th Marines in some of the hardest fighting of the Pacific war; and the Marine detachment aboard the battleship *Pennsylvania* at Pearl Harbor. A smart high school student in St. Paul, Cushman got his appointment to Annapolis as a high school junior and majored in electrical engineering, graduating tenth of 442 midshipmen in the class of 1935. His first overseas service had been with the 4th Marines in China from early 1936, and he had known Lew Walt, a fellow officer in the regiment, from that time. In Word War II Cushman earned the Bronze Star in the battle of Bougainville, the Navy Cross at Guam, and the Legion of Merit on Iwo Jima. There is no reason to suppose General Cushman lacked the fiber to take on Westmoreland.

The most likely explanation for Cushman's failure to make an issue of DYE MARKER was simply his determination to improve the frosty relations between Westmoreland and the Marines. Cushman was a new broom, he could start fresh, he did not need to fight the same battles Walt had. The failure to fight that intramural battle within the U.S. command, however, led directly to the frustration of Marine pacification strategy and contributed to the isolation of Khe Sanh.

The people who were prepared to do something about DYE MARKER were the North Vietnamese. Installation of the strong points and the cleared strip, or "trace," that were part of the DYE MARKER system meant prolonged Marine presence in the DMZ area. The NVA responded by bringing up forces of their own, including artillery of up to 152mm caliber, which they first used along the DMZ that year. Colonel Corson, who denigrates the barrier's construction as like a Depression-era "WPA project," observes that "at each step the Marines who were required to plow the 500-meter-wide strip have been shot at by North Vietnamese gunners like clay pigeons in a shooting gallery."

During the July 1967 battles the NVA employed artillery in direct support of infantry assaults for the first time. The actions began with operation BUFFALO, a Marine thrust north of Con Thien in early July. Repeated heavy contacts with the NVA during this period earned the 1st Battalion, 9th Marines the nickname "the Walking Dead." One company walked out of BUFFALO with only twenty-seven Marines still standing. On July 7, to make matters worse, a North Vietnamese shell scored a direct hit on the battalion command post at Con Thien. That place became a hot sector indeed.

Brewing trouble below the DMZ crystallized the III MAF command problem. General Cushman simply did not have the forces to be in strength everywhere at once. Though Westmoreland was augmenting Task Force Oregon, only nine U.S. battalions were available for the entire area from Hue–Phu Bai north, and two of them were at Khe Sanh. Division commander Hochmuth decided, and Cushman concurred, that Khe Sanh would have to give up some troops. Westmoreland was not happy with the thinness of Marine dispositions in Quang Tri and Thua Thien, the two northernmost provinces of South Vietnam. "Nor was I pleased," Westmoreland records, "with the semistatic defense that the shortage of troops imposed on the Marines at Khe Sanh."

It was in mid-1967 that Westmoreland began making quiet preparations to redeploy his 1st Cavalry Division (Airmobile) from the II Corps area north.

Reductions in force at Khe Sanh began in mid-August when the command group from the 3rd Battalion, 26th Marines plus Kilo and Lima Companies were sent to the Con Thien area to operate under the 2nd Battalion, 9th Marines. On August 20, the 3rd Battalion commander, Lieutenant Colonel Kurt Hoch, was rotated to an assignment at 3rd Division headquarters. Lieutenant Colonel Harry Alderman, his replacement, had just arrived in Vietnam. In September, when the NVA stepped up their activities near Con Thien again, the remainder of 3/26 came back from Khe Sanh as well. There was a two-battalion NVA attack on Con Thien that month, and the strong point would be hit by an average of two hundred rounds of artillery fire every day, but it held. For forty-nine days Westmoreland hurled a series of maximum-effort air strikes ("SLAM" strikes for "seek, locate, annihilate, monitor") at the NVA in the area, killing an estimated two thousand. Westmoreland believed it a Dien Bien Phu in reverse.

Regardless of the outcome at Con Thien, however, the reduction of the force at Khe Sanh had a marked impact on the operations of

Colonel Lownds's 26th Marines. As Westmoreland observes, theirs became a quasi-static defense. Since, given the necessity of holding the hill positions, there had hardly been a battalion available to operate when two held the base, it became difficult to operate at all with only a single battalion at Khe Sanh. Dave Lownds and his battalion commander, Jim Wilkinson, exercised considerable creativity in phasing, staging, and timing operations so as to temporarily free a company here, a platoon there, which could carry out patrol and sweeping missions. Yet their dance was a delicate one. With its airfield being reconstructed, Route 9 cut, and its second battalion withdrawn, Khe Sanh had truly become isolated.

"Thank God for Letting Me Be a CAC Marine"

Typical of the unusual breed of Marines who ended up in the combined action companies (CACs), Daniel Richard Kelley, Jr., had spent his first six months in South Vietnam with an infantry unit. His battalion had operated around Dong Ha with the first of the Marines to arrive in the DMZ sector, those who set up the defense of Con Thien. But Kelley was not cut out for the big unit war. He found himself protesting the callous and casually brutal treatment Americans sometimes showed to Vietnamese. In contrast, Kelley tried to befriend them and learn their language. The contrast became pointed one day when on patrol, passing through a village, Kelley witnessed a sergeant, a man who had been his instructor in advanced infantry training, grab an old woman and throw her down a well. The Marines forced the boy with her, young enough to be her grandson, to carry ammunition for them. No one protested and no charges were ever brought against the noncom. Corporal Kelley found himself pondering how the war was dehumanizing Americans.

Kelley had had visions of becoming a professional Marine, and he had served at Camp Lejeune in North Carolina and Guantanamo Bay in Cuba. But he was not getting along well with the Marines of his platoon, who were not too happy about his friendliness toward Vietnamese. His battalion seconded Kelley for the new combined action program, Kelley's platoon and company commanders nominated him, and one day the corporal found himself at the CAC school. Nothing came easily, however, and Kelley was disturbed upon graduation to be assigned to CAC Oscar at Khe Sanh; he worried that all the Vietnamese language he had learned would go to waste.

Instead Corporal Kelley, like other CAC Marines, became absorbed in the lives of the montagnards around him. Indeed, Kelley took the trouble to learn Bru well and eventually became the only Marine really fluent in that tribal language. Kelley also knew a little French, which he used in resolving a dispute when some 60mm illumination rounds fired from Marine mortars fell in orchards that belonged to the planter M. Simard. Kelley talked to Simard, whom he found very pleasant.

Later the Marines learned from Simard that his Bru laborers, to begin their day's work in the orchard, routinely dismantled the trip flares the combined action platoon (CAP) Marines set out so very carefully every night. If the ultra-sensitive flares could be taken down by Bru, they could hardly be of much use against North Vietnamese, in particular NVA sappers. Remarkably, when Marines themselves attempted to dismantle the flares, they repeatedly set them off instead.

Life among the Bru proved attractive enough that Kelley spent eighteen months there. At his initial assignment, with platoon Oscar-2, he began keeping a notebook of Bru vocabulary far more extensive than the essential words and phrases his CAP buddies would learn. Kelley's close rapport with the Bru developed into a relationship of trust. On one occasion a Bru Popular Force soldier came to Kelley to protest that his father had been taken by the police and was being tortured at district headquarters. The police chief, whose chain of command went directly to Saigon and so was independent of the district chief, indeed had the man. On his own initiative Kelley went to the building, found the room containing a hand-cranked electric generator, a chair for interrogation, and so forth, and exposed the evidence of torture, which was supposed to be illegal. The police chief was forced to release his prisoner. Kelley received an award for his action, but Vietnamese authorities made quiet complaints about him, and the corporal was reassigned to CAP Oscar-3.

Oscar-3 was the combined action platoon at Ta Cong, the hamlet just outside the wire of Khe Sanh combat base that was named after a kind of tree that grew thorns up to three inches long. Corporal Kelley continued quiet but effective work among the Bru, accompanying patrols that CAP Oscar-3 sent throughout the area, accomplishing civic action work with the montagnards. When, in the spring of 1969, Dan Kelley finally returned to the United States, he received a personal commendation from President Richard Nixon for learning the Bru language.

Corporal Kelley's devotion to the Bru was rather typical of CAP Marines. Among Oscar-3, for example, Marines Will, Talis Kaminskis, and Frank Iodice all wrote home to ask for packages of old clothes they could give the Bru people. Iodice went further and adopted Bahng, a ten-year-old Bru boy, as a sort of surrogate local family. "Here's a place where children grow up with a war, live with it and probably will end their life still fighting it," Frank Iodice wrote his mother. As for Bahng, "he already has scars from VC mortars, can arm a claymore mine . . . helps me clean my machinegun, can cuss like a 45 year old sailor and works as hard as any man knows about building a bunker."

Then there was Tim, a Bru man who could not be a soldier because he was the last surviving male of his family. Oscar-3 employed the man they called Tim as dishwasher and laundry man, paying him about thirty or thirty-five dollars a month, a princely sum among the montagnards. Tim had the only painted hut in the village, a place that became a rendezvous and sort of coffee shop for the fourteen Oscar-3 Marines during the summer and fall evenings. Once, when the cooking gear at the Oscar-3 compound was not working, Tim invited the whole platoon to his house for breakfast. The Bru was neither lazy nor selfish; he would work from sunup to sundown and thought nothing of spending half his monthly income to buy a pig for a Bru religious ritual. Tim's wife would cook for the Marines, and his niece Lam also lived in the house. The evening social scene was an engaging and lively one. "Thank God for letting me be a CAC Marine!" Frank Iodice wrote home.

Ta Cong was the village where Anha, the Bru tribal spokesman and assistant district chief, lived. Anha too was described in Frank Iodice's letters: "He is what I expected, an active personality, leader of a struggling people. Wore a white shirt with black jeans, shower shoes, and wearing a steel pot on his head, a flak vest with ammo magazines in its pockets. He addressed the PFs [Popular Forces] that work with us here, firm . . . yet funny and joking also." The things of which Anha had complained to Marines at the time of the battle of the hills remained issues for the Bru in the fall of 1967. The Vietnamese still hoarded the rice intended for the montagnards and then made them pay for it instead of giving it out as intended. Similarly the Vietnamese deducted an amount from Bru pay for ammunition issued to the montagnards. The Bru troops might be given one set of black pajama clothing every year or two. By comparison, CAP Marines wore out a set of sturdy, American-manufactured utility clothing in three months or so. Marines continued to be frustrated at Vietnamese attitudes toward the Bru.

The Marines loved the Bru, though over time they learned to make allowances for them in certain ways for military purposes. Corporal Grohman admitted, for example, that the Bru could not be given all their rations for a patrol before leaving, as Marines would, for the Bru would simply sit down right then and eat up all the food. Major Bruce B. G. Clark, now promoted to be the MACV district adviser, also complained that the Bru would waste their ammunition shooting at birds.

Still, Major Clark had more serious concerns. Far more upsetting was the district police chief, who Clark and former senior adviser Major James Whitenack suspected was somehow involved with the Viet Cong. Once when there was a mortar attack, Whitenack found impressions of the weapon's base plate in the ground in the police chief's own compound. The attack had occurred at a time when the police chief had been in his bunker. Equally serious, Whitenack recalls, "when the Air America helicopters came in and/or the Vietnamese came in on the airstrip, I started searching their belongings. And in one week's time I picked up about three beer cases full of syringes, scalpels, operating kits, penicillin in both tablets and syringe form, vitamin B-12, all kinds of stuff." Whitenack thought the police consignments were being sold to the Viet Cong and confiscated them. The traffic stopped because he was searching the shipments every day, but then retribution came in the form of protests from the police chief, his assistant, and three others, followed by charges by two Vietnamese women that Whitenack had molested them. The district adviser had taken the precaution of having one of his men present whenever he did anything, however, and the charges were readily dismissed. Still, the MACV advisory team, like CAC Oscar, knew that everything was not well in Khe Sanh village.

Platoon Oscar-2 of the company had its compound at the western edge of the village, a post with no electricity because none of the eighteen Marines with that CAP knew how to set up or wire the generator outside one of the bunkers. But the post benefited from a concrete Buddhist temple converted to a latrine, a pet parrot, a puppy, and one Marine who had bagpipes and was a skilled musician.

In early October Oscar-2 was hit one night by several hundred rounds of small arms fire and a half dozen grenades. Later a patrol had a contact with an unknown adversary force. With some apprehension Lieutenant Haines, the company commander, considered relocating the platoon to a hill between the hamlets Lang Con 1 and 2 where stood an old French concrete bunker. The situation remained unresolved through Christmas.

Bru proclivities were well illustrated by an incident that occurred at the compound of Oscar-3 in early December. During the graveyard shift on December 3 the silence was broken by a storm of fire from the Bru troopers manning the perimeter. The racket awakened CAP Marines Guillory and Roberts, who dashed out of their cozy bunker so quickly that the latter put on his pants backward. On the line the Bru were firing into the misty night air. No targets could be seen. Later they explained they had seen Panoah, an evil god who is said to devour people, and had fired to scare it away. Americans thought it all slightly funny but the Bru were perfectly serious. So spiritual, so much more aware than most people, perhaps the Bru *had* sensed something, for there were creeping demons afoot that would indeed soon be devouring lives at Khe Sanh!

Seventy-seven Pounds of Bricks

Whatever one thinks of the Bru spirits, there was a real presence in the hinterland, one so strong that Marines and Green Berets, not to say Bru montagnards, feared to move without the comfort of their artillery and airplanes. Even for reconnaissance teams the standard procedure was to prepare the place they would be dropped off by preliminary application of firepower. The hinterland was Indian country, the land of the North Vietnamese Army.

Americans said many things about North Vietnam during the war, and they say various things still today, but American grunts retain considerable respect for their opponents, the North Vietnamese soldiers who fought in the hills of Khe Sanh. The American and NVA soldiers shared an experience, wherever battle occurred in Vietnam, that set them apart from their compatriots, changed them, propelled them in directions they might never have thought of taking. Those on both sides who fought the war were not very different either — young, energetic, capable of excitement or disillusion, transported to a place that was alien space if not time.

In the heat of combat, in the flash of exploding shells and bombs, what Americans could see was the quality of the troops they called enemies, the élan, boldness, and determination of men some called the best light infantry in the world. In later years, with the dissipation of some of the fog of battle, it becomes increasingly apparent that the experience of North Vietnamese and American boys, at least around Khe Sanh, was actually quite similar in many respects. Marines groused continually about the state of their supply and felt that the Green Berets (who considered themselves to be working "in the bush") were supported on a lavish scale. North Vietnamese boys labored under similar shortages — of food, medicines, specialized equipment of all kinds — with the additional complication that their supply lines were under constant assault by the air and ground power the United States was able to muster in Laos.

One element that made the North Vietnamese experience even more enervating than the American was the necessity to walk to battle, walk tens and hundreds of miles south, traversing that same cauldron in which the Americans were attempting to destroy what came down the Ho Chi Minh Trail. The inferno was not a matter of a day or two of violence and then peace. Far from it. Passage down the Ho Chi Minh Trail typically took one to two and a half months, and at the end there was no assurance the nightmare would end. The NVA troops in South Vietnam were constantly vulnerable to ARC LIGHT strikes from B-52 bombers that flew so high they were both invisible and inaudible and to the lethal combination of forward air controller plus fixed-wing tactical aircraft. Then there were helicopter gunships, random artillery fire for harassment and interdiction, SOG booby traps and sabotage — the dangers of life in the NVA were both formidable and constant, and the danger of death in combat was not the greatest of them. Some Vietnamese still remember the bombings with terror — they are said to have "B-52 stare" as Americans are afflicted with "post-Vietnam syndrome" — while to others the terrors are mosquitoes and malaria. A MACV wartime intelligence study in 1966 observed that "NVA soldiers sent to fight in the south quickly discover that life is filled with hardship."

The North Vietnamese Army consciously adopted training programs designed to mitigate the difficulties of prosecuting war in the south. At the level of political indoctrination there was a constant emphasis on heroic themes, on striving for success despite obstacles, on the ability of revolutionary fervor to overcome them. Emulation campaigns encouraged soldiers to do as well as legendary heroes and other superachievers. Political officers monitored morale among the men, their task simplified by the creation of small cells throughout the army. The individuals in each cell, usually three, had a collective responsibility for one another. Methods ranged from the *auto da fé* of "criticism and self-criticism," which could be bogus and contrived or sincere and heartfelt, to cell members more surreptitiously informing political officers about their comrades. Contrived or not, the device of cells provided the NVA with a basic tool for creating cohesion at the small unit level and gave each trooper a set of companions who could become his buddies. Beyond structure there was formal indoctrination. Political officers told the men before leaving for the south that they would be welcomed joyfully by the people of South Vietnam.

Indoctrination was complemented by rigorous physical training. Men not only were trained to handle their weapons but were hardened for the trip south. Instructors built endurance with long route marches. A typical program described in the 1966 intelligence study involved three route marches weekly with trainees made to walk several hours while carrying loads of fifty-five to seventy-seven pounds of bricks.

Americans often assumed, like the author of the poem "The Hills of Khe Sanh," that the foe was very well acquainted with the terrain and had fought there for centuries. In fact, the northerners were no better off in this respect than the young Marines who faced them. Even the general conditions of hardship were unfamiliar except to the rapidly diminishing cadre of veterans of the anti-French war. Speaking of the NVA soldier arriving in the south, the 1966 MACV study noted: "It is usually his first contact with unfavorable terrain and climate . . . the vast majority of NVA infiltrators are from the coastal and delta lowlands of [the north]. They are no more accustomed to the hardships in the highlands than are ARVN or American troops."

In captured documents and prisoner interrogations the theme that came across again and again was difficulty and hardship. One diary entry by an NVA platoon leader reads:

Living in the jungle became exceedingly and terribly rough. At first, three balls of pressed rice mixed with salt and a canteen of water were given every day. Now, at each meal, only one ball of rice mixed with salt and a little fresh water are served. However, it is better than to eat moss as a rice substitute, taste ashes of straw as a salt substitute, and drink urine instead of water.

Similarly evocative is this account of a soldier's trip south with the 101st Regiment of the NVA 325-C Division:

> The cadre and soldiers . . . carried heavy loads, walked on foot two and a half months long, ate short rations of rice with salt only, and drank water from the streams, so some soldiers and cadre suffered malaria. Upon arrival in [the south] the total number of soldiers suffering malaria increased quickly. Within a month, 120 members of the 101st Regiment contracted malaria. A number of others began to contract this disease, but they still had to engage in combat. For lack of beds and mats in the dispensaries, all patients lay in hammocks fastened to trees. Treatment was not sufficient with two medics for 120 patients. Then . . . these two medics were sent to battle to give aid to wounded soldiers. No one took care of the patients. Thus the moderately sick patients looked after the serious ones. . . . As for healthy soldiers, their conditions were no better; when not in combat they were forced to work all day and night. For rations, each was given two cans of rice, some manioc and salt. Otherwise, they always worried about sudden US-RVN air attacks.

North Vietnamese soldiers dug fast and they dug deep in case of B-52 attacks. Viet Cong and North Vietnamese use of tunnels has become legendary. Around Khe Sanh the NVA made similar use of caves. When firefights occurred, more often than not the instant of contact found the North Vietnamese ensconced in bunkers, usually underground.

NVA fire discipline was also impressive. As a rule, the North Vietnamese did not engage in random fire, did not fire except en masse or when encountering the enemy, and were very steady when waiting to spring an ambush. These very qualities were what made credible the kind of herding-by-fire tactics that Sergeant Billy Waugh believes the North Vietnamese used to counter SOG patrols.

Thus we have the paradox of the antagonist: the North Vietnamese endure great hardships to reach the battlefield, are sparsely supplied once there, are forced to scrounge for a measure of what they keep, yet fight so well that Americans think they have been doing it for centuries. The argument that Vietnam's was a warlike society stumbles on the general lack of aggressiveness of the South Vietnamese Army, in sharp contrast to the northerners. That the NVA fought so hard for sheer ideological reasons seems far-fetched. The basic reason had to be that the North Vietnamese soldier *believed* in Hanoi's war aim of "liberating" the south. Only such a grand purpose could have propelled men of flesh and blood into the maelstrom that became Khe Sanh.

Postwar assessments notwithstanding, Marines at the time retained a healthy caution regarding North Vietnamese Army capabilities. Colonel Padley, for example, in his 26th Regiment after-action report for operation CROCKETT, noted that "the enemy in this Area of Operations [AO] proved well-led, well-fed, and well-equipped. Enemy forces have engaged in massive defensive engineering efforts, bunkering and camouflaging continuously along approach routes. By so doing, he is able to occupy and fight from excellent defensive positions upon the approach of friendly forces, and [has] prepared positions against air and artillery attacks." Padley observed that the time required by the Americans to summon helicopters and lift reinforcements into an engagement usually allowed the NVA to break contact and withdraw and that a favorite North Vietnamese tactic was to enter the AO very quickly by night, mortar or rocket U.S. positions, and then escape before anything could be done about it.

The appreciation that the North Vietnamese were capable of the kind of hit-and-run actions that John Padley feared gradually changed into a belief that the NVA might be able to mount sustained offensive activities. Rather than showing a reduction in NVA strength after the Marines' presumptive victory in the hill battles, intelligence estimates continued to show North Vietnamese in the Khe Sanh area as three to six battalions strong, with reinforcing heavy weapons units, all usually elements of the NVA 325-C Division. During the summer of 1967 Marine intelligence detected an NVA regiment move into the Co Roc massif just across the Laotian border. These troops came and stayed, very likely to cover the emplacement of NVA heavy artillery.

The official judgment of General Victor Krulak's command, Fleet Marine Force Pacific, rendered in late August, was that the North Vietnamese had attained the capability to attack either Con Thien or Khe Sanh, or other allied positions near the DMZ, with a reinforced division of troops backed with artillery, rockets, and mortars.

Khe Sanh's own intelligence wizards, the S-2 section of 26th Regiment staff, was the responsibility of Harper L. Bohr, Jr. On November 1, after three months on the job, Captain Bohr summarized the NVA

Khe Sanh village area typified the bifurcations between lowland Vietnamese and mountain tribal Bru. Both the village *(bottom)* and the Bru hamlet Breh *(center)* are visible. Route 9 runs through Khe Sanh village from the lower left center to the right edge of the picture. In the hills above Breh, the massive destruction inflicted by American airpower is visible as numerous craters covering the land. Taken by an Air Force plane on January 28, 1968. *(U.S. Air Force)*

Top: Khe Sanh village is quite clear in this picture taken in the summer of 1967. The triangular structure to the right center is Huong Hoa district headquarters. Below and slightly to the left are the Buddhist shrine and school, which North Vietnamese troops used for a firing position in the battle for the village. *(James Whitenack) Bottom:* Americans came to Khe Sanh in the fall of 1962. This is a group picture of Detachment A-131, the first Special Forces unit to spend its full tour at Khe Sanh. Detachment commander Robert Korchek kneels in the front row, farthest left. Next to him is weapons specialist Frank Fowler. The men are in front of the inherited bunker they called "The Alamo." *(Frank Fowler) Left:* Route 9 is clearly visible entering at the upper left edge and exiting on top to the right. The intersection toward the center is where Route 9 meets the road from Old French Fort, which is near the center of the photo. Note the coffee tree groves that begin just north of (above) Route 9. Taken by an Air Force plane on January 28, 1968. *(USAF)*

Special Forces camp Khe Sanh in 1965–1966, taken from near the CIDG barracks at the eastern end and looking toward the American building in the distance behind the truck. Camp headquarters is to the right; the structure in the left middle ground is the barracks of the 2nd CIDG Reconnaissance Platoon. *(Peter Morakon)*

With its somewhat exotic status as the northernmost Special Forces camp, Khe Sanh attracted a number of visitors other than military. Pictured here is actor Raymond Burr, better known as television's Perry Mason. *(Peter Morakon)*

Khe Sanh in the early days: Lieutenant Colonel Peter A. Wickwire *(left)*, commander of 1st Battalion, 3rd Marines, explains the situation to visiting Lieutenant General Lewis W. Walt in September 1966. Major General Ray Davis and Colonel Wilson *(right)* look on. *(USMC)*

John and Carolyn Miller, the Wycliffe Bible translators, at Khe Sanh village on October 23, 1967, being interviewed by CBS television reporter Robert Shackney. The footage aired in the United States on January 20, 1968, just hours before the first North Vietnamese attacks of the siege. *(Ray Stubbe)*

Above: Khe Sanh: the hill battles in the spring of 1967 culminated in assaults on significant terrain outside the combat base. Here, on April 30, 1967, Marines of Golf Company, 2nd Battalion, 3rd Marines, catch their breath during the assault on Hill 861. That day the company overran an NVA bunker complex. *Below:* At the height of the hill battles the NVA countered with an attack on the CIDG camp at Lang Vei, whose site is shown here in July 1967. This Lang Vei camp would be held until November, when Special Forces moved to an improved camp about a kilometer to the southwest. *(USMC)*

Khe Sanh combat base, September 3, 1967, looking directly down the runway, which was oriented east-southeast. Aircraft revetments are to the left, the parking apron on the right, along with the Ponderosa area. To the right beyond the apron lies the heart of the camp, including the combat operations center, FOB-1 launch point, Charlie Med, the main ammunition dump, and other facilities. *(Martin Kux)*

A Marine patrol struggles through elephant grass. The grass could cut like a knife, and wounds often festered. The adversary could be five feet away and a man might not see him. Here Marines are on the lookout while their patrol momentarily halts. Hill 861 towers in the background. *(Ray Stubbe)*

The outpost on Hill 861, looking north. Later outpost 861-A would be located on the knoll directly to the right. Hill 1371 is in the distance. *(Ray Stubbe)*

Above: Another, closer view of Hill 861, clearly showing the outline of the Marine outpost in July 1967. The 861-A knoll is at the right center. The knoll beyond 861 to the left is the position from which the North Vietnamese attacked in January 1968. The Rao Quan river valley is just visible to the upper right. *(Ray Stubbe) Below:* The view of Indian country from Hill 861 to the southwest. The forbidding hill mass at the center, truly dangerous indeed, is Co Roc in Laos, from which North Vietnamese artillery shelled Khe Sanh. Note the Marine mortar aiming stakes in the foreground. *(USMC)*

Above: A radio relay station atop Hill 950 provided Khe Sanh's communications with the reconnaissance patrols that radiated out from it, as well as fine visual observation from the South China Sea to the interior of Laos. An NVA attack one night in the summer of 1967 forced Marines to fight for their lives. Hill 950's defenses were subsequently improved and are seen here on September 3, 1967. *(Martin Kux)*
Below: Group portrait of the hills, showing relative positions of the Marine outposts in November 1967. Diagonally from the west, in the foreground lies Hill 881 South. Against the horizon to the right of center are Hills 950 and 1015; just below them, barely visible, is Hill 861. *(USMC)*

Summer pastimes: Marine helicopter pilots visit planter Felix Poilane *(left)* in July 1967. Poilane introduced the Marines to his pet deer, Bambi. Note that Poilane's fence is made from metal plates used in building the Khe Sanh airstrip. *(Ray Stubbe)*

The "Lion of Khe Sanh," Colonel David E. Lownds, who cultivated a mustache during the siege and pretended to reporters that he knew nothing about Dien Bien Phu. *(David Lownds)*

Lieutenant Colonel James B. Wilkinson, whose 1st Battalion, 26th Marines spent the longest time and suffered the most at Khe Sanh. Loved by his men, Wilkinson also seems to have been well regarded by the Marine Corps, which kept him in command of the battalion for an unusually long time. *(USMC)*

Above: In the summer of 1967 the newly forming MACVSOG component Forward Operating Base 3 took over the Old French Fort position. Worried about poor security, the MACVSOG unit soon relocated to a position just outside the wire of the combat base. *Below:* A moment of relaxation for the MACVSOG was this dinner with the Bru. At left, in tiger stripe camouflage, is Major Fred Patton, first commander of FOB-3. *(James Whitenack)*

Above: The Huong Hoa district headquarters was home to an Army advisory team, a joint CIA–military intelligence team, South Vietnamese authorities, and combined action company (CAC) Oscar. The compound, in Khe Sanh village, is shown in July 1967. *(USMC) Left:* Marines of CAC Oscar build an ammunition storage bunker in the district headquarters compound, September 1967. *(Ray Stubbe)*

Above: A CAC Oscar patrol makes its rounds: Marines enter Bru village of Tum Plang, September 26, 1967. A camera left on a tree stump, which even at Khe Sanh would readily disappear, was left undisturbed by the Bru. *(USMC) Below:* The Bru laundry chief and handyman Tim, who with his family did much to help the Marines of CAC Oscar. Tim survived the siege and is shown here at a Bru refugee camp near Cam Lo in May 1968. *(Ray Stubbe)*

Above: North Vietnamese observers could see Khe Sanh from many of the surrounding hills and ridges. This is the view from Hill 471 on September 26, 1967, looking toward the combat base, where a C-130 is just visible parachuting supplies. The Bru village of Areng is to the right, Lang Kat to the left. *(Ray Stubbe) Below:* Sergeant First Class James Perry of MACV Advisory Team 4 during a sick call at a Bru village in the summer of 1967. This kind of civic action was an important element of pacification efforts. *(James Whitenack)*

Above: Khe Sanh's eyes and ears were in reconnaissance patrols, which ranged far into Indian country. A group from Company B, 3rd Reconnaissance Battalion prepares to depart on a mission in late August 1967. *Below:* The patch worn by Vietnamese Special Forces troopers at Lang Vei was woven in silk. A white parachute and three white lightning bolts were superimposed on a green shield. The leaping tiger was woven in yellow with black detail and a red mouth. *(Ray Stubbe)*

Above: Local CIDG strikers gather at Lang Vei camp on August 1, 1967. At the left, smoking, is one of the American advisers of Special Forces Detachment A-101. *(Ray Stubbe) Below:* Navy Seabees at work on the reinforced concrete casting for the tactical operations center bunker at the new Lang Vei CIDG camp. At the center front is the foundation for the observation tower that loomed above the bunker. During the last desperate hours of the February 1968 battle at Lang Vei, American survivors would owe their lives to the strength of this bunker. *(U.S. Navy)*

Aerial view of the position at Hill 558. Colonel Lownds advanced his 2nd Battalion, 26th Marines to Hill 558 to block any NVA advance from the northwest down the Rao Quan valley. *(USAF)*

capability as sufficient for multibattalion coordinated attacks against the combat base, Hills 881 South, 861, and 950, Lang Vei Special Forces camp, the district headquarters, or CAC Oscar. Bohr thought the North Vietnamese could reinforce existing field forces within twelve hours with two additional battalions of the 95th Regiment of 325-C Division. For lesser options the North Vietnamese could draw U.S. forces into battle on terrain of NVA choosing, could conduct reconnaissance or counterreconnaissance, could infiltrate men and supplies past Khe Sanh to the north and south at will, or could withdraw from the Khe Sanh area. Bohr thought a multibattalion attack probable at some point and felt it unlikely the NVA would choose to withdraw.

Some indications seemed positively ominous. In early September, for example, Captain Bohr received an item from the CIA's JTAD group reporting the nearby movement of two very strong NVA battalions, together estimated at 1,600 men. Most startling was that six very tall Caucasian men, possibly Russian advisers, accompanied the NVA units. Bohr noted it was only the second report of Soviet advisers in the area and the first Soviets actually entering South Vietnam.

More ominous yet was what happened shortly before 10:00 P.M. during the night of October 29. An aircraft circled over Khe Sanh combat base and dropped a flare directly overhead. That would not have been too unusual except that the plane did not respond to radio calls from the Khe Sanh control tower. In addition "Landshark Bravo," the air support control center for the DMZ sector, located at Dong Ha, had no aircraft under its control aloft in the Khe Sanh area that night. The plane might have been a supersecret SR-71 spy plane taking photographs for Washington, but it could equally well have been Russian, Red Chinese, or North Vietnamese. Lending credence to the latter possibilities was the fact that the same kind of incident had occurred almost precisely a year earlier, at 3:00 A.M. on October 25, 1966. American photo reconnaissance planes would not have needed to hide in the night, and at that time there were not enough North Vietnamese immediately around the combat base for surprise nighttime photography to reveal much about their activities.

Certain documents captured by Marines in a firefight on December 1 seven miles northeast of Dong Ha also bear on Hanoi's intentions. One of these, mentioned earlier, was the notebook containing reference to a "Route 9 Front," not as a command, it turns out, but as a political committee. Highly suggestive, the notebook referred to orders for units to close down Route 9 by continual attacks. The front operational areas listed, however, were identical to those of the existing North Vietnamese DMZ front command. Marine intelligence interpreters noted that "there is no other evidence to substantiate the addition of another front in this area." The most likely explanation is that the author was making a colloquial reference to the DMZ front without using its formal name.

Another document captured during this time near Dong Ha was a set of notes by NVA political officer Nguyen Thanh Van. The Van notes too were suggestive: his unit's orders for the winter campaign were to operate along Route 9 to tie down U.S. and ARVN troops, enabling the Tri-Thien-Hue Military Region forces to launch a large-scale offensive; to attack bases along Route 9; and to apply pressure on Con Thien. Generalized to other NVA units along the DMZ, the second mission could be interpreted as threatening Khe Sanh. The first mission, however, clearly suggests that the role of the DMZ front would be diversionary. Hanoi's specific intentions with respect to Khe Sanh remain ambiguous in these documents.

Then there was the matter of truck traffic along the Ho Chi Minh Trail. Increases in the traffic became apparent from mid-October. By early November the CIA had noted them, as indeed did the mass media following a wire item carried by United Press International that reported the sighting of 2,500 trucks along the trail during November, a traffic level three times that of the year before. It was not coincidental that the National Security Agency, America's communications intelligence megalith, began making special reports on NVA troop movements along the trail in mid-November.

Retrospective analysis by MACV and the ARVN Joint General Staff in the spring of 1968 purports to have established that the 9th Regiment of the NVA 304th Division departed Tho Xuan of Thanh Hoa province in early November heading south, while the 24th Regiment of the division left Nong Cong and the 66th arrived at Dong Trai, both in Thanh Hoa. The handwritten notebook of Pham Ngoc Muon of the 5th Battalion, 24th Regiment, however, captured during the later relief of Khe Sanh by forces of the 1st Cavalry Division, demonstrates that his unit worked on construction projects in Yen Thanh district of Nghe An province through mid-October and departed on November 7. The battalion moved through Quang Binh and reached central Laos on January 1, 1968. The unit's travails summed up the North Vietnamese experience:

Muon complained that he became "extremely exhausted due to hardships and a critical shortage of rice."

Hanoi's dispatch of the NVA 304th Division, like so many other suggestive elements of this story, is a measure of the gravity with which it viewed the 1967–1968 winter–spring campaign. In many ways the 304th was the banner unit of the People's Army of Vietnam. Created in the crucible of the anti-French war, the division had been the first large regular formation of the army. It had existed in embryo even in the late 1940s as the 209th Doc Lap, or Independence, Brigade, which expanded following the arrival of the Red Chinese on Vietnam's northern border in December 1949. Afterward, with access to Chinese training bases, the Vietnamese merged their Independence Brigade with the 840th Regional Regiment and other elements to create the new 304th Division. It would be followed by five more of these big units, each with three regiments and a weapons battalion, at full strength perhaps 10,000 men.

Its first campaign, in the summer and fall of 1950, gave the 304th Division its first big taste of military victory. That campaign is known in French military history as the struggle for Route Coloniale (RC) 4, the road that wound its way along the Vietnamese-Chinese border. The French were dealt a stinging defeat when the 304th and other new People's Army divisions smashed the barrier line of French forts that extended along the road and then trapped and overwhelmed the relief column the French sent to meet their withdrawing garrisons. The situation in the 1950 campaign bore certain similarities to 1967's McNamara Line and the Khe Sanh combat base, though the parallel most frequently cited remains Dien Bien Phu, the climactic battle of the Franco-Vietnamese war.

The 304th Division had been at Dien Bien Phu too, as well as at the many battles and campaigns between the RC 4 and Dien Bien Phu high points of the French war. Indeed the division earned the honorific Nam Dinh for its role during a 1951 action along the southern edge of the Red River delta. The division's base was established in Thanh Hoa province, a place to which it returned repeatedly during and after the French war. Part of the division numbered among the triumphant People's Army contingents who marched into Hanoi in October 1954. Two years later the 304th helped suppress peasant unrest in Nghe An province, to the south of Thanh Hoa. Prior to fall 1967 only the 66th Regiment among the division's units was believed to have ever gone south to the new war. Hanoi's commitment of the 304th was putting a major piece into play.

American Marines around Khe Sanh had long faced another antagonist, the NVA 325-C Division. That formation too had its origins in the anti-French war, though it had not been activated as a division until after the war. In fact, the 18th and 95th Regiments, which formed the bulk of the division's strength, had long experience in the very area to which the U.S. Marines deployed during the Second Indochina war. Those regiments had defended the so-called Street Without Joy, basically the coastal strip between Hue and Quang Tri, against the French. Absorbing the 101st Regiment, which had fought the French farther north, the 325th Division came into being around Dong Hoi in 1955. Its units had experience in all three nations of Indochina, for the 101st had been deep inside Cambodia at the time of the 1954 Geneva agreement.

During the late 1950s the division remained around Dong Hoi, considered a second-line unit within the People's Army. With the exception of leading cadres and officers, original personnel were replaced by new recruits in a three-phase reorganization drive, while an effort was made to standardize unit weapons and equipment. The 101st Regiment intervened in Laos during 1961, fighting in the panhandle opposite the South Vietnamese provinces of Quang Nam and Quang Ngai.

In 1962 the North Vietnamese attempted to improve the education and skills of 325th Division personnel. Another drive began, this one to replace officers with individuals who had at least completed high school. In addition, two hundred division noncommissioned officers were reportedly sent to a school run by the military region. Beginning in 1963 the division conducted infiltration training for a succession of units sent south, the first open intervention by the People's Army alongside the Viet Cong. Between December 1964 and April 1965 all the 325th Division's regiments entered South Vietnam, making it the first combat division to enter the war.

Whatever this unit's early problems, nothing in its education or training dissuaded Hanoi from committing the 325-C in the south in 1965. Marines would have been surprised to learn the 325-C had been considered second rate. At Khe Sanh the North Vietnamese troops of this division seemed entirely professional and every bit as careful as their American opponents. The coming battle would test the mettle of men on both sides.

*   *   *

Hanoi made a decision during the summer of 1967, but what that decision was cannot be said with precision in the absence of authoritative documentation from the Vietnamese successor government. Actually, even if there were such an authoritative statement, historians and former participants on various sides of this debate would probably continue to dispute it, questioning the quality or veracity of the sources. The debate is rooted in the close relationship in time between what happened at Khe Sanh and the massive offensive the North Vietnamese and Viet Cong launched throughout South Vietnam at the moment of the 1968 lunar new year, or Tet. Either the Tet offensive was a diversion intended to facilitate NVA preparations for a war-winning battle at Khe Sanh, or Khe Sanh was a diversion to mesmerize Westmoreland in the days before Tet. Thus Hanoi's decision in summer 1967 was either to fight a battle for Khe Sanh or to conduct an offensive at Tet.

The first school of thought is led by Westmoreland himself and his chief of intelligence at the time, Brigadier General Phillip B. Davidson. In their estimation Hanoi intended a three-phase operation, beginning with attacks to divert MACV attention, proceeding to countrywide attacks on cities, towns, and villages, and winding up with the assault on Khe Sanh. This was the view Westmoreland propounded in his cables to Washington, and it is the one Davidson puts forward in his retrospective history *Vietnam at War*.

According to the memoir of senior Viet Cong official Truong Nhu Tang, as early as 1966 the Viet Cong political arm, the National Liberation Front, had resolved to prepare for a general uprising of the South Vietnamese people against the Saigon government. As most such actions came at the direction of, or at least in coordination with, Hanoi, it was apparent that constant attention was being given to this facet of North Vietnamese strategy and that the conditions necessary for such an attempt were under continual review.

In December 1965, at the height of the U.S. troop buildup, a plenum of the North Vietnamese Worker's (Lao Dong) Party had exhorted the state to seek victory within a relatively short time. The 13th party plenum, which Ho Chi Minh convened in early 1967, adopted a resolution specifically calling for a "spontaneous uprising" leading to "decisive victory in the shortest possible time." Ho Chi Minh and the Politburo confirmed this Resolution 13, General Davidson believes, by May, after which NVA and VC military and political staffs began detailed planning. On or about July 4 a surprise ARC LIGHT strike on the headquarters of the Central Committee for South Vietnam (COSVN), the shadowy VC high command, temporarily interrupted the effort. This bombing also had a direct impact because fragments mortally wounded the committee's commander, General Nguyen Chi Thanh, who was evacuated to the 108th Military Hospital in Hanoi by night flight. General Thanh's funeral on July 6 furnished an occasion for senior North Vietnamese military and political leadership to reaffirm its intentions.

General Thanh's replacement as executor of the Tet offensive was North Vietnam's chief of staff and minister of defense, General Vo Nguyen Giap, the victor of Dien Bien Phu. Giap happened to be a longtime rival of Thanh's; also over the previous two years Giap had been criticized as too conventional while Thanh had been arguing against mechanically copying past formulas and against reliance on modern military tactics, sure to play into the Americans' hands.

This coincidence leads some observers to conclude that Giap's involvement meant that Hanoi changed focus to Khe Sanh as an opportunity to repeat the success of Dien Bien Phu. Unfortunately, evidence here is fundamentally ambiguous. Thanh's opposition to modern military tactics can be read equally as advocacy of protracted guerrilla warfare, a course Giap was known to favor. Since the essence of guerrilla warfare is political, a series of attacks on cities and towns, a *political*-military offensive was not out of keeping with the nature of the strategy. Thus there is no necessary reason to assume that Giap and Thanh had opposing strategies or that Giap insisted on great changes in plans for the Tet offensive. Moreover, only such a political-military offensive held any chance of producing the spontaneous general uprising about which Hanoi liked to fantasize. A battle at Khe Sanh, no matter how successful, could not produce that result.

Most significant is the series of articles Giap wrote that are collectively known as *Big Victory, Great Task*. These appeared beginning in September 1967 in *Nhan Dan* and *Quan Doi Nhan Dan*, the newspapers of the Lao Dong party and the People's Army, respectively. Westmoreland writes that he dismissed the series as camouflage and planned deception. David Schoenbrun, the journalist who penned the introduction to the series when it was published in the United States, saw the thrust as advocacy and propaganda, "hortatory rather than expository," a mélange of "disappointing generalizations" to justify Hanoi's great task of holding off even greater American blows.

Both general and journalist saw Giap's series as further elaboration of a desire to pursue protracted war, guerrilla warfare.

These reactions perhaps miss important elements of General Giap's writing, in which the NVA chief of staff, exhorting to be sure, warned that achieving a *big* victory would be a *great* task. Specifically, Giap wrote that President Johnson's approvals of further troop deployments would give the United States over half a million troops in Vietnam by mid-1968 but that "the present mobilization level has far exceeded initial U.S. forecasts and is at sharp variance with U.S. global strategy." Thus Giap recognized a near-term risk in the growth of Westmoreland's forces and appreciated an opportunity to confront Washington with the dilemma of its Vietnam policy versus its global responsibilities. This sounds very much like the recipe for an NVA offensive, one that had to occur before those extra reinforcements reached Westmoreland, one, in fact, at Tet. "The American imperialists are now at a crossroad," wrote Giap, surely an expression of his view of the impending opportunity. The real purpose of *Big Victory, Great Task* was precisely to furnish all those NVA political officers with a detailed prospectus explaining the great demands that were shortly to be made on their men.

If one looked closely, the Giap articles even contained some hints about the military operations he envisioned. For one, Giap extolled "people's war" strategy as opposed to conventional military tactics. Second, the "Liberation Armed Forces," that is, the People's Army plus the Viet Cong, would "repeatedly harass the enemy and destroy many large U.S. and rebel units . . . scattering the enemy in order to fight him." Large-scale battles were not ruled out, but the military effort really was intended as a "bugle call" that would urge the southern people "to take advantage of their victories to surge forward."

Either it is an uncanny coincidence that North Vietnamese military operations in the fall of 1967 followed this formula so closely or the resemblance was quite intentional. During October NVA and VC forces offered pitched battle at Loc Ninh, northwest of Saigon. In November came a similar pitched battle in the Central Highlands, at Dak To. During the latter action the Americans captured a document that Westmoreland and Davidson were both aware of and that Westmoreland cites in his memoirs as evidence of Hanoi's intentions to launch a Tet offensive. Westmoreland even referred to the document at some length in a news conference in Washington on November 22, 1967, on a visit to the United States to help increase support for the war. The document was a front command directive providing roles and missions for the winter–spring campaign. North Vietnamese troops were to "annihilate a major U.S. element," but that was specifically made instrumental to the main objective, "to force the enemy to deploy as many additional troops to the Western Highlands as possible." Diversion was thus the key role — as Giap had put it, to scatter the enemy in order to fight him.

An NVA attack at Khe Sanh like the battles at Loc Ninh and Dak To may have been intended in mid-December 1967, as shall be recounted shortly. The attempt was forestalled by timely reinforcement of the combat base, but had it occurred, the diversionary intentions of the adversary at Khe Sanh would in retrospect have been much clearer. What bears repeating is that no general uprising was likely to flow from combat action at Khe Sanh and that it was Hanoi's intention to provoke such an uprising before arrival of Westmoreland's reinforcements.

General Westmoreland had always been sensitive about Khe Sanh, and he never believed that NVA activity aimed at the combat base could be a diversion. Phillip Davidson follows this line, ridiculing any notion that Khe Sanh could be a diversion as "obvious nonsense." To reach that conclusion he compares the combat strength of the Americans at Khe Sanh with that of the North Vietnamese. But Westmoreland explicitly described his border interdiction strategy to Washington in a cable on December 10, 1967: blocking the borders with *small* forces, sufficient to oblige the adversary to battle, striking the opponent "as soon as he is within reach," using *reserves* from the populated areas.

From the foregoing it is clear that the proper comparison is not opposing forces at Khe Sanh but rather opposing forces in the III MAF/I Corps area or, even more centrally, opposing forces in Quang Tri province. By this measure Westmoreland certainly did find himself drawn to Khe Sanh, battle or not, for good or ill. In his memoirs he acknowledges a move to the north as a principal theme of his Vietnam strategy. Between January and March 1968 the proportion of U.S. forces in I Corps increased from about forty percent to slightly more than fifty percent of MACV's *entire* force, with *every* corps area other than III MAF designated an economy of force zone, one in which MACV accepted calculated risks by using minimal forces. Over the same period ARVN deployment in I Corps remained static at about twenty-two percent of its total. We shall return to the reasons Westmoreland felt he needed to respond in this way, but the point is that these decisions were made at MACV, not in Hanoi.

We should also reverse the logic of General Davidson's argument about diversion. He argues the absurdity of tens of thousands of NVA troops diverting the much smaller garrison of Khe Sanh, concluding that an offensive at the combat base was Hanoi's intention. But at the time Hanoi made its decision, Khe Sanh was in fact held by two, or even just one, battalion of U.S. combat troops. Is it not absurd to think Hanoi would have focused the entirety of a multidivision, multiphase military offensive on eliminating a single battalion of U.S. Marines?

If a general uprising could not be forthcoming from a Khe Sanh attack and if Westmoreland could be perceived as highly sensitive about Khe Sanh, not to mention the DMZ barrier line, a diversion in northern Quang Tri, a diversion such as Khe Sanh, would appear to Hanoi to be quite a good proposition. Hanoi used the U.S. Marines at Khe Sanh combat base in service of its larger aims.

To cap this question we can refer to the MACV intelligence summary for November 1967, a product of Davidson's own intelligence section. The November summary described Hanoi's method as a "peripheral strategy" in which the enemy demonstrated presence "by keeping the majority of his main force units in being and positioned near border sanctuaries. This permits him to take advantage of exploitable opportunities by large-scale attacks, while evading Allied offensive operations and controlling his losses." Davidson's monthly estimate projected the most likely NVA course of action as continuing this strategy while bringing up units from its strategic reserve. The intelligence authorities were prepared to believe in the hypothesis of an offensive against Khe Sanh — it was an "exploitable opportunity" for a large-scale attack.

At the Defense Intelligence Agency in Washington, two analysts assembled a joint paper predicting that the North Vietnamese would only feint toward Khe Sanh. Among the more experienced Vietnam analysts, the DIA people had spent four years studying NVA methods and they based their conclusions on their understanding of Giap's techniques. The paper outlined the NVA alternative purpose: to draw American forces away from the coastal plain. When the analysts presented their paper at a DIA briefing, the audience was amused and listeners laughed when the analysts suggested that the Joint Chiefs be apprised of the analysis and that it be sent to Saigon as a DIA assessment. Their boss, an Army colonel, taped the paper to the wall next to his desk. The analysts were asked, "How could you possibly know more than General Westmoreland?"

"Every One of Them as Tough as Nails"

Matters of high policy in Hanoi, Saigon, and Washington hardly affected grunts on the ground at Khe Sanh, except in ways they would discover only in the future. For them the main task was living from day to day and their main trouble was the travails of that day. Hill 861, though it was most affected by weather, remained typical of the Khe Sanh experience in the summer of 1967. About a week after Bravo Company of the 1st Battalion, 26th Marines took over the hill in August, rain washed away the trench line on one side of the hill, caved it in on another, and collapsed at least three bunkers. Marines had to suspend their patrolling to rebuild the positions. Charlie Company took over Hill 861 on September 15 and two days after that, six inches of rain fell within twenty-four hours. This was all before the monsoon even began. Marines shuddered to think what that might bring.

One day the gunnery sergeant of Charlie Company, who had faithfully served the Marine Corps for fifteen years, announced he was getting out. The gunny was fed up with the Marines' slipshod supply system. He calculated that the Army had enough helicopters to furnish two to every single platoon in the field. At Khe Sanh the reinforced 1st Battalion had two helicopters to support the entire unit. Since there were four companies in a battalion and three platoons per company, not counting headquarters and weapons platoons, the comparison was rather stark. The gunny had men he could not send on patrol because they had no boots, and some were forced to wear sandbags instead. When 3rd Marine Division commander General Bruno Hochmuth visited the hill on October 25 he saw men without T-shirts and with unkempt hair and demanded explanations. The lieutenant in charge, proud of the way his men had reestablished their defenses despite the rains, was not very happy talking about haircuts. The next day there was a new company commander, Lieutenant Jay French, formerly the battalion intelligence officer.

The main business on Hill 861 was patrolling, the specified purpose

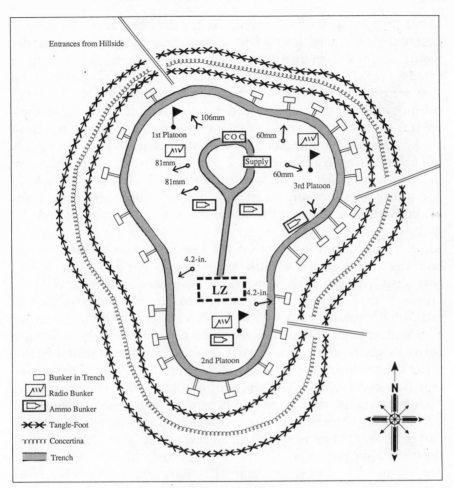

Entrances from Hillside

1st Platoon
106mm
COC
60mm
81mm
Supply
81mm
60mm
3rd Platoon
4.2-in.
LZ
4.2-in.
2nd Platoon

Bunker in Trench
Radio Bunker
Ammo Bunker
Tangle-Foot
Concertina
Trench

N

6 · Hill 861, August 1967

of the position as set by the directive for the operation. The routine eventually developed into a fine science: the company commander would simply designate a grid square on the map (see Map 12 for a sample portion of the Khe Sanh tactical map). The duty rotated so that one platoon patrolled every day, and a platoon got the job every third day. When the platoon leader with patrol duty got his assignment for that day, he would simply put his men in column, march to the assigned grid square, set up a command post, and put out squads of men radiating in all directions to cover the terrain. In the afternoon the men would pack up and return to their hill. The work was hard and it was not especially interesting. Though there were many signs of the North Vietnamese, the adversary was rarely encountered.

Merely a significant function for the Marine line companies, patrolling was the raison d'être of the recon Marines and the MACVSOG specialists. Always difficult, the job of the professional recon men got no easier as the spring of 1967 wore into summer and passed on to fall. Still, their task was vital. If the NVA could surprise and overrun Khe Sanh it would be a stunning success; recon made the difference between ignorance and knowledge. Frank Tomeo, regimental intelligence officer during the first part of this period, recounted that sightings had come everywhere during his tour, which ended in June. Tomeo estimated that there had been some thirty-nine attempts to insert recon patrols into the area, of which approximately fifteen had had to be aborted or extracted on an emergency basis. "It seems that the minute we put recon in," Tomeo reported, "it sort of draws the enemy, and we have these small sightings, and we have instances where our recon is surrounded."

Employing recon was always a delicate procedure. The men were tough and excellently trained, but they were not supermen and, unlike the noisy infantry patrols, recon often encountered the adversary. The difference between life and death could be as simple as whether the men had gotten enough rest. Life for the recon men was a microcosm of life at Khe Sanh, except that recon men most often lived on the edge. Recon and SOG people carried on a lively debate on the best procedure for inserting patrols. Whether these should walk in, go by truck, or ride aboard helicopters was one issue; each means carried implications for North Vietnamese ability to perceive the start of a patrol action. Then there was the question of preparation. Some insisted that it would be too dangerous to begin a patrol at an insertion point or landing zone that had not first been subjected to artillery or air bombardment. Others argued equally vehemently that such preparatory fires merely tipped off the NVA that something was coming. Khe Sanh tried things every kind of way: with preparation, without preparation, with simultaneous preparation of many insertion points and LZs, with random selection among several LZs. The dangers always remained.

If the North Vietnamese were not danger enough, there were dangers of another kind. Recon Marine Kevin Macaulay found out as much on his second patrol out of Khe Sanh. He was primary radio man on a patrol commanded by Sergeant Gary D. Trowbridge. Secondary radio man was Ernie C. Husted, point man was Roy T. Burns, and medic Grant Gilbert had volunteered to carry an M-60 machine gun. Macaulay recalls that it was a miserable patrol, but at least everything went smoothly until the day the team was to be extracted. Macaulay tells the story:

We were humping our backsides off. . . . We worked our way off the ridge line, staying off the paths that crisscrossed [it]. We had seen numerous signs of North Vietnamese activity . . . we had a couple of fire missions fired on the lights in the area, so they knew we were out there. We knew they were out there. We didn't know how close they were, but they knew how close we were.

Khe Sanh was socked in that day. We were coming out to the same LZ we had gone in on the patrol because there was nothing else in the area. The rest of it, for five or six thousand meters around, was just totally triple covered canopy. . . . I was cut to shreds [by the elephant grass]. I had forgot my gloves.

We called up Khe Sanh and said we were ready to move into the LZ, and they said, "Forget about it; we can't get choppers airborne." . . . We sat there and we set up our harbor site for the night. It was about four-ish in the afternoon. . . .

The next thing we know, Relay is calling us: . . . "ADULT GROUP make to the LZ. Your choppers are on their way."

Trowbridge said, "Pack up! Let's get going!" So we started to pack up and everybody was in a hurry because they wanted to get back to the base and take showers and get the hell out of the bush. . . . In my haste to get ready I left the [radio] handset out and left it dangling from the end of my pack. . . .

I got separated from the rest of the patrol, and they were three-quarters of the way into the LZ when I noticed movement up ahead of me, thirty to forty meters away. And I stared, and they stared.

I was running through the bush to catch up to the patrol, and the handset fell off the back of the pack, snagged in between two trees, and I ran out the full extension of eight feet of the handset cord and flipped over backwards. I landed flat on my back. At this point, I spotted the NVA and they spotted me.

Off to my right-hand side I could hear Ernie Husted, "Preacher" as we called him, "Mac! Down this way!" Before I could answer him I cracked off a couple of rounds at the two NVA I had spotted. One went down. It was sheer surprise, I don't think I hit him. . . .

. . . As I was running up the hill, I saw a rocket, or some type of ordnance, impact fifteen or twenty feet off to my left, and at that point in time I realized I'd better run fast because our own helicopters were shooting at me!

I finally got up into the LZ and joined the rest of the patrol . . . [the machine gun jammed]. . . . And Trowbridge was livid. He was about ready to hit [the machine gunner] over the head with his M-16. . . . And we started taking incoming rounds into the LZ. Luckily no one was hit. I felt I had been hit because I felt extremely warm on the front of my trousers until I realized I had urinated in my pants out of sheer fright.

The helicopters came in, picked us up. . . . We finally got back to the Khe Sanh base. And the fog cleared and the helicopters set down and this first lieutenant came running up to me and said, "Gee, I'm sorry, I'm so sorry," and I said, "What are you sorry about? You just saved my life!" He said, "No, I'm a gunship pilot," and then it dawned on me that he was the one shooting at me as I was running up to the LZ.

I said, "I must have looked like a Goodyear blimp out there. What's the matter with you? How could you mistake me for a five-foot Vietnamese?" And he looked at me and said, "Well you know, things look a little different from the air."

Macaulay and the pilot talked some more and finally had a laugh over their mishap, while in the recon area the machine gunner busily stripped his M-60 to see why the weapon had not fired in the last critical engagement. Gunner Burns found the reason: the M-60 had had no firing pin. Macaulay recalls, "Trowbridge looked at him, and I think if looks could kill, the telegram would have been on the way to Burns's parents."

Private Roy T. Burns of Garyville, Florida, was actually not all that bad. In fact he was a premier recon man, one of the best point men in the outfit, someone who virtually taught other recon Marines the realities of fieldcraft by his example. His cigarette lighter bore the inscription "To appreciate life you must experience death." Burns came to Vietnam a private first class and left with the same rank, despite being promoted about eight times: typically he would be promoted for action in the field and then busted for misdemeanors at base. Heavy drinking did not help. He was also a coffee aficionado, which led to trouble on one patrol when the recon team was hunkered down to avoid being seen but Burns could not resist igniting a small pellet of C-4 plastic explosive to heat water for his coffee. The freckle-faced Burns, problematic as he may have been and much as he kept to himself on base, was a Marine his buddies wanted to have with them when there was trouble.

Besides Sergeant Trowbridge, other recon men included Corporal "Peppy" Lopez, an experienced patrol leader due to leave soon who was much admired by his men and helped keep them out of trouble. Sergeant Bill Kaufman was a radio man who drew little posters and cartoons expressing the feelings of the men. Kaufman decorated the team bunker with an illustration of a voluptuous, bare-breasted woman. Ernest Clyde Husted, Jr., was known as "Preacher" because he had taught Sunday school before enlisting in the Marines. Husted came to recon from the 3rd Battalion, 4th Marines, which had had duty as a battalion landing team.

There were as many stories as there were recon Marines. Sergeant James L. Hutton coming in from the States had some idea he could establish dominance by snapping the men into shape. Soon after his arrival he took one of the most experienced recon teams, men who had spent days on end in the bush outpacing NVA search cordons, and ordered them out for some toughening, specifically a run around the airstrip.

"I want to hear those legs thunder, Marines!" Hutton called out as the men began their circuit.

Recon Marine Robert E. Pagano sets the scene: "So he ran us around the airstrip. Of course it was almost 110 [degrees] out. And by the time we got all the way around the airstrip he wasn't in too good a shape, and we were pretty OK. . . . We said, 'Come on, Sarge, let's *thunder* around one more time!' " Hutton never called physical training again. At Khe Sanh forever after he would be known as "Thunder Legs."

The Navy provided medics, called corpsmen, for Marine units, but being medic to Force Recon posed particular problems. With their small teams in the field, recon wanted every man to be a warrior. "Recon," observed the senior corpsman of the company, HM2 Packard, "really doesn't need a corpsman. They make their corpsman into a machine gunner. So I have a machine gun and we get into a firefight; somebody gets wounded. If I give up the gun we may get overrun and everyone dies, but that's what the rest of the team is for, not me. I should be there helping the wounded; that's my job." Another corpsman chimed in, "It's now SOP [standard operating procedure]: you don't treat any patients until in a cleared area."

Packard did not like recon's use of its medics, but there were things he appreciated at Khe Sanh: "The simple things suddenly take on great meaning — a smoke, a pause when you can think to yourself. And you see the sunset and say — it may sound corny but it's true — you say, 'I thank you Lord, for letting me see it.' I remember all the times during the day, the men wounded and the snipers still there, waiting for the corpsman, but I go anyway, and somehow the bullets miss me."

Hutton and Packard mounted twenty-four patrols in August, had ten sightings and nine contacts, and called eleven fire missions. During September twenty-two patrols aggregated fourteen sightings, fourteen fire missions, four air strikes, and two contacts. In October and November, on the average, three or four recon teams were on patrol at any time. During December Force Recon dispatched thirty more patrols. There were many sightings and nine contacts. Recon men were among the first to sense the growing danger. As early as August 3, Preacher Husted wrote in his diary: "Things aren't looking too good here at Khe Sanh. We're completely surrounded. Before long will be overrun."

It was in fact not long before Husted was overrun, but not in the way he imagined. First came an emotional onslaught, the result of his girlfriend's leaving him, an all too real danger for men in a high valley thousands of miles from home, with no possibility of getting there before their tours ended. Husted's team had been embroiled in a fierce firefight. The radio man, Husted had called artillery and air strikes to save his buddies in the three-hour donnybrook. Then, at Khe Sanh on September 5, after just a day or two to feel good about himself, came the bad news about his girlfriend.

Two days later, leaving on another patrol, Husted's emotions were still unresolved. It was a tough patrol, begun with a ten-foot jump from a hovering helicopter at the LZ. Marching up and down the hills he kept thinking of home. The patrol was extended an extra two days. They found caves, medical gear and food, an empty base camp, a mortar position.

On the fourth day the recon men noted that they were being followed. They tried to evade. Roy Burns was point man, Thunder Legs Hutton in command. Working their way down between two steep hills they found a stream and stopped to refill their canteens. Then they started up one of the hills. Suddenly, above them, they heard a noise. It was the sound of a weapon hitting the ground; someone had probably tripped. The Marines were underneath, on the side of the hill, sitting ducks in a firefight. Hutton ordered the men to make for the hill on the other side, a very steep one. The recon Marines moved out quickly.

The going was rough on the other hill, slippery and almost vertical. The men were clawing their way. Then Roy Burns upset a bees' nest and the insects swarmed around the hapless Marines. "As if in a dream," Husted later wrote, "I had no control over what was happening. The bees were all over my body, taking turns at attacking exposed skin. I tried to wipe them off my face and hands, but more took their place. The insects were trying to get into my nose and ears. I watched them squash themselves against my glasses." Everyone ended up with at least twenty or thirty stings, two had more than a hundred each and seemed ready to pass out. One of them, Robert Hatfield, on his second patrol, did lose consciousness. None of the men cursed or cried out, none made any sound at all; they were recon Marines. A medical evacuation by two H-34 helicopters from the hilltop got the patrol back to the combat base. Not all the perils at Khe Sanh were military ones.

The other major component of Khe Sanh's scouting forces was, of course, MACVSOG, which experienced considerable change during this phase of the campaign. With its agent nets, Spike patrols, and Hatchet teams, the SOG fought the NVA on the Ho Chi Minh Trail. At first located across from district headquarters in Khe Sanh, the newly formed forward operating base, FOB-3, initially augmented the FOB-1 launch site, providing an additional fifteen or twenty men under Major Fred Patton. It was not long before specialization developed: FOB-1 still aimed at the trail and the head of the A Shau valley; FOB-3 became the MACVSOG contribution to the McNamara Line. FOB-3 was charged with emplacing and maintaining sensor systems that extended the barrier into Laos. With the new mission came Major George Quamo to supervise what was called the "special project."

With its new mission FOB-3 also outgrew its quarters in Khe Sanh village and moved to Old French Fort through the summer. During that period Captain Wayne Snow's team returned to Phu Bai, replaced by the unit under Captain Lee Dunlap. Once at Khe Sanh, Dunlap worked with Quamo and the FOB commander, Major "Shaky" Campbell, to emplace the barrier system. This did not mean that FOB-3 collected no intelligence, but the days it had teams in the field solely for that operational mission, according to Dunlap, could probably be counted just on fingers and toes.

French Fort was not too secure. About the time the Snow detachment pulled out, Dunlap and other FOB leaders went up the chain of command to get approval for a new base site. At first they considered using Lao Bao, tucked right up next to the Laotian border, but that was outside easy support range and seemed too forbidding. At length the decision would be to base FOB-3 in a compound right outside Khe Sanh combat base. Major Campbell managed the move in such a way that there would be no diminution of operations or intelligence during the interval.

Work on a FOB-3 compound at Khe Sanh combat base began in late September. On the 29th, Air Force transports dropped huge 12-by-12-inch timbers to support bunkers. Marines on the combat base, who lost a man killed at about this time by the ceiling of a collapsing bunker, envied SOG their support. Sixty-five Seabees of Naval Construction Battalion 10 did the construction work, which progressed in spite of rain. The Seabees built four massive underground concrete bunkers, a helicopter pad, a medical dispensary, eight accommodation huts, and such service facilities as showers and nine latrines. The last Seabees returned to their home base at Gia Le on February 19, 1968. A Marine chaplain visited FOB-3 as early as November 8 to arrange Roman Catholic and Protestant services. He found Major Campbell very friendly but resistant to any special schedule. Those FOB-3 men who wished to attend services could simply walk to them at the combat base. The lavish FOB-3 supply stock became a kind of Mecca for hard-pressed Marines, for whom any number of items remained in short supply. The MACVSOG supply point even stocked a footlocker of hard liquor. At Khe Sanh that last fact was less well known than many things that were classified top secret.

Marines at the combat base never would have all they wanted, or even everything they needed. The Corps made a fetish of how "lean" it could be, priding itself on returning money to the U.S. Treasury every year. For the grunt Marines at Khe Sanh, however, that meant annoyance and misery, sometimes danger, even death.

One example of the perils of short funds is that the Marines were unable for a long time to obtain accurate maps of their own operating areas. Cartography and surveys for new maps were expensive. There was little motivation on the matter until June 26, 1967, when Marine gunners at the combat base tried a fire mission against targets on the north slope of Hill 950. Their shells, aimed over the peak of the hill on which Khe Sanh had its radio relay station, scored direct hits on the Marine positions instead. The men atop Hill 950 became frantic but managed to get the shelling stopped before anyone was hurt.

After the Hill 950 shelling incident the Marines brought a special survey party to Khe Sanh with sophisticated laser ranging equipment. In late July the survey team succeeded in determining that Hill 950 was actually 963.29 meters high. After that the survey team was kept on at the combat base through the fall to verify the accuracy of altitude readings of other key terrain features.

Meanwhile reduction of the forces at the combat base severely curtailed Khe Sanh's ability to saturate the operating area with patrols. In September there were just two company-size patrols, by A and D Companies of 1st Battalion, 26th Marines. During October there were again just two patrols, both by Bravo Company. None of these patrols made contact with the enemy. Then, in December, infantry patrols encountered the NVA three times.

Reduced patrols did not reflect the totality of military activity at Khe Sanh, however. During October, for example, reduced-strength companies carried on 17 operations, 94 night ambushes, 54 platoon-size patrols, 98 squad-size patrols, and 253 listening posts. During November there were 13 patrols by reduced companies, one search and destroy operation by a similar force, two dispatches of helicopter-borne reaction forces, 16 night ambushes, 49 platoon-size patrols, 48 squad-size ones, and 403 listening posts. Twice Marines swept Route 9 between the combat base and Lang Vei to remove mines. Usually it was the small-scale operations that found signs of the North Vietnamese. This happened often enough that toward the end of October the regimental intelligence officer, Harper Bohr, announced at a daily staff briefing, "We are now having more contact with the enemy than we've had in a long time."

One death that greatly affected subsequent events at Khe Sanh came on November 14, when Major General Bruno Hochmuth's UH-1E helicopter exploded and crashed in a rice paddy five miles northwest of Hue, leaving no survivors. Shortly thereafter the phone rang in Major General Rathvon Tompkins's quarters at the recruit depot in Parris Island, South Carolina. On the telephone was the chief of staff at Marine headquarters, Lieutenant General William Buse, who asked Tompkins how quickly he could leave for Vietnam to take over the 3rd Marine Division. Tompkins left for Southeast Asia on November 22, assuming command of the division five days later.

"Rath" Tompkins was a fifty-five-year-old fighting Marine who had won the Bronze Star on Guadalcanal, the Silver Star on Tarawa, and the Navy Cross as a battalion commander on Saipan. At the end of the war in Korea, Tompkins had commanded a Marine regiment. Most recently he had been deputy commander of Joint Task Force 122, the force the United States sent into the Dominican Republic in 1965. General Tompkins had been assistant commander of both the 3rd and the 2nd Marine Divisions and acting commander of the latter for four months in 1963. A native of Boulder, Colorado, he was well equipped to command the 3rd Division.

Most notable among the changes that had occurred in the situation around Khe Sanh by the time General Tompkins took command were those at Lang Vei. After the attack there in May it had been resolved to relocate the CIDG camp, and a new site was selected on a broad slope a few hundred meters to the southwest. Thus Lang Vei could continue to block one of the major approaches to Khe Sanh. Some of the last Rough Rider convoys up Route 9 brought in major construction supplies for the new Lang Vei camp, while the Air Force airdropped more than seventy tons of additional material. According to Green Beret commander Captain Frank C. Willoughby, a former Marine Corps NCO, it was the heaviest air drop for that size zone thus far in the Vietnam war.

The new Lang Vei compound would be built by Naval Mobile Construction Battalion 11. By the first week of September a quarter of it was finished, including exterior walls for an underground concrete bunker of the type Marines envied. The Green Berets, Vietnamese special forces, and CIDG strikers moved in during October when Lang Vei was largely complete. The redesigned camp featured an inner compound into which Vietnamese were not permitted, a perimeter compound around that to be held by Nung troops, and separate corner strong points, each with independent all-around defenses and barbed wire, for four CIDG companies. (See Map 7.)

Construction at Lang Vei was covered by a battalion-size operation by ARVN I Corps on September 23, the first in many months, utilizing nine Vietnamese H-34s plus twenty-eight U.S. Army UH-1 slicks to air assault the ARVN troops into an LZ near the new camp. The actual move into Lang Vei was similarly covered by two Mike Force operations along the Lao border to the west and south, one from October 25 to November 5, the other from November 5 to 14. Nevertheless one of the road clearance operations from Khe Sanh in late November suffered harassment. An SOG unit operation near Lang Vei also took fire from the Co Roc massif across the river in Laos.

Green Berets said their newly completed camp could hold out against the assault of an NVA regiment. According to them, more than a million dollars had been invested in the new Lang Vei, some $150,000 just for the concrete bunker. The predictions would soon be put to the test.

Meanwhile other changes were in progress on Hill 881 South. In contrast to the Marine positions on Hill 861, those on 881 held up very well to the rains of the fall. Water was still a problem, but here it was scarcity of potable water, which had to be flown up from the combat base. Marines could shave only on even-numbered days. The daily supply flow to the various hilltop positions averaged some 40,000 pounds. It was substantially higher on August 3, when the LZ of 881 South was jammed with three 105mm howitzers, each with 1,000 rounds of ammunition, that were being brought up to augment fire support. Another particularly good day was November 18, when 127,000 pounds were coptered up to the hills.

Hill 881 South was held by Alpha Company of 1/26 until September 9, when Delta Company relieved it. By this point in 1967 the 1st Battalion, 26th Marines had been in Vietnam for more than thirteen months, the standard length of tour for Marines in Vietnam. Thus that fall came large-scale turnovers in personnel. One of the new arrivals was Second Lieutenant Donald J. Jacques. A year before, Jacques had been in college at the University of Denver, rooming with the son of a television producer, perplexed by the growing antiwar sentiment. People said that kids went to college to stay out of Vietnam and Jacques didn't want any part of that, so he joined the Marines. He trained at Parris Island when General Tompkins commanded there and went on to the basic school at Quantico because of his college experience and high honors in training. He graduated and was commissioned an officer and Don went straight to Vietnam. At Khe Sanh in October 1967 Jacques was put in charge of the 3rd Platoon of B Company, 1/26, on Hill 881 South. Combat inexperienced, he sported that status on his sleeve, wearing a little piece of green material. Nevertheless Jacques was one of the first to volunteer for whatever mission company commander Captain Bruce Green might have.

Don Jacques sent letters home that describe in microcosm life on 881 South. "I have a great bunch of men here, every one of them as tough as nails," he wrote on October 21. "It is one of two extremes," Don noted four days later, "soaking wet or no water at all. . . . It can get pretty bad trying to keep the troops from wasting the water." Soon he was complaining that many of his men, including all his squad leaders and his platoon sergeant, were rotating home. At one point the platoon was down to fewer than thirty men; by early December it was up to more than fifty. By that time Jacques was practically an old hand and could write of his men: "They have a hell of a lot to learn." On November 8 Jacques wrote, "We are working hard to get the hill in shape so that the trench lines and hooches won't wash away in the monsoon." Then, a few days later: "The only way I could walk my lines was to slip and slide and use a bamboo stick for balance."

Meanwhile, at a higher, secret level, the situation and perceptions of it were changing. The sentry dogs the Marines had kept atop 881 South left on Halloween. Then or shortly thereafter arrived a small detachment of communications intelligence specialists of the 1st Radio Battalion, which contributed to National Security Agency reporting. They set up shop in an oddly shaped bunker near the LZ on the hill, one with a diamond-shaped revolvable antenna protruding above the ground. Inside was a large metal box with a compass indicator on top. Men who looked in were told the place was a restricted area.

On November 9 the brass descended upon Hill 881: Lieutenant General Cushman, accompanied by General Alfred D. Starbird, the mastermind behind the McNamara Line, plus a couple of brigadiers and assorted colonels and lesser fry. They walked to the north side of the hill and stood there a long time, gazing into Indian country. Occasionally Marines saw one or another of the generals pointing toward Hill 881 North or elsewhere. Then the generals got back into their helicopters and left.

The next day, Friday, November 10, was the Marine Corps' 192nd birthday, an occasion celebrated by Marines the world over. That day Colonel Lownds and Lieutenant Colonel Wilkinson flew up to 881 South through a pea soup fog. They brought cake, soda, and beer. The only ones who missed out were Don Jacques's 3rd Platoon, who were on patrol that day. The battalion commander told Delta Company that the NVA attached great importance to the hill and would try to capture it in the near future but that Marines would stand firm against them. Then Colonel Lownds asked the men to break ranks and gather round. Once the Marines were at ease the regiment commander delivered his own pep talk and wound up: "Men, we here at Khe Sanh are going to be remembered in our American history books!" Lownds's peroration chilled like the fog. At least one of the men wondered what the colonel knew that they did not.

"Escalatory Action Against the Out-of-Country Sanctuaries"

Henri Navarre, the French general who commanded at Dien Bien Phu, was once said to have an air-conditioned brain. William Childs Westmoreland was said to be an inevitable general. Much as air conditioning a brain is patently impossible, Westmoreland's military career was far from inevitable. In fact, his father wished "Rip" to become a lawyer and entertained visions of him at Yale Law School. Westmoreland first attended college at a military school, The Citadel in Charleston, South Carolina, but that was supposed to be preliminary to law school.

The path to law school apparently changed as a result of a trip to Europe and Westmoreland's chance encounter with a midshipman from the Naval Academy at Annapolis. Their conversation fascinated Westmoreland, who decided he wanted to be a sailor and tried to get an appointment to the academy. Instead South Carolina Senator James F. Byrnes offered Rip an appointment to the Military Academy at West Point and Westmoreland accepted it, eventually selecting field artillery as his service branch.

Westmoreland became a member of the class of 1936, along with Creighton W. Abrams, Harold K. Johnson, Bruce Palmer, and John P. McConnell, every one of whom rose to full general and became Army chief of staff, except McConnell, who would become chief of staff of the Air Force. At the Point Westmoreland acquired the nickname "Westy" by which he would be known throughout his military career and showed special talent for military evolutions, becoming first captain and a cadet regiment commander. He also won the coveted Pershing Trophy for leadership. In contrast, he had difficulty academically, leading his sister to joke that the greatest obstacle Westy faced during his military career was passing English at West Point. He also had problems with French and Spanish and placed in the bottom tenth of the combined economics/government course. William Westmoreland graduated 112th of 276 cadets and was commissioned a second lieutenant on June 12, 1936.

At Fort Sill, Oklahoma, for field artillery school, Westmoreland learned the intricacies of the guns that many thought had been the key weapons of World War I. When the Second World War began Westmoreland was a captain with the 34th Field Artillery battalion at Fort Bragg. In April 1942 he took command of that battalion and led it in the North African and Sicilian campaigns. The high points in the war for Westmoreland were probably the battle of the Kasserine Pass in North Africa, for which he was awarded a Legion of Merit, the Sicilian campaign, and the 9th Division's role in fording the Rhine at Remagen, for which Westy won a Bronze Star.

It was the Sicilian campaign of 1943, however, that probably had the most to do with William Westmoreland's future career, for it was during that interlude that he gained a patron. The adjoining unit, the 82nd Airborne Division, needing some heavier artillery support, was temporarily given operational control over the 34th Artillery Battalion. Brigadier General Maxwell D. Taylor, the airborne artillery commander, had himself once commanded the same type of guns and was impressed by Westmoreland's methods. Paratroopers like Taylor and General Matthew Ridgway were in the ascendency in the postwar Army. It was important to be a paratrooper and a coup to have a paratroop patron. Westmoreland went through jump school in 1946 and had Taylor looking out for him.

At the height of the Korean war, when Ridgway commanded the U.S. forces there, Westmoreland got the plum job of leading the 187th Airborne Regimental Combat Team, the sole paratroop unit in the theater. The 187th made only one air drop and Westmoreland led it. When Ridgway became Army chief of staff, Westy went to Washington for a Pentagon job. Then, when Taylor succeeded Ridgway, he appointed Westmoreland as secretary to the general staff, a key Army staff position. It was Taylor again who saw to it that Westmoreland got a solid divisional command, the 101st Airborne Division at Fort Campbell, Kentucky, from April 2, 1958, to June 30, 1960. After that

Westmoreland returned to West Point for three years as superintendent, followed by a stint as commander of the 18th Airborne Corps, the heart of the United States strategic reserve, at Fort Bragg. By that time Taylor was chairman of the Joint Chiefs of Staff and he had more kind words to say about forty-nine-year-old William Westmoreland when a deputy commander was needed in January 1964 for the newly created Military Assistance Command Vietnam. Westy got that job too and succeeded to the top command that summer. From the beginning of the United States ground combat role in South Vietnam, William Westmoreland was in command.

Never comfortable making small talk as a cadet or young officer, as a general in Vietnam William Westmoreland found himself in a situation where much depended on what he said and did. Westmoreland worked hard at it: he spent long hours with reporters at briefings, on trips, at intimate dinners, all the while sharing subtle confidences. Westmoreland also courted congressional representatives, administration officials, important business leaders, anyone he thought could further his cause. In 1967, in the effort to preserve public support for the war, Westmoreland was quite willing to lend himself to two extensive public relations trips home, one of them including an address to a joint session of Congress. Dressing faultlessly, carefully calculating everything he said, Westmoreland projected an image that seemed the very essence of generalship; perhaps that is why he seemed the inevitable general.

Behind the facade, however, the degree to which the image was calculated and contrived was impressive. For starters Westy monitored the press that reported the Vietnam war. His papers are full of clippings and cartoons about him from all over the country, the finding and collection of which must have kept a platoon of clerks busy almost full time. Moreover, Westmoreland actively considered ways to further positive coverage or counter negative. For example, when Ambassador Ellsworth Bunker passed Westmoreland a manuscript copy of an article Jonathan Schell wrote for *The New Yorker* on the brutality of the war in Quang Ngai province, an article later published in book form as *The Military Half,* Westmoreland complained in his diary notes that "the article is highly exaggerated and will definitely create major problems if published." It was "an obviously biased and distorted article" by an "avowed pacifist." Westy set MACV staffers to work on a sixteen-page critique of the Schell article, for which they

interviewed battalion commanders in Quang Ngai and even tried to
replicate Schell's experience, deliberately sending an inexperienced,
newly arrived foreign service officer out flying with the same hard-
bitten forward air controller who had flown Schell. Westmoreland
himself discussed the article with the commander of the Americal
Division, which controlled Quang Ngai.

Westmoreland worked equally hard to build and preserve staff
loyalty. Adept at the tricks of a politician, or indeed a division commander, Westy could recognize and remember the names of men who
had served in his units years before, a sure morale booster when he
greeted some soldier while visiting a unit. Old acquaintances were
also a source upon which to draw for MACV personnel. It was not
entirely coincidental that MACV's deputy commander, Creighton
Abrams, and his successor, Bruce Palmer, were both West Point class-
mates of Westmoreland.

The same sensitivity Westmoreland showed to his public image and
his service staff seemed to extend to operations. That is, certain elements of the military situation became staples with the MACV commander. John R. Chaisson, the Marine brigadier who had set up and
commanded the MACV combat operations center, observed that
some things could always evoke a response from Westy, almost like
pressing a button. The Central Highlands was one such area, the A
Shau valley another. The differences that developed between Westmoreland and Lew Walt and their persistence once Cushman replaced
Walt show that Khe Sanh and the DMZ were also among Westmoreland's sensitivities.

General Westmoreland had already attempted at least twice to get
approval for an invasion of Laos. He tried more successfully for authority to extend unconventional warfare operations in that country.
By 1967 it appears to have become an *idée fixe* with Westmoreland
that a Laotian invasion, which could be mounted only from Khe Sanh,
would seriously set back the North Vietnamese. There was some
support for this view within Lyndon Johnson's White House, where
national security adviser Walt W. Rostow believed that the worst
mistake made in Southeast Asia was when John Kennedy failed to
enforce the 1962 Geneva accords by using force while blocking the
Laotian panhandle. By 1967 Rostow had a special preference of his
own: an amphibious invasion of southern North Vietnam to block the
infiltration routes and, incidentally, "hold the area hostage against
North Vietnamese withdrawal from Laos and Cambodia." Rostow
felt that might be a more effective strategy than an invasion of Laos

in the dry season, though he would have supported an invasion in preference to no action at all.

Both alternatives were aired in the spring of 1967, after Westmoreland's request for an 80,000-troop increase in South Vietnam. Westmoreland proposed a second alternative, an "optimum" force increase of 200,000 troops, to comprise four and two-thirds divisions and ten air squadrons. The troop level decision could not be made without some examination of strategies such as the Laos versus North Vietnam invasion options, and LBJ called one of his "Tuesday Lunch" national security meetings for precisely this discussion. The meeting occurred on Thursday, April 27, as Marines at Khe Sanh fought their hill battles. Westmoreland personally made the case for the Laotian invasion in some detail.

Then Walt Rostow went to the map in the Cabinet Room. Rostow recalls it as one of only two times during his service with President Johnson that he intervened at a cabinet-level meeting. Rostow believed that the country would not take more of the same plodding approach and that decisive action might work. An invasion of North Vietnam, around Vinh, might very well work. It could be like the Inchon landing during the Korean war, the brilliant flanking move that changed the whole logic of operations. Unlike the Laos option, which would have to wait six months for arrival of the dry season, an invasion would neither have to be delayed nor depend on long cross-country supply lines. Westmoreland affirmed that he had developed contingency plans for such an invasion and there was some discussion of troop requirements and desirable weather factors.

President Johnson said nothing. Secretary McNamara, in his presidential memorandum a month later, if not at the meeting itself, advised against both a Laotian and a North Vietnamese invasion. McNamara believed there were no really attractive options. In the end LBJ approved neither strategy and also refused to give Westmoreland all the men he wanted, for the force augmentations could not be accomplished without some mobilization of U.S. reserves, which the president was not willing to sanction. Only 45,000 men would be added.

It was just as well that Lyndon Johnson held his counsel, for these escalation options were not as easy as they might have appeared on paper. Rostow is correct, in retrospect, that the probability of Chinese or Soviet intervention was overestimated at the time, although even here the record has become clouded with recent admissions by both the People's Republic of China and the Soviet Union that they did send combat troops to North Vietnam to play active roles. For example, the Soviets helped operate North Vietnamese antiaircraft defenses, and an invasion around Vinh could be expected to fight some of these anti-aircraft troops on the ground. What Moscow would have done once its troops had been shot at by Americans is unknowable, but it surely was not an insignificant factor for an American president.

Equally important was the military problem on its own terms. An invasion at Vinh or elsewhere in North Vietnam's southern provinces not only would have cut the flow of NVA supplies to the south but by the same token would have offered the NVA the target of American units placed squarely across a path already sustaining a flow of forces. Thus an NVA buildup against an American beachhead would have been *simplified*, not complicated, and NVA supply lines would have been shorter. Moreover, the action would have taken place on terrain and with a population actively hostile to the Americans, not one that was mostly quiescent and sometimes friendly. Rostow's invasion option sounds heroic but in actuality would have been reckless.

The North Vietnamese knew as much, both in retrospect and at the time. The calculation was not too difficult and Hanoi was perfectly able to make it. General Nguyen Xuan Hoang, chief of the historical office of the People's Army of Vietnam, told American interlocutor and former Marine William Broyles in 1983 that of all the American escalation options "the landing would have been the most foolhardy. We knew we could easily defeat as many as a hundred thousand men there." Plain to see, *at the time*, was Vo Nguyen Giap's comment in *Big Victory, Great Task:* "We have adequately prepared ourselves and are ready to deal destructive blows . . . if they adventurously send infantry troops to the north." Giap explicitly raised the specter of intervention, saying that invasion would be attacking "the mainland of a member country of the socialist camp." Finally, Hanoi's minister of defense rightly asked where troops for this hypothetical invasion were to come from. "Attacking the north means opening another large battlefield," Giap wrote. "The American imperialist forces would become more scattered and would be annihilated more easily."

Worst of all, invasion of the Democratic Republic of Vietnam would have meant conducting a major ground campaign that required air support squarely within the North Vietnamese air defense environment, which has been described as the most sophisticated since the defense of the Ruhr by the Germans in World War II. American aircraft would not have enjoyed the advantages they had in the south.

The best thing that can be said about the option of invading North Vietnam is that it is a good thing no one tried it.

As for Westmoreland's preferred option, invasion of Laos, that too had its problems. Hoang told Broyles that the NVA always kept some of its best troops, several divisions' worth (Broyles calls it a "corps"), in anticipation of just such a scheme. What happened when the South Vietnamese tried this option in February 1971 bears him out. A Laos invasion would have been a slugfest, not a relatively easy search and destroy mission. General Westmoreland expected this and wanted to mount a corps-size invasion, but that approach had implications of its own.

In U.S. military practice a corps is a formation of at least two, and usually several, divisions. Standard Army planning factors (which were proved inadequate by the Vietnam experience and would be substantially increased just a few years later) were that each division would require 411 tons of supplies for the first day of a meeting engagement, 835 tons for the first day of full-scale offensive combat, and 516 tons for each succeeding day. For 155mm artillery battalions the figure was 150 tons a day, and for 8-inch gun or howitzer battalions 145 tons; a corps would be supported by a number of these units. Assuming, for the purposes of this illustration, a three-division corps with five supporting artillery battalions, the supply requirement (using the older, inadequate planning factors calculated from World War II and Korea) for the first week of a Laos invasion would have been on the order of 16,500 tons, or 2,350 tons per day.

In a few months it would be apparent that Khe Sanh airstrip was fully utilized accepting deliveries averaging about 300 tons daily, and whatever tonnage it could take would also have to provide for the garrison at that place. The rest would have to come across Route 9, on which a truck couldn't even turn around between Ca Lu and Khe Sanh. The supply requirement translates into more than eight hundred truckloads daily, even assuming the airstrip was used to capacity. Such a degree of usage might have been sustainable for a few days before the road deteriorated too badly, but it also might very well have put an intolerable strain on the entire supply system. Either way there was no margin for anything except a Laos operation that went exactly according to plan. Moreover, Route 9 would be in use to overcapacity twenty-four hours a day, posing a mighty tempting target for ambush, and a single successful ambush would have left the entire Laotian invasion force out on a limb. Even rainy weather alone could take

Route 9 out of service. If ever there was an operations plan dangling by a shoestring, this was it.

General William Westmoreland nevertheless believed that an invasion of Laos was doable and he wanted to do it. During the summer and fall of 1967 he projected a series of four operations he collectively code-named YORK that would be carried out in 1968 to sweep to the Laotian border in the four northern provinces, clearing the way for the invasion. Though Lyndon Johnson resisted the latter, Westmoreland hoped his plan could be approved after the 1968 elections. But even he was not impervious to logistics considerations. When he met with top commanders and staff on December 9 to discuss YORK plans, the supply factors forced him to scale back the first phase from a division less a brigade to just a single brigade. At the new size, YORK was not going to have very much impact. Scaling back the preliminaries also reduced the feasibility of EL PASO, the Laotian invasion option.

This was the situation when reports began to come in of new movements of NVA divisions down the Ho Chi Minh Trail. Westmoreland probably theorized that one thing that could reduce the difficulty of his plan would be to defeat the main body of NVA forces *inside South Vietnam*. Khe Sanh was a good location — away from populated areas, U.S. firepower could be concentrated there with less fear of civilian casualties; the Saigon government was hardly active in the area, making coordination with it less important; the enemy seemed interested enough in the place to be drawn into combat. William Westmoreland *wanted* a battle at Khe Sanh. Contrary to previous accounts, which attribute the battle solely to Hanoi's intentions, the battle at Khe Sanh was not merely some plan concocted by the NVA. The Marines at Khe Sanh were about to be used by *both* sides for purposes that had little to do with the place itself.

Both Walt Rostow and his military aide and liaison with the Joint Chiefs of Staff, General Robert Ginsburgh, confirm in recent interviews that a specific decision was made in early December 1967 to have a battle at Khe Sanh. The decision was made in Saigon but approved by Washington in an exchange of cables between Westmoreland and Joint Chiefs chairman General Earle G. Wheeler. A search of the declassified records and other sources by the authors reveals that intelligence brought both Saigon and Da Nang to see opportunity in the reputed North Vietnamese threat to Khe Sanh.

The exchange between Wheeler and Westmoreland centered on the broader question of MACV's border interdiction strategy rather than narrow concerns with I Corps or Khe Sanh. Wheeler dispatched his cable early on December 7 (Vietnam time), a moment when Khe Sanh, fearing the NVA might try some gambit duplicating Pearl Harbor, was on full alert and blacked out. Wheeler asked a series of questions about strategy, to which Westmoreland responded on December 10 with a top secret cable (MAC 11956). The MACV commander opined that the reason the North Vietnamese were concentrating forces along the borders was to launch major attacks in the hopes of scoring psychological victories while retaining the ability to disengage and retreat into sanctuaries.

Westmoreland rejected withdrawal from the border zone as a counter to the NVA tactic. Withdrawal would have political, psychological, and economic impacts and "it is also unsound from a military stand point," he wrote. Indeed,

> If we do not violently contest every attempt to get NVA units into South Vietnam, we permit him to expand his system of bases in-country. . . . When we engage the enemy near the borders we often preempt his plans and force him to fight before he is fully organized.

Moreover,

> When the enemy moves across the borders we must strike him as soon as he is within reach, and before he can gain a victory or tyrannize the local population. We cannot permit him to strike the confidence of the South Vietnamese people in ultimate victory or to bolster his own morale with successes. To do otherwise would be to deliver to him, without contest, the very objectives which he seeks.

General Westmoreland did not intend to tie down his own forces manning border defenses, however. "We do not stand along the border and catch the enemy as he enters," the MACV cable read. "Rather, we take every step to meet him and stop him before he reaches his objectives." Westmoreland saw his mobility as permitting him to fight along the borders without seriously depleting forces on the coastal plain. Troops would engage in pacification missions until the moment of battle, be deployed swiftly to combat, and then be returned to other tasks. The November 1967 battle of Dak To was held out as an example. Thus, "I keep my reserves in the populated areas . . . where they can be productively employed to grind down the enemy while awaiting other missions." Westmoreland's explicit explanations belie the claims of former MACV officers regarding who was diverting whom at Khe Sanh. Although we agree with General Phillip Davidson's claim that U.S. forces in this area were not "tied down," his assertions that these forces were *not* supporting Khe Sanh by being there are plainly inaccurate. This kind of indirect reserve role was exactly what Westmoreland was describing to Wheeler in his cable.

One last point regarding Westmoreland's strategy described in his December 10 cable is that the MACV commander proved oddly defensive on his cherished notion of invading Laos. Wheeler had asked Westmoreland whether he thought fighting near the borders created "pressures for escalatory action against the out-of-country sanctuaries." Westmoreland attacked the very question as "reverse reasoning."

Neither Davidson nor anyone else should have made any mistake describing Westmoreland's strategy, for the MACV commander promptly leaked it. On December 14, 1967, Westmoreland allowed *Time* magazine bureau chief Sims Fentress and reporter David Greenway to read the top secret cable for background. It informed *Time*'s reporting later that month. The cable itself was declassified only on May 11, 1984.

The afternoon of the day he received Wheeler's cable, General Westmoreland was at III MAF for an update briefing on the DYE MARKER strong point program and the corps situation. Westmoreland cautioned that the NVA would try to make strikes somewhere around the DMZ area near Christmas for "emotional effect" on South Vietnamese and Americans. He ordered General Cushman to prepare a plan to minimize casualties. He repeated his concern at a MACV combined intelligence and staff meeting on December 9 and questioned whether there was adequate heavy artillery support available for Khe Sanh. The MACV commander suggested that additional 175mm guns be moved to Camp Carroll.

Meanwhile MACV intelligence and operations staffs had been asked to draw up a study or war game to identify what the NVA reinforcements might try to do. Westy had given this assignment as soon as the signs of North Vietnamese preparations began to come in. Phillip Davidson of intelligence, William Pearson of operations, and John Chaisson of the combined operations center teamed up to conduct the study. They did not actually play out any war game scenarios but decided that the NVA intended to attack somewhere in I Corps.

Westmoreland heard the briefing in November, probably on the 29th when he returned from his latest trip home, and directed that it be repeated for General Cushman and senior III MAF officers.

Davidson and his MACV cohorts flew up to Phu Bai with trepidation, he recalls, afraid the III MAF people would think they were being sold a bill of goods. The scenario was that the NVA would make a major effort in the two northern provinces and a secondary stab at Saigon and in the Central Highlands. The briefing went quite well. Cushman proved to be "one of the nicest guys I ever ran into," Davidson recalls, and the III MAF intelligence chief, Colonel Kenneth J. Houghton, was an old friend.

"Well, I think this makes a lot of sense," Cushman said.

The intelligence people fell to talking about where the blow might come. Some of the MACV people and other experts thought it would be Camp Carroll. Lieutenant Colonel Alfred M. Gray of the 1st Radio Battalion argued on the basis of his unit's communications intercepts that the target would be Khe Sanh. The argument went on all day and then recessed for dinner. Houghton recalls that Gray's people had done a traffic analysis of NVA communications networks and had some strong evidence. There were a couple of men, even generals, who resisted the analysis. That night Cushman decided to accept the hypothesis of a threat to Khe Sanh and reinforce it when the time came.

On Wednesday, December 13, the time came. Colonel Houghton went to Cushman with new intelligence and told the III MAF commander he needed to get an extra battalion to Khe Sanh before six o'clock that night. General Cushman promptly called Rathvon Tompkins at the 3rd Marine Division, described the need for reinforcements, and asked what was available. Tompkins had been planning an operation with the 3rd Battalion, 26th Marines and had the unit in motion.

Khe Sanh was informed forty minutes later, and within ten minutes of that, a full company was already on the airstrip unloading from helicopters. The rest of the battalion followed. So quick proved the arrival of Lieutenant Colonel Harry Alderman's 3rd Battalion that the regiment mess did not have food for all the men. Lownds's executive officer had to go to his opposite number of the 1st Battalion, 13th Marines to ask if the artillery unit's mess could feed an extra 250 men that night. There were no bunkers for the new men, no quarters, nothing. It had all been a quick improvisation.

Dennis Mannion's experience with Kilo Company of 3/26 suggests just how quick it was: Mannion had been in a truck with his buddies waiting to be driven up toward the Rockpile. Then a major ran up shouting orders to the drivers to get down to Dong Ha instead: " 'Back to the airstrip. They're going to Khe Sanh!' " Soon Kilo Company was in helicopters. "We flew in 'locked and loaded,' " Mannion recalls, "expecting the worst, and saw guys walking to chow with metal trays in hand."

Later the 3/26 operations officer, Major Matthew P. Caulfield, would recall: "In the last analysis, Khe Sanh was defended because it was the only logical thing to do. We were there, in a prepared position and in considerable strength. A well-fought battle would do the enemy a lot more damage than he could hope to inflict on us."

The die was cast. Reconnaissance radio man Kevin Macaulay got it perfectly in a letter he wrote home at the beginning of December: "I think all hell is going to break loose around Khe Sanh!"

chapter 7

Boxing in Darkness
(1967–1968)

AT THE BIG DAILY BRIEFING the day after the arrival of the 3rd Battalion, 26th Marines, Lieutenant Colonel Wilkinson announced that both Marine battalions would remain at Khe Sanh and the combat base was now free to begin conducting operations of almost a battalion in size. The 3rd Battalion immediately undertook a search and destroy mission toward Hill 918, about five kilometers west of Hill 881 South. It was a place where even the recon teams went with trepidation. Recon radio man Kevin Macaulay had predicted in a letter to his parents that an operation would be laid on to take Hill 918; now he proved to be right. Macaulay had also predicted the effort would be even bloodier than the hill battles of the previous spring.

Fortunately Macaulay's second prediction proved less prescient. Lieutenant Colonel Alderman's battalion used three companies for the operation, lifting them aboard helicopters to Hill 881 South. Troop arrivals were staggered so there would never be so many Marines on the LZ as to provide a good target for North Vietnamese mortars. As soon as each company assembled, Alderman sent it off to the operational area, the men moving in single file off the hill.

"We went several days," James E. Schemelia remembers. "We headed out towards Laos. . . . We found some old NVA fighting positions. We sat on the ridge lines at night and sent out ambushes. We just made no contact. . . . I look back now and try to reflect sort of how crazy it was for just a company to be that far out of Khe Sanh, knowing later that there was just thousands of North Vietnamese just hiding there, just waiting, not wanting to make contact with us. It's . . . amazing that any of us came back."

About a kilometer northwest of the objective, India Company found a regular installation consisting of about twenty well-built reinforced and camouflaged bunkers. Meanwhile Lima Company with Colonel Alderman's command group worked along another ridge line. On the last day Lima, under Captain Richard D. Camp, who had just returned from a short leave in Hawaii, got orders to return along a parallel route through the jungle, at lower elevation, while the main body of 3/26 kept to the ridges. The trek went smoothly until Lima found a well-beaten trail, as much as five feet wide, which clearly had been in recent use. Following that for a distance, the company found a bunker complex too, a big one with forty or fifty bunkers of every sort, then another, and then more. Camp figured *each* of those bases could support a full 250-man NVA infantry battalion. They were all empty. It was even worse than the first day of the operation when, ascending the ridge, Camp had smelled the enemy, or rather his pungent fish sauce and burning wood. Lima Company rejoined the main body of the battalion.

Far from a bloodbath, the sweep out to Hill 918 produced no contact at all. Only one man was killed, a Marine reportedly blown up in his own booby trap when he attempted to recover the M-26 grenade he had set out. There was just one other casualty: a Marine who fell off a stump on which he had been sitting. The battalion was back in Khe Sanh on December 24 in time to celebrate Christmas.

"How Good Do You Have to Be to Get into Heaven?"

The big 3rd Battalion operation, before it went out, had had plenty of people concerned, not least the Marines who would have had to do the fighting. One Lima Company Marine went to chaplain Ray Stubbe and solemnly asked him, "How good do you have to be to get into heaven?" Suddenly it was a time for big thoughts. Among the rumors that were current, aside from the perennial one that the base would be attacked that night, was one that the 2nd Battalion, 26th Marines (which had never fought alongside the rest of the regiment) would be coming up too. Then there was the rumor that 3rd Battalion was going to keep going right into Laos. One colonel later said he had been told by a general that the reason for the buildup at Khe Sanh was precisely to go into Laos but that at the last moment permission had been denied. Highly classified as Westmoreland kept his plans, grunts on the ground had an inkling of them.

Like the big operations, nothing came of the big thoughts, at least in the short term. Small operations, on the other hand — it was as if the North Vietnamese chose to engage only the smallest formations. Mortar and small arms fire hit the Khe Sanh village headquarters of CAC Oscar on December 19. On December 22 recon team 3-B-2 observed points of light near the Laotian border about six kilometers north-northwest of Hill 918. They requested artillery fire, but no barrage proved forthcoming because the targets were out of range of anything Khe Sanh could shoot. The closure of Route 9 and the failure to get 175mm guns through to Khe Sanh now told against the Marines.

Recon team 2-B-1 got its turn on Christmas Eve, inserting by truck at a point just past Poilane's coffee trees a few kilometers northwest of the combat base. Corporal William McCreight led the patrol, which ran into the NVA six kilometers from Khe Sanh in the late afternoon. They formed a perimeter and asked for air support; UH-1E gunships arrived within twenty-five minutes. The firefight lasted more than an hour, with the team extracted by helicopter at 5:58 P.M., just two minutes before the scheduled start of the Christmas truce. The recon members, between them, had only two grenades and about thirty rifle bullets left. Recon radio man Kevin Macaulay back at the combat base wrote, "I was praying so hard at the time that I was about crying."

The truce was not much at Khe Sanh. Not only did the recon patrol action spill over into the truce period, but there was an attack on Hill 950's radio relay post two hours later. Martin Kux, engineer chief of the naval construction crews who had relaid the airstrip, expressed the general feeling when he noted in his diary that Christmas Eve: "Merry Christmas! Bah! Here we sit in the office, while Hill 950 is under small arms attack and the base is completely blacked out. . . . Truce my foot! Another political gimmick to get Americans killed."

Christmas was observed in different ways that day, but with special meaning to men at war. During the afternoon of Christmas Eve some Air Force planes with loudspeakers orbited overhead playing carols like "Joy to the World." That evening there were services for the CAC Oscar Marines at their mess in the village. The only light came from perhaps a half dozen beeswax candles. Every Marine of the detachment was there. Next day the Catholic chaplain of the 3rd Battalion faced a service crowded with men just returned from the Hill 918 sweep. Over a hundred received communion. Protestant services attracted an overflow crowd, some 168 Marines.

Services were also held on Hill 950, where a collapsible Christmas tree had been passed along to the top sergeant to give to one of the line companies.

With 3/26, Jim Schemelia recalls Christmas night as "the first time I really got a feeling that I was part of India Company. I didn't feel like a stranger anymore. We sat around a camp fire at night . . . that was kind of unreal — there were a lot of camp fires around Khe Sanh that night." Schemelia had a sumptuous Christmas dinner — soup, hot turkey, cranberry sauce, mashed potatoes, vegetables, and all the trimmings. Captain Camp of Lima Company, by contrast, wrote that his unit got only C-rations on Christmas Eve but organized an impromptu celebration with cookies and other goodies in the mail from home. Colonel Lownds, with a young enlisted volunteer dressed as Santa Claus, drove over to Khe Sanh village where they distributed candy.

Just after the truce and holiday, on December 26 India Company was sent to Hill 881 South to replace Company B of the 1st Battalion. Similarly, Kilo Company went to Hill 861 in substitution for Company D. The regrouped elements of the 1st Battalion were to be used for another battalion-size operation beginning December 28. Colonel Wilkinson intended to place companies of his battalion on two LZs north and northwest of Dong Tri mountain and Hill 950 and sweep to the northwest to connect with his fourth company, which would hold a blocking position near Hill 743.

Charlie and Delta Companies air assaulted into the main landing zone, LZ Crow beneath Hill 632. A photo reconnaissance mission over the area the previous day had shown the hill to be heavily fortified. But Wilkinson's battalion encountered no opposition. The worst impediment was eight-foot-tall elephant grass. Someone got the bright idea of igniting flares to clear the grass, but the grass fires quickly grew out of control, burning toward the Marines' line of march as they ascended the hill. From back in the column men yelled to get out of the way, but no one would give the order. The battalion sergeant major later remarked, "We're so trained that even I didn't want to break the formation." Eventually they did, scrambling across the hillside and then upward to the summit, where everyone arrived exhausted. The sergeant major, First Sergeant J. D. Williams, complained that the exertion had set off his migraine headache. Fortunately he found a foxhole already dug and thus could sit down and rest. The men bedded down. For more than eight hours the horizon was lit by the flashes of ARC LIGHT strikes.

Just because Colonel Wilkinson's battalion could make little contact with the North Vietnamese did not mean the NVA was not out there. A classic counterpoint was the experience of "Clemson Song," reconnaissance team 1-B-2, dispatched to probe the area west of Hill 689.

The vegetation in that area seemed incredibly thick; the recon team decided to follow the trail. Following a trail was not a normal procedure; it was rarely done in Vietnam (especially by recon) because it was not conducive to remaining undetected. But there seemed no alternative here. If they had gone through the brush paralleling the trail, dense as it was, the noise would inevitably have alerted anyone on the trail itself. On the trail the Marines could move more quickly and quietly, and if they did see someone, they could fade back into the jungle alongside. The idea might not be prudent, but it seemed the lesser of two evils.

In any case, all went well initially. Clemson Song marched ahead until they came to a point where the trail forked. A quick exploration revealed that farther along the two forks merged, making the area between a sort of jungle island. To the recon men it seemed a natural harbor site. The Marines left the trail, sat down to eat, check their camouflage, and ready their gear. After a time they rose to continue the patrol. The point man had gone only three or four feet when suddenly he froze, raised his rifle, flicking the selector to automatic fire. The other recon men realized he was getting ready to fight, and all tried to make themselves scarce in the foliage.

The point man had seen a North Vietnamese force, men in green uniforms carrying heavy packs, each with three rockets tied to his back. There were plenty of them — later the Marines would report forty but some thought there were more than a hundred. The North Vietnamese marched down the trail and reached the fork and then continued along both sides. The NVA for once had no clue to the presence of Americans.

Radio man for this Marine recon team was "Preacher" Husted, who was struck by the physical attributes of the enemy. The North Vietnamese wore different colored uniforms and their equipment was designed differently, but it served the same purposes as gear the Marines themselves carried. The NVA were revealed as young men just like Marines, no longer shadows in the night or muzzle flashes from some tree line. North Vietnamese were perhaps people too.

As the Americans watched breathlessly, one of the NVA soldiers took out a cigarette. The man's idea was plain as day — he might catch a smoke unseen by the officers or NCOs. Evidently the smell quickly alerted a superior, however, and the cigarette was promptly yanked out of the man's mouth. Chagrined as any Marine would have been, the soldier kept his place in the column, which marched on. Moments later the man behind in the column reached forward and pushed the soldier's hat forward over his eyes. All the North Vietnamese men laughed. Yes, they *were* people too! "I had the unpleasant feeling," Husted recalls, "that the memories of what I was doing now would not end when I left Vietnam."

Once the NVA force passed, the Marine recon team backed up a little and Husted put up his whip antenna at maximum extension. The Marines' PRC-25 radios broadcast on a line of sight, and Hill 689 towered over the area where the team had been operating. Until now radio communications with the combat base had been spotty at best, but suddenly contact was crystal clear and the company commander, Captain Phillip Reynolds, wanted the team to *follow* the NVA column.

In the jungle the team leader and radio man looked at each other in consternation. Husted tells the story:

> I looked over to the team leader, and he shook his head, and I shook my head that I understood. I had found out — purely by accident one day because I wasn't a trained radio operator — [that the PRC-25 has] a control plug on the top right corner of the radio that you . . . put a jeep plug into when it's on a jeep for external power so you don't run your batteries down. If this plug is loose or out, it cuts off the power supply.
>
> So I started calling back to the base asking for clarification on the message, and the whole time I was loosening and playing with the plug. You could hear by the crackling that the radio was going out. The other radio was normally kept on a secondary frequency. It seemed to have the same trouble only it had it quicker because we didn't have anyone on the net talking to us on it. We just pulled that plug right out. And then we backed up to where we were, and just stayed for quite a few hours.

When Husted reconnected his plug, communications were instantly restored. Reynolds quickly asked whether they had followed the North Vietnamese seen on the trail but Husted replied that he had had radio problems and had not understood the orders. Captain Reynolds asked to see the radio batteries so he could inspect them, but the patrol responded that the batteries had been cut open and the individual cells destroyed and buried, a standard recon procedure. Husted had no doubt that if the Marines had followed the NVA column none of them would have returned from the mission.

Faces in the Rain

In line with his expressed concern that the North Vietnamese might attempt a big push to inflict casualties on Americans over the Christmas holiday, William Westmoreland worked constantly to prevent the action or, failing that, to limit NVA potential. He tried to get the Christmas cease-fire cancelled and did succeed in getting it limited to just twenty-four hours in northern I Corps. At one session with top subordinates and staff, Westmoreland even considered a suggestion that MACV draw the venom in advance by putting out a press release on projected NVA activities in the DMZ area that might negate the psychological advantage of the feared offensive.

A major part of Westmoreland's effort, belying his claims to have lost interest in the McNamara Line, was precisely on DYE MARKER, the strong point obstacle program. In December, just two days after returning from his U.S. visit to drum up support for the war, Westmoreland sat down with his operations staff to discuss MUSCLE SHOALS, the air component of the barrier system, which depended on electronic sensors. On December 7 he met with III MAF staff at Da Nang specifically about DYE MARKER. On Saturday, December 16, the MACV commander returned to the area, to Hue/Phu Bai, where he again met with General Cushman and III MAF staff, followed by a helicopter tour above the DMZ. Westmoreland alighted at strong point C-2 and at Dong Ha.

Westmoreland's discussions at Hue/Phu Bai that day concerned advance preparations for deploying the 1st Cavalry Division into northern I Corps. He wanted the necessary base facilities completed by January, and he ordered a conference to be held the next day to ascertain whether III MAF had all the resources for the job. The latest intelligence "suggests we should greatly accelerate these efforts," Westmoreland recorded. He also noted that "this project is in effect an acceleration of the requirements which grew out of YORK II." These comments from Westmoreland's own diary show both that he was reacting to the presumptive threat along the DMZ and that the basic thrust of his interest was to preserve the option of an invasion of Laos, an obsession he continued to pursue.

Westmoreland's interest in northern I Corps was not confined to broad questions of strategy. At MACV's request in September, staffers at III MAF had worked up an analysis of casualties to be expected in installation of the barrier line (672 Americans killed and 3,788 wounded, plus 112 ARVN killed and 642 wounded). On December 16 at Dong Ha, Westmoreland was still reviewing details of construction. He was gratified to learn that "the bunkers in the DMZ seemed to be moving rapidly" but was surprised that sandbags had had to be flown into one position and upset that materials were inadequate to build both living quarters and firing positions. "I directed that this matter be looked into as a matter of urgency," Westmoreland recorded. He did not know, as General Tompkins later told debriefers, that the Marines had deliberately diverted some DYE MARKER fortification materials to Khe Sanh.

Another reason why fortification materials appeared insufficient for all the planned installations Westmoreland discovered on Christmas Day, when he returned to I Corps and visited several units, including the 2nd Battalion, 1st Marines at Con Thien. There he learned that the Marines were building installations for a complete U.S. battalion — about nine hundred men — despite the fact that Con Thien was supposed to be taken over in the spring by an ARVN battalion, typically half the size. Westmoreland worried that the Marine-built positions might require garrisons of two ARVN battalions rather than one, "which we can ill afford."

General Westmoreland's comments in his diary, which he called "history notes," are not the words of a man who had given up on the McNamara Line: "I've had no end of problems with the strong-point obstacle system. The reason seems to be that the Marines have had little experience in construction of fortifications and therefore lack the know-how to establish them in the way I had visualized. I thus have been remiss in taking for granted that they had the background; hopefully it is not too late to get this project on a solid track." In

Saigon the day after Christmas Westmoreland met with his chief of staff, Major General Walter T. Kerwin, plus operations and logistics officers and gave them instructions for a directive that would "clarify the philosophy behind the defense line and the concept of construction."

The MACV commander continued to take an active interest in DYE MARKER. On January 3, 1968, he listened to observations from a follow-up trip report on DYE MARKER. He had the 3rd Naval Construction Brigade at Da Nang build sample bunkers of the desired design and attended a demonstration of them on January 14. There were many more discussions of DYE MARKER.

Given the intelligence that rather little NVA infiltration came across the DMZ, one needs to look elsewhere to explain Westmoreland's continued drive to put the strong point obstacle system in place. His *idée fixe* that he could create conditions for an invasion of Laos is the most likely explanation. In fact, his work on DYE MARKER continued in close parallel with his efforts to prepare for Laotian operations. At his weekly intelligence and strategy conference on Christmas Eve, for example, he noted, "I gave some guidance for the preparation of a plan to be implemented approximately a year hence. The plan (move into Laos to cut the Ho Chi Minh Trail) is predicated on certain assumptions and is designed to be prepared to exercise options if political considerations permit."

In a cable on January 8, 1968 (MAC 00321), General Westmoreland explained to superiors his concept of operations for EL PASO, the plan for Laotian operations. Evidently the knowledge alarmed Washington; Lyndon Johnson had never approved any Laotian invasion and remained sensitive to the suggestion. Protests from that quarter led Westmoreland to defend himself in a second cable (MAC 00686) dispatched from Saigon shortly after 8:00 P.M. on January 14:

> I detect there may be some misunderstanding about operation EL PASO. This exercise is in the category of advance planning and involves an operation that could be conducted not sooner than the end of the northeast monsoon season in the late fall or early [w]inter of this year. The purpose of this exercise is to develop a plan, determine its feasibility, and refine it between now and the November election so that we could have a military plan that could take advantage of a possible change in national policy. This exercise has no immediacy, but I reported it to inform higher headquarters as a matter of information. It

will be several weeks before it is developed to the extent that it could
be given any meaningful review.

EL PASO was indeed at the planning stage, but it was more than a
mere contingency, or there would have been little reason for the
MACV commander to deflect review by higher headquarters. Saigon's
ticklish response to the inquiry indicates awareness of the lack of
enthusiasm for the Laotian option in the White House. In fact, there
is *no* evidence in the available records that MACV had been given the
authority to plan an invasion of Laos.

Permitted or not, an invasion would be possible only under certain
conditions, as General Westmoreland had told his staff on Christmas
Eve. Change of the monsoon was a necessary condition; so was completion of the McNamara Line, which would shield the right flank of
the invasion forces. A sufficient condition, however, without which
there could be no invasion, was that Americans continue to hold Khe
Sanh.

New Year's was the perfect day. At least Dick Camp thought so. His
company, Lima of 3/26, had been having a hard go of it since arriving
at Khe Sanh. The 3rd Battalion came without its field kitchens, its
most sophisticated medical gear, even its chaplain. So Captain Camp
and his men had been existing on a diet of C-rations even though Khe
Sanh had mess halls and such things for other units. Similarly, much
as the Special Forces had consigned the first Marine battalion ever to
come to Khe Sanh to the area outside its perimeter, the area now called
"The Ponderosa," regiment had had 3/26 settle outside the perimeter
too, expanding it toward the northwest. Thus Lima Company initially
had no perimeter defenses of its own, no accommodations, nothing.
The first night the men spent under ponchos in the rain.

After that Captain Camp had his men get busy on defenses and then
bunkers. He had some difficulties with battalion staff over whether the
bunkers should be built above or below ground and how they ought
to be designed. Basically the situation seemed pretty miserable. On
New Year's Day Camp woke up determined to do something about
the plight of Lima Company.

What could be done? Dick Camp decided to take his men down to
base central for showers. It had been more than two weeks that Lima's
men had spent in the field or in the mud of their position at the combat
base. Showers seemed just the thing. The Marines did not think so,

and there was a certain amount of grumbling until they were actually on their way, trotting down the road chanting cadence. Then they actually showered and were given freshly cleaned utilities — morale soared.

Later, back at their area, Camp called for a football game. By then the Marines were ready to get physical and so many wanted to play that Lima Company ended up with sixty to seventy men on each side. Even the battalion chaplain, Roy Swift, a former semipro football player, showed up to take part. That evening the battalion managed to organize a hot meal.

The only thing that could possibly have made the day better happened the next night. As dusk approached, the company prepared its night defense, among other things setting out listening posts. One of these, "Dunbar County Lima," was located about four hundred meters from the west end of the airstrip. Four men and a scout dog made up the post. Everything went well until the early morning hours, when suddenly the dog picked up a scent.

Back at Lima's command post, Captain Camp coincidentally woke up at about this time, just as the company radio man sought him out with news of the listening post contact. Camp listened in on the company radio net, asked for clarification, but could get no response from the listening post. Assuming they must wish not to make noise, Camp asked Dunbar County Lima to key their radio set if they had a contact. A couple of clicks confirmed suspicions.

Camp summoned Corporal Brady, leader of his mortar section, to get together the Marines who usually carried ammunition for the mortar crews. They would be a reaction force the Lima commander could use without taking any of his riflemen off the line. Lieutenant Nile Buffington of the 1st Platoon, which had provided the original listening post team, took over the reaction force as they reached his position.

Buffington led the mortar men out and contacted the listening post, which reported seeing six men walk past them. Buffington put his men on line for a sweep of the area, and Lima's mortars illuminated the scene with starshells. Army 40mm Dusters began to fire and Buffington's men saw and challenged the enemy. Though a Marine monograph contends the adversaries were dressed "like Marines" and Buffington says they wore green uniforms, Dick Camp remembers all of them in black pajamas wearing sandals. In any case, Buffington challenged the men in English, got no reply, and when one seemed to go for a weapon, the Marines opened fire, instantly killing five and wounding the sixth. The North Vietnamese seemed like faces in the rain.

Pandemonium broke out over the combat base. The Duster fire was only part of it, but Camp worried about his own men being hit by the American fire. Someone on the combat base perimeter fired a pop-up flare, the kind Marines derisively called "jack-offs," and it was followed by many more. One flare fell in the FOB-3 wire and set off a trip flare. There was shooting, people running, excitement charging the air. Meanwhile Captain Camp had made his way to the 3/26 combat operations center with the real story of the encounter that had started it all, only to find that no one seemed especially interested.

Buffington, his scratch force, and the listening post team spent a little while nosing around in the dark but found nothing that night. Lima Company stood down. In the morning Buffington, Camp, the Marines who had been in the firefight, and others went out beyond the perimeter. No one expected to find much because the NVA were always so good about policing battlefields, but the five bodies were there. A trail of blood indicated that the wounded man had dragged himself off. An empty map case suggested that the man had retrieved some documents before getting away. The bodies were minus their shoulder straps, further evidence that at least one had made off and also that all the dead had been officers. That so many officers had come out together and walked so close to the Marine perimeter was an indication that the NVA were making a reconnaissance before finalizing plans for an attack on the combat base.

Once the NVA bodies had been found, the battalion called in intelligence, specifically Gunnery Sergeant Max Friedlander of the 17th Interrogation-Translation Team. The intelligence people looked around carefully and even made plaster casts of the faces of the dead. One body, which seemed unusually tall for a Vietnamese, was suspected of being Chinese, and regiment called for that one to be brought back for medical examination. That body was later sent on to Phu Bai while the others were processed at Khe Sanh's graves registration unit. Friedlander meanwhile took a dog and started to follow the bloody trail left by the wounded North Vietnamese. After about sixty yards he stopped and returned to the Marines hovering around the battle site. Later the Americans received information that the tree line in front of them had been occupied by an NVA company ready to fire if the Americans came any closer. Friedlander accompanied the bodies back to Charlie Med, where they were examined, the tall one by dentist as well as doctor.

Friedlander recalled in a recent interview being able to identify the units and ranks of all the North Vietnamese dead. Camp recounts that the deceased were all identified *by name*. But regimental intelligence officer Harper Bohr insisted at the time that, while he agreed one of the bodies might have been Chinese, "I don't recall, even after evaluating other intelligence information, that one . . . was a regimental commander." The Bohr comment did not dissuade Marine historians from recording in a monograph on Khe Sanh that the NVA casualties included a regiment commander, his operations staff officer, and his communications officer. A last piece of significant information, which Captain Dick Camp has revealed only recently, is that officers from FOB-3 who monitored the NVA radio nets told him the North Vietnamese erupted in a spate of frantic calls about an hour or so after the firefight. Whoever the NVA dead had actually been, this little engagement was noticed right up the American chain of command.

Concerns about Khe Sanh went right to the highest levels after the January 2 North Vietnamese reconnaissance incident. Just a few days later, Walt Rostow reported to President Johnson that there was "increasingly solid evidence of major North Vietnamese buildup against I Corps area" and that General Westmoreland's "best estimate" was that the NVA were "massing for another major offensive in this area, perhaps targeted this time on Khe Sanh."

The query Westmoreland received on January 11, though it came from the Joint Chiefs of Staff, very likely owed something to Lyndon Johnson's doubts. Earle Wheeler and the other chiefs would not have asked some of the elementary questions the cable contained. The January 11 cable (JCS 00343) inquired about plans to reinforce Khe Sanh and asked whether an attack against Khe Sanh could be preempted by an offensive into Laos or forestalled by withdrawal of the combat base. The cable also asked about reopening Route 9, plans to control the high ground commanding the base, NVA artillery, and the relationship between MACV and Marine headquarters in Da Nang.

The next day Westmoreland was in Da Nang accompanying Marine Corps commandant General Leonard F. Chapman at a reception hosted by III MAF. That morning Westmoreland, his chief of staff, and General Frederick Weyand had listened to a special intelligence briefing on the apparent North Vietnamese buildup. That evening

Westmoreland discussed the situation with III MAF commander General Robert Cushman at the III MAF function. Late that night he replied to the Joint Chiefs' cable.

General Westmoreland's response (MAC 00547) listed Cushman's contingency plans for reinforcing the combat base: on eight hours' notice Khe Sanh could be augmented by a Marine battalion, and a second could be sent with twelve hours' warning; beyond that were Special Landing Force troops. Having heard what Cushman had available, Westmoreland ordered him to alert a brigade of the Americal Division to move to the Hue/Phu Bai area, where it could replace Marine troops and make them available for northern Quang Tri. Westmoreland was also prepared for reinforcement of the area with a brigade of either the 1st Cavalry or the 101st Airborne and he ran through a list of additional measures.

The MACV commander correctly rejected an invasion of Laos as a means of disrupting an NVA offensive: "Preempting a Khe Sanh area assault by an offensive into Laos is neither logistically nor tactically feasible at this time." Airlift capability was inadequate for both Laos and other areas of South Vietnam that were threatened, and while an air line of communication would be essential, flying weather was marginal. Moreover, air assaults west of Khe Sanh would encounter heavy antiaircraft fire and Westmoreland doubted that this could be neutralized within a short time. Further, a brief campaign would not be likely because of the size of the NVA forces around Tchepone.

At the opposite extreme Westmoreland equally rejected any suggestion of withdrawal from Khe Sanh: "This area is critical [t]o us from a tactical standpoint as a launch base for SOG teams and as flank security for the strong point obstacle system, it is even more critical from a psychological view point. To relinquish this area would be a major propaganda victory for the enemy. Its loss would seriously affect Vietnamese and U.S. morale. In short, withdrawal would be a tremendous step backwards."

As for his relationship with Robert Cushman, Westmoreland insisted they had no problems: "I reject out of hand any implications to the contrary. This is absurd."

With its field commander rejecting both preemption and withdrawal, Washington could only conclude that MACV *wanted* to fight a battle at Khe Sanh.

On January 15 Westmoreland followed up with a further cable, in which he discussed EL PASO and returned to the many actions being taken in support of Khe Sanh, including the beginning of B-52 strikes around the combat base. "The odds are 60-40 that the enemy will launch his planned campaign prior to Tet," Westmoreland estimated. "My objective is to preempt this attack."

According to records kept by the deputy chief of staff at MACV, Khe Sanh questions preoccupied the weekly intelligence and strategy conference of January 13. Westmoreland asked his 7th Air Force commanders to check stocks of bombs in the north. General Creighton Abrams, Westmoreland's deputy, asked for a thorough evaluation of airlift requirements for major 1st Cavalry Division operations around Khe Sanh. Westmoreland also asked his Air Force staff to evaluate the potential of electronic sensor equipment, code-named "DUMP TRUCK," if diverted from MUSCLE SHOALS to Khe Sanh. Various troop movements to I Corps were considered. Finally, someone questioned the adequacy of the defenses of Lang Vei. Westmoreland asked that Cushman be queried on the defensive preparations; he wanted an answer by January 15.

The next afternoon, over Westmoreland's signature, MACV operations staff dispatched a message to III MAF directing a "maximum effort . . . to insure the defense posture of the Special Forces camp at Lang Vei leaves nothing to be desired." Also, "any assistance required to accomplish contingency reinforcement of Lang Vei which is beyond your tactical support capability should be reported to this headquarters without delay." General Cushman forwarded the message to 3rd Marine Division and asked to be notified of any additional assistance or support necessary. General Rathvon Tompkins forwarded the queries to Khe Sanh. Something went wrong along the way.

Preparations

As long as there had been a Marine command at Khe Sanh, the Marines had been responsible for the Special Forces camp. That had been as true for Franchise Rep as it was for the 26th Marines. Part of the responsibility was planning for support of the CIDG camp should it be attacked and for reinforcement or relief of the camp if it should be endangered. The MACV and III MAF questions about plans for assistance to Lang Vei, therefore, were hardly breaking new ground. They replied that existing plans were fine. On January 20 General

Tompkins reported up the line that "plans for initial support and reinforcement of Lang Vei have been reviewed. Plans [were] written [in] September 1967 and remain valid." In fact this optimistic assessment cloaked a host of difficulties.

No military service likes to admit it cannot accomplish a mission; the Marines were reluctant to report they could not accomplish the Lang Vei mission. Higher levels of III MAF command may also have been more optimistic than personnel at Khe Sanh. The 26th Marines staff had little confidence in the regiment's ability to reinforce outlying posts such as Lang Vei, perhaps especially Lang Vei. In November there had been a couple of mine clearing operations out to the CIDG camp and a couple of marches to rehearse a relief attempt. All had taken a very long time. In December, on a company-size operation to the northwest of Khe Sanh village, Captain Camp's Lima Company had had the experience of dense, impenetrable growth, consuming hours in walking a few hundred meters. At night, against the NVA ambushes that were sure to be set for a relief force en route to Lang Vei, it would be worse. Air assaulting a relief force in by helicopter would be impossible on the scale necessary to turn back a real threat to the CIDG camp. Either a small, first-echelon relief column would be engulfed in a surging NVA tide or a larger force would be decisively delayed while Marines marshaled their helicopters for the lift. Lang Vei would be in trouble regardless.

The slim chances for Lang Vei's survival are highlighted by the concrete content of the relief plan. The 26th Marines OPLAN 5-67, dated September 18, 1967 (Ser 0042-67), explicitly assumed that NVA ambushes would occur and that any NVA attack would take place at times of restricted visibility or weather. The ground force envisioned was a single reinforced rifle company, with other companies to follow as required and a battalion command group available if necessary. It was also assumed that these forces would be provided by the 3rd Marine Division rather than by the 26th Marines from internal resources. The plan assigned the relief force merely to carry out "such operations as directed," and it was vague on how a relief force should get to Lang Vei and on what it should do once there. By far the longer portion of the OPLAN was that detailing the planned defensive artillery fires and those that might assist a ground operation.

At one time the 26th Marines had as many as two companies in reserve that might be called upon to act as part of a relief force. That was as much as Colonel Lownds had ever had in reserve and was possible only after the 3rd Battalion joined the 1st Battalion in mid-December. Then Lownds had one company from each battalion. Mike Company, the 3/26 unit on reserve, would be sent up to Hill 881 South to permit the garrison there to undertake a company operation in January. The unit then remained engaged in the hills. Delta Company of 1/26, under Lieutenant Ernest E. Spencer, was the other reserve formation in early 1968. Spencer's company became the regiment's only reserve, for an emergency on the hills, at Khe Sanh combat base, or at Lang Vei. That his unit would be sent off to relieve some outlying strong point was by no means self-evident. Spencer was never told his company would not be sent to the relief of Lang Vei but privately he had his doubts.

Of course, Lang Vei CIDG camp, to the extent that it was an American facility, was an Army installation, not a Marine one, and some are tempted to see every difficulty arising between the services as a product of interservice politics. The evidence suggests this was not the case at Khe Sanh, however, for Marine positions received identical treatment. For example, one of the more significant assignments for Spencer's Delta Company during November had been a six-day mission out toward Hill 881 South for the specific purpose of developing alternatives for reinforcement, resupply, and evacuation of casualties from the hill strong point. The mission was like the route marches out to Lang Vei.

Not only was the mission similar, the results were identical. Delta had been accompanied by specialists from the truck detachment (from the 3rd Motor Transport Battalion), the ONTOS section, and engineers. They were specifically interested in vehicular trafficability. The conclusion was that not even fully tracked vehicles could reach 881 South without extensive engineer work. The high point of the exercise came early one morning when Delta's 1st Platoon was charged by five water buffalo, one of which pinned the platoon commander to a tree. The buffalo had to be driven off with small arms fire. Just as there were obstacles to a reinforcement mission to 881 South, so there would be problems getting to Lang Vei. This was not a Marine or an Army mission; it was an impossible mission.

While asking questions about Lang Vei, the high command had in hand a number of other preparations for a potential battle of Khe Sanh. Westmoreland's most important idea was to make the combat base the scene for a major air campaign. Massive bombing of the environs of Con Thien during the summer and fall of 1967 seemed to have canceled the threat to that place just south of the DMZ. Westy code-named that operation NEUTRALIZE and he thought that the bombing, a so-called SLAM operation (for "seek, locate, annihilate, and monitor"), had been very successful. Now he proposed to give Khe Sanh the same treatment, in a SLAM operation called NIA-GARA. Westmoreland envisioned a virtual cascade of bombs and aerial munitions that would smite his enemies. He ordered a plan for such an air campaign in early January.

The NIAGARA concept provided for a campaign in two phases, the first of which would be an intensive scouting and reconnaissance effort to gain maximum information about the adversary. The recon-naissance phase would utilize every available man — from air recon-naissance to MACVSOG — to find all the NVA forces around Khe Sanh and target them for aerial bombardment missions. In the second phase the bombers would come after the newly discovered targets.

Westmoreland's decision to conduct a SLAM operation around Khe Sanh resulted in the formation in Saigon of a SLAM committee to coordinate further tasking. General William W. Momyer, West-moreland's deputy for air and concurrently commander of the 7th Air Force, the top air boss in the theater, also formed a special intelligence staff to review results of the initial phase of NIAGARA. Only after Westmoreland ordered preparations for NIAGARA on January 6 would Cushman and the III MAF staff at Da Nang be informed of the plan and its new intelligence requirements.

Detailed plans for bombing and interdiction operations were dis-cussed between January 9 and 15. Both Saigon and Da Nang played active roles. The SLAM committee dispatched representatives of MACV intelligence, MACVSOG, 7th Air Force, 5th Special Forces Group, and MACV combat operations center to Da Nang to correlate intelligence with III MAF for the ARC LIGHT and tactical air strikes. Momyer briefed Westmoreland on the plans on January 15.

What threatened to derail NIAGARA was a classic conflict of ser-vice roles and missions. Saigon had not taken into account Marine combat procedures and command relationships in creating the oper-ations plan. The Marines contained organic air forces, not only he-licopters and light aircraft but fighters, strike aircraft, even medium transports like the C-130. The Marines prided themselves on the way all their forces were oriented to support their ground elements, and they had developed a unique air-ground team concept under which a

Marine air wing would act in concert with a Marine infantry division. The Air Force had no such intimate relationship with ground forces, either Army or Marine, and its close air support mission, though developed to cooperate with the ground forces, was not integral to its service role.

Because III MAF had long had command of the American war effort in the northern provinces and because Marines formed the original basis of the force deployed there, the air management system was the Marine system. In operation NEUTRALIZE, the Con Thien SLAM action that was the model for NIAGARA, the scale of effort had been just small enough that ad hoc measures sufficed. The Marines and Air Force had established additional liaison and exchanged air controllers to work in existing air support control centers. But for NIAGARA to be the cascade of bombs that General Westmoreland wanted, large-scale Air Force activity in the III MAF area was going to be necessary.

There were two aspects to the NIAGARA command and control problem. Operational control was the most obvious. The existing Marine system provided an air control center at Dong Ha, called "Landshark Bravo," with a forward detachment at Khe Sanh. The Marines divided the airspace around Khe Sanh into five strike zones. Available strike aircraft would be assigned their missions by the control center responsible for the area to which they were dispatched and then guided by forward air controllers. Higher headquarters would "frag," or allocate, sorties among the areas requiring them. Khe Sanh's control center had responsibility for the immediate zone, with final navigational guidance available from Air Support Radar Team Bravo. Strikes in a further band to the northwest and southeast were also to be controlled by Khe Sanh, but artillery would not be used in them. Strikes to the east and along the DMZ were the responsibility of Landshark Bravo at Dong Ha. The northwest corner of south Vietnam and the mountain area toward the A Shau valley to the southeast were free strike zones. Laos could be considered a sixth strike area, one already controlled by 7th Air Force.

General Momyer disliked the Marine system, which he thought less flexible than 7th Air Force procedures. In his own air management system sorties were fragged by a center at headquarters in Saigon, were controlled by airborne command aircraft, and received final assignments from forward air controllers over the battle zone. Because he had the SLAM committee in Saigon, and especially because he had formed a special intelligence staff under Colonel George E. Keegan, Momyer felt that only 7th Air Force had the big picture necessary to properly frag the daily sorties.

The Marines disagreed, and here a second thorny issue complicated NIAGARA preparations. In the Marine system the III MAF commander had final authority over air components in his force. Thus the 1st Marine Aircraft Wing, under Major General Norman J. Anderson, which acted as a team with the 3rd Marine Division, belonged to Cushman. If Momyer were to frag the Marine aircraft, they would be under control of 7th Air Force, whose command link went straight to Hawaii and the CINCPAC, Admiral U. S. Grant Sharp. General Anderson adamantly opposed such an arrangement for his wing, and Cushman was not too comfortable with it either. William Momyer, however, was determined and took the issue to General Westmoreland.

When Momyer brought the problem to Westmoreland in mid-January, the MACV deputy for air insisted that centralized control of air assets was absolutely essential and that Khe Sanh could well be lost without it. "After considerable soul searching," Westmoreland recorded on January 18, "I concluded I would be remiss in carrying out the responsibilities of my office if I did not effect arrangements that would most effectively and efficiently use the total assets available to me, regardless of service cognizance or past doctrine."

After meeting with Momyer that day, Westmoreland sent a cable to Admiral Sharp citing the changing situation and the "premium on the need for rapid decision-making" as justifications for his giving Momyer operational control of the 1st Marine Aircraft Wing, less helicopters. "It is no longer feasible nor prudent to restrict the employment of the total tactical air resources to given areas." Admiral Sharp was lukewarm to the initiative for a month or more. Momyer obscures this timing in his own account, which states that CINCPAC approved Westmoreland's ideas after being briefed by 7th Air Force's chief of staff for operations, Major General Gordon F. Blood. In fact, the Blood briefing of Sharp and his further briefing of Joint Chiefs Chairman Earle Wheeler occurred only in late February.

In the meantime, on January 19 General Westmoreland flew to Da Nang to visit III MAF headquarters. That afternoon he met for two hours with Generals Cushman and Anderson and other key officers. Westmoreland stressed the importance of NIAGARA and the need for cooperation. He argued that a single manager should control all air striking forces. He cited the necessity for rapid air strike clearances, such as could be provided by airborne command planes, and for secure procedures. Westmoreland declared that he was appointing General Momyer as the single manager.

The Marines' reaction at the January 19 meeting has gone unrecorded, but it was negative. General Cushman escalated the dispute up the chain of command to Washington, where the commandant of the Marine Corps made the MACV action an issue for the Joint Chiefs of Staff. There bureaucratic political considerations further complicated the dispute. The Army chief of staff, General Harold K. Johnson, felt vulnerable on the issue of air command of organic forces because the Air Force had long sought operational control over the Army's force of light transport aircraft. Johnson refused to set a precedent that would weaken Army claims to control *its* transport force and therefore did not support Westmoreland's action.

The further evolution of the dispute over the air campaign is a story for another page. For the present it is sufficient to note that a dispute had emerged but that this did not prevent higher authority from approving the NIAGARA operations plan. In fact, U.S. Ambassador to Laos William Sullivan concurred on January 16 with those aspects of NIAGARA that involved Laos. The following day CINCPAC gave its approval as well. General Westmoreland ordered the execution of the second phase of NIAGARA, bombing NVA targets, to begin on January 21. That same day the North Vietnamese began heavy shelling of Khe Sanh combat base.

"Aggressive Hardening Measures"

Khe Sanh on the eve happened to be a very busy place. All sorts of preparation were in train. Some of the tougher ones were those of the radar navigation unit, the air support radar team, which was being provided by Marine Air Support Squadron 3. Air Support Radar Team Bravo was building itself bunkers behind the Gray Sector of the combat base perimeter. First Lieutenant Timothy Allen led the detachment.

Bunkering in the van containing the sensitive and fragile electronics and computer proved especially difficult. A number of NVA mortar and gun shells and rockets would explode in this area during the battle. One rocket even made a direct hit on top of the bunker. The computer van, however, would stay operational throughout. It was all built within three days of the unit's arrival at Khe Sanh on the evening of January 16. The radar team was up and on line in two; during its first month at work the unit guided more than 4,200 sorties delivering more than 20,000 tons of ordnance against 2,880 targets in the Khe Sanh area. American combat power proved awesome.

The late reinforcement was part of a wave that strengthened the combat base, filling it out just before battle. General Westmoreland issued no direct orders for troops to be sent to Khe Sanh, but he did instruct Cushman not to exceed force levels that could be fully supplied by air. Rathvon Tompkins takes credit for the next major reinforcement. The 3rd Marine Division commander believes that Colonel Edward J. Miller, intelligence chief on the division staff since late September 1967, was a superb intelligence officer, often twenty-four hours or more ahead of Da Nang in his assessments. If his intelligence officer and III MAF's had disagreed, Tompkins says he would have believed Miller. And Miller saw a threat to Khe Sanh. On January 16 Tompkins told General Cushman that, unless otherwise directed, he was going to deploy another Marine battalion to the combat base. Cushman had no objection, so Tompkins sent the 2nd Battalion, 26th Marines under Lieutenant Colonel Francis J. Heath, Jr.

Once again the reinforcement action proved unexpected. The telephone rang at Colonel Lownds's combat operations center at Khe Sanh; it was 3rd Division staff.

" 'I'm sending 2/26 back to you,' " Lownds recalls the caller, probably Tompkins, saying.

"When?" Lownds asked.

"Look up in the sky and you'll probably see 'em coming in," was the reply. Lownds left to greet the battalion commander about five minutes later.

Private First Class Hennie G. Vandervelde, a 2/26 man, remembers that the battalion left Phu Bai for Dong Ha. Expecting to stay at Dong Ha, the men worked hard to pitch camp, putting up more than a hundred tents. Then Colonel Heath came and made a little speech, after which everyone began packing up again. They would be going to Khe Sanh. In the middle of the night the men were awakened to re-form their working parties. Staff labored through the night to constitute a mobile command group and repack the battalion for shipment.

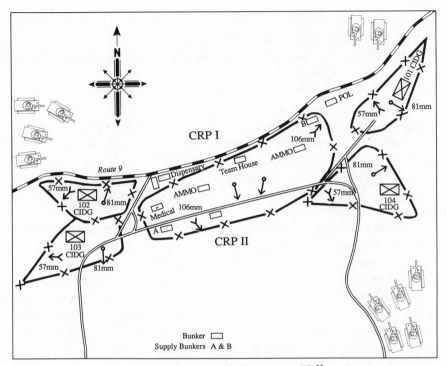

7 · 2nd Battalion, 26th Marines, Hill 558

Colonel Lownds met Heath and his 2/26 officers as soon as they set foot on the ground at the airstrip. He took them back to the combat operations center for a secret briefing. Among the Marine officers present was Captain Earle Breeding. More than a decade before, Breeding had been an enlisted Marine scout in a regimental intelligence section led by then Major David Lownds. Now the 26th Regiment commander recognized Breeding in the crowd and remembered him. Lownds startled his audience when, at a climactic moment in the talk, he interrupted himself to exhort: "We will hold! Won't we, Captain Breeding?" The young officer shot back, "Sir, with Echo Company, Khe Sanh will be held!"

At the moment 2/26 moved in, Colonel Lownds was doing what he could to block likely North Vietnamese avenues of approach to the main combat base. The hill strong points furnished a shield of sorts to the northwest, though there was nothing up the Rao Quan valley. That was where Lownds sent the 2nd Battalion, with Fox Company moving out immediately to occupy the position while the remainder of the battalion assembled that night and followed next morning.

Colonel Heath's battalion took over a low hill, 558, that effectively marked the edge of the Khe Sanh plateau.

The Marines of 2/26 were under no illusions about what awaited them. "I can still recall the day we got to Khe Sanh," writes Chuck Hoover. "It was like a place that God forgot. You knew that death was around." Lance Corporal Daniel Tougas voiced similar sentiments: "The first time I saw [Khe Sanh] it really kinda scared me: everybody wearing flak jackets and helmets and all those weird-looking bunkers — all big barrels and everything." For several days fire discipline at Hill 558 was forgotten as shaky Marines fired at every shadow in the night. Eventually the men settled down and established a strong defensive perimeter.

By now Khe Sanh was a beehive of activity as it prepared for battle. For days Colonel Lownds had been talking about digging in deeper. At the evening staff meeting on January 13 he ordered the building of fighting holes for every Marine at both his work site and his hootch, each to be stocked with rations. All water cans were to be kept full at all times, internal barbed wire would be laid within the combat base, and all Marines had to begin wearing flak jackets within two days.

General Tompkins issued his own instructions on January 15. He ordered Khe Sanh to maintain constant aggressive patrolling all around its positions; to search west and south for suitable outpost locations; to improve the defenses of outlying positions; to strengthen fighting holes, especially against blast effects; to prepare to receive reinforcements in battalion increments; and to prepare counterattack plans based on current forces and on augmentation of one to three additional battalions. The division commander also diverted selected engineering items, such as razor barbed wire, from available DYE MARKER stocks.

First Lieutenant William K. Gay, of Alpha Company, 3rd Engineer Battalion, was the detachment commander charged with developing the defenses. Though he worried about the bunkers built with local materials — likely as not to be supported by wood that was rotting — the perimeter had to be his first concern. When Gay arrived in mid-November the perimeter consisted of a single barrier of triple concertina barbed wire. The barrier was in extremely bad repair, fronted with elephant grass, often up to eight feet tall, which grew right up to the wire. "If we had been hit by a large force at that time," Gay recalled, "I have absolutely no doubts that Khe Sanh would of been easily overrun."

Gay redesigned the perimeter. He reversed the usual order of building inward to make the existing wire barrier the final protective wire. In addition, the engineers cut back the grass, clearing all vegetation from a trace 150 to 200 meters wide. Gay's six-man detachment supervised as three platoons on rotation provided the manpower. They ringed Khe Sanh with another triple concertina layer, a ten-meter-wide swath of tangle-foot wire, and then an outer perimeter of double apron wire strung from eight-foot-tall posts that made it difficult to use mats for crossing. Between some of the barriers the engineers purposely left behind spools of wire stuffed with explosives that could be detonated as improvised fleshette bombs, and inside the old concertina they emplaced a ring of Claymore mines. This new perimeter was a fairly sophisticated obstacle system.

Other preparations at the combat base included preregistering all the defensive artillery concentrations, carefully making sure that map grid coordinates were understood and artillery guns precisely calibrated for each potential target. A forward observer went to Lang Vei for this purpose in the second week of January. For the hill positions — 881 South, 861, and 950 — defensive fire plans were approved on January 13 and preregistered by the 15th. Captain Lawrence B. Salmon led the Fire Direction Center that controlled all artillery barrages. Controlling air missions was Major C. D. Goddard and his Direct Air Support Center. Both were components of the fire Support Control Center under Khe Sanh's artillery commander in the 26th Regiment combat operations center. As artillery commander Khe Sanh had Lieutenant Colonel John A. Hennelly, who was in charge of the resident artillery battalion, the 1st Battalion, 13th Marines.

Khe Sanh's preparations were watched from a high level. In mid-January, General Cushman came to take a long look and was mightily impressed with the artillery fire plans, especially those for counter-battery fire. Cushman thought the plan outstanding, thought it ought to be copied throughout the division, and promised to recommend similar procedures to the 1st Marine Division as well.

General Cushman walked the trench lines of the combat base with Colonel Lownds and Lieutenant Colonel Wilkinson. The local leaders, perhaps putting their best foot forward, took Cushman through the Gray Sector, the southern face of the perimeter. Next day the commanding general of III MAF sent a dispatch to Lownds and Tompkins commending the defenses, on the whole, as "excellent" but observing that perfection was required. "As viewed from the air," Cushman noted, "it seems to me that I visited the most advanced part of the defenses, and that the western and northern defenses are behind and need concerted effort." Cushman was also concerned that the first hundred feet or so of the airstrip were outside the perimeter and there seemed to be no preparations for any kind of mobile barrier that could block the strip and be covered by fire.

Another pair of visitors to Khe Sanh were the intelligence chiefs, Colonel Kenneth J. Houghton of III MAF and Brigadier General Phillip B. Davidson of MACV. They visited on January 20. Houghton and Davidson were friends but there was little love lost between Houghton and Rathvon Tompkins. Houghton apparently thought Tompkins complained too much, while the 3rd Division commander thought Houghton a poor intelligence officer. Houghton indeed considered himself a fighting Marine, not an intelligence man. In any case, Houghton and Davidson listened to a 3rd Division briefing at Dong Ha and then continued on to Khe Sanh, where they met with Colonel Lownds. Davidson was struck that Lownds would not go beyond a single regiment in his enumeration of the NVA threat, especially once he saw pinned to a bulletin board some of the same communications intercepts MACV and III MAF had used to decide that the North Vietnamese had two full divisions near the combat base.

Davidson claims both he and Houghton tried to break through the seeming complacency, insisting there really were two NVA divisions out there.

According to Davidson, Colonel Lownds replied, " 'Maybe, maybe not.' "

Unlike Cushman, General Davidson does not profess to have been very impressed with the quality of fortifications at the combat base. As he left with Houghton, he noted that most of Khe Sanh was constructed above ground. That evening at 7:30, Davidson, by now back in Saigon, briefed Westmoreland and Abrams on what he had seen at Khe Sanh. Davidson mentioned Colonel Lownds's apparent skepticism regarding the scale of the threat.

According to Davidson, Westmoreland appeared upset and heatedly commented to Abrams that he had lost confidence in the Marines, in Cushman's ability to cope with conditions in his area. Westmoreland ended by saying, "Abe, you're going to have to go up there and take over."

"Yeah, I guess you're right," General Abrams responded.

Westmoreland's history notes confirm his decision on January 20 to establish a MACV forward headquarters in the northern provinces to supervise III MAF and work with the ARVN I Corps. Westy made this decision while considering Khe Sanh in advance of the opening of the battle. He could not have known that the first blows were just hours away.

The discussion at the weekly intelligence and strategy meeting on the morning of the 20th, just before General Davidson left for Khe Sanh, is quite revealing of the attitude in Saigon on the eve of battle. There was considerable talk about the care and evacuation of wounded from Khe Sanh during an attack. General Westmoreland ordered his operations staff to prepare a command message for III MAF on the subject and directed that the message also reemphasize the need for "aggressive hardening measures" at the combat base. Westmoreland discussed emplacement of electronic sensor equipment with General Momyer and the air staff. Then Davidson presented an intelligence special estimate on the anticipated NVA attack. Westmoreland ordered this briefing repeated for General Cushman, for the U.S. embassy, for the Joint Chiefs of Staff and CINCPAC in message form, and for the press in a sanitized version. By Westmoreland's explicit order, all the briefings were to make the analogy between Khe Sanh and Dien Bien Phu.

It was only now, on January 20, that MACV finally ordered III MAF to halt work on the cleared trace for DYE MARKER. Thus Saigon pushed completion of the strong point obstacle system until the very cusp of battle.

Most significant was the back-channel cable that General Westmoreland directed be prepared for CINCPAC and the chairman of the Joint Chiefs of Staff. This message was to flag various aspects and problems of the situation around Khe Sanh and in northern I Corps and enumerate the actions under way to counter them. In this cable, Westmoreland told his subordinates, "There should be discussion on [the] need for unanimity and solidarity against any pressure to abandon the Khe Sanh area."

General Westmoreland was awfully serious about Khe Sanh. He was prepared not only to put his deputy in charge of the zone, superimposed over III MAF authority, but also to enlist the Joint Chiefs chairman to help deflect demands for withdrawal. Westmoreland wanted that battle.

Prelude to Battle

As General Davidson, Colonel Houghton, and the Marine major accompanying them prepared to leave Khe Sanh in the early afternoon of January 20, they noticed a commotion at the eastern end of the airstrip. This turned out to be one of the most important incidents in a very eventful day, a day in which large-scale combat occurred for the first time in several months. In any case, the incident began with the appearance of a North Vietnamese soldier who appeared carrying a white flag.

It was the 2nd Platoon of Bravo Company that first reported a white flag. At the time, company commander Captain Kenneth W. Pipes was checking his lines in the Gray Sector. In addition, one of the ONTOS assault vehicles happened to be in the area preparing for practice fire toward Hill 1015. The man appeared to the northeast of the runway.

Captain Pipes immediately took a fire team from his 2nd Platoon and moved toward the figure, accompanied by the ONTOS and its range safety officer, a Marine lieutenant. As they walked, Pipes shouted several times in Vietnamese that he was a Marine captain. About three hundred meters outside the perimeter the man with the white flag reappeared and surrendered. The man turned out to be a senior lieutenant in the North Vietnamese Army named La Thanh Tonc. He gave himself up to Lance Corporal Lou Boria of Bravo Company, 1/26.

Initially turned over to battalion commander Wilkinson, the north Vietnamese deserter, after brief questioning, went on to the 17th Interrogation-Translation Team, located near Charlie Med. There he was interrogated by Gunnery Sergeant Max Friedlander and Staff Sergeant James Brown. La Thanh Tonc identified himself as commander of the 14th Antiaircraft Company of the 95-C Regiment, 325-C Division.

Tonc opened up after a cigarette and a meal. In fact, Friedlander recalled him as "kind of anxious to start telling me why he had surrendered." Disgruntled after being passed over for promotion, disillusioned with superiors who told him things he knew were not true, demoralized with the endless casualties, Tonc seemed to have stopped believing in what he had been fighting for. Married with several children, the NVA officer had not been able to send them a letter in two years.

Tonc's information was of vital import: the NVA officer told his interrogators that attacks would commence that very night, beginning with an assault on Hill 861. Tonc claimed that the assault force would comprise the 6th Battalion of his own regiment reinforced by the 29th Sapper Company. Once the hill had fallen, the combat base itself would be hit by a regiment-size force from the northwest (presumably the 29th Regiment) plus the 4th battalion of 95-C, while another regiment (101-D) struck from the south. The 5th Battalion, 95-C Regiment was to hold Hill 1015 to interdict helicopters coming up from Dong Ha. Meanwhile a mortar platoon on 1015 would mask Marine heavy weapons on Hill 950 while another mortar platoon bombarded the airstrip.

Upon hearing Tonc's initial revelations, Friedlander ran down to the combat operations center to pass the word to Colonel Lownds as Sergeant Brown continued the questioning. Friedlander was sent to Lang Vei by helicopter to tell the Special Forces there, while an officer courier flew down to 3rd Marine Division to inform General Tompkins. The latter, as he reported to a U.S. congressional committee afterward, felt there was little to lose but much to gain from regarding Tonc's information as accurate. Colonel Lownds made a similar determination. Days before, Lownds had ordered everyone into flak jackets and helmets; now he alerted Hill 861, recalled India Company, then fighting on the slopes of 881 North, and ordered units at the combat base to go on fifty percent nighttime alert.

Meanwhile Tonc had more to say, both to Friedlander and others, when they took time to speak with him. The 29th Regiment of 325-C Division would be in reserve, and he had heard that three battalions of tanks positioned in Quang Binh province north of the DMZ could support the attack. Other support would be provided by artillery guns, the first time this kind of ordnance had been used around Khe Sanh. According to Tonc the NVA soldiers were eager to fight and were encouraged by an array of rewards: an outstanding soldier could be sent to officers' candidate school, could be furnished a letter of appreciation, or could have his name appear in North Vietnamese newspapers.

The North Vietnamese deserter also brought a larger message. Political indoctrination that the 95-C Regiment had received was that the campaign beginning at Khe Sanh would be the most important NVA effort since U.S. ground forces intervened in South Vietnam. The campaign would be designed to force the United States out of the war through negotiations, and Hanoi would gain bargaining leverage through the conquest of every U.S. base between the Laotian border and Con Thien, liberating Quang Tri province. Tonc further reported that the campaign was being controlled directly by the North Vietnamese ministry of defense, that is, by Vo Nguyen Giap.

Finally, the NVA officer told Friedlander that on January 2, in the now celebrated incident of the NVA commanders who had been caught outside the perimeter, an entire North Vietnamese company had been in place the next morning just a few tens of meters away as Americans went over the bodies. The revelation chilled Friedlander, who had been among the Marines hovering around the dead North Vietnamese commanders. He realized now that he had been close to being killed that day when he began to follow the trail of blood that led away from the bodies.

If Tonc's account of the aftermath of the January 2 incident was accurate, the North Vietnamese had deliberately refrained from firing at a bunch of Americans who were exposed and vulnerable. It was almost as if the NVA wanted the Marines to find the bodies and had stationed a detachment nearby to report the reaction.

In fact, counterintelligence mavens could have had a field day with Tonc and his story. For starters, Tonc's eagerness to talk would have been held against him. Then there was the matter of the extent of Tonc's information — much greater than one might expect from an antiaircraft lieutenant in the security-conscious NVA. According to Robert Pisor in his Khe Sanh history *The End of the Line*, Tonc revealed details of NVA dispositions and plans even for units north of the DMZ and in the coastal plains. Marine accounts credit Tonc with great revelations, though the details become fuzzy except for what he said about Khe Sanh. The unparalleled timeliness and convenience of Tonc's intelligence would also have been suspicious to a counterintelligence specialist.

One individual who thought Tonc's professed reason for defecting — slow promotion — was dubious for such an extreme action was CIA man Robert Brewer, the Quang Tri province senior adviser. He had been in place since early 1967, originally dispatched to help sort out the problems between South Vietnamese officials and the resident U.S. advisers. Brewer had been with the 101st Airborne Division in World War II and later joined the CIA, being detached during the Korean war to Far East Command headquarters, where he served in special operations.

In Quang Tri the CIA officer recruited and ran a North Vietnamese double agent, a man he called "X-1," who supplied Brewer in late 1967 with a copy of Lao Dong party Resolution 13, the document that supposedly underlay North Vietnamese preparations for an offensive in early 1968. Not only that, the agent subsequently gave Brewer a revision of the document, so-called Resolution 13a. According to Brewer, the documents explicitly referred to attacking Khe Sanh and other points in the northern provinces. Despite this intelligence, which ought to have predisposed Brewer to believe in the information from Tonc, the CIA man recalls, "I didn't think much of it." Nonetheless Brewer kept his mouth shut and said little as the Marines and others lent credence to Tonc's story.

Brewer makes his objections for the record, not having expressed them at the time. He may have been influenced by the sequence of North Vietnamese operations, in which, two days after the defection of Tonc, the NVA attacked Khe Sanh village, where Brewer's district advisory team was housed. Despite his detailed revelations, Tonc does not seem to have said anything about attacks on the village.

One officer who takes an opposite tack on the subject of the Tonc intelligence is Rathvon Tompkins. The 3rd Marine Division commander reflects that knowledge of Tonc's defection may have actually led the North Vietnamese to advance their timetable and attack before completion of all their preparations. In the end it is not possible to say one way or the other, for there were certain Marine operations in progress around Khe Sanh that can also be regarded as having triggered the siege of the combat base. Either way, the battle was about to begin. The adversaries' pieces were in place on the board; North Vietnamese intentions and capabilities were no longer so opaque as before. Marines continued to grapple with the NVA, but not in darkness.

8

Contact

THE FIRST ACTION FOR MARINES of the 2nd Battalion, 26th Marine Regiment, once they arrived on January 16, was not battle at all but a struggle with nature that would have been highly amusing if it hadn't been so annoying. These Marines moved to Hill 558 and established a new strong point. The first few nights, every night, they thought themselves under attack. Rocks would land among them in their foxholes or hit the men in the open. After several nights of broken sleep and panicky shooting, the Marines realized the rocks were not being thrown by the enemy but by apes that inhabited the area. Once the men became accustomed to the apes, they began noticing the local fauna more than ever. One Marine of Fox Company's 3rd Platoon emptied an entire M-16 magazine into a goat that wandered into their perimeter in the night. No one knew how to gut it or skin it until enlisted man Mike Dagner, a deer hunter at home, got together with a few friends and managed to butcher the goat, later cooking it over an open fire. The fresh meat tasted as good as anything they could have gotten at home.

Another animal encounter back at the combat base on January 9 had proved more fateful. David Doehrman of the 3rd Reconnaissance Battalion infiltrated the mess hall and filched two cases of steaks from a locked freezer. He and his buddies cooked them on camp stoves, gorged themselves on the steaks and then flopped down on their bunks to sleep. Doehrman's hand dangled over the metal tray containing the remaining steaks, and he was bitten by a rat in the night. The next morning Doehrman went on medical hold to receive a series of rabies shots. The encounter was fateful because "Dockleaf," the patrol on which he had been scheduled to go, was decimated in the field.

Possibly the last man to see all the Dockleaf Marines alive was Jim Schemelia of 3/26. Schemelia had adopted the routine of waking up early so he could go over to the warming tent and boil water for tea. By getting in early, the Marine avoided the crush in the tent that occurred later when men attempted to heat breakfast rations on the stove. Schemelia became acquainted with the recon Marines as a result of his custom and used to talk with whatever patrol might be on its way out in the morning. On the morning of January 11, 1968, the team happened to be Doehrman's scheduled patrol, led by Lieutenant Randall Yeary, a young, well-respected officer. Dockleaf flew up to Hill 881 South and moved toward 881 North with Lance Corporal Richard C. Noyes on point. The second man in line spotted an ambush about halfway to 881 North and Yeary stopped the patrol, radioing back for instructions to India Company commander Captain William H. Dabney on 881 South. Dabney ordered the team to his hill. That night another man suffered a rat bite before continuing the patrol.

On January 14 the team was working their way along the slope of 881 North, making for 881 South, when they were caught in a second ambush. Several were wounded and then the defense was disrupted when a rocket-propelled grenade killed Lieutenant Yeary and a second man and wounded three more. It was not long before everyone had at least one wound. Gunship helicopters finally helped the Marines extricate themselves, though they were obliged to leave the two bodies behind. The survivors arrived at Khe Sanh covered with blood. Some men rearmed, mounted helicopters, and went back out to find the bodies. India Company Marines retrieved the dead recon men and conveyed them to an LZ from which they were taken back to Khe Sanh. A tearful David Doehrman met the returning helicopter and helped carry the stretcher with Yeary's remains. Some veterans credit Dockleaf with actually triggering the siege of Khe Sanh, revealing the NVA's dispositions and thus forcing them to attack sooner than planned.

"They're Shooting at Us!"

By now the North Vietnamese around Khe Sanh were becoming so numerous that the indications of their presence could hardly be avoided. On January 15 an India Company patrol from Hill 881 South found fresh footprints and then old fighting holes. That evening Kilo Company on the sister outpost, Hill 861, reported that one of its listening posts had seen a trip flare go off in the perimeter wire. Outside the combat base a Marine patrol manning an ambush position heard movement only a couple of hundred meters away. The NVA seemed to be probing American positions throughout the area. Next morning the chief of CIA's Joint Technical Advisory Detachment 101 in Hue informed III MAF of intelligence of the presence of an unusual NVA unit spearheaded by a platoon of montagnards.

Things were equally hot for MACVSOG along the border and in Laos. On January 5 tragedy had struck an SOG team being inserted about thirty kilometers south of Lao Bao when NVA antiaircraft opened fire on the transport helicopters. The second ship in the formation, hit at 2,000 feet, began an uncontrollable spin and went down, exploding on impact. Staff Sergeant John T. Gallagher of SOG was noted as missing in action. A week later SOG suffered another MIA when a Spike team was ambushed south of Khe Sanh just one mile inside Laos. The team broke contact, escaping through a gully to a low hill where they set up a perimeter and called for extraction. Staff Sergeant James D. Cohron, second man from the rear, plus two indigenous strikers, did not make it. The evading Spike team could not see them through the elephant grass and also could not raise them on the tactical radio net. Cohron too would be listed as MIA.

On Hill 881 South on January 18, Captain Dabney sent Lieutenant Tom Brindley's 3rd Platoon on a patrol toward 881 North. Part of their mission was to provide cover for the Dockleaf detail, which was supposed to split off along the way and disappear into the jungle. Brindley made it to 881 North and set up a patrol base there, with a squad for perimeter security and two 60mm mortars to support his other units. The 3rd Platoon searched to the west and southwest of the patrol base, while the recon team hunkered down on the slopes of 881 North and tried to be as inconspicuous as possible. Brindley's men finished their sweep and returned to 881 South, little knowing how soon they would be back.

The recon team on 881 North was Lieutenant Yeary's ill-fated patrol, whose first ambush has already been recounted. Brindley's platoon of India Company was the force sent to help them, returning to the hill immediately after reaching their home base. It was an emergency, with recon Marines wounded and dead. Brindley ordered his men to remove flak jackets, packs, everything except water, weapons, and ammunition. The 3rd Platoon practically double-timed to 881 North in three squad columns. Despite not knowing just where the recon team was, Brindley reached them and set up an LZ in less than two hours.

In the panic of the moment and the heavy NVA fire, the wounded Marines were unable to salvage the radio and code "shackle" sheets used by Corporal Richard J. Healy, Yeary's dead radio man. The equipment, especially the code sheets, was considered vital. Consequently, India Company mounted a further operation toward 881 North on January 19. This time Captain Dabney sent Lieutenant Harry E. Fromme's 1st Platoon, reinforced with extra sections of M-60 machine guns and 60mm mortars, plus an 81mm mortar forward observer. At noon Fromme's platoon had reached a point about five hundred meters from the crest of 881 North when it came under fire from an NVA force on the same finger of the hill. Fromme estimated the North Vietnamese at a platoon in size.

Fromme moved to the head of his column for a closer look and then deployed his men and moved among their positions encouraging them. Private First Class Leonard L. Newton, a machine gunner, cleared two jams on his M-60 and kept up a steady fire, even standing to shoot more effectively. Newton became the sole Marine killed in this action when an NVA bullet hit him in the head. He received credit for suppressing at least three NVA automatic weapons, enabling the 1st Platoon to maneuver, and was awarded a Silver Star posthumously. Fromme got a Bronze Star. Dabney extricated Fromme's force by committing a further platoon of India Company to cover their withdrawal.

After firefights on the 881 North slopes two days in a row it was clear that, despite the negative search results, something was going on. Captain Dabney requested permission from battalion on January 20 to conduct a reconnaissance in force to Hill 881 North. He wanted a company-size operation with his full force. Colonel Harry Alderman agreed. To cover 881 South, he dispatched Mike Company, the battalion reserve, to the hilltop outpost, with two of its platoons plus the company command group.

Also present for the foray was another recon team, a seven-man patrol with the call sign "Barkwood" under Corporal Charles W. Bryan. Barkwood had been sent up to conduct a search along the western face of 881 North and was to depart from Dabney's hilltop strong point. Intending to take the field himself, Captain Dabney suggested to Bryan that Barkwood accompany Lieutenant Brindley's 3rd Platoon and then detach at a suitable point. As the recon men and India Company checked their gear and assembled for the sortie, the weather was fair, the temperature seventy-five degrees, and the visibility good, though some morning fog hung in the valleys. India moved out.

Dabney deployed his company in two columns separated by about five hundred meters. On the left were Harry Fromme's 1st Platoon, leading, with Lieutenant Michael H. Thomas's 2nd Platoon in reserve. Brindley's 3rd Platoon and the recon men made up the right-hand column, with Dabney's own command group.

Fromme's platoon advanced toward the place where Brindley's men had seen action the day before. Dabney called this Objective No. 5. It seemed the most likely point of contact, so Fromme put two of his squads on line. Sure enough, as the force reached a point only twenty or thirty meters from the crest of Objective No. 5, heavy rocket-propelled grenade and automatic weapons fire cut into them like a scythe. In less than a minute twenty men were down and out of action, most with leg wounds, while the Marines saw no one. Dabney ordered Fromme to pull back so artillery and mortars could plaster the objective.

The confusion is mirrored in the story of Chester W. Wilson, Jr., a Marine who was saved by a buddy named Provanzano:

> I was busy loading and firing when I hear some movement behind me and I thought to myself, Charlie got behind us. What had happened was that both guys to either side of me had been hit, and when the word was passed to pull back, I didn't get it. Here I am all alone on the side of the hill fighting a one man war. The noise to my rear was Provanzano coming back to tell me they had all pulled back. He asked me if I was trying to win the battle all alone, so I hauled my rear out of there, back to the others.

To cover his disengagement Fromme called up 1st Platoon's machine gun section, led by Sergeant James L. Moore. The M-60s deployed and Moore directed their fire, but one was hit almost immediately by a rocket-propelled grenade. All but two men of the team were wounded, including Moore, hit in the leg. The section leader nevertheless kept firing, refusing treatment and medical evacuation until everyone else was taken care of.

The 1st Platoon recoiled down 881 North. Jim Schemelia saw them coming, crawling — he didn't see anyone walking. Corpsmen used a bomb crater near Schemelia as a casualty collection point, and a little while later a CH-46 from squadron HMM-262 came to retrieve wounded. The slope was so steep that the helicopter piloted by Lieutenant R. R. Ropelewski and Captain S. R. Stegich could not land. The ship had to back into the hill and hover just above the ground.

Schemelia pitched in to help move the wounded. He grabbed one man who had been shot in the leg and had gotten shrapnel in the face. The Marine got the casualty aboard the helicopter and walked him all the way to the front to leave room for plenty more. He turned back to the door, assuming by then that additional casualties would be at the door ready to be loaded. Instead no one had reached the helicopter.

Suddenly machine gun rounds ripped through the ship, cutting a fuel line, which spewed aviation gas everywhere. Fire burst out. The helicopter crew chief ripped off his burning flak jacket and flung it out the door. The helicopter began to wave uncontrollably, and Schemelia realized they were drifting down the side of the hill, so he grabbed the wounded Marine and attempted to get them both out of the helicopter.

"It was like trying to climb back up a mountain," Schemelia recalls. "The ramp was still down. I looked out — we were about thirty feet from the side of the hill and I just pushed him out. By the time I jumped, [the ship] was a lot further." Schemelia luckily landed in some brush, which broke his fall. Then he found the wounded Marine and took him back to the crater. There was nothing else to do.

Ropelewski meanwhile managed to ground his copter at the base of the hill bare seconds before it became completely engulfed in flames. He and the copilot jumped to safety. Stegich then turned back to the ship looking for the gunner but found no trace of him. A helicopter from a different squadron retrieved the remaining survivors.

India Company's other column had difficulties of its own. Lieutenant Brindley was deploying his men to assault Objective No. 2, about 400 meters to the west, when the fog cleared and the 3rd Platoon came under immediate fire, killing the point man and wounding others. Because the platoon was not yet ready to attack, Dabney decided India would take Objective No. 5 first and ordered Brindley to pull back a few hundred meters to a point that would make a good landing zone. The company executive officer asked recon team Barkwood to select and secure the LZ. Brindley supervised the disengagement, throwing grenades and directing support fire.

In due course Dabney ordered resumption of the attack on Objective No. 2. Brindley combined the remnants of his decimated third squad with the Barkwood team and made Corporal Bryan the squad leader. With the improvised squad plus another, fire support from wounded men, one remaining M-60, machine guns from the 1st Platoon, and artillery and mortars, Brindley led the assault. The NVA were well entrenched, seventy-five meters distant up a thirty-degree slope. At about 2:30 P.M. Bryan's squad made it around the right flank of the objective, only to find more North Vietnamese about to envelop the Marines. The squad fought them to a standstill and also silenced one of four .50-caliber machine guns that were lashing out at the 3rd Platoon. Losses were considerable: only six Marines were left from the squad; except one man, all the original Barkwood Marines were wounded or killed.

Corporal Bryan died of wounds a few hours later. Moving fearlessly among his men, Bryan had gone to help his radio man, Lance Corporal Robert E. Pagano, who had been hit in the right leg while calling support fire. The squad leader was actually attending to Pagano's wounds when hit himself. Bryan's death greatly affected his recon platoon commander, who considered him an excellent team leader, as well as his buddies. Corporal Bryan was awarded a posthumous Navy Cross for the battle on Hill 881 North.

Another posthumous Navy Cross went to Lieutenant Brindley. The platoon commander from St. Louis kept his men going from sheer force of example, up and over the objective. "It was right out of the pages of Chesty Puller or something," recalled battalion operations officer Matt Caulfield. "He went from flank to flank, knocking each one of his Marines on the back." The comment was significant as it pertained to one of Bill Dabney's officers, for Dabney happened to be married to Chesty Puller's daughter. Puller, a famous Marine leader in World War II and Korea, could not have run the assault better. Brindley was shot down as he crested the rise where the NVA held their position. The platoon's squad leaders went down too. Brindley's radio operator reported back to Captain Dabney that he himself had become the most senior surviving Marine.

Brindley's men were reinforced after a time by Thomas's 2nd Platoon, which had been in reserve. Thomas skillfully maneuvered his unit from its place in the other column to a position behind the 3rd

Platoon and then pushed forward. Once he linked up, Thomas consolidated the position and organized a rescue party to move the wounded. When he discovered eight Marines missing, Thomas put together a search party that found six of them. The others were found by other Marines, inspired by Thomas, who himself was first wounded and then killed in action. He too received a posthumous Navy Cross.

From the hilltop strong point on 881 South, the battalion commander and key staff officers observed the action on Hill 881 North. Colonel Harry Alderman saw that India Company had cracked the center of the NVA defenses but worried about its heavy losses. Major Caulfield felt frustrated that it had taken nine cursing conversations with the regimental air officer and seven hours to get fixed-wing air support for the 881 North battle. Alderman conferred over radio with Colonel Lownds, informing him that India Company needed reinforcement to exploit the success. The regiment commander refused to commit any additional forces. That afternoon Lownds had learned from North Vietnamese defector La Thanh Tonc that the NVA were supposed to begin their attack during the night. Rather than reinforcing India Company, Lownds wanted it to come back.

Caulfield felt awful relaying the recall order to Captain Dabney and projected that feeling to Dabney. India Company had spent more than five hours in pitched battle with the NVA with little to show for it but four dead and forty wounded Marines. The predominant emotion among India Company Marines was anger, for they wanted to finish the job and avenge their fallen comrades. But Dabney is reported to have felt drained, surprised that the whole day had been consumed by this combat action. Still, if there was going to be an NVA assault that night, regrouping would be the safest course by far. "I'll never forget standing down by the gate of 881 that night," Major Caulfield says, "and watching these young Marines walk in."

One of the last reconnaissance patrols to make it out of and back to Khe Sanh was mission Nurse, dispatched that same day, January 20. Team 3-B-1, consisting of an officer, six enlisted men, and a Navy corpsman from the 3rd Platoon, Company D, 3rd Reconnaissance Battalion, left the combat base on foot at about 8:00 A.M. Their task was to scout the northeast slope of Hill 552 and the eastern slope of 689 before returning.

The patrol was hiking across 552 early that afternoon when they spotted half a dozen North Vietnamese soldiers on the bank of a nearby stream. The NVA wore green uniforms and had packs and rifles. They disappeared in the direction of Route 9 before any action could be taken. Patrol Nurse resumed its mission, progressing a couple of kilometers farther to Hill 689. That evening they settled into a harbor site on the far slope of the hill.

It was at 9:35 P.M. that recon men detected perhaps eight or ten dim figures moving toward their position. When the leader reached a point just five or ten feet away, one of the Marines opened fire. The adversary suddenly withdrew and enveloped the harbor site, moving counterclockwise. Within just ten minutes the Marines found themselves surrounded by an NVA force of seventy-five to a hundred troops.

By radio the recon men asked Khe Sanh for artillery support. Despite other commitments that night, Marine cannon cockers from the combat base fired very effective box barrages, putting a ring of steel between Team 3-B-1 and the North Vietnamese. Some 2,400 rounds were expended to assist the patrol. Nurse also got help from two flareships and a Spooky gunship that remained overhead until early morning fog made the patrol's strobe light impossible to see.

The recon men saw nothing more and heard no further movement. They did furnish Khe Sanh with useful warning when rockets began to fly over them on trajectories aimed at the combat base. In the morning the patrol broke contact and returned to friendly positions around the Rock Quarry, where they learned that their battle had by no means been the major action of the night.

It was midafternoon that January 20, Dennis Mannion told one of the authors, when he spotted five or six NVA on a rise about half a kilometer west of Hill 861. Captain Norman J. Jasper, Jr., commander of Kilo Company on 861, asked him to call in an artillery mission. Corporal Mannion, a forward observer for Battery C of 1/13 at the combat base, did just that.

Afterward Jasper decided to send a platoon to check the results of the fire. Mannion volunteered to go with the patrol, so at ease he forsook his combat boots in favor of low-cut black sneakers. The patrol would be under observation from the hilltop strong point for its entire sojourn and there seemed to be no special reason for concern. Yet just as the men reached the ridge line they wanted to search, just when they could smell the cordite and see the craters, word came over the radio to pull back to Hill 861.

The platoon lieutenant objected to the new order — his men had just reached the impact area; given ten minutes they could do a good search. Captain Jasper suddenly came up on the radio net himself.

"Get the f—— back now! Six Out!" Jasper said, using the numeric designator for a unit commander.

Before 5:00 P.M. the entire platoon was back at 861. Given the urgency of the orders and the sequence of actions, it seems clear that Jasper was responding to the directive that came from regiment right after Colonel Lownds learned of the intelligence from the NVA defector. Mannion's conclusion remains appropriate: "I shudder to think of what lay on the other side of that ridgeline, because it was only eight or nine hours later that we got attacked — and from that very location."

Once Kilo Company had been regrouped on 861, its commander called in his officers and NCO staff to get the lowdown. As artillery observer, Mannion attended the meeting and learned that the hilltop outpost most likely would be hit that night. Everyone went on full alert at sunset, but as the early evening wore on, nothing happened. There were a few probes but nothing more serious than had happened other nights; it began to seem like a false alarm.

Corporal Victor Martinez had duty that night in one of the listening posts outside the perimeter. Shortly after 11:00 P.M. Martinez heard movement outside the wire. The listening post threw one grenade, and 60mm mortars at the outpost fired on the target. Subsequently the listening post heard moaning, but they assumed it had been just the usual probers. By half past midnight sounds of people in the outer wire had become certain. Grenades were thrown and fired from M-79s to prevent the NVA from breaching the wire.

Dennis Mannion made four or five trips from his own position down to the trenches at the northwest corner of 861 to listen to the noise of the North Vietnamese in the wire. There was not much to see — fog had already gathered in the folds of the land below the hilltop — but the North Vietnamese seemed unable to keep quiet that night. "It was an unsettling thing to hear people go about the business of trying to penetrate the wire oblivious to the hand grenades," Mannion wrote. "At some points they were even laughing among themselves." Mannion and his radio man, Private First Class David Kron, hardly knew what to think.

Back at their bunker, situated next to a fairly elaborate latrine, Mannion and Kron heard noise once more, but it turned out to be Malcolm Mole, a Navy corpsman who hoped to become a disc jockey when he left the service. The artillerymen challenged Mole, who was en route to relieve himself.

"Oh, this is KWN in Miami, Florida! Weather 71 degrees."

Mannion and Kron laughed. "Oh, doc, come on. Give us a break!"

Moments later, as Mole walked back down the exposed northern face of 861, the North Vietnamese opened fire. A direct hit from a rocket-propelled grenade instantly killed the corpsman.

Elsewhere, Lance Corporal Dale R. Flaherty saw two red cluster flares arc up into the sky. Manning a .50-caliber machine gun with the 1st Platoon, Flaherty wondered who had broken light discipline. Then all hell broke loose.

At another point on the perimeter stood Sergeant Michael R. Stahl, a forward observer for the 4.2-inch mortars of 1/13, a man with almost two full Vietnam tours already under his belt. Stahl was just calming one of the new Marines by telling him no NVA were out there when the bombardment began. "It was the heaviest barrage I have seen to date," Stahl told Marine debriefers later. "Their accuracy was almost uncanny. I'm sure their [forward observers] had pre-plotted our bunkers. . . . [Not] one bunker [was] standing the next morning due to this barrage."

Suddenly the North Vietnamese added intense automatic weapons and small arms fire from the ridge line immediately west of 861, a position that was actually perhaps ten meters *higher* than the Marine outpost. Kilo Company replied with .50-caliber machine guns and 106mm recoilless rifles. Lance Corporal Flaherty had managed to get off about fifty rounds when his weapon jammed. Before it could be cleared, the NVA scored a direct hit on a 106mm gun just ten yards to the left, blowing up the gun and its ready ammunition. Flaherty went down to the lines and joined the infantry, doing the best he could. He and Sergeant Michael H. Lyons, who had been with the .50-caliber as a forward observer, took the gun team and spread them out on the perimeter. "Actually we didn't have any support but 60 [mm] mortars," Lyons recalled, "because the 81 [mm] mortars were out of ammunition. The 60 mortars were doing a good job up there."

Meanwhile at the Kilo command post Captain Jasper got a report that maybe thirty NVA were just outside the wire at the southern tip of 861. Jasper sent Dennis Mannion and his radio man over there in hopes of their calling in a fire mission for Khe Sanh's artillery. But Mannion saw nothing and started back up the hill. Just then the command post suffered a direct hit. Jasper was grievously wounded and later was evacuated, and Gunnery Sergeant Himmel died in Mannion's arms. Command devolved upon First Lieutenant Jerry Saulsberry, fresh out of Marine basic school after being washed out of flight school at Pensacola. The 3/26 operations officer, Matt Caulfield, himself atop 881 South after observing India Company's attack that afternoon, was trying to run the battle by remote control, in tandem with the 3/26 alternate command post back at the combat base. Caulfield got Saulsberry on the radio.

Caulfield told the young lieutenant to work closely with his gunny, only to be told the gunnery sergeant was dead. Then Caulfield mentioned the Kilo first sergeant, Stephen L. Goddard, "a real legend in the battalion and a tremendous Marine." Caulfield was shocked when told the first sergeant too had wounds and was dying. (In fact the sergeant, shot in the throat, had the willpower to keep his jugular vein pinched together, limiting his loss of blood. He survived.)

None of this simplified Saulsberry's immediate problems, however. Indeed, an unknown force of North Vietnamese had begun its assault on Hill 861. "They crept as close to our lines as possible under the cover of supporting arms," Saulsberry later said, "then began to throw sticks of dynamite with pyrocaps over the wire to simulate mortars still landing. As these sticks of dynamite were thrown into our perimeter the mortar barrage was lifted. However, a good many of our personnel still believed we were under mortar barrage and were seeking cover. . . . This enabled the enemy to get much closer to our lines than they would normally have been able to."

The brunt of the assault fell on the northwest corner manned by 1st Platoon. Lieutenant Linn Oehling's 2nd Platoon, covering the lower portion of 861 that contained the LZ, was not attacked at all. But Marines in the assault sector were in dire straits. Corporal Mannion discovered that his artillery radio frequency was jammed but later reestablished communications. Both the platoon corpsmen were down, killed or wounded, as were a number of other Marines. The North Vietnamese swarmed over the position. Mike Stahl, back at the 4.2-inch battery position with 2nd Platoon, called for starshells, which opened above their trenches. "You could see hundreds and hundreds of NVA coming up our hill, up the slopes. They were yelling, firing. It looked kind of like a football game where you [are] observing it from the air."

Oehling sent two of the mortar men and four of his own Marines up the hill to seal off the hole in 1st Platoon's sector. They returned to his position.

"Lieutenant, they're shooting at us!"

"No kidding," Oehling thought. He told his Marines, "It's not a one-way war; you can fire back at 'em!"

"You want us to go back up there?"

"You got small arms and you got grenades," Oehling replied. "Use the best tactics you know and kick the shit out of them!"

The six — Lance Corporals Huff and Wheeler and Privates First Class Lonza, Pangel, King, and Wasilewski — went back, killed three North Vietnamese in the trenches they wanted to occupy, and then held like rock. Oehling said to Marine debriefers later, "I can't tell you how proud of them I was. Of course, Stahl, I'm very proud of him too. . . . No one likes to do a job like that; somebody has to do it. And they did a fine job."

Sergeant Stahl received a Navy Cross for his role in the action. Useless while his gun teams were engaged, Stahl worked his way around the position repeatedly, moving to 3rd Platoon, back to 2nd, up the hill, down the hill, taking other Marines with him and depositing them in key positions. At one point he took over a 3rd Platoon .50-caliber whose crew had been killed and fired it as best he could. He contemptuously regarded his several shrapnel wounds as minor and stayed in action.

According to North Vietnamese defector Tonc, Hill 881 South had also been scheduled for attack that night. Marines there were all on alert but nothing happened. After a time, therefore, India Company went into action in support of Hill 861 with its 60mm and 81mm mortars. In fact, gunners worked the pieces so hard they began to glow red hot and had to be cooled by pouring water, then fruit juice, and finally by urinating over them. The barrage from 881 South put a curtain of fire between the NVA assault troops and their reinforcements, which proved crucial in the battle for the hill. Down at the combat base the specialists at FOB-3 monitored the NVA radio nets and heard the North Vietnamese commander calling for reserves, so often that he began screaming in desperation. None ever arrived.

On the hill the battle raged through the night. Five or six 105mm shells from the combat base hit the southeast sector of Marine lines as Mannion tried to get the artillery to pump its rounds just over the hilltop to hit the valley from which NVA reinforcements would have to come. The 105mm guns couldn't do it, and neither could the Army 175mm weapons firing from Camp Carroll. Mortars proved truly vital that night, in particular the exactly 680 81mm rounds from 881 South.

Lieutenant Saulsberry may have been inexperienced, but he fought like a pro. Major Caulfield decided Saulsberry was "a real trooper." The lieutenant led his platoon leaders well, allowed the kinds of unconventional tactics that met this desperate situation, and marshaled his forces to knock the NVA back once their penetration had been sealed off. The platoon leaders were also tops, exercising great initiative and finely honed judgment. Best of all were the Kilo Company Marines who proved resolute fighters in adversity, moving and shooting by ones and twos, stopping an adversary who seemed to have thought through all the angles.

Nonetheless everyone wished hard for morning, which seemed slow coming. The last hour, from 6:00 to 7:00 A.M., was the longest. First Sergeant Goddard, still holding his vein shut but now, incredibly, back on his feet, found two mortar crews singing the Marine Corps hymn as they slung shells into their weapons as fast as they could. Marines in the trenches put heavy pressure on the North Vietnamese still in place on 861. Finally, about 6:30, a green flare rose into the sky, apparently the signal for NVA withdrawal. After that the North Vietnamese melted away. Miraculously Kilo Company had suffered only four killed. Though official claims admit but eleven wounded, corpsman Roderick J. Lyons reports evacuating about thirty wounded that morning even though he was keeping behind Marines with minor wounds. The 1st Platoon had had such severe casualties that one entire side of 861 was undefended and the remaining platoons had to thin out their lines to cover the sector. By midafternoon of January 21 Colonel Lownds had sent a platoon from Alpha Company, 1/26, to replace the losses. A few days later Echo Company of 2/26 was sent to occupy the slightly higher hill from which the NVA had attacked. Henceforth that was called Hill 861-A. Its defender, Captain Earle Breeding, was the man who had promised Lownds that Khe Sanh would hold with his company.

Marines recovered much North Vietnamese equipment from the slopes of 861 and counted forty-five dead NVA. There must have been many more NVA casualties, however, for numerous drag marks were seen and for weeks a horrible stench rose from the slope the NVA had attacked where most of their bodies lay unburied. The decomposing bodies eventually became a health threat to Marines on the hill who, in some places, were obliged to wear gas masks.

One North Vietnamese prisoner taken as a result of the battle was Duong Van Ha, a private in the 1st Company, 4th Battalion, 95-C

Regiment. Ha confirmed the intelligence provided by La Thanh Tonc except for supplying a different identification for the attackers at Hill 861. The NVA themselves had expected to take prisoners — most of the bodies Marines found bore literature printed in English. A pamphlet, reportedly printed by pacifists in the United States, carried a superimposed statement promising American captives they would be well treated and supplying them certain rules for behavior. That was just not the way it turned out.

Secondary Explosions

As the Hill 861 fight reached its climax, disaster came to Khe Sanh combat base. The beleaguered reconnaissance team Nurse, out beyond Hill 689, were among the first to realize what was about to happen. They radioed a report of rockets launched and flying toward Khe Sanh. Soon there were plenty of rockets and mortars too, in the stiffest bombardment the combat base had sustained in many weeks. Certain moments at Khe Sanh everyone would remember, this night among them. There would be many days of siege, and numerous bombardments heavier than the one this night, but the rockets and mortars of January 21 could never be forgotten.

Lance Corporal John Seitz had the artillery liaison radio watch for 1/26. With call sign "Blackbud Bailey," he had gone on duty just after midnight of January 21 in the battalion combat operations center. Just a few other Marines were there at the time, including a radio operator for the infantry and one for air liaison. The action that night was at the 3rd Battalion alternate combat operations center; the 1st Battalion command post was quiet. Lieutenant Reeves of the 81mm mortar section was the watch officer. Suddenly the Marines began to hear the "crump" of exploding mortar shells and someone yelled, "Incoming!"

One of the luxuries of the combat operations center was that it had light at night, so Seitz had been writing to his cousin, Laura Lee. When the bombardment began, he put the letter aside to pick up later. Seitz never found it again.

Marines of Alpha and Bravo Companies had been enjoying a different luxury that night — beer. David Leverton, a Navy corpsman with Alpha, remembers it as the first opportunity for the men to let their hair down after rotating back from sixty days manning Hill 861.

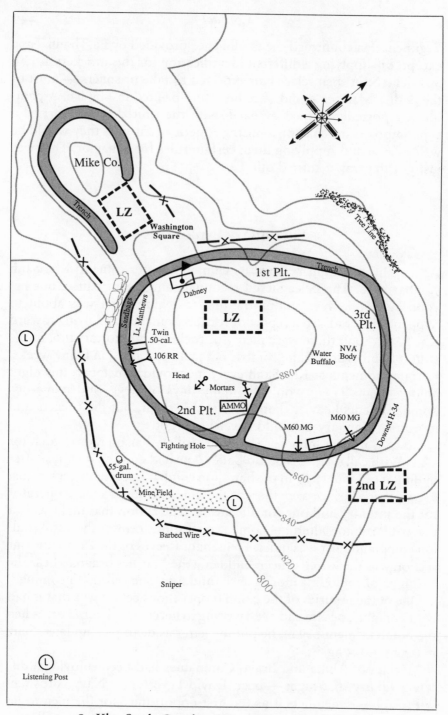

8 · Khe Sanh Combat Base, January 28, 1968

He turned in about 11:00 P.M. only to awake to a sound, or perhaps it was some imperceptible change in the air. Leverton writes, "I swear like in slow motion I must have raised three feet laying flat on my back and screamed 'Incoming!' out of a sound sleep. Why, I don't know, but less than thirty seconds later the first rocket hit. Nobody in that tent was still sleeping." At Bravo, Captain Kenneth Pipes had just completed a check of his lines. Tom Quigley remembers Pipes suddenly exclaiming, "That sounds like incoming!"

The company gunnery sergeant, from Georgia, would have none of it. He woke up and shot back, "Hell, no, Captain, that ain't incoming."

Just about then, two or three shells landed right outside the bunker. The gunny was *definitely* wrong.

The Bravo corpsman, supply specialists, and radio operators lived in a tent near the command post bunker. When the first shells landed, everybody dashed out. Then Lance Corporal Steven L. Hartwig, apparently thinking he had forgotten something, turned back for the tent. A shell landed very close and cut him in half. Hartwig never knew what hit him.

Marines later calculated that between 5:00 and 5:30 A.M. the combat base was hit by approximately a hundred rounds of 82mm mortar shells and sixty 122mm rockets. Though not an especially fierce bombardment by later Khe Sanh standards, what made the shelling of January 21 so awesome and memorable occurred fifteen minutes after it began. At that moment one or more North Vietnamese shells fell in the base's main ammunition dump. The effect was devastating.

At the 1st Battalion combat operations center, Lieutenant Reeves walked over to Lance Corporal Seitz and warned, "The ammo dump is on fire and it's going to blow up any minute." Not more than five seconds later, Seitz remembers, "it was like watching on the TV set — they simulate an explosion. You'll see the picture shake, at least in the old movies, and you're sitting still. That's exactly what I felt like. I was just watching the whole world shake and I was sitting still."

James Kirk was probably one of the first casualties. His bunker directly faced the ammo dump. The blast wrecked the bunker, and something took his right leg off. Kirk was traumatized; aware something bad had just happened, he screamed. Lance Corporal Kenneth W. Claire, the squad leader, moving along the trench line encouraging his men, quickly arrived on the scene. Claire got corpsman John A. Cicala to put on a temporary dressing and then rustled up a couple of clerks to carry Kirk to Charlie Med. The quick action undoubtedly saved Kirk's life. Claire worked equally hard for the rest of his men throughout the bombardment, for which he was honored with a Bronze Star.

Another man Claire assisted, for example, was Private First Class Alexander Tretiakoff, who had been returning from listening post detail. As Tretiakoff reached the perimeter he got entangled in the barbed wire and was stuck in the open as rockets and mortar shells exploded all around. Claire left his own covered position and dashed across thirty meters of open space to free Tretiakoff from the wire and help him to the trenches.

The danger from the ammunition dump was not simply injury from its explosion. That was bad enough, but just as bad was the danger of ignition of the many munitions blown out of the dump by the explosion, shells that could have become unstable as a result. Edward I. Prendergast, Jr., of Bravo Company recalls, "Hot rounds were landing in the trenches. They were whole artillery and 106 rounds still glowing red." Prendergast and others had to take off their shirts, which they used gingerly to pick up the shells from both ends and toss them out of the trench. The work went on for hours, during which the Marines continued on the alert against attack as well. Captain Pipes recalled: "The men: I just can't say enough about them. They stayed in their positions. In certain areas of the trench lines, ordnance was within the trench line one to three feet deep." At the Bravo Company command post 105mm shells kept rolling through the door, propelled by the periodic explosions of munitions in the dump. Bravo Marines took the shells back out into the open, where some of them later exploded. Pipes had to move his headquarters several times that night and next morning before danger abated.

The 81mm mortar platoon of 1/26 was also emplaced near the ammunition dump and continued to deliver counter-mortar fire throughout the bombardment. Its fire direction center was hit and partially destroyed at least three times by NVA fire or exploding munitions. The platoon lost all lights and communications. Gunnery Sergeant James A. Morris, assistant commander, was knocked down by concussion or blast at least twice as he stood at the plotting board in the fire direction center. Each time he got up and went back to work. When the lights went down, Morris lit a candle. When he lost communications, he set up a messenger relay. In the midst of the barrage, he moved among his mortar crews to encourage them. Morris received a Bronze Star.

Marine artillery remained active, indeed heroic, through the bombardment. First Lieutenant Marion H. "Hank" Norman, an artillery forward observer with Bravo, left the safety of his bunker to try to find the NVA firing sites. With the exploding ammunition supply point just fifty meters away, Norman stayed outside to analyze the trajectories of the incoming rockets. Though knocked to the ground several times by concussion, Norman performed skillful crater analyses and passed the results to the artillery.

Some of the most effective artillery were the three 105mm howitzers of Battery C, 1/13 (the unit's other three guns had been moved to Hill 881 South). Just twenty-five meters behind the combat base perimeter and only fifty or seventy-five from the exploding dump, the battery kept working its guns. Because the unit had lost all electrical power in the first moments of the shelling, the fire commands were being scribbled on scraps of paper and carried to the guns by runners. Meanwhile, Corporal David E. Courtney moved from gun to gun to repair communication lines, while the battery executive officer, First Lieutenant William L. Eberhardt, Jr., and the supply chief, Sergeant Ronnie D. Whitenight, combed the gun pits for dud shells being thrown over from the dump. These two carried almost a hundred shells to a safe area. Gun number 2 went out of action for fifteen minutes after a dud mortar round landed in its emplacement; later gun number 5 sustained a direct hit by a white phosphorus shell thrown out of the maelstrom of the dump. The shell ignited the gun's ready ammunition and killed Lance Corporal Jerry O. Stenburg. The section chief sent his remaining crew to another emplacement and stayed behind to put out the fire. Subsequently he received leg and head wounds from another NVA shell that hit the gun area. The battery command post took five direct hits, which miraculously wounded no one. Battery C fired until about 8:00 A.M., by which time it had expended 3,000 shells and had lost all the aiming stakes used to verify gun deflection.

Yet another danger was gas, the Marines' own CS tear gas, the stockpile of which was in the blown-up ammo dump. With the first shells battalion commander Jim Wilkinson donned his flak jacket and helmet and made a dash for the combat operations center, sliding through the doorway at the last second as a mortar shell hit nearby. The command post was heavily affected by the dump fire, and when the gas shells went off the entire area was filled with CS gas as thick as fog. The stuff wafted right into the center. Wilkinson had previously been worried about NVA gas and had ordered his men to have gas masks ready; now that precaution became vital to protect against the Marines' own gas. Despite the precautions, the CS proved so thick that the masks were only partially effective.

Hours after the bombardment actually ceased the combat base was still in danger from burning ammunition. In fact, one of the worst moments of all came at about 10:00 A.M., when the fire ignited a large quantity of C-4 plastic and other explosives. The shock wave cracked a large timber that supported the roof of the battalion combat operations center bunker. Several of Wilkinson's staff were knocked to the ground, and they all were afraid the bunker would collapse on them. After a time it became clear the roof had settled but would not collapse, and the men breathed a sigh of relief.

The North Vietnamese defector had been guarded in shifts by Marines of the 26th Regiment's Scout-Sniper Platoon. Sergeant Franklin D. Jones had been scheduled to take the evening shift, but the noncom on the graveyard shift, who felt sick, switched with him. Jones and another Marine handcuffed themselves to Tonc when the NVA officer asked to go to the latrine. They had quite a time coming back, for it was at that moment that the bombardment began. The Marines guarding Tonc sat through it in a sturdy bunker but were shocked to return to their area later and find it nearly leveled. Frank Jones's own tent was completely destroyed and Sergeant Terence Smith, the man who had switched shifts with him and used his bunk, was dead. The line between death and life was thin at Khe Sanh that night.

Colonel Lownds emerged from the regimental operations center and began to check out the base soon after the bombardment died down, while the dump was still burning and munitions were exploding. There was plenty to see. At the airstrip the navigational aids were out of action, two CH-46s had substantial damage, two UH-1Es were damaged, and one was destroyed. Also damaged were H-34 and CH-53 helicopters. Living quarters for the Marine air contingent had been destroyed. All the weather equipment was destroyed, the control tower inoperative, the runway cratered.

The scout-sniper area had been heavily affected, as had the Gray Sector of the defense perimeter and the emplacement area of Battery C of 1/13. Surviving guns of that battery were evacuated to the Ponderosa area of the combat base (see Map 8) so that work parties could remove hundreds of shells that were scattered all over. Only several days later did Battery C move back, with a new gun to replace the

105mm howitzer whose recoil mechanism had failed. A further Marine howitzer battery reinforced Khe Sanh to stiffen its artillery, while General Tompkins also sent the 1st Battalion, 9th Marines to increase infantry strength.

In the Seabee and supply areas much equipment had been damaged, including perhaps fifteen percent of the heavy construction machinery that would have to be used to repair the airstrip. Aboveground communications facilities were mostly destroyed, as were telephone wires. The Air Force pulled its TIGERHOUND project out of Khe Sanh on January 21, 1968, leaving behind Majors Hartentower and Keskinen to function as air liaison officers between the 26th Marines and the Air Force.

Ammunition had suddenly become critical, though fortunately not nearly as much as it could have been. Just days before, a proportion of the ammunition had been moved to a second dump in the Ponderosa, both to make it more available to artillery units emplaced there and to make the artillery supplies less vulnerable. That action now turned out to have been fortuitous. The exploded dump had contained some eleven thousand ordnance items. Almost six thousand additional rounds had been expended during the night of January 20–21 either in counterbattery or in aid of Hill 861 or recon team Nurse. The day before, the artillery commander, Colonel Hennelly, could confidently look at stocks of about twenty thousand shells. Now he had less than four thousand.

From his own standpoint Colonel James Wilkinson would agree that Khe Sanh seemed most vulnerable that day in the wake of the bombardment. Casualties had not been too bad, but the destruction of the ammunition dump was a great reminder of mortality. The almost immediate arrival of Lieutenant Colonel John F. Mitchell's 1st Battalion, 9th Marines was a useful restorative for morale. Wilkinson took another morale action all on his own: he posted an armed guard over the remaining beer stocks. Thereafter beer would be parceled out at a rate of two cans per man every other day. Khe Sanh was going to be a different sort of place.

Death in the Village

The sounds of the North Vietnamese barrage died away, succeeded by desultory mortaring through the day, the major noise and action now

coming from the inferno of the ammunition supply point. The re-
prieve mirrored what was happening in Khe Sanh village, then enjoying restored calm though its hour, too, had struck. At the village
the Marines of CAC Oscar, the district advisory team, and Regional
Force troops were fighting for their lives.

Long before January Bob Brewer, the Quang Tri province U.S.
pacification chief, had come to an arrangement with the Marines
whereby the combat base would furnish reinforcements if ever district
headquarters were attacked. As already related, Brewer had disturbing indications in late 1967 that he interpreted as a threat to Khe Sanh.
Being a CIA man and, as pacification chief, more attuned to the
political aspect of the war, Brewer worried more about the Huong
Hoa district headquarters than he did about the combat base. At the
New Year he flew from Quang Tri to Khe Sanh and spent two or three
days at the village. There he spoke with the district senior adviser,
Army Major Bruce B. G. Clark, about what to do if the threat crystallized. Brewer also checked his existing emergency arrangements
with Colonel Lownds, at least according to Brewer.

In early January missionaries John and Carolyn Miller left for the
coast to get out of the way of what might shortly happen. The Millers
actually had no desire to go, but Colonel Lownds ordered them out.

Major Clark did not receive any intelligence information directly
from the 26th Marines but he could not miss what had been happening around him. The spooks of MACVSOG had moved their FOB-3
compound to under the guns of the combat base; the CIDG camp had
also moved and had been reconstructed to defend against a heavy
attack; the combat base had put out more outposts and organized
internal security; and battalions had come to reinforce Khe Sanh.
Bruce Clark made up his mind that something was definitely up and
reorganized some of his own defenses. Just outside the wire stood a
storage building that had not been included in the defense perimeter.
Clark put a fighting position on top of that building and added more
wire around it. "We changed just enough of our fortifications that it
was not the same district headquarters the NVA had rehearsed
against," he remembers.

Talk of changing the platoon locations was common at CAC Oscar
also. That unit had had a leader, Lieutenant Elmore, who had been
sent precisely because Khe Sanh was supposed to be a quiet sector and
he had already been wounded twice. Under existing policy Elmore
would automatically be sent home if wounded a third time. That was

exactly what happened. First Lieutenant Thomas B. Stamper, his replacement, took over CAC Oscar on December 27. Stamper arrived to reports of recent contacts and night incidents and discussions of relocating Oscar's 2nd Platoon. The proposed site was a few hundred meters north of hamlets Lang Con 1 and 2. Colonel Lownds told Stamper not to make the move, but when asked his justification, he replied, "I can't tell you why."

Shortly thereafter, on January 11 or 12, that area was obliterated by an ARC LIGHT strike. Stamper quickly surmised why the site was unsuitable for CAC Oscar.

As a result of not making that move, however, on the night of January 21 there were still two platoons of CAC Oscar in Khe Sanh village. In addition there were two Vietnamese platoons of the 915th Regional Forces Company, and there was Captain Clark's advisory detachment, with about four Americans. According to Brewer, total strength was slightly more than 175 men. The position was also a difficult one, with a hill that swept down into the village, overlooking the barracks and district headquarters. An effort had been made to solve this problem by incorporating the hilltop into the defense perimeter, but the field of fire was poor, with vegetation right up to the perimeter wire, while manpower was divided, with CAC Marines in their own compounds, not quite sufficient for the defensive position.

In their discussions Clark and Brewer always recognized the difficulty of holding the Khe Sanh district headquarters. Brewer anticipated that the post would require reinforcement, and he wanted to put the relief force in just over the hilltop, in the coffee trees of Simard's plantation. Most of the trees were just six to eight feet tall and Brewer thought fighter-bombers with heavy ordnance could clear out instant landing zones where helicopters could insert the troops. Brewer's plan miscarried.

On January 20 Major Clark was on patrol six or seven kilometers south of the village when he got a cryptic warning from Special Forces to clear the area. He did so and three hours later an ARC LIGHT strike devastated that map grid. When he got back to the village he found that the local representatives of the CIA-Vietnamese Joint Technical Advisory Detachment had gone. "It's almost as though they knew it was coming," Clark recalled.

By that night it seemed clear the North Vietnamese were moving in around Khe Sanh village. Fortunately, for what it was worth, radio communication conditions improved at night and those were the times Major Clark could best use his single sideband radio to talk with Bob Brewer at Quang Tri. Clark reported that the village was being invested by an NVA force he estimated at a battalion in strength. Later, based on body count and abandoned weapons, that estimate would be increased to a regiment.

It also proved fortunate that the CAC Marines had spent several days digging new trenches and that they had just received an especially large consignment of ammunition and sundry equipment. All of it would now be used. That night Lieutenant Stamper put out a listening post on Route 9. Though no report came during the eight hours the post was on duty, MACV analysts later concluded that this had been one of the main routes the 8th Battalion, 66th Regiment, NVA 304th Division used to get into position. Some analysts also believe that although the main attack would be delivered by a single regiment, even solely by the 8th Battalion, all the rest of that NVA division took position to ambush whatever reinforcements the Americans sent to district headquarters.

When the bombardment of the combat base began in the early morning of January 21 the CAC Oscar Marines went on full alert. Stamper woke up Clark before heading for his own command post. He settled in long enough to decide he wanted some coffee. Stamper had just suggested to one of the Marines that they walk together to the mess hall for some coffee when the entire perimeter erupted in gunfire. Having begun to climb out of the trench, Stamper quickly flattened himself into it. The harsh crack of AK-47 fire was all around them.

By this time, approximately 6:55 A.M., Clark had taken one of the Bru platoons of the CAC, just thirteen troopers, and was crossing a bridge over the nearby waterfalls to begin a patrol of the sector. Clark miraculously got back to the perimeter and under cover without anyone's being hurt.

At the western edge of the village, CAP Oscar-2 now learned about the threat, as corpsman John R. Roberts describes:

> The warning came in over the radio. . . . Our team leader, Sergeant Roy Harper, sounded the alert. . . . There was little time to sit and think what might happen, already we could hear a rapid volume of automatic weapons fire in the direction of our sister unit [CAC–district head-quarters]. We did not have to wait long before our company com-mander, Lt. Stamper, called to confirm that they were under a massive ground attack. Almost simultaneously we began to get small arms fire from the front and to the right flank of our own compound.

Oscar-2 was taking fire from planter Simard's house and the Buddhist pagoda. The nine Marines, one Navy corpsman, and ten Bru soldiers braced for assault. They had Claymores, two Browning automatic rifles, a 60mm mortar, and one M-60 machine gun. Roberts continues his account:

> It was still dark. A[n] RPG [rocket-propelled grenade] slammed into our front observation bunker. LCpl. Sergeant and Sgt. Harper were in the top of the tower. . . . Harper was the first serious casualty. He had been hit in the face with shrapnel. Cpl. Sullivan remained calm and returned fire to the front and sides while LCpl. Sergeant and I pulled the sergeant into the trench. As the sun began to rise the NVA pulled back. Lt. Stamper radioed the base . . . requesting air support. In a short while, the jets came in dropping napalm so close we could feel the intense heat as though we were in an oven.

Back at district headquarters things were even worse. Because of the numerous civilians in the village, the CAC Marines had emplaced their Claymore mines inside the perimeter wire. Now they did not dare detonate them for fear of destroying the wire barrier. The lack of clear fields of fire crippled the defenders. Regional Force soldiers holding the building rooftop fighting position fled, but they dropped just enough grenades to break the momentum of the NVA attackers. Major Clark asked Khe Sanh for a ring of steel, a last-ditch artillery defense, and the combat base also used deadly variable-time (VT) fuses for air bursts over the defense wire.

Bruce Clark recounts the climax this way:

> I had told the montagnards to keep down, but some of them by the main entrance didn't and were killed — about five of them. Despite the heavy artillery the enemy kept assaulting the perimeter. We took a lot of sniper fire from the pagoda, where it appeared the dead and wounded were being taken. We knocked that out by artillery — on the third round. We took a lot of sniper fire from the "bus stop" right outside the main entrance and brought in "quick action" fuse 105s but they kept sniping. We also took some small arms fire from the Howard Johnson's across the street and then knocked them out. There appeared to be a blocking force by the entrance of the gate of the perimeter to prevent us from leaving the compound. We fired at least five hundred rounds of 81s, all without increments. They landed and exploded right outside our wires.

In addition, the artillery support from the combat base was substantial, including more than one thousand VT shells, and direct fire kept the NVA back. Sergeant John J. Balanco, squad leader and senior adviser, roamed the fighting positions to distribute the dwindling ammunition and encourage the men. When he discovered casualties he told others to cover those fire sectors and found men elsewhere on the perimeter to replace them. Balanco won the Silver Star for his role that night. Corporal Verner R. Russell also won a Silver Star for his skillful use of a machine gun to counter NVA pressure on weakened portions of the line. Already a dozen Regional Force soldiers were killed and twice that many wounded. At 8:11 A.M., after a Marine A-6 aircraft accomplished a spectacular precision bombing, laying twenty-eight 500-pound bombs right on the North Vietnamese, the adversary assault force broke and melted back into the jungle.

There were pieces to pick up on both sides. An aerial observer who came on station about two hours later reported seeing a long line of NVA troops and porters bearing the dead and wounded toward Laos. More air strikes resulted in an estimated additional two hundred NVA killed. At the combat base at 11:00 A.M. Colonel Lownds ordered Delta Company of 1/26, in regiment reserve, to relieve beleaguered Khe Sanh village. After second thoughts about NVA ambushes and the difficulty of getting men cross-country to the village, the orders were countermanded. This action took place just as Delta Company's lead elements were entering Khe Sanh village.

Captain Clark reported to province pacification chief Robert Brewer that district headquarters might hold another night but that ammunition was extremely low. Brewer pulled out the stops, since the village defenders had no LZ and now had no control over their former drop zone; he got helicopters that would fly in low and simply kick the resupply of ammunition out the door. The attempt was only partially successful and the helicopters took numerous hits from NVA automatic weapons surrounding the village. It was clear that that tactic was going to work just once.

On the night of January 21–22, only sniper fire broke the silence; there was no assault or even a bombardment. Having taken better stock of what he had left, however, Clark told Brewer he could hold another night *if* reinforced.

At Quang Tri Bob Brewer organized a council of war. The group that met included ARVN province chief Colonel Nguyen Am, ARVN tactical operations center director Major Tuyen, his U.S. adviser Major Sanders, economic development adviser James R. Bullington, psychological warfare adviser Marine Lieutenant Colonel Jean T. Fox, intelligence adviser Air Force Captain Warren Milburg, and Regional Forces/Popular Forces (RF/PF) adviser Army Major John B. Oliver. Brewer himself and his deputy, Army Lieutenant Colonel Joseph Seymoe, plus his special assistant, John M. Uhler from USAID, rounded out the group. Brewer's conviction carried the day and the group agreed on the need to reinforce Khe Sanh village. With the approval of ARVN 1st division commander Major General Ngo Quang Truong, Colonel Am provided one of his best RF companies for the mission. A helicopter unit from Da Nang provided nine UH-1E ships to carry them. The slicks lifted off from Quang Tri city at 5:10 P.M. on January 21 with the 256th RF Company.

Brewer's deputy volunteered to lead the relief mission. Given the shortness of time and impossibility of extensively briefing the pilots, the CIA man thought it might be good to have someone along who knew his plan, so Brewer approved the inclusion of Seymoe. The deputy, originally from the Air Force, was a brave man who held a Distinguished Flying Cross for his actions in the Korean war. He had been grounded because of injuries, however, including some loss of hearing, and had then transferred to the Army. Seymoe's poor hearing had fateful effects on the relief expedition.

In addition to Seymoe, Brewer sent along a forward air controller (FAC) on his staff, Captain Cooper. Flying an L-19 observation plane, Cooper was to mark the orchard of coffee trees so that fixed-wing aircraft could blast down the trees to create the LZ for the relief force. Instead there was a classic foul-up. Brewer tells the story best in a video interview he gave in 1989:

> When Cooper got up, there was another L-19 in the vicinity. It was a Marine Corps . . . FAC, but Cooper couldn't get him on the radio. So he's chasing around the sky, trying to tell that guy to get down, get out of the way. And meantime he radioed to the oncoming choppers lumbering in: "Hold up, we couldn't get the fighter strike in yet."

Now Cooper had four flights of fighter-bombers ready to level the coffee grove, but Seymoe with his bad ear understood that Cooper was reporting that the strike had been canceled. Seymoe then ordered the slicks to land his relief force at the Old French Fort. That place, since the departure of FOB-3, had become an NVA stronghold. The result was a massacre.

Flying the lead chopper, Captain Tommy Stiner happened to be celebrating his thirtieth birthday that day. His best present was going to be his life. Stiner brought in his slick, disgorging the Vietnamese RF troops. Just as he lifted off, an explosive shell, either mortar or rocket, hit the front of the helicopter, propelling it sideways and over the lip of the hill, where it descended, rolled over, and crashed. One side gunner was dead, crushed by the weight of the ship. Seymoe was alive, but he was pinned by an aluminum bar normally used to secure stretchers and was unconscious and threatened by the fire starting in the wreckage.

Tommy Stiner's day turned into a nightmare. It had begun with a surprise birthday party thrown by his buddies of the 282nd Assault Helicopter Company. About twenty had been with him in the operations building when orders for the Khe Sanh mission came through. Stiner protested because the 282nd had lost three ships recently. Now he himself was down and, with his copilot and surviving gunner, desperately attempting to free Seymoe from the wreckage. Meanwhile the flames grew until they encountered fuel or hydraulic fluid and then the fire just incinerated the slick.

Stiner had to give up the effort to save Seymoe. He decided to make a run for it, though he had no survival gear, map, compass, not even a canteen. "I picked up two grenades and clips for my carbine and started downhill," he said later. "Then I bumped into an enemy force. I surprised them as much as they surprised me. They were walking and I ran through them. I kept running. They were chasing me and firing and yelling. It didn't sound too friendly. I would run until I just couldn't run anymore. So I would find a bushy area and hide, then run more."

Getting away from the North Vietnamese turned out to be only half the problem. The other half was finding some Americans and joining up with them without being taken for an enemy. That was the worst of all. After thirteen hours of terror Stiner found Ta Cong hamlet before first light of January 22. As he walked toward it in relief, unknowing, he entered one of the Marine minefields. First Stiner stepped on a mine and was wounded by shrapnel, then a Marine guard shot him, and then Marines on the line opened up thinking him to be the NVA. It took Tommy Stiner some time to convince the Marines of Oscar-3 to take him in. Even then they could not believe Stiner was on their side, perhaps thinking him some Russian adviser to the NVA, so the Army officer spent the next night tied up.

For all his pain, Stiner was the lucky one. So was Specialist-4 How-lington, who made it to Khe Sanh. Efforts to warn off the other choppers before they set down at French Fort were unsuccessful, and survival in that place was distinctly precarious. The ships went in and the RFs jumped out, only to face immediate opposition. They formed a perimeter but never had much of a chance. Thirteen American pilots, fourteen other crew, and seventy-four RF soldiers went dead or missing. Months later Bob Brewer returned to the site and recovered Seymoe's body. There was not much left of it. In terms of propor-tionate casualties and equipment losses, this air assault at Old French Fort would be the worst military debacle of the entire campaign at Khe Sanh.

A couple of RF soldiers who evaded and made it to Khe Sanh district headquarters told Major Clark what had happened. That night Clark talked to Bob Brewer at the Quang Tri tactical operations center. Also present was Brigadier General Ngo Quang Truong, commander of the ARVN 1st Division, who held the military responsibility to the South Vietnamese government for territorial defense of northern Quang Tri, including Huong Hoa district. Brewer argued that he could not defend the district headquarters if the Marines were unwilling to reinforce and support it. Truong resisted any withdrawal since he believed the NVA objective was not to capture Khe Sanh, as certain Americans in-sisted, but precisely to take a political seat such as Huong Hoa district. Silence reigned for a good half hour in the operations center, the only noise that of the radio chatter in the background. Finally Truong ap-proved and Brewer told Clark to get out of the village.

At the combat base David Lownds faced the parallel dilemma of whether to reinforce CAC Oscar. "After long consideration and proper evaluation of the facts," Lownds told debriefers, "it ap-peared . . . that this unit should be withdrawn and that the seat of the district government be moved within the perimeter of the Khe Sanh combat base." Those were the orders Lownds gave Lieutenant Stamper, who informed his own men that the Marine reinforcements had not been able to get through because of NVA ambushes, that they would have to hold through the night, but that the next morning they would evacuate the village. "It had been a soul-searching night for us all," corpsman John Roberts said later.

In the morning the North Vietnamese began to fire artillery guns at the village. It was the first time the NVA had used anything heavier than mortars or rockets. Marines and others at Oscar-2 made a mad dash to district headquarters. Helicopters diverted from supply missions to the hill outposts came in to pick them up on an improvised LZ. The choppers took out thirty-four wounded and then lifted thirty-four CAC Marines. However, given the constant fire on the LZ, the Marines refused to provide helicopters to lift out the 915th Regional Forces troops. As a result Major Clark and his advisory team refused to be evacuated and instead walked out with their RFs, an LLDB officer, and thirteen CIDG strikers who happened to be in the village when the battle began. Lang Vei offered to supply a Mike Force company for support, but this offer was rejected. Luckily Clark and his men reached the combat base safely.

As one of his last actions before evacuating the village, Lieutenant Stamper warned Oscar-3 to get out of the way. That platoon, with eleven Marines and thirty Bru PFs, was at Ta Cong village, where Tommy Stiner had ended up, just outside the combat base. Stamper told his men that eight or nine *thousand* NVA were headed their way and that they should pull back to join with FOB-3. The Oscar-3 men got together their fighting gear, put C-4 plastic explosives in all the bunkers, emptied a fifty-five-gallon drum of gasoline into the hootches to make sure, and then blew up their compound. Henceforth Marines of CAC Oscar defended a sector of the FOB-3 line at the combat base. Many civilian refugees filtering back later endured special problems as the entire area became one huge battlefield.

Meanwhile the CAP Marines who had pulled out left a good deal behind them — not only weapons but stocks of rice. An FOB officer estimated there was enough to feed a division. The northern area MACVSOG commander, Lieutenant Colonel Daniel L. Baldwin III, was visiting FOB-3 at the time of the fall of the village and ordered a patrol to go in and destroy some of the supplies before the NVA could get to them. Baldwin called up Lownds and asked that Khe Sanh village temporarily be made a no-fire zone, then grabbed a helicopter. The FOB-3 operations officer, Major Thomas Simcox, led the patrol on the ground, accompanied by Captain Clark, who led the way while Colonel Baldwin remained aloft in the chopper to spot any approaching enemy. The patrol blew up rice and captured some weapons, including the first sample of the RPG-7 weapon ever taken by the United States. Then the SOG troopers got out of the village. The North Vietnamese, apparently awaiting nightfall to enter the village, were caught flatfooted. Baldwin won the Vietnamese Cross of Gallantry with Palm for that foray.

For the Americans, the loss of the village went a good way toward sealing the fate of Lang Vei, reducing almost to zero any possibility of getting a relief force through to the CIDG camp. Conversely, with the NVA in Khe Sanh village, Hanoi attained some political objectives without directly engaging the combat base. General Truong of ARVN had feared this very eventuality. General Westmoreland did not. He had prepared a battle royal for Khe Sanh.

"Khe Sanh Already Shows Signs of Battle"

BOB BREWER HAD AT LEAST ONE THING IN COMMON with South Vietnamese General Ngo Quang Truong — both believed the main threat in the Khe Sanh area was to the district seat of Huong Hoa, not necessarily the combat base or its outlying strong points. Colonel Lownds and Generals Tompkins, Cushman, and Westmoreland obviously thought otherwise. Khe Sanh combat base buttoned up in preparation for major battle simultaneously with and immediately after the fight for the village.

Then (and now) the adversary's true intentions were known only in Hanoi. Marine combat intelligence officers at the time (and historians today) were limited by the available evidence, largely confined to general knowledge of North Vietnamese troop movements and dispositions. Anything that could make those movements and dispositions more transparent, more susceptible to detection, would be a boon in the developing engagement. The revelations of Lieutenant La Thanh Tonc promised just that, and this is what made them so attractive to American ears. At the same time, the Americans were on the verge of a technological leap that promised some transparency also. In a sense the days that followed the Khe Sanh village battle were a race between the North Vietnamese Army getting into position and the Americans emplacing their new instruments of detection. The winner of that race might well become victor of the battle of Khe Sanh.

Shadows Across the Battlefield

The intentions of those North Vietnamese soldiers who hovered like shadows in the night beyond Marine perimeters were moderated by an entire command structure different from, but with the same function as, the Marine chain of command. The Tri-Thien-Hue Military Region, intermediate command authority for the NVA at Khe Sanh, established objectives in 1967 that it confirmed in a resolution studied in its party committee on January 16, 1968. The resolutions figured among documents later captured by American and South Vietnamese forces. Both resolutions envisioned establishing a front line that extended from Khe Sanh clear down to the Hai Van Pass, which separated Da Nang from Hue and Quang Tri province. The potential prize could be the capture of Quang Tri province, and victory might become a turning point in the war.

To accomplish the Khe Sanh portion of its aims the North Vietnamese moved serious forces into position around the combat base. The NVA 304th Division showed its hand in the attacks on district headquarters. Given the length of time necessary to deploy from North Vietnam down the Ho Chi Minh Trail, the 304th was probably sent into action almost immediately after arrival. With standard strengths for an NVA division estimated at roughly seven to eight thousand men, major elements of the 304th on location included all three of its regiments, 9th, 24th, and 66th, the 68B Artillery Regiment, and the 14th Antiaircraft Battalion. Attached in support was the 24th Artillery Battalion. One North Vietnamese artillery unit was armed with 122mm guns; another, possibly from the 367th Artillery Division, had 85mm weapons.

Significant discrepancies exist between American and South Vietnamese documents on the status of the other major component of the NVA siege force, the 325-C Division. A Khe Sanh analysis compiled by MACV in July 1968 credits the NVA, perhaps following the La Thanh Tonc interrogation material, with having the entire division in place. However, a study of two thousand pages of captured documents, completed by the ARVN Joint General Staff just weeks after the end of the battle, places just a single regiment (18/325-C) at Khe Sanh. Instead the JGS study concludes that two regiments of *other* North Vietnamese divisions supplemented the siege force by holding strategic blocking positions along Route 9. According to the South

Vietnamese these were the 31st Regiment of the NVA 341st Division and possibly a regiment of the 324-B Division. Units of the 18th Regiment (also known as E29 or the 29th) later moved east to Route 9, and two battalions were sent as far south as Hue, where they participated in the last stages of the battle for that city.

Antiaircraft support was formidable for the infantry of the 325-C Division. In addition to their organic 14th Battalion, the 74th and 75th Battalions from Military Region 4 were identified as attached to the division. At a minimum these units were armed with 12.7mm machine guns and 37mm cannon. The MACV Khe Sanh analysis notes that the presence of 14.5mm machine guns was suspected but not confirmed, while the ARVN JGS analysis not only credits the North Vietnamese with these weapons but notes the presence of 75mm, 80mm, and 100mm antiaircraft guns with full loads of ammunition. In February and March these guns would shoot down eight aircraft in the Khe Sanh area.

Artillery support for the North Vietnamese came essentially from the units assigned to the 304th Division. Possible but not confirmed was augmentation by the 4th Battalion, 84th Rocket Artillery Regiment, believed attached to the 325-C Division. In any case the big guns were mostly emplaced in caves or well-dug-out positions on the Co Roc massif in Laos, perhaps ninety-six gun tubes in all, at least as estimated by National Security Council staffers for President Johnson. Beyond gun artillery, LBJ was told the NVA might have some forty-eight 120mm mortars and sixteen launchers for 122mm rockets.

Although the MACV analysis of the Khe Sanh battle contains little regarding North Vietnamese construction and logistics activities, which were central to the preparation of the battlefield in NVA doctrine, these are covered in some detail in contemporary CIA reports and in the ARVN study. Preparations included construction of two new roads paralleling Route 9 to the north and south and extending from Ban Dong (in Laos) and from Laotian Road 92 to the Vietnamese border, essentially giving access to two of the five avenues of approach to Khe Sanh. Marines began to call this improvement the Santa Fe Trail. The southernmost road extension led to the vicinity of Co Roc and featured large bunkers and storage areas. Numerous new depots and distribution points were built in Laos east of Tchepone during the last months of 1967. In addition a chain of way stations or supply points that crossed the DMZ was established roughly sixteen to twenty-four kilometers east of the Laotian border.

Transportation Group 559, which ran the Ho Chi Minh Trail, was known for its use of *binh tram* units, special depot and transport formations that moved supplies and managed activity on the network. Associated with the Khe Sanh effort, according to the ARVN study, were at least thirteen transportation companies, of which the study identified eleven: the C-1, C-2, C-3, C-4 C-5, C-6, C-11, C-12, C-13, C-14, and C-15. In addition there were at least two civilian labor battalions composed of North Vietnamese from Ha Tinh province, one of natives from Nghe An, and unknown numbers of laborers impressed locally in Quang Tri. The network was believed to operate seven hundred of its own trucks. Supporting the combat and logistics forces were six specialized medical units. Documents indicated that in late January alone the Santa Fe Trail network moved two hundred tons of ammunition and eight hundred tons of provisions to one terminus, presumably Khe Sanh, plus an additional fifty tons to a related destination.

Around the combat base there had been extensive work on fortifications ranging from simple foxholes to bunkers, entrenchments, camps, large strong points, and gun positions. Every photo reconnaissance mission that went out brought back new indications. The regiment that had remained in the Khe Sanh area through the fall of 1967 had maintained at least some of these positions in fighting trim. Others were newly constructed, such as the strong points in the hill mass south of Route 9. By the beginning of February 1968 all the 37mm antiaircraft guns discovered had been sited to protect rear depots, but 12.7mm machine gun positions were found north and northeast of the Khe Sanh combat base and within 1,500 meters of its airfield. Emplacements for 152mm guns were detected beyond the maximum range of Marine artillery.

The CIA calculated that the North Vietnamese forces concentrated in the Khe Sanh area would require thirty-two to thirty-seven tons of supplies each day under sustained heavy combat conditions. A two-regiment force (which the CIA believed to be drawn entirely from the NVA 320th Division) blocking Route 9 would add another requirement of seventeen to twenty-one tons daily. Given observed NVA traffic rates on the trails, the intelligence agency credited the North Vietnamese with a stockpile, accumulated since mid-November or before, sufficient for sixty to ninety days of combat, plus the daily resupply capacity necessary to maintain reserves at that level.

Scanning the full panoply of North Vietnamese preparations, the CIA in February 1968 drew the conclusion that seemed appropriate:

> The Communist forces are prepared to defend the areas they now hold, to encircle U.S. positions completely, to extend their positions closer to ours in siege fashion, and to prepare in advance assembly areas from which assaults can be mounted. If these positions are subsequently connected by communications trenches, the Communists will be able to maneuver their forces from one portion of the battlefield to another under cover from friendly fire. They would also be in position to block movement from the main base at the airfield to outlying U.S. positions on the hills to the northwest. These techniques are similar to those employed by the Communists in their prolonged siege campaign at Dien Bien Phu.

This was the threat the CIA saw from the 22,000 NVA troops it believed around Khe Sanh at that time.

There are no North Vietnamese archives, oral histories, or memoirs with which to compare these appreciations. The single official commentary that exists is an informal one, albeit from an official source, General Cao Pha of the North Vietnamese Institute of Military History, which hosted a retrospective conference on the war that brought together Vietnamese and American historians in November 1978. General Pha gave the American interlocutor who questioned him about Khe Sanh the impression he had been there, mentioning four or five places that the American, a Marine, had also been. Pha commented that Hanoi initially assembled a force of two divisions plus ten artillery and antiaircraft units in the Khe Sanh area, which tallies almost precisely with American intelligence estimates and the MACV and ARVN analyses. Pha also noted that, as the battle progressed, the North Vietnamese Army decided to send in a third infantry division.

Meanwhile the North Vietnamese continued preparing the potential battlefield. One more necessary preparation was to do something about the Laotians at Ban Houei Sane. Whatever arrangements the Laotian unit BV-33 may have had with the NVA, its position astride Route 9 blocked one of the most important approaches to Khe Sanh. If there was to be a serious battle the Lao troops could not be permitted to remain in place. On the night of January 23–24 the North Vietnamese moved to do something about it, sending three battalions backed by seven tanks against the BV-33 positions. The attack opened with a barrage of perhaps 150 rounds from guns of 100mm or larger.

This action at Ban Houei Sane, not the battle two weeks later at Lang Vei, marked the first time in the war that the NVA committed armor in a conventional assault role.

The Laotian battle had special significance for American air forces, for BV-33 had been a valued intelligence resource for forward air controllers and airborne command centers. The controllers, in particular, had not only gotten information from the Laotians, whose radio call sign was "Elephant," but had often landed their planes at Ban Houei Sane's airstrip to confer with the Laotian commander, Lieutenant Colonel Soulang, and his officers. The Americans attempted to support Soulang the night of the NVA attack but adverse weather severely hampered their efforts. For example, two B-57 bombers were available in the area that night, but Captain Charles Rushforth was unable to send them in because he couldn't see the battle on the ground. Even radar-controlled approaches (assisted by the Marine element ASRAT Bravo from Khe Sanh) were of limited use because strike requests were overtaken by events as the NVA rapidly sliced through the BV-33 positions. By 7:00 A.M. the North Vietnamese had captured the Laotian defenses and consolidated their new positions.

Survivors and refugees fled along Route 9 toward Lang Vei CIDG camp. American forward air controllers stayed in contact with Soulang and hovered over his column all day long. The NVA made no further effort to obstruct the Laotians. American aircraft destroyed a bridge once the Lao troops had crossed it to prevent pursuit. At Lang Vei the Green Berets disarmed the Laotians. American suspicions had been aroused by how clean the Laotians' guns seemed to be in spite of their pitched battle. Following argument and remonstrations by Colonel Soulang, however, some equipment was handed back and Special Forces instructed the Laotians to assume positions at the abandoned CIDG camp, the old Lang Vei, situated about a kilometer to the north. There were 519 Lao soldiers accompanied by some 2,270 civilians. William H. Sullivan, the U.S. ambassador to Laos, argued that evacuation and repatriation of the Laotians would be militarily unsound, coming under artillery fire and at a critical moment in the reinforcement of Quang Tri province. A movement through Khe Sanh would also be certain to attract press coverage, while a "decision to remain at Lang Vei lessens the risk of publicity of presence of Lao forces in SVN."

Radio Hanoi waited a month before commenting on the battle at

Ban Houei Sane. In English at 10:55 P.M. on February 24 it broadcast a Pathet Lao news agency report that went to some length to disguise the particulars. Hanoi reported that the Laotian troops had fled their border post in July 1967, had gone to Khe Sanh, and had been turned away and told to defend Lang Vei for the Americans. However, it was true, as the Hanoi report stated, that the Laotian post had been inside a "liberated" zone.

While some considered Colonel Soulang a usually reliable intelligence source, eyebrows went up when he said the North Vietnamese had used tanks in their attack. A Pacific Command study later concluded that the disbelief came primarily because there had been no tank sightings prior to the action. However, the morning after the attack aircraft discovered marks in the earth around the battle site clearly made by vehicles with cleated treads, though they saw no tanks. A plane off to the southwest, nearer Co Roc, actually reported five tanks that day. At Lang Vei American officers were sufficiently concerned that they sent for a hundred light antitank weapons. Others continued to disbelieve the tank reports or to not take them seriously. It would not be long before the Americans would see the NVA tanks with their own eyes.

"Wars Are Won by One Guy Beating the Other Guy"

Though it might have waited weeks as with the Laotian news, after just a few days Hanoi crowed about its Khe Sanh bombardment and the ammunition dump disaster. At the time the Marines were still digging out from the effects of the explosions, with men at the combat base shaking their heads in relief that they were all right. Colonel Lownds, stoic, perfectly poised, inspired confidence, making the rounds to see the damage firsthand. As the battle became a siege and then wound on, Lownds adopted the practice of daily walks around the combat base. Marines were impressed to see their regimental commander up close; some admired the handlebar mustache Lownds had begun cultivating.

A daily occurrence of equal or greater inevitability was the shelling. Some days the North Vietnamese bombardment would be intense, others just enough to harass. Marines had to be ever alert for the noise of incoming gun, mortar, or rocket rounds. Soon the defenders became adept at what they began to call the "Khe Sanh shuffle" or "trot," the halt and flatten, then run like hell technique of making for cover at the first sign of bombardment.

Lownds was capable of great compassion toward his Marines faced with the NVA shells. Kevin Macaulay of the 3rd Recon saw it one day as he and his buddies hustled a grievously wounded comrade to Charlie Med. Macaulay had barely noticed the new lieutenant crossing in front and descending into the combat operations bunker, as was customary for newly arrived officers, so Lownds could look them over. The man saw Lownds, got his assignment, and exited the bunker. At that precise instant a 122mm rocket whooshed through the air and exploded in the street squarely between the bunker and the area of Recon Company Bravo. The new lieutenant caught the full force of the blast, which left him lying on the ground, one of his feet at an impossible angle, practically severed.

The recon men moved the wounded lieutenant as soon as they finished taking their buddy to the medical unit. As they did, Macaulay noticed Colonel Lownds come out of the combat operations center and watch them. When Macaulay returned with the empty blood-stained stretcher, Lownds yelled, "Hey Marine, how's he doing?" Macaulay shook his head.

"You could see the look that came across Colonel Lownds's face, you could see how visibly he was affected by this man's death," Macaulay remembered later. The incident left him thinking that Lownds really cared for his men, not just about his command writ large, the combat base encircled by twenty to forty thousand North Vietnamese.

The Marine commander had to make many command decisions during the battle of Khe Sanh. The first of them, which Lownds decided in the negative, was whether to reinforce the village when it came under attack. The consequence was to require a further decision of whether to evacuate the Bru and Vietnamese villagers, of whom perhaps fifteen hundred stood at the base's main gate the morning after the village fight began. With shelling sporadic that day, Lownds agreed to permit an aerial evacuation.

This decision to evacuate was not made without difficulty. South Vietnamese I Corps commander General Hoang Xuan Lam, insisting there was no place to put the Bru, opposed evacuation, but had no problem agreeing to take in the twelve hundred Vietnamese villagers. American pacification chief Bob Brewer was equally vehement that the villagers had to be provided for. Marines took the problem into their own hands when General Tompkins sent Captain James G. Collins, a G-5 (civil affairs) pacification field representative, up to Khe Sanh to organize the Vietnamese villagers to move from the combat base to a site the Marines selected near Dong Ha. Air Force and Marine supply flights, once they had disgorged their cargoes, were sent back loaded with Vietnamese villagers. When military aircraft and helicopters completed their scheduled missions into the combat base the Marines brought in Air America to continue the civilian lift. Some 1,115 of the civilians were evacuated on January 22, among them five Vietnamese nuns and the family of Felix Poilane. The whereabouts of M. Simard and other French planters were unknown. Captain Collins managed to convince the Bru to return to their villages temporarily while arrangements were made for them. As a result, despite the impending battle, eight thousand Bru montagnards still populated the area.

Another vital decision Lownds had to make that day was where to place his latest reinforcement, the 1st Battalion, 9th Marines, which began to arrive at about 5:00 P.M. The reinforcements brought difficulty as well as relief, as Lownds observed to Marine debriefers: "It started off as a one-battalion show. I was a battalion commander really, or a supervisor of a battalion commander. . . . We had prepared positions for one battalion . . . [not for the] five battalions I ended up with. . . . The units came at a moment's notice and we put them in as best we could." For 1/9 the ideal positions might have been on Hill 689 or 471, where they could have precluded NVA artillery observers looking down into the combat base. The North Vietnamese were already in the valley, however, and were showing considerable interest in the Rock Quarry the Seabees had used to rebuild the airstrip. Lownds determined to send the new battalion there, blocking a likely avenue of approach for an NVA attack. The location, Lownds observed, "proved that it served a worthwhile purpose since they've been probed many times."

Priming his defenses was action Lownds knew he could sink his teeth into. This was not the routine of body counts so prevalent in Vietnam. For David Lownds body counts were a waste of time and effort. "Wars are not won on body count," he said. "Wars are won by one guy beating the other guy." Lownds wanted to count only the bodies he could put his foot on. Defending prepared positions against NVA assault was a way to inflict casualties of that type. Colonel Lownds relished the opportunity, much as did William Westmoreland.

Of course the French too had talked about inflicting casualties by defending positions, and that strategy had only led them to Dien Bien Phu. That was the analogy everybody made, both in the chain of command and in the press. Lownds reacted, especially with the reporters, by claiming he had no idea what they were talking about. Yet 26th Regiment Marines claim to have seen a copy of Bernard Fall's *Hell in a Very Small Place* in the colonel's hootch. A staff officer candidly told one reporter that the 26th Marine commander had a talent for "jerking off the press."

Indeed, Lownds seemed insensitive to the scale of the NVA threat, not just to reporters but to generals like Phil Davidson. Some of the press privately referred to him as the "Lion of Khe Sanh." Plenty of reporters saw this act, for almost the whole Vietnam press corps made it to Khe Sanh, and the siege generated enormous attention. According to a tabulation of Vietnam coverage by correspondent Peter Braestrup, during the sixty-day period of February and March 1968 Khe Sanh accounted for thirty-eight percent of all Vietnam stories filed by reporters with the Associated Press, a quarter of the Vietnam clips on TV evening news (for CBS the figure rose to half), and the headlines and lead paragraphs of the Vietnam wrap-up stories in the *New York Times* on seventeen of the sixty days. David Lownds was playing to a big audience.

The 9th Marines had provided the very first infantry combat unit the United States sent to South Vietnam. It was woven into the unit's history that it should always be called upon and would frequently give of itself. First created at Quantico for World War I, the 9th Marines had not made the battlefront in that conflict, serving instead at Guantanamo and in Texas. Reactivated for World War II, the 9th fought in the northern Solomons, Bougainville, Guam, and Iwo Jima. After a second hiatus, it had duty on the China coast at the height of the civil war, including tense missions at Tsingtao and Shanghai. Reactivated once more for Korea (though it never fought there) the 9th became part of the Marine Corps permanent establishment, stationed in Japan after 1953 and on Okinawa from 1956. This regiment provided the Marines sent to Thailand in the Laotian crisis of 1962; for Vietnam in 1965 President Johnson once again called upon it.

Landing at Da Nang, the Marines immediately began to provide security for the major air base there. The 1st Battalion, 9th Marines arrived on June 17, 1965, to replace the unit the regiment had originally sent. Thus that battalion had one of the longest Vietnam histories of any American unit. Time and again the battalion had been sent into harm's way until the men called themselves the "Walking Dead" and others suspected them of being a hard-luck outfit. Its Bravo Company had been at Khe Sanh as garrison in the spring of 1967 and its patrols had run into the NVA and ignited the hill battles. At Con Thien, 1/9 had also been in the thick of the fighting. In fact Bravo Company had had to fight its way out of a massive ambush near Con Thien in July 1967, with only twenty-seven Bravo Marines walking out of the action. The battalion sustained more than three hundred casualties at Con Thien, including nine men missing in action. The nickname began to seem very appropriate.

The move to Khe Sanh on January 22, as was so frequently the case for the reinforcements, came on short notice. "We got the word midmorning of the day we were going to go," recalls Corporal Bert Mullins, a radio man. "It was a fairly bright, sunny day. The word that we were given was that we were going to a place called Khe Sanh and we'd be there a maximum of three days. . . . We went up there pretty light." Corporal Otis H. Glenn, a machine gun squad leader of 1st Platoon, Company B, had a similar experience: "Gunny came down one day and told us to pack up. We got packed up and went back to Camp Evans. The [executive officer] came around and told us we had fifteen minutes, that we're going to war. Nobody didn't know where we was going. Everything was kinda a mix-up." Glenn too got the word they would be out about three days and figured it must be some kind of operation. He would be at Khe Sanh for three months.

Marine records show that 1/9 received its preparation orders at noon, January 22. Lieutenant Colonel John F. Mitchell, battalion commander, planned to move his command group and companies Delta, Alpha, and Bravo in that order, while Charlie Company held the Camp Evans positions between Phu Bai and Hue pending arrival of 2/4, which would be deployed from battalion landing team duty to replace Mitchell's unit. The move began at 2:20 P.M. with the Marines boarding helicopters that had just disgorged civilians being evacuated from the Khe Sanh area.

Khe Sanh had a big helicopter pad located at FOB-3 behind the lines of its Red Sector, the northernmost extension of the combat base, held by Captain Dick Camp's Lima Company of 3/26. Camp noticed a large helicopter formation coming in that afternoon. Marines in full combat gear jumped out, formed up, and marched to the Ponderosa.

They wore towels around their necks. Camp, who had friends in 1/9, knew that was a distinctive badge of the Walking Dead. "The new arrivals were so effective at getting under cover that I didn't see any signs of them until the next morning," he recalled, "when the entire battalion marched up the road leading out to the . . . Rock Quarry."

In fact the Walking Dead had simply flopped down wherever they could for the night. Corporal Mullins, for example, ended up in a concrete bunker being used by one of the 13th Marines artillery units as a fire support coordination center. The main things he remembers were the radios going all night, the coldness of the floor, and the enormous quantity of junk scattered around. When he asked about it, Mullins was told about the ammunition dump fire. Being good Marines, the men of the bunker had scavenged among the debris for anything they thought might ever be needed and now the stuff was waiting to be used.

The morning march was not without its own difficulties. Moving out the main gate, past FOB-3 and Lima Company, the Marines moved north and then west. There was a little confusion. They marched past the Rock Quarry and to the top of a low hill just beyond. There was no way to put an entire battalion on the hill. Colonel Mitchell declared that they must be in the wrong place, and the Walking Dead went back down the hill and finally found the intended destination. Mitchell sent Alpha Company back to the small hill to establish an outpost.

At midafternoon of January 23 Captain John W. Cargile's Charlie Company, the last element of 1/9, arrived at Khe Sanh and was sent to join the rest of the battalion, assuming part of the perimeter defense at Mitchell's main position.

"Those first few nights were very hairy," remembered Lieutenant James R. Talone. "We had no wire; elephant grass was right up to the road; you had approximately ten to fifteen meters of cleared area; one corner of my sector was heavily wooded; we were on high ground looking down into this woods; many, many noises at night; spent many sleepless nights with people hearing things out there." The Marines pitched in to clear fields and lay out wire. Within two weeks, with the aid of a bulldozer, they had cleared a strip a hundred meters wide. Corporal Mullins again:

Everything was in short supply. No one had brought field jackets up there that I can recall because it really wasn't that cold down at Camp

Evans. It was darn cold up there at Khe Sanh. We had brought rain suits and they served to be a real good wind jacket. But other than that things were in real short supply. And, foolish as I was, I didn't even bring my toothbrush up there. . . .

We didn't have any engineer stakes. We didn't have any overheading materials. We didn't have anything up there to really build anywhere near adequate bunkers with. We did get some sandbags up there initially. We used those to build what we could in terms of shelter.

It took three weeks before the Marines received any toothbrushes.

North Vietnamese radio broadcasts made no distinction between their mortars and rockets and "heavy" artillery, asserting that it was the latter that had caused Khe Sanh's ammunition dump fire. Marines knew better, as no doubt did North Vietnamese soldiers. The combat base dug out from the effects of the munitions explosions, and stocks were partly made up with the priority resupply of 200,000 pounds of ordnance on January 23.

The heavy artillery was coming, however, and the Laotians' battle at Ban Houei Sane was only the beginning. Its first use against the Americans was at Hill 881 South later in the day on January 24. Captain Dabney happened to be talking to India Company's gunnery sergeant.

"Skipper," said Gunny De Armond, "I just heard something I haven't heard in a bunch of years."

"What do you mean?" Dabney asked.

"Somebody is firing heavy artillery, and the way my ears are working, it ain't us."

Pandemonium ensued on the hill; Marines practiced their Khe Sanh shuffle to get under cover. Bill Dabney recalls:

I'd never had heavy artillery fired at me, so I didn't really know what to keep listening for; but he had been at the Chosin Reservoir and in the big fighting in Korea, so [the gunny] had some experience with it. I listened more closely and after a while, during these rocket salvos, more or less coincident with them, if you listened very closely you could hear way, way out, to the west, a kind of pop, boom, that sort of thing, and . . . if you listened fifteen, twenty seconds later, over the hill, you'd hear this . . . like a squirrel running through dry leaves.

Well, we reported it . . . down to Khe Sanh by radio. The response we got back initially was, "Oh, they don't have any heavy artillery out there."

Marine records indicate that between 5:30 and 7:10 P.M., beginning on Hill 881 South, the NVA bombarded that hill, 861, and the combat base. The North Vietnamese used rockets, 82mm mortars and 100mm and 152mm guns; the combat base alone received some 250 rounds. In the Red Sector held by Lima Company, where the battalion operations officer had insisted the bunkers be built aboveground, one Marine was killed and four wounded. A 152mm shell left a crater inside which a man could stand and still not see past the lip; it was clear not only that Khe Sanh had to rebuild underground but that no bunker could be proofed against shells of this caliber. One 152mm shell turned out to be a dud. Examination proved beyond any doubt that heavy artillery had come to Khe Sanh.

The worst problem with NVA use of 152mm guns, though their destructive power was great, was their range. The gun was capable of firing four rounds per minute to a range of 17,260 meters, about ten and a half miles. The 130mm gun, introduced later, was even more formidable, firing a 74-pound shell out to 31,000 meters, almost nineteen miles. The heaviest Marine ordnance at Khe Sanh, the 155mm, ranged to 14,955 meters, about nine miles. Thus the U.S. artillery was outranged and the NVA took advantage by emplacing their guns in locations from which they could shell Khe Sanh while being impervious to return fire. The Co Roc massif was one such location, out of range for the heaviest U.S. artillery, the 175mm pieces at Camp Carroll and the Rockpile. Thus counterbattery work was left to air forces.

In view of the rapidly increasing seriousness of the situation, 3rd Marine Division issued new orders following the Hill 861 battle. General Tompkins wanted Lownds to reduce drastically his use of patrols, fearing they could be subject to piecemeal ambush. Tompkins ordered that patrols not be allowed more than five hundred meters outside friendly positions, a decision that brought a virtual end to patrol activity. From Hill 558, 2/26 managed one last patrol in almost company strength to investigate a lower hill to the northwest, an operation that made contact and only confirmed Tompkins's opinions. As for the 3rd Recon, their patrol Frostburg, out to the southeast of the combat base, was scheduled for recovery on January 21 but had to wait three extra days for a helicopter extraction. In the interval the recon patrol saw NVA troops so confident that they were making a road march, carrying their packs and other equipment, right up Route 9.

Frostburg turned out to be the last Marine reconnaissance mission mounted from Khe Sanh before the siege. The recon men stayed on as part of the garrison. Ironically they would suffer more casualties from NVA shelling than they ever had on their patrols.

General Tompkins's decision on patrolling was and would remain controversial. As a young artillery officer, William M. Smith, notes:

> We had no idea what was out there. I would have felt much more secure — and this gets back to its really being a company commander's war. I hate to say it but a lot of the field grades weren't in touch with what was going on. We were having things like guys shot filling sandbags on the lines by sniper fire. All of that could have been precluded by aggressive combat patrols within a reasonable distance that we could support . . . with direct fire weapons from the base. And all of that tunnel-digging activity — it could have been effectively kaboshed. The order not to conduct patrols outside the base I think was absolute foolishness.

Major Jerry Hudson notes, however, that a subsequent attack by 1/9 on Hill 471 captured a diary whose writer, evidently either an NVA company commander or political officer, plaintively and repeatedly asked when the Marines were going to "come out" from their base. The NVA company apparently had been deployed in ambush positions during both the Khe Sanh village attack and the Lang Vei attack. This evidence suggests that General Tompkins was quite right — that the North Vietnamese were ready and waiting for Marine patrols. The one time a patrol went beyond Tompkins's artificial boundary, a clear disaster followed.

Most desirable was to find targets while holding position in the Khe Sanh fortifications. Though this did not exercise the troops, it could boost their morale. The new battalion, 1/9, got a taste of what Khe Sanh's firepower could be like on January 28 when they spotted an odd procession: an NVA vehicle leading groups of elephants, the first of which were carrying mortars. Forward observers called in artillery missions that dispersed the elephants; one took a direct hit on its hindquarters by a 4.2-inch shell. The animal staggered but walked off. Several months later the elephant, which had apparently made it only to the bank of a nearby stream to die, got its revenge: Marines of 1/9 who had not had a bath for months used that stream to bathe, only to discover afterward that upstream of them the water had been flowing through the elephant's rotting carcass.

Two could play at the game of spotting. Marines learned at the morning staff meeting on January 27 that an NVA radio transmission had been intercepted from a North Vietnamese recon unit that reported it was inside a U.S. position. Background noise included the sound of steel sledgehammers hitting engineering stakes. A check revealed that the only place such activity had been taking place was *inside the combat base itself!* Marines redoubled their precautions.

Later that day Khe Sanh received its last major reinforcement, the ARVN 37th Ranger Battalion under Captain Hoang Pho. A regular ranger unit normally assigned to I Corps, the 37th was moved up from Phu Loc. In deciding how to place the new troops Lownds noted that superiors repeatedly commented on how the end of the runway at Khe Sanh extended beyond the defense perimeter. The perimeter here, the Gray Sector, was also disturbingly close to artillery positions and the main ammunition dump. Lownds determined to gain more elbow room by using the 37th Rangers to push out the perimeter another hundred meters, not quite to the end of the runway. Captain Pho was cooperative, though his men were effectively being placed outside the American combat base, as if the Marines did not trust them.

Actually the Marines of Bravo Company, 1/26, who manned the adjacent portions of the American perimeter, soon came to like these Vietnamese with their tiger patches. Kenny Pipes, Bravo's commander, noted that his men "quickly gained a high regard and deep respect for the rangers and their officers." Bravo and the 37th Rangers shared ammunition and kibitzed with one another. Pipes believed that ARVN had able leaders, professional NCOs, and soldiers who were individually brave and dedicated. Marine Ray Strischek similarly recalls:

> Food got scarce and for three to five days (I can't really remember) we went to one C-rat[ion] per day. Well I with my telephone and pliers and a Vietnamese ranger with his carbine and floppy shower shoes aspied some fool dumping what looked like hundreds of cans of C-rats into a barrel. We and the Viet ranger eyed each other, eyed the barrel, and ran for it. We were running along, elbowing each other and laughing. (We didn't know each other.) Apparently neither of us could really believe someone would throw food away. When we got to the barrel it was full of C-rats all right. The Viet ranger picked up a can, I picked up a can. All ham and lima beans. The ranger grunted, cursed and spat, and said "Chit numba Ten Thou." . . . We walked away from Ham and Lima beans. He pulled out some Viet rations; a clear plastic bag, I guess, of

fried fish eyes and minnow like parts. I had a can of fruit cocktail. Couldn't understand a word he said and vice versa. Whatever it was tasted pretty good. We parted friends.

Many such experiences brought men together, closer perhaps than with some of their own buddies. Strischek, for example, learned only months later that a good friend, cocaptain with him of their high school wrestling team, had been at Khe Sanh too, in a bunker only eighteen feet behind his own!

The ARVN Rangers settled in, using trenches begun for them by Marines, which also helped establish some rapport. In addition, as the shelling continued, Marines and corpsmen made nightly trips to the ARVN positions to carry wounded back to the medical area. It did not help the ARVN that they had not been paid in several months or that they never received any replacements to cover their casualties. Just a few days later worries for their families would intrude as the Tet offensive erupted throughout South Vietnam. Ken Pipes wondered if American troops could have done as well under similar circumstances. Captain Pho's men actually planned and conducted a daring daylight raid that netted the first medium recoilless rifle captured during the siege. Pipes, for one, concludes, "It was a privilege to have served with officers and men of such an outstanding allied unit."

Hoang Pho sent some of his rangers out on patrol on the morning of January 29. Toward noon an unidentified voice came up on the Rangers' radio frequency to say, in a northern Vietnamese accent, that they had the ARVN patrol in sight but would refrain from firing because of the imminent Tet holiday, suggesting that the patrol return to its lines. The ARVN troopers changed their radio frequency instead. Late the next afternoon the rangers spotted an NVA platoon-size or larger force on the move to the northeast and opened fire with 60mm and 81mm mortars. Such action was permissible because South Vietnamese and U.S. authorities had earlier canceled the planned Tet cease-fire.

The North Vietnamese continued their shelling every day, sometimes more, sometimes less, but always just enough to interrupt sleep, to harass, to start the gnawing fear. On January 30 they scored again, during the noon hour, when one of a barrage of rockets ignited a fire among a stack of damaged high-explosive projectiles in the main ammunition dump. A repeat of the disastrous munitions fire threatened.

Sheltering from the barrage in their bunker were the members of the airfield crash crew, including Master Sergeant George J. Edwards, Sergeant Sittner, and Gunnery Sergeant Donald H. McIntyre. Suddenly Sergeant Jesus R. Vasquez burst into the bunker to tell them of the fire. Without time to consult their commander, Major John Havlik, the men rushed to prevent the dump fire from getting out of hand. They were joined by more of the crash crew: Lieutenant Eugene L. Keiter, Corporal Gregory W. Zemanek, Lance Corporal Glenn D. Pike, Master Gunnery Sergeant John P. Driver, and Corporal Paul R. Carmean, Jr. Firefighters and explosives disposal men, these Marines averted what could have become a tragedy. Vasquez was wounded, along with Keiter, Driver, McIntyre, Pike, and Zemanek. Driver tried to save Vasquez by applying a tourniquet to his mangled arm, but he died later. Vasquez won a posthumous Navy Cross, while Driver and Edwards received Bronze Stars.

Though the allied command canceled its Tet cease-fire, the North Vietnamese seem to have observed it, at least at Khe Sanh. At the hour it would have taken effect, the NVA dropped six 60mm mortar rounds into the combat base and then the guns fell silent. The calm at Khe Sanh belied the storm throughout Vietnam, at MACV, and in Washington.

"I Don't Want Any Damn Dinbinphoo!"

William Westmoreland was worried, not so much about the North Vietnamese and whether they were mounting a feint but about whether his own superiors would permit him to fight a battle at Khe Sanh. That was the basic meaning that lay behind Westmoreland's remarks at the morning staff meeting on January 20, when he talked about "solidarity" against pressures to abandon Khe Sanh. The comment must have seemed cryptic to many, at least to those who did not know the avenues by which MACV and the Joint Chiefs of Staff managed the Vietnam war.

Westmoreland knew there was a problem not because of any message from the White House or President Johnson, not from any complaint from Secretary McNamara, but from his private, back-channel cable traffic with Joint Chiefs chairman General Earle Wheeler. Whenever there was a problem, even frequently when there was not, when he simply wished to apprise field commanders of impending matters, Wheeler's custom was to fire off "eyes only" back-channel messages. He could warn on the back channel and then inform in a routine cable, or solicit answers privately and then ask the questions on the front channel. The system was convenient and confidential.

Despite the decisions made in December to fight at Khe Sanh, Westmoreland learned in the second week of January that two differing views of Khe Sanh permeated Washington. Wheeler described the views in a cable on January 11. Only one corresponded to the view Westmoreland held — that a battle could be turned to American advantage. The opposing view held that the United States ought to withdraw from Khe Sanh while it still could without much public notice. Wheeler attributed this view to "non-military quarters" around Washington. In his return cable Westy thundered, "I regard the non-military expressions as tantamount to desperation tactics on the one hand, and defeat on the other." The exchange served notice to the MACV commander that things were not quite what they seemed — Washington's support for his battle was shallow and tentative.

Thus there was an important element of relief for Westmoreland at the defection of the NVA officer and then the attacks on the hills and the village. These events in effect fulfilled his predictions and confirmed, for him, that the battle would take the course he had ordained. Late in the afternoon of January 21 he reported to Wheeler and Admiral Sharp in Hawaii: "The anticipated enemy attack on Khe Sanh was initiated last evening. . . . There is a buildup north of the DMZ and . . . west of Quang Tri. The next several weeks are destined to be active."

General Westmoreland sent his deputy to III MAF to visit General Cushman and assess the situation at Da Nang. On January 22 Westy dispatched an "eyes only" cable of his own outlining his assessment of the presumed NVA campaign plans for the winter and spring. Feeling that the North Vietnamese were going to mount a major effort in Quang Tri or Thua Thien, the MACV commander wrote of the adversary: "He has made determined attempts to gain a spectacular victory, and is now preparing for another attempt in northern First Corps. I believe that the enemy sees a similarity between our base at Khe Sanh and Dien Bien Phu and hopes, by following a pattern of activity similar to that used against the French, to gain similar military and political ends." Later that day, while reporting the NVA assault on the district headquarters in Khe Sanh village, Westmoreland's cable noted, "These actions were probably preliminary to a full-scale attack."

The reports, speculations, and warnings were accompanied by a growing stream of comment from Westmoreland warning of an even larger-scale purpose that Hanoi might have. The MACV commander began to predict that just prior to or just after Tet the adversary might attack Da Nang and Quang Tri city, and they might launch a multibattalion assault on the imperial city of Hue.

At Saigon Westmoreland and Ambassador Bunker huddled on January 24 to discuss the Tet cease-fire as well as the NIAGARA air operations around Khe Sanh. The MACV commander and the ambassador recommended that, at least in I Corps, the cease-fire be canceled. Westy preferred countrywide action but settled for the narrower cancellation. His continued focus on Khe Sanh, however, vitiated wider concerns. For example, after warning of a number of possible attack targets throughout South Vietnam, on January 25 Westmoreland declared that the Khe Sanh situation was critical and could represent the turning point of the Vietnam war.

This is not the place to recount the story of the Tet offensive, which began when some Viet Cong and NVA units prematurely launched attacks on January 30. On the night of January 31 massive attacks followed all over the country, *except* at Khe Sanh, where the guns remained strangely silent. By then the cease-fire had been canceled and American and ARVN troops were reacting as best they could, largely preventing the VC from gaining their military objectives. Even then, at the height of Tet, William Westmoreland would not allow himself to be distracted. A press release that he prepared (but did not use) on January 31 contains this revealing language: "The enemy is attempting to confuse the issue. . . . I suspect he is also trying to draw everyone's attention away from the greatest area of threat, the northern part of I Corps. Let me caution everyone not to be confused."

The man to be influenced by all the back-channel maneuvers was the president of the United States. Lyndon Baines Johnson closely followed the events in Southeast Asia, managing the war through his Tuesday lunches. Copies of most major cables routinely went to the White House. Johnson remained attentive to Vietnam events and kept his first team on top of the situation. Thus the president, his national security adviser, the adviser's military assistant, and the National Security Council staff man for Vietnam were all intimately aware of the run up to the Tet offensive, the doubts and beliefs of MACV, and the general progress of preparations at Khe Sanh.

Closest to the situation among the White House people were the president's special military assistant and the national security adviser's military aide. Johnson's special military assistant was none other than General Maxwell Taylor, who had been brought back to the White House after completing his stint as ambassador to South Vietnam. Taylor was retired and served in a civilian capacity as an overseer of the military. LBJ constantly sought out Taylor for commentaries on Vietnam strategies — from bombing plans to military interface with negotiations to strictly military questions.

The military aide to Walt Rostow, the president's national security adviser, was Brigadier General Robert Neville Ginsburgh. An Air Force officer who had started out in the Army, graduating from West Point in 1944 and then officers' basic training on D-day, Ginsburgh had won a Silver Star as an artillery observer with the 89th Division in the race across the Rhine. He switched to the Air Force after his father went over in 1947, and both enjoyed rapid promotions in the new service. Ginsburgh had gotten a graduate degree at Harvard and had served with Earle Wheeler on the NATO command staff for southern Europe and with the air staff in Washington.

When Walt Rostow headed the policy planning council at the State Department and insisted that the Pentagon send him a capable and talented military aide, they gave him Ginsburgh. When Rostow went on to the White House as national security adviser, Ginsburgh remained at State until Colonel Robert C. Bowman, military aide to the security adviser, came to the end of his tour, and then Rostow brought Ginsburgh over to the White House. Wheeler, now chairman of the Joint Chiefs of Staff, thought Ginsburgh could be his own liaison officer to Rostow. The arrangement worked very well throughout the last three years of the Johnson administration. Ginsburgh had weekly private meetings with Wheeler and similar sessions with Rostow two or three times a day.

Though Ginsburgh might be liaison to Wheeler, his boss remained Walt Rostow. The fifty-one-year-old Rostow, an economist by profession, had been in the national security business since John Kennedy brought him to Washington in 1961. Rostow had first served Kennedy as deputy national security adviser and then moved to the policy planning job, which he had held for more than four years, quietly advising Secretary of State Dean Rusk and coming to LBJ's attention through his seeming ability to produce new ideas for the president at the drop of a hat. Rostow was no military expert, though he did know something about bombing, having spent the latter portion of World War II in London working with an OSS office that advised on targeting policy. As Johnson's national security adviser Rostow had been most active on Vietnam bombing policy, though he did not hesitate to comment, often on the basis of advice from Ginsburgh, on other subjects.

Rostow, Ginsburgh, and Wheeler had all gotten involved at the beginning of the discussions about Khe Sanh and Tet. Since December 1967 they had been exchanging cables and memos, with one another and with Bunker and Westmoreland, about North Vietnamese strategy, expectations of an offensive, and plans to defend Khe Sanh. Once Westmoreland reported the initial NVA attacks on Hill 861, Washington's expectations went up another notch. Westmoreland's phraseology — the "anticipated" attack — and his prediction that the next several weeks were destined to be active ones certainly encouraged this response. So did his comment that the Khe Sanh fight could herald a turning point. White House expectations soared higher still.

Where General Wheeler had the background and experience to interpret the MACV cables, not to mention the back-channel knowledge of what they would say and why, White House understanding had to be based on the literal content. Only Ginsburgh and Taylor were military men. The NSC staff specialist for Southeast Asia, Bill Jorden, had been seconded from State and was in fact a reporter by trade. Rostow was a generalist. Lyndon Johnson, the most interested spectator, worried about the approaching attacks but kept his own counsel.

Johnson had reason to worry. Not only the press but even Westmoreland and Wheeler were making liberal use of the Dien Bien Phu analogy, and LBJ had had a central role in that earlier episode of Vietnam's history. Then Senator Johnson had been minority leader when the Eisenhower administration had wanted to intervene to help the French at Dien Bien Phu. Examination of LBJ's personal papers for that era demonstrates conclusively that he had accepted at face value many of Eisenhower's arguments for the intervention and had repeated them in his own constituent newsletters. LBJ's mail had run nine to one against such an intervention. As many as fifty-seven of his constituents had signed one of the letters. Despite his inclination to go along with the Eisenhower administration, LBJ had turned away when it developed that the scheme lacked allied backing and had not been thought through.

Lyndon Johnson remembered Dien Bien Phu. In 1965, when he had begun his first full term as president and stood on the verge of making a major commitment of American ground troops to Vietnam, Under Secretary of State George Ball effectively raised questions in the president's mind by referring to the French experience. McGeorge Bundy, then Johnson's national security adviser, had felt compelled to assemble a memorandum, one of the longest he ever gave the president, specifically rejecting the Dien Bien Phu analogy for the Vietnam commitment. Now, less than three years later, Westmoreland was preparing to fight a battle everyone said looked just like Dien Bien Phu.

"I don't want any damn Dinbinphoo," rasped Johnson.

The president was concerned and he expressed his preferences, but he supported his military commanders and the men in the field. LBJ met with the Joint Chiefs of Staff on January 29 to make sure they were prepared for battle. Contrary to previously published accounts, President Johnson did *not* insist that the Joint Chiefs make promises signed in blood that Khe Sanh would be held. LBJ may have bragged later that he had such promises and used that phrase, but the truth is rather more prosaic: Johnson never said anything about getting a promise from the Joint Chiefs. Rather, aware of the president's concerns, Walt Rostow and Bob Ginsburgh spoke to Earle Wheeler; they told the chairman how desirable it would be to have some statement on record from Wheeler about Khe Sanh. Wheeler volunteered to make it a statement from all the chiefs. He went back to the Tank, the famed JCS conference room at the Pentagon, and came up with a suitable document.

The document, titled "The Situation at Khe Sanh" (JCSM-63-68), was prepared in Wheeler's office on January 29 (Washington date), the day the Tet offensive began. Wheeler signed it "for the Joint Chiefs of Staff"; it was not in fact signed by anyone else. Far from a promise "signed in blood" that Khe Sanh would be held, JCSM-63-68 states simply that "the Joint Chiefs of Staff have reviewed the situation at Khe Sanh and concur with General Westmoreland's assessment. . . . They recommend that we maintain our position at Khe Sanh." The bulk of the Joint Chiefs' memo, in fact, consists of Wheeler reporting his telephone conversation with Westmoreland (only about five hours before the initial Tet attacks) in which the MACV commander recited his many preparations for battle at Khe Sanh and gave his judgment that the United States could and should hold the place, insisting that "everyone is confident" and that "this is an opportunity to inflict a severe defeat upon the enemy." Wheeler further improves upon Westmoreland's statements by recalling MACV's cable of January 12 that had supplied reasons why the Khe Sanh position was important.

Within forty-eight hours the situation changed greatly, not because of anything that happened at Khe Sanh but because the onset of the Tet offensive engulfed Washington. The morning of the fighting at the U.S. embassy in Saigon, January 31 (Saigon date), Rostow went so far as to call Saigon directly for news. Wheeler evidently became enraged at this foray outside the chain of command and Rostow felt obliged to apologize later. The next night, when Wheeler, Rostow, and LBJ were conferring in the White House Situation Room, by mutual agreement they sent Ginsburgh out to call Westmoreland for more news.

As the Tet offensive began and built to a crescendo, Washington waited breathlessly for the other shoe to drop. That shoe was the assault on Khe Sanh. The Situation Room went on round-the-clock shifts, with at least one senior official, either Rostow, Ginsburgh, or Situation Room director Art McCafferty, present at all times. On the evening of February 2 LBJ called General Wheeler for news, bypassing his own NSC staff, and asking Wheeler to send up a written Khe Sanh report. Wheeler complied and inaugurated a series of daily secure transpacific telephone conversations with Westmoreland on which he based the Khe Sanh report. Rostow found it so useful he asked Wheeler to send reports every day.

President Johnson was not a mere observer. LBJ asked specific questions and sought particular answers. On February 1 Wheeler cabled Westmoreland with one set of the president's inquiries. Johnson wanted to find out what the MACV reinforcement capability would be if bad weather closed in once the NVA had begun the assault. Wheeler had argued that MACV possessed substantial helicopter assets and that reinforcements would not be a problem. Westmoreland seconded Wheeler's argument, adding that the United States had additional artillery outside the immediate battle zone that could "reinforce" Khe Sanh by fire, much greater capacity for aerial resupply than the French had had at Dien Bien Phu, and air support assets greater by "orders of magnitude."

All this was reassuring for a president who had told General

Wheeler he did not want anyone coming to him after the battle claiming it would all have turned out better if the military had only had this or that. Westmoreland seemed properly reassuring. But what the MACV commander appeared to give in one hand, he simultaneously took away with the other.

In a cable he sent General Westmoreland and Admiral Sharp on February 1, a different "eyes only" cable than the one just mentioned, Wheeler informed his theater and field commanders that there was "a considerable amount of discussion around town" comparing Khe Sanh to Dien Bien Phu, most delicately with respect to nuclear weapons planning. Though Wheeler himself considered the use of nuclear weapons an unlikely eventuality, some thought had apparently been given to the matter at the Pentagon. The Joint Chiefs chairman now solicited "your views as to whether there are targets in the area which lend themselves to nuclear strikes, whether some contingency nuclear planning would be in order, and what you consider to be some of the more significant pros and cons." Wheeler explicitly acknowledged that MACV might have to "put a few of your bright planners on this" issue.

Westmoreland writes in his memoirs that this query came about as a result of a question LBJ asked Wheeler on the telephone about whether he might be faced with any decision regarding nuclear weapons. The Wheeler cable, however, contains no reference to the president or any such query, whereas his cable about reinforcements and weather does. It is more likely that Wheeler's cable resulted from planning recommendations at the Pentagon or from congressional inquiries.

In any case, Westmoreland's formal reply to the question of nuclear weapons, rendered breezily the very next day, was that the United States ought to consider weapons of greater effectiveness. Carefully Westmoreland cabled that "the use of nuclear weapons should not be required in the present situation." But that did not preclude them. "Should the situation in the DMZ area change dramatically, we should be prepared to introduce weapons of greater effectiveness against massed forces. Under such circumstances I visualize that either tactical nuclear weapons or chemical agents should be active candidates for employment." At MACV the general formed a small planning group to study the question.

Westmoreland writes in retrospect that because the region around the combat base was "virtually uninhabited," civilian casualties from nuclear weapons would have been minimal. If Washington was so intent upon sending a signal to Hanoi, "surely" nuclear weapons could convey it.

Though it is not clear that Westmoreland was an enthusiast for nuclear attack, from his cable it is apparent that he certainly was not ruling it out. That attitude must have jarred Lyndon Johnson and robbed Westmoreland's cable of the reassuring effect he presumably had intended it to have. The president may have discussed nuclear weapons with his top advisers at a White House meeting on February 9, the day LBJ had his press secretary put out a statement that no *recommendations* had been received for the use of nuclear weapons in Vietnam.

On February 9 the issue became public as a result of a question put to Dean Rusk during testimony before the Senate Foreign Relations Committee. Rusk denied the existence of any plans for nuclear use or of stockpiles of nuclear weapons in Vietnam. The question had been put by Senator J. William Fulbright and reportedly was based on an anonymous phone call to his committee's offices. Today Fulbright, who suffered a stroke in late 1989, is unable to say whether he had more specific suspicions than this anonymous tip.

The White House denial of February 9 seems clearly intended to reinforce the Rusk testimony. A few days later, however, Earle Wheeler sounded a more sour note when he refused to go beyond saying he did not *think* nuclear weapons would be *required*. This, like Westmoreland's cabled opinion, represented the narrowest possible basis for reply, in effect a gambit to keep the option open. Westmoreland defended himself later to researcher Colonel William Y. Schandler, saying that he had been worried about the uncommitted NVA forces in the north and the possibility of a mass attack across the DMZ. Wheeler's opinion may have been similarly based. In any case the episode once more illustrates Westmoreland's uncommon sensitivity over the DMZ.

Lyndon Johnson himself took a hand in the effort to dampen speculation at his news conference on February 16. "The President must make the decision to deploy nuclear weapons," Johnson said, insisting that he had never been given a recommendation about deploying nuclear weapons. "No recommendation has been made to me," LBJ declared once more. "Beyond that, I think we ought to put an end to that discussion."

It is instructive that President Johnson too was capable of narrowly focused commentaries. On February 16, 1968, his key words were "deployment" and "recommendation." *Deployment* of nuclear weapons in Vietnam was not at issue; *use* was. Similarly, a recommendation exists at the presidential level only when it has reached the president, but that does not necessarily mean that none was in the works. Lyndon Johnson may have been speaking with great care that day. It is suspicious that as late as the 1980s, when private think tanks were preparing studies for a Pentagon history of nuclear decisions, a paper on nuclear weapons at Khe Sanh, prepared from open sources, was promptly classified by responsible authorities.

The authors personally believe that President Johnson had no intention of using nuclear weapons at Khe Sanh but we are unable to demonstrate this from presently available evidence. This continues to be a mystery of Khe Sanh.

One of the more lurid bits of rumor that appeared as news during these fervid days in Washington was that President Johnson wanted to quash all nuclear weapons activities in South Vietnam and accordingly sent out a secret mission composed of four scientists, including Richard L. Garwin, a noted nuclear weapons specialist. Reporters probably picked up on Garwin's name and then added it up wrong. There was a scientific mission, Garwin was on it, as a member of the Defense Science Board, but it had nothing to do with nuclear weapons. The scientists were visiting Vietnam to assay progress on DYE MARKER, the strong point obstacle system to protect the DMZ, and its Laotian electronic extension. They had in fact been prevented from landing at Tan Son Nhut Airport in Saigon by the fighting there at the outset of the Tet offensive and had had to divert to Thailand. That was at the end of January, before the nuclear question had arisen, so Lyndon Johnson could not have sent them on such a nuclear quest.

Incidentally, the scientists' impression during their visit was that General Westmoreland remained wholly committed to DYE MARKER.

Meanwhile Lyndon Johnson began other efforts to reassure himself regarding Khe Sanh at the end of January, when he summoned Maxwell Taylor and gave the general orders to monitor the situation. Taylor's activities would have consequences we shall see later.

President Johnson made one command decision affecting the impending battle at this time: permitting the use at Khe Sanh of so-called controlled fragmentation (COFRAM) munitions, shells and grenades, some containing submunitions, that exploded with very lethal high fragmentation effects. COFRAM was very hush-hush, "special compartmented information" to the security specialists, and not for foreign knowledge. David Lownds, though a full colonel in the Marine Corps, knew practically nothing about COFRAM, which had been given highest national priority in a national security action memorandum in 1967. On January 12, 1968, almost as an afterthought in a cable arguing against any withdrawal from Khe Sanh, Westmoreland had asked for permission to use COFRAM in the battle. The request was unusual in that COFRAM ordnance stocks in Southeast Asia were far below the levels the logistics people considered necessary for use. LBJ decided to allow it anyway.

Meanwhile the White House Situation Room was on full alert, a measure that had not been taken for Tet. President Johnson was apt to call downstairs for the latest information at any hour of the day or night; sometimes he even came down himself, looking haggard and gray. The night shift tried to meet LBJ's thirst for information by feeding it to him before he called.

Bob Ginsburgh had the watch on Sunday, February 4, when he sent up three memos to the president. Reaching for a proper historical comparison to still LBJ's qualms, Ginsburgh selected D-day:

> As we wait for some word of what may be happening at Khe Sanh, it helps to remember that these are always trying periods for Commanders (or Commanders-in-Chief).
>
> General Eisenhower, after refusing to allow Prime Minister Churchill to accompany the D-Day invasion forces expressed his thoughts: "Nevertheless my sympathies were with the Prime Minister. Again I had to endure the interminable wait that always intervenes between the final decision of the high command and the earliest possible determination of success or failure."

The metaphor of the invasion of northwest Europe in 1944, clearly one of the major if not *the* major U.S. combat action of World War II, suggests that at Washington as much as in Saigon, it was Khe Sanh and not Tet that was considered the key contest. The alert posture of the Situation Room conveys the same impression.

It could hardly be otherwise, for William Westmoreland had repeatedly informed Washington that he saw Khe Sanh as the culmination of Hanoi's multiphase campaign. At the same time the MACV commander had done everything he could to prepare a battle of annihilation at Khe Sanh such as Vietnam had never seen. In short, Westmoreland had determined that Khe Sanh was going to be the most important battle of the war. If he was lucky, after it was over he would be allowed to invade Laos to crown the achievement.

At the White House, Bob Ginsburgh did not have such a grand vision, but he tried to analyze for LBJ why the NVA had not yet begun their assault on the combat base (because of the success of U.S. bombing or of an intention to synchronize with a further round of attacks on South Vietnam's cities). Ginsburgh also sent up the latest reports from the National Military Command Center on the battle for Hill 861-A, where the North Vietnamese *were* fighting that night. "We might expect the battle for Khe Sanh to start," he informed President Johnson, "within the next three days."

"To Prompt Me to Consider Resigning"

William Westmoreland reports that during all his time as Commander, U.S. Military Assistance Command Vietnam, there was just one matter contentious enough "to prompt me to consider resigning." That concerned an important aspect of U.S. preparations for Khe Sanh, the command and control over air support assets. This matter was stalled at CINCPAC, where Admiral Sharp had refused to go ahead with the centralized arrangement Westmoreland desired, so MACV proceeded at first with a less ambitious scheme to improve coordination between Marine and Air Force units.

Representatives from General William W. Momyer's 7th Air Force met with Marine air officers at Da Nang on January 22. The conferees agreed on the Marine geographical delineation of the area around Khe Sanh into air zones and accepted that Marine air assets, actually ten squadrons of strike aircraft in the III MAF command, would concentrate in the strike zones closest to Khe Sanh, preserving the integrity of the Marine air-ground team concept. This decision much favored Major General Norman J. Anderson of the 1st Marine Air Wing who, Westmoreland thought, had become very emotional on the issue. In addition all strikes in the close-in air zone, whether run by Marine aircraft or not, were to be cleared through the Khe Sanh fire support control center and directed either by a Marine tactical air controller or an Air Force forward air controller. The Khe Sanh center was also to review all strikes plotted into zones where air and artillery might collide. General Momyer was placated in that the January 22 agreement provided for a new link between the Marine control network and 7th Air Force through a C-130 airborne battlefield command and control center.

The ink was barely dry on the agreement when Westmoreland went to I Corps on January 23 to visit the 1st Cavalry Division (Airmobile), almost always called "the Cav" in Vietnam, which had just redeployed two of its brigades to new operating areas west of Hue. At division headquarters Westy learned that these Army troops were having difficulties obtaining air support and that they had no direct communications link with the Marine air control network, which had a control center barely a kilometer away. Moreover, Marine General Anderson had not even visited the Cav to ascertain their needs. Westmoreland went on to Hue/Phu Bai where he hit the ceiling: "Needless to say," he recounts, "I raised hell about this situation and reminded [III MAF commander] Cushman of my conversation with him," the discussion of January 19 regarding aerial cooperation for NIAGARA.

Meanwhile the air people swung into the firepower phase of the SLAM operation NIAGARA. Westmoreland instructed Cushman to have Lownds confine his patrols to close-in security, giving the aircraft an open field of play. Westmoreland thought the command arrangements "not optimum nor fully practical." Furthermore, "during the days and weeks that followed, there was a general erosion of the arrangements." Some 7th Air Force staffers complained that the Marine air zones put too much emphasis on geography, were too rigid. General Momyer complained that just as his own aircraft could be "fragged" to any force requiring air strikes throughout South Vietnam, Marine planes should also be available for these missions. Conversely, strike aircraft should be able to hit targets anywhere around Khe Sanh as required, not be restricted by Marine arrangements. Operational commanders groused that Marine pilots were ignoring instructions from the C-130 flying command posts. There was bound to be more trouble.

Despite their command impediments, air forces were doing work vital to the men on the ground at Khe Sanh. Indeed, one of the NSC staff explanations to President Johnson for why the North Vietnamese assault had not already begun was precisely that the success of the air attacks had set the NVA back. The pattern was established early and continued from day to day: almost three hundred fighter-bomber sorties plus thirty-odd from the heavy B-52s would blast known or suspected North Vietnamese positions.

Bare statistics hardly convey the impact of the air effort, but they do give an idea of the weight of Khe Sanh in U.S. strategy. Over the length of the siege, 7th Air Force fighter-bombers flew 9,691 sorties into the Khe Sanh area and delivered 14,223 tons of bombs, rockets, and other munitions. Planes of the 1st Marine Air Wing flew 7,078 sorties and loosed 17,015 tons of ordnance. Air support from naval aircraft depended on the weather and tactical situation over North Vietnam, for most Navy planes were fragged for missions there, diverted only when conditions were unsuitable or special orders were in effect. Nevertheless, Navy planes made 5,337 sorties into the Khe Sanh area with 7,941 tons of munitions. Then there were the ARC LIGHT B-52s from Guam and Utapao in Thailand. These bombers flew 2,548 sorties but delivered a staggering 59,542 tons of ordnance. Only 881, or about a third, of the B-52 sorties were flown before mid-February. Thus the bombing was being considered effective long before it had reached its apex of destructiveness.

Summarized differently, tactical aircraft delivered 39,179 tons against the 59,542 brought by B-52s. That amounted to almost 1,300 tons of bombs around Khe Sanh, the equivalent of a 1.3-kiloton tactical nuclear weapon, *every day of the siege.* Allied aircraft were delivering approximately five tons of bombs for every one of the 20,000 NVA soldiers initially estimated to be in the Khe Sanh area, or more than 15 tons per man measured against roughly 6,450 Marines and ARVN troops in the garrison. This was indeed a cascade of bombs.

Despite its massive weight the bombing was by no means blind or indiscriminate, though the target criteria seem to have been stretched on occasion. Strikes were targeted on the basis of reports from patrols on the ground, aerial photography, radio intelligence, visual sightings, and a variety of electronic sensors. Forward air controllers provided immediate targeting for tactical aircraft, the ARC LIGHT strikes were approved directly by Westmoreland on the basis of strike recommendations fed up the chain of command or studied and originated by a special staff at MACV. The special staff, called the Khe Sanh Red

Watch, worked around the clock in a small plot room next to West-moreland's own conference room.

According to Army Lieutenant Bruce E. Jones, an intelligence specialist for I Corps assigned to the Khe Sanh Red Watch on January 20, the staff were told MACV intended to put more tons of explosives around Khe Sanh than had been used in all of World War II. That proved an exaggeration but the effort was nonetheless quite substantial. The Red Watch had a quota of sorts to fulfill — to provide targets for a cell of three B-52s every ninety minutes. No doubt in the interest of operational flexibility, this was later changed to six every three hours. It was in meeting the quotas, as always in Vietnam, that the criteria were fudged. On one occasion the major in charge of the staff plotted an ARC LIGHT strike on a footpath crossing a stream, calling it an indicator of troop concentrations. Another time a strike would be plotted when the sole observed target was a single machine gun nest.

Other raids benefited from very good or at least very suggestive intelligence. One of the most notable, the biggest ARC LIGHT strike of the war until that time, occurred as a result of radio intelligence. Intercept stations had detected an unusually large volume of radio transmissions from one source, and direction finding indicated a location just across the Laotian border near Khe Sanh. At Saigon, MACV intelligence became convinced the radio source represented a major headquarters, perhaps that of the putative Khe Sanh front, perhaps with Giap personally in command. General Westmoreland approved a major air strike.

The Red Watch staff plotted every target it could find near the radio source but could not use up all the B-52 loads on its available list. The men were called back for another targeting session. Jones suggested that the target be hit a second time; that became the strike plan. The Air Force balked at being asked to hit the same target twice, but finally Major General Selmon W. Wells, commanding the 3rd Air Division, accepted the assignment. ARC LIGHT went in with thirty-six B-52s in a morning strike, followed by nine that night.

A number of sources, both official monographs and popular histories, confirm that the big headquarters strike occurred on January 30. It was judged highly successful: the radio emissions stopped. However, William Westmoreland wrote (dictated) the following passage in the memorandum for the record where he describes his January 24 meeting with Ellsworth Bunker, in which he briefed the ambassador on the progress of NIAGARA: "I reported to him that the firepower phase had started and I thought we had located *and inflicted great damage on* the control headquarters in Laos, which could conceivably be manned by Giap, or at least his representative." This contemporary record suggests the headquarters strike occurred earlier than has previously been disclosed.

Meanwhile tactical air conducted a headquarters strike of its own that it could brag about. Confirming the suspicions of a number of people after the NVA takeover of Khe Sanh village, on January 24 an unidentified source reported seeing a flag with three stars flying from the district headquarters building. Another time an American prisoner was conducted to the village to what he felt was a headquarters because of the large number of NVA officers scurrying about. The key indicator, however, again resulted from radio intelligence, this time from FOB-3, which also housed a detachment of an Army radio research unit.

Larry Henderson, a MACVSOG officer who retired from the Army as a colonel, recalls the day two of his men were monitoring the NVA radio frequencies and identified one emitter as a command post. Suddenly a North Vietnamese on the radio reported they were being attacked by helicopter gunships. The FOB men contacted the helicopter flight leader and discovered that the gunships were shooting at the district headquarters. Then FOB contacted Khe Sanh command with the find. The reaction came quite rapidly: "They went in there with A-4s. They put a massive amount of air strikes in there and he [the NVA emitter] just went off the air."

Henderson believes it was a regimental headquarters that was destroyed.

Whatever the case, something happened that stirred up the North Vietnamese. On February 7 American sensors detected six hostile aircraft, including transport types that could hold up to twenty passengers, over the Khe Sanh area. One of the planes appeared to have parachuted its people, the others turned back. General Momyer had an air strike run against Tchepone, the apparent destination, the next morning. Later Momyer phoned Westmoreland and reported that the NVA men on the transports "may have been replacements for staff members lost at headquarters hit previously."

Though it is fascinating to speculate on the effects of the headquarters strikes, these apparently did not prevent the North Vietnamese Army from prosecuting operations around Khe Sanh. In fact, the very day the Americans detected the transport planes, before replacement staff could have arrived and begun to accomplish any useful work, the NVA soldiers on the ground fought their biggest battle yet.

Some of the best intelligence supporting the air strikes would come from fields of electronic sensors sown around Khe Sanh in a plan originally developed under General Alfred Starbird for the Laotian extension of the McNamara Line. At a staff meeting on January 13 Westmoreland had asked the 7th Air Force to study sensor employment near the combat base. The MACV commander returned to the subject at a meeting a week later and also inquired about the anti-personnel Gravel mines. Westmoreland soon ordered emplacement of the sensors.

At this time the sensor system had been active for about six weeks along the Ho Chi Minh Trail, its intended point of deployment, and specialists were just beginning to learn how to use the equipment. In charge of the array was Task Force Alpha, a unit at Nakhon Phanom in Thailand under Air Force Brigadier General William P. McBride, working under the code name DUTCH MILL. Upon receiving MACV orders to employ sensors at Khe Sanh, McBride took his intelligence officer, Colonel William L. Walker, and made a quick trip to Dong Ha to confer with General Tompkins of the 3rd Marine Division. The DUTCH MILL specialists tried to describe the sensor system, point out its advantages, and tell the Marines what their center could do for Khe Sanh.

In the MUSCLE SHOALS system, sensors emplaced in the area broadcast their readings of troop movements to a repeater aircraft, a modified EC-121, that forwarded them to the DUTCH MILL integration and interpretation center. Because the readings were being broadcast, they could be monitored at Khe Sanh, which would be the focal point for the Marines' own effort. The 3rd Division detached an officer from its intelligence staff to work with the sensor system. DUTCH MILL would help Khe Sanh interpret the sensor data and provide warning of attacks by groups of a hundred or more North Vietnamese.

Though a variety of sensors were used for MUSCLE SHOALS, the two main types were acoustic (Acoubuoy) and seismic (ADSID). Acoubuoy used a converted Navy antisubmarine device from which the hydrophone had been removed, replaced by a sensitive microphone that passed on the actual sounds around it. The ADSID (for "air delivered seismic intrusion device") was a miniature seismometer capable of recording minute vibrations. Measures were taken to filter out random noises; the signal was not activated, for example, unless there were four steps recorded within six seconds. The explosions of Gravel mines would also activate the devices. Whenever the sensors were activated their data, code-named SPOTLIGHT, would be repeated to the target information officer at Khe Sanh and DUTCH MILL.

Sensor emplacement for MUSCLE SHOALS began on January 20 when CH-3 helicopters of the 21st Helicopter Squadron dropped the first ADSIDs. Colonel Walker of DUTCH MILL had estimated that about 250 sensors would be required to seed the Khe Sanh area; of these 104 were emplaced north and west of the combat base in just the first two days. The emplacement missions benefited from data developed from soil samples previously gathered by Marines of the 3rd Reconnaissance Battalion. By the end of January Navy and Air Force aircraft had flown 72 sorties to drop 44 strings totaling 316 sensors in nine arrays or modules. In just the first ten days, acoustic sensors were activated 105,007 times and seismic ones 197,501 times; there were 52,356 assessments performed by DUTCH MILL computers, and Khe Sanh selected 99 targets based on the SPOTLIGHT data.

The first big problem with the MUSCLE SHOALS sensor array was that the readouts could have no meaning unless the position of each sensor was known with a great deal of precision. The sensors could record information accurate to within ten meters of their locations. But officers plotting the data discovered that the locations could be off by as much as two hundred to a thousand meters. Originally the sensors were equipped with an additional seismic device that was supposed to alert the inserting aircraft when the sensor penetrated the earth below, enabling crews to plot the locations of the sensors. The shock of impact, however, frequently disabled these devices. Later, crews simply pitched an additional acoustic device out the door as the sensor was released to provide location information. As the days passed, photographic intelligence and radio direction finding furnished more precise location data.

Learning to use the SPOTLIGHT data properly was a second problem central to the Khe Sanh target information officer, Captain Mirza Munir Baig. He had been clandestine intelligence coordinator for the division before this special assignment to the combat base. He knew nothing about MUSCLE SHOALS at first but arrived with four assumptions in mind: that the NVA would invest Khe Sanh in accordance with a master plan prepared by someone other than the field force conducting the siege; that the NVA commander on location would not be able to modify this plan to any significant degree; that the North Vietnamese modus operandi would be predictable; and that the plan would reflect the classic siege tactics of Dien Bien Phu, as modified by NVA experience at Con Thien during the fall of 1967. Baig applied this analytical framework in interpreting SPOTLIGHT's indications of movement.

At first there was a general tendency to regard the sensor data as indicating point targets rather than a progression activated by passage of something or other. During this early phase firepower brought to bear on the supposed targets proved useless because whatever had activated the sensors would have moved away before arrival of the bombs or shells laid down in response. Moreover, sensors were often activated by air strikes, elephants, tigers, even rock apes. Baig, divisional intelligence representative Major Robert B. Coolidge, and regimental intelligence officer Major Jerry E. Hudson soon learned better: the key to detecting real targets lay in watching the progression of movement from one sensor to another. There was "a definite pattern," notes Marine historian Moyers S. Shore:

> Preceding each assault, the devices around the point of intended attack showed heavy movement after remaining relatively quiet for several days. This indicated that the enemy was marshalling his forces. When the North Vietnamese moved forward, the sensors to the Marines' immediate front suddenly became hyper-active and that was the signal for the [fire support coordination center] to put its defensive fire plan into effect.

Kenneth Houghton, III MAF intelligence chief, was more graphic:

> Dave Lownds gets immediate readout in the CP [command post]. We can hear people moving. We fire artillery and hear the screams. It's just beautiful. It's music to my ears. They're really blood-curdling. And we can pick up tracks. We can tell if it's artillery or tanks. So it's really great.

A problem in the early days of MUSCLE SHOALS was partial data. Since the progression of detections was critical and needed to be collated with intelligence knowledge of NVA positions, assembly areas, trail networks, and the like, during the interval before all the arrays were in place it was possible to miss or misinterpret significant movements. The DUTCH MILL specialists had thought a week or ten days necessary to put the arrays in place. General Tompkins had wanted it all done in four days. That deadline was met with difficulty and possibly at the expense of full effectiveness. For example, the Red Watch staff at MACV on the first day of Tet received a set of infrared photographs revealing massive NVA troop movements around Khe Sanh. A Red Watch specialist interpreted this as North Vietnamese troops moving *away* from the combat base. Officers examining the SPOTLIGHT data apparently interpreted it as showing the NVA *closing in* for a massive attack. In fact, *nothing* happened at Khe Sanh for several days.

The North Vietnamese, who would later become relatively sophisticated about masking U.S. sensors, also had a lot to learn from this early encounter. Data from microphones showed the adversary to be more interested in recovering the parachute silk used to emplace the things than in the sensors themselves. Colonel Franklin W. Pippin recalled: "We have cases where they've put one up against a tree and executed it — shot it right there! And you have one guy begging, 'Let me shoot it; it's my time to shoot it!' "

It has been estimated that the MUSCLE SHOALS sensor system around Khe Sanh cost something on the order of a billion dollars. All agree it was worth it. Colonel Lownds later told a congressional committee that but for MUSCLE SHOALS he might well have had twice as many Marines killed at Khe Sanh.

"When My Bad Dreams Started"

Captain Baig soon got the opportunity to show just what MUSCLE SHOALS could do, when the NVA massed to attack another of the hilltop outposts. Again the pattern of operations dovetailed neatly with previous information provided by a North Vietnamese defector. This time the defector was a private, Lai Van Minh, who had deserted from the C-23 (possibly C-13) Transportation Company supporting the 95-C Regiment. Minh walked up the lines of Charlie Company of 1/26 holding his hands in the air on the morning of January 22. After furnishing various information about his unit, recent truck shipments, and a hospital complex, Minh told his interrogators something that probably perked them right up.

Private Minh declared that his company political officer had told the men that if the initial attack on Khe Sanh failed, North Vietnamese forces would pull back into Laos until after Tet. The commissar claimed the NVA would then return to the attack around February 3, using twice the previous number of troops as well as artillery and tanks. It was the first explicit mention of tanks by a *chieu hoi*. The North Vietnamese company commander reportedly told his men that Khe Sanh would be for the Americans what Dien Bien Phu had been for the French and that, after taking the combat base, NVA troops should press on until all of Route 9 was captured. The men were admonished not to worry about B-52 attacks because NVA combat elements would be so close to the Marines that the Americans would be unable to risk using the air strikes.

At MACV the initial reaction of the Red Watch staff to defector La Thanh Tonc's story had been that the North Vietnamese lieutenant knew too much. One wonders what the staff thought of Lai Van Minh. Sure enough, on the night of February 3–4 Captain Baig's sensor arrays began to light up with the first indications of what eventually developed into a large-scale turning movement north of Hill 881 South, soon joined by a second and third movement north of Hill 861. Baig initially evaluated the activity as resupply operations, and artillery missions were ordered on the targets as they appeared. The following night, February 4–5, the movements resumed. Baig now suspected the NVA present in regiment strength, from 1,500 to 2,000 troops, and preparing to attack Hill 881 South or 861. In fact, there were no sensors right around 861 and the recently occupied adjoining hill, 861-A. It was perhaps this factor that led Baig to lose track of some of the North Vietnamese while he focused on the force that appeared to be closing in on 881 South.

Captain Baig warned regiment of an impending attack and Colonel Lownds ordered defensive artillery fire. Quite remarkably, the artillery completely smashed the NVA units in their assembly areas, breaking up the intended attack altogether. DUTCH MILL later told Baig the acoustic sensors had picked up men screaming in panic and sounds of the troops beginning to flee. This incident on the night of February 4–5, 1968, is one of the earliest instances in warfare of a ground attack opposed and entirely broken up solely on the basis of remote sensor data.

One or possibly two North Vietnamese battalions, however, had separated from the larger force and moved toward Hill 861-A. The object, which Captain Baig afterward castigated himself for losing sight of, was apparently to launch an assault in tandem with the aborted attack on 881 South.

Unlike officers watching the sensor data or Marines in the regimental combat operations bunker, the men atop Hill 861-A, preoccupied with the routine of daily life and of turning their hilltop into a strong point, had no idea they were in for it. The unit on the hill was Captain Earle Breeding's Echo Company of 2/26, detached from the battalion to occupy 861-A following the NVA attack on Hill 861. Breeding's hill was important in that it overlooked 861 and Hill 558 in the Rao Quan valley, which in turn dominated one of the most important avenues of approach to the combat base. Recognizing this, Lownds had ordered the battalion commander, Lieutenant Colonel Heath, to get someone to the summit of 861-A. The luck of the draw fell on Echo Company, for, as it turned out, nothing worse than stray shells and periodic probes ever happened to the Marines who went to 558.

Captain Breeding had led his men away from the battalion column, ascending the foothills to the west. Larry E. Jackson went part of the way as point man: "I remember saying to myself that I couldn't believe that any type of grass could grow this high. It was about six to seven feet high. Each blade would cut you as you walked across it. . . . I would have to take my M-16 rifle and put it in front of me and lean forward with all my weight to open a trail." As Echo Marines climbed the hill, their equipment began to weigh heavier. "Fellow Marines started throwing away mortar shells, extra rounds, C-rations, etc.," Jackson recalls. Afraid the North Vietnamese would recover the stuff and shoot it back, Jackson picked up discarded items until he felt overloaded.

Hill 861-A was a fresh position. No Marines had ever occupied it before, so Echo had to start from scratch building defensive positions. Supply was also a problem, particularly water. Jackson recalls:

We started cutting bamboo trees around the surrounding area to drain the small amount of water from each section. We gathered probably eight or ten canteens of water which contained leech larvae that we had to strain off. We boiled the water and split it between the company. A couple of days later we received a load of water from a chopper which had to virtually drop it from about twenty feet in the air. We only salvaged five containers . . . [then] we were told by radio communication that they didn't know when we would receive water again. The five containers were kept in the CP area. We were [given] a half canteen cup of water a day for about five days. With this ½ cup of water you had to drink it, shave with it, and also brush your teeth with it.

Other features of life on 861-A were constant fog, damp mornings and evenings, and low morale, because the North Vietnamese seemed to be shooting often at the combat base but never bothering with the hill.

The Marines began stringing barbed wire around their perimeter. By February 4 they had four or five strands completed. It made Larry Jackson, for one, feel more secure, though he had sweated over the wire all day. A hot day degenerated into really dense fog in which Marines literally could not see past their wire barriers. The men were on three-hour watches. One man in each foxhole would be asleep, one awake. The attack came that night; it was the moment, Jackson recalls, "when my bad dreams started."

The sole indication of anything untoward was a pungent smell that the Marines atop 861-A detected from about midnight on. Some likened it to marijuana, others to unwashed troops. Shortly after four o'clock on the morning of February 5 came a tremendous volley of 82mm mortar fire simultaneous with a battalion-size assault. The wire barriers were professionally blown. North Vietnamese troops quickly closed with Lieutenant Edmund R. Shanley's 1st Platoon. They seemed to know the locations of weapons pits and other support positions and fired into them. Echo Company was in trouble immediately.

Earle Breeding told debriefers later that most of his casualties occurred during the initial mortar barrage, primarily because Echo had not been in place long enough to have really good fortifications. Typical of this phase of the battle was the experience of Corporal Eugene J. Franklin, with the mortar squad of Shanley's platoon:

All I heard was one shot go off, and I thought that was just somebody, like they thought they saw something in the wire and they just fired. And all of a sudden mortar rounds . . . dropped all around the gun pit and around my hootch. And I had one man that got trapped inside his hootch when they busted the lines. And myself, I was still inside my hootch. And I seen the flashes of light from the inside . . . 'cause I had a tunnel-way . . . leading from my hootch straight to the gun pit. And

I seen different colors of light. I didn't know exactly what it was — come to find it was shrapnel flying around inside the gun pit. And as I tried to get out [of] my gun pit, I got right up in it and concussion from one of the rounds knocked me back. . . . Then I tried to get out again, that's when I see a couple of enemy troops coming up on [the] side of the hill.

Meanwhile the mortar section leader, Corporal Billy E. Drexel, braved the heavy fire to get another squad with a second 60mm mortar into the battle area. Private First Class Newton D. Lyle came with the reinforcing mortar:

We went over there and you could actually see the Gooks running around on the lines, laughing and throwing [grenades] in bunkers, and you could hear the screams of your buddies, your friends, and we was running around out there firing mortar rounds out in front of the wires, and after a while they come and told us that all the men had been wiped out in the trenches directly in front of us and we was to fire directly into the trenches.

The mortar's targets finally were so close that the shell blasts sent shrapnel right back onto the Marine crew.

Then there was Tom Eichler, a machine gunner moving toward Shanley's platoon positions to provide more help:

Making my way down the trench line I found three of my machinegun crew lying severely wounded. Thinking they had been hit by a mortar shell, I took off my ammunition belt, laid down my rifle and placed one of the wounded Marines on my back. Making my way back through the trench line I suddenly came face to face with an NVA soldier. Instinctively I turned and began running down the trench. . . . The NVA soldier opened fire and I could feel the bullets striking me in the back, but they were not penetrating. The wounded Marine was absorbing the rounds in his flak jacket. I ran right into another NVA soldier who was firing a rocket down the trench line. With the wounded Marine on my back I strangled the NVA soldier with the strap from his rocket pouch. During this incident the young Marine on my back who was now close to death was whispering directions in my ear. Funny, I had started out saving his life, now he had saved mine. Then and only then did I realize that we had been overrun.

There were many harrowing moments, such as when Eichler saw bloody marks on the wall of a hole from a mortally wounded Marine trying to claw his way out. But there were humorous incidents too. Eichler recounts one that occurred with the Marines in their last defensive perimeter:

I was in the process of throwing grenade after grenade out of the position when I thought, this is taking too long. So, in my haste to speed up the process I pulled the pin on two grenades and laid them behind the Lieutenant [Shanley] who was directing supporting fire from Hill 881. The Lieutenant turned around just as I came to my senses and had barely managed to get the grenades out of the trench line before they exploded. To this day he believes that I saved his life by throwing enemy grenades out of the position. At the time I was afraid to tell him what really happened.

Support meanwhile came to Echo Company in abundance. The mortars on 881 South were just the beginning of it. Those weapons technically lacked range for targets on 861-A, but they happened to be located at a relative altitude about twenty feet higher that provided them just enough extra range to shoot. By the end of the battle the mortars on 881 South, it is said, had just five shells left. Artillery also played a major role, with about two thousand shells fired in barrages boxing in 861-A, cutting the NVA assault battalion off from the estimated additional battalion behind it in reserve, and firing patterns designed to trap and eliminate the North Vietnamese. The long-range Army 175mm guns and Marine weapons from the combat base cooperated and coordinated their fire. Mortars and 106mm recoilless rifles from Hill 558 also contributed. Colonel Lownds put the combat base on red alert to guard against any NVA attack on Khe Sanh itself.

On top of 861-A North Vietnamese assault troops lost some of their momentum trying to loot Marine bunkers. Several Marines mentioned subsequently that NVA soldiers were caught sitting down looking at copies of *Playboy* and other magazines left behind by Marines out on the firing line. Captain Breeding also used CS gas grenades, although they did not seem to do much good — wind blew the gas back on the Marines, while the adversary seemed so excited that no effect could be observed; indeed some speculated that the North Vietnamese were drugged and thus avoided the effects of gas.

In the final contest it came down to hand-to-hand fighting, after Breeding gathered some troops and made a counterattack. Breeding recalled:

The M-16 didn't come into play too much because of the hill we were on. There were really no fields of fire to speak of, and it turned out to be a hand grenade war. And then when Charlie got inside the wire it was just like a World War II movie with . . . knife-fighting, bayonet fighting, hitting people on the nose with your fist and all the rest of that, and Charlie didn't know how to cope with it at all. We just walked all over him once we were able to close with him.

Five Navy Crosses and many other awards were given for actions on 861-A that night. Lieutenant Don Shanley, who rallied his platoon in spite of a painful head wound, received a Bronze Star. The company lost seven Marines with another thirty-five wounded seriously enough to be evacuated.

The North Vietnamese tried a last gasp assault from the south at 6:10 A.M. on February 5 but were quickly beaten back. Behind them were left many bodies, 109 according to the official Marine monograph, as many as 150 by other counts. Larry Jackson, put on a burial detail, had to toss nineteen bodies of North Vietnamese soldiers into one hole, but Captain Breeding allowed policing of the battlefield only within the Marine positions. No one was permitted outside the perimeter, either to count bodies or to do anything else. As the sun burned off the fog that morning, it looked as if Captain Breeding had redeemed the promise he had made to Colonel Lownds that his company would successfully defend Khe Sanh.

After the battle Earle Breeding kept waiting to see the battalion or regimental intelligence officers. The Echo Company commander supposed they would come up to Hill 861-A and have a look around. He was wrong, as was Captain Dabney on Hill 881 South, who also had expected the intelligence debriefers. Breeding wanted to pass along some information that did not lend itself so well to a communications and reporting system that emphasized numbers. One piece of information was what Breeding felt about the attack on his position. The man who had defended 861-A thought the adversary assault troops had been too well groomed to be NVA, and they also had seemed bigger and more muscular than Vietnamese. Earle Breeding suspected that his Marines had fought Chinese troops but no one ever came to listen.

In fact, things were difficult at the combat base just then. The word at the combat base was that February 6 would be it, and Khe Sanh remained under bombardment, while the threat to Hill 881 South seemed to have been renewed. The race to install the remote sensor systems before the North Vietnamese completed preparations had ended in a dead heat, but it was the Green Berets and montagnards who would next feel the North Vietnamese fury. The scene of battle was about to shift to the CIDG camp at Lang Vei.

CHAPTER

10

The Fall of Lang Vei

THOUGH NOT SUPERSTITIOUS, even before he left for the Nam and before completing his training at Fort Bragg, John A. Young had had the feeling he was not coming back. Young was a weapons expert ranked Specialist-4 with the Green Berets. Initially assigned to the Special Forces B detachment at Da Nang, he supervised Nung security teams who guarded the compound. With just a month in country, on the evening of January 26 a clerk told Young he would be going up to Lang Vei to work with the Laotians. Young knew nothing at all about either Lang Vei or Laotians, and there was no one at the Da Nang operations center to brief him; Young speculated that everyone had gone to the club.

There were any number of hard luck assignments in Vietnam, but surely this was one of them. For starters, relations with the Laotians of BV-33 were very delicate following the incident in which Green Berets had disarmed them. Laotian commander Lieutenant Colonel Soulang was now refusing to take orders from company grade officers of Special Forces. Consequently the Special Forces commander, Lieutenant Colonel Daniel F. Schungel, leader of the C detachment at Da Nang, had to fly up to Lang Vei every other day, alternating with his deputy, Lieutenant Colonel Hoadley, to meet with the Laotians. Still restive at their treatment, the Laotians barely accepted a small unit of three Green Berets as advisers. According to Young, the first team that drew the assignment left in disgust after the Laotians, who were being issued food but little in the way of arms or ammunition, refused to mount any patrols. Young himself was not wanted by his own Green Berets. When the team sergeant of A-101, William T. Craig, heard he was being sent a Specialist-4, he protested. The C detachment sergeant major explained that he had no one else to send up as weapons expert, whereupon Craig replied he would do without. But Young was already on his way.

Flying over the combat base en route to Lang Vei, the replacement could see how the place was embattled and felt glad he was not going to Khe Sanh. But Lang Vei, which he thought only slightly better situated, was invested just as tightly. One glance at the intelligence map in the tactical operations center bunker told Young that. In the meantime at Lang Vei, as in Da Nang, no one showed up to orient the young weapons specialist, who, after a beer at the team house, went on to old Lang Vei and joined two Special Forces medics who constituted the remainder of his team.

Nearly five hundred Lao soldiers were crammed into dug-out firing holes that doubled as accommodations, Young found at his destination. The vegetation that had grown since the spring had ruined the fields of fire around the old CIDG camp, while what passed for a bunker was the corner of a partially collapsed building, where the American team had their bedrolls. A young black medic told Young, "Man, we're in trouble."

He was quite right.

The Special Forces men had one interpreter, while Soulang was the sole Lao who spoke English. Young gave Soulang a pair of binoculars, trying to establish some familiarity. Soulang proved no more optimistic than his American advisers. The Laotian troops were armed with an assortment of weapons, even including French Browning automatic rifles and a few modern Communist AK assault rifles. The men were limited to one grenade each. Young began to gather the oldest weapons, trading them for M-1 carbines he scrounged from A-101 at the new Lang Vei camp, repairing rifles when necessary. That took two days.

The main action at the Laotian camp on January 29 was a mass inoculation against cholera carried out by a doctor flown up from Da Nang. That evening Young got orders to report to Lang Vei, and the sun was just setting over the hills as he entered the operations bunker there. Captain Frank A. Willoughby, A-101 commander, who had just returned that day from a month's leave in the States, ordered him to lead a patrol out to Lang Bu, about two kilometers northeast of Lang Vei, the next day. No one had been anywhere near it since CAC Oscar had been driven out of Khe Sanh village.

Young believes that Willoughby just wanted to stir things up. The

Special Forces officer simultaneously refused to permit any other Americans to go out on the patrol with Young, though the standard procedure with CIDG strikers was to have at least two, and usually three, Americans. Craig has a different version of the origin of this patrol, saying that it was Young's idea, that he wanted to go on a patrol, and that the first mention of it was when the senior noncom with the Laotians, Sergeant First Class Eugene Ashley, Jr., called on the radio to report Young's desire. Craig says he permitted Young to go out only with a listening post and only if it kept within sight of the BV-33 camp. Craig apparently believes Young talked the Laotian troops with him into walking into Khe Sanh village.

Young recounts that he had to return to the Laotian camp in the dark, knowing the area was infested with NVA. Hoping that Soulang would give him a company to conduct this patrol, all Young got was a unit of seventeen men under a Laotian sergeant. They moved out in a column of twos down the road leading to Khe Sanh soon after sunrise on January 30. After walking along the road for about forty-five minutes they went left to enter the jungle. The point man, twenty meters in front of the patrol, suddenly went down with a bullet in his head. The Laotians evaporated. John Young was wounded by a bullet that shattered both bones in his lower left leg. North Vietnamese soldiers captured him. It was a bad portent for A-101 at Lang Vei.

A View to a Kill

As John Young put it, "The North Vietnamese wouldn't hit a Special Forces camp on three or four days notice." The NVA base he was taken to had an air of permanence and was obviously considered a rear area. Young saw North Vietnamese officers and troops nonchalantly strolling without weapons. Throughout the sector the adversary quietly shifted troops in preparation. Hoang Ba, a private from the 304th Division, probably from the 8th Battalion of the 66th Regiment, noted in his diary that his unit began staging on the afternoon of January 26. At night, to counter the darkness, the troops picked up dead leaves and rotten wood in the forest and smeared phosphorus from them over their hats or packs as a means of following each other. Ha, a friend of Ba's, was so affected by the hardship and malnutrition, the leeches, and the pain of fording rocky streams that he lost his rifle without even noticing it. As Ha went back to look for the weapon, an artillery officer collared him and asked him to relay orders for his unit to speed up its movement.

Another diary captured from an unidentified soldier of the 7th Battalion, 66th Regiment, discloses how the unit analyzed its battle experiences. The initial attack on "strongholds" in Khe Sanh village was considered a valuable lesson because a number of the troops had had no previous combat experience. The writer's platoon suffered heavy casualties owing to this inexperience. On January 25 the unit went to the village stronghold to recover husked rice left behind by the defenders. On the 27th, the diarist notes that division command foresaw that the subsequent phase of fighting could be even harder because the Americans had the capability to lift the entire air cavalry division into the area.

On January 30 Luong Dinh Du, who claimed to be a master sergeant with the 8th Company, 8th Battalion, 66th Regiment, rallied to the Special Forces at Lang Vei. Du recounted that his unit had lost half its strength to bombing and desertions during the trip south, had had to head back north for replacements, and had then returned to Khe Sanh just in time for the attack on district headquarters, in which the battalion once again lost more than half its strength. The *chieu hoi* pegged the current strength of his unit at just two hundred soldiers, that of the entire division at only about three thousand, and the whole of 66th Regiment at only about a thousand troops. He supplied map coordinate locations for the command post and all three battalions of his regiment.

According to the rallier, the mission of the 66th Regiment was simply to ambush American or allied forces along the stretch of Route 9 between the combat base and Lang Vei. This was to be the task until about February 15; after that the unit was to assault Lang Vei with its 8th Battalion in the lead. In the actual assault on Lang Vei, which occurred more than a week before the date predicted by Luong Dinh Du, the 8th Battalion was in fact in reserve. The strike elements, as reconstructed by the ARVN Joint General Staff, were the 7th Battalion of the 66th Regiment and the 4th Battalion of the 24th Regiment, also from the 304th Division. One battalion of each regiment (5/24 and 9/66) would have support roles while one each (6/24 and, as noted, 8/66) would make up the reserve.

The rallier finally reported that a squad of sappers, North Vietnamese specialized assault engineer troops, along with his battalion executive officer had reconnoitered the Lang Vei defenses on the night of January 28. That preparations of this sort were made is also indicated by what John Young reports of his interrogation. Young, who turned against the war later as a POW and is sometimes disbelieved, insists that he did not give away anything about Lang Vei to the NVA. The North Vietnamese *had it already*. They showed him telephoto pictures of the bunkers, gun pits, and other features of the CIDG camp. Such photographs might very well have been taken by a mission such as the one described by Luong Dinh Du. As for Young's providing aid to the enemy, there is no denying his point that he was not at the CIDG camp long enough, or briefed well enough, to give the NVA anything they did not already know.

A day after the North Vietnamese captured John Young, Captain Frank Willoughby reacted by ordering out a patrol of the MIKE Force company at Lang Vei. To the minds of headquarters scribes, the MIKE Force unit was "exploiting" the contact in which the American adviser had gone missing. For the platoon leaders of Lieutenant Paul R. Longgrear's MIKE Force, the concern seemed more immediate: it could easily have been any of them in the same predicament. For the Hré montagnards, men from the Central Highlands whom CIDG recruiters had never expected to serve against North Vietnamese regulars in Quang Tri, the patrol was a trying ordeal.

The patrol probed carefully up Route 9. In the early afternoon of January 31, at a place where a trail intersected with Route 9, the fog cleared enough for MIKE Force to see what they initially estimated as a platoon of North Vietnamese. The patrol backed up a little and hunkered down, calling in gunships and fixed-wing air support. When the strikes hit the NVA, who were evidently camping, it became clear that their force was nearly a battalion in size. Once aircraft had plastered the target, the patrol followed up with small arms and grenades.

When the smoke had cleared, the extent of the success became more apparent. Colonel Jonathan F. Ladd, 5th Special Forces Group commander and Lang Vei's top boss, told MACV the next day that the combat result had been fifty-four North Vietnamese killed, forty wounded (an unusual report because enemy wounded could almost never be counted), and eight weapons captured. Unfortunately the patrol found no trace of the missing Green Beret.

This encounter had immediate consequences at Lang Vei, where

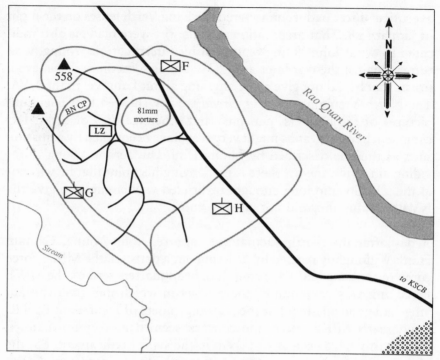

9 · Lang Vei

Captain Willoughby reevaluated the proximate threat and changed his dispositions as a result. Before, mainly because the Bru CIDG strikers did not get along well with the Hré MIKE Force, Longgrear's company had been deployed to an observation post on Route 9 almost a kilometer west of the main camp. Now Willoughby pulled back the MIKE Force, sending just a single platoon forward each night to man the observation post. The rest would defend the central redoubt (see Map 9) of the camp, their strength variously given as 170 or 196 men. Also defending the central area would be three combat reconnaissance platoons (CRPs). The MIKE Force beefed up the defenses with eight M-60 machine guns and four special short-barreled 60mm mortars.

At the ends of the elongated lozenge that made up the main position were fully organized strong points for each of the four CIDG companies at Lang Vei. The positions were internally wired, the fields of fire clear, and the bunkers and fighting positions strongly sandbagged on all sides and overhead. Willoughby's largest unit, the 101st, manning the northeast redoubt with eighty-two Bru, he considered weak because of poor leadership. More typical were the 102nd and 103rd Companies, with forty-two and forty-three Bru respectively. Different figures have been given for total CIDG strength, which is carried at 282 in the after-action report but is given as 342 elsewhere. (The latter figure may include the recon platoons, who are not enumerated in the after-action report.) Also at Lang Vei were a dozen ARVN Regional Force soldiers for general security plus the Vietnamese team with the CIDG, composed of nine enlisted men and three officers under Lieutenant Quan, the theoretical commandant of Lang Vei.

Captain Willoughby's A-101, the counterpart team to the ARVN special forces, consisted of fourteen Green Berets. Lieutenant Longgrear had five more Special Forces men with him in the MIKE Force company, and there were the three additional men advising the Laotians. During early February, engineer Lieutenant Thomas E. Todd came up on temporary duty to survey construction requirements at Lang Vei. Finally, there was the daily alternating liaison between 5th Special Forces Group and the Laotians. In all, that made twenty-five Americans in and near Lang Vei.

Firepower assets at the camp (exclusive of the MIKE Force) were also significant: two 4.2-inch mortars with 800 rounds; six 81mm mortars with 2,000 rounds; fifteen 60mm mortars with 3,000 rounds; two 106mm and four 57mm recoilless rifles with more than 3,000 shells (including 2,800 of the canister type); two .50-caliber machine guns with 17,000 rounds; forty-seven .30-caliber machine guns with 275,000 rounds; twelve M-60 machine guns with 60,000 rounds; and thirty-nine Browning automatic rifles with 200,000 rounds. All of this was in addition to the men's small arms.

Not knowing what to expect, Captain Willoughby in early February shifted to patrol patterns in addition to his dispositions, mounting small recon and ambush patrols. These radiated in all directions from Lang Vei but went no farther than one to three kilometers from the camp. The patrols had several contacts. In all the minor actions between January 31 and February 5 the losses amounted to four killed and seven wounded, with only three known North Vietnamese killed.

Toward midmorning on February 6 North Vietnamese artillery began to shell Lang Vei, disrupting the camp routine. Eight strikers were wounded. That afternoon Lieutenant Colonel Schungel arrived to take his turn as liaison to the Laotians. Starting at 6:10 P.M. for about an hour, the NVA sent forty to sixty 152mm shells into the camp, damaging two bunkers and wounding two strikers. The first

shells landed in the 104th Company area. Sergeant Nickolas Fragos
went there to aid the wounded while Staff Sergeant Peter Tiroch tried
to spot the flashes for counterbattery. After a few moments Tiroch
went over to one of the 4.2-inch mortar emplacements to try some
return fire. He found Colonel Schungel and Lieutenant Longgrear
already there. Together the three men moved the heavy mortar as far
forward as they could. Then, while others carried ammunition, Tiroch fired at maximum elevation with the strongest charges possible,
sending out six to eight shells. Each time he fired the North Vietnamese seemed to stop shelling; then the NVA shelling became less accurate, and finally the adversary began to shift targets to concentrate on
Khe Sanh combat base. Only toward the end of the shelling, it seemed,
did Marine guns begin to reply. About 7:00 to 7:30 P.M. the shelling
died out altogether.

Meanwhile the MIKE Force platoon at the observation post, about
forty soldiers under Sergeant First Class Charlie Lindewald and Sergeant Kenneth Hanna, began to report sounds like diesel engines.
Lindewald had a reputation as a man who liked his liquor — even
under siege the sergeant was paying an old Bru woman three hundred
piastres a bottle to bring him Ba Mui Ba beer through the NVA lines.
Lindewald's report might have been discounted. But about the time
the NVA shelling stopped, Bru strikers of the 104th Company also
reported noise from the direction of Lang Troai hamlet. The noises
sounded like vehicle engines.

An hour and a half later three trip flares went off in the wire surrounding the observation post. The mobile strike force troopers and
many at Lang Vei opened fire then, shooting at shadows, at animals,
at anything they saw, convinced a battle impended. After fifteen minutes or so the strikers sheepishly stopped, but Lindewald and Hanna
had trouble with their restive men after that. The strikers talked of
seeing "beaucoup VC" and wanted to get out. Some probably did
leave, but when the attack actually began a number of the MIKE Force
men were still with the two Americans.

At Lang Vei itself things began to seem increasingly creepy starting
about 10:00 P.M., February 6, when a trip flare went off in the wire
outside the position of the 104th Company. Again the strikers opened
fire. No results could be observed. Sergeant John Early, a MIKE Force
platoon leader who was manning the observation tower above the
tactical operations center, called out that he could see lights on the
road from Lang Troai.

Khe Sanh combat base meanwhile found itself distracted by NVA diversions, beginning with the evening bombardment. After that a light ground attack from the north and southeast began against Breeding's Echo Company on Hill 861-A. Even at the time, regiment evaluated that as a diversion. But the combat base also received 82mm mortar fire, rockets, and a probe at the southeast end (Blue Sector) of the position. Listening posts and ARVN Ranger patrols were pulled back into the perimeter. Regiment operations staffers estimated that two battalions of NVA were moving toward Khe Sanh.

Instead, at 11:25 P.M., the attacks on Hill 861-A stopped. Five minutes later, at Lang Vei, the 104th CIDG Company reported North Vietnamese troops in the wire. The real battle had begun.

"I've Got a Tank Sitting on Top of My Bunker"

Those who thought they heard engine noises in the distance were entirely correct. North Vietnamese armor was about to spearhead the assault on Lang Vei. A threat that had been discussed in hushed tones by GIs, mostly late at night in harbor sites or hootches, that had been denied more than once, was about to become concrete. The NVA tanks were Soviet-built light amphibious vehicles designated PT-76s. Intelligence never established the exact identity of the NVA armored units at Khe Sanh, which ARVN carried as a battalion and MACV as a company, but it was known that the North Vietnamese Army possessed two tank regiments, the 202nd and 203rd, and that a battalion of the former had been armed with PT-76 amphibious tanks.

In contrast to its inability to identify the NVA armor, thanks to aerial photography, intelligence did quite well at establishing retrospectively how the NVA massed armor for the battle. Simply advancing down Route 9 with tanks would have been foolhardy. That was the kind of move the Americans watched for and would have been well prepared to deal with. Instead, according to a CIA report and an analysis of February 13 by the National Photographic Interpretation Center, the NVA armor made a wide circuit to the south, traversing the new road they had built and then following a trail the last few kilometers to the Xe Pon river. The tanks entered the river eleven kilometers south of Route 9, swam a kilometer or two, and then mounted the west bank of the river. For about six kilometers the NVA tanks apparently drove overland up the Laotian side before entering the river once more to swim perhaps four more kilometers to the Vietnamese village of Lang Troai.

Such a difficult and time-consuming approach march was necessary to maintain the element of surprise. Greatly facilitated by the qualities of the PT-76, a true amphibian, the movement probably consumed several nights. This was possible because the PT-76, according to analyst David C. Isby, possesses an unrefueled range of 100 kilometers over water and 260 on roads. Water propulsion was from two rear-mounted hydrojets.

In other respects the PT-76, introduced as a reconnaissance vehicle and to provide armor support for the Soviet army during river crossing operations, was not all that sophisticated. Its straight six-cylinder diesel engine, engineered from half the twelve-cylinder V-type used in the medium T-54 tank, is rear-mounted and protected by light internal armor. The transmission is mounted in the front, a type known to have problems causing poor acceleration. In general, armor coverage is light, thickest on the turret front at seventeen millimeters and then fourteen on the hull side and lower front. Armor plate so thin can be penetrated by weapons down to the .50-caliber machine gun, of which the CIDG camp had two. The plate on the hull upper rear was just seven millimeters and that on the belly only five.

The PT-76 was also a relatively old weapon, its design probably dating from the late 1940s. Prototypes had begun testing as early as 1952, and large-scale deliveries to the Soviet army had begun in 1955. By the time of Lang Vei its protection, which had been reasonable in the 1950s, was no longer up to the standards of 1960s antitank weapons. Among the armament at Lang Vei, we should note, were a hundred of the more recent light antitank weapons (LAWs).

Offensively the PT-76 mounted a 76.2mm, .42-caliber gun capable of elevating to thirty degrees or depressing some four degrees from the horizontal. With the gun at maximum elevation and the tank parked on an incline, the D-56T main gun could reach a range of 12,100 meters. The tank also featured a turret-mounted 76.2mm machine gun. There was no externally mounted machine gun, nor any in the hull. Though this tank did not qualify as a wonder weapon, for montagnard strikers on the night of February 6, 1968, men who had never faced tanks, the PT-76 added an element of terror to the North Vietnamese assault.

*   *   *

Fifteen minutes after midnight, another trip flare went off where the road came up from Lang Troai. Green Beret medic Fragos saw two men in front of the perimeter of the 104th CIDG Company cutting through the barbed wire. Behind them stood a vehicle Fragos could not identify — one of five tanks that hit this sector. Defenders promptly shot down the men, but to no avail — the tank briefly flashed a spotlight and then simply rolled over the wire barrier. Fragos quickly ran to the inner compound to the Special Forces tactical operations center. He reported what he'd seen to Captain Willoughby and Lieutenant Colonel Schungel.

Willoughby got a second report from Sergeant Early in the observation tower: two tanks appeared to be sitting in the wire beyond the 104th Company. Schungel ordered Willoughby to call for air support and for artillery fire directed at Lang Troai and to request help from a flareship.

The 104th Company compound became the initial focus of the battle, with the NVA deploying for a tank-infantry assault. North Vietnamese troops appeared from the darkness, firing at targets illuminated by the PT-76 searchlights or tracer rounds. Just a few hours earlier, Lieutenant Quan, the ARVN camp commander, Lieutenant Quy, his operations officer, and Colonel Schungel had carefully inspected all camp positions, including these. Now the CIDG strikers were already wavering.

A welcome assist came from the 106mm recoilless rifle located in the central compound in the area held by the 2nd Reconnaissance Platoon. Manned by Sergeant First Class James W. Holt, senior medic of A-101, the gun fired on the NVA tanks, immobilizing both lead tanks with hits at point-blank range (less than 350 meters). Holt reloaded with Beehive fleshette rounds, each containing about nine thousand small steel darts, and tried to wipe out the NVA infantry. In the meantime Schungel sent Fragos to collect all the LAWs he could carry — these were single-shot disposable launcher-warhead combinations — while the Special Forces commander and all the CIDG riflemen he could muster tried to stop the penetration. With Schungel was ARVN Lieutenant Quy, Lieutenant Paul Longgrear, and Specialist-4 William G. McMurray, a radio operator. They were later joined by First Lieutenant Miles R. Wilkins, the A-101 executive officer.

Near Holt in the recon platoon area was a 4.2-inch mortar in a pit. That was manned by Staff Sergeant Dennis L. Thompson; Sergeant

First Class Earle F. Burke, a MIKE Force platoon leader; and Specialist-4 Franklin H. Dooms, a radio man back in the Army for the second time after finding work with the CIA too tame. They were joined by Sergeant First Class William Craig, the team sergeant, and Staff Sergeant Emmanuel E. Phillips, a radio operator. Soon the crowd in the mortar pit grew again with the arrival of the team intelligence specialist, Staff Sergeant Peter Tiroch, who had been awakened by shouts of "Tanks in the wire!"

Tiroch saw there were plenty of men with the mortar, so he dashed across to Holt's position to help load the recoilless rifle. When he got to the gun Tiroch could see two burning tanks and a third moving around them into the compound. Just then light faded as a flare burned out. When another illumination round burst and Holt could aim again, he hit the tank on the first shot, but by then the tank had destroyed several CIDG bunkers. Tiroch now discovered they had only one more antitank round for the 106mm gun, and Holt used it to make sure the third tank was knocked out. The NVA crews of the three tanks abandoned their machines. Three of the nine crew members seemed to be women.

Once the antitank ammunition ran out Sergeant First Class Holt sped toward the ammunition bunker to get some LAWs while Tiroch returned to the mortar. Holt was never seen again. A fourth tank appeared up the Lang Troai road and fired at the 106mm gun, destroying it. Within about forty-five minutes North Vietnamese troops overran the remainder of the 104th Company position.

According to Colonel Schungel in the Lang Vei after-action report, by 1:00 in the morning, just fifteen minutes after he had gone to try and set up some tank killer details, one of the NVA tanks "was practically on top of us." The colonel's party fired LAWs but needed at least five to immobilize the PT-76. "On each impact," Schungel recalled, "there would be a shower of orange spar[k]s."

Considering that LAWs had been designed specifically to combat Soviet armor, even tanks heavier than the PT-76, the poor performance of this weapon is one of the mysteries of Lang Vei. Questioned on this point, David Isby and Steven J. Zaloga, another expert on Soviet armor, both agree the most likely reason the NVA light tanks proved so survivable is that the large amount of interior space in the PT-76 made it more difficult for antitank rounds to hit their vital machinery.

Schungel finally stopped the tank he had been fighting and the three-man NVA crew bailed out. Before they could use their AK-47s, Schungel and Lieutenant Quy downed them with grenades and small arms fire. By then another tank had flanked the immobilized combat vehicle and took Schungel's party under fire with both its gun and machine gun. Sheltering behind some oil drums filled with rocks, Schungel sent Paul Longgrear off to get more LAWs. Before he could return, the NVA tank hit the position and also collapsed the entrance to the tactical operations center bunker, the big fancy one that the Seabees had built out of concrete. Longgrear mistakenly concluded that Schungel and the others had been killed. In fact, Quy remained unscathed, though everyone else had been wounded, and he kept firing to shield his comrades. Lieutenant Wilkins was crushed between barrels, Specialist-4 McMurray had both his hands mangled, and he could not see. Schungel was knocked head over heels by concussion but received only a light wound in his right hip and a cut across his left cheek and ear.

In the meantime things had gone no better at the advance listening post manned by the MIKE Force. They reported heavy mortar and automatic weapons fire at about the same time the action began in the 104th Company area. Sergeant First Class Hanna estimated at least a company and possibly two more tanks. The NVA closed in. Hanna called for two artillery missions near his position. Then he reported that Charlie Lindewald was gravely wounded, hit by machine gun fire in the stomach. Kenneth Hanna, a weapons specialist, now had to administer first aid. He radioed that they were still under heavy attack. That was the last ever heard from him. Hanna is believed to have been captured but he did not return in the postwar prisoner exchanges.

As the battle swelled, another NVA force with four tanks advanced from the west and hit the 102nd Company compound. Then two more tanks backed more North Vietnamese who attacked down Route 9 from the northeast, the direction of Khe Sanh combat base. They assaulted the 101st CIDG Company. Lang Vei clearly had been invested on all sides.

Survivors of the 104th CIDG Company eventually withdrew into the central compound. This exposed the southern flank of the 101st Company area, now under attack from the two tanks to the northeast. The 101st Company crumbled in only fifteen minutes. Sergeant Harvey Brande, on his third Vietnam tour, was wounded in the right hand and injured in his left leg; he lapsed into unconsciousness and later was further wounded in both legs and his chest. The North Vietnamese captured Brande, who was taken to the camp where the NVA already held John Young.

The two CIDG companies whose compounds flanked the western face of Lang Vei were also smashed in short order. With four tanks backing their assault, the NVA advanced confidently. Another material innovation they introduced in the battle, its use confirmed by men on the ground, forward air controllers, and relief elements the next day, was flame throwers. The CIDG bunkers were shot to pieces or burned out. The 102nd and 103rd Companies broke up. Some fought a rear-guard action and pulled back into the central compound, others tried to escape and evade toward Route 9.

The NVA tanks forged ahead into the central compound. Thus while fighting outside the tactical operations center (TOC) bunker, Schungel suddenly realized there were tanks attacking from his rear also — from the western flank of the camp. The tanks seemed impervious to the grenades and small arms fire that were all Schungel had at that moment to fight with. Then the lead tank flamed — it had fallen victim to a strike from the rear, and Schungel and Quy were able to wipe out its crew. The destruction of this tank revealed that other tank killer details were also at work.

Miles Wilkins led one of these brave teams. Like Schungel they seemed condemned to rely on inadequate weapons. One after another the LAWs failed to fire, bounced off the PT-76s, or hit and did not stop them. Wilkins had three misfires with one barrage of LAWs against one tank. The other two weapons hit but did not halt it. At one point he was momentarily nonplussed when a Vietnamese appeared alongside a tank and shouted "CIDG! CIDG!" Wilkins felt relief for a second that they had a tank on their side too now, until it dawned on him that strikers knew nothing about tanks and could not operate them the way this tank was maneuvering inside Lang Vei. Earle Burke, who worked with Wilkins, dashed off to get another armful of LAWs. The tank proved similarly impervious to grenades, including the M-79 shots that Dennis Thompson fired at it.

Nickolas Fragos had been working along with Schungel after his initial warning of the enemy assault. He had gone for the first batch of LAWs from the TOC and then got another from the 4.2-inch mortar pit, dragging four LAWs by their straps toward Schungel. Seeing one tank looming dangerously, Fragos tried to take it out himself. His first LAW misfired, and his second fell short and buried itself in the ground. Finally he made it to the colonel, only to be sent down into the TOC to free the balky safety of another LAW. He left the weapon in the operations center after telling Captain Willoughby the defenders were beginning to take fire from the northern wire. Willoughby called for artillery fire. Fragos went with Schungel and Specialist-4 James L. Moreland, a MIKE Force platoon commander, on a tank killing foray. Schungel's LAW misfired again. The men tried to stop the tank by firing into its apertures but that had no effect. This was the tank that suddenly ground to a halt when a second team hit it in the rear.

Pete Tiroch, after his initial work on the recoilless rifle, had run back to the 4.2-inch mortar. There he spotted a tank, grabbed a LAW, and shot — another misfire. He made it to a .50-caliber machine gun from which he fired a full belt of armor piercing bullets. Tiroch defended the position until he ran out of ammunition and then evaded through the northern perimeter wire to old Lang Vei. There he worked with the Laotians to get a relief force back into the CIDG camp. Tiroch later received a Purple Heart for his wounds, the Bronze Star, and the Vietnamese Cross of Gallantry.

Special Forces with the Laotians at old Lang Vei tried to help as best they could — with illumination rounds and high explosives from their 81mm mortar. The Laotians made no effort at that stage to mount operations. Specialist-4 Joel Johnson spotted two tanks sitting on the supply drop zone between the two positions. Then, at 1:36 A.M. support aircraft accidently put a bomb on the Laotian positions. Fortunately no one was hurt by the blast.

Another who would be helped at the Laotian camp, where he would finally get first aid, was Colonel Schungel, who made his escape after daylight. Fighting outside the TOC, Schungel suddenly found himself alone except for the wounded Wilkins. North Vietnamese soldiers were roaming at will through the camp. Flares were going off, air strikes and artillery were hitting, and so the NVA were confused. Schungel and Wilkins managed to cross to the team house near Route 9 on the northern edge of the camp. When five NVA troops approached with satchel charges, Schungel shot them down, emptying a full magazine. With the adversary now alerted, Wilkins suggested they run for the dispensary and hide out underneath it until daylight. This they did, staying under cover even while North Vietnamese ransacked the medical supplies in the building above them. Schungel and Wilkins stayed put until well after dawn, when the NVA seemed to disappear; they finally joined team sergeant Craig, by then operating with some of the Laotians, who got them to old Lang Vei.

The massive American firepower that so many counted on for so much did not save Lang Vei. Khe Sanh got its first reports of the attack at forty-two minutes past midnight of February 7. Just three minutes later the North Vietnamese began a vicious mortar and rocket barrage on Khe Sanh to suppress the Marine artillery. Shells hit at an average rate of six per minute; by morning the total stood at about a hundred rockets and 450 rounds of mortar fire. It had been the heaviest bombardment yet.

Despite the bombardment the American artillery did shoot, and with a fair degree of effectiveness. But the effort was hampered by initial incredulity, by delays in responding to calls for fire missions, and by communications difficulties. Each of these factors merits some comment, but together they added up to critical lapses in support.

At the very beginning of the battle, strong fire on the preplanned targets in the direction of Lang Troai might have caught the NVA armor moving into position. Instead Khe Sanh wanted confirmation of the reports it was getting. Lang Vei radio had called "Jacksonville," the call sign for the 1/13 Marines, the combat base artillery, to report "armor in the wire."

"This is Jacksonville," replied Khe Sanh. "Are you sure about that armor?"

"Roger, roger, that is affirm. We have tanks in the perimeter!"

But the Marines only came back: "Can you see them from your position?" The question was silly since the Lang Vei communicators were in the TOC, a windowless underground bunker, and could see nothing. Seventeen minutes passed before the first salvos of artillery shells came crashing down. In that interval the North Vietnamese tanks had crossed the wire and entered the camp.

In less than two hours Lang Vei would have to report, to a forward air controller overhead, "I've got a tank sitting on top of my bunker." That vehicle happened to be one of the last successfully knocked out. Later the NVA would rock a tank on top of the bunker with impunity in their effort to force out the last defenders.

The time had come for COFRAM, the top secret special fragmentation weapon. At least Rath Tompkins thought so; at 1:50 A.M. the 3rd Marine Division commander ordered Lownds to employ COFRAM against the tanks at Lang Vei. But Lang Vei protested against using "Firecracker," the radio euphemism for COFRAM, worrying that its use might compel airborne controllers to curtail air support, which Lang Vei wanted to keep overhead at all costs.

About an hour after these exchanges, the 26th Marines operations officer reported to division that NVA troops were inside the wire at Lang Vei and that tanks were moving both inside and outside the compound. The officer, Lieutenant Colonel Edward J. A. Castagna, also mentioned Lang Vei's reasons for resisting the use of COFRAM. General Tompkins now advised sequencing the firepower, using Firecracker, then conventional artillery munitions, and then air. Before any decision was made, at 2:45 A.M. III MAF advised that its information indicated that everything moving above the ground at Lang Vei, at this point, was enemy. Tompkins converted his suggestion into an order. Khe Sanh began to shoot "packages" of twenty-eight COFRAM shells followed by five minutes of high-explosive or VT-fused shells, alternated with air strikes.

The forward air controller on station in the Lang Vei area at the moment the battle began carried the call sign "Covey 235." He was soon joined by a "Puff the Magic Dragon" flareship. The airborne command post "Moonbeam" was orbiting to control operations. With variable cloudiness and low overcast, air support became less effective than it could have been. In addition, the strike aircraft initially available packed loads of large bombs, less useful in resisting an infantry assault than comparable loads of rockets and cluster bombs. Moreover, Covey 235 quickly expended his flares and rockets marking the earliest targets. Covey 232 launched from Da Nang at fifteen minutes past midnight, but it was 1:00 A.M. before he arrived over Lang Vei. The controller who normally flew as Covey 230 volunteered to come along on this mission and flew the right seat, providing two sets of experienced eyes to spot targets in the darkness. The pilots found it very difficult to orbit in a single position because of antiaircraft fire. The report of a tank atop the bunker was their last radio contact with the men inside Lang Vei's tactical operations center.

A North Vietnamese shell that set afire the oil tank near the east end of the CIDG camp provided the airmen their best navigational reference. Covey marked targets with rockets and then sent in a flight of B-57 bombers. These seemed to destroy two tanks. Still Covey 232 felt he could not direct strikes right into the CIDG camp because, without radio contact with Lang Vei, there was no way to tell what was friendly among the movements they spotted on the ground. As dawn approached, Covey 688 came up from Ubon to support the hesitant relief operations beginning from old Lang Vei.

Primary beneficiaries of all this effort were the men trapped inside the tactical operations center at the CIDG camp. These included Lieutenant Longgrear and Sergeants Fragos and David M. Brooks, who had gone inside to get more ammunition or LAWs; the Green Beret commander, Captain Willoughby; radio men Emmanuel Phillips and Frank Dooms; medic Wes Moreland; MIKE Force platoon leader John Early; Vietnamese Lieutenant Quan, the camp commander; a CIDG communications man; and twenty-five other strikers. Some were wounded or worse, and they became trapped when the NVA tanks fired into the bunker entrance and exit. They lost primary communications with Khe Sanh at 3:10 A.M. and with Da Nang headquarters ten minutes afterward. Only an hour later, on secondary radio channels, was contact regained. About then the NVA began throwing satchel charges down the entrance to smoke out the defenders, and they also impersonated Lieutenant Wilkins in an attempt to deceive the Americans. Thermite grenades started a fire, gas grenades followed, and then satchel charges from both ends of the TOC. This hell went on for more than four hours. The best that could be said about it was that the fire did not spread very much since there was so little air in the battered bunker.

As Lang Vei shuddered, Walt Rostow planned for a National Security Council meeting. Deputy Bromley Smith suggested that General Wheeler be asked to summarize the latest reports on Vietnam. This suggestion proved more timely than Smith could have known; about the time he made it, the battle began at Lang Vei. President Johnson had recently received a study by Bob Ginsburgh comparing the Khe Sanh situation with that at Dien Bien Phu. Rostow, who had asked Ginsburgh to do the report, had passed it along with the comment that "the numbers suggest why our military are confident."

Now the North Vietnamese were striking and the moment all awaited seemed to have arrived. At 2:55 P.M. of February 6 in Washington, about the height of the battle, Situation Room manager Art McCafferty sent LBJ word:

> We have just received information that the ARVN unit at Lang Vei, to the west of Khe Sanh, was under heavy ground attack at 2:20 P.M. this afternoon. Initial reports indicate that the enemy employed seven tanks; at least one of the tanks had been knocked out.

McCafferty also noted that COFRAM had been fired in defense of the position.

That evening the Associated Press carried a wire item from Saigon baldly reporting that "a Special Forces–Green Beret camp in the northwest corner of South Vietnam was overrun and occupied early Wednesday morning by communist troops using tanks and armored cars." Knowing that Johnson monitored the wire services quite closely — indeed, he had tickers in his office — the Situation Room took immediate steps to verify the report. The White House called the National Military Command Center, which in turn called MACV. At 8:30 P.M. Bromley Smith reported to the president that the AP bulletin "is *not* true. The camp has *not* been overrun and occupied." Instead, the NSC staff aide noted, "South Vietnamese forces and our forces at Lang Vei are in their bunkers."

In this instance the Pentagon was clearly misinforming the White House. At the time of the exchange all that was left at Lang Vei were a handful of desperate, half-suffocated men clinging to life inside the command bunker. The rendition given to President Johnson implied that the camp was buttoned up, on the alert, many bunkers manned, confidently defending itself, with just a hint that things might come out all right. In reality, by midafternoon (Washington time) III MAF had known, and MACV certainly knew too, that everything aboveground at Lang Vei belonged to the enemy — that the CIDG camp had been overrun and occupied.

The president's eyebrows must have lifted the next morning when he got Earle Wheeler's daily report on Khe Sanh, which supplied times for key events that clearly contradicted what he had been told the previous evening. The attack had opened at 11:45 A.M. (Washington time), the JCS chairman noted, simultaneous with the bombardment of the combat base. By 1:50 P.M. at least five tanks had been destroyed, and by 10:00 P.M. the battle had died down. All buildings at Lang Vei were said to have been destroyed. Wounded survivors had been evacuated from the bunker at 2:00 A.M. The Wheeler memo (CM-2971-68) reported a reaction force en route by 3:30 A.M.

The Joint Chiefs of Staff reporting was reinforced very quickly by a spot report (SC 07681/68) from the Central Intelligence Agency. This noted that the NVA had gained control of the camp by the morning of February 7 (Washington time), that defenders were evacuating under cover of intensive aerial and artillery bombardment, and that six of twenty-four Americans plus more than three-quarters of the indigenous personnel "have not yet been accounted for." The CIA

had not yet established the identity of the attacking unit but speculated it might have been the 66th Regiment of the 304th Division,
possibly assisted by elements of the 101D Regiment of 325-C. For the
first time this report clarified for LBJ what had really happened at
Lang Vei: "Earlier in the day, an estimated company had controlled
the camp above ground while friendly personnel were entrenched in
underground bunkers."

It was only at 7:15 A.M. (Washington time) of February 7 that
MACV told Washington that thirty men, sixteen of them American,
had been evacuated from Lang Vei. This was the first Saigon command admission that Lang Vei was doing anything other than repel-
ling the adversary. Rostow sent the information to LBJ at 8:40 A.M.
Less than two hours later he reported from a garbled secure telephone
call from MACV to the National Military Command Center that *all*
personnel had evacuated Lang Vei.

Rostow's notes, the Wheeler daily memo, and the CIA intelligence
report all mentioned relief forces. The CIA furnished the best information, mentioning two columns converging on the scene, noting that
one was the Laotian battalion, the other comprising Special Forces
troops helicoptered from Khe Sanh. According to the CIA, "Neither
had entered the camp-site at last report." What had happened to the
relief of Lang Vei?

After the Fall

It had always been anticipated that Lang Vei would come under attack
someday, and the Marines had a contingency plan to reinforce the
CIDG camp and had plotted artillery fire points to support it. MACV
and III MAF had had the contingency plan reviewed just a few weeks
before. Yet on the night of the attack, save for the artillery fires, no
effort was made to carry out the plan. The story of Lang Vei relief
efforts is a sad tale indeed.

In actuality, Saigon's insistence that the defense be ensured had
come after General Tompkins, concerned about being able to support
the camp, recommended that Lang Vei be abandoned. The Marines
were convinced reinforcement would prove to be impossible. The
previous November Colonel Wilkinson, 1/26 commander, had sent
Captain John W. Raymond on an imaginary relief mission from the
combat base to Lang Vei, just to establish the time and space factors

for planning. Wilkinson told Raymond to avoid the roads and trails as if he were moving tactically in combat. The battalion commander considered Raymond a highly qualified, very dedicated, very brave Marine and his Alpha Company a fully capable unit. It had taken Raymond and Alpha Company nineteen hours to execute the move.

In the interval between that mission and the attack, a number of things happened to complicate the situation. Most important, the North Vietnamese closed in around Khe Sanh. Now Captain Mirza Baig was carrying no less than three thousand active targets on his electronic arrays of adversary threats around the combat base. The NVA had taken Khe Sanh village, directly between the combat base and the CIDG camp. They could be presumed to be lying in wait for a relief force; indeed, all Marines knew it was standard tactics for the North Vietnamese to make attacks specifically to draw out relief forces that could then be ambushed. A photo reconnaissance mission on February 5 yielded pictures indicating an ambush site being prepared along Route 9. An actual ambush had already occurred in the area, too — the action in which Green Beret John Young had been captured.

On the night of the Lang Vei attack the available reserve was First Lieutenant Ernest E. Spencer's Delta Company of 1/26. Spencer's company was under strength, missing its 3rd Platoon — thirty-six men under Lieutenant Hanna — which had been deployed to replace Echo Company casualties on Hill 861-A. In any case, the operations plan called for use of a second company and a battalion command group in case of a major threat, which this certainly was. General Tompkins rasped to an interviewer that he would not have risked even a full battalion out toward Lang Vei. An operation would have been dangerous enough in the daytime, but now it was night.

With such difficulties in the way of an overland move, an air assault also seemed too risky. Nighttime helicopter operations were inherently dangerous, more so if being staged into areas where opposition might be encountered. The best potential landing zone in the vicinity of Lang Vei was the clearing that served as its supply drop zone. The North Vietnamese could read the terrain as well as anyone and put two tanks on the area. Once the spotting report by a Green Beret at old Lang Vei reached the combat base, the Marine command rejected the air assault option as well. The presence of tanks alone practically precluded any reaction force since Marine infantry in this role, shorn of their own armor backing, would have been in peril.

That Marines refused the role did not end all prospects for a reaction force, however. There remained the Special Forces' own chain of command, deathly worried about their comrades at Lang Vei. Colonel Jonathan Ladd of the 5th Special Forces Group asked Saigon to permit a relief operation. Westmoreland directed that the decision be left to Cushman and Tompkins. The entire force of Project DELTA, the Special Forces elite scout unit, led by detachment B-57, volunteered to go in. At Da Nang the I Corps MIKE Force gathered 150 strikers under Major Adam Husar for the same purpose. The MIKE Force people asked for helicopters to fly them in at first light. To be in readiness about a hundred of the strikers got on board a C-130 that was cleared to leave for Khe Sanh. At 3:35 A.M. III MAF confirmed to Khe Sanh a C-130 would be coming in shortly. Khe Sanh, however, had suffered damage to its runway in the NVA bombardment and could land only light planes. While the damage would be repaired in the morning, that was too late for a dawn assault.

At 4:00 A.M. several officers met at Da Nang on the matter. Special Forces Captain Edwards asked that a relief force be sent at dawn. Colonel Richard B. Smith and Major Saimon of III MAF were more cautious. Smith, the operations watch officer at III MAF headquarters, spoke to General Tompkins by telephone at 3:50 A.M. and the division commander asked how the proposed relief force would make its way to Lang Vei and protested the C-130 flight. Now Smith decided Tompkins had to talk to Cushman, which he did at 4:05. A minute later Tompkins refused a MIKE Force intervention.

This early morning exchange did not end the matter, however, for by midmorning William Westmoreland had left for Tan Son Nhut to get a plane to Da Nang. Westmoreland was airborne by 10:45, in place by noon, and after a quick lunch spent three hours closeted with III MAF staff and division commanders, representatives of his MACV forward echelon, and General Cushman of III MAF. Westmoreland called it a "historic meeting" and saw himself countering Cushman's "absence of initiative" in "dealing forcefully with the situation."

Colonel Ladd from 5th Special Forces was present. His operations officer, Lieutenant Colonel Hassinger, briefed the group on the situation and the need to move immediately to evacuate survivors. Lieutenant Colonel Daniel L. Baldwin III, senior MACVSOG commander in the north, volunteered FOB-3 for a relief mission but needed helicopters for the job. There was considerable argument. Some feared a larger relief force could be endangered by an effort to rescue the ten Americans and roughly forty CIDG strikers thought to be still trapped inside Lang Vei. Baldwin had a plan and thought he had the answers.

"Give him the helicopters," Ladd pleaded.

"Well, I can't do that," a Marine air officer replied. "We may need these for our own evacuation."

General Westmoreland broke into the conversation.

"You need helicopters, Baldwin?" Westmoreland turned to Cushman: "General, give him the helicopters!" Norman Anderson was to furnish strike aircraft as well. Ladd's own plan, under which two MIKE Force companies had been authorized to stage from Nha Trang in II Corps to Da Nang, one of them prepared to drop by parachute, would be passed over in favor of the MACVSOG alternative. Baldwin's men were Green Berets just as much as Ladd's. "I decided that the Special Forces would conduct a raid," Westmoreland recounts, "from Khe Sanh to the vicinity of Lang Vei."

The most important characters in the final hours of the Lang Vei drama were its own defenders, the Laotians, and the Green Berets at FOB-3 next to the Khe Sanh combat base. It was, in fact, not true that everything moving above the ground was North Vietnamese. By ones and twos, sometimes larger groups, the men outside the TOC bunker made their escape or rallied. Most rallying occurred at the old Lang Vei camp, for the Laotian BV-33 compound was the sole friendly position in the area. Ironically, the much-denigrated Laotian troops were now to be the last hope for the Americans surrounded at Lang Vei.

Team Sergeant Craig, with Vietnamese Sergeant Major Day, led the largest survivor group. They started out in the 4.2-inch mortar pit with a few companions, among them Tiroch, Thompson, and Burke. A column of forty or fifty CIDG strikers from the 102nd Company area soon joined them. They made their way quickly over Lang Vei's inner wire barrier and were about to cross the outer one when they came under fierce fire from machine guns. Craig, Tiroch, and perhaps ten of the strikers went to ground while the others made it out. When the light from flareships and artillery died down, Craig's party made its break to a stand of bamboo about a hundred meters away. The group hid for perhaps half an hour until aircraft began dropping bombs all around them. Craig, Tiroch, and one of the strikers were wounded by fragments. The strikers took off then, leaving the two Americans by themselves. Craig and Tiroch moved along a dry streambed and hid out until dawn. Observing the camp in daylight, they saw troops maneuvering in the open, decided they might be friendly, and revealed themselves.

For a moment, as they got closer, Craig and Tiroch had the scare of their lives, for they saw NVA field caps and AK-47s. But then they saw camouflage fatigues and carbines too and realized this might be an element of BV-33. The group turned out to be Special Forces with Laotians, including Sergeant First Class Eugene Ashley, Jr., Sergeant Richard H. Allen, and Specialist-4 Joel Johnson.

All night Ashley had been trying to get Colonel Soulang to give him troops for relief operations. Some suspect that Soulang had been receiving messages from the NVA to stay put and do nothing and that he had followed that advice. However, the coolness with which Captain Willoughby's detachment had treated BV-33 when the Laotians retreated into the area can itself account for the Laotians' reticence. In addition, the standard of combat efficiency in the Royal Laotian Army remained far lower than that in the U.S. Army or ARVN, and the intensity of the battle may simply have scared Soulang. The Laotian had told Ashley to wait until morning and, once morning came, was willing to allow Laotians to fight for Lang Vei. The Lao troops proved equally gun shy, and it took more than an hour to muster just about a hundred men.

Now Ashley with this little band was trying to mount assaults into Lang Vei from the outside. They were in touch with the TOC on its secondary radio frequencies and knew of the growing danger for the survivors — the NVA had finally blown a six-foot hole in the wall of the bunker with explosives they buried in the ground next to it. Craig and Tiroch joined Ashley's group for their action, which proved to be the beginning of a curious minuet. The Americans would push, beg, cajole, even threaten to get the Laotian soldiers to join in the assault. At one stage Ashley apparently was almost turning his gun on the allied troops. Then the air strikes would come in and hit the area, following which the assault force would move out. When the NVA opened fire to halt them, the Laotians would run away and the whole thing started over again.

Five times the little force tried to make its way to the center of Lang Vei. They made their best progress during a foray after Johnson had brought up a 57mm recoilless rifle from old Lang Vei and silenced an NVA machine gun that had been harassing them. On one thrust the band recovered Colonel Schungel and Lieutenant Wilkins, who were sent on to old Lang Vei. On the fifth attempt Ashley was wounded in the chest. Given first aid, he was then placed in a jeep sent up to take Schungel, but just inside the Laotian perimeter a mortar shell exploded nearby, killing Ashley and wounding his medic, Sergeant Allen. Ashley was awarded a posthumous Medal of Honor.

Another American on the loose was Staff Sergeant Dennis Thompson, a fine soldier and free spirit on his second Vietnam tour. Escaping from Lang Vei, he received wounds in the legs and back and elected to stay behind so as not to slow down the others. He returned to the central compound only to be accosted by a large group of desperate montagnards who begged him to lead them to safety. Finding a radio, Thompson organized the party into four groups suitable for helicopter evacuation. Before he could do much else the strikers were surrounded by a force of NVA; then, apparently attracted by this concentration on the ground, an A-1 Skyraider dropped a canister of gasoline that ignited just feet from the American.

When Thompson regained consciousness North Vietnamese soldiers were dragging him along the road. He was eventually placed with another Lang Vei prisoner, Sergeant Harvey Brande.

Back at Da Nang Colonel Baldwin boarded an ARVN H-34 chopper for the flight to FOB-3. The ship had no navigational aids and only UHF radio, but that did not become a problem until it took hits en route. The helicopter lost power and made an emergency landing in a valley. Later the crew were able to get it restarted but they insisted on returning to base. Baldwin ended up back at Phu Bai talking to Major George Quamo at Khe Sanh over the single-sideband radio. Baldwin told Quamo just where to go and what to do and the FOB-3 deputy activated the plan.

Quamo first asked for volunteers. There were many, and ten Americans and about forty strikers were chosen. Captain Heckman, the Air Force forward air controller then flying over the CIDG camp, heard that a "Mission 87" had been slated for the Lang Vei mission. The transport choppers assembled at FOB-3 by 3:00 P.M. and their pilots alighted for a briefing. The air assault would lift off at 4:30.

In the meantime Colonel Schungel, now at old Lang Vei, established radio communication with Quamo and also had contact with the Americans remaining in the TOC at Lang Vei. Schungel knew things were desperate at Lang Vei. That morning, after the NVA had blown in the bunker wall, they had called down to the defenders to surrender. The Americans indignantly refused, but the Vietnamese Special Forces and montagnards had had enough. They filed out, never to be seen again. That left just eight men, including two badly wounded and Captain Willoughby, whom the others thought dead but who regained consciousness that morning. The Green Berets prepared to go down fighting the last assault but it never came. Perhaps the repeated relief attempts by Ashley's group and the Laotians did divert the North Vietnamese after all.

By afternoon the Americans in the bunker decided they must make a break for it. Everyone was wounded except two communications men (Emmanuel Phillips and Frank Dooms), and Wes Moreland seemed so bad the others decided to leave him behind. Until then Nick Fragos had had his hands full trying to calm the semiconscious and delirious Moreland, who screamed whenever anyone touched him. John Early, the other most seriously wounded man, was carried out. Willoughby arranged with Schungel that the Americans would run for it after another set of air strikes. They did. There was some NVA fire but it didn't come close.

Paul Longgrear led the procession. "So I'm the first one out," he recalled. "So I take off running, and I get maybe 30 or 40 yards and I see an automatic weapon and two guys, so I knew he would kill us all. So I figured, well, I'll just take it out. So I went for the weapon and I knocked out the weapon. But I had been wounded in the ankle, and so my ankle snapped. I just flipped through the air and landed on my back."

The others saw what had happened and assumed Longgrear had been killed. In fact, Longgrear had an eerie experience of speaking to God amid a sudden silence on the battlefield. After that he got up and, using his rifle as a crutch, began to hobble to safety. He later converted to Christianity and became a minister.

The party made its way painfully past a supply bunker to Route 9. Near Lang Vei's old east gate they encountered Vietnamese Special Forces Lieutenant Quy, who had been captured by the North Vietnamese but had escaped. Quy had a ¼-ton truck, on which he loaded the thankful Green Berets and drove them to old Lang Vei. It was about 4:00 P.M.

At 5:15 Major Quamo and the FOB-3 reaction force helilifted into old Lang Vei to mobilize the Laotians and make a combined strike into the CIDG camp. Helicopters circled and would not land until Quamo in his UH-1 swooped in ahead of them. The maneuver was supported by an air armada that included two forward air controllers, six A-1E propeller-driven aircraft, four jet fighters, and five or six

Army and Marine helicopter gunships. As the transport CH-46s came in, they were mobbed by frantic Laotian and Vietnamese troops who had to be physically ejected so the dozen wounded Americans and the most seriously wounded indigenous troops could be loaded first. Quamo's reaction force was undoubtedly pleased to find all these Americans already at the Laotian site.

There was one American so far left behind, however. He was Lieutenant Thomas Todd, the engineer officer who had come up on temporary duty. At the height of the battle, when he could fight no more, Todd took cover in the medical bunker, where he remained undisturbed. At about 5:00 P.M. he decided to join the Americans he assumed were still inside the TOC, but he found the bunker a mass of rubble. He saw Moreland, who appeared to have died, and then glimpsed a helicopter taking off from old Lang Vei and ran off in that direction. Todd was recovered by helicopter.

Perhaps a half hour later a station came up on the radio calling itself "Elephant" and requesting helicopter extraction for fifteen persons. This too was accomplished, but Colonel Soulang and his BV-33 had apparently expected more. When Todd arrived at old Lang Vei on foot, followed soon by a helicopter to recover him and the fifteen others, many Laotians tried to crowd aboard. There was trouble and some of the crew later stated that they believed many of the hits they suffered were from Laotians being left behind. In any case, Soulang and the survivors of BV-33 evacuated old Lang Vei and began to march toward Khe Sanh at about 6:30 P.M.

The battle of Lang Vei was over. A total of 2,476 rounds of artillery fire had been expended to help the CIDG camp, together with two ARC LIGHT strikes with twelve B-52s and sixty-seven Marine air sorties delivering 125.9 tons of ordnance. The number of Air Force and Navy fixed-wing sorties is not known, but it is not negligible.

As had happened with Saigon's tardy reports to Washington during the early hours of the battle, the special message reporting the recovery of the survivors to the National Military Command Center apparently was dispatched about three hours after Major Quamo's force had made its helilift. Walt Rostow would finally be able to modify his initial reports to President Johnson.

Though the battle for Lang Vei had ended, there remained plenty of loose strings to tie up. Ten Green Berets were missing or dead along with five Vietnamese Special Forces and five interpreters. Only fifty to seventy of the montagnards were at first accounted for, although eventually 117 CIDG strikers and 127 of the MIKE Force troopers straggled in from the hills. Many of those who did make it, including all but one of the Americans, were wounded. No one had any notion what North Vietnamese losses might have been. The after-action report estimated NVA losses at seven tanks destroyed and about 250 killed in action. These figures were repeated in the summer 1968 MACV analysis.

Aside from losses and lost positions, the most serious outcome of the Lang Vei fight was to uproot once more the Laotian troops and refugees and terrify the Bru villagers remaining in the combat zone. Colonel Soulang's later account to a military attaché in Laos was that BV-33, after losing about twenty-six men to NVA fire or U.S. bombs in the relief efforts, got very little help from Americans. Soulang claims the Americans promised him two helicopters to carry Lao troops but picked up only Americans and Vietnamese. When asked again, the United States sent two ships that carried a load each but on the second trip picked up only one load. Altogether only forty Laotians were lifted out. Once arrived at Khe Sanh they were disarmed and put into shell craters outside the combat base.

Soulang told his unit commanders to break up into small groups and either make for Khe Sanh or evade across the Laotian border. The colonel and seventy-four of his men went to Khe Sanh. There they too were disarmed and put into craters, guarded by Marines. The Laotian colonel says his men felt more like prisoners of war than allies and were especially upset that no food was issued either to them or to the civilian refugees who were arriving in growing numbers. On February 8, after strong protests, a Special Forces major returned the Laotians' weapons, but they were still required to remain outside the perimeter wire. Except for individual Americans who shared with them, the Lao received no food whatever, and on February 10 Lao civilian refugees decided to return to Laos and disappeared down Route 9.

Colonel Soulang and 113 men were flown to Da Nang aboard a C-130 on February 11. There they were fed, bathed, clothed, and treated well by an Air Force civic action team. Soulang and two officers went to the Laotian embassy in Saigon to make arrangements for repatriation of their men. They were flown back to Savannakhet on February 15 by Royal Laotian Air Force C-47 transports.

After hearing Soulang's report, General Boun Pone, Laotian southern region commander, remarked that his army now "must consider South Vietnamese as enemy because of their conduct."

Even more than the Laotian troops, the appearance of masses of civilian refugees triggered panic among American commanders and demoralization among the troops at Khe Sanh who could do so little for them. Westmoreland first discussed the problem with General Cushman on the telephone at 9:25 P.M. of February 7, the same conversation in which Cushman reported recovery of sixteen Americans from the Lang Vei area. Westmoreland proposed flying the refugees out to Savannakhet, but Cushman noted there were too many for air transport. Westmoreland then asked about air dropping rice to the refugees but again Cushman referred to the problem of air transport — available tonnage was fully occupied carrying supplies for the combat base. Then Cushman warned that he "may be forced by tactical considerations to use CS [gas] to chase them out."

Ten minutes later Westmoreland was on the phone to Ellsworth Bunker to say he needed guidance on the matter. Bunker drew up a cable to Washington reporting that six thousand refugees were outside the combat base (the number had already grown from the five thousand Westmoreland had estimated on the telephone) and that this represented a serious tactical problem because of worries that the civilians might be used as a shield for an NVA attack. Bunker proposed to send the Laotian chargé d'affaires in Saigon to speak to the refugees and urge them to leave the area.

Actually the refugee problem was even thornier than anyone thought. Scattered among them were CIDG and MIKE Force strikers whom no one would recognize or admit to the combat base. Moreover, Laotians could have made up only a small portion of the masses of refugees, since only about 2,200 had entered the country in the first place. The larger fraction of refugees had to be Bru, and talking to the Laotian chargé was not going to do much for them. In addition, officers naturally feared that the North Vietnamese would try to insert agents among the crowd.

Special Forces worried that not taking care of the CIDG and MIKE Force strikers would affect their ability to recruit indigenous forces in I Corps. Colonel Ladd protested to MACV, dragging in Westmoreland's hobbyhorse, operation YORK, claiming that an invasion of Laos would be impeded if nothing were done. General Cushman conceded that these friendly soldiers ought to be provided for but reiterated that there was no one to identify them. He also reported that the strikers had been advised to stay in an abandoned hamlet "until such time as verification of their status could be made." General Westmoreland ruled on February 9 that a special evacuation would be made of these troops and their dependents, as had been done for the BV-33 soldiers.

At midday of February 9 Westmoreland met with Ambassador Bunker. He told Bunker, only about an hour after his message directing the specialized evacuation, "We have a problem with refugees at Khe Sanh among the [Laotian] tribesmen. We cannot afford the helicopters to evacuate them but will get them out on a space-available basis to the extent possible." The U.S. embassy in Vientiane, Westmoreland reported, "is very concerned about this and somewhat unrealistic in their appraisal of the situation." When the Laotian refugees left on foot it became evident they were the smaller part of the problem. It was the Bru who needed help.

Looking at the refugee mass and considering the military problem, General Tompkins instructed his deputy chief of staff for operations to notify Khe Sanh of the procedure he wanted used if the NVA launched an attack behind a human wave of refugees. First the Marines were to fire CS gas to disperse the civilians, then they were to fire over their heads, and finally they should shoot into the crowd.

"This is a sticky one," Colonel Lownds told one reporter at Khe Sanh.

> There's no right answer. Here are these people whom we organized, trained, gave weapons to, and promised we would help defend. . . . They come to my gate and ask me to take them in. They have fought bravely on our side and have been overrun. They are hurt and beaten and they need help. . . .
>
> On the other hand, the fact is I don't know really who any of these people are. Even if most of them are Vietnamese and montagnards who worked with our Special Forces people at Lang Vei, I know they are certainly infiltrated with VC. I can't let them in without also letting in several thousand civilians out there whom I know even less about.

The dilemma was a sharp one, not made any easier by the decision of ARVN I Corps commander Hoang Xuan Lam that no Bru be permitted to evacuate to the lowlands. General Lam based his order on claims that there was no place to put the refugees and nothing to feed them, but it was privately held to be another reflection of Vietnamese attitudes toward the montagnards. When about 1,500 Bru nevertheless tried to walk out of the area on Route 9 they were stopped, this time by the North Vietnamese near Ca Lu.

Such evacuation by air as was carried out finally moved eight

ARVN Special Forces soldiers, 104 MIKE Force men, and 112 CIDG strikers. In addition, the aerial evacuation at the end of January had moved another 91 Laotians or their dependents and 90 MIKE Force or CIDG troops. The Bru tribesmen were left out in the cold. CAP Marine Frank Iodice says: "We stabbed them in the back. I wake up and I look in the mirror every morning and I think of that. Had I not been so naive and immature, I would have saw that 'set up' coming and I would have started moving those people earlier. But I still believed in the Marine Corps' ability to do the right thing."

Linguist Daniel R. Kelley, just back from leave in the States, witnessed these events with the rest of CAC Oscar. He was often angry at the Marine Corps and ashamed at how little the Americans were willing to do for the Bru. Kelley was asked to question Bru who worked in the FOB-3 compound about what they would do if their families were made to parade in front of a North Vietnamese assault force. Some of the Bru simply said they would shoot. Kelley was surprised. Here the United States stood in the midst of a war for the loyalties of Vietnamese citizens, who included the Bru, yet for all its power America seemed unwilling to show as much loyalty as the Bru themselves. Americans were lost in an exotic culture many could not appreciate. Vietnam was an unusual war in which white could sometimes be black, or black white. Without understanding the special character of the Vietnamese war, it would be difficult for Americans to win hearts and minds. A corollary was that the single-minded focus on making Khe Sanh a battle to annihilate the North Vietnamese Army meant the sacrifice of the pacification of this upland district.

Within twelve hours of the peak of the Lang Vei fighting, the so-called South Vietnam Liberation Radio began to broadcast a special communiqué. The message correctly recounted the initiation of the assault at fifteen minutes past midnight, calling Lang Vei "an important position of the U.S. aggressors on Highway 9 in the Khe Sanh defense system." The terse North Vietnamese account noted:

At [12:15 A.M.] on 7th February, the liberation armed forces' artillery furiously shelled this position. Their shock infantry force, in several prongs, rapidly thrust at the enemy position, dividing them into many sections and wiping them out one after another. The defending enemy were unable to resist the mighty attack.

The communiqué, signed by "The Command of the Liberation Armed Forces of the Khe Sanh Front," commended the cadres and fighters of "different armed services" for close coordination and brave fighting. The reference to "different armed services" was the only allusion to the participation of armored forces. Other than inflating the garrison of the CIDG camp to a thousand "U.S. puppet troops" and claiming that Lang Vei had been "completely annihilated" by 2:30 A.M., the description of the main features of the battle was accurate. Shorn of its propaganda content, the communiqué, which took pains to put the battle into the larger context of the Tet campaign, does not suggest that Khe Sanh was the major focus of North Vietnamese operations. Parts of the communiqué were rebroadcast in English by Radio Hanoi just before midnight of February 7.

The same Radio Hanoi program the following night publicized the commentary that appeared that day in *Quan Doi Nhan Dan*, the official paper of the People's Army. That commentary emphasized that Lang Vei had been "a first-rate annihilation battle," a "very good example of how well . . . regular units can conduct a lightning, neat attack, and how quickly they can take control of the battlefield."

In Vietnamese earlier in the day Radio Hanoi carried a longer article from the People's Army newspaper. Themes drawn from the first communiqué are again clearly in evidence:

> The Lang Vei victory is a striking example by the main force Liberation Armed Forces of quick attack, complete annihilation, and holding the initiative on the battlefield. With a determination to fight and close coordination from various armed branches, the Liberation Armed Forces, coming from many directions and various points, quickly divided the enemy, destroyed position after position, and in a short time annihilated a strong U.S. defensive position. That was a strong blow smashing the enemy snake, cutting defensive Route 9, and throwing the enemy into great turmoil.

More laconic are the notes recorded by North Vietnamese cadres Vu Xuan Mau and Le Viet Yeu in their notebook. They simply wrote that they had "liberated Lang Vay." As for Khe Sanh the notes read, "continued to tighten . . . encirclement."

11

The Khe Sanh Shuffle

THE FALL OF LANG VEI CLEARED AWAY the last obstacle preventing the North Vietnamese from closing in on Khe Sanh from the southwest. The next act occurred in the valley itself, barely twenty-four hours later, while just a few kilometers away Marines struggled to cope with the refugee masses. This was the first North Vietnamese assault action in the immediate vicinity of the combat base and also the first time the NVA dared continue a battle action into daylight hours. In combination with the events of the preceding days the new action seemed to presage an immediate threat to Khe Sanh. At a minimum it highlighted the vulnerabilities of the position as the campaign lengthened, stretching into a battle of days, and then a siege of weeks.

On February 8 the object of the firefight was Hill 64, the little knob that the 1/9 Marines had mistakenly climbed near the Rock Quarry. When the battalion relocated, its commander, Lieutenant Colonel John F. Mitchell, put an outpost on Hill 64. On January 23 the 1st Platoon of Company A occupied the knob along with a section of the battalion weapons company. Second Lieutenant Terence R. Roach led forty-five infantrymen, and twenty weapons specialists were under the command of Second Lieutenant Francis B. Lovely, Jr. Within ten days the Marines had built bunkers and a perimeter trench around the knob, and after that they began to lay barbed wire. The position was oriented roughly northwest–southeast, about forty meters long and twenty wide. One machine gun was emplaced at the northwest end of the position, the most likely avenue of attack because it was the only slope with a gradient less than forty-five degrees; there was a second machine gun at the northeast tip.

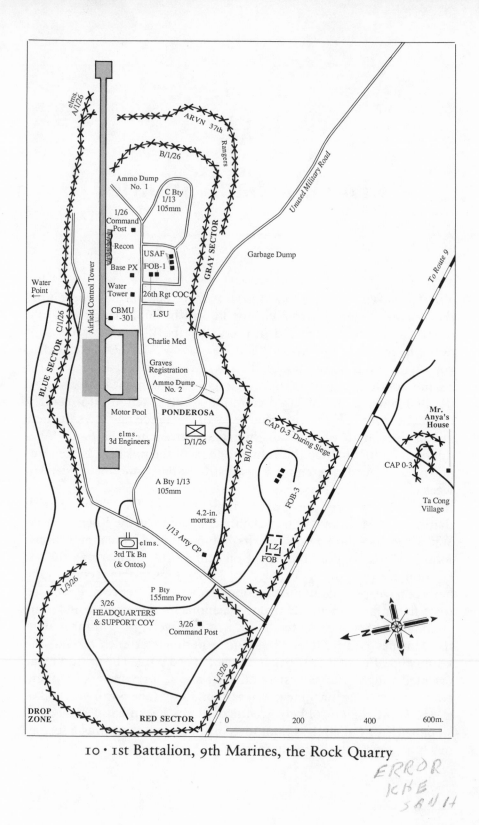

elms.
A/1/26

ARVN 37th Rangers

B/1/26

Ammo Dump
No. 1

C Bty
1/13
105mm

1/26
Command
Post

Recon

Base PX

Water
Tower

CBMU
-301

USAF

FOB-1

26th Rgt COC

LSU

GRAY SECTOR

Garbage Dump

Unused Military Road

To Route 9

Water
Point

BLUE SECTOR C/1/26

Airfield Control Tower

Charlie Med

Graves
Registration

Ammo Dump
No. 2

Motor Pool

elms.
3d Engineers

PONDEROSA

D/1/26

B/1/26

CAP 0-3 During Siege

Mr.
Anya's
House

CAP 0-3

Ta Cong
Village

A Bty 1/13
105mm

4.2-in.
mortars

FOB-3

3rd Tk Bn
(& Ontos)

elms.

1/13 Arty CP

LZ
FOB

P Bty
155mm Prov

L/3/26

3/26
HEADQUARTERS
& SUPPORT COY

3/26
Command Post

L/3/26

DROP
ZONE

RED SECTOR

0   200   400   600m.

10 · 1st Battalion, 9th Marines, the Rock Quarry

ERROR
KHE
SANH

Sergeant Edward W. Welchel figured the Alpha Company outpost was a sitting duck so long as a huge NVA force sat out there. His fears rose in early February when a chaplain visited and held a prayer meeting. Then, Welchel recalls, "the corpsmen started giving classes on first aid, and we knew it was coming."

Here, just a few thousand meters from the combat base, the North Vietnamese seemed so confident they were willing to parade in plain sight. On February 3 Marines called in an artillery mission when they saw forty or more North Vietnamese marching by. An air observer called another strike nearby when he sighted NVA in a tree line changing from field uniforms to black pajamas. Another mission was called in similar circumstances on February 7. That afternoon an artillery forward observer, Private First Class Lawrence J. Seavy, got involved in a contest of wills with a North Vietnamese gun that seemed to constantly fire on the Marines. Finally, in the last hour of the evening twilight, Seavy managed to spot its muzzle flash well enough to adjust grid coordinates. Calling in another fire mission, "I was finally rewarded with a secondary explosion," he recalled.

Seavy and Roach also spent part of that afternoon registering artillery targets with the fire support control center at Khe Sanh. Intending merely to ensure availability of preplotted artillery fire, the Marines on Hill 64 had no idea how soon they were going to need it. The evening passed quietly.

Unknown to the Americans, at that very time an estimated battalion of the 101D Regiment of the NVA 325-C Division had quietly moved into assembly positions for an assault against their outpost. The North Vietnamese opened with a barrage of mortar and artillery fire at the Marines' Rock Quarry positions and then went into the attack. The battalion positions reeled under the impact of about 350 shells.

At the Alpha outpost the actual time of the attack was 4:45 A.M. on February 8, according to Sergeant Welchel. He remembers "because my bunker was the first to be attacked and at that time I was looking forward to [five o'clock], as I was going to get one more hour of sleep." Three grenades exploded inside the bunker, one a red smoke grenade, apparently a signal to trigger the attack. Welchel could barely breathe in the smoke and dived out of the bunker.

The North Vietnamese assault came with considerable shock and power. Three to four minutes after the barrage began, wire barriers on the northwest perimeter were breached with bangalore torpedoes.

Other NVA tossed rolls of canvas across the wire to bridge it. By 5:13 A.M. the NVA were inside the position. Most of 1st Platoon's casualties occurred during these first moments of the firefight.

On the southwest side Lieutenant Roach quickly left his command post bunker, ordering his radio man, Lance Corporal James P. Rizzo, to take cover in the bunker along with another Marine. Roach raced across the top of the hill and tried to organize his men, providing cover fire for surviving Marines who were wounded or trapped. Two or three squads of NVA soldiers were already in the trenches in the northeast sector. One North Vietnamese leaped up and shot Roach, who was killed instantly. He was awarded a posthumous Bronze Star.

Rizzo fared no better. Initially he had helped Roach by shining a penlight on NVA, whom the lieutenant then took under fire. Ordered into the command post bunker, Rizzo was supposed to maintain communications with battalion. Inside he found Corporal Fisel getting more ammunition. Fisel failed to convince Rizzo to stay put. There was firing right outside the bunker. Rizzo had barely exited when he took a burst of automatic weapons fire in his chest.

"This is the CP [command post] radio operator," Rizzo broadcast. "I'm hit. I've been shot. I'm dying. This is my last transmission."

Fisel heard North Vietnamese moving outside the bunker. They called out in English, "Come out; we know you are in there. Give yourself up!" Instead Fisel climbed up on a supply shelf suspended over the entrance and perched there. The NVA tossed grenades into the bunker. Fisel lost consciousness. Later he discovered that the handset wire of Rizzo's radio had been cut. Evidently North Vietnamese had entered the bunker after the grenades and either had not seen Fisel or presumed him dead.

Private First Class Michael A. Barry on the north side of the outpost engaged in a hand grenade duel. That was what he was doing when the 1st Squad Marine felt a plonk on his helmet and a Chinese-manufactured grenade fell at his feet. Barry stooped to pick up the grenade and drew back to throw it when the thing went off in his hand. Chinese grenades frequently produced an uneven fragmentation pattern and this one was no exception — the force of its blast was mostly down and away from Barry's body. Though the Marine received metal fragments in his right arm, leg, and back, he did not lose even a finger and remained in action. Had Barry's mishap occurred with an American M-26 grenade, he would most likely have been killed.

Meanwhile Private Seavy, the artillery observer, was initially in a bunker just behind the northeast perimeter. With grenades going off all around, he quickly decided Hill 64 was being overrun and tried to call for the artillery missions he had registered the previous afternoon. But with the danger, excitement, and noise, Seavy was unable to recall the exact registration numbers. Ordinarily this would have been no problem, for the numbers were written on his map, but it was night, there was no light inside the bunker, and Seavy had lent his penlight to Lieutenant Roach. Seavy figured the artillery fire was urgent and lit a match to try and read the numbers. His radio operator promptly blew the thing out, warning Seavy not to light any more.

This tiny amount of illumination, glimpsed from behind the poncho, which was not quite large enough to cover the entire bunker entrance, clued the NVA that someone was inside. Two grenades rolled into the bunker just as Seavy called in the artillery numbers. The two Marines were lucky to be able to roll the grenades back through the door. With the explosions, however, Seavy's ears were practically numb and he could hardly hear Khe Sanh on the radio; he had to virtually shout on his end. The combat base refused to fire artillery without approval from the local unit commander, Lieutenant Roach, who, unknown to all in this drama, was already dead.

Seavy's radio man was unable to raise Roach or Rizzo on the PRC-25. That left no alternative but to go out and look for them. It was the beginning of a hazardous venture during which Seavy's rifle jammed and he repeatedly became the target of NVA grenades, fought a hand-to-hand duel with a North Vietnamese infantryman, and was almost captured during his initial egress from the bunker.

By now Hill 64 was under command of the weapons officer, Lieutenant Lovely, who had also been in his bunker when the action began. Lovely ran out into the trenches and into several NVA who were already through the perimeter wire. Shooting at them, he saw or heard that Roach had fallen and assumed command. He was able to find perhaps fifteen Marines and by 5:00 A.M. had staked out a new perimeter, not quite to the crest of the hill, including just about a fifth of the former position. A few more Americans staggered in, giving Lovely twenty-two fighting men. They were all that remained of a sixty-five-man garrison.

The battle degenerated into a stalemate. The North Vietnamese seemed unable to complete their conquest of 1st Platoon's outpost, while Lovely's band of Marines lacked the strength to eject the NVA from the knob. Support came from the mortars of 1/9, most important starshells, flares that lit up the entire area. Lovely believes the battalion would have run out of these had the action lasted another hour.

Many stark, brave actions were taken on Hill 64 that morning. Lance Corporal Arnold Alderette won a Silver Star for his work with an M-60 machine gun, waking up in the first heat of the assault and then using the gun constantly, even after wounded, racing from one position to another to help repel the NVA. When Marines with Alderette ran out of grenades, he told them to throw rocks and yell to fool the North Vietnamese. Private Seavy was also all over the battlefield, making at least fifteen forays into the abandoned northern section of the position to retrieve weapons, ammunition, grenades, and other combat gear left by the dead and wounded. This was a critical function because many of the men on Lovely's improvised perimeter were disarmed or burdened with damaged rifles. Seavy brought back at least twenty M-16s, which Corporal Edward H. O'Connor worked to fix and clear for the defenders. Shortly after 6:00 A.M. the remaining NVA regrouped and made a further assault to drive off the last Marines. Seavy had never seen so many grenades; they were practically raining down on the Americans. To spare their comrades, Seavy and Alderette began to move around, setting up the M-60 and firing a few bursts, as if the machine gun were assuming a new permanent position. The NVA repeatedly focused on the automatic weapon while other Marines on the line went unscathed.

At the Rock Quarry Colonel Mitchell determined to dispatch a relief column at first light. Alpha Company's commander, Captain Henry J. M. Radcliffe, no less determined, chose Second Lieutenant Michael P. Hayden's platoon for the effort. Radcliffe accompanied the force when it moved off at 7:40 A.M. Delta and Bravo Companies with a section of tanks furnished savage support fire, hitting the edges surrounding the moving relief force. Nevertheless heavy NVA fire opposed the Marines. Captain Radcliffe led the force, knocking out two NVA positions with M-26 grenades. When an enemy grenade landed between him and another Marine, Radcliffe tossed it back at a North Vietnamese soldier, killing him.

Radcliffe's column reached the base of Hill 64 a few minutes after 8:00 A.M. Twenty minutes later they had climbed to the crest, joining Lovely's survivors, who were beginning to consolidate the position. Fighting continued for almost three hours against the NVA rear guard.

Delta Company fired with all its weapons at the North Vietnamese they saw streaming away from the outpost.

Alpha and Delta Companies counted 150 bodies of fallen adversaries. Perhaps thirty were actually atop Hill 64. Sergeant Larry L. Powell's job was to examine North Vietnamese bodies for items of intelligence interest. "It was quite a scene up there," Powell told Marine debriefers. "Didn't really believe it. . . . I *know* they fought hard on that hill. Men that made it had to do some real good fighting."

One of the NVA dead yielded a map that proved quite interesting to Khe Sanh's intelligence specialists. Markings indicated every tank and position suitable for armor on the combat base perimeter. Sergeant Patrick J. Fitch recalled that "this map showed, almost to a bunker, that they knew where everything we had was, including the positions of our underground ammo bunkers. If they had hit, I'm sure an initial wave of RPG [rocket-propelled grenade] men would have been in the area, and they would have decimated many of these positions."

Among the NVA weapons captured were three heavy machine guns, nine light ones, and a 60mm mortar. There was also one prisoner of war. The weapons taken amounted to half the total heavy weapons captured in all of the Khe Sanh siege to date. The map was highly valuable. Marine losses were twenty-four dead and twenty-nine wounded.

General Westmoreland's daily report to Washington noted these events quite laconically: "The enemy penetrated the wire of the platoon outpost but was repulsed. The enemy broke contact." The report admitted casualties of *one* Marine killed and *two* wounded and evacuated.

Battles in Saigon and Washington

For William Childs Westmoreland the easy fight was the one in Saigon. There it was merely a question of the MACV staff, and his writ would be law. "The state of mind at that time with respect to our posture at Khe Sanh," Westmoreland noted in his diary, "was so tenuous that I wanted to put to bed once and for all any defeatism or negative attitude." Westmoreland therefore requested his command historian's opinion comparing Khe Sanh with Dien Bien Phu, plus a more general assessment of Khe Sanh against classic sieges.

Classic sieges were high military science to Colonel Reamer W. Argo, command historian. Argo assembled a team and went to work on an analysis that he presented at a meeting in the late afternoon of February 11. The audience comprised denizens of the so-called Pentagon East, chief among them Westmoreland plus a few outsiders such as the visiting General Bruce Clarke.

In his historical presentation Colonel Argo reached back to the siege of Constantinople in 1453 and listed a total of thirty-nine sieges. Argo concluded that in the medieval period fortresses had had a fair record of withstanding sieges but that the advent of gunpowder reduced the time necessary to breach a fortress to an interval within the endurance of the investing force. Indeed, "so well was it recognized that a fort could not withstand a siege that formalized rules for surrender were observed by all commanders."

Of the fifteen sieges Argo identified during the twentieth century, defenders resisted successfully in only *two* instances: the Soviets at Leningrad between 1941 and 1944 (when the siege lines were never perfected) and the Americans at Bastogne in 1944 (when a strong relief force had been available). In the hundred years preceding, from the Napoleonic Wars to World War I, Argo had found only two more successful defenses of a fortress — both of them Union armies defending locations during the American Civil War. Though one might dispute some of Argo's characterizations, such as the defense of Na San during the Franco-Vietnamese war (1952) as "unsuccessful," Argo's list also left out a significant number of additional "unsuccessful" defenses, such as Kut el-Amara during World War I and Richmond-Petersburg in the Civil War. There was little point to disputing the substance of the analysis.

The briefers maintained that the inability of fortresses to withstand siege could be attributed to the tendency to forfeit the initiative, to supply problems that developed, and to the demoralization that often beset besieged forces. Success was attributed to the dispatch of relief forces or to such negative factors as withdrawal of the investing adversary or the beleaguered force itself. "It appears that Khe Sanh is following the pattern of previous sieges," the briefing paper observed. It discounted reinforcing Khe Sanh as merely raising the ante and American firepower by noting that the NVA had "undoubtedly taken into account and made allowances for the attrition [they] will suffer." The bottom line recommendation was that "urgent consideration be given to employing an outside force in offensive action against the enemy's forces devoted to the siege."

General Westmoreland felt "the whole presentation was frought [*sic*] with gloom." He looked around and his staff was stunned. Westy quickly intervened, saying that it was good they had heard the worst but that Khe Sanh was different because of the available air and artillery support and because other troops could easily be diverted there, either by air or land. According to Westmoreland's diary, he thanked Argo but "made it unequivocally clear that the decision had been made to hold Khe Sanh." He also "made it absolutely plain that I wanted no talk that we could not hold it, since we were going to do just that."

"We are not, repeat not, going to be defeated at Khe Sanh," Westmoreland quotes himself as saying. "I will tolerate no talking or even thinking to the contrary." After that the MACV commander stalked out of the room.

These weeks of February 1968 very likely were William Westmoreland's worst days in Vietnam. First the Tet offensive exploded in his face, upsetting all calculations in spite of his anticipation. Then the maddening on-again, off-again pattern of the long-awaited set piece battle for Khe Sanh, combined with the gloom and doom among his staff and in Washington, surely upset the general. Of course Colonel Argo's conclusions could hardly have been a surprise to the MACV commander, for Westmoreland had known for weeks that his subordinates were very uncertain about Khe Sanh and he himself had insisted on solidarity in previous staff meetings. It may be that Westmoreland deliberately intended the Argo briefing to provide him a platform to rally the troops with a dramatic statement like the one he made. Westy probably saw himself as struggling to conduct a battle against all odds, impeded by uncertain subordinates and Washington's sensitivity.

General Westmoreland could not but be aware of the changed perceptions of Vietnam in the United States, where, for the first time ever, some prominent figures and segments of the media had begun to call for replacement of the MACV commander. President Lyndon Johnson, quick to see dangers in such press speculation, cabled Westmoreland "literally eyes only" to castigate the "irresponsible talk in the newspapers" and assure the general of his confidence.

For his own part, however, General Westmoreland continued to use his somewhat diffident technique of reporting with assurances but preparing for the worst case, a technique that could only shake Washington's faith. At the beginning of February, when Joint Chiefs chairman Earle Wheeler had asked him to form a study group to plan possible use of nuclear weapons, Westmoreland's mere mention of these weapons in a subsequent cable had raised White House eyebrows.

With the Argo briefing, Westmoreland effectively ordered solidarity. However, he began to think seriously about an operation to relieve Khe Sanh by opening Route 9.

That Westmoreland was quite capable of keeping his own counsel is demonstrated by the back-channel dialogue he conducted in deep secrecy with Wheeler and also by the curious episode of his French military advisers. The United States, of course, had replaced France in Vietnam, and Americans never tired of explaining how the United States was not France, was not fighting like the French, had nothing in common with the French, and so forth. Yet Westmoreland regularly consulted, as often as three or four times a year, with French Indochina veterans who came to Saigon to give advice. While telling Colonel Argo, and indeed President Johnson, that Khe Sanh was not Dien Bien Phu, Westmoreland was privately talking to French advisers about Dien Bien Phu. So private were the consultations that General Phillip Davidson, Westmoreland's own intelligence chief, says he did not know about them at the time and only recently got confirmation from the MACV commander that they took place.

The chief French military adviser was General Paul Vanuxem, a lion of the Red River delta who had commanded French mobile groups under famed Marshal Jean de Lattre and others but who had been passed over for command of Dien Bien Phu. Vanuxem had started out as a student of philosophy, though he had won his spurs in Italy during World War II and had gone on to the Algerian war. His experience was in counterinsurgency and clearing operations, not sieges. Of the three sieges Colonel Argo's study cited from the Franco-Vietnamese war, Vanuxem had not been present at any. Always small, Vanuxem's consultant group varied in size and grew to as many as seven in years after Westmoreland's departure from Vietnam. It was Vanuxem himself who revealed its existence.

On February 9 General Westmoreland told Washington that NVA attacks in the Khe Sanh area indicated a strength of two divisions there and that "a major offensive is imminent." In a longer message predicting a second wave of Tet attacks, the MACV chief reported that two North Vietnamese officers captured in Laos had said the date for the renewed offensive would be February 10. In a further cable

Westmoreland sent shortly after midnight on February 10 he emphasized "an enemy threat of major proportions" to I Corps, the considerable forces he had sent north, and the tasks his troops must
accomplish. "Needless to say," Westmoreland stated, "I would welcome reinforcements at any time they can be made available." Reinforcements acting in conjunction with the 1st Cavalry Division could
clear the coastal road and "effect a land link-up with Khe Sanh."

It was not Westmoreland, or Cushman, Tompkins, or Lownds for
that matter, who sat at the center of the maelstrom. The man in that
unenviable position was Lyndon Baines Johnson. He had been told
repeatedly that Hanoi's multiphase strategy was aimed not at Tet but
at an attack on Khe Sanh. The final arbiter of U.S. policy, President
Johnson wanted more information on exactly what was happening.
That was why, on February 3, he had Rostow cable General Westmoreland to request a special Khe Sanh report daily, for which
Johnson would be the basic audience. Rostow also asked General
Wheeler to submit daily reports on the Vietnam situation based on his
conversations with Westmoreland over a secure telephone line. The
MACV reports on Khe Sanh began to flow on February 5.
   Though the president held ultimate responsibility for this most
important battle in the highlands, it was the function of government
to advise him; heavy responsibility lay in the fulfillment of that task.
Johnson's basic protection against the judgments of history resides in
the quality of the advice and information provided him. Lyndon
Johnson was not above letting that be known. Thus it was Johnson
himself, at a session in the White House with reporters on February
2, who had revealed the existence of the Joint Chiefs of Staff memorandum on Khe Sanh, which LBJ called "a letter saying they were
ready for this offensive."
   Clark Clifford, an intimate private adviser whom President Johnson
had convinced to succeed Robert McNamara at the Pentagon, closely
observed these events while preparing for his new job. Clifford became increasingly uncomfortable with the advice LBJ was getting. At
none of the meetings with his military advisers, Clifford notes in his
recent memoir, did any of the generals warn that the Khe Sanh activity
might be part of a plan to divert American attention. Westmoreland
and Wheeler had decided that Khe Sanh was going to be the major
battle of the war. Wheeler carried that message to the White House
when LBJ met with his advisers over several days in late January to

review preparations for the engagement. By early February Clifford saw the problem as a "Khe Sanh obsession," one that Lyndon Johnson, concerned for American boys at risk in South Vietnam, could hardly help sharing.

President Johnson's essential problem at this tense moment of the Vietnam war involved intuiting the interrelationship between events at Khe Sanh, the countrywide Tet offensive, and the seemingly remote incident off Korea in which the U.S. intelligence ship *Pueblo* had been taken over by North Korean naval forces. These events could be related or they might not. They could presage a global or continental war or they might not. The Vietnam situation alone might or might not require massive U.S. response. The *Pueblo* incident turned out to be of passing import, but for a few days all three matters appeared to be deadly serious.

The existence of this strategic conundrum is the reason for the series of detailed interrogatories that went to Westmoreland from Rostow and Wheeler just after Tet, questions that sharpened as the moment of decision appeared to approach at Khe Sanh. Westmoreland held to his analysis that Hanoi intended to mount a military operation in three phases culminating in the Khe Sanh action. President Johnson accepted the essentials of that analysis and conducted himself accordingly. In this he is not to be faulted, though some chose to do so. Columnist Marquis Childs, for example, published a piece on February 7 complaining that LBJ "increasingly . . . cites the authority of Westmoreland for his personal judgments on Vietnam. And he backs this up by reciting what the Joint Chiefs of Staff tell him. He seems at times to be reversing the Constitution of the United States which holds that the President as Commander-in-Chief exercises the supreme authority."

Whatever his understanding of the Constitution, Childs at least got it right in perceiving President Johnson as keenly interested in what the military had to say at this stage of the war. On LBJ's instructions, Rostow's deputy Bromley Smith asked Wheeler to open the National Security Council meeting the day of Childs's column with a Vietnam briefing. Wheeler told the group what the Pentagon had just learned — that Lang Vei had had to be evacuated after heavy combat against an adversary armed with tanks. Subsequently the NSC meeting, originally intended to focus primarily on military aid programs, concentrated largely on Vietnam instead. After discussion of various aspects of the situation, talk turned to Khe Sanh.

"How do things look at Khe Sanh?" President Johnson asked. "Would you expect to have to move out of Lang Vie [*sic*]?"

General Wheeler answered, "It was not planned that we would hold some of these outposts. We may have to move back that company on Hill 861."

Johnson then turned to Secretary of Defense Robert S. McNamara. "Bob, are you worried?"

"I am not worried about a true military defeat," McNamara responded.

"Mr. President," Wheeler then interjected, "this is not a situation to take lightly. This is of great military concern to us. I do think that Khe Sanh is an important position which can and should be defended. It is important to us tactically and it is very important to us psychologically. But the fighting will be very heavy, and the losses may be high.

"General Westmoreland will set up the forward field headquarters as quickly as possible. He told me this morning that he has his cables and communications gear in. He is sending a list of his needs, including light aircraft. We are responding to this request."

"Let's get everybody involved on this as quickly as possible," the president ordered. "Everything he wants, let's get it to him."

The subject came up again in a more general discussion of Tet and Vietnam political issues that Johnson held on February 9. The president told his advisers to assume the United States would need more troops in Vietnam and to plan what could be done in minimum time to meet a crisis request. Regarding any call-up of reserve forces, LBJ wanted to "make the preparations now so that we do not have to do it in the middle of the night."

Only toward the end of the session did Khe Sanh come up. "Let's hope for the best but expect the worst," President Johnson told the group. That could entail more troop requests. LBJ asked if U.S. air support was deterring Hanoi "around Khe Sanh and elsewhere."

Secretary McNamara replied in the affirmative. "If they need more air support they will have it."

Secretary of State Dean Rusk wanted to know if there was "some way we can turn this around and take the offensive ourselves."

"The answer from the Joint Chiefs," McNamara replied, "will be to try a false offensive or an actual invasion against North Vietnam above the DMZ."

"This is more of a political decision than a military one," Rusk observed. The ball was in Lyndon Johnson's court.

"As near as we can make it out," Rostow then summarized, "the reserves now being held back would go in somewhere outside of Khe Sanh. They would from an outside point level pressure on the attacking forces. We may not have the people to take care of unexpected situations around Khe Sanh."

McNamara noted that Washington could accelerate dispatch of four additional rifle battalions scheduled to leave for Vietnam in April.

President Johnson then asked that the Joint Chiefs, who had been waiting in another room, enter to join the discussion. After more talk of troop levels, ARVN and South Korean troop quality, and Hanoi's strategy, President Johnson came back to Khe Sanh. "How is the supply problem at Khe Sanh?" he asked General Wheeler. "Will artillery and rockets knock this out? Can we rely on roads?"

"There is no road available up there," McNamara said.

"We moved in 214 tons of supplies yesterday," Wheeler added in reply to the president. "As long as we use B-52's and tactical air, we will be able to keep our resupply up. They are keeping about 10 to 12 days supplies in storage."

"Wouldn't we have one big problem if the airfield at Khe Sanh was out?" the president followed up.

"Yes," said Wheeler. "We would have to link up by road some way. Of course we can use air drops and helicopters. The airstrip will be used from time to time."

"If you lost the airstrip," LBJ asked, "would you evacuate Khe Sanh?"

Wheeler answered, "That depends on the course of the fighting and their ability to resupply."

"Nobody can give a categorical answer," Army Chief of Staff General Harold K. Johnson opined. "We think we have a 50–50 chance of sustaining our actions out there."

The president, Generals Johnson and Wheeler, and Rusk talked more about the airfield and the weather, and then the meeting went on to other Vietnam subjects like Tet. The Chiefs were probably not aware at that point of the degree to which President Johnson had relied for his questions on material from his special military adviser. Rusk and McNamara were. LBJ had told them, just before the Joint Chiefs entered the Cabinet Room for that February 9 meeting, "General Maxwell Taylor says he has some very deep concerns. We must at least be prepared."

*   *   *

In fact, Lyndon Johnson's questions for his advisers on February 9 closely paralleled a list of "Questions Related to the Military Situation in Vietnam" that Maxwell Taylor had sent the president the previous day. Johnson's questions about weather, about the adequacy of airlift forces, about Westmoreland's available mobile reserves, about North Vietnamese air capability, even about the Khe Sanh airstrip, followed Taylor's eight-point list. Dean Rusk raised a very significant question about the advisability of substituting something stronger for the Gulf of Tonkin Resolution, the government's basic authority to conduct war in Vietnam, which did not have the legal force of a declaration of war. This question too was prefigured by Taylor, who wrote, "Should we reconsider the question of a declaration of war?" Taylor also suggested asking about how the Marines had organized the Khe Sanh position for defense, how many days of supplies were in the perimeter, and whether these were protected from hostile fire. Only the query regarding the organization of Khe Sanh's defenses failed to receive an airing at the February 9 meetings.

Former chairman of the Joint Chiefs of Staff, Army chief of staff, special military representative to John F. Kennedy, intimate of presidents since Dwight D. Eisenhower, not to mention ambassador to South Vietnam, Maxwell Davenport Taylor had a perfectly sound basis for raising those questions. Familiar with Taylor's work for President Kennedy, LBJ had brought him back as a military adviser in the fall of 1966. Since then Taylor had been furnishing Johnson with a steady stream of commentaries — on Hanoi's intentions, on plans for bombing halts, reinforcements, annual campaigns, anything LBJ took an interest in. Max Taylor's role at Khe Sanh would be especially striking because William C. Westmoreland was his protégé.

During the Kennedy administration Taylor played important roles in the Berlin Wall crisis, the Cuban missile crisis, and early U.S. involvement in Vietnam. Some believe he first came prominently to Lyndon Johnson's attention in the Cuban affair, when Johnson as vice president sat in on Taylor's expositions on the military situation and options. At that time Taylor had just become JCS chairman, a job he held until LBJ asked him to be ambassador to South Vietnam in 1964. Taylor presided over the Saigon embassy during the crucial months when President Johnson made the decisions committing American ground forces to a combat role in Vietnam; now he sat at the right hand of the president at the climax of the war.

Previously published accounts maintain that LBJ asked Taylor to monitor the Khe Sanh situation in late January, about the time of Tet.

The evidence from declassified documents of Taylor's strongly held views and their longevity suggests that he had been watching longer than that. It is quite possible that Taylor himself was the "high non-military quarter" pressing for evacuation from Khe Sanh to whom Earle Wheeler referred in a January 11 cable to Westmoreland. In any case, following President Johnson's session with the Joint Chiefs on February 9, Walt Rostow and Robert McNamara were instructed to pass along to Taylor the gist of the discussion. Taylor was to comment, and he was also given the opportunity to study Westmoreland's cable that conceded an NVA threat "of major proportions" north of the DMZ and around Khe Sanh.

Taylor's reaction was a memorandum he sent the president on February 10. While agreeing to the general proposition that Vietnam should be reinforced, Taylor coupled that with a recommendation that Westmoreland and Admiral Sharp should be sent new directives giving them "strategic guidance . . . in broad terms" for the upcoming months.

Referring to the Westmoreland cable, Taylor noted, "I did not find in the cable how he expects to react to the offensive in the north which may strike the Third Marine Division units across their forty-mile front from the coast to Khe Sanh. . . . If [Hanoi] uses [its] imposing force with full effectiveness in a battle of attrition for the widely separated Marine positions, he can seriously disrupt the plans which Westy describes in his cable." In consequence, and in allusion to Khe Sanh, Taylor thought that the new strategic guidance he proposed ought to say, "We should not seek battle close to the cross-border sanctuaries of the enemy but rather try to entice him out of the sanctuaries even at the sacrifice of some terrain in order to get him into favorable killing zones. We should not undertake to hold exposed outposts unless their value is equal to the anticipated cost and unless reinforcements are available if needed for the defense." Maxwell Taylor discussed his view in a Tuesday Lunch meeting with the president on February 11.

Although Taylor made his points in private, in papers that presumably did not circulate beyond the White House, the Westmoreland cable provided a major focus for discussion at the Tuesday Lunch, attended by McNamara, Rusk, Taylor, Rostow, Wheeler, Clark Clifford, and Richard Helms of the CIA. Afterward Wheeler passed the main points to Westmoreland in a secret cable. Disguising Taylor's identity behind the tag line "one conferee," the JCS chairman noted the man's comments at the meeting — an exact summary of Taylor's position:

> [The "conferee" said] that Priority 1 should be to clear the cities; Priority 2, give away no territory of value but avoid combat with the enemy in terrain and weather favoring him. You will perceive the thought in Priority 2 that perhaps we are making a mistake by attempting to hold the Khe Sanh area and perhaps should concentrate our defenses further to the east.

In case Westmoreland missed the point, Wheeler spelled it out for him, further saying that he wished to hear Westy's views on some points in their next secure telephone conversation. He wanted a return message on the full subject, including the excerpt just quoted.

General Westmoreland sent a cable, dispatched from Saigon barely five hours later, that reviewed his postulated NVA three-phase plan and then passed to a description of a proposed operations plan: MACV would prevent the "general erosion" of Quang Tri and Thua Thien by opening up Highway 1 north from Da Nang and Route 9 west to Khe Sanh. "These two tasks are not unreasonable, provided that I can divert the troops to provide security and commit the engineers to the task," Westmoreland wrote. He needed to make "a down payment in troops" to provide adequate support to the deployed forces plus expected reinforcements, including "a regiment or brigade to secure Highway 9 to the Khe Sanh area."

Significantly, the MACV cable noted that "we are now in a new ball game where we face a determined, highly disciplined enemy . . . in the process of throwing in all his military chips to go for broke." Lyndon Johnson had used an almost identical phrase — that Hanoi was "putting all of their stack in now" — in the February 9 meeting with the Joint Chiefs. Of the North Vietnamese Westmoreland said, "He realizes and I realize that his greatest opportunity to do this [go for broke] is in Quang Tri-Thua Thien. We cannot permit this. . . . We must seize the opportunity to crush him. . . . Time is of the essence."

In his history of the Vietnam war Phillip Davidson claims that the Wheeler cable quoted here represented Washington "playing coy" on the question of reinforcements. The content of this cable and the reply, the time-date groups of the two messages, and the entire context of the exchange make clear that this was not the case. Washington at no time sought to deny MACV the small reinforcements (a Marine regiment and an Army brigade) Westmoreland had requested, as is demonstrated by the NSC and Tuesday Lunch meetings and even Max Taylor's memoranda. Rather the exchange centered around Khe Sanh, cloaked by a discussion of general strategy and triggered by Westy's penchant for taking both sides of every question in his communications. Davidson is simply mistaken. In a February 12 memorandum to the president, Wheeler stated that the MACV cable was *not* a reply to his own message, but the content of the Westmoreland cable makes that assertion appear to have been made precisely because someone in the White House thought otherwise.

Maxwell Taylor's opinion of the latest Westmoreland message was that "it is hard to believe that this cable is written by the same man as the preceding one. . . . This new one is clear, crisp and sounds like an unambiguous call for additional help in minimum time." Taylor agreed it had become a new ballgame and a great opportunity "if we use our resources correctly." However, "I am a little afraid that Westy feels he is responsible for holding every square foot of these two provinces and that he will regard terrain as important per se. I would encourage him to make a flexible defense of these provinces yielding worthless terrain without reluctance and avoiding major combat on unfavorable terrain or under unfavorable conditions of weather."

As for Westmoreland's intention to reopen Route 9, Taylor wrote: "I am doubtful . . . that he will be able to open these roads before the main attack of the enemy, and am particularly dubious about the ability of one brigade to open Highway 9 and keep it open to the Khe Sanh area. As you know, this road runs parallel to the DMZ from which enemy forces can debouch with surprise and cut the road pretty much at will. If Khe Sanh is to be supplied by ground, this overland operation will require a lot more troops than Westy has available for the purpose."

Taylor warned, "There is a real danger that the defense of Khe Sanh will require resources better used elsewhere. It is often very costly to rescue an outpost as remote as Khe Sanh once it is under heavy attack."

That day, February 12, came the first crack in MACV's heretofore solid front on holding Khe Sanh. This was reported, fittingly enough, by General Wheeler after another secure phone conversation with Westmoreland. Wheeler noted in his memo to the president: "As to

Above: Aerial view of Khe Sanh combat base on January 28, 1968. The airstrip and Ponderosa are clearly visible, along with the perimeter of much of the Gray Sector. The area of the main ammunition dump, the headquarters of 1st Battalion, 26th Marines, and recon billets is less distinct or in shadow. The road down the center intersects with Route 9. *Below:* Center right is the Red Sector of the Khe Sanh combat base, defended by 3rd Battalion, 26th Marines; just below it is the FOB-3 compound. The Bru village of Ta Cong is in the lower right and, left of center, are the Rock Quarry positions of 1st Battalion, 9th Marines. Also visible throughout are the Poilane plantation road and several tracks ascending from it into the hills or up the Rao Quan valley to Hill 558. *(USAF)*

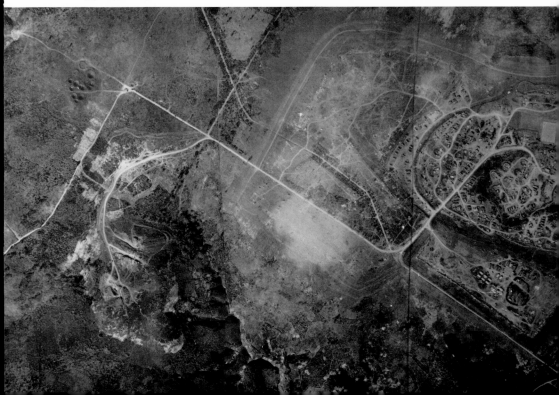

Above: Chaplain Ray W. Stubbe conducting worship services just behind the Blue Sector perimeter at Khe Sanh. The peak of Hill 1015 is directly above the head of the Marine from Chicago. *Below:* A typical supply locker at Khe Sanh. By March 1, 1968, this one was a sieve from shrapnel holes. Marines learned the Khe Sanh Shuffle, techniques for seeking cover they had never thought of before, in their efforts to stay safe on the base. *(USMC)*

Above: The Khe Sanh Shuffle in action on January 25, 1968, as Marines run for cover. Forty-five mortar rounds and eight rockets hit Khe Sanh that day. Note that a camouflage parachute covers a bunker and that one of the Marines is completely airborne. *Time* magazine reported, "The dash for cover is part of every man's routine." *Below:* Marine "cannon cockers" of 1st Battalion, 13th Marines preparing their 105mm howitzer. The artillerymen were notably steadfast and often remained in action right through the North Vietnamese barrages. *(USMC)*

Above: A Marine throws an expended 105mm shell casing on the growing pile at Khe Sanh. Artillerymen would fire some 158,891 rounds during the siege, making refuse such as casings a real problem. Welded casings turned up as flagpoles, water collectors, tent and bunker supports, and in other incarnations. *(USMC) Below:* North Vietnamese artillery remained a serious threat. This crater was made by an NVA 152mm shell on the airfield runway. The crater was actually less serious than the 152mm usually caused because the runway was a more hardened target than most of Khe Sanh. Ensign Kux, who stands inside the crater, and his repair crews became so adept that they could repair the damage from such a hit in just forty minutes. *(Martin J. Kux)*

Two views of the key White House meeting on February 9, 1968, where President Johnson considered Khe Sanh in conjunction with the Joint Chiefs of Staff. *Above:* The full group in the Cabinet Room. Walt Rostow sits in the left foreground, assiduous notetaker Tom Johnson to the right. *Below:* The Joint Chiefs sit across the table from LBJ, who is flanked by Robert McNamara and Dean Rusk. Joint Chiefs from the left: General Harold K. Johnson, Army; JCS chairman General Earle G. Wheeler; Admiral Thomas H. Moorer, Navy; General John P. McConnell, Air Force; General Leonard F. Chapman, Marine Corps. *(White House)*

Above: President Johnson and his advisers study a map of Vietnam, February 12, 1968. From the left: Walt Rostow, Richard Helms of the CIA, LBJ, General Maxwell Taylor, and Clark Clifford. Critical papers by Taylor on this day and on February 14 questioned the rationale for the defense of Khe Sanh. *Below and opposite page:* Lyndon Johnson makes up his mind about Khe Sanh on February 14 and 15, about the time a CIA-produced terrain model of the Khe Sanh area arrives at the Situation Room in the White House. These three views of the model were taken on February 15. Walt Rostow and General Robert N. Ginsburgh locate the action for their later briefing of the President.

Above: Ginsburgh points out the situation as LBJ and Rostow look on. *Below:* The group is joined by press secretary George Christian, who will later speak to reporters about what he is now learning. *(White House)*

Above: The air remained Khe Sanh's lifeline to the outside. Here a C-130 parachutes supplies to the defenders. Some 8,120 tons of supplies arrived by parachute or extraction methods over the period of the siege, compared with about half as much landed and unloaded. *Below:* Helicopters were the main supply source for the hillside outposts, though routing through Khe Sanh combat base eventually had to be abandoned in favor of direct supply from Dong Ha. A Marine CH-46A helicopter brings in a cargo sling of supplies at the airfield. Khe Sanh received 461 tons of supplies in this fashion during February 1968 alone. *(USMC)*

Above: Khe Sanh airfield would remain a very dangerous place. On February 10, a Marine KC-130 transport crashed and burned next to horrified recon Marines in their positions. *(Ernest C. Husted, Jr.) Below:* Hill 881 South during the siege, where Bill Dabney's India Company held a colors ceremony every day. The right-hand portion is the India Company position. On the left side a spur of 881 was held by two platoons of Mike Company, 3rd Battalion, 26th Marines. *(USAF)*

North Vietnamese trenches approach the Khe Sanh perimeter in these two interpreted aerial photographs of February 28, 1968. *Above:* The area southeast of the combat base shows the Gray Sector and the end of the runway, the area where Donald Jacques's ghost patrol disappeared. *Below:* Similarly extensive trench networks elsewhere in the Khe Sanh area, probably just northwest of Hill 558. *(USAF)*

Above: Marine defenses proliferated as the siege continued. These positions were held by Charlie Company, 1st Battalion, 26th Marines, in the Blue Sector of Khe Sanh combat base. Picture taken on March 15, 1968. *(USMC) Below, left:* The tiger was a frequent theme on unit identification patches worn by ARVN infantry, special forces, and Ranger units. Here it appears on the patch worn by Captain Pho's 37th Ranger Battalion at Khe Sanh. *(Ray Stubbe) Below, right:* Unidentified members of the ARVN 37th Ranger Battalion in a group portrait at Khe Sanh. In the center rear is American artillery observer Ted Golab. The group is posed in front of a pole, fashioned from 155mm shell casings, that is used to string communication lines. *(Ted Golab)*

Above: Day by day, life for the Marines became a matter of eternal vigilance against the moment the North Vietnamese might emerge to storm the combat base. Here Marines watch for NVA movement next to their machine gun. *Below:* Among more than 22,000 fixed-wing aircraft sorties providing close air support for Khe Sanh was this strike by an F-4 Phantom jet on March 15, 1968. Note the intrepid Marine who, instead of taking cover, is taking pictures! *(USMC)*

As the siege wound down, some of the Bru montagnards were finally moved out of the Khe Sanh area. Here a Bru family hurries away from the lowered ramp of a Marine Air Group 16 helicopter that has airlifted them to Dong Ha on March 31, 1968. *(USMC)*

Above: Operation PEGASUS jumps off on April 1 in a bid to reopen Route 9 to Khe Sanh. Army vehicles, in particular a quadruple .50-caliber machine gun mounted on a truck, provide security for engineers during bridge building. Note the narrow width of Route 9. *(U.S. Army) Below:* Foxtrot Company of 2nd Battalion, 1st Marines moves along a ravine water course as PEGASUS slogs its way toward Khe Sanh on April 2, 1968. *(USMC)*

Above: The only point to PEGASUS was to enable the engineers to restore Route 9. Lance Corporal Henry Riddel of B Company, 11th Engineer Battalion, bulldozes at a bridge site about eleven kilometers east of Khe Sanh. *Below:* Khe Sanh, once it had been relieved by operation PEGASUS, was intended to become a maneuver base for Marine operations. Near Khe Sanh on April 29, 1968, a Marine tank fires at suspected North Vietnamese positions. *(USMC)*

Right: A North Vietnamese postage stamp commemorating the battle of Khe Sanh. Notable features include American figures crouched in a trench as the NVA fires mortars. It is interesting to note that, unlike contemporary North Vietnamese newspaper accounts, which often claim any type of indirect fire (including mortars) at Khe Sanh as "heavy artillery," the postage stamp clearly gives credit to the lighter NVA weapons. *(Ray Stubbe) Below:* Looking along the runway, a Marine gazes into the distance during a special memorial service held at Khe Sanh in November 1968. *(USMC)*

holding Khe Sanh, [Westmoreland] has prepared on a close hold basis contingency plans to execute a tactical withdrawal if this becomes desirable and necessary." Once again Westmoreland reiterated his strong belief that holding was necessary, this time to afford him an opportunity "to exploit the enemy's commitment of troops in and around Khe Sanh." And once more he also took both sides of the issue; it is difficult to escape the impression that the general made such assertions because he felt they would make his strategies more palatable to superiors. Questioned in an interview about the Taylor papers, Westmoreland recalled, "I think one time I got a telephone call from General Wheeler . . . based on a conversation he [had] just had with the president. And I told him — I think I have this in [my] book — I said, Buz, don't worry about it; tell the president I'm not that concerned; he shouldn't be concerned either."

This telephone call is not in Westmoreland's book; it also does not sound very much like what Wheeler in fact reported Westmoreland had said. Taylor's reaction was that, although he had not seen Wheeler's February 12 memo before writing his own to LBJ, he did not think "that the memo requires any significant change to my comments."

Late on the afternoon of February 13, Walt Rostow drafted a memo of his own for President Johnson observing, "General Taylor again raised the question of whether we should hold Khe Sahn [*sic*]. He believes we could protect the coastal cities of I Corps further to the west. . . . If we decide to pull out, he believes we should not pull out when Khe Sahn is under maximum siege, but sooner — to upset the enemy's plan by moving west after he's dug in, emplaced his guns, and then has to follow westward.

"If we did such a thing," Rostow noted, with one phrase added in his own hand, "we would, in my judgment, require a plan to attack the enemy's I Corps force, at our initiative, at a time and place of our choice."

The issue would be posed most starkly the next day, February 14, when General Taylor sent LBJ a memorandum focused solely on Khe Sanh. "I know that Khe Sanh is very much on your mind as it is on mine," Taylor opened. "It may be too late to do anything about the situation; if so, we should put all doubts behind us and prepare for the fight. On the other hand, if there is still time to exercise a useful influence, we should move quickly." This Taylor paper, the last of the series, is of historical importance and deserves quotation at length:

I have reviewed what General Westmoreland has said about Khe Sanh in his recent messages. To paraphrase his cables, he points out that the original occupation of the position was justified by the need to establish a forward operating base to permit operations against the key infiltration routes in Eastern Laos. More importantly, he also considers that its occupation has blocked the route of enemy advance into Quang Tri and has kept the fighting away from the populated coastal belt of I Corps. *He concedes that Khe Sanh has not had much effect on infiltration from Laos and it is not clear whether he regards the role of blocking the Quang Tri approach as of current or of past importance.*

Thus, General Westmoreland does not appear to argue strongly for the defense of Khe Sanh *because of its present value* either in relation to the infiltration routes in Laos or in defense of major areas of the northern provinces. Although he mentioned to General Wheeler in a telephone conversation [reported in Wheeler's February 12 memo] his belief that the maintenance of our position in the Khe Sanh area would offer us the opportunity at some time of dealing the enemy a severe blow, he has not amplified the point and, in his cables, he stresses rather the difficulty of getting out of Khe Sanh at the present time and the adverse psychological effects of a withdrawal. . . .

My review of Westy's cables does not convince me of the military importance of maintaining Khe Sanh at the present time if it is feasible to withdraw. *Whatever the past value of the position it is a positive liability now.* We are allowing the enemy to arrange at his leisure a set-piece attack on ground and in weather favorable to him and under conditions which will allow us little opportunity to punish him except by our air power. The latter can be neutralized to some degree by the favorite Communist tactic of closing tightly around our positions in areas which our forces, particularly the B-52s, can not attack with safety to our own forces.

General Westmoreland recognizes the difficulties of air supply of Khe Sanh and indicates an intention to open Highway 9 to provide an overland line of communications. To do so will require a large number of troops to keep Highway 9 open in the face of intermittent road-cutting operations which can be expected from the enemy.

My present opinion is that Khe Sanh probably *can* be held but that it will be at a heavy price in terms of casualties and in terms of other ground troops necessary to support and reinforce it. I have real doubt that we can afford such a defense in view of the limited reserves which General Westmoreland is likely to have in the time frame in which these events may take place.

I make the foregoing comments in full realization of how wrong one can be at a distance about a military situation such as this. I have the utmost confidence in General Westmoreland and am sure that he sees possibilities in the situation which are not visible from here. Nonetheless, I would feel greatly relieved if the Joint Chiefs of Staff would see fit to send General Westmoreland guidance which would contain some of the following points:

"In view of the strong likelihood of a heavy enemy attack along the DMZ and against Khe Sanh, accompanied possibly by other attacks in the cities and along the Kontum-Pleiku border, the Joint Chiefs of Staff wish to provide the following comments for your guidance (i.e. General Westmoreland's). They are impressed by the many tasks which you may be called upon to perform concurrently with limited reserves and appreciate your problem in establishing priorities among these tasks as they arise. To assist you in making your decisions, they wish you to understand that, in their opinion, you should not hesitate to give up terrain in remote areas in order to meet the enemy on ground favorable to your scheme of maneuver. . . .

"In this connection, Khe Sanh appears to the Joint Chiefs of Staff to be an exposed position difficult to supply by air and expensive to supply overland in terms of lines of communications forces. Khe Sanh has already well-fulfilled [its] purposes . . . it is less clear that its present value now justifies the cost of an all-out defense.

"While the Joint Chiefs of Staff recognize the adverse psychological consequences of a withdrawal which you mention, the effect of a costly defense absorbing forces badly needed elsewhere could in the end be far more disadvantageous to our cause than a withdrawal now. Indeed, the latter could prove to be a useful stratagem nullifying the laborious logistical build-up of the enemy around Khe Sanh and upsetting his winter-spring schedule.

"The Joint Chiefs of Staff are not prepared to assess the feasibility or the desirability of a withdrawal at this late date but wish you to know that they will support you completely if you decide to pull back from what may prove to be a disadvantageous position. They will support you equally in a decision to defend Khe Sanh." [Emphasis added]

There it was: the president's special military adviser voicing opposition to the plans of the Vietnam field commander at the height of a decisive battle — surely the stuff of potential tragedy. Until now no attention whatever has been given to these very real differences over Khe Sanh. In a biography of his father published in 1989 John M. Taylor quotes an excerpt of this February 14 memorandum but fails to supply the context or follow the Washington policy debate on Khe Sanh. The Davidson history provides much commentary on Tet but just a few pages on the entire Khe Sanh campaign, none of it on this aspect. Robert Pisor's book on Khe Sanh devotes some space to Washington's interest before the battle but none to this crucial command decision.

A tactical withdrawal from Khe Sanh would have been a whale of a military problem. It was no wonder that Westmoreland was loath to consider one or that Taylor, in his language for a draft JCS cable, had the Chiefs refusing to judge feasibility of the operation. Most difficult would have been pulling the Marines out of the hilltop outposts. The combat base represented less of a problem because the North Vietnamese had not yet closely invested it. The Americans had enough aircraft and helicopters and other friendly positions nearby where troops could be dropped off that the physical problems of moving the garrison could be solved. But North Vietnamese troops were present throughout the Khe Sanh area in sufficient strength to inflict air losses on a withdrawing garrison. That would have been a minimum. The NVA might also move to assault the Marine positions at the first sign of the pullout. Any mistakes could turn withdrawal into a debacle.

An experienced military leader, General Maxwell Taylor was by no means ignorant of these factors. It is probably for this reason that he never recommended that MACV be *ordered* to withdraw from Khe Sanh even as he pressed for Westmoreland to be *encouraged* to do so. Taylor also had a fine appreciation of the time factors and conceded that it might already be too late, in which case he was prepared to put all doubts behind and fight the battle. Of course, Taylor's proposals were only recommendations; the decision was up to Lyndon Johnson.

Maxwell Taylor's advice was only a part of the stream of material with which the president had to cope. He was also reading General Westmoreland's cables, the Wheeler and Westmoreland daily reports, summaries from the National Military Command Center, supply and casualty summaries, CIA reports, a daily intelligence checklist, and other items. Then there were aerial photographs to view and communications intercepts or radio broadcast summaries from the organizations responsible for those functions. All this was in addition to the advice the president received from Walt Rostow and the members of his National Security Council and apart from LBJ's task following other national security, foreign policy, and domestic issues, not to say other Vietnam-related work.

President Johnson could see he had to make a decision, but these kinds of esoteric military subjects were not easily illuminated by advice in the absence of information. Understanding the information in the various reporting cables and memoranda, in turn, was made more difficult by their use of military terminology and map grid coordinates. Many times the president came down to the Situation Room and stood before the maps, while Bob Ginsburgh or Art McCafferty tried to explain things to him. Other times aerial reconnaissance photos were the key. "President Johnson came to appreciate a good aerial photo," wrote a former CIA officer, "but, like many people who grew up in flat country, he had a tendency to envision landforms in Vietnam as being flatter than they actually were. This was especially true of the terrain encompassing Khe Sanh."

Director of Central Intelligence Richard Helms saw Johnson struggling to cope and tried to help. He called the National Photographic Interpretation Center (NPIC) at the Washington Navy Yard and spoke to its director, Arthur C. Lundahl, a pioneer in aerial photo interpretation. Lundahl had been with the Navy in World War II, when he had specialized in working with photography of invasion beaches. In many instances, preparations for an invasion had included making detailed models of the terrain using data from maps, photos, and other sources. Now Lundahl suggested to Helms that a terrain model of the Khe Sanh area might prove very useful to the president.

It took NPIC only three days to construct the model. Briefers described the advantages of the terrain relief presentation of the model to Rostow, noting that the military grid system was laid out on a glass cover that fit the model. Thus it could be used to locate the action in any of the messages the president received. On February 13, Rostow told LBJ of the terrain model and invited him to come to the Situation Room to see it. Johnson was very pleased, making the model a centerpiece of subsequent Situation Room briefings on Khe Sanh.

Thus, owing to a coincidence in time, Lyndon Johnson may very well have been standing over the terrain model when he made his final decision on Maxwell Taylor's advice. Former members of the NSC staff agree that Taylor seemed to have a special relationship with the president, who would listen to Max when he might dismiss many others, because of Taylor's great credibility and long career. On the other hand, the terrain around Khe Sanh spoke for itself.

William Westmoreland knew something was up, though perhaps not exactly what. On February 12 (13 in Saigon) he complained to Wheeler about being asked by Taylor to prepare "a special report

completely off-cycle from other reports." Westmoreland drafted a
letter to Wheeler and Sharp, the gist of which he conveyed instead by
phone. Westy evidently thought Max Taylor had been "detailed to
run the White House war room" and saw the request for a report as
evidence of "oneupmanship" among those striving to be first to bring
information to the president. In fact, Art McCafferty remained in
charge of the Situation Room; Taylor never had anything to do with
it. According to both Rostow and Ginsburgh, moreover, Wheeler
never complained to LBJ about either Taylor's relationship and access
to him or any reporting requirement Max may have levied on MACV.

When President Johnson received Taylor's February 14 Khe Sanh
memorandum, he held it briefly and then phoned Robert McNamara.
Later that day Rostow sent McNamara a copy of the memo with a
cryptic cover note that said simply, "This is the paper the president
wished you to handle in the way he indicated." Former Secretary
McNamara has refused an interview that might clarify this point.

What happened to Taylor's advice? There exists a second version of
the February 14 memorandum, in which its provenance from Maxwell Taylor is disguised while Taylor's suggested language for a JCS
cable is modified by substitution of the word "we" or "us" for "Joint
Chiefs of Staff" wherever they appear, very much as if the paper were
being sanitized for wider circulation. We do not yet know what happened after that, but we do know what happened in November 1967,
when Robert McNamara sent LBJ a paper arguing for a halt in the
bombing of North Vietnam. In *that* instance the McNamara paper
was sanitized and circulated among senior officials, and LBJ collected
comments on it, after which he rejected the advice. A similar thing
could well have occurred with Taylor's Khe Sanh memo. In this regard
it is suggestive that General Westmoreland told one of the authors he
thinks some of the Taylor papers reached Ambassador Bunker,
though Westmoreland does not recall having seen any of them himself.

Still, Westmoreland need not have worried. The terrain favored
him, so to speak, as the model demonstrated to Lyndon Johnson, a
bigger than life Texan who was hardly likely to walk out on an
opportunity to nail a coonskin on the wall. In their regular transpacific telephone talk on February 15 (Washington date), Earle Wheeler
told Westy that McNamara had talked to the president. Wheeler once
again referred to "civilian armed-chair strategists" and remarked that
they were "extremely nervous about the Khe Sanh situation." *But,*

Westmoreland noted Wheeler telling him, "the President has full confidence in my judgement and actions with respect to Khe Sanh . . . if I ever feel it desirable to withdraw, he would like to get forewarning so that he can prepare the political defenses." William Westmoreland replied a little stiffly that he assumed "full responsibility" for Khe Sanh.

At a news conference the following day Lyndon Johnson reiterated his confidence in Westmoreland in the strongest terms: "If I had to select a man to lead me into battle in Vietnam, I would want General Westmoreland." And "Just before he goes into battle there in Vietnam — Khe Sanh or whatever engagements may follow — I would not want to have him in doubt for a moment, or a single one of his men in doubt, about his standing with his Commander-in-Chief." Westmoreland was in the midst of the most important battle of annihilation of the U.S. war in South Vietnam, and Lyndon Johnson would let him fight it.

As General Robert N. Ginsburgh later observed, "Westy could not have had a more solicitous commander-in-chief."

Nonetheless the president, being Lyndon Johnson, also was not dismissing Max Taylor out of hand. Rather, LBJ was accepting only the *immediate* battle at Khe Sanh. The evidence suggests LBJ bought Taylor's longer-term strategic argument, undermining Westmoreland's dream of conducting an invasion of Laos. On February 19, with LBJ preparing to consider the questions Earle Wheeler should carry on a visit to Vietnam, Taylor suggested that Wheeler ask about MACV's plans to evacuate Khe Sanh under attack and also ask just what was Westmoreland's concept of how defending Khe Sanh would contribute to a major defeat for Hanoi.

Taylor's tenacity would not allow the evacuation option to die. In early March Westmoreland found himself responding to the question — probably Taylor's question left by Wheeler on his departure — of whether evacuation and formation of a defense line farther to the east would improve or worsen the I Corps situation. "There are no advantages of military significance accuring [*sic*] from abandoning Khe Sanh if it is indeed our purpose to eject or destroy the invading NVA forces," Westmoreland replied. Unspoken in this eyes-only cable was that the official U.S. objective in Southeast Asia was to preserve an independent, non-Communist South Vietnam. Neither the defense nor the fall of Khe Sanh would affect that in any way. It was a subtle reinterpretation and Westmoreland apparently felt sen-

sitive enough about it that he quietly asked his chief of staff for a note
identifying U.S. aims in Vietnam. Objectives, however, were the province not of MACV but of Washington.

In the third week of March, as the actual siege of Khe Sanh drew
toward its close, the evacuation option reared its head once more. By
then President Johnson had asked a group of distinguished former
officials, the so-called Wise Men, to come to Washington and assist
him in reviewing Vietnam policy. Walt Rostow sent a list of the alternatives to be considered over to the State Department, where the
group was meeting. Third among the alternatives was "Redeployment
of the troops at Khe Sanh to other areas which might be regarded as
having greater strategic importance."

Life on the Line

Maxwell Taylor would have been much less worried about Khe Sanh
had the combat base not depended so much on its airfield. Disaster
could easily follow simply from the daily flow being choked off: supplies and replacements in, wounded and men completing their tours
of duty out. Maintenance of Khe Sanh airfield and its supply in turn
depended on the skill and bravery of air crews, managers, ground
crews, engineers, and the weather. Always tinged with danger, life on
the flight line for the units supporting Khe Sanh would be a challenge
for all. The high stakes involved in this most important battle of
attrition and the fierce combat environment saddled life on the line
with great danger indeed.

Hanoi was as aware of the stakes as the Americans and apparently
resolved not to depend entirely on the weather to close down Khe
Sanh. Though its air force of just a few dozen aircraft was no match
for the American aerial armada, it seems the North Vietnamese had
some intention of making air power their secret weapon in the Khe
Sanh campaign. So vulnerable that many of its planes were obliged to
hide out on bases in the People's Republic of China, the North Vietnamese air force nevertheless gamely conducted training exercises,
revealed here for the first time, in which its MiG interceptor jets
practiced dropping bombs. In late January and early February U.S.
intelligence detected North Vietnamese efforts to upgrade air defenses
and rehabilitate airfields in the region just north of the DMZ.

On February 5 American aircraft downed a MiG over the north, on the 6th they got another; the pace of air engagements was up. On February 7 Air Force radar installations detected six North Vietnamese aircraft in the DMZ and Laotian panhandle, an unheard of development. At 5:30 P.M. on February 8 Khe Sanh went to condition red alert when three unidentified flying objects were detected coming toward the combat base from the DMZ area. Naval ensign Kux, the airfield construction specialist, wrote in his diary, "Dunno *what* happened there." It was like science fiction, some thought, like the Twilight Zone; anything might come next.

But there were no flying saucers at Khe Sanh. What the grunts on the ground did not know about was a source of concern for the high command. At the White House that day (February 7 Washington date) General Wheeler told the group assembled in the Cabinet Room: "We are concerned about stepped up MiG activity. . . . MiGs may be used for the first time in support of ground action or in an effort to shoot down our B-52s. They may also attempt to attack an air base, like the one at Da Nang. I sent a message to all field commanders alerting them to these possibilities."

Dean Rusk asked about the dangers of MiGs attacking aircraft carriers in the Tonkin Gulf. Wheeler thought it unlikely.

"Go in and get those MiGs at Phuc Yen," Lyndon Johnson ordered, referring to a North Vietnamese air base near Hanoi. Wheeler said he would as soon as he got some decent weather.

"The MiGs would have negligible military effects but they would have spectacular psychological impact," Secretary McNamara remarked. "We do get the feeling that something big is ahead. We do not know exactly what it is, but our commanders are on alert."

In Vientiane, Laos, Ambassador Sullivan got wind of the MiG report, attributed to Hanoi's interest in intercepting the B-52 missions into the Khe Sanh area, and cabled to offer alternative explanations. One was that "Hanoi, in anticipation of cessation of U.S. bombing activity in North Vietnam, is preparing for [the] eventuality that we will, however, continue bombing [the] Ho Chi Minh Trail." Bases might therefore be intended to harass U.S. aircraft in the panhandle. The second alternative offered, "if cessation of bombing takes place before [repeat] before major assault against Khe Sanh," was that "Hanoi might find it useful to have [a] MiG sanctuary in order [to] render air environment around Khe Sanh as hazardous as possible."

The subject came up again at the White House on February 9

(Washington date) at LBJ's session with the Joint Chiefs, right after he had brought up Maxwell Taylor's question about the impact of weather. President Johnson asked, "Have you anticipated air support from any of the communists?"

"There is no evidence of any movement except the training flights and the Soviet bombers which were seen at Khe Sanh," Wheeler replied. Hanoi had only eight obsolete IL-28 bombers, he added a little later. Its "capability in using air is a nuisance and has propaganda value rather than any great military threat."

Nevertheless, Pacific theater commander Admiral U. S. Grant Sharp ordered a cruiser equipped with antiaircraft missiles into the Tonkin Gulf to beef up offshore defense capability. Again Lyndon Johnson issued a direct order. "Keep those MiGs in sight," he said.

In his study of the press coverage of Khe Sanh and the Tet offensive, later published as *Big Story*, Peter Braestrup is very critical of reporters who wrote on the subject of the IL-28s, the MiGs, and air base preparations in Laos or the southern part of North Vietnam. "These bomber reports were a one-day wonder," Braestrup writes, and the *New York Times* story on the subject was "the most imaginative newspaper story of the Tet period." The bomber reports were "irrelevant to Khe Sanh or the larger course of the Vietnam war." These conclusions no longer seem valid in light of the foregoing account of National Security Council deliberations. Far from irrelevant to Khe Sanh, the MiG sightings were real and caused concern up the chain of command and then orders back down to alert antiaircraft units and move a warship. Press reports appeared precisely because these latter orders led MACV to brief reporters regarding the putative bomber threat on February 10. In this instance Braestrup's critique of the press goes too far. The press was not simply making smoke and waving mirrors in search of headlines; rather it reported relatively straightforwardly exactly what MACV was putting out. The *Times* even managed to get a whiff of the high-level fears that the North Vietnamese were building an airfield in Laos that William Sullivan had discussed in his classified cables just a few days earlier.

The aircraft reports were a "one-day wonder," as Braestrup puts it, in the sense they never again figured in the battle action or press reporting. But that does not mean Hanoi's planes played no part in the battle. The few actual missions we know of have already been mentioned, but the real role was psychological, as McNamara observed. Washington could, and did, take into account the *threat* of North

Vietnamese aircraft. That was a valid response. Hanoi never made any known air attacks, probably precisely because it wished to continue to threaten in this fashion. Had the North Vietnamese air force gone out to battle, it would surely have been a death ride.

When Major John Havlik arrived at Khe Sanh on January 27 he was appalled at what he saw. A management specialist for the 1st Marine Air Wing, Havlik discovered that at Khe Sanh the ground element consisted of a haphazard collection of forward detachments of units located elsewhere. One unit ran the control tower, one the fuel system, another the crash unit, a different one the unloading section. One detachment did communications, another the local weather reports. All the detachments reported directly to their (remote) parent outfits. There was no overall task organization.

"None of these people had ever been formed into a cohesive organization," Havlik later told debriefers. He changed all that. "On the morning of the 28th of January was the first and last time I gathered all the people and personnel attached to the airfield at Khe Sanh in one group. I informed them that although I did not possess Article 15 [authority], that I was officer in charge of the airfield . . . that there was a definite chain of command." Within two days Major Havlik had convinced Marines and Air Force alike to leave the management to him. He established himself just in time to play an important role mobilizing his crews to fight a dangerous ammunition dump fire on January 29.

That Khe Sanh airstrip was a dangerous place to be. The North Vietnamese knew perfectly well it was vital to the defense and that if they could knock it out the Marines would be in deep peril. Planes were called "mortar magnets" or "rocket bait." To work the field, where the sound of aircraft engines drowned out the vital warning sounds of guns firing and rockets or mortar shells igniting, required iron will and plenty of guts.

Being anywhere around the airstrip carried the same dangers; this was one of the reasons the men of the 3rd Reconnaissance Battalion, who were positioned in a switchback line to protect the interior of the combat base should the NVA come in across the airstrip, suffered so many casualties. The airstrip stories were many, and many were sad. Sergeant Edward E. Brown, a short-timer aviation electronics operator with Marine Air Support Squadron 3, went over to the strip one day to see if his relief was coming in. Most of those waiting for the plane were standing right across from Charlie Med. "I didn't feel like standing out there," Brown said, "so I went into a little bunker right along the airstrip. And sure, as the [H-]34 came in . . . a couple rounds were thrown in right on the pad . . . there were around three killed and fifteen or sixteen wounded."

It was the same in reverse for men arriving at the airstrip. "We had just landed and were walking across the airstrip when enemy rocket and mortar rounds started falling all around us," said Captain Steve Dickey, a pilot with HMM-262. "We all managed to squeeze into a drainage pipe just along the strip. We stayed there for the next forty-five minutes while the enemy fired rounds into the zone." Sergeant T. M. Kane was a radio relay expert with the 1st Marine Air Wing who volunteered to go to Khe Sanh carrying several badly needed antenna parts. "We got off the plane and [some] guy says 'Run!' Well, I ran! And they were hitting all around us. I got to really hand it to the pilots; they got some kind of courage! Because I tell you what: it takes courage to land that big baby in there and take off again!"

Major Havlik did the best he could to make things better for the fliers. He designed a special procedure for coordinating his air controllers and the fire support control center (FSCC). In bad weather planes were controlled by radar until they reached the three-mile mark and then were talked down over the critical final approach. Havlik himself tried to be present at these times and would call in the fire support at the mile-and-a-half point. At night the fire support control center also would use three mortars in battery to fire illumination rounds over the heads of the adversary. "If all three worked," Havlik recalled, "we were in clover; if only two worked, it was satisfactory; if one worked we were in trouble. But it did provide sufficient illumination for the helicopter to see the runway and land. Upon landing I immediately notified the FSCC to cease firing. This procedure worked extremely well, and we lost no helicopters on . . . departure from Khe Sanh for the entire two and a half months that I was there."

Aircraft had a time of it on the daily runs. The basic force supporting Khe Sanh consisted of Marine KC-130s of Aerial Refueler Transport Squadron 152, helicopters from Marine Air Groups 16 and 36, and Air Force C-130s, C-123s, and C-7s of the 834th Air Division. By far the largest commitment, at least in terms of deployed forces, came from the 834th under Brigadier General Burl W. McLaughlin. In late January McLaughlin had on hand six squadrons of C-7As with eighty-one aircraft, four of C-123s with fifty-eight aircraft, and three detachments of C-130s with seventy-two planes. Westmoreland requested and the White House approved the dispatch of two additional C-130 detachments. (All the C-130s, incidentally, actually belonged to the 815th Air Division in Japan.)

The official supply requirement for Khe Sanh, set by III MAF, stood at 235 tons per day. Air Force deliveries over the last eight days of January averaged 250 tons daily, with the high for the entire campaign, 310 tons, occurring on January 27. At the direction of the White House, Air Force operating orders specified that flights earmarked for Khe Sanh should be programmed at 120 percent of requirements, that no such flight could be diverted without special authority, and that C-130 flights bound for north of Da Nang could not be scheduled for intermediate stops.

Even with these special priorities, deliveries dipped in early February. The constant NVA shelling was taking its toll. The combat base would be the target of two hundred shells on February 4, 5, and 6, and of six hundred on the 8th. The daily average of eleven C-130 landings dropped precipitously to three on February 9 and six the next day. Three times during the first week of February the airstrip had to be closed for repairs. Ensign Kux's construction crews got so expert they could fill a typical hole in just forty minutes, including patching the metal plates. Still the constant pounding made it rougher for the transports. One key statistic that shows how tough Khe Sanh field had become is that the average longevity of C-130 aircraft tires for all of 7th Air Force declined from forty sorties to just eighteen precisely in February 1968.

On the morning of February 4, General Momyer of 7th Air Force told Westmoreland by telephone that all operational requests were being satisfied. Momyer believed *six* more C-130 squadrons were necessary, not two, and he was trying to get them through Air Force channels. Two evenings later Momyer told Westmoreland that a C-130 had been hit by mortars just as it was taking off from Khe Sanh. The plane was expected to have to land at Tan Son Nhut without its landing gear after flying off all excess fuel.

Other serious incidents occurred on the ground at Khe Sanh. On February 5 a C-130E based at Tuy Hoa on the central Vietnamese coast had a breathtakingly close call landing at Khe Sanh with a cargo of ammunition. The plane came under machine gun fire on its final approach, perhaps from an NVA antiaircraft squad that had taken up position alarmingly close to the end of the runway. The bullets ignited a fire in wooden ammunition boxes in the cargo compartment. As his crew used hand extinguishers to fight the flames spreading through the interior of the plane, pilot Lieutenant Colonel Howard M. Dallman brought the plane down and then backed it up to the end of the runway to minimize damage to the base if the cargo exploded. Dallman's crew managed to put out the fire and swiftly unloaded the ammunition, but by that time the C-130 had suffered more hits, one of which punctured a main landing gear tire. Maintenance men and air crew changed the tire while fixed-wing aircraft tried to suppress the NVA artillery. The air strikes slowed but could not stop the barrage, and a mortar shell landed directly in front of the C-130, showering it with fragments and knocking out one engine.

Dallman finally managed to take off on just three engines, even though his plane was low on fuel and still receiving hits. Dallman was awarded an Air Force Cross, the highest award given a transport pilot thus far in the war.

The conventional wisdom is that what Dallman did was impossible: Colonel Thomas Sumner, another C-130 pilot, puts it succinctly in an account of a mishap of his own: "A three-engine take-off from that strip was impossible — not enough runway."

On February 11, another Tuy Hoa–based C-130 suffered mortar damage just after landing. The plane was simply not flyable — the hydraulic system was badly damaged, the engines holed by shrapnel, the tires blown. Two passengers had been killed. Air crew went to work to restore the plane, helped by a mechanic from Da Nang. At 7:45 P.M. General Momyer reported to Westmoreland by telephone, describing the grounded plane as damaged severely and still needing four or five hours' work plus spare parts.

Momyer ordered the aircraft commander, Captain Edwin Jenks, to move his plane in the night so that it did not sit in one place as a target. Meanwhile one of the mechanics worked on the tail with only a flashlight as illumination. Five other men completed the repairs alongside him. On the 12th, an NVA mortar shell hit just fifteen feet from the C-130 and further damaged an engine. Then the workers noticed that the NVA opened fire only when other planes were landing. General Momyer issued orders for no further landings until the C-130 was gotten out. The plane was still at Khe Sanh, Momyer told Westmoreland, at 9:00 P.M. on February 12. Soon after that Captain Jenks lifted out. Maintenance men at Da Nang found 242 holes in the C-130 before they gave up counting.

Though Air Force C-130s had been lucky, the Marines suffered a loss on February 10 when a KC-130 was hit in both the cockpit and crew compartment. Gasoline spewed throughout the plane's interior and a fire began at the rear, engulfing the plane before it had completed its landing roll. Several more explosions completed the destruction of the aircraft. The pilot, Chief Warrant Officer Harry Wildfang, and his copilot escaped through an overhead hatch with minor burns. Major Havlik's crash crew, wearing special heat suits, rescued several, but six passengers perished.

The C-123Ks, with a shorter landing roll and auxiliary jet engines to assist them on takeoff, had an easier time of it. They usually were able to stop and turn off the runway at the first entrance to the loading ramp on the left. If coming down high or fast, the C-123s could still make the second entrance. The C-130s often had to roll out the full length of the runway and then taxi back to the loading ramp, a procedure that left them quite vulnerable. Sumner's experience was representative of that of C-130 pilots: making about twenty trips into Khe Sanh, he suffered damage every time but one. Sumner's most memorable flight was the time he became delayed on the loading ramp because a cargo pallet jammed on the guide rails as it rolled down. Rockets began to land all over the area. Then an engine warning light went on, threatening to force the crew either to stay at Khe Sanh or to attempt a three-engine takeoff. When the jam cleared they got out of Khe Sanh as fast as they could. By then the shelling was really close and chunks of debris were flying everywhere. Sumner always remembered that trip "because it was one in which I did not get a single hit but by all odds should have been blown to pieces."

As a result of such incidents with the big planes, on February 12 Khe Sanh was closed to C-130 landings. The C-123Ks, whose use of the airstrip would increase by a factor of five through the rest of February, took up the passenger traffic. Freight was delivered by C-130s using other means such as by parachute. The C-130s typically originated at Tan Son Nhut, Cam Ranh, or Tuy Hoa and flew their last minutes into the drop zone under ground radar control. The vulnerability of this system was demonstrated on February 19 when the North Vietnamese hit the radar facility, killing three Marine air controllers. The next day a new radar system got its initiation. The first plane to use it overshot the drop zone but eight other C-130s dropped accurately.

General Momyer's ban on C-130 landings applied only to the 7th Air Force. During the interval it remained in force — until February

25 — Marine KC-130s still made occasional landings. The bulk of air traffic was smaller planes, though. From February 12 to 17 C-123Ks made fifty-three sorties into Khe Sanh for a daily average delivery of forty-eight tons. Eight C-7A flights brought an additional thirteen tons. The weather then closed Khe Sanh completely. From February 20 to the end of the month, weather improved sufficiently that C-123Ks averaged three landings per day.

The bigger aircraft continued to have their share of problems. On February 22 two Marine KC-130s were damaged while on the ground at Khe Sanh. Momyer lifted the ban on Air Force C-130s on February 24, but it was two days before any made the attempt. Two landed that day, one of which suffered fifty-seven hits and was forced to depart without unloading. Over the last four days of February, fifteen C-130s came, delivering more than 160 tons to the combat base, but the risks were simply too great. With the beginning of March, C-130s stopped landing at Khe Sanh for the duration of the siege.

Novel techniques substituted for aircraft landings to solve Khe Sanh's supply problem. One suggestion, whose rejection by Colonel Lownds would be upheld at higher levels, was to land the C-130s at night. Radar-guided parachute drops became the mainstay of the airlift effort. Used on a more limited scale, but of incomparable precision and convenience, were two even more radical delivery systems called the low-altitude parachute extraction system (LAPES) and the ground proximity extraction system (GPES).

LAPES and GPES both involved techniques for delivering supplies without landing an aircraft. Though LAPES utilized a parachute for extracting the load, it was not a true air drop system since the parachute at no time supported the load in the air. The GPES system required installation of equipment on the ground while LAPES did not. The systems had been developed earlier in the 1960s when there had been much concern over "brushfire wars" and the ability to supply forces in remote areas. The Army and Air Force both worked on the systems, but the Army had never had much interest in them. Some Air Force officers felt the Army had been restricting its thinking to airborne operations and, consequently, parachute drops. In any case LAPES and GPES development went forward through systems engineering to prototype production to field testing at the Tactical Air Warfare Center at Eglin Air Force Base in Florida. When the McNamara Pentagon forced the services to choose which system should be deployed, the Army opted for LAPES, which at least used a parachute though it did not depend on it. The Air Force also chose LAPES and experimented with it at Khe Sanh in the fall of 1967 while Ensign Kux and his men were refinishing the airstrip.

Using the LAPES system, which returned to Khe Sanh on February 16, 1968, transport planes could avoid making an actual landing. The planes, usually C-130 Herky Birds, would fly in very low as if landing and open the rear cargo ramp. The load would be on roller pallets rigged to a drag parachute. A loadmaster would activate this drag chute by firing a "squib," a small explosive charge that freed the main parachute to be pulled out after a drogue chute. This greatly slowed the velocity of the cargo relative to that of the aircraft so the pallets would literally be pulled right out the door.

The physics of the idea were wonderful, though from a practical flying standpoint LAPES seemed a little more difficult. The pilots had to fly very low — typically within about five feet of the ground — and very near stalling speed. A simple gust of wind might drive a plane into the ground. In case of difficulty, however, the expedient of putting down the landing gear during the approach enabled aircraft to make just a momentary touchdown and then scramble back into the air. Planes using LAPES were far less vulnerable to North Vietnamese fire than those that landed.

The system used at Khe Sanh was a LAPES variant designed by the Aerospace Research Corporation and so called ARC-LAPES. It improved on the original by having the plane tow a reefed main parachute that would be opened by the squib, thus avoiding the vagaries of parachute deployment. A further improvement called 1528 LAPES was in development but not yet available in the field.

Tragedy struck on February 21, six days after the system's inauguration, when a Herky Bird inadvertently hit the ground during its extraction maneuver. The shock ripped off the rear ramp, the cargo was shaken out, and the load broke up. On the ground one man was killed and five more injured. Major Michael Rohrlick of the Tactics and Systems section of the 834th Air Division had been in on the original testing of both LAPES and GPES and knew the systems had been designed to get loads onto the ground in forest clearings, where planes would have to pull up very abruptly to clear trees. Pilot training had naturally conveyed this maneuver as a standard for extraction. At Khe Sanh, of course, there was no forest cover and the maneuver became superfluous. Yet Rohrlick could not get the pilots to stop pulling up too abruptly, though it made deliveries more risky for them, and he also could not get the crews to stop making their approaches so late they wasted the first thousand feet or so of runway.

On March 9 came another incident in which a cargo did not budge even after the parachute became fully inflated. A loadmaster who had little experience with LAPES was too slow to jettison the chute. As the C-130 gained speed and began to climb, its load finally rolled out — now a ten-ton missile that slid 1,500 meters until it crashed into a bunker and killed a Marine. There were three more incidents of this sort, though none of the others caused serious injury.

The best safety record of all was compiled by GPES, the system that had been discontinued. Here Mike Rohrlick again played an important role. At Eglin in 1966 the gear was put in storage. Major Rohrlick, in Saigon with the 834th Air Division, participated in discussions in late 1967 about how Khe Sanh could be supplied in adverse circumstances, and he stood up for GPES in addition to LAPES. When he learned that Eglin had intentions of condemning the GPES equipment for scrap, he arranged for the 834th to store it in Vietnam instead.

The brigadier general who headed the Tactical Air Warfare Center subsequently learned of the GPES gear in Vietnam and denounced the move, which had been made in just two days. General Burl McLaughlin, 834th Division commander, found out Rohrlick had been perpetrator of the deed. Though usually a fine gentleman, McLaughlin was almost ready to lash out at Rohrlick until he thought about it — the Air Warfare Center commander had been a LAPES enthusiast and thus became angered by efforts to save the GPES system. It turned out to be fortunate the equipment made it to Vietnam.

In essence the GPES system worked much the same way that aircraft carriers recover their planes, with ground-anchored heavy cable combined with an extraction hook joined to the cargo pallet. Like the carrier plane's tail hook catching onto arresting gear, the GPES hook would catch the ground cables and be brought to a halt, yanking the cargo out of the plane. It worked famously at Khe Sanh: cargo runaway became impossible; all cargoes usually came to rest at the same spot, both reducing damage to the airstrip and simplifying recovery. Nine sets of GPES gear were used at Khe Sanh, and the first delivery by the method came in mid-March. To demonstrate GPES capabilities, Major Rohrlick suggested including a crate of eggs in the pallet load. Only two broke on landing. On the second GPES delivery, one end of the ground cable pulled loose from its mooring but the cargo still landed perfectly. There would be fifteen GPES deliveries to Khe Sanh and fifty-two by LAPES.

Ultimately both techniques, novel as they were, could not compete with the old standard air drop. Some 496 air drops succored Khe Sanh. Statistics showed that C-130s had made 148 sorties on instruments in bad weather, while 308 sorties dropped in good weather. The average circular error was just 110 yards. Volume was also quite considerable: 8,120 tons delivered by parachute, LAPES, or GPES. This compared with 4,310 tons of cargo and 2,676 passengers delivered by 273 C-130, 179 C-123, and eight C-7A landings. The planes also lifted out 1,574 passengers, including at least 306 wounded.

Of course the supply effort was not without cost. The 311th Troop Carrier Squadron lost three of its C-123Ks in just a few days of early March. The most serious air loss of the campaign came on March 6 when a transport had to abort its initial approach because of an unannounced Vietnamese aircraft in the landing pattern. When the C-123 circled back to try again it was hit by ground fire and crashed. Killed were forty-three Marines, a Navy man, and four Air Force personnel. In addition, on March 1 a C-123 hit by mortar fragments crashed on takeoff, while another plane was destroyed on the ground by bombardment that day and the next. Eight C-123s and at least eighteen C-130s incurred heavy damage on sorties into Khe Sanh.

Khe Sanh Marines were frequently annoyed that reporters always seemed to choose the wreckage of the Marine KC-130 on the side of the airstrip as backdrop for their eyewitness stories from the combat base. Overfrequent television viewing of this one wreck conveyed the misleading impression that Khe Sanh was an embattled garrison. To those who flew the Khe Sanh route regularly, however, the opposition was no joke. In early March, to equalize the risks for C-123 crews, the 315th Air Division ordered *all* its squadrons of this type to contribute planes and crews to the detachment of the 311th Squadron deployed at Da Nang.

Da Nang was one world, Khe Sanh was another. One a place where men complained they had to eat strawberry ice cream five days in a row, the other where men had not had any ice cream in five *months*. A third world entirely was the world of the hilltops, the outposts where the cans on the wire rattled in the night. The Herky Bird pilots could go home to beds at night, and the garrison at the combat base at least had heavy construction equipment; the Marines on the hills had only their hands. Where fancy extraction methods and parachute drops were fine for getting supplies to the combat base, on the hills an average error of 110 yards meant that vital supply loads landed in Indian country. For the world of the hills, only helicopters sufficed, and life on the line for helicopter pilots was especially difficult and challenging.

When the siege began, supplies for the hills were funneled through the combat base. They would be landed, unloaded, and repacked into smaller loads by the logistics support unit and then carried by helicopters from the base. The Marine command typically assigned Khe Sanh a "direct support package" of two UH-1E slicks, two to four CH-46 cargo carriers, and a couple of H-34 utility ships. Their primary mission was medical evacuation and resupply for the hilltops.

The flights were not easy ones, as Colonel Franklin E. Wilson recalls:

> When the dense monsoon clouds rolled into the valley, the mountain tops were the first to become submerged and, as the overcast lifted, the last to reappear. During these periods the North Vietnamese took advantage of the reduced visibility and emplaced heavy automatic weapons along the neighboring peaks and waited for the ceiling to lift which invariably heralded the arrival of the helicopters. As a result, the UH-1Es, UH-34s, and CH-46s were pelted with a hail of enemy bullets during each mission.

This began at the beginning of each flight, as the NVA fired on the ships and cargo handlers trying to prepare the missions and continued right through the flights to the hills.

Marines tried every kind of gambit to get the supplies through; tactics were completely fluid. Helicopters never dropped supplies twice in succession at the same landing zone; they would feint at one hill and then make for another. For landings at Khe Sanh itself the copters could use bad weather to their advantage, deliberately staying up in the clouds, above the aircraft glide path, following altitude and heading calls from the ground control approach facility at the airstrip. With a descent at forty knots begun just after crossing the field edge, helicopters usually broke out of the clouds about mid-field. Marines assumed the NVA would be listening in on the radio nets, so they developed a practice of informing pilots of their destinations simply by signs held up by ground personnel. The pilots would acknowledge with thumbs up. The receiving end had its stratagems too. Captain Dabney at Hill 881 South had one of the larger hilltops, giving him the luxury of picking his LZs. Dabney would do so at the last moment and use false signals with colored smoke to outfox the NVA.

Despite all the tactics, the dangers remained — or perhaps the tactics were necessary *because* the risks were so immense. The NVA on surrounding hills had excellent observation of both the outposts and the airfield. Either on the hills or at the combat base, a helicopter could not afford to remain stationary for longer than twenty to twenty-five seconds. More than that and the NVA mortar rounds and rockets began to land. This was especially painful for attempts at medical evacuations. If the casualty was not ready to go or his litter was delayed in any way, after about thirty seconds the helicopter pilot had no choice but to take off without the evacuee. In that case the ship would have to cycle for another landing and recovery attempt.

Having a helicopter detachment based at Khe Sanh became more difficult as the battle progressed. Revetments or not, the ships on the strip attracted fire, while the crews had problems of their own. Marine air units made no arrangements to accommodate their people at Khe Sanh, so crews were on their own. Most bedded down with FOB-3 because, having furnished helicopter support to MACVSOG so often, the crews had friends there. However, crossing from the FOB-3 compound to the airstrip then assumed the proportions of a major trial. Pilots became adept at the "Khe Sanh Shuffle" — from trench to culvert to bunker to ditch to reach helicopters that might themselves be shot up and useless. Getting across the combat base often took forty-five minutes, sometimes twice that long.

What was hard for the men was no better for the ships. In fact, a point came when the copters had to be kept flying all day, every day, whether or not they had work to do, just to keep them off the ground and less vulnerable. Marine crews and staff officers did not like that at all. "It became alarmingly apparent," Major Arthur C. Crane told debriefers, "that keeping aircraft at the base at Khe Sanh was utter folly. We were losing aircraft on the ground up there at a rate faster than we could replace them. However, the ground commander at Khe Sanh and the Third Marine Division [were] adamant that they wanted aircraft to remain . . . it took an almost knock-down-drag-out fight and loss of a CH-53, which is what finally, I believe, triggered the Wing to say: This was it." Similarly the assistant operations officer of

VMO-6, Major William A. McGaw, Jr., recalls, "I think the record's going to show that Khe Sanh cost us about a squadron of airplanes destroyed in the period January to March . . . for prestige purposes, or for a show of support, or for some reason, we had to keep aircraft parked in the revetments."

Finally Harry Alderman, commander of 3/26, much of whose strength could be found on Hills 881 South and 861, recommended to Lownds that Khe Sanh no longer attempt to supply the outposts and that this function be taken over directly by division at Dong Ha. The air liaison officer at Khe Sanh, originally the manager of all this local air activity, was overloaded by the increasing tempo of operations. Control eventually passed to the Direct Air Support Center at Khe Sanh, which put the helicopters in the higher-level chain of command, making transfer of the supply function all the more logical. Colonel Lownds affirmed Alderman's recommendation and passed it along. General Tompkins approved.

Something still had to be done about tactics, and for that 1st Marine Air Wing commander General Norman Anderson went to III MAF. Anderson and General Cushman conceived the idea for really large-scale operations by helicopters to replace individual sorties. The details were worked out at 1st Marine Air Wing headquarters by three talented officers, Colonel Joel B. Bonner, Lieutenant Colonel William J. White, and Lieutenant Colonel Richard E. Carey. The latter, who drafted Operation Plan 3-68, which incorporated large-scale formation tactics with air support plans, coined the term "supergaggle" to describe the tactic. Supergaggle derived from the Marine practice of calling any formation of helicopters in flight a "gaggle," as in a group of geese.

A typical supergaggle might include a supply element of a dozen CH-46s covered by a dozen or more A-4 attack jets. The copters themselves would have a close escort, in this case four UH-1E gunships, that would provide additional suppressive fire. The initial supergaggle operation was run on February 24.

The mission assumed a requirement for 32,000 pounds of supplies per outpost per day. Because of the small LZs on the hills, only the CH-46D was really suitable to fly resupply, which made supergaggle essentially a job for Squadron HMM-262. By the time the technique went into use, HMM-262 had already lost more than half its helicopters. The Marines solved the problem for the short term by transferring thirteen pilots for temporary duty from HMM-364. For the longer term the problem solved itself: following introduction of this tactic, the Marines lost no more helicopters. There were, however, twenty-eight aircraft damaged and fifty fire incidents, but skillful flying, the electronics and other technical assistance available to the Americans, and the carefully coordinated air support combined to make these resupply missions as safe as could be, given the circumstances of a garrison under siege.

General problems included radio discipline, for troops on the ground often cluttered the air tactical nets with appeals and questions about when their requests would be serviced and about the weather. The latter was truly significant. At Hill 950 and at 861, there were periods of a week or more when nothing could get in or out because of the weather. Supplies evaporated quickly. At one time stocks for the garrison on 950 were down to less than two gallons of water for about seventy-five Marines.

Between January and the end of July, helicopter support teams of the 3rd Shore Party Battalion, with detachments at Dong Ha, Camp Evans, Quang Tri, Ca Lu, and Khe Sanh, coordinated 11,591 lifts, which carried 24,147 passengers and 40,975,113 pounds of cargo. Statistics for flights specifically to assist operation SCOTLAND, the code name for Khe Sanh activities during the siege, show 9,109 sorties by MAG-36 and MAG-16, which transported 14,562 passengers and 4,661 tons of freight. Khe Sanh received 465 tons by helicopter in February and an average of forty tons daily once the weather began to improve. Helicopters were an indispensable component of the team that won the battle of Khe Sanh.

As novel measures were introduced to spark the aerial resupply operation, air managers continued to resist novelty in the NIAGARA bombardment campaign. By mid-February CINCPAC Admiral Sharp had not even replied to Westmoreland's proposal to designate a single air manager for I Corps. Westmoreland consulted General William Momyer of the 7th Air Force on February 17 regarding a further message Westy was going to send Sharp. The proposed text was "too vague," Westmoreland complained; when Sharp saw it, he was going to "wonder what I want you to do that [you are] not doing now." Westmoreland asked Momyer to draft the instructions he wanted to govern the air campaign, which the MACV commander could then incorporate in his cable to CINCPAC.

On February 20 Momyer flew to Da Nang to present his concept at a full dress staff meeting with III MAF. That evening Momyer phoned Westmoreland with the results: "Had [a] good session. . . . Most of [the] problem came from Anderson — as expected. If [I] could have talked to [III MAF commander] Cushman alone would have had no problem."

Momyer was apparently putting the best face upon a stormy conference, however. He had declared he was not attempting to disrupt Marine doctrine, and he promised the effect would be to guarantee III MAF everything it needed. General Cushman would be put in a stronger position than before, but none of the promises stilled Marine objections. Momyer resorted to veiled threat: he finally told Norman Anderson and the others (disingenuously) that 7th Air Force *already had* the directive to run the air campaign. As reported to Westmoreland, he said, "There would be no argument about whether or not [this] would be done, but only how to do it." Momyer promised to incorporate Marine objections in a detailed paper and told Westmoreland he would hand carry the paper to Cushman and then bring it to MACV.

A couple of hours after Momyer's phone call, MACV received a "special category, exclusive" message from Cushman to Westmoreland. The Marine commander found it troubling that the briefing had failed to specify his own command authority in the contingency of the deployment of multiple corps forces to I Corps, as was occurring. He pointed out that Momyer's proposal inserted "at least" two additional levels of approval authority into the existing system, inevitably reducing responsiveness. Moreover, Cushman observed, 7th Air Force estimated that the new system would overturn Marine Corps air requests, on the average, just once a month. General Cushman turned this around to argue: "Accordingly, to insist upon a more complicated request system for the exception, rather than the rule, appears to be neither necessary nor desirable."

Further objections included that, as a matter of U.S. law, Marine air belonged to the Corps. His air-ground system, Cushman pointed out, was designed to provide a certain number of sorties per battalion. "To follow the system proposed by General Momyer," the message went, "would, in effect, dilute the number of sorties required for the support of each Marine battalion. On the other hand, the integral air support of the U.S. Army is untouched [since] under the proposal, helicopters are not affected." Momyer had in fact told Westmoreland on the telephone that III MAF had a fair gripe here and that he had asked Cushman to calculate how many sorties would compensate.

General Cushman's bottom line was that "there is no compelling reason for changing a system that is presently working well." In fact, Cushman insisted, III MAF's own air system was "the finest air control system existing in the world today." He offered to assume responsibility for coordination of the entire air effort in the I Corps area.

Thus, far from the good session Momyer thought he had had with Cushman, III MAF seemed in virtual revolt on the air control issue. Momyer and Westmoreland discussed the matter again at 10:50 A.M. on February 21. Momyer opined that the III MAF message had been written by Norman Anderson and others, not Cushman, and that the Marine commander had failed to "expand his perspective" to consider he now had under him a full corps in addition to his own force.

That day the 7th Air Force and Brigadier General John Chaisson of the MACV Combat Operations Center worked up a new message to III MAF to pour oil on the troubled waters. Chaisson accurately feared that Marine Corps zealots in Washington would try to make the air manager issue a cause célèbre in Washington. The new message emphasized there was no notion of trying to break up the Marine air-ground team.

Westmoreland had previously complained to Marine air commander Norman Anderson about the 1st Marine Air Wing's responsibility for providing air support for all formations under III MAF control. Now, on February 25, Westmoreland learned that the air wing was indeed running air strikes into the A Shau valley. He asked Momyer whether 7th Air Force had known of the operation and what it would have to do to send air support into the same area. Momyer said he would have to ask the Marine air wing's permission. That evening Westmoreland sent a cable to General Earle Wheeler, then in Bangkok, complaining, "I am even more prone than ever to describe the present situation as a 'dog's breakfast.' I could also apply other adjectives, such as unprofessional and even dangerous." On February 27 Westmoreland complained anew to CINCPAC that the existing system resulted in "haggling" with the 1st Marine Air Wing and in "coordination problems" over the A Shau valley and that it was taking too long to muster B-52 raids.

At this juncture Saigon sent a 7th Air Force representative to Honolulu to brief Admiral Sharp. The man was Momyer's operations officer, Major General Gordon F. Blood. The quiet mission turned into an extended sojourn as Momyer's man awaited CINCPAC's decision. A few days later General Wheeler weighed in supporting the Westmoreland-Momyer position. On February 29 Blood was asked to remain at CINCPAC in anticipation of the edict.

A staff memorandum went to Sharp on the afternoon of March 2. Scuttlebutt in Honolulu held that Sharp was going to approve all the MACV–7th Air Force recommendations. In fact, Sharp approved, ordering a single change. On March 8 General Westmoreland duly designated William Momyer his single manager for all air assets in the I Corps area.

As the battle continued at Khe Sanh, the air support remained massive and effective. The procedures for air management went into effect in early April and almost immediately resulted in tragedy. The larger roles and missions question, however, went to the Joint Chiefs. Acrimonious debate continued there long after the problem ceased to have any operational significance. Westmoreland would be directly questioned on this by Lyndon Baines Johnson after his return to Washington. Perhaps it is not so surprising that the dispute led Westmoreland to consider resigning.

Anxious for a personal look at the NIAGARA air operations area, on February 26 Bill Momyer himself hopped aboard a plane and overflew Route 9, following it all the way out to Tchepone in Laos, cutting through the A Shau valley on his way back. It was obvious the North Vietnamese were making heavy use of the road, despite the fact that all five bridges were out between Khe Sanh and Tchepone. Momyer figured the NVA must be using mobile bridges erected only at night.

The 7th Air Force commander also detected a new trick he had not seen before which the North Vietnamese clearly expected to reduce vulnerability on the Ho Chi Minh Trail. Now they were placing drums of gasoline along the sides of the road at intervals of one and a half to two miles. Using these, trucks could refuel anytime and could avoid truck parks, which attracted attention from U.S. aircraft. Moreover, the new technique reduced the necessity for large fuel dumps, very vulnerable targets. Route 9 itself Momyer found to be in excellent condition and capable of sustaining heavy truck traffic. Returning to Tan Son Nhut Momyer ordered his tactical commanders to have their pilots strafe along both sides of the road to get the dispersed fuel. The single air manager was determined to win.

"The Main Ground Contest Remains to Be Fought"

There were as many expressions of defiance of the North Vietnamese as there were Americans at Khe Sanh. One of the best known and most obviously defiant gestures was one Captain Dabney's men made atop Hill 881 South. Early during the siege the Marines began to raise an American flag over their position every morning and night. The gesture may have been patterned after the battle of Iwo Jima, at which it had also been the 26th Marines who raised the American flag atop Mount Suribachi, in the process cutting an image that became an icon of heroism in the Pacific war and indeed an enduring symbol for the Marine Corps. In any case, on top of 881 South, this flag-raising ceremony occurred twice a day, at first using a small flag that belonged to one of the men and a radio aerial. The raising of the colors always followed the prescribed ceremonial procedures, but the time was varied to fool the NVA.

One day Dabney found one of his platoon leaders crouched in a foxhole sobbing. The young lieutenant had arrived only three days before and already twenty-nine of the thirty-three men in his platoon had become casualties. While commiserating Dabney discovered that the man could play the bugle, a skill for which he had long been searching. After that the young officer would run to a knoll on 881 South at each ceremony. In the morning he would play "To the Colors"; in the evening, "Retreat." Two Marines would run with the flag and raise it while everyone else stood in their positions and saluted or presented arms. Marines rotated the flag detail so that every man could have a chance to participate.

It was a fine piece of calculation. The NVA replied to the flag ceremonies with mortar fire, and Marines could hear the shells inserted in the tubes an instant before firing. India Company worked out its ceremony and bugle call so that precisely twenty-nine seconds elapsed, after which every man dived for cover. The North Vietnamese shells took thirty-one seconds to arrive on target.

A constant hazard on 881 South, the NVA mortars meant misery for plenty of Americans. At least once the 1/13 artillerymen got back at the enemy, a couple of days into the siege at midmorning, when gunners Ronald Pierce and James E. Payne were trying to get wiremen to replace the severed telephone link from their 105mm howitzer to the artillery commander. Suddenly an officer holding forward observ-

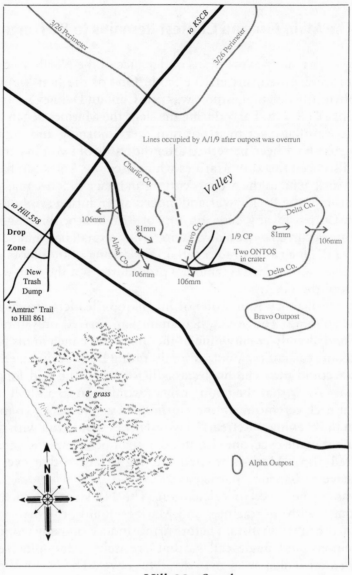

3/26 Perimeter

to KSCB

3/26 Perimeter

Lines occupied by A/1/9 after outpost was overrun

Charlie Co.

Valley

106mm

81mm

Delta Co.

to Hill 558

Drop
Zone

Alpha Co.

Bravo Co.

1/9 CP

81mm

106mm

New
Trash
Dump

106mm

106mm

Two ONTOS
in crater

Delta Co.

"Amtrac" Trail
to Hill 861

106mm

Bravo Outpost

8' grass

River

N

Alpha Outpost

11 · Hill 881 South

er's (FO) field glasses ran into their position. "Pointing toward 881 North," Payne remembered, "he jams the FO glasses in my face screaming, 'Look down my f—— ing arm! That's a f—— ing gook mortar tube out there in that f—— ing crater!' " Payne looked and saw figures moving near the lip of a crater on the slope of 881 North; the officer repeated that that was the mortar position. Payne and Pierce had their howitzer trained close to the alignment needed for this target, and they quickly adjusted its aim. The NVA mortar was so close there was no question of using a gun sight. Payne simply opened the breechblock and cranked the gun's handwheels until the figures in the crater appeared just below the center of the gun's bore. Pierce loaded a white phosphorus shell. The Marines fired. Shouts of encouragement went up from other nearby Marine positions; Payne and Pierce continued pumping 105mm shells into the target. It was a moment of exhilaration, to be exceeded by despair later in the siege when their gun suffered a direct hit, one of the few Marine guns destroyed at Khe Sanh. Payne, who would be on 881 South throughout the siege, was the sole survivor.

Another flag that flew on 881 South was "Maggie's Drawers," the signal traditionally used on the firing range to denote a complete miss of the target. This was for a North Vietnamese sniper in the trees below who seemed unable ever to hit anyone. Every morning Marines' heads appeared above the trench line as they had their flag ceremony, every morning bullets flew from the sniper's rifle, and never was anyone hit. Finally one day Privates First Class James Schemelia and Charles Reed turned to each other and said, "We'll fix 'em!" They thought of Maggie's Drawers. Schemelia and Reed got a section of tent pole and Schemelia came up with a pair of 3rd Marine Division swim trunks the men had been issued at Khe Sanh but had never used. They nailed the trunks to the pole. After that, each morning the sniper missed, the Marines would raise Maggie's Drawers.

On February 15 Hill 881 South underwent heavy automatic weapons fire and bombardment by 122mm mortars. The Marines suspected that the NVA had emplaced some of these heavy mortars underground, sighted so as to fire only on one single target (something the Viet Minh had done quite a bit at Dien Bien Phu), for the hilltop received a good deal of 122mm fire but when Marines ventured off it they never got any. Five Marines were wounded in the February 15 bombardment and the Mike Company commander, First Lieutenant John T. Esslinger, immediately ran to the impact area and helped get

the wounded to safer positions. Esslinger received shrapnel in both
legs from another mortar round but personally directed the incoming
medevac helicopter and then carried three of the wounded Marines to
the chopper. Only then did he get his own wounds treated. Esslinger
remained in command of Mike Company until March 23, when Captain Walter R. Jenkins replaced him. Esslinger received a Bronze Star
for his actions.

Over the following weeks Hill 881 South several times would be
subjected to bombardment from what were thought to be self-
propelled artillery guns. Though the pieces themselves were never
seen, the guns were heard firing and dust clouds rose as if guns were
rapidly switching positions to avoid counterbattery fire. On one occasion an officer of the Laotian BV-33 actually reported seeing a
convoy of no less than 1,200 self-propelled guns, tanks, armored
personnel carriers, and other vehicles. That was undoubtedly an exaggeration, although an NVA artillery regiment moved into the Khe
Sanh area around this time, making up for North Vietnamese infantry
who were moving away.

With the supply situation as bad as it was, the predicament of
outlying positions like 881 South was complicated because there was
little flow of personnel from the combat base. Thus it was difficult to
request specific supplies in a secure fashion. Dabney was reduced to
talking over the radio deceptively, saying things like "my horse is
hungry," meaning he needed 106mm ammunition for his recoilless
rifle, or whistling the tune "Stout Hearted Men" to indicate he wanted
replacement personnel.

Letters from Lieutenant William R. Ammon on the Mike Company
spur of 881 South caused a ruckus at home in late February when his
parents had them published in the *Cincinnati Enquirer*. The letters, as
any letters from 881 South would have done, spoke of the paucity
of supplies and delays in receiving letters. Marine senior
commanders defensively explained away the complaints, accused
Ammon of being "guilty of minor exaggeration" and "the victim of
poor judgment on the part of his parents." In fact, as General Victor
Krulak conceded to Marine commandant General Leonard F.
Chapman, 881 South *had* completely run out of supplies at least
once — for two days in February — *had* suffered from poor mail
delivery — Major Matthew Caulfield recalls it got no mail for
twenty-six or twenty-seven days — and the combat base had had a
deficit of 1,037 tons in scheduled supply deliveries during February.

Krulak also admitted that no less than thirty-three helicopters had been destroyed or permanently disabled in resupply activities between January 21 and March 22.

Air support continued to be controversial not only at the command level but in the field. A quintessential example was an experience of Echo Company of 2/26 on Hill 861-A. Captain Breeding's men detected the North Vietnamese beginning to tunnel into the side of their hill, only about fifteen meters from the edge of the Marine perimeter. For almost two weeks they begged forward air controllers to direct fixed-wing air strikes at this target. The controllers consistently refused. It happened that virtually all of these cases had involved either Air Force air controllers or strike aircraft or both, and the Air Force rigidly adhered to the restrictions set on distance from friendly forces at which various sizes of ordnance could be used. Then one day a Marine forward air controller was on station with Marine air coming in and the controller was talking on the radio with Captain Breeding. Told of the seriousness of the tunnel threat, the air controller agreed to buzz the target himself to judge whether it could safely be hit. After that the controller agreed to take on the target, asked Breeding to get his men under cover, and sent in a flight of four fighter-bombers one by one. There were secondary explosions on the very first pass and before it was over the target was belching yellow smoke and finally blew up with a tremendous explosion. Whole boulders were thrown into the air.

Another device of great use to Marines was the Starlight Scope, a mechanism that optimized ambient light to permit viewing at night. These early low-light sighting devices were huge — more than forty pounds — and were not used during the first several weeks of the siege, perhaps because of how cumbersome they were, perhaps because of the poor weather. In mid-February Corporal Dennis Mannion, a forward observer on 861, decided to use the scope and see how well it worked. He trained it on the adjoining ridge shortly after midnight one night. He recalled:

> I could not believe what I saw. There were at least twenty or twenty-five NVA digging into the top of the ridgeline. It was a regular stateside working party. Some guys digging, some squatting and resting, some guys bringing up logs and branches. To stare out into the dark at that ridge 500 yards away and see nothing, then use the scope and see twenty of the enemy was a real jolt.

Mannion called Captain Paul L. Snead, who organized a fire attack with an M-60 machine gun and a 106mm recoilless rifle, based on estimates of the range and declination of the target. Mannion watched the North Vietnamese "with sinister and eager anticipation," but when the Marines fired, the flashes of their shells so overloaded the Starlight Scope with their brightness that its circuits blanked out for minutes afterward. Subsequently Marines on 861 used the scope many times but were never able to observe results with it.

The North Vietnamese may have had some surprise weapons of their own. A defector from the 72nd Local Force Battalion in mid-February told Marines his unit commander had said the NVA was going to use ground-to-ground missiles at Khe Sanh. The rallier, Nguyen Ngoc Thanh, described a missile with a configuration similar to an SA-2 SAM but longer and wider, sounding very much like the Soviet FROG (for "free rocket over ground"). The man told interrogators the missile had a technical deficiency such that it would require about *thirty days* to do the cartographic work to target the missile and complete its electronic prelaunch sequences.

Toward the end of February, Captain Dabney recalls, one night the NVA themselves fired illumination rounds, a string of parachute flares ignited on a line north of 881 South. Fearing assault, Dabney called an immediate artillery mission into that area and then had the eleven mortars on his own hill fire in all directions at different ranges. The North Vietnamese used more illumination. It was extraordinary for the NVA to give up the advantages of darkness. Once the illumination stopped,

> it was quiet, just like a church mouse. About a minute after everything stopped and the last flare burned out we heard what I could best describe as what sounded like standing in a New York subway station when an express train that is not going to stop in your station goes by . . . coming out from . . . around Co Roc. The noise got louder until it sounded as if what was making it had passed right over the hill from south to north, and then, about a thousand meters to the north of us, there was a horrendous explosion. And that was it.

No further FROGs, if that was indeed what the weapon was, were launched at the Marines.

Americans and North Vietnamese, locked in a delicate dance with death, embraced anything they thought might help in the hour of need. For all that, the basic fact remained that American firepower was more supple, flexible, and powerful than that of the adversary. It was the North Vietnamese who had to tiptoe around the opponent, never quite daring to come to grips. Aware of American advantages, the NVA showed signs of getting in so close that they too could benefit from the restricted bomb zones. Then there might be a real battle. Until then the fact remained, as General Cushman put it to Colonel Lownds the day after the Lang Vei attack, "the main ground contest for Khe Sanh remains to be fought . . . a continued effort of vigilance is still necessary."

No Place to Go

As Khe Sanh waited for whatever might come, Hanoi stepped up its propaganda rhetoric. The daily newspaper *Nhan Dan,* noting the arrival of the 1st Cavalry Division and other American reinforcements in I Corps, nevertheless insisted that NVA and local force actions in Quang Tri province and at Khe Sanh had "shown . . . the aggressors that they cannot avoid not only one but many Dien Bien Phus." As for General Westmoreland, North Vietnamese Army paper *Quan Doi Nhan Dan* opined on February 26 that he had been retained in command because dismissal would have been too clear an admission of defeat. The NVA paper termed "braggadocio" Westmoreland's statements at his news conferences and compared the general "to the frog who wished to become as big [as a] bull."

While a good deal of this rhetoric was plainly febrile, it draws attention to Hanoi's more or less open desire to score a major victory. The locale for this could be wider than just Khe Sanh, as suggested by the reference to Quang Tri, but at Khe Sanh the very texture of the siege looked very much like Dien Bien Phu. One prominent feature of the earlier French battle, for example, had been the use of trenches dug to within just a few meters of the defenders' positions. Trenches now appeared at Khe Sanh also, increasingly blanketing the western and southern sides of the battlefield.

On February 25 an aerial observer noted a trench running almost due north to within twenty-five meters of the combat base perimeter. This was an extension of a trench network that already existed on Hill 471 and represented an addition of some seven hundred meters in just one night! The trench appeared to be about two feet wide and four deep and terminated in a trench parallel to the Khe Sanh perimeter

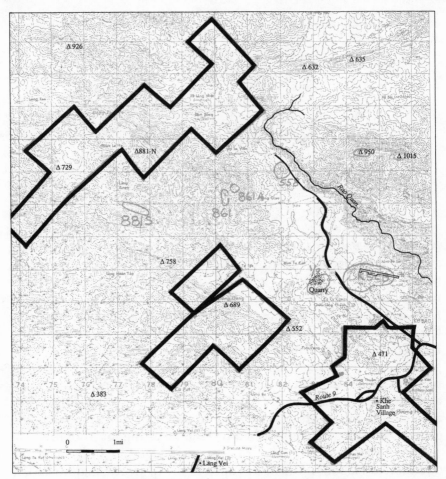

12 · NVA Trench System, March 1968

approximately fifty meters long. It appeared to be a preparation of the departure line for an assault.

The following day, of course, more trenches could be seen, paralleling the lines of Bravo Company of 1/26 in the Gray Sector of the combat base. Aerial photos the next day disclosed an entire system of trenches and bunkers extending from some 1,500 meters south of Khe Sanh and ending close to it. "We watched with some fascination and no small apprehension, day by day, as the trenches crept closer in to our perimeter," wrote Robert P. Keller, a senior air officer whose men tried to think of ways to neutralize the trenches. The air units tried everything from napalm "baths" to 2,000-pound bombs. Artillerymen speculated about using the Army 175mm guns to do the job at long range, but the possible aiming errors at that distance made them too risky so close to Marine positions. Marine artillery at the combat base tried delayed time fuses but the job remained a tough one (French experience in Indochina had been that a thousand 105mm hits were necessary to destroy a hundred meters of trench).

In Washington others played at the same sorts of possibilities. There was even a suggestion to stymie the trench system by filling it with quick-drying concrete. A Marine colonel on the Joint Staff showed the impracticality of this idea by calculating that to fill a trench two feet wide and three deep that was six hundred yards long would require eight hundred tons of concrete (four hundred cubic yards) to be carried by 116 aircraft sorties ranging from C-130 to CH-46. To fill a system of trenches around Khe Sanh that might ultimately total fourteen thousand yards in length would take about 2,400 aircraft sorties. This scale of air effort would obviously not be possible.

General Cushman finally asked for C-47 "Spooky" gunships on a rotating basis to lace the trenches with constant fire.

North Vietnamese probes occurred on both the Gray and Red Sectors and were detected by both Lima Company of 3/26 and Bravo Company of 1/26. Intelligence reported a diminution of truck traffic in Laos, interpreted to mean the NVA had completed their logistics buildup. The moon began to wane on February 20, entering a phase felt to favor NVA attack since it would make nighttime air support more difficult. On February 19 a photo recon flight returned evidence of a large underground complex inside the Laotian border a few kilometers south of Co Roc. The facility appeared to have both radio aerials and radar antennas. Large quantities of supplies had been stacked outside it. Early in the afternoon of the 19th, NVA radios resumed communicating after maintaining silence for more than seventeen hours. Once more this suggested impending attack.

North Vietnamese bombardment, however, remained relatively light. On February 17 only forty rounds of mortars and thirty-five of artillery were fired at Khe Sanh. As Walt Rostow summarized Westmoreland's daily report of February 19 for President Johnson, mortar fire was even less. What attack?

Weather continued to be poor, almost "zero-zero" — zero ceiling and zero visibility — perfect conditions for an NVA attack.

The action, such as it was, came on February 21. Suddenly the North Vietnamese escalated their bombardment, that day unleashing 50 rounds of artillery, 70 of rockets, and 250 of mortars on the combat base. Shortly after noon and for about two hours afterward, the shelling was supplemented by an estimated battalion assaulting the lines held by Captain Pho's 37th ARVN Ranger Battalion. The South Vietnamese held on quite well, with few casualties. Some Rangers were knocked down by shelling, one was thrown against a wall and broke his wrist, and an estimated twenty or twenty-five NVA died on the battlefield. Saigon's daily situation report given to LBJ listed the attack as a company-size probe that was over before dark.

The Ghost Patrol

Intelligence reported to Lyndon Johnson that the North Vietnamese artillery regiment moving toward Khe Sanh reached battle positions near the village on February 23. The next day the combat base was hit for the first time by shells of 130mm caliber. At Khe Sanh, Marines worried over the North Vietnamese capability to intensify their bombardment, in particular any efforts (of which there were none) to interdict drawing supplies from the water point outside the Blue Sector of the perimeter. On February 24 the combat base itself had just five hundred gallons in its water supply.

North Vietnamese artillerymen lost no time manifesting their new power. On February 23, the day the North Vietnamese trenches became noticeable, Khe Sanh underwent its peak bombardment. The combat base suffered ten killed and fifty-one wounded. Once again bombardment ignited a fire at one of the ammunition dumps, cooking off, detonating, or otherwise ruining 1,120 90mm shells, of both high explosive and canister types, and 500 "Beehive" rounds for 106mm recoilless rifles. Some Marines insisted the real count that day rose to more than 1,400 shells, while a FOB-3 officer maintained that if shells hitting their unit area were included, the total count numbered more than 1,700. Official tally was 1,307.

Everybody wanted to know what was going on outside the wire. Major Mirza Baig's sensor systems were a terrific source of information while the adversary was in motion, but once the NVA were in position there was not much movement to sense. The road convoy approaching with the NVA artillery regiment had been sighted by aircraft, so many vehicles that observers couldn't put a number on them, but the North Vietnamese were hardly seen at all from the bunkers and fighting holes of the combat base. Are there two or three or four NVA divisions out there, wags began to ask, or just a couple of guys with a bicycle and a radio?

Colonel James B. Wilkinson of 1/26 had the main responsibility for defense of the combat base perimeter and he needed to know more about Indian country. So Wilkinson planned a reconnaissance patrol that would follow a diamond-shaped pattern to points A, B, and C and then return to origin. He cleared it with regiment, as usual, getting approval from Colonel Lownds right down to the fire plans for support of the patrol should things go awry.

"In hindsight," Jim Wilkinson now says, "that patrol should have been a much smaller patrol. It should have been probably a squad patrol. It was a reconnaissance patrol. It was not supposed to have been a combat patrol."

But the patrol of February 25 looked like a fighting patrol and it acted like one. Led by Lieutenant Don Jacques, who had gained the confidence of company commander Captain Ken Pipes by his willingness to take on any mission and his constant motion, the 3rd Platoon of Company B got the call for the foray. Pipes suspected a site along the old access road as the location of three NVA 82mm mortars that were giving the Marines trouble. Previous patrols had tried to find the mortars but had seen nothing. Perhaps Jacques would have better luck. Pipes briefed him late on the afternoon of the 24th. He was to take two squads, heavily reinforced with weapons men and forward observers, a total of forty-seven Marines. Jacques was given three checkpoints to make the diamond, and a two-squad force of Company C under Second Lieutenant Skip Wells to deploy about two hours into the patrol to cover the return of the detachment. The plan looked quite straightforward, but Don Jacques had a strong force and, having been initiated to combat in the heavy metal environment of the hilltop outposts, he was not averse to using it.

Four months before, Jacques had been a green second lieutenant trying to get experience on 881 South. Now he was considered a seasoned officer well able to lead a patrol outside the perimeter. The evening before his patrol the twenty-year-old Jacques spent quietly writing letters to his sister and parents. To his sister Jacques wrote:

> We're just sitting here waiting for all hell to break loose [;] with each day that goes by the incoming increases and the 3rd [Platoon] digs deeper. We are already for them in my opinion but no matter how well prepared you think you are there is always something more you can do. We have been lucky so far and I hope that the good fortune holds for us. Although my platoon has had 30 wounded since Jan. 21st, none have been too serious and the majority of the men are still on duty. . . . They seem to think Khe Sanh will be the turning point to the negotiations tables. I hope so but if not we will go on until this is over one way and the only way.

With his parents Jacques went into more detail on his daily life at Khe Sanh:

> The days go by quite quickly but the nights are long around here. I haven't been getting too much sleep as I've said before and am getting quite use to that also. I stay awake all night sometimes and others not. We get our sleep in the day a couple of ours at a time. That is if the work load isn't to great. It is a constant digging deeper and the work really never stops. It can't.

These were the last written words of young Donald Jacques.

In preparation for the patrol, early the next morning Corporal Gilbert Wall came to the 3rd Platoon area. A Blackfoot Indian from Montana, Wall was a forward observer for 81mm mortars who had spent the night with the ARVN Rangers. Believing the NVA were probing their lines, the South Vietnamese had kept up a vigorous fire in the darkness. Wall alone figured he must have shot about seven hundred bullets and had no time to clean his M-16 before being sent out on patrol with Jacques's platoon. Ironically the dirty rifle, by dissuading him from the temptation to slug it out with the NVA, would save Wall's life.

Many were the patrols Gil Wall had shared with Don Jacques, so when the lieutenant saw the forward observer he invited Wall into his bunker for coffee and breakfast. It was the least they could do on a Sunday morning. Jacques introduced Wall to his new platoon sergeant, George McClelland. Wall joked about the late breakfast — he had eaten hours before.

Wall spoke with some of the Marines before the patrol moved out. He knew some of the men but most were new — lacking the red skin tone from Khe Sanh's mud. The new men looked ten years younger than everyone else. "Everybody was in a surprisingly good mood," Wall recalls. "They were all happy, loose and relaxed. It was a nice day, and just to move outside of base for a while gave you a good feeling."

The patrol consisted of two squads of 3rd Platoon reinforced by Wall's forward observer team, a scout from the battalion intelligence section, a Kit Carson scout, two M-60 machine gun teams, and a rocket team. In the briefing Corporal Kenneth Claire, whom Ken Pipes and some others considered the best squad leader in the company, told his men they were going on a sweep with the basic purpose of checking the perimeter, determining whether the wire had been cut or sabotaged, chasing out NVA observation posts, that kind of thing. They were not to venture farther than 1,000 meters from the combat base. The mortars Wilkinson wished the patrol to spot, however, were estimated to be located at 1,200 or 1,300 meters outside the base. Another concern would be the NVA trenches suddenly sprouting along this face of Khe Sanh.

The patrol left about 8:00 A.M., before the latest reports at the battalion staff briefing, which had been moved back to 9:30 on this Sunday morning. The February 25 briefing never happened; before the scheduled hour, Lieutenant Jacques's patrol had made contact and become embattled.

As the Marines approached a tree line, they saw several North Vietnamese running along the plantation road that met Route 9 farther on. Jacques called in for permission to attempt capture of prisoners. Pipes had the impression the patrol had gotten off its assigned route but wasn't certain. Sergeant Patrick Fitch later told Marine debriefers the patrol was actually almost four hundred meters beyond its second checkpoint. In any case, prisoners were very valuable and Pipes, mistakenly believing the patrol to be on the road past the trash dump, not west of it on the one that led past the Poilane house, warned Jacques to be careful but to go ahead and get the prisoners if he could.

Lieutenant Jacques ordered his men forward. Private First Class Clayton J. Theyerl had just taken over as point man. The Marine he relieved, Calvin E. Bright, recalls: "I remember the word was passed back that we had found [the NVA], and the Kit Carson scout that was with us begged and pleaded not to go; he said, 'Don't go any farther!' "

Jacques drew his pistol and then dropped his hand in the silent signal for a charge. He turned and smiled at Gilbert Wall, who smiled back. Seconds later, as Marines crossed the road and set foot in the brush on the other side, heavy automatic weapons fire began from tree lines both in front and to the side. There was virtually no cover. The North Vietnamese were in fortified positions and trenches. It was a classic L-shaped ambush. The shock could not have been greater. Theyerl was killed instantly.

Jacques ordered Claire's squad and a machine gun to the right to try and envelop the ambush force, hooking into their rear to outflank them. Ken Claire tried his best. The rugged squad leader, who in childhood had started summer mornings in California's Sierra Nevada with the Tarzan yell, was a great outdoorsman and rugged son of a retired professional football and baseball player. Claire had plenty of drive and gumption, but the NVA fire was murderous. George McClelland stood in the middle of the field yelling at Claire to get his squad up and moving to the cover of some trenches, about forty meters away. Claire stood too, hollering at his men to forget about maneuvers, just run and get in that trench. In less time than it takes to tell it, Claire's squad was decimated. Bright, who had been to the left of the line, moved to the aid of wounded comrades. Corpsman Frank V. Calzia found some of the men just wounded, though the Marines out front had all perished.

Sergeant Ronald L. Ridgway, Lance Corporal Charles G. Geller, a radio man, and Private First Class James R. Bruder all made a dash to the trench at the edge of the wood. When they looked back, nobody was following. They shot several incautious North Vietnamese, but Bruder took a chest wound and Geller one in the face. Ridgway was hit in the leg and shoulder and broke an arm, as did Private First Class Willie J. Ruff, whom Ridgway reached in the field just before collapsing. A jet struck the trench the Marines had left, spattering them with some napalm they managed to brush off. Drifting in and out of consciousness, Ridgway was finally taken prisoner by the North Vietnamese. He was held until March 1973, after the Paris agreements, when American prisoners were released.

While Claire's squad broke right, Jacques and Wall moved left on the line. Wall wanted to call an 81mm fire mission in front of Claire's men, but the trees confused him, blocking his vision. Not willing to take the risk of calling fire on Marines, Wall selected a different target. Men were getting hit all around him. "The screaming and shouting was so loud you couldn't hear your own voice," Wall said. He threw a grenade into an NVA trench and got three of the enemy, but more North Vietnamese took their places in no time. "I couldn't believe how many of them there were."

Jacques came over, firing an M-79 grenade launcher, telling the men to pull back. Some Marines helped the wounded, and Wall provided cover fire and then grabbed two boxes of machine gun ammunition. Some of the North Vietnamese were following. Jacques had almost made it back to the combat base when he suffered a severe wound in the groin. Wall was with him at the time and tried to bandage the lieutenant's wound, but Don Jacques died holding his arm. He lost blood so fast it instantly soaked through the inch-thick bandage Wall applied to the wound. John Watashay dragged the body back to the perimeter. A photographer caught that instant on film, the picture was printed in *Newsweek*, and Jacques's father inevitably saw it to compound his pain.

As the Marines pulled back, the patrol lost its cohesion. Many were dead and wounded, and the survivors knew little about the others. Captain Pipes sent out his 1st Platoon to cover the withdrawal, and he asked for tank and ONTOS support, which was granted. Later he asked for Delta Company to make a full-scale thrust to recover the wounded and the bodies of the dead. That kindled an agonizing debate at the battalion command post over whether to commit more Marines to the battle. Jim Wilkinson faced a tough decision because, as had been the case during Lang Vei, Company D was the regiment's only operational reserve.

Colonel Wilkinson avers that had he based his decision solely on pride, guilt, and emotion, not only would he have sent another unit after the Jacques patrol, he would have led it himself. In fact he considered grabbing whatever unattached Marines he could and leading the force. But the radio reports, confirmed by Lieutenant Ernie Spencer (since February 14 the battalion intelligence officer), indicated the patrol had lost many of its casualties quite quickly and that there was not really much to be saved. Wilkinson's mission was to defend Khe Sanh combat base; getting a company or half a battalion into a serious firefight as night approached was "a very tenuous position." Reliving the decision in years since, Jim Wilkinson remains convinced he did the right thing.

At the time, Wilkinson went to Colonel Lownds, explained the situation, and took full responsibility. He made it clear that the company commander, Captain Kenneth Pipes, was not at fault and would be retained in command. Although it has been written that Wilkinson was himself relieved as a result of the loss of the patrol on February 25, and although the Marine historical monograph on Khe Sanh lists Wilkinson as having been relieved on March 1, in a 1989 interview the former commander recalled that he remained in command until the 15th or 16th. That gave Wilkinson about eight and a half months in charge of the 1st Battalion, 26th Marines, probably some kind of record for 3rd Marine Division battalion commanders in Vietnam. He was posted later as executive officer to the 4th Marine Regiment, hardly a sign of ill repute.

The atmosphere in the battalion command post was confused and explosive that day. There were arguments, recriminations, staffers at each other's throats. Staff tried to reconstruct who had been on Don Jacques's patrol, where exactly they had been, not only which road they had crossed but where they had been along the road. "Everybody was at a loss for what to do," recalls staffer Bill Smith. "Half the people wanted to send out a heavy relief force, but we were under orders not to run any combat patrols off the base at that time. That pissed everybody off. It was a good thing that we didn't at that point because everybody wanted blood, and at that time I think we would have very hastily run a battalion-minus [operation] out there and gotten really in shit . . . and gone piecemeal to our oblivion."

As the stragglers wandered in, Marines discovered that even the survivors didn't know exactly who had gone down or where. Battalion waited a long time before doing the tactically correct thing — calling in artillery and air on the ambush site — and even then the staff felt none too good about it. Marines filtered back by ones and twos, most wounded. The Kit Carson scout who had warned against the adventure came back holding what he was convinced was the only gun that could ever kill him — one he took off a North Vietnamese soldier who almost had. Other survivors included Gilbert Wall, Ed

Rayburn, Ted Golab, Johnny Belina, Tom Detrick, most of them wounded. The platoon's well-appreciated "doc," John A. Cicala, Jr., dragged himself back to the perimeter wire grievously wounded.

Don Jacques's patrol never came back. Like a band of ghosts, their fate nagged at the Marines at Khe Sanh, who wanted desperately to discover the bodies, recover the wounded, get the real story of this incident. But Saigon's daily report to Washington listed the action drily as "a mid-morning patrol [that] engaged an estimated NVA company . . . [until] the contact broke at noon." Casualties were reported as one dead, twenty-one wounded, and twenty-five missing in action.

Such certainty was not felt at Khe Sanh. Almost two weeks later, following considerable study, casualties were established as nine dead, fifteen wounded but not evacuated, ten seriously wounded, and nineteen missing.

Radio Hanoi broadcast its version of events on the morning of March 14. The dispatch, credited to a Liberation Press Agency correspondent, claimed that "two U.S. companies made a desperate sortie at the southern end [of Khe Sanh combat base] but were caught in a fierce ambush." Playing on the standard MACV-style press release, the report noted that a "body count" (by the NVA) verified 120 dead Marines. One Marine officer, it was claimed, had been captured. Squad No. 7 received credit for having "wiped out 30 Marines" all by itself.

The best last word is what Jeff Culpepper wrote, having left 3rd Platoon on February 23 to attend a weapons course on Okinawa. "This whole damn war became too real today," Culpepper told his mother. "As soon as I got to Phu Bai I found out that my entire squad was killed along with almost my entire platoon. . . . Every buddy I had is dead. . . . Nothing can stop me now! If I die I'll feel proud to be back with them."

Khe Sanh 207 Red

Aside from the beckoning ghosts, the episode of the Jacques patrol may have had a positive military aspect. The North Vietnamese trench system that became the locus of this firefight had, of course, materialized in the context of preparation for a real or feigned assault on Khe

Sanh combat base. The NVA forces were present in strength that may well have been for the same reason. Heavy bombardment of the area by artillery and air power that followed immediately after the patrol battle could have broken up the planned NVA assault. Alternatively, whatever the North Vietnamese got out of the prisoner they captured, Ron Ridgway, may have led them to delay their attack. Ridgway had found the NVA desperate for data about the combat base, so he had indulged them: "One day they were trying to interrogate me and I inflated the numbers. I inflated the truth — the number of men on the base, the number of rows of concertina, and everything else. I made it worse than it was." Such disinformation may have had a chilling effect on North Vietnamese officers poised to execute their assault. If so, the interval of delay permitted American firepower to further wear down the NVA assault troops.

Already in motion, the development that would prove crucial in halting the attack had been under examination in Saigon and elsewhere for some time. This was the mounting of ARC LIGHT strikes in close proximity to American positions. Basic procedures for ensuring safety of friendly forces set exclusion zones around them that varied with the type of ordnance used; B-52 strikes had never been allowed closer than three thousand meters from friendly positions. Remembering Con Thien, North Vietnamese officers expected this restriction. They confidently reassured their men that precisely by getting close to the Americans they would neutralize the B-52 threat.

Unfortunately for the NVA, the Con Thien experience could be read different ways. At MACV someone remembered that an ARC LIGHT strike on Con Thien had accidentally been made just 1,400 meters outside U.S. lines without adverse results. By late January Westmoreland was asking Momyer and Cushman for a special effort to strike all close-in targets within forty-eight hours. On February 13 Westmoreland advised CINCPAC that the tactical situation would require that all types of firepower be used against close-proximity targets; he recommended that the existing B-52 restriction be rescinded. Admiral Sharp approved the change for emergency contingencies five days later. Technical preparations had been in train since January 29, when a 3rd Marine Division planning group recommended installation at Khe Sanh of X-band radar guidance that would ensure accurate weapons delivery at distances of less than one thousand meters.

For assurance, the Americans decided to do a test strike. "Khe Sanh 207 Red" became the target, an area 1.2 kilometers north of Hill 881

South that ran generally northeast and included Hill 881 North. Bill Dabney's Marines on 881 South were quite used to firepower. They had seen large amounts of it applied near their hill and had contributed to the pyrotechnics the night of the NVA attack on Hill 861-A. They regularly hosed down their own hill with their mortars, and at times Dabney had all his men toss grenades at the same time. As he put it, "We reacted to every movement, we reacted to every noise, even every smell with massive amounts of indirect fire." But the ARC LIGHT would be something new, and precautions were taken.

One Marine recounts the moment well:

We got in word that B-52s were going to attack that ridge line. We kinda looked at each other kinda strange. I mean, B-52s flying high level, and they were going to drop 500-pounders just across from us! They expected the impact from these bombs to be very severe. Of course, they were. Everyone was ordered inside their bunkers and to stay in there, and it was passed over the radio the moment the bombs were dropped. We were told to place our fingers in our ears and pull our knees up to our chests and scream as loud as we could during the bombing. . . . This was . . . to prevent anyone from getting shock. And even though we did this, many of us got nosebleeds from the concussion of the bombs being dropped.

Air buffeted the Marine positions but the target box looked devastated. Close-in ARC LIGHT strikes became an accepted tactic, though still regarded as a departure from normal target criteria that was reserved for emergencies.

The new tactic achieved acceptance just in time. During the last week of February intelligence began to show remarkable NVA supply traffic between Tchepone and Khe Sanh, as if the NVA was attempting a rapid logistics buildup. Then the MUSCLE SHOALS sensor arrays lit up.

Before the start of the siege, while familiarizing himself with the battle zone, David Lownds had trudged the dust of Route 9 to the Laotian border. This "personal previous reconnaissance" told Lownds the time required to reach various points along the road. Sensors now confirmed the early estimates and also, by computing the time required for the full NVA column to pass each array, enabled the Marines to estimate the force at regiment size. By then the sensor activity was in two directions — along Route 9 and east of Hill 881 South. "It became obvious to me that an enemy regiment was trying

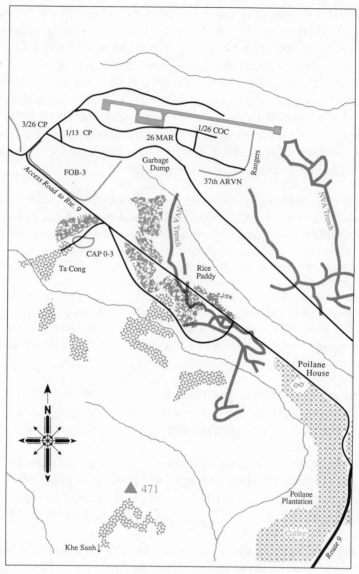

13 · ARC LIGHT Strikes

to close the base," Lownds later testified to a Senate subcommittee.

Majors Mirza Baig, the target officer, and Jerry E. Hudson, 26th Regiment intelligence officer, put together what they knew of local paths, the most desirable assembly areas for an assault, and the NVA trench system. They concocted a list of suitable targets. Lownds relayed the target data to 3rd Division headquarters. One target lay near the Poilane house, another near the combat base garbage dump. Colonel Lownds felt strongly that, because of the high rate of sensor activation and movement along two axes, "this might well be the main attack," he told Marine debriefers. "I called up Division and I said, 'I need a B-52 strike NOW; any later than two hours from now, forget it because he's going to have closed with me.'"

The sense of foreboding was considerable at Khe Sanh that last day of February. Ensign Kux noted an evening phone call from Jerry Hudson predicting an infantry attack that night, preceded by a heavy artillery bombardment beginning at 9:00 P.M. Ernie Spencer, the intelligence officer for 1/26, alerted his battalion for an attack, exact target unknown, to be expected at 8:00 P.M. The actual bombardment began at 10:00 P.M. and went on until midnight, apparently in desultory fashion, for only 157 rounds were recorded falling at Khe Sanh.

In the meantime there happened to be B-52 bombers in the air and these were diverted on an emergency basis to hit the targets the 26th Marines requested. "This was the only time that the kids on the lines told me . . . that they actually saw bodies being thrown in the air," Lownds recalled. "I sincerely believe . . . that those strikes caught at least two battalions. We were already in contact on the perimeter . . . with a battalion, so I feel we had a regiment."

What was left of the North Vietnamese force went ahead and made its attack against the sector held by the ARVN 37th Rangers. The anticipated big assault, for which Khe Sanh went to condition red alert at 10:15 P.M., resolved itself into three simple probes against the Ranger sector. The ARVN line had been secured by 4:30 A.M. None of the attacks even reached the barbed wire barriers, much less breached them. South Vietnamese troops reported killing just seven NVA, although an early morning patrol discovered a total of seventy-eight bodies and recovered twelve rifles and a number of bangalore torpedo–like devices clearly intended for use against the wire.

The spooks of FOB-3 had a very special contribution to make to the events of February 29–March 1. They always seemed to have a few extra moments of warning whenever the North Vietnamese fired their heavy artillery. It turned out that most of the NVA artillery fired on radio command and FOB-3 constantly monitored the circuits. The NVA were not so security-conscious as Americans and did not constantly change their radio frequencies; in fact, they used the same ones for months on end. The *pièce de résistance,* according to Staff Sergeant Harve Saal, was that the North Vietnamese had listed their radio frequencies, *all* their operational codes, and the keys to their cyphers in a single codebook and FOB-3 had a copy of it. This led directly to the FOB-3 contribution. Harve Saal takes up the story:

> One day a[n] NVA message was intercepted and decrypted. The message said that a ground attack, using armor, would take place in the near future. The code book listed the use of hand-held pyrotechnics for their anticipated ground attack. . . .
>
> Well, as any good tactician could estimate, it was just the thing to do — give all the FOB [Special Forces troopers] the "Cease Fire/ Retreat" flares.
>
> Then one night the still was shattered with the commencement of an artillery and rocket barrage. I could sense that this was the "BIG" night! The incoming artillery and rocket rounds now pounded further away from the perimeter's defensive wire. The shifting of the impacting explosions now revealed other sounds in the night, the sound of armor rolling towards us. Then the NVA signal for "ATTACK" lit up the sky. The impacting artillery and rocket fire shifted another 300 meters. . . . The ground shook — or was it me?
>
> I fired my "Cease Fire/Retreat" handflares in the correct order (I hoped). I looked into the sky's darkness. "Pop" — "pop" — "pop," the colors shone brightly. But just then, "pop" — "pop" — "pop" — more flares! . . . Who? Why? The colors filled the sky's horizon.
>
> The other [Special Forces] had fired their flares too! There was such confusion within the NVA attacking ranks that the attack was halted.

Saal's story is intriguing; moreover, the CIA reported tanks within 1,500 meters of the Khe Sanh perimeter around this time. But existing accounts pass over this battle in just a few sentences or even words. Thus there is no detailed recounting of *any* of the events of the night of February 29. As early as January North Vietnamese defectors had spoken of plans to use armor against the combat base but these tanks had not heretofore materialized. The operation of North Vietnamese armored forces throughout the siege remains one of the enduring mysteries of Khe Sanh.

Westmoreland's official report to Washington for February 29 described artillery fire as "slackening . . . paralleling enemy ground activity." Moreover, the Saigon official report for the *next* day declared that "for the second successive day, enemy activity at Khe Sanh was limited to small probes and comparatively light incoming." To hear MACV tell it, nothing, not even a victory, had happened at Khe Sanh. The close-proximity ARC LIGHT strikes became a big plus for Khe Sanh's defense, and ultimately 589 sorties of this type would be conducted, but the battle of February 29 well illustrates one of their perverse effects: paradoxically, the more successful the air intervention, the more difficult it became to tell what had happened.

The people who best knew what did happen were the commanders of the North Vietnamese Army. Such dangers as existed in conducting a siege of Khe Sanh did not remain hidden through the advent of close-proximity ARC LIGHT strikes. Rather, those dangers were apparent early in the campaign, certainly by the time of the battles at Hill 861-A and Lang Vei. It must have been clear after those actions that the cost of a full siege would be high indeed. Had Hanoi not intended Khe Sanh as a feint from the first instance, these early frustrations furnished the NVA renewed opportunity to reconsider its position.

Depending on one's reading of the evidence, the abortive assaults of mid- and late February were either gambits to keep the Americans in place or genuine efforts to mount a mass assault. The strangest thing was that despite the sensor data and communications intercepts, few North Vietnamese were actually *seen*. In fact, at the end of the campaign, after a slew of hotly contested combats, the total count of enemy bodies (that dubious benchmark of success) stood at just 1,602. This was the very stuff of which doubts are made.

Like the NVA commanders, those who must have had a few doubts were the rank and file of the North Vietnamese Army. Documents captured later that contained strength returns have been analyzed to indicate that in early March only 283 soldiers of the 554 on the rolls of 1st Battalion, 9th Regiment, 304th Division were actually available to fight. Sixty-four of the rest had died, eighty-three were wounded, and eighty-five more had deserted. The high number of desertions was unusual but a continuing phenomena — a few days later a return showed sixty-one more. Similarly, 300 replacements of Infiltration Group 926 deserted before the unit arrived near Khe Sanh, where remaining personnel were assigned to the 9th Regiment. The motivating factor in many of these desertions was fear of air power.

Captured diaries give the flavor of the fears felt by North Vietnamese soldiers. In one, a March 10 entry describes an incident in which a passing aircraft dropped a balloon at the location of the unit rice depot. As soldiers rushed to look at it, "they were discovered and the whole area was turned into a mass of fire by enemy aircraft." Another NVA soldier, passing through Laos on his way farther south, recorded on March 7 that he was "very close to Khe Sanh and some 3 to 4 kilometers from Route #9. From here I can hear the roar of guns on the battlefield and our men from Khe Sanh come here to rest. We can see the lights on enemy aircraft during the night."

Quite pointed is the comment by Hoai Phong, a 9th Regiment cadre who titled his last diary entry, recorded on March 21, 1968, "The 60-day fighting," in evident reference to the length of the siege of Khe Sanh up to that time. Phong wrote:

> Fifteen days after the siege began, things turned out to be more atrocious than ever and even by far fiercer than Go Roong and Dien Bien Phu. We retreated to our trenches and left our friendly units to perform the mission. From the beginning until the 60th day, B-52 bombers continually dropped their bombs in this area with ever growing intensity and at any moment of the day. If someone came to visit this place, he might say that this was a storm of bombs and ammunition which eradicated all living creatures and vegetation whatsoever, even those located in caves or in deep underground shelters.

At length, whether or not the siege was meant as a diversion, the North Vietnamese command decided it had to reduce losses and modified tactics accordingly. Not only did the trenches sprout, but tunnels allegedly did as well. Although the Marines were quite sensitive to the possibility of tunnels, kept a watch for them, and even brought up special equipment for detecting them, none were found. Yet an NVA prisoner from the 9th Regiment, captured during April, told interrogators his unit had been assigned the task of tunneling under Khe Sanh, beginning from the Poilane plantation about two kilometers southeast of the combat base and proceeding in two main branches. According to the POW statement, by the time his regiment was relieved and withdrawn for rest in Laos, on March 20, the tunnel had been completed to a point fifteen meters *inside* the wire perimeter of the base. Both Marine and MACV sources conclude, however, that neither trench nor tunnel efforts at Khe Sanh were as sophisticated as those at Dien Bien Phu.

The most effective method of reducing losses, of course, was to withdraw from the battlefield. At least one analyst, the senior I Corps specialist at the Combined Intelligence Center, Vietnam, thought he had found indications of withdrawals from Khe Sanh even before Tet. Elements of one NVA division at Khe Sanh were identified in combat in the battle of Hue. By late February, more or less coincident with reinforcement of the North Vietnamese battle force by the 468th Artillery Regiment, additional indications of withdrawal appeared.

Robert Pisor reports that General Westmoreland concluded on March 6 that the NVA had turned its attention away from Khe Sanh. If Westmoreland made such a statement it must have been at the background news conference he gave that day, where he compared North Vietnam's gains from Tet with those of the Germans at the Battle of the Bulge.

The statement may have been for public consumption, but its real basis was intelligence information available in both Saigon and Washington. The previous day, in fact, the CIA had circulated its tentative conclusion that the NVA might be pulling units out of Khe Sanh to send elsewhere. Walt Rostow and Bob Ginsburgh had already reviewed the reports with LBJ. Rostow cautioned on March 6 that the evidence was *"extremely fragile"* and that "I would *not* yet draw the conclusion that [the North Vietnamese] have given up on an attempt to take Khe Sanh."

Another memorandum prepared for President Johnson that day presented a far different construction of enemy intentions than the three-phase buildup to a Khe Sanh attack so often reiterated by MACV. The memo quoted a captive taken at Tet, as reported by Ellsworth Bunker at the end of February. According to the prisoner, the initial phase was Tet itself. Then,

if Phase I failed, Viet Cong troops during Phase 2 would besiege the cities and, at the same time, lure U.S. troops into the Khe Sanh area. Phase 3, which was expected to coincide with the establishment of a coalition government, would involve a decisive battle in the Kontum-Pleiku or Saigon area. In support of this new strategy, the North Vietnamese/Viet Cong planned to increase activities in southern Laos to permit infiltration into South Vietnam of most regular North Vietnamese Army units. The latter would try to avoid pitched battles with U.S. troops and, instead . . . confine them to their bases.

North Vietnamese withdrawals from Khe Sanh fitted far more closely with this construction of Hanoi's intentions than with the MACV view.

A report out of Saigon on March 9 indicated that NVA troop strength around the combat base had fallen to just 6,000 to 8,000. This was apparently accepted by the White House Situation Room but immediately questioned at a higher level. Art McCafferty checked and found that intelligence still believed about 14,000 NVA to be in the Khe Sanh area. All agreed that most of one regiment had moved to Hue and that the North Vietnamese no longer had the capability to reinforce with the 320th Division because they had moved it east and north to the DMZ. A more extensive CIA intelligence memorandum on March 13 gave "perhaps as many as 20,000" for North Vietnamese strength, rating the 304th Division at full strength (10,000) and the 325-C at "at least 6,000."

Departure of a portion of the North Vietnamese siege force from the Khe Sanh area received intelligence confirmation only on March 15. In the meantime Westmoreland reported the NVA no longer repairing its trench system. At III MAF General Cushman advised Saigon of his belief the North Vietnamese attack had been blunted and declared his desire to seize the initiative. He told Marine colleagues that he wished to avoid any appearance the siege had had to be broken by outside forces. Hanoi put on the best face it could, issuing a statement through the ostensibly southern Liberation Press Agency, that at Khe Sanh since January 21 it had "put out of action" 4,120 troops, including 2,580 "Yankees," capturing "many" Americans and "puppet soldiers," and destroying or damaging 218 aircraft. But the siege had not ended. There would be one final try against Khe Sanh. Still, it would be a curious finale for the most important battle of the war.

The story of the final attack actually begins at Tet. A North Vietnamese prisoner taken during that offensive told his captors that the signal for timing the offensive had actually been given right over Radio Hanoi. It had been an open code, a certain number of beeps during a regular broadcast that would be meaningless except to someone listening for it who also knew what it meant. In that case the signal meant that units should attack the following night, at the hour corresponding to the number of beeps broadcast. Intelligence took note of the report and put a radio watch on both Liberation Radio and Radio Hanoi, and then Saigon went about its business.

Scuttlebutt regarding a North Vietnamese pullback reached the ears of Marines at Khe Sanh, but little slackening of the battle was actually perceptible. Every day brought shelling, harassment of the airstrip, minor incidents of various kinds. Inevitably there arose a certain ennui, but not the degree of demoralization Hanoi hoped to suggest when it quoted an Associated Press report filed on March 17. According to the North Vietnamese newspaper, ARVN Captain Pho of the 37th Rangers had complained: "If my men hold on to Khe Sanh much longer, they will lose morale and give way to despair."

Perhaps reports like this encouraged the NVA command to try one more gambit. The notebook of Trinh Khao Lieu, of a unit identified elsewhere as the 9th Regiment, 304th Division, records that his battalion received orders on March 18 to move into positions within two hundred meters of a target that MACV analysts concluded was Khe Sanh. Then Lieu's unit got orders to prepare an attack for the night of March 22–23. During those preparations Lieu's unit suffered from the attentions of Khe Sanh's artillery.

On March 21 Captain Pipes, to see what had happened in the North Vietnamese trenches in front of Gray Sector, sent out a patrol of Bravo Company. Unlike the ghost patrol, this detachment received support from the instant of its sally — 1,300 rounds from Khe Sanh's artillery. The NVA responded with 82mm mortar fire, wounding nine Marines, only three of them enough to be evacuated; but no actual ground contact materialized. On March 22 a forward air controller sent in several flights of fighter-bombers against targets within four hundred meters of the perimeter. Again no North Vietnamese could be seen, and absolutely no ground fire opposed the strikes.

Despite these contrary indications, there were NVA troops out there. Suddenly, on March 22, Marines received word to expect an artillery barrage and a possible ground assault that night. The combat base once again went to condition red.

Late the previous night Radio Hanoi had broadcast in English a report on Khe Sanh full of the usual false hyperbole, including the exhortative assertion that "holding firm the initiative, the armed forces and people in northern Quang Tri have launched an all-out offensive on the Highway 9 battlefront." North Vietnamese practice was often to broadcast identical reports on Radio Hanoi and Liberation Radio, frequently in Vietnamese as well, in addition to domestic reports that would not be repeated in foreign languages. There would typically be multiple broadcasts of a given item. It may thus have been this very report that was being broadcast on Liberation Radio at 1:22 P.M. on March 22 when three beeps occurred during the transmission.

Sure enough, beginning about 6:30 P.M. came a heavy bombardment with a high proportion (about a third) of shells from the NVA
big guns at Co Roc. The shells fell at a rate of about a hundred an
hour, with 642 before midnight and 534 more between then and 6:00
A.M. It was the heaviest shelling of the month and a complete transformation from the immediately preceding days (the combat base had
not been shelled at all on March 19 or 20). Effects included damage
to two Marine guns, one gun destroyed, fires in four berms of one of
the ammunition dumps, and the destruction, for the second time in a
month, of the command post of Charlie Company of 1/26. Five men
died and four were injured in the collapse of the command post
bunker. Overall thirty-nine Marines were wounded or injured, of
whom seventeen required evacuation. The combat base replied to the
North Vietnamese fire, going round for round, shooting 2,042 shells.

Meanwhile the sensor system lit up in Indian country. Readings,
measured by the number of activations, were the highest they had ever
been and ran 200 percent higher than the March average.

It happened that four ARC LIGHT strikes, totaling twenty-four
B-52s, were in the air at the moment the Americans saw these suspicious indications of an attack. Meanwhile the 7th Air Force had created a mechanism for rapid diversion of ARC LIGHT strikes as a
result of orders General Westmoreland had given at a March 2 staff
conference. These four strikes were now diverted on an emergency
basis to Khe Sanh targets, the closest just 1,100 meters from friendly
positions.

For good measure some Marine ground units opened small arms
fire to their front at 3:00 A.M., the time suggested by the purported
signal on Liberation Radio.

General Creighton Abrams told the story to Earle Wheeler later,
noting, "of course, we will probably never know if we did block the
attack, but [there] is some evidence that we did so."

One bit of evidence is the notebook of 304th Division men Vu Xuan
Mau and Le Viet Yeu. "At Khe Sanh on 23 March," reads its final
entry. "A day full of bitter hardships and bloodshed."

13

The Winged Horse

ON JANUARY 25, the day after Westmoreland told Ambassador Bunker he was preparing plans for an amphibious feint attack north of the DMZ, other orders went to Major General John J. Tolson, commander of the 1st Cavalry Division (Airmobile). Division staff were to begin preparation of a contingency plan to relieve or reinforce Khe Sanh. Since his division was already being redeployed to I Corps, and since the Cav featured mobility and firepower combined, selection of Tolson's troops for a Khe Sanh relief expedition seemed logical and straightforward.

The reopening of Route 9 became a theme in Westmoreland's dialogue with Washington regarding reinforcement of MACV in the wake of Tet. A number of the relevant cables have been cited in their proper contexts at various points in this narrative. By mid-February, at the latest, a thrust to reopen Route 9 had become a firm element in MACV strategy, so much so that Maxwell Taylor found it appropriate to question whether the single brigade Westmoreland associated with Route 9 in his cables on reinforcements was really a sufficient force.

In the meantime General Tolson continued his planning and had gone far enough by March 2 to present a briefing at Da Nang for Generals Abrams and Cushman and for III MAF senior staff. Several competing concepts existed, and the whole question of future plans was ventilated at Phu Bai on March 10, on the occasion of Westmoreland's official activation of his MACV forward headquarters. Staff presented three offensive options: to clear the coastal plain from Dong Ha north to the DMZ; to attempt the destruction of the NVA in the A Shau valley; and to attack and reopen Route 9.

Cushman argued it was necessary to conduct the Khe Sanh campaign as a matter of priority, that now, with the combat power in I Corps to seek a decisive battle, it was no time to divert to the DMZ. That could follow Khe Sanh, not precede it. Also, Cushman had little taste for major operations into the A Shau. General Westmoreland spoke up at that point, essentially agreeing with Cushman. While the adversary should be kept under continuous pressure in the lowlands, and the valley mouth of the A Shau blocked, he wanted to get onto the Khe Sanh plateau and open up Route 9. Westmoreland wished it done in April or early May and thought it ought to take priority over the Con Thien–Dong Ha sector. Engineering preparations for the Route 9 operation could begin immediately, along with the lowland and A Shau mouth activities, and SOG or DELTA Force operations could saturate the A Shau to compile a target list for air suppression.

In an executive session immediately following the afternoon meeting, attended by Abrams, Cushman, Provisional Corps commander designate Lieutenant General William R. Rosson, and lesser generals such as Chaisson, Pearson, Flanagan, and Hoffman, Westmoreland looked even further ahead. He wanted a contingency plan for brigade-size cross-border operations into Laos in conjunction with the Route 9 clearance, and he wanted a force posture study to identify the dispositions necessary to maintain northern I Corps in the period beginning in September. This posture study specifically was to include retention of the Khe Sanh position, and Westmoreland also wanted it to provide for greater ARVN participation in the Khe Sanh area.

Other points Westmoreland made during the staff meeting or executive session illuminated several aspects of the Khe Sanh problem. He pointed out that the entrenched camp could expect at least ten inches of rain during June and asked that serious thought be given to drainage. In conjunction with the Route 9 clearing operation, soon to receive the code name PEGASUS, after the winged horse of Greek mythology, Westmoreland asked why an alternate road could not be constructed up the Ba Long valley to intersect with Route 9 in the vicinity of Ca Lu. The top engineer of Provisional Corps Vietnam replied that such a project "would be difficult to conclude successfully." When Abrams suggested that the 1st Cavalry Division should be prepared if necessary to commit a brigade directly to the Khe Sanh fighting, Westmoreland endorsed the idea and finally set the target date for PEGASUS at April 1.

Thus, as of March 10, MACV explicitly intended to be prepared for a coup de main thrust into Laos in conjunction with the relief of Khe Sanh, and he wanted to continue the occupation of Khe Sanh into the fall of 1968 and later. This sheds light on the depth of William Westmoreland's commitment; he was not, as has been argued, simply avoiding some NVA psychological victory by fighting at Khe Sanh. This also shows the transformation that would occur in MACV strategy over the ensuing weeks, for Khe Sanh, as shall soon be seen, would not be held very long at all.

General Tolson began detailed planning for PEGASUS on March 11. The air cav commander reports he was given complete freedom, a mission plus the forces to carry it out. These included his own division, the 1st Marine Regiment with two battalions, and the ARVN 3rd Airborne Task Force. Tolson would also have operational control over the 26th Marines at Khe Sanh and support from Army artillery in the lowlands. In all, there would be more than thirty thousand troops under his command, including ten thousand Marines and nineteen thousand Army soldiers, with 300 helicopters and 148 heliborne artillery pieces. It was going to be the biggest III MAF offensive of the war. The myriad planning tasks proceeded under the supervision of Tolson's chief of staff, Colonel George W. Putnam.

Five days into the planning cycle, General Westmoreland reported to Washington on offensive plans for I Corps for the coming period. Terming his effort a review of Cushman's plans, Westmoreland recounted the most salient points of the Phu Bai staff discussions. On March 17 he did a circuit of I Corps locations, including stops at Phu Bai, near Hue, at Camp Evans, and at Dong Ha. Tolson briefed him on PEGASUS at 1st Cavalry headquarters. The most difficult problem was creation of a large operating base from which the division could air assault into its initial objectives. A site had been selected near Ca Lu, however, and engineers were already preparing a strip for helicopters and short takeoff and landing aircraft. With air cav swagger the place would be called "Landing Zone Stud." Having heard what Tolson had done to prepare the offensive, Westmoreland went on to 3rd Marine Division headquarters where Rathvon Tompkins briefed him on the terrain and North Vietnamese dispositions. Marines suspected the NVA might be tunneling underneath Hills 861 and 558. The only other sour note was the belief expressed that the ARVN 37th Rangers had had too many self-inflicted wounds and ought to be rotated out of Khe Sanh a company at a time. (Observers at Charlie Med recall no special incidence of self-inflicted wounds among the

Rangers. Instead, their worst problem seemed to be that ARVN sent them no replacements so the battalion kept getting smaller and having to retract its sector of the combat base defenses.)

Toward the end of March, with facilities at LZ Stud complete by the 26th, Westmoreland refocused on the impending offensive. He returned to Da Nang on March 28 for a final conference with Cushman and Rosson. He issued new instructions on DYE MARKER fortifications and reviewed PEGASUS. Westmoreland discovered that Rosson, in view of the fading NVA threat to Khe Sanh, was now recommending that PEGASUS be of shorter duration, just two weeks, so the Cav could be sent into the A Shau. Though Westmoreland did not rule out a Cav swing past Hue into the A Shau, he believed it "imperative" that "with the extensive resources which have and will be committed to Khe Sanh . . . PEGASUS forces exact maximum destruction of enemy personnel and facilities." Westmoreland decided the duration should be determined by the evolving tactical situation, though he thought more than two weeks might be needed. PEGASUS would have support from ten ARC LIGHT strikes per day commencing four days before the operation.

There was more talk of operations in Laos. At Da Nang the talk focused on "hot pursuit" that might flow from PEGASUS. General Rosson discussed the specific plans for brigade-size operations drawn up after Westmoreland's instructions at Phu Bai. Westmoreland commented that the plans were proper but now asked that objectives be limited to Co Roc, Route 9, and the small Vietnamese salient into Laos, essentially the area of Lao Bao. Pursuit would have to be cleared with both Ambassador Sullivan in Laos and with Washington, and Westmoreland estimated this might take as much as two weeks. In Saigon two days later Westmoreland would be briefed on plans for operation EL PASO CITY, his dreamed-of major advance into the Laotian panhandle. Westmoreland provided new instructions to restudy EL PASO and reduce its troop (and hence supply) requirements. He still hoped to carry it out. For his historical notes Westmoreland commented: "The plan is a feasible one and with authority could be carried out to the great benefit of the war effort." Still lacking Lyndon Johnson's approval, Westmoreland would be going to Washington soon to be one of the Joint Chiefs. He would be able to campaign actively for the approval he coveted.

As the countdown to PEGASUS began, Landing Zone Stud bristled with armament and bustled with activity. Assistant division commander Brigadier General Oscar E. Davis supervised preparation of facilities by Navy Seabees, the Marines' 11th Engineer Battalion, and the Army 8th Engineers. In only eleven days the engineers leveled and graded a 450-meter airstrip complete with parking ramp. They also improved Route 9 between the Rockpile and LZ Stud to permit stockpiling of supplies, built a logistics complex, ammunition storage bunkers, a communications center, and vehicle and aircraft refueling facilities. The Marine engineers, barely rested after finishing their share of this work, redeployed to carry out the mission of refurbishing Route 9 behind the advancing assault troops.

Combat reconnaissance became the province of Lieutenant Colonel Richard W. Diller's 1st Squadron, 9th Cavalry, known as the "Headhunters." This unit operated three troops of helicopters, each having but a single platoon of infantry for such emergencies as covering extractions and securing downed ships. Then there was Delta Troop, composed of three recon platoons, each containing scout, mortar, infantry, and antitank squads. During the six days before the attack the Headhunters ranged up and down Route 9 marking important targets and hitting urgent ones immediately. Diller coordinated his scouting with artillery fire, air strikes, and ARC LIGHT flights.

The day before PEGASUS General Tolson moved to the Cav's forward headquarters established at LZ Stud. The attack was on. That day in the lowlands northeast of Con Thien, the 3rd Marine Division began a regiment-size offensive toward the DMZ, an operation intended as a diversion to keep the North Vietnamese from appreciating what was coming on Route 9. The diversion featured an armored battalion, paratroop elements, ARC LIGHT support, heavy artillery, and all the other trappings of big U.S. operations.

Generals Westmoreland and Cushman had their final pre-PEGASUS exchanges on March 30 and 31, centered on the media. Westmoreland learned on the 30th that reporters returning from I Corps knew of the impending offensive. He worried that the adversary might learn, either through the grapevine of the Caravelle Hotel bar in Saigon or elsewhere. Westmoreland wanted to play PEGASUS in as low a key as possible and have the results speak for themselves.

Cushman pointed out in a message to General Rosson which he forwarded to Westmoreland that the knowledge of PEGASUS had in fact been very closely held. The press was not even told they needed to move from Da Nang's press center to the operating area until one day before the operation and then they were being told only that "it was in their interest" to go, without any other information. The fact of PEGASUS would be disclosed only when reporters were in the field and dependent on military beneficence. Yet at least eight reporters left Da Nang on March 28 and 29 for the 101st Airborne and 1st Cavalry Divisions and "a number of them returned . . . with questions indicating they knew the location, date, and general size of the operation." The knowledge was too detailed and precise to have been speculation. Clearly the reporters had looked up friends in the field and had been able to put it all together themselves. An investigation followed as the brass tried to figure out how PEGASUS had leaked.

In actuality there was no intention and little possibility of keeping secret anything so big. The plans for PEGASUS, "our most significant forthcoming operation" had always included "taking advantage of the inherent elements of newsworthiness in an appropriate manner," as General Cushman himself noted. That reporters had found out sooner than intended was merely one more round in the public relations game MACV had long been playing with the press, which had led reporters to develop contacts of their own in the first place. General Tolson, the operational commander, provides testimonial that none of this mattered too much: "I must mention the element of surprise. Certainly the enemy knew we were in the area. Our own reporters let the whole world know the situation as they saw it. . . . However, the inherent capabilities of the airmobile division presented the enemy with a bewildering number of possible thrusts that he would have to counter, all the way to the Laotian border."

As Tolson put it, "The initiative was ours." Despite last-minute worries from forecasts of bad weather, PEGASUS took wing at precisely 7:00 A.M. on April 1.

No Siege Today

Two factors were in play for Marine commanders as March wore on and the high command ruminated on operation PEGASUS. The dawning realization of a diminishing North Vietnamese threat encouraged a desire to begin pushing out from the combat base. A second factor, for good or ill, was the gnawing thirst for knowledge of what had happened to the Jacques patrol. The expressed wishes of III MAF — to avoid any appearance that Khe Sanh was being saved from the outside — merely strengthened the convictions of commanders in the field.

Bill Smith, an artillery officer with 1/13 who worked up fire plans in conjunction with Mirza Baig, repeatedly heard of the need for operations, the wish for operations, the relish for operations, most aimed at discovering the truth about the Jacques patrol. He recalls:

> Regiment was talking about it all the time. It got to be almost . . . the bastard child of 1/26 and the horrible family secret that you didn't want to talk about. . . . There was the stigma of the ghost platoon or the lost platoon, leaving your dead on the battlefield, all those Marine Corps myths that you just didn't dare . . . everything was there. And everything got blown way out of proportion.

When Lieutenant Colonel Frederick McEwan, long ago a 26th Regiment staff officer, came in and replaced Jim Wilkinson, planning for a renewed foray became concrete. McEwan and battalion staff envisioned a strong force that would follow in the footsteps of the ghost patrol. Smith recalls:

> They planned methodically, and regiment was spurring it on. . . . We hadn't patrolled outside the base in so long, it was making everybody real nervous, because everybody knows that you don't [just] sit in an area like that. . . . We had no idea what was out there. . . . There was in the battalion this kind of "beef everybody up" [attitude] because it was a 1/26 vengeance raid and all that shit — going to get back its bodies and that kind of thing.
>
> There were a lot of good reasons not to do it, an awful lot of good reasons. . . . First of all, after that period of time, getting the bodies simply wasn't that important. I mean the thing had happened. It was over with. We'd left the bodies. No matter whether you get the bodies back at that point or not, you still [had] left your bodies out there. There was a lot of dispute about whether it was sound tactically to do it. If in fact they knew we were coming, the shit was going to hit the fan and you were going to suffer heavy casualties. What good was it going to do? Would it have been better to send out small reconnaissance patrols and really case the joint and find out what we could expect? We never did that. . . . To me that was a big tactical error. We should have been using the recon people or our own small unit. . . . I felt they were rushing headlong into the flame like a moth.

Smith, together with Mirza Baig, whom everyone called Harry, nonetheless went on to establish very detailed artillery fire plans. Smith and

Baig took the range of NVA 82mm mortars and plotted every useful firing position for this weapon in front of the Gray Sector plus every potential observation point. Then they selected combinations of weapons and ordnance types suited to the neutralization of each target. The mixture of support fires became intricate and Baig took to calling himself a composer; Smith then termed himself the maestro and the two mixed their fires with great aplomb. Targets were grouped by area into specific plans each of which got the name of a fruit; the entire support plan would be called "the fruit basket." When the day came Marines on the line would be able to get any area plastered by simply reciting the name of a fruit into the radio.

As befit a vengeance raid, the assault mission was given to Ken Pipes's own Bravo Company, presumably champing at the bit to get at the enemy though half its men were fresh replacements. There would be two objectives: a North Vietnamese fortified position just beyond the point where the bodies of the Jacques patrol presumably lay and an NVA trench, the two forming a line roughly from the lowest slopes of Hill 471 to the Poilane plantation road. Captain Pipes would move his company outside the Khe Sanh perimeter just before first light and then, following artillery preparation, Lieutenant John W. Dillon's 2nd Platoon would advance, two squads up and one echeloned to the rear, to capture the NVA trench. Once Dillon secured his objective he would become the rear echelon while the balance of Bravo advanced to the high ground. Pipes would then set up a defensive perimeter while a recovery team searched for the Marine bodies. Finally, Bravo would return to the combat base.

The action that followed from this plan has been described as classic in the Marine official monograph on Khe Sanh and brilliant (or at least successful) in previous accounts of the battle. Bravo Company received a meritorious unit citation from MACV. In actuality, Ken Pipes's Marines found themselves in a mean scrap with an adversary tentatively identified as the 8th Battalion, 66th Regiment, 304th Division. The battle would be successful in the sense that the North Vietnamese suffered great losses, but the price was much of Bravo Company, and in the heat of the action there was not time to recover the bodies of Don Jacques's patrol.

Lieutenant Dillon's platoon crossed its line of departure at 7:25 A.M. on March 30, encountered no initial resistance, and secured its objective without incident in just thirteen minutes. Pipes pushed off with Bravo Company at 7:34. A platoon of FOB-3 Cambodian strikers cooperated by holding nearby high ground. Bravo's maneuver impressed Ted Golab, the Marine forward observer attached to FOB-3 at its request: "Everything looked like it should be in the book. They all had fixed bayonets; they got flak jackets on; they got helmets on. They looked good. They had all their formations down pat. And you could see the NVA walking in their trenches, just nonchalantly. One guy had a cup in his hand. Then it looked like [Hill] 471 was beginning to wake up. And I called artillery on 471."

It was not long before Golab noticed a line of trees in the distance filled with smoke, puffs of smoke like weapons firing. That turned out to be the NVA mortar emplacements. Before fire could be brought down on the target, Bravo Company had been pinned down, starting with its 1st Platoon. Direct hits decimated the company command group, with Pipes, his artillery observer and radio men all killed or wounded. Pipes remembered the mortar shells flew so thick he could actually *see* them in the air.

That began a four-hour firefight, in which Marine artillery fired fiercely. Between preparation and the fruit bowl fires, the guns shot 2,608 rounds, and American mortars added another thousand shells. By 11:30 A.M. Ken Pipes, still directing his company despite wounds, had his men back inside the combat base. The North Vietnamese battalion that Bravo had faced seemed devastated — its radio had reported a *battalion* of Marines, its commander had appealed for reinforcements and been refused, and the unit's transmissions had subsequently ceased. But Bravo Company did not come out a whole lot better off: the Marines' official report claimed 115 NVA dead against nine Americans killed, 42 seriously wounded, 29 wounded but not evacuated, and three Marines missing in action. The official Marine monograph obscures these losses by referring only to the nine men killed. Pipes wrote later that Bravo had suffered approximately *a hundred* wounded. As for the recovery phase of the mission, only *two* bodies of members of the ghost patrol had been found before Pipes got orders to pull back.

Ted Golab and his redheaded radio man from Texas, nicknamed "Roach," discovered when attached to FOB-3 that there were even greater differences between MACVSOG and the Marines than they had ever anticipated. Marines in general were slightly leery of the spooks and that feeling prevailed at Khe Sanh. At the high point of discomfort in February, Marines had refused artillery support for FOB patrols, FOB had sealed itself off from the combat base, and Khe Sanh had reciprocated by having Marine tanks train their guns on the FOB compound in the expectation that the indigenous strikers would desert and leave a hole in the defenses. None of that came to pass and Golab became the beneficiary of the improved relations. He thought the FOB compound one of the "Seven Wonders of the Nam," a whole different world from Khe Sanh. Where the Marines endured muddy, collapsing bunkers, FOB had a vast complex of secure concrete facilities. Where the Marines existed on C-rations and a single canteen (or less) of water a day, the spooks had refrigerators from which they fed on steak and ice cream.

Golab's visit the night before the Bravo Company sortie had been all too brief. It was not certain he would ever get another chance. The nature of SOG's work was such that it was always on the move, not often needing or wanting artillery observers. The spooks never stopped their patrols, unlike the Marines, and at the height of the NVA threat had had forty teams in the field in northern Quang Tri and adjoining parts of Laos. When the Marines of CAC Oscar had fought for and been driven from Khe Sanh village, SOG had had a team in there *after* them, and of course they had been crucial in efforts to recover survivors from Lang Vei.

As the day for PEGASUS approached, SOG's efforts were again critical. In mid-March FOB-3 numbered 588 men including 131 Americans, of whom 20 officers and 105 enlisted men were from the Army. On April 1, the initial date of PEGASUS, Major David Smith commanded the unit.

In late March or early April SOG team Michigan became the first patrol to reenter Khe Sanh village. Larry Payne was a member of the team. "You could tell where there was foundations and stuff and that was about it," Payne recalls. "Most of the walls were gone. And there were CBUs [cluster bomb units]! It looked like somebody had come in there with rye grass and sowed it. . . . You couldn't hardly step without hitting one of them!"

Not long after, Michigan, still operating from FOB-3, was inserted atop Co Roc in Laos. Payne remembers:

I was the first recon team on top of it. . . . There was lots of tall elephant grass. They put us up there to find the caves. We never did find them. We wasn't in there long enough! The enemy was still there. When they put us in they said, "We're going to try something new." Now they usually put us in about seven or eight o'clock in the morning, and you had all day to get covered up and so on and so forth before night hit. So they said, ". . . we're going to put you in [at] four o'clock, 5:30 in the evening." And we said, "Oh?" So they put us in. We moved for about an hour and a half. There was nothing around us but elephant grass about five foot tall. So we got out into a good clump of elephant grass and the five of us (three "yards" [montagnards] and two Americans) just sat down, back to back, sat down there for the night.

All of a sudden a montagnard woke me up and said, "Beaucoup VC!" and I said, "Where?" And he said, "All around!"

We stood up and looked, looked over the grass. We counted in excess of sixty flashlights walking around the top of Co Roc looking for us. We was about fifty to a hundred meters back from the cliff. And we were going to head down and then see what we could find as far as the tunnels, but — the next morning, I told them what we had around us, and they finally brought in some gunships and stuff, backed [the NVA] off, and picked us up. I was only in there eighteen hours.

Whatever else may be said about the spooks, they definitely tried some things no one else did, and they got their men out too!

Without MACVSOG, the battle of annihilation the Americans fought in the highlands would have happened under much less favorable conditions, and PEGASUS too would have been affected. Without MACVSOG the high command might have been blinded, or at least afflicted with much dimmer vision, during the most important battle of the war. The difference would have been palpable for everyone except, perhaps, the South Vietnamese ARVN, whose role in PEGASUS would be designed to be cosmetic.

Along Route 9

In actuality the long-anticipated flight of PEGASUS, the winged horse, began with an old-fashioned ground advance conducted in the traditional manner by the 1st Marine Regiment under Colonel Stanley S. Hughes. This happened because April 1 dawned overcast and foggy at LZ Stud and General Tolson was determined he would not begin airmobile operations until the weather was favorable. Thus at 7:00 A.M. Marines opened the big offensive across Route 9 by advancing from Ca Lu. Two battalions formed the main strength of the road-bound force: 2nd Battalion, 1st Marines and 2nd Battalion, 3rd Marines. The 1st Regiment actually controlled a third unit, the 1st Battalion, 1st Marines, but this would be committed later.

One of the Marine battalions advanced to the north of Route 9, the other immediately to the south of it. On the road itself, thus protected on both flanks, were the Marine 11th Engineers, who were to repair Route 9 while advancing along it. "One thing that amazed me," recalled Lieutenant Richard J. Wheeler of the engineers, "is how beautiful this country is out here, and it's too bad it's marred by all this fighting right now." The heavy construction equipment of Wheeler's 1st Platoon, A Company, 11th Engineers, at least temporarily, deformed the land even more.

Toward midday the sun finally burned off the fog and the 1st Cavalry Division swung into action. Good weather was to be a relative thing during PEGASUS — Tolson noted ruefully that "good weather" would be considered any condition in which the ceiling was at least 500 feet and visibility more than a mile and a half. On most days these minimal flying conditions did not obtain until 1:00 P.M. or even later. But few of the PEGASUS forces would be subjected to emergency conditions that might have tempted tactical commanders to challenge the weather.

For the initial air assault General Tolson had planned to use his 3rd Brigade under Colonel Hubert S. ("Bill") Campbell. The brigade had been operating west of Hue until relieved by the 2nd Brigade of the 101st Airborne Division. Campbell lifted his troops into LZ Stud only the day before the offensive, March 31. Campbell had the 1st Battalion, 7th Cavalry (Lieutenant Colonel Joseph E. Wasiak), the 2nd Battalion, 7th Cavalry (Lieutenant Colonel Roscoe Robinson, Jr.), and the 5th Battalion, 7th Cavalry (Lieutenant Colonel James B. Vaught).

Wasiak's battalion opened the airmobile phase of PEGASUS with an air assault into LZ Mike on Hill 248, a position surrounded on three sides by the Quang Tri river and its tributaries. After the 1st Battalion, 7th Cavalry had secured the landing zone, the 2nd Battalion helilifted into the same LZ. (On Maps 14 and 15 accompanying this section an inverted helicopter is used to denote troops taking off from an LZ for an air assault, a level helicopter symbol for troops landing at an LZ, and a troop unit symbol for troops already on the ground at the indicated location.) To the north of Route 9 in a symmetrical position on the slope of Dong Chio mountain, Colonel

Vaught's 5th Battalion, 7th Cavalry assaulted into LZ Cates. Batteries of 105mm howitzers of the 1st Battalion, 21st Artillery were lifted into both landing zones while Colonel Campbell set up brigade head-quarters at LZ Cates.

Despite the late start, things went so well the first day that before it ended General Tolson decided to accelerate his operation, commit-ting Colonel Joseph C. McDonough's 2nd Brigade a day earlier than planned.

On April 2 Colonel Hughes made a Marine air assault with two companies into LZ Robin north of Route 9, protecting the flank of forces operating along the road. Meanwhile Campbell catapulted the 2nd Battalion, 7th Cavalry into a new LZ, Thor, south of but near the old Bridge Site Marine garrison. Robinson's battalion radiated around LZ Thor, but as had been the case throughout the area, encountered little NVA resistance. Poor weather restricted tactical air support to just twenty-three sorties, delivering forty-seven tons of ordnance, but there were seven ARC LIGHT strikes involving forty-two B-52s.

As the Cav flitted about in their Hueys, the Marines hacked their way forward along Route 9. "The terrain on PEGASUS was very mountainous and heavily wooded," recalled Wayne T. Haaland, a platoon commander with Hotel Company of the 2nd Battalion, 1st Marines. "It was jungle — the worst kind you can find. . . . After operating a few days in the area [we found] that it was almost im-possible to walk from objective to objective. The terrain was so rough and the growth, the underbrush, was so thick that we had to use helicopter[s]." In any helicopter match, of course, the Cav, a forma-tion that had been designed to use and depend on helicopters and had been lavishly provided with them in comparison to the Marines, would have automatic advantages.

Though few North Vietnamese opposed the advance, the signs of their presence were numerous and had to be treated carefully. The 1st Battalion, 1st Marines captured many documents pertaining to the NVA 29th Regiment and especially the 8th Battalion of that unit. The Cav found much material from the NVA 66th Regiment. Everyone encountered empty fighting positions near hilltops, bunkers, some-times elaborate camp facilities, and many kinds of supplies and equip-ment. During the course of PEGASUS (which the South Vietnamese called LAM SON 207-A) the operating forces recovered 13,890 tons of NVA materiel. Curiously, all but 264 tons of this amount repre-

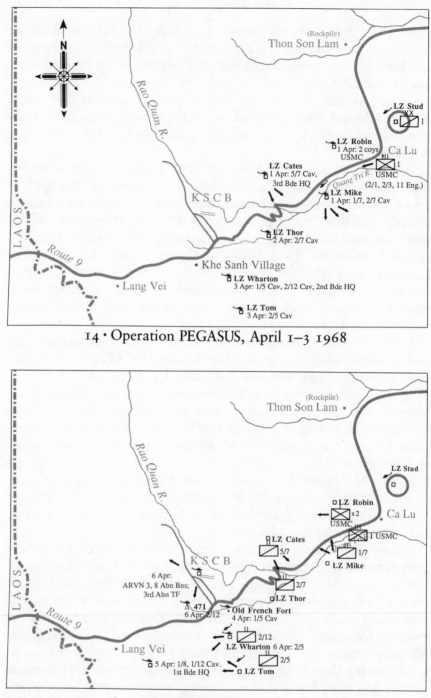

14 · Operation PEGASUS, April 1–3 1968

15 · Operation PEGASUS, April 4–6, 1968

sented food. A MACV analysis speculates that the malnourished NVA had been denied access to their caches by U.S. firepower, and the Marine monograph that the decimated NVA units had been unable to carry off the cached supplies. Equally likely was that the finds represented the accumulation of many months (and even years) of caching in an area never previously subjected to large-scale search and destroy operations. If the claims about the amount of supplies uncovered are accurate, this raises further questions as to how the defense of Khe Sanh was supposed to prevent North Vietnamese access past the Laotian border.

In any case PEGASUS forged ahead. On April 3 (D + 2) General Tolson committed his 2nd Brigade, opening up two new landing zones. Colonel McDonough with his command group plus 1st Battalion, 5th Cavalry (Lieutenant Colonel Robert L. Runkle) and 2nd Battalion, 12th Cavalry (Lieutenant Colonel Richard W. Sweet) air assaulted into LZ Wharton, south of the French Fort. North Vietnamese gunners shelled the LZ but otherwise the movement was largely unopposed. About two and a half kilometers to the southeast, Lieutenant Colonel Arthur J. Leary's 2nd Battalion, 5th Cavalry opened up LZ Tom. Again, except for shelling, there was little opposition. Troop A of the Headhunters, the 1st Squadron, 9th Cavalry, spotted a battalion-size force of NVA about three kilometers southwest of Khe Sanh village and engaged them with gunships.

The most significant action that day involved established LZs. Robinson's 2nd Battalion, 7th Cavalry pushing out from LZ Thor encountered a North Vietnamese company in blocking positions south of Route 9 near the hamlet of Lang Khoai 2. By evening the newly established LZs were being supported by all three batteries of the 1st Battalion, 77th Artillery, while ten heavier pieces — six 155mm and four 8-inch howitzers — were brought into the area of operations. That made a total of 102 guns supporting PEGASUS, not counting the 16 Army 175mms at Cam Lo and the Rockpile. That day III MAF artillery fired 796 missions for a total of 10,814 rounds. The NVA response was feeble: approximately twenty 130mm shells fell on LZ Wharton that night.

On April 4 the North Vietnamese appeared in greater force. Colonel Robinson tried to move his 2nd Battalion, 7th Cavalry west along Route 9 but ran into opposition immediately, probably from the same NVA troops that had held him back the previous day at Lang Khoai. By midafternoon the battalion returned to LZ Cates. "The NVA here are dangerous," noted Lieutenant Joe Abodeely, of Delta Company, in his diary. "I don't like this area. I hope we all get out alive."

That day began the battle for French Fort, in which Lieutenant Colonel Robert Runkle lost his life. Runkle's 1st Battalion, 5th Cavalry air assaulted the position from LZ Wharton only to find an estimated battalion of North Vietnamese. An Army aircraft flying over the battle area suddenly crashed, killing one soldier and wounding another. The fight continued through that day and into the next, Runkle being succeeded by Lieutenant Colonel Clarence E. Jordan. After significant losses, 1st Battalion, 5th Cavalry was replaced in the assault by Lieutenant Colonel Leary's 2nd Battalion, 5th Cavalry, attacking from the northeast after another helilift. French Fort held out until April 7.

Along Route 9, on April 5 Golf Company of the 2nd Battalion, 1st Marines discovered a North Vietnamese complex capable of housing a full battalion. It included seventy-five bunkers, one a combined mess hall and kitchen, another a command post. Many had porches or thatched roofs with sun decks. There was furniture outside, running water, even a bathtub — all for bunkers capable of stopping an 81mm mortar round. Marines marveled at the lengths to which the North Vietnamese had gone to make their camp comfortable. This complex, at which Americans captured a full ton of rice, yielded fewer than a thousand mortar shells, 150 grenades, and 6,000 rounds of small arms ammunition. Such supply levels were clearly inadequate for a force of the size and sophistication of the one that created and used the complex. The evidence suggests the North Vietnamese *were* saving some of their supplies, the ones that enabled them to fight!

In conjunction with PEGASUS, leading the Marine breakout from Khe Sanh would be the 1st Battalion, 9th Marines, which moved out of the Rock Quarry to capture Hill 471. This was effectively the action of a new Khe Sanh, for much was different between the units that had defended the combat base and those same organizations when the moment came to break out. Most obvious was the difference in command control; General Tolson of the 1st Cavalry had superceded Tompkins of the 3rd Marine Division beginning April 1 and for the duration of the offensive. The 1st Battalion, 9th Marines, about to make its assault, also had a new commander, Lieutenant Colonel John J. H. ("Blacky") Cahill, in place only three days before his battalion went against Hill 471.

Given the Khe Sanh experience of the past two months, perhaps only new men could have accepted the plan for the April 4 attack. In this scheme Cahill's battalion was to move out under cover of morning fog, leave behind one rifle company (Bravo), a quarter of their strength, to guard the command post and the Rock Quarry, and make a three-kilometer approach march to an attack position at the foot of 471. There was to be *no* artillery preparation and only a short blast of fire at the instant of the final assault. Marines imbued with the Khe Sanh Shuffle must have thought the plan fanciful.

The battalion started out with Delta and Charlie Companies moving abreast. Alpha and the headquarters and support companies were behind the lead elements. Everything went well at first, with nothing more than occasional sniper fire to oppose the approach march. About noon, when Cahill's men were just reaching their final assault position, the fog lifted and the NVA began to fire 122mm mortars. Cahill's command group took bad hits, seriously wounding the operations officer, Major Ted R. Henderson, and killing the air staff officer, Captain Walter C. Jones III. Cahill and his artillery staffer, Lieutenant John LeBlond, were both wounded but remained in the action.

Lead elements of Delta Company meanwhile noticed several North Vietnamese on top of 471. The plan was to leapfrog the rifle companies up the hill, with Delta to secure a rise immediately adjacent to 471 and then cover an assault by Alpha. Forward observers saw more and more disturbing signs, including twenty to thirty NVA and a fortified area. Abandoning the original intention of a lightning strike, from 12:30 to 2:00 P.M. the Marines settled down while substantial amounts of air and artillery were poured onto 471's slopes.

Unfortunately the fire seemed far less effective than hoped. As Lieutenant Francis B. Lovely moved up the slope with his 1st Platoon of Alpha, they were hit by NVA mortars. Fire came close enough to Lovely and his right-hand flanker that they had to be sent to the rear for a time with concussion. As the platoon reached the crest, company commander Captain Henry D. Banks committed 1st and 3rd Platoons to the left and right of the first wave. First Lieutenant Paul H. Wallace kept his 3rd Platoon men from bunching up, standing on the slope without regard for his own safety. As he reached the crest Wallace fell with an AK-47 bullet that went completely through his neck. Though he could have gotten medical evacuation at any time, the platoon commander stayed to lead his men. Wallace received the Silver Star for his work that day.

Bill Lanier, a 1/9 battalion scout who happened to be with Alpha

Company on the assault, was crawling up the hill on all fours but found himself veering off to the right as he reached the top. With NVA fire at his heels, he dashed for a bomb crater and dove headlong into it. Only then did Lanier realize the crater was occupied — by three North Vietnamese soldiers. It turned out the NVA were mere boys, thirteen to fifteen years old, terrified of the huge six foot three Marine. They immediately surrendered! Lanier called his accompanying Kit Carson scout, put empty sandbags over the heads of the boys, and sent them to the rear. The NVA turned out to be from the 66th Regiment and told interrogators their unit had suffered heavy losses, had low morale, and had not eaten for three days.

The 3rd Platoon secured the eastern half of Hill 471 at about 3:30 P.M. The remainder was in Marine hands a half hour later. Captain Ralph H. Flagler's Charlie Company then climbed up to help defend the place. Within only about twenty minutes, an extremely rapid response, the NVA began shelling Hill 471, through the rest of the day and night raining artillery shells, rockets, and mortar rounds on the crest. American losses in the assault and subsequent shelling amounted to ten dead and fifty-six wounded and evacuated. Thirty North Vietnamese soldiers died defending their positions on the hilltop.

About 3:30 A.M. a starshell that burst over Hill 471 revealed NVA troop movements on the forward face of the hill. An hour later the 7th Battalion, 66th Regiment counterattacked. Some thought its strength no more than a company. The well-equipped North Vietnamese were brave and had good discipline but proved unable to get closer than fifteen or twenty meters from Marine lines. The NVA broke contact about 6:30 A.M., leaving 148 bodies behind. Three more NVA prisoners fell into Marine hands. The soldiers reported they had previously been sent to Hue but had been brought back in a thirty-six-hour forced march when the NVA command heard Hill 471 had been taken. This latter report is possibly apocryphal since only about twelve hours elapsed between the Marines taking Hill 471 and the NVA counterattack. North Vietnamese troops may have been recalled from Hue on more general news of PEGASUS or the report may have been entirely fabricated.

Later on April 5, Cahill's battalion endured a lapse of the much-touted "single air manager" system which had now been in operation at Khe Sanh for five days. The mistake might have annihilated the whole force on 471. Origins of the error lay in a request 26th Marines had submitted the previous day for a preplanned visual close air support attack on Hill 471 to assist their tactical plan. The request had been canceled at 2:00 A.M. on the 5th, but with the additional layers of authority in the new management system the cancellation did not have time to move up the chain of command and down to operating units. At 12:05 P.M. on the 5th a flight of aircraft under radar (not visual) control delivered twenty-four 500-pound bombs on Hill 471. Luckily for the Marines, the bombs failed to detonate and no one was hurt. Colonel Lownds was furious.

At noon the following day some of Tolson's Cav troops linked up with 1/9 on 471. Soon afterward Cahill's battalion got orders to attack farther west toward Hill 552. Captain Charlie B. Hartzell, now battalion operations officer, believed in not leaving the night to the NVA. The original plan to take 471 owed something to his ideas, and now he had free rein. Soon after receiving orders at 2:00 A.M. on April 7 the battalion moved and occupied the objective without incident. Hill 552 turned out to be something of an oasis on the battlefront: the NVA neither defended it nor counterattacked and the Marines were left undisturbed.

Having taken 552, on April 8 Cahill's battalion received orders to capture Hill 689. Once again the approach came under cover of darkness, with the assault beginning at 6:00 A.M. of April 9, Charlie Company leading. The sole untoward incident was artillery fire that seemed to be coming from behind the left flank. This turned out to have come from guns supporting the ARVN 3rd Airborne Task Force, then operating in the vicinity of Lang Vei. The South Vietnamese troops had seen figures on Hill 552 at first light and mistook them for North Vietnamese.

The worst NVA resistance occurred only *after* Hill 689 had been captured. About ten minutes later the NVA began a mortar bombardment that resulted in about twenty Marine casualties before the source could be found and silenced.

Another breakout action the Marines took involved 2nd Battalion, 26th Marines, still under Lieutenant Colonel Francis Heath. On April 5 the battalion's Golf Company (Captain Lee R. Overstreet) conducted a company-size combat patrol to the southwest of Hill 558, the first since late January. The mission was to be a reconnaissance — to check whether the NVA occupied a ridge that overlooked Hill 558 from about 1,800 meters to the west.

The battalion maneuver uncovered an NVA hornet's nest. Golf

Company stumbled into a reinforced North Vietnamese company atop its objective. A lot of things went wrong, including a two-hour delay in support fire because of a supergaggle of helicopters that refused to vacate the area. When Heath called the company back to 558 for the night, the toll stood at three killed, eleven missing, forty-nine wounded and evacuated, plus eleven wounded but not evacuated.

On Palm Sunday — April 7 — Heath tried again, this time with two companies. To Golf he added Foxtrot under Captain Charles F. Divelbiss. The men struggled forward under an extremely hot sun, through dense foliage and up steep slopes. There were a number of heat casualties before the Marines even got close to the NVA ridge line. The assault itself would be equally tough. In Foxtrot both officers leading forward platoons were shot. One platoon was reduced to fourteen Marines led by a corporal, Rudy de la Garza. Captain Overstreet with Golf was wounded twice. Golf was again repulsed, and Foxtrot had to be withdrawn with eight dead, two Marines who later died of their wounds, and fifty-one others wounded. As for Golf Company, it now had only 120 of the 210 Marines it had had a couple of days before.

Two days of aerial and artillery bombardment followed as Heath drew up a plan for an attack by his entire battalion. Not wanting to begin prematurely, he rejected the offer some helicopter pilots made of inserting a force of riflemen directly on top of the ridge. Also, Echo Company under First Lieutenant Joseph R. Meeks was sent to Hill 861 on April 9, where it became the battalion reserve for the attack on the ridge opposite. Heath, like Cahill, made a night move to put the battalion into assault positions before first light. At 6:30 A.M. they attacked with three companies on line.

The rest was anticlimax. Having fought so hard against the earlier forays, the North Vietnamese decided they had had enough and pulled out. Marines found the bodies of the missing and an American PRC-25 radio still tuned to Golf Company's frequency.

Over the succeeding days the 2nd Battalion, 26th Marines mounted additional patrols to the northwest, north, northeast, and south. On April 14 Captain Charles O. Broughton's Hotel Company reopened the road between Hill 558 and Khe Sanh combat base. Again there was no opposition. Broughton's Marines found only two Chinese-made antitank mines and a crude device built around C-4 plastic explosives.

*   *   *

South Vietnamese participation in PEGASUS had been under discussion throughout the planning of the operation. All were conscious of the desirability of giving ARVN a role, and the plan featured commitment of an ARVN force on the fourth day of operations. The unit was the 3rd Airborne Task Force consisting of 1,740 paratroopers of the 3rd, 6th, and 8th Airborne Battalions. On March 30, in a late preoperation review message to General Cushman, General Westmoreland had made plain his concerns: "It would be beneficial to the image of the Vietnamese if they were committed at the time that heavy contact begins or a link up is made so they will be obviously in the thick of the battle and an important part of it. I do not suggest that we make last-minute changes in the plan, nor commit the airborne task force under circumstances that they are not capable of coping with, but I do feel we should consider their role as more than a military one." Westmoreland clearly expected PEGASUS to yield a public relations bonus.

On April 5 Colonel Nguyen Khoa Nam's 3rd Airborne Task Force at Quang Tri received instructions to prepare a rifle company to insert at Khe Sanh and link up with the 37th Rangers. Lift of the 84th Company of 8th Battalion actually occurred the next day and the linkup came at 1:20 P.M. of April 6. While the ARVN troops landed on the airstrip, the NVA began one of their inevitable mortar barrages. Captain Wesley B. Taylor, an American adviser with the 8th Airborne, was almost killed when a shell ripped out a piece of the metal runway mat and flung it into the air and squarely onto the top of his helmet and pack.

The linkup with the Rangers still seemed an obvious publicity stunt. Though Cav units had not yet made contact with the combat base, 2nd Battalion, 12th Cavalry had already relieved the 1st Battalion, 9th Marines on Hill 471. PEGASUS forces were operating all over the area and virtually outside the gates of Khe Sanh. By contrast, no ARVN troops were engaged at all, and the airlift was happening on the fifth day, a day *later* than envisioned in the planning. The Americans tastefully delayed their own formal linkup with the combat base until April 8.

The real fighting the ARVN troops would be let into was the pursuit. Tolson committed the 3rd Airborne Task Force on April 7, when Colonel Nam's lead battalion air assaulted into LZ Snake, about two kilometers southeast of the combat base. The other two battalions followed, including 84th Company with Captain Taylor. They were to block escape routes toward the Laotian border. Soon after their arrival came an NVA barrage in which eighteen ARVN soldiers were wounded.

Tough as they presumably were, the South Vietnamese paratroopers were being stiffened by Delta Troop of 1st Battalion, 9th Cavalry. Recoilless rifle teams of this Headhunter unit were parceled out among the ARVN airborne battalions. Sergeant Richard MacLeod led one of these teams atop Hill 400, where they got the fright of their lives: "Shortly after dark, we could see headlights to the west of us heading our way. We assumed they were tanks. . . . I was nervous. I knew our gunners were good, but what were the odds if the NVA guns had a longer range? And how many tanks were there? . . . Since the headlights kept coming but didn't seem to be getting any closer, we decided that what we saw was probably a supply column inside Laos. We all breathed a sigh of relief."

Another ARVN battalion faced a threat that became concrete. North Vietnamese troops assaulted their position at 3:50 A.M. of April 8. The attack was quickly defeated and the NVA broke contact within twenty minutes, leaving behind seventy-four of their dead and thirty-nine individual weapons. South Vietnamese casualties included eleven killed and thirty wounded.

Down on Route 9 things were approaching a climax with Roscoe Robinson's 2nd Battalion, 7th Cavalry. A twenty-six-year-old officer with the battalion, Joseph DeFrancisco, had been mightily impressed when his unit staged through LZ Stud and he saw the rows and rows of helicopters. "To me, being a young guy, moderately gung ho," he recalled, "it was very inspirational." Now, on April 6, DeFrancisco sat with Robinson in the command helicopter while the battalion ran into a pitched battle below them, seven kilometers east of Khe Sanh village. An estimated company of North Vietnamese held a prepared position while Robinson maneuvered his battalion in a firefight that went on most of the day.

Robinson's chopper took hits serious enough that he returned to the LZ to get another and help some of the men who required medical evacuation. With DeFrancisco along to call artillery missions, Robinson went back to pick up the wounded. Their ship attracted fire as it landed, and once they got the wounded to a secure LZ, Robinson had to take over yet a third helicopter. The command group returned to the scene for the last hours of the battle. The NVA finally broke and ran, leaving behind ten heavy weapons, 121 other weapons, and eighty-three bodies, while the 2nd Battalion also took a prisoner.

Moving even closer to the combat base the next day, some of the battalion elements air assaulted into a location just five hundred meters from the Marines, Lieutenant Joe Abodeely's 2nd Platoon of Delta Company, which had been last in the order of march but had been leapfrogged past the lead company when that unit encountered resistance. The remainder of the company followed, and then the battalion closed up and camped that night right outside the combat base. They uncovered more NVA equipment and an old French bugle for which they made a tassel. Abodeely had played trumpet for his high school band so the company commander asked if he knew how to play "Charge" on a bugle. The next morning Abodeely took up the tune as the 2nd Platoon led the 2nd Battalion, 7th Cavalry's final march into Khe Sanh.

Juan Fordoni, a private first class from San Juan, became the first trooper to reach the Marines when he shook hands over the wire with a lance corporal. Specialist-4 Joe La Russo was the first Cav trooper through the gates. Abodeely tried to say something dramatic as he led the platoon up to a Marine captain, but the officer simply told him where to deploy his men. Unthinking grunts in the field exacerbated already simmering interservice jealousies — Army and Marine veterans still argue over whether Marines broke Khe Sanh's siege or were relieved by PEGASUS. "In reality," notes former Marine company commander Dick Camp, "the NVA broke the siege by leaving."

Indeed, pursuit was the name of Tolson's game at this stage of the operation. Campbell lifted his 3rd Brigade headquarters into the combat base the day the Cav arrived to control units already west of Khe Sanh. The 1st Brigade of the Cav under Colonel John E. Stannard had already opened LZ Snapper southeast of Lang Vei, moving in on April 6 with the 1st Battalion, 8th Cavalry (Lieutenant Colonel Christian F. Dubia). Snapper was reinforced with the 1st Battalion of the 12th Cavalry, under Lieutenant Colonel Robert C. Kerner, which put the cap on PEGASUS by recapturing Lang Vei CIDG camp against light resistance on April 12.

By that time the ground had already begun to shift under PEGASUS and Khe Sanh. Even before the relief expedition began, Lieutenant General William Rosson, Provisional Corps Vietnam commander, who now exercised tactical control over the two northern provinces, had advised that PEGASUS be curtailed in favor of a 1st Cavalry offensive into the A Shau valley. Westmoreland resisted the suggestion at the time, preferring to see how PEGASUS developed. As the North

Vietnamese melted away, however, so did MACV's objections to an A Shau campaign.

On April 10, just as a helicopter of A Troop of 1/9 made the first confirmed tank kill, calling in an air strike on a hapless PT-76, 1st Cavalry Division received orders to plan for an assault into the A Shau as quickly as possible. General Tolson states that these orders came "without warning." Limited Cav operations continued in the Khe Sanh area until April 17 and then the winged horse flew away. Left unaccomplished were more than thirty-eight additional operations Tolson had projected to extend control in the Khe Sanh region.

In the course of his operation, General Tolson's forces captured 207 heavy weapons, two antiaircraft guns, and 557 other weapons, and they captured or destroyed seventeen vehicles, from trucks to PT-76 tanks. There were 1,304 NVA in the body count plus another 21 captured. Tolson's forces had had support from 1,625 tactical air sorties and 45 ARC LIGHT strikes. Allied losses were far from insignificant: 51 Marines were killed in action and 459 wounded; 33 ARVN troops were killed and 187 wounded. There are discrepancies in the tally of 1st Cavalry Division losses, which have been reported as 41 or 59 killed in action, 207 or 251 wounded, and five missing, for a total of up to 1,045 allied casualties. Against a withdrawing adversary who turned to skirmish only a few times, PEGASUS losses show that the North Vietnamese fought quite hard when they chose to do so.

Perhaps the most heroic role in all of this fighting was that of Lieutenant Colonel Victor A. Perry's 11th Engineer Battalion. In all of PEGASUS the object had been to enable Perry's construction crews to refinish Route 9. If the engineers did not succeed, the rest of the operation might as well not have taken place. Perry had a truly daunting task, and whereas the combat battalions could take out their frustrations on the North Vietnamese, the engineers had to endure both the enemy and the work.

Their task commenced with a warning order issued on February 16. The 11th Battalion planned to assign elements to different sections of the road, so when the execute order came on March 8 the first phase was the dispatch of A Company to open the road from the Rockpile to Ca Lu. Even in this area three culverts and a bridge had to be restored, and after that the engineers helped finish Landing Zone Stud.

The main effort began on April Fool's Day with D Company of the

11th Battalion spearheading and B Company following to widen the road, improve bypasses, clear both sides of the road, and generally upgrade things. A Company stayed at LZ Stud until April 8 when it was flown to Bridge 33 to improve its approaches. At Dong Ha, C Company fabricated steel stringers for the bridges. Meanwhile, the 3rd Platoon, 3rd Bridge Company, 7th Engineer Battalion accompanied the main force and handled the actual placement of the steel bridges. The bridge company motto was "Erections Are Our Business!"

During this effort the 470th Aviation Company of 1st Cavalry Division used its CH-54 "Flying Crane" helicopters to bring up sections of prefabricated bridge spans, such as the M4T7 bridges that went to three sites, greatly simplifying the work. Bridge 9-29 was the first placed using material transported by the Flying Cranes. The CH-54s lifted a completely assembled thirty-foot bridge weighing 16,500 pounds, as well as prefabricated loads of components for thirty-eight-foot bridges weighing 16,000 pounds. Other bridges included nine fixed steel-section bridges, a culvert overpass, and a pontoon bridge. Three of the steel-section bridges and the pontoon bridge were assembled by a platoon of the 7th Engineers Bridge Company before being helilifted forward. Four old French bridges still intact received repairs.

The last bridge went in on April 11. By dusk the next day Route 9 had become trafficable from the lowlands. Although further improvement remained to be done, in a dozen days the 11th Engineers and attached units had cleared landslides, filled numerous craters, built ten bridges, and made major repairs to three others. It was fitting that the first vehicle to make the trip from Dong Ha to Khe Sanh since the summer of 1967 should be a jeep from the 11th Engineers. Riding in it were Lieutenant Colonel Perry, the battalion operations officer Major Joseph C. Thorp, and D Company commander Captain Randy Brinkley. The company gunny, Gunnery Sergeant Lonnie Roberts of Dunbar, West Virginia, thought the countryside as desolate as the land "after the battle in a World War I movie." Someone else described the land as "like a graveyard scene in a Frankenstein movie."

There was one man whose return to Khe Sanh indeed became a horror like a scene from *Frankenstein,* and that was Felix Poilane. The coffee planter, eager to check his trees, was a passenger aboard Air Force C-130 mission 603 on the afternoon of April 13. The plane missed its first approach and came around for another landing run.

On the second approach it touched down but went out of control, sheering to the left off the runway, through GPES equipment and six waiting loads, a truck, and a forklift. Gas tanks in the right wing caught fire, which soon spread to the interior of the aircraft. A dozen passengers emerged dazed, and two crew plus three passengers were injured. Felix Poilane died. That was Khe Sanh.

"Get on Line in Classic Marine Fashion"

Virtually simultaneously with the end of PEGASUS came a change of command at the 26th Marines. With a commendation from General Cushman to put in his pocket, Colonel David Lownds packed up and left, replaced by Colonel Bruce F. Meyers. The new regiment commander was familiar with Khe Sanh as a result of monthly visits in his former capacity of operations staff officer for the 9th Marine Amphibious Brigade, of which the 26th Regiment formed the main element. He actually had orders now to close down the combat base. Meyers, a Marine who had had a major role in the creation of Force Reconnaissance, undoubtedly preferred the kind of offensive maneuvering stance that Marine and MACV brass now thought should be assumed by the forces at Khe Sanh.

Meyers would have had no argument from Tolson and his Cav troopers, but the role grated on others. The night before his relief, Colonel Lownds called Ensign Kux to his bunker to mobilize naval construction men for perimeter defense — the *entire* 1st Cavalry force that had funneled in to hold the Blue Sector of Khe Sanh had left to continue their operations, without a word to the Marines. Kux assigned six men — all he could spare — to stand perimeter watch in front of his unit's area. Worst of all, at least in Kux's view, was that he had been asked to estimate how long it would take to *completely tear up* Khe Sanh airfield and load the metal plates on trucks for convoy out. That someone was serious about the idea was underlined by the fact that Kux was also asked to inventory his own equipment to estimate requirements for airlift or road convoy.

Things were indeed changing at Khe Sanh, even before the formal end of PEGASUS. In line with the maneuver concept, General Tompkins wanted a higher commander in the area and gave verbal orders to his assistant division commander, Brigadier General Jacob E. Glick, to form a task force of all units operating at Khe Sanh. Activated on April 11 for planning purposes, Task Force Glick actually took the field four days later when the 1st Cavalry Division formally terminated PEGASUS. At that point the forces around Khe Sanh amounted to Colonel Meyers's 26th Marines and a reduced 2nd Brigade of the Cav that would be withdrawn over the following two days.

The next maneuver, which Marines came to call their "Easter Egg Hunt," would be a foray to take Hill 881 North, from which more than five thousand rockets had been fired during the course of the siege. Lieutenant Colonel John C. Studt's full 3rd Battalion, 26th Marines was detailed for the operation, carried out on April 14. The troops, in pretty bad shape after months spent virtually below ground in bunkers, assembled on Hill 881 South. Marines were being asked to hump at night over ground, the same ground Bill Dabney's India Company had not been able to win through in the daytime at the very dawn of the siege. But there was a carefully coordinated fire support plan and Colonel Meyers himself flew into Hill 881 South to observe the attack and personally coordinate the fire.

Matt Caulfield had been quite worried about the condition of the 3/26 Marines. Once the moment came, though, they proved raring to get at the North Vietnamese. One company commander whose men took off after the NVA with fixed bayonets reported that he could not hold them back. By midafternoon 881 North had been secured and Meyers went forward to officiate with Captain Dabney at a flag raising ceremony on the erstwhile enemy hill. Moderate NVA opposition had been completely trounced. Marine casualties were six killed and nineteen wounded. Some 106 NVA bodies were found while Colonel Studt estimated opposing losses at three times that many.

The next morning Task Force Glick officially began operation SCOTLAND II, under which offensive activities were to proceed in tandem with rotation out of the elements of the 26th Marines. Colonel Hughes's 1st Marines would become the major tactical formation at Khe Sanh. Work began on dismantling the combat base, with all materiel in place to be removed within one week. A series of seven ARC LIGHT strikes right on the old combat base was planned to destroy anything left behind that might be of value to the North Vietnamese.

Then came intelligence that the NVA were sending nine more tanks into the area. The plan to reduce the combat base to a support facility of less than a thousand men was shelved temporarily on April 15.

Ensign Kux wrote in his diary of suspicions that President Johnson himself had countermanded the withdrawal order when told of it. In any case, Kux and others had to dig out holes they had already filled, replace communications wire, and unstack equipment packed for shipment. Kux thought they would need a week just to regain their previous position.

For a few days Task Force Glick operated practically a division of troops on the plateau. But the Cav moved out while the 26th Marines were scheduled to rotate out battalion by battalion to the lowlands. On April 18 the 1st Marine Regiment assumed operational control of units that had not yet left. Principal among these elements were 2/26 and 1/9, which had been holding outlying positions. Bruce Meyers took 26th regimental headquarters to Quang Tri where he was supposed to conduct a sector offensive.

Meyers had not wanted to leave Khe Sanh, thinking he was being forced to abandon a subordinate unit in mid-operation, for the fact was that men of the 1st Battalion, 9th Marines were just then fighting for their lives. Their crisis perfectly highlighted the irony of Vietnam — the war where men changed but the battle remained essentially the same — for they were engaged on the slopes of Hill 689, one more fight on a hill that would have meant nothing except for someone's desire to keep Americans at Khe Sanh.

Even more, the death ride of the 1st Battalion, 9th Marines happened scant days *after* the relief of Khe Sanh, fewer than a hundred hours since the largest U.S.–South Vietnamese offensive of the war in the northern provinces.

All this occurred simply because Marines kept running into NVA around Hill 689. There was one contact on April 13, another two days later. For April 16, Captain Henry D. Banks got orders to take his Alpha Company and clear the area. They came under sniper fire as soon as they began climbing the rise adjacent to 689, and then Lieutenant Francis Lovely's 1st Platoon was pinned down by heavier fire. Banks deployed another platoon but the NVA, much stronger than thought, had been holding their fire. Lovely was forced to take temporary command of both units after the officer and sergeant with 2nd Platoon were killed. Banks radioed Colonel Cahill, the 1/9 commander, to ask for help. Cahill sent John W. Cargile's Delta Company to assist. He couldn't get artillery or air into the fight because Alpha had become too closely intermixed with the North Vietnamese. Later Cahill had Larry Himmer's Charlie Company maneuver to take the supposed NVA position from another direction.

Cahill's maneuver failed miserably. The NVA were awaiting them in a second bunker complex that had gone entirely unnoticed. Charlie Company too was pinned down and suffered heavy casualties. Just to disengage they had to attack. The wounded leader of 1st Platoon, Second Lieutenant David O. Carter, told debriefers, "The only choice for Charlie Company was to get on line in classic Marine fashion with bayonets . . . and come up the hill at them."

Colonel Meyers was under orders to move 26th Regiment headquarters to Quang Tri, but he tarried to help Cahill's battalion. There was some justification in that the relief unit, 1st Regiment headquarters, was still back on Route 9 somewhere, perhaps as far back as Ca Lu. Meyers did not relish leaving his men in the lurch. Division insisted — the Quang Tri operation it had planned took precedence. When the Marine Corps later investigated the tragedy, it would be Bruce Meyers who paid the price.

Meanwhile near Hill 689 the situation was a mess: with night nearing, Cahill had two companies pinned down plus a third in the area of which higher command remained completely ignorant. At Khe Sanh Richard R. Blair, the Task Force Glick operations officer, could hear the tension in the voices on his radio. Meyers did everything he could short of relieving Cahill, taking all artillery supporting other forces in the vicinity and putting it behind 1/9 once they could back off a bit. Cahill ordered his men back to Hill 689, figuring he would get the live ones under cover and go back for the casualties later. Charlie Company could not make it back until about 3:00 A.M. of April 17.

Wounded Marines still lay out in no-man's-land, some of them calling out to buddies. Patrols returned a few but missed at least one wounded man, Corporal Honeycutt. Army choppers covered by the spectacular suppressive fire of eight Cav gunships brought out one more man, but it turned out not to be Honeycutt, who was finally retrieved by two platoons of Charlie Company on April 18.

A casualty summary enumerated the heavy toll. Alpha Company registered five dead, thirteen wounded, seven missing, and four non-battle casualties. Charlie had just one man dead, but twenty-two wounded and twenty-five missing. Delta Company had three dead, five wounded, two missing, and one nonbattle casualty. Even headquarters had losses: six wounded, two missing, and seven nonbattle casualties. Once again the 1st Battalion, 9th Marines justified its nickname, the Walking Dead.

On April 19 India Company of the 3rd Battalion, 4th Marines

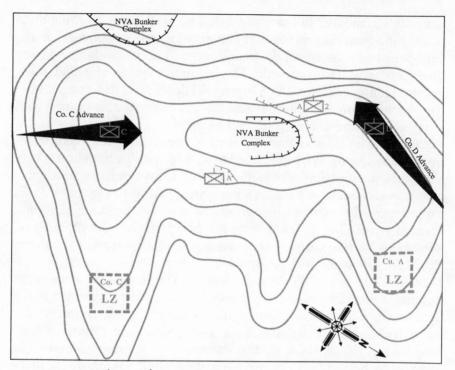

16 · Area of 1st Battalion, 9th Marines Contact

arrived at Hill 689. The worn-out 1st Battalion, 9th Marines helilifted to Cam Lo, completing the move on the afternoon of April 21.

The 2nd Battalion, 26th Marines spent its last days at Khe Sanh sending men to replace other units that were pulling out. At the end, augmented by its Company B, the battalion held *four* of the hilltop outposts: 558, 861, 881 South, and 950. At the latter, once the object of a fierce battle to preserve American positions, Marines found that Army troops had simply flown away and deserted the place when their relief had to be delayed because of weather. The 3rd Battalion, 26th Marines took more casualties leaving Khe Sanh than in many battles for that place — repeated use of the same LZs and repetition of helicopter tactics were as dangerous as ever. Returning to Quang Tri on April 16 along with the ARVN airborne troops was like entering Paradise. The Marines got fresh uniforms and fresh food — broiled steaks, vegetables, cakes, and so on. But for months afterward Khe Sanh Marines felt funny elsewhere, without their bunkers, in tents that weren't sandbagged; it was like they were just waiting for the incoming.

In the afterdays Colonel Hughes held Khe Sanh with his 1st Marines, initially controlling four battalions: 1/1, 2/1, 2/3, and 3/4. The intelligence specialists put North Vietnamese strength nearby at twelve battalions; that is, intelligence recorded *no change* in projected NVA strength between the beginning of PEGASUS and the putative maneuver warfare phase the Marines called operation SCOTLAND II.

Intelligence uncovered other disturbing indications as well. Living on the adversary's doorstep, so to speak, would never be easy. Planes found the North Vietnamese building another road into Vietnam south of Co Roc, an extension of their Road 92, which inside Vietnam turned north toward Khe Sanh. The last big Marine operation, for which the 4th Marines deployed to reinforce the 1st, went into this area. If anything, this phase of mobile warfare proved even costlier than the siege. Marine casualties between April 16 and July 11 totaled 301 killed, 1,489 wounded and evacuated, 242 wounded and not evacuated, and three missing. Army casualties added another 25 dead, 123 serious and 34 minor wounded, and two missing. North Vietnamese losses included 2,440 killed, 33 prisoners, and other estimated casualties.

By late June III MAF and General Rosson's northern provinces command, Provisional Corps Vietnam, were united in their preference for this mobile warfare over further efforts to hold Khe Sanh. A battalion or more had been tied down holding open Route 9, and both security and engineering requirements would be reduced considerably by making Ca Lu the forward supply point. There were early thoughts of retaining a couple of fire bases in the Khe Sanh area but that notion too was abandoned. It is notable that the III MAF concept of operations under which Khe Sanh was abandoned, that is, the formal plan underlying the military move, is dated June 12, 1968. This is significant because William Westmoreland had relinquished his command of MACV the day before. Westy would be going to Washington to become Army chief of staff.

Marines who had fought at Khe Sanh, the men who had held the place by dint of bravery and resourcefulness, were furious that the combat base would be abandoned. Some Marines with 1/26, at that moment at Wunder Beach on the coast, blamed Westmoreland for the withdrawal and were almost in open revolt.

The truth may never be established, although the weight of evidence indicates that Westmoreland intended to hold Khe Sanh indefinitely. Equally likely is that the seed for the withdrawal was planted by Maxwell Taylor and cultivated by Lyndon Johnson when MACV deputy commander General Creighton Abrams visited Washington during March 1968. President Johnson had certain private conversations with Abrams of which no known record exists. Abrams and LBJ are both dead and other records for the period are yet to be opened or remain classified, so for the moment analysis of the withdrawal must remain speculative. Our speculation is this: President Johnson wanted no more nonsense about defending exposed positions or pressures to invade Laos. LBJ adopted Taylor's advice and quietly told General Abrams to get out of Khe Sanh as soon as Westmoreland had left the scene for his new post in Washington. This explanation most directly accounts for the timing of the withdrawal plan and its execution before Westmoreland could become fully established as Army chief of staff in Washington.

News of the withdrawal first appeared in the U.S. press on June 27, before the move had been made, a scoop for which John S. Carroll of the *Baltimore Sun* lost his military accreditation. Within twelve hours of the report, shelling increased in the Khe Sanh area and a strong ground probe was directed at Hill 689. The NVA tried to block Route 9 but were prevented. The last Marines left Khe Sanh on July 6, 1968.

Colonel David Lownds made his final appearance on the Potomac, not the Rao Quan, at the White House on May 23. He appeared with regimental Sergeant Major Agrippa W. Smith to receive the Presidential Unit Citation in behalf of the 26th Marines. Lyndon Johnson made the award to the regiment and attached units with evident pride and pleasure. "Despite overwhelming odds," the citation read, "the 26th Marines remained resolute and determined, maintaining . . . its positions and inflicting heavy losses. . . . By their gallant fighting spirit and their countless individual acts of heroism, the men of the 26th Marines (Reinforced) established a record of illustrious courage and determination."

The South Vietnamese government made a like determination when, as the regiment prepared to leave Vietnam in March 1970, Saigon awarded it the Vietnamese Cross of Gallantry with Palm. This was the last act of the most important pitched battle of the U.S. war in Vietnam.

Only the men of Khe Sanh can say if it was worth it.

chapter 14

Then Is Now

ON MARCH 27, 1968, General Earle Wheeler summed up the latest developments for a meeting of the National Security Council, a meeting attended by Creighton Abrams, with the words: "Khe Sanh appears to have served the NVA's purpose." He pointed out how the North Vietnamese were pulling out their troops and suddenly seemed primarily interested in Hue and Saigon. Inside the White House the president was being told that MACV systems analysis specialists had calculated, using three different methods, that North Vietnamese killed around Khe Sanh must total between ten and fifteen thousand. These figures are far greater than any confirmed body count, but they are consistent with statements in captured documents and postwar comments by North Vietnamese officers noting the hardships and costs of the Khe Sanh campaign.

Nevertheless, with that peculiar quality of double meaning that seems to touch everything related to the Vietnam war, Wheeler's comment to the 583rd National Security Council meeting can also be read to suggest he felt Hanoi had achieved its goals at Khe Sanh — that is, that the battle was a victory for the North Vietnamese Army. That is most emphatically not the view of William Westmoreland. The former MACV commander told an interviewer in 1988 that of all the decisions he had to make during the Vietnam war, he was proudest of his decision to hold Khe Sanh. Implicit in this is the notion that Khe Sanh constituted a substantial U.S. victory.

What is the real story? Was Hanoi defeated? Did Westmoreland thwart its plan to overrun the two northern provinces and set up a provisional government, as he maintained in the 1988 interview? Did Hanoi ever intend to fight a battle at Khe Sanh? Did Khe Sanh serve

Hanoi's purposes, diverting MACV while the North Vietnamese went on to launch their Tet offensive? Who lost? Who won?

Sadly, even this history must settle for answers that are not quite definitive. Hanoi's original intentions are not knowable now and may never be. Furthermore, the development of the battle suggests that North Vietnamese intentions changed over time. Before Tet the evidence is not conclusive. At the time of Lang Vei, the hill fights, and the battle for the village, it looks very much as if the NVA intended to pursue a real siege. In later February and March the North Vietnamese seem to have alternated hot and cold on the idea of a major assault. Some of the later action also smacks of deception. Perhaps the true answer is that Hanoi did not have a fixed plan at all but a set of strategic goals toward which it aimed, modifying battlefield actions as appropriate. If this be so, the North Vietnamese ought to receive some credit for their flexibility in the field.

Hanoi *was* defeated at Khe Sanh. That is, a demonstrably large North Vietnamese army absorbed tremendous losses while achieving little concrete beyond the capture of Huong Hoa district headquarters and the Lang Vei CIDG camp. In the sense of thwarting a purported scheme to overrun provinces and set up an alternative government, Khe Sanh also has to be seen as a setback for Hanoi. Creating such a provisional government had *always* been an aim of North Vietnamese strategy, however, not just at Khe Sanh. That was a political strategy, an action continuously impending that could not be rendered impossible by a single military setback, however great. That Khe Sanh thwarted such a strategy is not possible. Military difficulties may have delayed Hanoi's political moves, but to gain a decent interval is not to inflict a decisive defeat.

As for the military situation in specific terms, the North Vietnamese defeat that we assume occurred had little measurable impact on the security situation. The estimated scale of threat — twelve battalions in the region — remained identical after Khe Sanh to what it had been before PEGASUS. If anything, this scale of threat was greater (double) than that during the summer and fall of 1967 when the security situation had already been considered serious. It is significant that the South Vietnamese government made no effort to regenerate the administrative structure extant before the battle or to mobilize new local forces.

There was more than one defeat at Khe Sanh. Also defeated was William Westmoreland's long-cherished dream of mounting an invasion of Laos. Hanoi may not have attacked Khe Sanh in a serious way, but by the force of its arms it demonstrated clearly that it intended to block the road into Laos. The losses of American lives that occurred even in the absence of major assault suggested that an offensive foray, at a minimum, would be politically impossible in the post-Tet climate. Saigon may not have taken the point — MACV continued to plan for a Laos invasion and other contingencies — but Washington did. Lyndon Johnson gave medals to Khe Sanh's defenders but emerged determined never again to commit Americans in this kind of vulnerable situation. Richard Nixon appreciated the point too; though one day he would sanction a Laotian incursion, it would be by South Vietnamese forces alone. What happened to the ARVN on that occasion fully confirmed the point Hanoi had made at Khe Sanh.

A good deal of obscurantism also has surrounded the cost of Khe Sanh. Official casualty figures are 205 killed in action, 816 wounded and evacuated, 852 wounded but not evacuated, and one missing. Unfortunately these figures do not reflect the full toll of the battle. They include only Marine casualties, and only for the combat base and hilltops. Not included are losses in the village battle, at Lang Vei, in aircraft, and in operation PEGASUS, which properly belong in any full accounting. In addition one may well ask, since it is a campaign under discussion here, whether losses prior and subsequent to the siege proper should be included. Moreover, the Marines' own casualty figures, in the heat and confusion of battle, may be incomplete and inadequate. For example, Khe Sanh's Charlie Med log records 903 casualties treated just between January 21 and February 24, a figure that does not include Marines treated by regimental or battalion aid stations, the number of which would have been considerable. It seems difficult to reconcile these figures with the official tally. An analysis by coauthor Ray Stubbe, based on memorial service bulletins and 3rd Marine Division casualty records, identifies by name some 353 Marines killed between January 20 and March 31, 69 between then and the end of PEGASUS (April 15), plus 54 killed on April 16 and 17. There is reason to believe official Marine casualty claims are in error.

The picture becomes even more complicated when allowance is made for other losses. Most notable are the 219 killed, 77 wounded, and one missing in the fall of Lang Vei, approximately 25 killed and 40 wounded in Khe Sanh village, and PEGASUS losses of at least 125 killed, 853 wounded, and five missing. Another 52 assorted Army and Marine personnel died in plane crashes, shellings, and other incidents not counted in the official figures, which also do not include Air Force personnel, whose fatalities probably number between five and twenty. A consolidated figure, even one that uses the (low) Marine official numbers as a base, would suggest losses of roughly 650 killed, 2,598 wounded, and seven missing in action. Using the higher figures for Marine fatalities in the siege and Army losses during PEGASUS would give totals of 730 battle deaths, 2,642 wounded, and seven missing. These figures are far higher than official claims, yet there is still reason to suspect the number of wounded to be understated, even in these adjusted estimates.

If one went further to enumerate losses in the full Khe Sanh campaign by including also those suffered during SCOTLAND II, the period of mobile operations following the siege, casualty numbers rise once more. It is worth noting that casualties from the mobile operations, which lasted about as long as the siege itself, are higher than the casualties the Marine Corps has admitted for the siege. These losses amount to 326 killed, 1,888 wounded, and three missing. Adding these to siege losses would give a round total of 1,000 dead and 4,500 wounded, about 200 dead and 500 wounded per month. By comparison, U.S. losses during the two-month invasion of Cambodia in 1970 amounted to 284 killed, 2,339 wounded, and 13 missing. Cambodia would be the biggest offensive of the war, yet Khe Sanh losses are comparable. Khe Sanh had been a costly campaign.

However great their losses, the North Vietnamese learned some important lessons from the Khe Sanh campaign. This battlefield became the place where the North Vietnamese first practiced coordinating different combat arms in a conventional, modern warfare setting. The maneuvers of armor with infantry would assume increasing importance as the Vietnam war continued and would finally provide Hanoi the key to victory in the conflict. In Laos in 1971 and during the Easter offensive of 1972 the NVA relied to a great degree on these methods. Without the experience gained at Khe Sanh, the North Vietnamese forces would have had a much harder time of it later.

Khe Sanh also became the locale where the NVA introduced a significant number of its technical and tactical innovations other than armor. Long before the siege they introduced the 122mm heavy mortar at Khe Sanh. During it the innovations included the 130mm gun, possibly the FROG surface-to-surface missile, flamethrowers — in all, a significant panoply of conventional military technology. As we have seen, Hanoi may also have exercised the threat of its own air force. Although none of these weapons except the heavy mortars and big guns acquired significance in the NVA order of battle, Khe Sanh gave Hanoi the opportunity to test and select technologies, and that was significant.

In the last analysis Khe Sanh represented William Westmoreland's battle. Khe Sanh was an attempt to make the definitions of other wars apply in Vietnam; it was a large, conventional engagement, a set-piece battle in a conflict dominated by fleeting guerrilla encounters. Westmoreland wanted to fight the biggest battle of annihilation of the Vietnam war, a battle to open the way for his Laotian plans, a battle to sap the strength of the North Vietnamese Army. The test followed logically from Westmoreland's focus, since the earliest months of the war, on the northern provinces. Now, here, Westmoreland matched wits with the adversary. To bait the trap he dangled a Marine garrison and was willing to yield the initiative. That it was a trap seems clearly indicated by the carefully controlled conditions the MACV commander strived to establish surrounding his proffered bait. Despite North Vietnamese technological adventurism at Khe Sanh and regardless of their having exercised tactical initiative there, Khe Sanh was Westmoreland's battle. Tet was Hanoi's.

A countrywide offensive for which they took the initiative all across South Vietnam, Tet figures as a clear strategic move by Hanoi. Khe Sanh was ambiguous. There was no possible payoff for the North Vietnamese at Khe Sanh comparable to what MACV stood to gain from a conventional victory there. It is ironic that North Vietnamese losses in the offensive they chose turned out to be much greater than any they suffered in the engagement Westmoreland intended as the biggest battle of the war. It is doubly ironic that the American military gains at Khe Sanh (and Tet as well) were wiped out by the political losses at Tet, especially since Westmoreland had pointed to political and psychological effects as reasons for holding Khe Sanh in the face of the adversary.

Khe Sanh veterans remain bitter at the way they were treated, especially men from the 1st Battalion, 26th Marines, who were there the longest and suffered the most. It was not so much that the Marines were left unsupported, which they certainly were not, but that they were beleaguered at the end of a tenuous supply line. If Khe Sanh was supposed to be the most important thing happening in Vietnam, in

this view, it was unconscionable to have Marines defending the place
while wearing rags and starving, and without benefit of the materiel
that could have turned Khe Sanh into a true fortress. Westmoreland,
as the senior commander, bore the ultimate responsibility. Years later,
when Westy gave the keynote speech at a special session of the 3rd
Marine Division Association marking the twentieth anniversary of
Khe Sanh, some Marine veterans boycotted the assembly.

There is also the matter of the apparent animosity between Westmoreland and the successive Marine commanders, Lew Walt and
Robert Cushman. We take Westmoreland at his word, expressed to
Washington in 1968, that there were no difficulties between him and
Cushman. Yet there was a constant tension between MACV and III
MAF that has been a repeated theme in interviews and can be detected
as an undertone in messages and in the air control dispute. If Westmoreland and his Marine colleagues had no personal problems, yet
the difficulties were so real, the conclusion must be that the competition between Army and Marine Corps continued through the Vietnam war, long enough to be live and well at Khe Sanh.

Finally, William Westmoreland's retrospective view of his steward-
ship, as expressed in his memoirs, naturally presents an idealized
account of events. This too has been a repeated theme among veterans
interviewed for this book. It is not unusual for accounts by participants, of course, and as a work of history this book has tried to show
a few instances where the record ought to stand corrected. We should
point out, however, that Westmoreland wrote from a large collection
of background materials and his daily diary notes. His account is
more than the simple self-serving tract that some veterans see, and his
problems at MACV were more complex than previously appreciated.
Westmoreland was not simply managing the war but also was per-
forming a delicate dance between the Pentagon, the White House, the
South Vietnamese government, and other centers of influence as well.
Yet former MACV officers who attribute all their difficulty to Washington also oversimplify the reality. The emerging documentary
record is a rich lode, revealing hidden dimensions to the Vietnam war,
which will ultimately force reinterpretation of the conventional wisdom drawn from Vietnam.

Just as there was more than one defeat at Khe Sanh, so too there was
more than a single victory. In an important sense there was a victory
of technology at Khe Sanh, for the siege heralded a new era in methods
of warfare. Technology affected both the strategy and tactics of com-

bat engagement and the scale and effectiveness of service support. Experiments with methods in embryo form at Khe Sanh we see as standard operating techniques today in the Persian Gulf and other conflicts.

Khe Sanh occurred at the dawn of the complex of related technologies later to become known as the "electronic battlefield." Lessons learned at Khe Sanh made more feasible the tracking and engagement of an adversary never seen but simply detected by remote sensors. These lessons were put to use in the interdiction campaign over the Ho Chi Minh Trail. Today the lessons of Khe Sanh, now become the conventional wisdom, are expressed in the constant thrust for real-time intelligence capabilities. Marine commanders at Khe Sanh estimated that their casualties would have doubled but for the sensor systems. That may serve as a crude measure of the value of these mechanisms in the campaign.

Equally important to Khe Sanh, and of lasting importance to the Vietnam war, were the techniques developed during the siege to introduce flexibility into the ARC LIGHT strike — the tactical use of strategic aircraft. The close-in strikes that proved so vital in breaking up suspected North Vietnamese assaults would become the cutting edge of the American war effort in South Vietnam in 1972, when the use of U.S. ground troops to help ARVN was no longer possible. The notion of using strategic bombers in such a tactical role has since become standard United States doctrine for meeting conventional contingencies.

Contrary to the expressions of the pundits, the "armed chair" strategists, as Earle Wheeler liked to call them, it was *not* in 1991, in DESERT STORM in the Persian Gulf, that air power first won a ground campaign virtually by itself. This is precisely what happened at Khe Sanh; the distinction properly belongs to operation NIAGARA. In 1972 also, a good argument can be made that air proved decisive in a ground war, and this development built directly on the experience of Khe Sanh.

America's Persian Gulf adventure that began in the summer of 1990 also underlines another feature of the Khe Sanh experience — the deliberate reliance on airlift as a mechanism for hauling supplies, equipment, and personnel. Though there was in general great use of air supply techniques in Vietnam, at Khe Sanh these were refined to a considerable degree. Sadly, the GPES system which proved so useful at Khe Sanh would quickly be retired afterward, but other refinements have been retained. Air drop and air delivery techniques utilized at

Khe Sanh are still at the heart of America's tactical and strategic airlift capabilities. Without the Vietnam experience, the mass airlift carried out during the 1973 October War would not have been possible, and without both of these opportunities to refine and define requirements, the Persian Gulf buildup in Saudi Arabia prior to DESERT STORM would have been much slower and less decisive.

The general richness of the fire support for Marines at Khe Sanh allowed them to prevail in the battle. In this respect that battle furnishes counterpoint to the fashionable postwar argument that American tactics are flawed because they rely on firepower to the exclusion of maneuver. Not only did the Marines win at Khe Sanh without maneuvering, if they *had* been maneuvering, in motion all across the battlefield, the mass application of firepower that won the battle would not have been possible. Furthermore, at Khe Sanh, after literally months of life in their bunkers, Marines took the offensive and maneuvered very well, even by night, traditionally the province of the North Vietnamese. Fashionable arguments mislead: warfare is not a matter of firepower *versus* maneuver; rather, the ageless truth is that the role of firepower is to bring troops to the point of contact in such fashion that their maneuvers carry the day. This truth too received confirmation anew in the Iraq-Kuwait operation DESERT STORM.

At the instant of decision the men behind the bayonets have always mattered. It is they who should have the last word on Khe Sanh, the battle for the valley of decision.

These are some of the things those who were at Khe Sanh now say. The authors consider it appropriate for this peroration that the various veterans here quoted shall remain anonymous. Their commentaries are what matters.

> If someone told me at Khe Sanh that seventeen years later I would still be affected by what I experienced, I would have told him he was crazy. In those days we fought to stay alive physically. Today . . . you and I . . . have waged far worse battles to stay alive mentally.

> Khe Sanh is a big presence that looms over my thoughts and emotions even sixteen years later. The days from January 21 to April 14 in any year are particularly tough. . . . Now I'm sixteen years removed and yet there isn't a day that goes by when I don't think of Nam or Khe Sanh in particular.

[A dream:] I am alone on the airstrip. Suddenly there are Gooks all around me. I am about six feet tall and they are like ten feet tall. It is as though I am in a fishbowl and they are looking at me ready to smash me like a bug.

One of the things I felt and still feel . . . the friends: I always wanted to know what happened to them . . . there's a feeling that I guess all of us feel that served time over there, fought in combat, that kinship and that feeling of love. . . . I never really identified it as love while I was over there. But now, reflecting back on it, it was just as intense as what I now feel for my family. Because they were my family. Each and every one of them meant so much to me. There were guys I didn't like, but the feeling I have for them right now, for the guys who didn't make it home, and the guys who did make it home, is just a feeling of total kinship.

Each and every man left a part of himself at Khe Sanh. Khe Sanh in turn left a part of itself inside of us.

I hurt then and I still hurt today, but it is from the pain that I have gained an awareness of war's real change. The real pain is not on the battlefield, it is on the land and the people afterwards. Nothing can extinguish the horror of war. . . . As a small boy I looked upon war as glamorous, without pain, no one hurt, returning home a hero. That's the way I went to Nam. The biggest realization that affected me . . . was when I realized that the person who I considered a monster, one to be destroyed, was another person, one who also had feelings, friends who got killed, a family who loved him. . . . In that moment all my childhood dreams and myths lay shattered. The real enemy in war I feared was not my enemy, but myself. . . . Blatant warfare and hatred — where death was the solution to a problem that did not exist. . . . Now innocence was replaced by knowledge. How short, how deceitful, how surprising, life's promises can be.

So much has happened since we were young Marines at Khe Sanh. The transition of coming back to the "World" has taken so many years for many of us. I think I have been one of the fortunate ones. Once you allow yourself to stop being so full of hatred and rage and let some people get close to you. . . . It's amazing how long it took me to figure it out.

As time passes it seems as if all those fine young men who died in Vietnam was just so much cannon fodder. What a loss! What a shame! Not much can be done. I remember those I can each day.

It's been so long since Khe Sanh and yet it was only yesterday!

In fact it *is* like yesterday. The Bru returned to their sacred mountains. So did Bible translators John and Carolyn Miller; the children they had then are grown up now. As before, the tribes are the butt of the lowlanders, the latest version of their tale being that gold has been discovered near Khe Sanh and the Bru are being made to mine it.

All in all I don't know really how to account for the war, as far as the way I feel about it. I think it was a senseless thing. And I know right now that if there was another, I've a son who is fifteen right now. And if he were seventeen and there were another outbreak as Vietnam was — a political action and so forth — I know that I would be the first — *the* first — to drive my son to Canada or whatever it took, to keep him from going. But if it was a declared war, I would be the first to coach my son to volunteer.

When you're in the Corps, everything is last names or nicknames, and I couldn't remember his first name. And when I read it on The Wall, it shattered me! I felt like a CRUDBALL that I couldn't remember his first name. He knew me more than I knew myself, and I couldn't remember the guy's first name. It *hurt* me!

When they abandoned the base in midsummer of '68, I lost all hope and belief in the war. Too many of my friends bled and died at Khe Sanh — and a few months later it was deemed "not important anymore." After that I just wanted to survive Nam . . . and get back to being a college student once again.

In conclusion, I'd just like to say that the Marines who served at Khe Sanh were about as fine a bunch of men as anybody could ever have the opportunity of serving with. They went through some pretty hard times. . . . But they never lost their spirit, they never lost their courage. . . . It was indeed a privilege to have served with them, to know them, to have known them.

Amen!

Notes
Bibliography
Index

Notes

Short titles are used for works cited in the Notes; complete publishing information can be found in the Bibliography. The following is a list of abbreviations used in the Notes. Details about the sources are given in the Bibliography.

BBC	British Broadcasting Corporation
CDEC	Combined Documents Exploitation Center (jointly run by ARVN and MACV)
CFVN	Country File, Vietnam (in LBJP)
DSDUF	Declassified and Sanitized Documents from Unopened Folders (in LBJP)
Fonecon	MACV, Record of COMUSMACV Fonecon
GMT	Greenwich mean time
LBJL	Lyndon Baines Johnson Library
LBJP	Lyndon Baines Johnson Papers (at LBJL)
MACV	Military Assistance Command Vietnam
ms.	manuscript
NSC	National Security Council
NSF	National Security File (in LBJP)
III MAF	III Marine Amphibious Force
USMC	United States Marine Corps
VNA	Vietnam News Agency

CHAPTER I. THE ENCOUNTER

1 "The distance covered today" et seq.: MACV, CDEC, Bulletin 11,456, April 16, 1968 (declassified October 28, 1981). LBJL, LBJP, NSF, CFVN, box 155, folder "Vietnam: Khe Sanh."

3 "There were some powerful": Ernest Spencer interview (Stubbe, January 4, 1987).

4–6 Animal encounters: Kevin Macaulay interview (Stubbe, August 22, 1984).

8–9 "Westmoreland thought Khe Sanh": William Broyles, Jr., *Brothers in Arms*, p. 89.

9 "Westmoreland had adopted the view": Nguyen Van Ba, "Evolution of the Military Situation in 1968," in Nguyen Khac Vien, ed., *American Failure*, pp. 94–95.

10 "it is conceivable": William C. Westmoreland, "Answers Prepared for Wes Gallagher [Associated Press]," ms., February 24, 1968. LBJL, Westmoreland Papers, box 16, folder "History Back-Up File v. 29 [II]."

10 "a major terrorist-guerrilla campaign": Memorandum, Hugh Cumming–Christian Herter, December 7, 1960. *Vietnam, 1958–1960,* vol. 1 of Foreign Relations of the United States series, pp. 717–18.

10 "plug up [the] porous border": Cable, Elbridge Durbrow–Christian Herter, December 8, 1960. Ibid., p. 719.

10 "The sparsely settled and rugged jungle terrain": Letter, General Lionel McGarr–Robert McNamara, October 30, 1961. *Vietnam, 1961–1963,* vol. 1 of Foreign Relations of the United States series, p. 448.

11 "raised the question as to why": Draft memorandum of conversation, May 4, 1961. Ibid., p. 118.

11 "the proposal to put forces along the border": Ibid., p. 328.

11 "free access to the Vietnam border": Memorandum, Admiral George W. Anderson–Robert S. McNamara, October 9, 1961. Ibid., p. 329.

12 "to infiltrate large numbers": Joint letter, Commanding General, Philippine Army Commander, Seventh Fleet, "Instruction for SEATO Amphibious Exercise TULUNGUN," December 13, 1961 (ltr FF/7/LWW:ml, 3,500, Ser. N32-00184). USMC Archives, file VE 23.2-N121615.

14 "We were told when we went in there": Jacques Standing interview (Stubbe, March 20, 1989).

14 "Any kind of security patrol": Gerald J. Howland interview (Stubbe, March 20, 1989).

14 "Neither the Vietnamese": Ibid.

14 "The whole situation": Jacques Standing interview (Stubbe, March 20, 1989).

15 "That was a very uncomfortable feeling": Ibid.

15 "It really makes you feel good": Frank Fowler interview (Stubbe, March 21, 1989).

15 "One time we went into the village": Ibid.

16 Hughes recollection: Hughes's comment to Stubbe during the battle of Khe Sanh. Captain Hughes was killed in action on May 9, 1968.

17 "Every time we sent a patrol out": Allan B. Imes interview (Stubbe, October 14, 1988).

17 "Those are hillacious mountains": Ibid.

18 "looked like a gypsy band" et seq.: Francis X. Harrison interview (Stubbe, February 26, 1989).

18 "They would not participate": Allan B. Imes interview (Stubbe, October 14, 1988).

20 "When we came out": Alfred M. Gray, Jr., interview (Stubbe, April 25, 1989). General Gray is the just-retired commandant of the Marine Corps, who led the Corps during Operation DESERT STORM.

21 "The threat got really bad": Ibid.

22 "I'm convinced that because I had that platoon": Allan B. Imes interview (Stubbe, October 14, 1988).

22 "Everything got real edgy" et seq.: Allan B. Imes interview (Stubbe, October 23, 1988).

23 "If we didn't trust them": John T. Wheeler, "Special Forces Men Live with Treachery," *San Juan Star*, March 4, 1965.

24 "After a first flurry": William C. Westmoreland, *A Soldier Reports*, p. 148.

CHAPTER 2. THE ANTHROPOLOGY OF DEATH

PAGE

26 "some say by the VC": Conversation, Madeleine Poilane–Ray Stubbe, Stubbe Diary, January 1, 1968.

28 "because we needed every bit of help": Letter, Daniel Kelley–Ray Stubbe, March 28, 1970.

28 "had cells in one area": James Whitenack interview (Stubbe, October 4, 1988). Whitenack served at Khe Sanh from Christmas 1966 to Christmas 1967.

29 "If Jesus Christ were to be walking": Comment by Harper L. Bohr noted in Stubbe Diary, December 16, 1967.

32 "the inclination of the Bru to fight aggressively": Joan L. Schrock

et al., *Minority Groups in the Republic of Vietnam*. The foregoing Bru material is based largely on this source supplemented by individual recollections.

32 "You mean they're different people?": Ray W. Stubbe, "Khe Sanh Chaplain" (ms.), p. 220.

36 "their families, chickens, and everything else": Peter Morakon interview (Stubbe, July 21, 1985).

36–37 "We knew it would only be": Ibid.

42 "Surprisingly, the Special Forces commander": Jack Shulimson, *An Expanding War, 1966*, U.S. Marines in Vietnam series, p. 141.

42 "based on someone's intel[ligence]": Letter, John D. Waghelstein–Ray Stubbe, August 20, 1985.

43 "It was territory hitherto untouched" et seq.: Jack Shulimson, *An Expanding War, 1966*, U.S. Marines in Vietnam series, p. 142.

43–44 "We started our hike at midnight": Chaplain John J. Scanlon, End of Tour Report. USMC Archives.

CHAPTER 3. "ONE OF THE BUSIEST PLACES AROUND"

PAGE

46 "When you're at Khe Sanh": Jack Shulimson, *An Expanding War, 1966*, U.S. Marines in Vietnam series, p. 196.

46 "I still hoped some day": William C. Westmoreland, *A Soldier Reports*, p. 198.

47 "attacks are most likely to occur" et seq.: OPLAN 415-66, "Relief of Special Forces Camp," p. 1. In 3rd Marine Division, Command Chronology, September 1966, USMC Archives.

47–48 "I notice you haven't made any comment" et seq.: John R. Chaisson, Marine Oral History no. 327. USMC Archives.

48 "We didn't want a force": Ibid., p. 374.

48 "I gained the impression": William C. Westmoreland, op. cit., p. 198.

49 "unprecedented rapid buildup": Cable, William Westmoreland–U. S. Grant Sharp, 291409Z, September 1966. III MAF, Combat Operations Center Records, Journal and File 29 September–1 October 1966, item no. 114. USMC Archives.

49 "far too much emphasis" et seq.: Letter, Lew Walt–H. W. Buse, December 29, 1966 (serial 0002000966), appended to III MAF OPLAN 121-66, "Practice NINE." USMC Archives.

51 "I . . . ordered the U.S. Navy's Seabees": William C. Westmoreland, *A Soldier Reports*, p. 198.

51 "You can't let a beautiful hunk of equipment": News Release, Naval Mobile Construction Battalion 10, September 1966. Stubbe Collection.

52 "gave every last bit": "Seabee Detachment Upgrades Vital Airstrip, Khe Sanh Special Forces Camp," News Release, Naval Mobile Construction Battalion 10, November 1966. Stubbe Collection.

52 "I have been impressed": Message, COMUSMACV-COMNAVFORV, 181331Z, October 1966. Ibid.

52 "I later wondered": William C. Westmoreland, *A Soldier Reports,* p. 198.

52 "we were going up there": George W. O'Dell interview (Stubbe, May 11, 1986).

52 "I am confident the walls of Jericho": G. R. Witt, Chaplain's End of Tour Report. USMC Archives.

53 "We never worked much outside": George W. O'Dell interview (Stubbe, May 11, 1986).

53 "I believe that along with combat pay": G. R. Witt, Chaplain's End of Tour Report. USMC Archives. "Utilities," daily use field uniforms, are also called "cammies" if the material is printed in a camouflage pattern.

55 "My memory of that place": Thomas M. Horne interview (Stubbe, January 11, 1987).

55 "They were playing both sides": Bill Steptoe interview (Stubbe, October 6, 1988).

59 "orange men": Ronald J. Lauzon interview (Stubbe, June 1, 1986).

59 "As a matter of fact, we were getting": Kenneth D. Jordan interview (Stubbe, June 2, 1986).

61 "He cut my hair": James Capers interview (Stubbe, May 24, 1986).

61 "I can tell you we were outside the border": Kenneth D. Jordan interview (Stubbe, June 2, 1986).

62 "You're not going to leave us" et seq.: Capt. Gordon M. Gunniss Statement in Support of Award of Distinguished Flying Cross for 1st Lt. Robert W. Hein, Jr. USMC Records.

65 "there were two helicopters down there": Kenneth D. Jordan interview (Stubbe, June 2, 1986).

66 "I was sitting there" et seq.: Fred Locke interview (Stubbe, May 6, 1989).

67 "to slow the enemy down" et seq.: James Capers interview (Stubbe, May 24, 1986).

67 "Believe me, we were making contact": Ibid.

70 "We had only one company there": Thomas Ryan interview (Stubbe, August 24, 1986).

71 "enemy activity increased": MACV J-2 Intelligence Staff, Periodic Intelligence Report, March 25, 1967. III MAF Command Chronology, March 1967. USMC Archives.

72 "He would ask me where I was going": Bruce B. G. Clark interview (Stubbe, May 17, 1989).

72 "Unknown to us": Donald E. Harper, Marine Debriefing, tape no. 567.

75 "I got on the radio": James Whitenack interview (Stubbe, October 4, 1988).

76 "I have always been a great believer": James M. Reeder interview (Stubbe, May 7, 1989).

76 "It is my personal belief": Letter, Michael W. Sayers–Marine Historical Division, May 28, 1981. Comments File, 1967 Vietnam History. USMC Archives.

76–77 "was preoccupied with keeping the dust down": James Capers interview (Stubbe, May 24, 1986).

77 "quite a continuing battle" et seq.: James M. Reeder interview (Stubbe, May 7, 1989).

77 "We found heavily used trails": Lawrence Keen interview (Stubbe, May 31, 1986).

78 "I remember a couple of times we went over": David Rogers interview (Stubbe, June 8, 1986).

79 "Since Khe Sanh has been closed": Message, Lew Walt–William Westmoreland, 280346Z, March 1967. III MAF Command Chronology, March 1967. USMC Archives.

CHAPTER 4. "THESE HILLS CALLED KHE SANH"

PAGE

83 "He had the whole thing doped out": Lee Klein interview (Stubbe, July 22, 1989).

84 "The colonel on the base had said" et seq.: Tom Ryan interview (Stubbe, August 24, 1985).

85 "I kept seeing those poor guys' faces": United Press International dispatch, "When Your Buddies Are Dead, Run like Hell!" in *Pacific Stars and Stripes,* May 1, 1967.

85 "We heard a couple of guys get hit": Michael A. Brown, Marine Debriefing, tape no. 1017.

86 "We got bombed by our jets": Tom Ryan interview (Stubbe, August 24, 1985).

87 "Look back": Ibid.

87 "I couldn't believe it": Michael A. Brown, Marine Debriefing, tape no. 1017.

88 "At first nobody knew where we were going": Henry Rose, Jr., Marine Debriefing, tape no. 1131.

90–91 "Why do you continue to attack?" et seq.: William R. Corson, *The Betrayal*, pp. 72–73, 74.

92 "Look, Dave" et seq.: David G. Rogers, Marine Debriefing, tape no. 3533.

92 "we didn't know exactly what was up on top": Ibid.

93 "The most impressive thing I saw": Quoted in Mick Dunten, "The Initiative of an Officer on Hill 881," *Pacific Stars and Stripes Sunday Magazine,* July 23, 1967, pp. A8–A9.

93 "You couldn't hardly hear yourself think": Larry W. Umstead, Marine Debriefing, tape no. 1126.

93-94 "I can still remember coming back": David G. Rogers, Marine Debriefing, tape no. 3533.

95 "He did it on the orders of somebody": Bill Steptoe interview (Stubbe, October 6, 1988).

95 "We got hit that night": Ibid.

96 "I heard the first rounds": Ibid.

97-98 "We have to be very leery": John J. Padley, Marine Debriefing, tape no. 1504.

98 "The NVA would hit Lang Vei": G. Golden, Marine Debriefing, tape no. 2584.

101-102 "They took 861-881 now": Letter, Samuel A. Sharp–Parents, May 7, 1967. Stubbe Collection.

102 "the cost of stopping the Communist effort": Maj. Gary L. Telfer, LtCol. Lane Rogers, and V. Keith Fleming, Jr., *Fighting the North Vietnamese, 1967,* U.S. Marines in Vietnam series, p. 45.

102 "The destruction of the base and forces": Report, Fleet Marine Force Pacific, Situation Report 768 (070105Z, May 1967). FM-FPAC SitReps File, USMC Archives.

103-105 William Stoss, "Home from the Woods," March 29, 1984. Used by permission. Mr. Stoss died in April 1989. The excerpt used here is roughly one-third of the complete poem.

CHAPTER 5. THE ADVENT OF THE 26TH MARINES

PAGE

108 "I had never seen anybody who had been in combat": Bruce Jones interview (Stubbe, February 25, 1989).

112 "Nobody working with the LSU": Quoted in GySgt. T. Donaldson, "Khe Sanh Marines Supplied: Support Group Doubles Effort," *Sea Tiger,* May 19, 1967. Also see GySgt. T. Donaldson, "Khe Sanh Sergeant Has Many Talents," *Sea Tiger,* June 9, 1967.

114 "I don't think the battle is necessarily over": William Westmoreland quoted in "Vietnam I: The Battle of the Hills," *New York Times,* May 7, 1967.

114 "I think the attack on Khe Sanh": Thomas M. Horne, Marine Debriefing, tape no. 1539.

114 "We've had no rest": Frank M. Tomeo, Marine Debriefing, tape no. 1194.

116 "There was nothing there": James Whitenack interview (Stubbe, October 4, 1988).

118 "We had a little trouble with the Marines": William D. Waugh interview (Stubbe, October 30, 1988).

120 "Captain Joe Bain, sir" et seq.: Lee Dunlap interview (Stubbe, April 8, 1989).

121 "If you can remember in your lifetime": Charles Minnicks interview (Stubbe, April 26, 1990).

121 "They flew sideways": William D. Waugh interview (Stubbe, March 18, 1989).

122 "If you go by helicopter": William D. Waugh interview (Stubbe, October 30, 1988).

125 "We were flying along": James Garvey interview (Stubbe, March 30, 1989).

129 "Incoming grenades!": Quoted in Sgt. Boo Pitner, "Early Marine Attack by NVA Stopped by Radio Relay Crew," *Sea Tiger,* July 7, 1967, p. 1.

130 "They were like eyes coming out of the fog": Richard W. Baskin, Marine Debriefing, tape no. 1196.

132 "If I see one" et seq.: Ibid.

134 "Nobody was sure where the hell": Paul E. Freese, Marine Debriefing, tape no. 3556.

135 "It was something like falling down a hill" et seq.: Donald W. Rogers, Marine Debriefing, tape no. 1195.

137 "Operations there should be": John J. Padley, Marine Debriefing, tape no. 1504.

CHAPTER 6. TO SOME A FORTRESS

145 "operations . . . conducted from a series": III MAF, OPLAN 11-67, "I Corps, ARVN–III MAF Defense of Northern Quang Tri Province," 18163OH, June 1967. USMC Archives.

146 "To have gone through with constructing": William C. Westmoreland, *A Soldier Reports*, p. 200. Westmoreland's context implies that the McNamara press conference occurred in 1966, which is not accurate, and that "reporters" coined the "McNamara Line" argot. *U.S. News & World Report* (January 1, 1968, p. 24) attributes the name to anonymous GIs in the field on the day of the press conference. What McNamara *had* done in 1966, which the Pentagon kept secret and never revealed to Hanoi, was to telescope the original JASON Group recommendation, which had simply been that a barrier line system should be *studied* by a combined civil-military group, into a *decision* to proceed with the system.

147 "He was a delightful man": James M. Reeder interview (Stubbe, May 7, 1989).

148 "Please excuse me": Ray Stubbe recollection of a comment by chaplain John McElroy, who was contrasting perspectives in the rear with those on the battlefront, within a week of the latter's arrival at Khe Sanh. Ray Stubbe, "Khe Sanh Chaplain" (ms.), p. 88.

149 "Our 1/26 battalion aid station is infested" et seq.: Stubbe Diary, July 31, 1967.

149 "If Jesus were alive today": Stubbe Diary, August 26, 1967.

154 "Gilbert and I talked about it": Bruce Jones interview (Stubbe, February 25, 1989).

155 "real Indian country" et seq.: Richard D. Camp, Jr., with Eric Hammel, *Lima-6*, p. 61.

155 "great stuff like concrete": Ibid., p. 63.

157 "resented the prostitution of his talents"; "They must be smoking hashish": William R. Corson, *The Betrayal*, p. 78.

158 "WPA project" et seq.: Ibid. The Work Projects Administration (WPA) was a Depression-era entity that engaged in large-scale public works projects.

159 "Nor was I pleased": William C. Westmoreland, *A Soldier Reports*, p. 204.

162 "Here's a place where children grow up with a war" et seq.: Letter, Frank Iodice–Parent, September 25, 1967. Stubbe Collection.

162 "Thank God for letting me be": Letter, Frank Iodice—Parent, November 9, 1967. Stubbe Collection.

162 "He is what I expected": Letter, Frank Iodice–Parent, September 25, 1967. Stubbe Collection.

163 "when the Air America helicopters came in": James Whitenack interview (Stubbe, October 4, 1988).

165 "NVA soldiers sent to fight": MACV, J-2, Combined Intelligence Center Vietnam, Research and Analysis Study ST67-013, *Update: The NVA Soldier in South Vietnam,* October 31, 1966, p. 34. *Westmoreland vs. CBS* trial documents.

166 "It is usually his first contact": MACV, *Update: The NVA Soldier in South Vietnam,* p. 34.

166 "Living in the jungle": Ibid., p. 36.

167 "The cadre and soldiers": Ibid., p. 34.

168 "the enemy in this Area of Operations": 26th Marine Regiment, "After Action Report, Operation CROCKETT," p. 14. USMC Archives.

170 "there is no other evidence to substantiate": Fleet Marine Force Pacific, Situation Report #998, December 26, 1967, section 6, p. 2. FMFPAC SitRep File. USMC Archives.

170 "extremely exhausted due to hardships": MACV, J-2, CDEC, Bulletin No. 11,439, April 16, 1968 (declassified October 28, 1981). LBJL, LBJP, NSF, CFVN, box 155, folder "Vietnam: Khe Sanh."

174 "hortatory rather than expository": Vo Nguyen Giap, *Big Victory, Great Task,* p. xi. Westmoreland's comment that the series was deception is in his *A Soldier Reports,* p. 313.

175 "the present mobilization level": Vo Nguyen Giap, *Big Victory, Great Task,* p. 90.

175 "The American imperialists are now at a crossroad": Ibid., p. 94.

175 "repeatedly harass the enemy": Ibid., p. 104.

175 "bugle call" . . . "to take advantage": Ibid., p. 105.

175–176 "annihilate a major U.S. element" et seq.: MACV, J-2, CDEC, Full Translation 11-1591-67, "Directives by B-3 [Front]," p. 1. LBJL, LBJP, NSF, CFVN, box 143–157, folder "Press Releases on Captured Documents."

176 "obvious nonsense": Phillip Davidson, *Vietnam at War,* p. 444.

176 "as soon as he is within reach" et seq.: Cable, William Westmoreland–Earle Wheeler (MAC 11956), December 10, 1967 (declassified May 11, 1984), pp. 2, 4. LBJL, Westmoreland Papers, box 15, folder "History File, v. 26."

177 "peripheral strategy" et seq.: MACV, J-2, Intelligence Summary, November 1967, Annex A, (c) Large Scale Significant and Large Scale Attacks (declassified July 25, 1983), p. 12. LBJL, LBJP,

NSF, DSDUF, box 4, folder "Vietnam, b. 69, 2C (3) General Military."

177 "How could you possibly know more": Patrick McGarvey, *CIA: The Myth and the Madness*, p. 128. Also see Patrick McGarvey, "DIA: Intelligence to Please," in Morton Halperin and Arnold Kanter, eds., *Readings in American Foreign Policy*, p. 324.

180 "It seems that the minute we put recon in": Frank M. Tomeo, Marine Debriefing, tape no. 1194.

181–182 "We were humping our backsides off" et seq.: Kevin Macaulay interview (Stubbe, August 29, 1984).

183 "I want to hear those legs thunder" et seq.: Robert E. Pagano interview (Stubbe, October 22, 1988).

183–184 "Recon really doesn't need a corpsman" et seq.: Stubbe Diary, November 29, 1967.

184 "Things aren't looking too good": Ernest Husted Diary, August 3, 1967.

185 "As if in a dream": Ernest Husted, Jr., "The Silent Ambush," p. 59.

187 "We are now having more contact": Stubbe Diary, October 29, 1967.

190 "I have a great bunch of men": Letter, Donald Jacques–Parent, October 25, 1967.

190 "It is one of two extremes": Ibid.

190 "They have a hell of a lot to learn": Letter, Donald Jacques–Parent, December 1, 1967.

190 "We are working hard to get the hill in shape": Letter, Donald Jacques–Parent, November 8, 1967.

190 "The only way I could walk my lines": Letter, Donald Jacques–Parent, November 11, 1967.

191 "Men, we here at Khe Sanh": Stubbe Diary, November 10, 1967.

193 "the article is highly exaggerated" et seq.: William C. Westmoreland, History Notes, December 5, 1967. LBJL, Westmoreland Papers, box 15, folder "History File v. 26."

194 "hold the area hostage": Walt W. Rostow, *The Diffusion of Powers*, p. 513.

196 "the landing would have been the most foolhardy": William Broyles, Jr., *Brothers in Arms*, p. 97.

196 "We have adequately prepared ourselves" et seq.: Gen. Vo Nguyen Giap, *Big Victory, Great Task*, pp. 101–2.

199 "it is also unsound from a military stand point" et seq.: Cable, William Westmoreland–Earle Wheeler (MAC 11956), December 10, 1967 (declassified May 11, 1984). LBJL, Westmoreland Papers, box 15, folder "History File, v. 26."

200   "tied down": Gen. Phillip B. Davidson, *Vietnam at War*, p. 522. General Davidson attributes the argument that Hanoi was attempting a diversion at Khe Sanh to reporters and to "ivory-tower generals," presumably a reference to General David R. Palmer, a former military history instructor at West Point who supported the diversion thesis in his Vietnam history *Summons of the Trumpet*, pp. 227–29, 232–33.

200   "emotional effect": Memorandum, "CIIB Meeting, 9 December 1967" (declassified November 5, 1984), Brigadier General William E. Bryan, Jr., for the Chief of Staff, MACV, Action Memo no. 67-167. (This series of memoranda recorded orders given and important points made at staff conferences Westmoreland regularly held with his senior intelligence and operations officers and top subordinate commanders). LBJL, Westmoreland Papers, box 15, folder "History File v. 26."

201   "one of the nicest guys" et seq.: Phillip Davidson interview (Stubbe, May 6, 1989).

201–202 " 'Back to the airstrip' " et seq.: Letter, Dennis Mannion–Ray Stubbe, May 29, 1984.

202   "In the last analysis": Matthew P. Caulfield, Marine Debriefing, tape no. 6157.

202   "I think all hell is going to break loose": Letter, Kevin Macaulay–Parents, December 1, 1967. Stubbe Collection.

CHAPTER 7. BOXING IN DARKNESS

PAGE

203   "We went several days" et seq.: James E. Schemelia tape, July 1984. Stubbe Collection.

204   "How good do you have to be": Stubbe Diary, December 20, 1967.

205   "I was praying so hard": Letter, Kevin Macaulay–Parents, December 25, 1967. Stubbe Collection.

205   "Merry Christmas! Bah!": Martin Kux Diary, December 25, 1967.

206   "the first time I really got a feeling": James Schemelia tape, July 1984. Stubbe Collection.

206   Christmas at Lima Company: Richard Camp with Eric Hammel, *Lima-6*, pp. 211–12.

206   "We're so trained": Stubbe Diary, December 28, 1967.

208   "I had the unpleasant feeling": Ernest Husted, Jr., "The Looking Glass" (unpublished ms.). Stubbe Collection.

208 "I looked over to the team leader": Husted interview (Stubbe, August 21, 1984).

210 "suggests we should greatly accelerate these efforts" et seq.: Westmoreland Diary, December 16, 1967. LBJL, Westmoreland Papers, box 15, folder "History Notes v. 26."

210 "which we can ill afford" et seq.: Westmoreland Diary, December 25, 1967. Ibid., folder "History Notes v. 27."

211 "clarify the philosophy": Westmoreland Diary, December 26, 1967. Ibid.

211 "I gave some guidance": Westmoreland Diary, December 24, 1967. Ibid.

211–212 "I detect there may be some misunderstanding": Cable, William Westmoreland-U. S. Grant Sharp (MAC 00686), 151214Z, January 1968 (declassified May 9, 1984). Ibid., folder "History File, v. 28."

213 "like Marines": Moyers S. Shore, *The Battle for Khe Sanh*. This is the Marine official monograph on the Khe Sanh battle. In the absence of the long-delayed history volume(s) for the year 1968, it remains the only official Marine commentary on Khe Sanh. The question of the bodies on January 2 is but one example of the many issues a Marine official history would be useful in addressing. Captain Camp writes (p. 228) of pajamas but prints in his own book photographs taken by interrogator Sergeant Max Friedlander (following p. 204) that seem to show the NVA to be uniformed.

215 "I don't recall": Letter, Harper L. Bohr, Jr., December 18, 1968. Khe Sanh Monograph Comments File, USMC Archives.

215 "increasingly solid evidence": Cable, Walt Rostow–Lyndon Johnson (CAP 80119), January 5, 1968 (declassified November 28, 1982). LBJL, LBJP, DSDUF, box 3, folder "Rostow Memos, b. 56."

216 "Preempting a Khe Sanh area assault" et seq.: Cable, William Westmoreland–Earle Wheeler (MAC 00547), January 12, 1968 (declassified September 5, 1984). LBJL, Westmoreland Papers, box 15, folder "History File v. 28."

217 "The odds are 60-40": Cable, William Westmoreland–U.S.G. Sharp (MAC00686), January 15, 1968 (declassified May 9, 1984).

217 "maximum effort ... to insure" et seq.: Message, William Westmoreland–Robert Cushman, 140801Z, January 1968. 3rd Marine Division Files, "Messages, Etc., January 1968," Item #34.

218 "plans for initial support": Message, Rathvon Tompkins–Robert Cushman, 200808Z, January 1968. Ibid., Item #53.

218 "such operations as directed": From the Lang Vei relief plan, 26th Marine Regiment, OPLAN 5-67, September 18, 1967, p. 3. USMC Archives.

222 "After considerable soul searching": Westmoreland Diary, January 18, 1968. LBJL, Westmoreland Papers, box 15, folder "History Notes v. 28."

222 "premium on the need for rapid decision-making" et seq.: Cable, William Westmoreland–U. S. Grant Sharp, cited in William W. Momyer, *Airpower in Three Wars,* p. 309.

224 "I'm sending 2/26 back to you" et seq.: David Lownds, Marine Debriefing, tape no. 3139.

225 "We will hold!" et seq.: Earle Breeding interview (Stubbe, July 18, 1984).

226 "I can still recall the day": Letter, Chuck Hoover–Ray Stubbe, March 23, 1987.

226 "The first time I saw [Khe Sanh]": Daniel Tougas, Marine Debriefing, tape no. 2775.

226 "If we had been hit": William K. Gay, Marine Debriefing, tape no. 3216.

228 "As viewed from the air": Message, Robert Cushman–Rathvon Tompkins, 161200Z, January 1968. III MAF Records, SpeCat, Exclusive Message File, January 1968, item no. 20. USMC Archives.

228 " 'Maybe, maybe not' ": Phillip Davidson interview (Stubbe, April 19, 1989).

228–229 "Abe, you're going to have to go up there" et seq.: Phillip B. Davidson, *Vietnam at War,* p. 556.

229 "There should be discussion": MACV, Chief of Staff Action Memo 68-23, January 20, 1968 (declassified August 11, 1988). This is a CIIB meeting record. LBJL, Westmoreland Papers, box 15, folder "History File v. 28."

230 "kind of anxious to start telling me": Max Friedlander quoted in Eric Hammel, *Khe Sanh,* p. 57.

233 "I didn't think much of it": Robert Brewer interview (John Wright, February 5, 1989).

CHAPTER 8. CONTACT

PAGE

239 "I was busy loading": Letter, Chester W. Wilson–Ray Stubbe, February 26, 1986.

240 "It was like trying to climb back up a mountain": James Schemelia tape, July 1984. Stubbe Collection.

241 "It was right out of the pages of Chesty Puller": Matthew P. Caulfield, Marine Debriefing, tape no. 6157.

242 "I'll never forget standing down by the gate": Ibid.

243–244 Mannion recollections: Letter, Dennis Mannion–Ray Stubbe, May 29, 1984.

244 "It was an unsettling thing": Letter, Dennis Mannion–Ray Stubbe, August 20, 1984.

245 "Oh, this is KWN in Miami": Dennis Mannion interview (Stubbe, August 31, 1986).

245 "It was the heaviest barrage": Michael R. Stahl, Marine Debriefing, tape no. 2776.

245 "Actually we didn't have any support": Michael H. Lyons, Marine Debriefing, tape no. 2776.

246 "a real legend in the battalion": Matthew P. Caulfield, Marine Debriefing, tape no. 6157.

246 "They crept as close to our lines": Jerry N. Saulsberry, Marine Debriefing, tape no. 2776.

246 "You could see hundreds and hundreds of NVA": Michael R. Stahl, Marine Debriefing, tape no. 2776.

247 "Lieutenant, they're shooting at us!" et seq.: Linn Oehling, Marine Debriefing, tape no. 2859.

248 "a real trooper": Michael P. Caulfield, Marine Debriefing, tape no. 6157.

251 "I swear like in slow motion": Letter, David Leverton–Ray Stubbe, May 11, 1985.

251 "That sounds like incoming" et seq.: Tom Quigley interview (Stubbe, May 11, 1986).

251 "The ammo dump is on fire" et seq.: John Seitz tape, December 11, 1985. Stubbe Collection.

252 "Hot rounds were landing in the trenches": Edward I. Prendergast, Jr., unpublished ms., November 1988.

252 "The men: I just can't say enough about them": Kenneth W. Pipes, Marine Debriefing, tape no. 2537.

256 "We changed just enough of our fortifications": Bruce Clark interview (Stubbe, October 15, 1988).

257 "I can't tell you why": Tom Stamper interview (Stubbe, 1969–1970).

257 "It's almost as though they knew": Bruce Clark interview (Stubbe, October 15, 1988).

258–259 "The warning came in over the radio" et seq.: Letter, John R. Roberts–Ray Stubbe, December 27, 1972.

259 "I had told the montagnards": Bruce Clark interview (Stubbe, October 15, 1988).

261 "When Cooper got up": Robert B. Brewer interview (John Wright, February 5, 1989).

262 "I picked up two grenades and clips": *New York Times,* Feb 21, 1971.

263 "After long consideration and proper evaluation": David E. Lownds, Marine Debriefing, tape no. 2621.

263 "It had been a soul-searching night": Letter, John R. Roberts–Ray Stubbe, December 27, 1972.

CHAPTER 9. "KHE SANH ALREADY SHOWS SIGNS OF BATTLE"

PAGE

271 "The Communist forces are prepared to defend": Central Intelligence Agency, Intelligence Memorandum SC 02144-68, "Construction and Logistic Activities in the Khe Sanh Area," February 7, 1968 (declassified July 25, 1985), p. 4. *Westmoreland vs. CBS.*

272 "decision to remain at Lang Vei": Cable, William Sullivan–Dean Rusk, 260811Z, January 1968.

274 "Hey Marine, how's he doing?" et seq.: Kevin Macaulay interview (Stubbe, August 29, 1984).

275 "It started off as a one-battalion show" et seq.: David Lownds, Marine Debriefing, tape no. 3139.

275 "Wars are not won on body count": Ibid.

276 "jerking off the press" et seq.: Michael Herr, *Dispatches,* p. 144.

277 "We got the word mid-morning": Bert Mullins tape, January 8, 1984.

277 "Gunny came down one day": Otis H. Glenn, Marine Debriefing, tape no. 2803.

278 "The new arrivals were so effective": Richard Camp, *Lima-6,* p. 249.

278 "Those first few nights were very hairy": James R. Talone, Marine Debriefing, tape no. 2803.

278–279 "Everything was in short supply": Bert Mullins tape, January 8, 1984.

279 "Skipper, I just heard something" et seq.: William R. Dabney interview (USMC, May 20, 1982).

281 "We had no idea what was out there": William M. Smith interview (Stubbe, March 16, 1985).

282 "quickly gained a high regard": Letter, Maj. Kenneth W. Pipes, undated. Khe Sanh Monograph Comments File, USMC Archives.

282–283 "Food got scarce": Letter, Ray Strischek–Ray Stubbe, March 4, 1986.

283 "It was a privilege": Letter, Maj. Kenneth W. Pipes, undated. Khe Sanh Monograph Comments File, USMC Archives.

285 "non-military quarters": Cable, Earle Wheeler–William Westmoreland (JCS 00343), January 11, 1968 (declassified July 29, 1983).

285 "I regard the non-military expressions": Cable, William Westmoreland–Earle Wheeler (MAC 00547), January 12, 1968 (declassified September 5, 1984). LBJL, Westmoreland Papers, box 15, folder "History File v. 28."

285 "The anticipated enemy attack": Cable, William Westmoreland–Earle Wheeler (MAC 01049), January 22, 1968 (declassified November 30, 1983). LBJL, LBJP, NSF, NSC Histories, box 47, folder "March 31 Speech, v. 2."

285–286 "He has made determined attempts" et seq.: Cable, William Westmoreland–Earle Wheeler (MAC 00967), Eyes Only, January 22, 1968 (declassified December 16, 1983). Ibid.

286 "The enemy is attempting to confuse": Statement by General William C. Westmoreland, January 31, 1968. LBJL, Westmoreland Papers, box 16, folder "History Notes v. 29 [I]."

289 "I don't want any damn Dinbinphoo": Hugh Sidey, "The Presidency: A Long Way from Spring," *Time*, February 9, 1968, p. 16. It is this column also that first asserted the claim that Lyndon Johnson had "made" each of the Joint Chiefs sign a promise that Khe Sanh would be defended.

289–290 "The Situation at Khe Sanh" et seq.: Memorandum, Earle Wheeler–Lyndon Johnson (JCSM 63-68), January 29, 1968 (declassified March 29, 1979). LBJL, LBJP, NSF, NSC Histories, box 47.

290 "orders of magnitude" et seq.: Memorandum, Earle Wheeler–Lyndon Johnson (CM 2944-68), February 3, 1968 (declassified March 16, 1979). LBJL, LBJP, NSF, NSC Histories, box 47, folder "March 31 Speech, v. 6."

291 "a considerable amount of discussion around town" et seq.: Cable, Earle Wheeler–William Westmoreland (JCS 01154), February 1, 1968 (declassified March 29, 1979). LBJL, LBJP, NSF, NSC Histories, box 47, folder "March 31 Speech, v. 2, Tabs A-Z & AA-ZZ."

291 "use of nuclear weapons": Wheeler memo, CM 2944-68. Ibid. This Wheeler memo reports Westmoreland's view stated in a telephone conversation.

292 "virtually uninhabited" and "surely": William C. Westmoreland, *A Soldier Reports*, p. 338. Westmoreland's comment to Herbert Y. Schandler that appears further down on page 292 is cited

in Schandler, *The Unmaking of a President* (Princeton: Princeton University Press, 1977), p. 90.

292 "The President must make the decision" et seq.: Johnson's news conference of February 16, 1968, in *Public Papers of the President: Lyndon Johnson, 1968* (Washington: Government Printing Office, 1970), vol. 1, p. 234.

294 "As we wait for some word": Memorandum, Robert Ginsburgh–Lyndon Johnson, February 4, 1968 (8:25 P.M.). LBJL, LBJP, NSF, NSC Histories, box 4, folder "March 31 Speech v. 2, Tabs A-Z and AA-ZZ."

295 "We might expect the battle for Khe Sanh": Memorandum, Ginsburgh–Lyndon Johnson, February 4, 1968, Ibid.

295 "to prompt me to consider resigning": William C. Westmoreland, *A Soldier Reports,* p. 344.

296 "Needless to say, I raised hell" et seq.: Westmoreland Diary, January 23, 1968. LBJL, Westmoreland Papers, box 16, folder "History Notes v. 29 [I]."

299 "I reported to him": William Westmoreland, Memorandum for the Record, June 21, 1968. LBJL, Westmoreland Papers, box 15, folder "History File v. 28."

299 "They went in there with A-4s": Larry Henderson interview (Stubbe, March 10, 1990).

299 "may have been replacements for staff members": Fonecon, 1855H, February 8, 1968. LBJL, Westmoreland Papers, box 31, folder "Fonecons, February 1968."

302 "a definite pattern" and "Preceding each assault": Moyers S. Shore II, *The Battle for Khe Sanh,* draft manuscript, p. 86.

302 "Dave Lownds gets immediate readout": Kenneth J. Houghton, Marine Debriefing, tape no. 2528.

303 "We have cases where they've put one up": Franklin W. Pippin, Marine Debriefing, tape no. 2907.

305–306 "I remember saying to myself" et seq.: Tape, Larry E. Jackson, November 16, 1984.

306 "when my bad dreams started": Ibid.

306–307 "All I heard was one shot": Eugene J. Franklin, Marine Debriefing, tape no. 2775.

307 "We went over there": Newton D. Lyle, Marine Debriefing, tape no. 2775.

307–308 "Making my way down" and "I was in the process": Letter, Tom Eichler–Ray Stubbe, September 3, 1986.

309 "The M-16 didn't come into play": Earle Breeding, Marine Debriefing, tape no. 2621.

309 Suspicious of Chinese in 861-A attack: Earle Breeding interview (Stubbe, May 29, 1985).

CHAPTER 10. THE FALL OF LANG VEI

PAGE

312 "Man, we're in trouble": Zalin Grant, *Survivors,* p. 192. This source contains Young's version of the Lang Bu patrol.

313 Craig's version of Lang Bu patrol: Bill Craig interview (Stubbe, October 4, 1988).

313 "The North Vietnamese wouldn't hit": Ibid., p. 189.

314 "strongholds": MACV, J-2, CDEC, Bulletin 11,839, April 27, 1968 (declassified October 28, 1981). LBJL, LBJP, NSF, CFVN, box 155, folder "Vietnam: Khe Sanh."

318 "beaucoup VC": Peter Tiroch Statement, 5th Special Forces Group After Action Report, "Battle of Lang Vei," February 22, 1968. U.S. Army, Military History Institute, Carlisle Barracks, PA.

322 "Tanks in the wire": John A. Cash, "The Battle of Lang Vei," quoted in John Albright et al., *Seven Firefights in Vietnam,* p. 120.

322 "was practically on top of us": Daniel Schungel Statement, 5th Special Forces Group After Action Report, "Battle of Lang Vei," February 22, 1968. U.S. Army, Military History Institute, Carlisle Barracks, PA.

324 "CIDG! CIDG!": Cash, "The Battle of Lang Vei," p. 124.

326 "armor in the wire" et seq.: John Early, "Armor in the Wire!" p. 74.

326 "I've got a tank sitting on top of my bunker": Warren A. Trest, "Khe Sanh (Operation NIAGARA) 22 January–31 March 1968," Headquarters, Pacific Air Force, Tactical Evaluation Directorate, Project CHECO, DOTEC 68-50, p. 31.

328 "the numbers suggest why our military are confident": Memorandum, Walt Rostow–Lyndon Johnson, February 5, 1968 (8:50 A.M.). LBJL, LBJP, NSF, NSC Histories, box 47, folder "March 31 Speech, v. 2."

328 "We have just received information": McCafferty, Situation Room Memorandum, February 6, 1968 (2:55 P.M.) (declassified August 29, 1980). Ibid., folder "March 31 Speech, v. 2. Tabs A-Z and AA-ZZ." We are unable to establish why the report to the president erroneously referred to Lang Vei's defenders as Vietnamese (ARVN) troops.

329 "a Special Forces–Green Beret Camp" et seq.: Note, Bromley Smith–Lyndon Johnson, February 6, 1968 (8:30 P.M.), with enclosure (declassified August 29, 1980). Ibid. Italics in the original.

329–330 "have not yet been accounted for" et seq.: Central Intelligence Agency, Intelligence Memorandum SC 07681/68, "Spot Report on the Situation in the Khe Sanh Area," February 7, 1968 (declassified September 3, 1986). Ibid., box 48, folder "March 31 Speech, v. 5."

330 "Neither had entered the camp-site": Ibid.

331–332 Rathvon McC. Tompkins, USMC Oral History, April 13, 1973.

332 "historic meeting" and "absence of initiative": Westmoreland Diary, February 7, 1968. LBJL, Westmoreland Papers, box 16, folder "History File v. 29 [I]."

333 "Give him the helicopters" et seq.: Daniel L. Baldwin interview (Stubbe, September 8, 1990).

333 "I decided that the Special Forces would conduct a raid": Westmoreland Diary, February 7, 1968. Westmoreland Papers, box 16, folder "History File v. 29 [I]."

336 "So I'm the first one out": Paul Longgrear interview, (Stubbe, January 7, 1989).

338 "must consider South Vietnamese as enemy": Warren A. Trest, "Khe Sanh (Operation NIAGARA)," p. 41 (see note to p. 326).

339 "may be forced by tactical considerations": Fonecon, William Westmoreland–Robert Cushman, 2125H, February 7, 1968. LBJL, Westmoreland Papers, box 31, folder "Fonecons, February 1968."

339 "until such time as verification": Message, Robert Cushman–Victor Krulak, 091218Z, February 1968, in III MAF Outgoing SpeCat Exclusive File, 4 February–1 March 1968, Item #15. USMC Archives.

340 "We have a problem with refugees" et seq.: William Westmoreland, Memorandum for the Record, June 21, 1968 (declassified January 29, 1990). LBJL, Westmoreland Papers, box 16, folder "History File v. 29 [I]."

340 "This is a sticky one": *Boston Globe*, February 22, 1968, pp. 32–33.

341 "We stabbed them in the back": Frank Iodice interview (Stubbe, May 18, 1986).

341 "an important position of the U.S. aggressors": Special Communiqué, South Vietnam Liberation Radio, 0501 GMT, February 7, 1968. BBC, Summary of World Broadcasts, Pt. 3, Far East, no. 2690, February 9, 1968, p. 10.

342 "a first-rate annihilation battle": *Quan Doi Nhan Dan* Commentary, "Lang Vei Proves Futility of All U.S. Efforts," Radio Hanoi, VNA, International Service in English, 1658 GMT, February 8, 1968. Foreign Broadcast Information Service, Daily Report, Asia and the Pacific, February 9, 1968, p. JJJ2.

342 "The Lang Vei victory": *Quan Doi Nhan Dan*, February 8, 1968.

Hanoi Domestic Service in Vietnamese, 0430 GMT, February 8, 1968. Ibid., p. JJJ3.

342 "liberated Lang Vay" et seq.: MACV, J-2, CDEC, Bulletin 11,357, April 13, 1968 (declassified October 28, 1981). LBJL, LBJP, NSF, CFVN, box 155, folder "Vietnam: Khe Sanh."

CHAPTER 11. THE KHE SANH SHUFFLE

PAGE

345 "the corpsmen started giving classes": Letter, Edward W. Welchel–Ray Stubbe, March 17, 1987.

345 "I was finally rewarded": Lawrence J. Seavy–Cioffi, "Our Victory for Alpha One," p. 9.

345 "because my bunker was the first": Letter, Welchel–Ray Stubbe, March 17, 1987.

346 "This is the CP radio operator" et seq.: Lawrence J. Seavy-Cioffi, "Our Victory for Alpha One," pp. 23–25.

349 "It was quite a scene": Larry L. Powell, Marine Debriefing, tape no. 2803.

349 "this map showed": Patrick J. Fitch, Marine Debriefing, tape no. 2398.

349 "The enemy penetrated the wire": Text of William Westmoreland cable, retyped and appended to Memorandum, Walt Rostow–Lyndon Johnson, February 8, 1968. LBJL, LBJP, NSF, NSC Histories, box 49, folder "March 31 Speech, v. 6: Khe Sanh Reports A-S."

349 "The state of mind at that time": Westmoreland Diary, February 11, 1968 (declassified January 26, 1990). LBJL, Westmoreland Papers, box 16, folder "History File, v. 29 [I]."

350 "so well was it recognized": "A Summary of Sieges," n.d. (presented on February 11, 1968). LBJL, Westmoreland Papers, box 16, folder "History File v. 30 [II]."

350 "It appears that Khe Sanh is following" et seq.: Reamer W. Argo, "Analysis of the Khe Sanh Situation in Light of Previous Sieges," March 3, 1968 (declassified July 5, 1984). Ibid.

351 "the whole presentation was frought with gloom": Westmoreland Diary, February 11, 1968 (declassified January 26, 1990). LBJL, Westmoreland Papers, box 16, folder "History File, v. 29 [I]."

351 "made it unequivocally clear": Ibid.

351 "We are not, repeat not": William C. Westmoreland, *A Soldier Reports*, p. 338.

351 "literally eyes only": Cable, Lyndon Johnson–William West-

moreland (CAP 80390), February 5, 1968 (declassified July 22, 1988). LBJL, Westmoreland Papers, box 16, folder "History File, v. 29 [I]."

352 "a major offensive is imminent": Retyped text of William Westmoreland cable, February 8, 1968 (declassified December 16, 1983). LBJL, LBJP, NSF, NSC Histories, box 47, folder "March 31 Speech, v. 2, Tabs A-Z and AA-ZZ." The Saigon date of this cable was February 9.

353 "an enemy threat of major proportions" et seq.: Cable, William Westmoreland–Earle Wheeler (MAC 01858), Eyes Only, February 9, 1968 (declassified July 22, 1988). Westmoreland Papers, Ibid. Local Saigon date of this cable was February 10.

353 "a letter saying they were ready": Notes of the President's Discussion with Correspondents, February 2, 1968 (declassified November 14, 1984). LBJL, LBJP, Tom Johnson's Notes of Meetings, box 2, folder "February 2, 1968 — 4:30 P.M." See the note on Tom Johnson's methods in connection with his February 7 NSC minutes (note to p. 355).

354 "Khe Sanh obsession": Clark Clifford with Richard Holbrooke *Counsel to the President,* p. 477; compare p. 469.

354 "increasingly . . . cites the authority of Westmoreland": Marquis Childs, "On Westmoreland, Generals, and War," *Washington Post,* February 7, 1968.

355 "How do things look" et seq.: "Notes of the President's Meeting with the National Security Council," February 7, 1968 (declassified August 14, 1985). LBJL, LBJP, Tom Johnson's Notes of Meetings, box 2, folder "February 7, 1968 — 12:29 P.M." A young man who had impressed Lyndon Johnson and had then been snapped up for the White House staff, in much the same fashion LBJ had once hired Bill Moyers, Tom Johnson became entirely consumed by his function of taking notes at meetings the president held. Johnson lacked experience, knew no shorthand, and yet had to take notes by hand; for these reasons he himself has always warned that this series of meeting notes is incomplete and not entirely accurate. However, Johnson's notes arguably capture the flavor of meetings, including many direct quotes. In instances where other official records exist that cover the same material as the Johnson notes, these have been shown to be largely accurate after all. Moreover, when compared to NSC summaries of discussions for the Johnson and Eisenhower administrations, the Johnson method of notetaking conveys an immediacy that is invaluable. For these reasons, the Tom Johnson notes are used as is in this narrative. The reader should be aware, however, that

words, sentences, and perhaps more may be missing from the discussions as recorded. Nevertheless the notes remain as the sole official record of these particular meetings.

355–356 "make the preparations now" et seq.: "Notes of the President's Meeting with Foreign Policy Advisers," February 9, 1968 (declassified July 7, 1980 and October 19, 1979). LBJL, LBJP, NSF, NSC Histories, box 49, folder "March 31 Speech, v. 7, Meeting Notes."

357 "Questions Related to the Military Situation in Vietnam" et seq.: Memorandum, Maxwell Taylor–Lyndon Johnson, February 8, 1968 (declassified October 19, 1979). Ibid.

358 "strategic guidance . . . in broad terms" et seq.: Memorandum, Maxwell Taylor–Lyndon Johnson, February 10, 1968 (declassified March 19, 1979). Ibid., folder "March 31 Speech, v. 8, Excerpts and Taylor Memos."

359 "that Priority 1 should be to" et seq.: Cable, Earle Wheeler–William Westmoreland (JCS 01695), February 12, 1968 (declassified July 22, 1988). LBJL, Westmoreland Papers, box 16, folder "History File v. 29 [I]."

359 "general erosion" et seq.: Cable, William Westmoreland–U. S. Grant Sharp/Earle Wheeler (MAC 01975), February 12, 1968 (declassified July 22, 1988). Ibid.

359 "playing coy": Phillip B. Davidson, *Vietnam at War,* p. 496. Davidson's purpose here seems to be to suggest that a panicked Washington was pushing Westmoreland to request immediate reinforcements, while a confident Westmoreland wished to delay pending availability of logistics support, thus annoying Wheeler, who was pursuing a private agenda of inducing LBJ to call out the reserves and enable the Army to refit the U.S. strategic reserve. This does not square with the actual cable traffic and declassified documentation of the period. The cables clearly show that General Wheeler wished to *separate* action on reinforcements required to meet the current crisis from that on the larger reinforcement program. On February 9 Wheeler specifically instructed Westmoreland (cable JCS 01589) by the back channel to *delay* his front-channel submission of supplementary troop requests for the coming year. Westmoreland agreed (MAC 01849) the same day. This exchange took place at precisely the moment we are asked to believe that Washington was trying to stampede MACV into urgent requests. With respect to the troops requested to respond to the crisis, the NSC meeting notes show conclusively President Johnson's entire support for MACV. Westmoreland informed Wheeler on the telephone on February 11 (recorded in CM 3003-68) that he *did* have the spare logistic capacity to support the forces he was requesting.

The reasons for whatever degree of urgency may have been reflected in MACV's actual troop requests must be sought elsewhere.

360 "it is hard to believe" et seq.: Memorandum, Maxwell Taylor–Lyndon Johnson, February 12, 1968 (declassified March 19, 1979). LBJL, LBJP, NSF, NSC Histories, box 49, folder "March 31 Speech, v. 8, Excerpts and Taylor Memos."

361 "As to holding Khe Sanh" et seq.: Memorandum, Earle Wheeler–Lyndon Johnson (CM 3003-68), February 12, 1968 (declassified March 29, 1979). Ibid., box 48, folder "March 31 Speech, v. 2, Tabs A-Z."

361 "I think one time": Westmoreland interview (Stubbe, June 2, 1989). The only presidential conversation and Wheeler telephone call to which Westmoreland refers in his memoirs concerns the potential use of nuclear weapons at Khe Sanh.

361 "that the memo requires any significant change": Postscript to Maxwell Taylor February 12, 1968, memorandum, cited on p. 360.

361 "General Taylor again raised": Memorandum, Walt Rostow–Lyndon Johnson, Eyes Only, February 13, 1968 (declassified August 29, 1980). LBJL, LBJP, NSF, NSC Histories, box 48, folder "March 31 Speech, v. 2., Tabs A-Z." Rostow reported that Max Taylor was *not* recommending that Westmoreland be *instructed* to withdraw. Note also that the direction "west" is mistaken: the coastal cities lay to the *east* of Khe Sanh and Taylor was also arguing that they be defended from a point farther to the east.

361–363 "I know that Khe Sanh is very much on your mind" et seq.: Memorandum, Maxwell Taylor–Lyndon Johnson, February 14, 1968 (declassified March 19, 1979). LBJL, LBJP, NSF, NSC Histories, box 49, folder "Excerpts and Taylor Memos."

365 "President Johnson came to appreciate": Dino A. Brugioni, "The President, Khe Sanh, and the 26th Marines," p. 24.

365–366 "a special report completely off-cycle" et seq.: Draft letter, William Westmoreland–U. S. Grant Sharp/Earl Wheeler, n.d. (a marginal note indicates that Westmoreland relayed the essence of the complaint to General Wheeler on the telephone on February 13). LBJL, Westmoreland Papers, box 16, folder "History File v. 29 [I]."

366 "This is the paper": Memorandum, Walt Rostow–Robert McNamara, February 14, 1968. LBJL, LBJP, NSF, NSC Histories, box 48, folder "March 31 Speech, v. 2, Tabs AA-W."

366 "civilian armed-chair strategists" and "the President has full confidence": Memo for the Record, William C. Westmoreland, "President's Position on Khe Sanh," February 16, 1968 (declassified

November 12, 1990). LBJL, Westmoreland Papers, box 16, folder "History File v. 29 [II]."

367   "If I had to select a man" et seq.: *Public Papers of the President: Lyndon Johnson,* (Washington: Government Printing Office, 1970), vol. 1, pp. 233–34.

367   "Westy could not have had": Robert N. Ginsburgh interview (Prados, October 27, 1989).

367   "There are no advantages": Cable, William Westmoreland–Earle Wheeler (MAC 02954), March 2, 1968 (declassified October 19, 1979). LBJL, LBJP, NSF, NSC Histories, box 48, folder "March 31 Speech, v. 4, Tabs C-M."

368   "Redeployment of the troops": Attachment to Memorandum, Walt Rostow–John Walsh, March 22, 1968. LBJL, LBJP, NSF, NSC Histories, box 49, folder "March 31 Speech, v. 7, Meeting Notes." As Maxwell Taylor summed up his efforts for Herbert Schandler, "I tried rather feebly to make the point that Khe Sanh was only an outpost, and no one should expect an outpost to be a Verdun" (Schandler, *The Unmaking of a President,* p. 91).

369   "Dunno *what* happened there": Martin Kux Diary, February 8, 1968. Italics in the original.

369   "We are concerned about stepped up MiG activity" et seq.: Tom Johnson, February 7 Meeting Notes (see note to p. 355).

369   "Hanoi, in anticipation of cessation": Cable, William Sullivan–Dean Rusk (Vientiane 4398), February 7, 1968 (declassified March 29, 1979). LBJL, LBJP, NSF, NSC Histories, box 47, folder "March 31 Speech, v. 2, Tabs A-Z and AA-ZZ."

370   "Have you anticipated" et seq.: Tom Johnson, February 9 Meeting Notes (see note to p. 355).

370   "These bomber reports were a one-day wonder" et seq.: Peter Braestrup, *Big Story,* pp. 316–17.

371   "None of these people": John Havlik, Marine Debriefing, tape no. 3298.

371–372 "I didn't feel like standing out there": Edward E. Brown, Marine Debriefing, tape no. 2936.

372   "We had just landed": "Khe Sanh Aviators Tell Tales," *Sea Tiger,* February 16, 1968, p. 10. (*Sea Tiger* was the Vietnam-era newsletter of the 3rd Marine Division.)

372   "We got off the plane": T. M. Kane, Marine Debriefing, tape no. 2840.

372   "If all three worked": John Havlik, Marine Debriefing, tape no. 3298.

374   "A three-engine take-off": Philip D. Chinnery, *Life on the Line,* p. 114.

375   "because it was one in which I did not get a single hit": Ibid.

380   "When the dense monsoon clouds": Letter, Col. Franklin E. Wilson, January 6, 1969. Khe Sanh Monograph Comments File, USMC Archives.

381   "It became alarmingly apparent": Arthur C. Crane, Marine Debriefing, tape no. 3294.

382   "I think the record's going to show": William A. McGaw, Marine Debriefing, tape no. 3293.

383   "wonder what I want you to do": Fonecon, William Momyer–William Westmoreland, 1755H, February 17, 1968. LBJL: Westmoreland Papers, b. 31, f. "Fonecons February 1968."

384   "Had [a] good session" et seq.: Fonecon, William Momyer–William Westmoreland, 2000H, February 20, 1968. Ibid.

384   "special category, exclusive" et seq.: Message, Robert Cushman–William Westmoreland, 201416Z, February 1968 (declassified May 9, 1984). LBJL, Westmoreland Papers, box 16, folder "History File v. 19 [II]."

385   "expand his perspective" et seq.: Fonecon, William Momyer–William Westmoreland, 1050H, February 21, 1968. LBJL, Westmoreland Papers, box 31, folder "Fonecons February 1968."

385   "I am even more prone than ever": Cable, William Westmoreland–Earle Wheeler (MAC 02674), February 25, 1968 (declassified January 29, 1990). LBJL, Westmoreland Papers, box 16, folder "History File v. 29 [II]."

385   "haggling" et seq.: Fonecon, William Westmoreland–William Momyer, 1758H, February 27, 1968. LBJL, Westmoreland Papers, box 31, folder "Fonecons February 1968."

389   "Pointing toward 881 North": Letter, James Payne–Ray Stubbe, December 30, 1988.

390   "guilty of minor exaggeration": Message, Victor Krulak–Leonard Chapman, 220314Z, February 1968. File "HQMC Supply Situation Khe Sanh," USMC Archives.

391-392 "I could not believe what I saw" et seq.: Letter, Dennis Mannion–Ray Stubbe, August 27, 1985.

392   "it was quiet, just like a church mouse": William Dabney interview (USMC, May 20, 1982).

393   "main ground contest": Message, Robert Cushman–David Lownds, 080112Z, February 1968. III MAF SpeCat/Exclusive File (Outgoing), 4 February–1 March, item #5. USMC Archives.

CHAPTER 12. NO PLACE TO GO

PAGE

395   "shown . . . the aggressors that they cannot avoid": *Nhan Dan,* February 17, 1968.

359 "to the frog who wished to become": *Quan Doi Nhan Dan,* February 26, 1968.

397 "We watched with some fascination": Letter, Brigadier General Robert P. Keller, Khe Sanh Monograph Comments File, USMC Archives.

399 "In hindsight, that patrol should have been": James B. Wilkinson interview (John Wright, July 14, 1989).

400 "We're just sitting here": Letter, Donald Jacques–Jeanne, Bob, and Billy [Jacques], February 24, 1968.

400 "The days go by": Letter, Donald Jacques–Parents, February 24, 1968.

401 "Everybody was in a surprisingly good mood": Gilbert Wall interview (Stubbe, August 26, 1988).

402 "I remember the word was passed back": Calvin E. Bright interview (Stubbe, August 1, 1988).

403 "The screaming and shouting was so loud": Gilbert Wall interview (Stubbe, August 26, 1988).

404 "a very tenuous position": James B. Wilkinson interview (John Wright, July 14, 1989).

404 "Everybody was at a loss": Bill Smith interview (Stubbe, March 16, 1985).

405 "a mid-morning patrol": Cable, Walt Rostow–Lyndon Johnson (CAP 80577), February 26, 1968 (declassified June 25, 1979). LBJL, LBJP, NSF, NSC Histories, box 49, folder "March 31 Speech, v. 6, Khe Sanh Reports, T-Z & AA-QQ."

405 "two U.S. companies made a desperate sortie": Radio Hanoi in English, 0213 GMT, March 14, 1968. BBC Summary of World Broadcasts, Pt. 3, Far East, no. 2721, section A-3, p. 1.

405 "This whole damn war": Letter, Jeff Culpepper–Mrs. Madalyn Culpepper, March 18, 1968. Stubbe Collection.

406 "One day they were trying to interrogate me": Ronald Ridgway interview (Stubbe, February 21, 1989). Ridgway is the first to dismiss the potential impact of the false intelligence he fed the North Vietnamese. Told, "Ron, you may have saved us!" he replied, "Oh no, I really don't think so."

407 "We reacted to every movement": William Dabney interview (USMC, May 20, 1982).

407 "We got in word that B-52s were going to attack": James Schemelia tape, July 1984. Stubbe Collection.

407 "personal previous reconnaissance" et seq.: United States Congress, *Hearings: Investigation into Electronic Battlefield Program,* p. 87.

409 "this might well be the main attack": David Lownds, Marine Debriefing, tape no. 3139.

409 "This was the only time": Ibid.
410 "One day a[n] NVA message": Harve Saal interview (Stubbe, May 20, 1989).
411 "slackening . . . paralleling enemy ground activity": Cable, Walt Rostow–Lyndon Johnson (CAP 80629), March 2, 1968 (declassified June 25, 1979). LBJL, LBJP, NSF, NSC Histories, box 49, folder "March 31 Speech, v. 6, Khe Sanh Reports, T-Z & AA-QQ."
411 "for the second successive day": Message, White House Situation Room (Hayden)–Lyndon Johnson (CAP 80639), March 3, 1968 (declassified June 25, 1979). Ibid.
412 "they were discovered": MACV, J-2, CDEC, Bulletin 11,456, April 16, 1968 (declassified October 28, 1981). LBJL, LBJP, NSF, CFVN, box 155, folder "Vietnam: Khe Sanh."
412 "very close to Khe Sanh": MACV, J-2, CDEC, "Infiltrator's Notebook" (Document Log no. 04-2278-68), April 21, 1968 (declassified October 28, 1981). Ibid.
412 "Fifteen days after the siege began": MACV, J-2, CDEC, Bulletin 11,439, April 16, 1968 (declassified October 28, 1981). Ibid.
413 "*extremely fragile*" and "I would *not* yet draw": Memorandum Walt Rostow–Lyndon Johnson, March 6, 1968 (11:50 A.M.) (declassified September 29, 1984). LBJL, LBJP, NSF, NSC Histories, box 48, folder "March 31 Speech, v. 4, Tabs C-M." Italics in the original.
413 "if Phase I failed": Memorandum, "The Enemy Offensive," March 6, 1968. Ibid., folder "March 31 Speech, v. 4., Tabs N-KK." This paper was most likely prepared by Robert Ginsburgh.
414 "perhaps as many as 20,000": Central Intelligence Agency, "The Continuing Communist Military Threat in Northern South Vietnam" (SC 01936/68), March 13, 1968 (declassified September 18, 1984). Ibid.
414 "put out of action" et seq.: *Vietnam Courier*, March 25, 1968, p. 1. The *Vietnam Courier* was Hanoi's official foreign-language newspaper, published weekly in English, French, and other languages.
415 "If my men hold on": *Vietnam Courier*, April 1, 1968, p. 6.
415 "holding firm the initiative": Radio Hanoi in English, 1541 GMT, March 21, 1968. BBC Summary of World Broadcasts, Pt. 3, Far East, no. 2728, section A-3, p. 2.
416 "of course, we will probably never know": Cable, Creighton Abrams–Earle Wheeler (MAC 04339), Eyes Only, March 31, 1968 (declassified August 21, 1981). LBJL, LBJP, NSF, NSC His-

tories, box 48, folder "March 31 Speech, v. 4, Tabs LL-ZZ & A-K."

416 "At Khe Sanh on 23 March": MACV, J-2, CDEC, Bulletin 11,357, April 11, 1968 (declassified October 28, 1981). LBJL, LBJP, NSF, CFVN, box 155, folder "Vietnam: Khe Sanh."

CHAPTER 13. THE WINGED HORSE

PAGE

418 "would be difficult to conclude successfully": Message, Robert Cushman–William Westmoreland, 120954Z, March 1968 (declassified May 9, 1984), p. 5. LBJL, Westmoreland Papers, box 16, folder "History File v. 30 [I]."

420 "with the extensive resources": Message, Robert Cushman–Westmoreland, 290448Z, March 1968 (declassified September 11, 1984). Ibid., folder "History File v. 30 [II]."

420 "The plan is a feasible one": Westmoreland Diary, March 30, 1968. Ibid., folder "History Notes v. 30 [I]."

421–422 "it was in their interest" et seq.: Message, Robert Cushman–William Rosson, 310305Z, March 1968 (declassified September 11, 1984). Ibid., folder "History File v. 30 [II]."

422 "our most significant forthcoming operation": Ibid.

422 "I must mention the element of surprise" et seq.: John J. Tolson, *Airmobility, 1961–1971*, pp. 172–73.

423 "Regiment was talking about it" et seq.: Bill Smith interview (Stubbe, March 16, 1985).

425 "Everything looked like it should be": Ted Golab interview (Stubbe, April 22, 1986).

426–427 "You could tell where there was foundations" et seq.: Larry Payne interview (Stubbe, September 17, 1988).

428 "One thing that amazed me": Richard J. Wheeler, Marine Debriefing, tape no. 2756.

429 "The terrain on PEGASUS": Wayne T. Haaland, Marine Debriefing, tape no. 3949.

431–432 "The NVA here are dangerous": Eric Hammel, *Khe Sanh*, p. 419.

437 "It would be beneficial": Message, William Westmoreland–Robert Cushman, March 30, 1968 (declassified July 5, 1984). LBJL, Westmoreland Papers, box 16, folder "History Notes v. 30 [II]."

438 "Shortly after dark, we could see headlights": Matthew J. Brennan, ed., *Headhunters*, p. 218.

438 "To me, being a young guy": Ivan Prashker, *Duty, Honor, Vietnam*, p. 143.

439 "In reality the NVA broke the siege": Richard D. Camp, Jr., with Eric Hammel, *Lima-6*, p. 283.

440 "Without warning": Tolson, *Airmobility,* p. 178.

441 "Erections Are Our Business!": Stubbe Diary, April 12, 1968.

441 "after the battle" and "like a graveyard": III MAF News Release 1246–68, reprinted in *Sea Tiger,* May 10, 1968, p. 3.

445 "The only choice for Charlie Company": David O. Carter, Marine Debriefing, tape no. 3950.

449 "Despite overwhelming odds": Presidential Unit Citation to 26th Marines (Reinforced), May 23, 1968. Quoted by Moyers S. Shore II, *The Battle for Khe Sanh,* back cover.

CHAPTER 14. THEN IS NOW

PAGE

451 "Khe Sanh appears to have served": Memorandum for the Record, 583rd Meeting of the National Security Council, April 4, 1968 (declassified July 8, 1980). LBJL, LBJP, NSF, NSC Histories, box 49, folder "March 31st Speech, v. 7, Meeting Notes."

451 of all his decisions Westmoreland is proudest: Laura Palmer, "The General at Ease," p. 33.

Bibliography

DOCUMENTARY COLLECTIONS

· *U.S. Marine Corps Records*

These include casualty cards on Marines killed in action; presidential unit citation files; awards recommendations files; Operation HOMECOMING and related debriefing files for certain individuals; end of mission debriefings (as noted under "Interviews and Oral Histories"); files of comments, correspondence, and other materials related to the Khe Sanh monograph by Capt. Moyers S. Shore II; miscellaneous messages, situation reports, and monthly operations files for Fleet Marine Force Pacific; command center, miscellaneous message, personal message, eyes only message, COC Journal, and other selected files for III MAF; command center, COC Journal, operational situation report files plus special intelligence studies for 3rd Marine Division; command center and other selected files for 1st Marine Air Wing, 1st Marine Regiment, 3rd Marine Regiment, 4th Marine Regiment, 9th Marine Regiment, 11th Engineer Battalion, 13th Marine Regiment, 26th Marine Regiment, Marine Medium Helicopter Squadron 262, Task Force Hotel, and subordinate units. Some of these records were collected at the time by the authors but most were consulted at the Library or Reference Section of the Historical Division, Headquarters, Marine Corps.

· *U.S. Army Records*

These include after-action reports and periodic summary reports from 5th Special Forces Group; after-action reports from 1st Cavalry Division (Airmobile); message traffic, some memoranda, command history excerpts, XXIV Corps histories, ARVN documents, and the Khe Sanh combat analysis by MACV. These materials were accessed through the Freedom of Information Act at the Center for Military History and at the National Archives.

· *U.S. Air Force Records*

These include summary histories for relevant periods from the 3rd Air Division, 504th Tactical Air Support Group, 12th Tactical

Fighter Wing (557th TFS), and 834th Air Division; reports from the Project CHECO series from the Pacific Air Force; and the unit history for Task Force Alpha at Nakhon Phanom Royal Thai Air Force Base. These materials were obtained directly from the Air Force at Bolling Air Force Base, Washington, D.C.

• *U.S. Navy Records*

These include end of deployment reports, annual operations reports, monthly reports, news releases, and yearbooks for Naval Mobile Construction Battalion 10 and Construction Battalion Maintenance Unit 301. These materials were collected at the time or subsequently from veterans of these units or were requested from the Navy.

• *Department of Defense Records*

These include memoranda by the assistant secretary of defense for international security affairs along with intelligence bulletins and excerpts from daily intelligence summaries from the Defense Intelligence Agency. These were accessed through the Declassified Documents Reference System and directly through the Freedom of Information Act.

• *Lyndon Baines Johnson Library Presidential Records*

These include a wide variety of declassified documents originating in the White House and all other parts of government including the Central Intelligence Agency, the Department of Defense, Joint Chiefs of Staff, MACV, the Army, and the National Security Council. The locus of these records at the LBJ Library lies in the collections called National Security File, Agency File; National Security File, Country File, Vietnam; National Security File, NSAMs File; National Security File, NSC Meetings File; National Security File, NSC Histories, March 31st Speech File; Meeting Notes File; and the Tom Johnson Notes of Meetings Series. Also at the LBJ Library are the papers of William C. Westmoreland from which we used materials from the History File; the Fonecons Series and the Eyes Only Message series. These records were consulted at the LBJ Library.

• *Trial Documents, Westmoreland vs. CBS* (1982)

These include a variety of declassified documents originating with the CIA, the Department of Defense, the U.S. Army, and MACV. The collection was consulted at a CIA reading room and at the

National Security Archive; the actual collection is held by Yale University.

INTERVIEWS AND ORAL HISTORIES

• *Marine Debriefings*

The Marine Corps maintained an active program of collecting comments and recollections from its men in the field during the Vietnam war. This is an enormously rich source never before tapped by historians, to the authors' knowledge. The tapes are of three types: individual debriefings, group debriefings, and individuals' comments on specific subjects. The Marine tapes are identified by number and by name or subject heading and are fully indexed at the Historical Division, Headquarters, USMC. A full listing of every tape, subject, and name consulted would be prohibitive in terms of space. Instead we list only those debriefings that we actually used or quoted in the narrative. (Note that "oral histories" retrospectively conducted by Marine historians are included under "Interviews.") The debriefing tapes are cited in the Notes as "Marine Debriefings," with tape number.

The total number of individual debriefings consulted is 798. Of these, the following were used or quoted in constructing our narrative: Capt. Andrew B. Adams (#2555); LtCol. Harry L. Alderman (#2535); 1/Lt. James M. Alexander (#2394); SSgt. McChurty G. Allen (#2775); GySgt. Roy A. Allen (#3557); Pfc. William R. Alyward (#2775); Cpl. Alonzo Barbett (#3081); Lt. Thomas A. Bailey (#1768); Sgt. Richard W. Baskin (#1196); Maj. Carl F. Bergstrom, Jr. (#2832); Lt. Alec Bodenweiser (#2775); 1/Lt. Haldon D. Bohlen (#3081); Capt. Earle Breeding (#2621); Pfc. James M. Bridge (#2810); LCpl. Derek E. Brockway (#2775); Sgt. Edward E. Brown (#2936); HN James R. Brown (#2810); Cpl. Michael A. Brown (#960); SSgt. Leon R. Burns (#993); HM3 Frank V. Calzia (#2621); Capt. John W. Cargile (#2803); Pfc. Carl Carter (#2775); 1/Lt. David O. Carter (#3950); LtCol. E. J. A. Castagna (#2621); Maj. Matthew P. Caulfield (#2535, #6157); Gen. John R. Chaisson (#327); Pfc. Donald E. Chandler (#2621); LCpl. Donald A. Clark (#959); 1/Lt. Gary M. Costello (#2803); Maj. Arthur C. Crane (#3294); Capt. Albert R. Crosby (#951); Pfc. Larry W. Curado (#2775); Capt. Richard W. D'Ambrosio (#2621); Cpl. Paul T. Dargan (#3168); Cpl. Rudy de la Garza (#2775); Sgt. Genor B. Dickson (#2810); 2/Lt. John W. Dillon (#2768, #3716); Capt. Charles F. Divelbiss (#2775); Capt. Robert J. Dougal (#2664); 1/Lt. James M. Doyle (#2977); Sgt.

Thomas E. Dubroy (#2803); LtCol. Billy Duncan (#3662); 1/Lt. William L. Eberhardt (#2536); Cpl. Michael E. Elrod (#2809); Cpl. David D. Faifer (#2775); Sgt. Patrick J. Fitch (#2498); LCpl. Dale R. Flaherty (#2776); Pfc. Herbert L. Flanagan (#2621); Cpl. Eugene J. Franklin (#2775); HMC Paul E. Freese (#3356); LCpl. David R. Ford (#2803); 1/Lt. William K. Gay (#3216); Maj. Clarence U. Gebson (#1193); Cpl. Otis H. Glenn (#2803); Maj. George Golden (#2584); LCpl. Francis Gonway (#2755); Cpl. James H. Grimsley (#3081); LtCol. Louis A. Gulling (#3417); Capt. Walter A. Gunn, Jr. (#2538); 1/Lt. Wayne T. Haaland (#3949); 1/Lt. Kenneth L. Harman (#2803); Sgt. Donald E. Harper, Jr. (#567), Capt. Charles B. Hartzell (#2803); LtCol. Harvey M. Harper (#2535); Pfc. Robert M. Hatfield (#1706); Maj. John Havlik (#3298); Cpl. John Hays (#949); LtCol. Francis J. Heath (#2779); Pfc. Ronald E. Hines (#1128); Gen. Carl W. Hoffman (#2535); Col. Thomas M. Horne (#1539); SSgt. James L. Hutton (#1739); Sgt. T. M. Kane (#2840); SSgt. Bruce E. Kates (#2751); Sgt. Timothy B. Keady (#2621); 2/Lt. Charles W. King (#2776); 2/Lt. Thomas G. King (#994); Maj. Gerald F. Kurth (#2775); Pfc. Stephen D. Lopez (#1115); 2/Lt. Francis B. Lovely, Jr. (#2803); Col. David E. Lownds (#2621, #3139); Maj. James L. Lumsden (#2830); Pfc. Newton D. Lyle (#2775); Sgt. Michael H. Lyons (#2776); LCpl. Michael H. McCaulay (#2810); Cpl. Mark P. McDonald (#3368); Maj. William A. McGaw, Jr. (#3293); Cpl. Larry E. McKee (#2991); LtCol. Bertram A. Maas (#3422); Pfc. Herbert E. Manager (#2810); LCpl. Jose A. Martinez (#2775); Cpl. Victor Martinez (#2776); Maj. Ron E. Merrihew (#2686); Col. Bruce F. Meyers (#2777); Sgt. Gary G. Miller (#2921); Cpl. George E. Moore (#3165); LCpl. Jesus M. Moreno (#3081); Pfc. Danny T. Nelson (#3081); 2/Lt. Michael H. Norman (#2768); Sgt. Milton G. Norwood (#992); LCpl. Richard C. Noyes (#2621); Capt. William J. O'Connor (#2535); 2/Lt. Linn Oehling (#2589); Pvt. Marcos M. Orozco (#2621); Col. John J. Padley (#1504); LtCol. Victor A. Perry (#2755); Sgt. Duane E. Petree (#2803); Capt. Kenneth W. Pipes (#2537, #2810); Col. Franklin N. Pippin (#2907); Sgt. Larry L. Powell (#2803); Sgt. Robert E. Powell (#2621); Cpl. Edward I. Prendergast (#2810); HN Carl K. Price (#2921); LtCol. Robert W. Rasdal (#2627); Col. Benjamin S. Reed (#1529); SSgt. Dennis W. Ritchie (#995); Capt. David G. Rogers (#3533); Cpl. Donald W. Rogers (#1195); 1/Lt. Duane L. Rogers (#2808); LCpl. Henry Rose, Jr. (#1131); Cpl. Larry G. Ruiz (#2991); SSgt. Ruben Santos (#949); 1/Lt. Jerry N. Saulsberry (#2776); Cpl. Steven Scarborough (#2776);

1/Lt. Roy W. Schmitt (#2688); Sgt. Robert H. Scott (#2775); LCpl. William P. Shafer (#2810); Maj. Glen J. Shaver, Jr. (#2663); Maj. John A. Shephard (#2621); Cpl. Kenneth W. Shields (#1130); Cpl. Larry E. Soper (#2775); Lt. Michael R. Stahl (#2776); Cpl. Robert E. Stanton (#1702); Sgt. Harry W. Steere, Jr. (#949); LtCol. Melvin J. Steinberg (#3423); Pfc. Edward Steward (#2775); Sgt. H. E. Stroud (#2452); Maj. William J. Sullivan (#2935); Cpl. A. Summey (#2921); LCpl. Fred W. Swets (#2621); 2/Lt. James R. Talone (#2803); Pfc. Frank C. Tanner (#2810); Cpl. Frank D. Thompson (#1677); Maj. Joseph C. Thorp (#2755); LCpl. Lance E. Tibbett (#2572); Capt. Frank M. Tomeo (#1194); Gen. Rathvon McC. Tompkins (#2535, #3627); HM3 Raymond Toombs (#2768); Cpl. Robert E. Torter (#949); LCpl. Daniel Tougas (#2775); Pfc. Alexander Tretiakoff (#2621); Cpl. Winfield Trivette (#2775); Cpl. Dewey E. Troup (#2803); LCpl. Larry W. Umstead (#1126); Col. John C. Vance, Jr. (#2909); Pfc. Hennie G. Vandervelde (#2775); Pfc. Robert F. Vermalion (#2921); Cpl. Gilbert L. Wall (#2768); LCpl. Lawrence Walsh (#1125); Cpl. James H. Ward (#997); Cpl. Paul Ward (#2803); Maj. George F. Warren (#2921); Pfc. William W. Waters (#2776); Pfc. Walter H. Weber (#1017); 2/Lt. William M. Wentworth (#2779); Lt. Richard J. Wheeler (#2756); Sgt. Ronnie D. Whitenight (#2536); Capt. James L. Williams (#1759); Capt. John P. Williams (#2803); 2/Lt. John T. Williamson (#2535); LCpl. James E. Wilson (#2810); HM3 Richard L. Woodard (#2775); Capt. Clyde E. Woods (#3662); Capt. Peter A. Woog (#4726).

• *Interviews*

Ray Stubbe conducted most of the interviews for this book. Except as noted in the following list, interviews are by Stubbe. John Prados conducted a number of interviews, while the authors also benefited from interviews and oral histories done by others.

Chuck Allen; David Assum; Fred Baker (Sept. 24, Oct. 16, 1988); Daniel L. Baldwin III (Jan. 4, Sept. 8, 1990); Brad Barton; Merlin "Russ" Bean; Johnny Belina; Richard R. Blair; Richard Blanchfield (Oct. 1, Oct. 9, 1988); Harper L. Bohr, Jr.; Pat Bonnell; Pat Brady; Earle G. Breeding (July 18, Nov. 5, 1984; May 29, 1985); Robert Brewer (Nov. 1, 1987; Sept. 11, 1988; by John Wright, Feb. 5, 1989); Calvin E. Bright; Edward Burns; Thomas W. Bystrom; James Capers (May 24, 1986; Sept. 11, 1988); Leo G. Cauley (by Prados, Jan. 3, 1990); Paul Camacho (by Prados, July 7, 1989); Jon R. Cavianni; Wilfred Charette (Apr. 30, May 7,

1989); John Cicala (May 29, 1984; Mar. 22, 1987); Frank Cius; Richard Claire; Bruce B. G. Clark (Oct. 5, 7, 1988; May 17, 1989); Jack Corbett; Tom Corcoran; Nancy Costello; Bill Craig; Richard Cruz (Aug. 19, Nov. 10, 1984); Jeff Culpepper (July 13, 23, 1984; Jan. 30, 1987); William H. Dabney (Sept. 11, 1988; USMC oral history, May 20, 1982); Richard Darling; Phillip B. Davidson (Apr. 19, May 6, 8, 1989); David Doehrman (Feb. 4, Aug. 12, 1984); Douglas Dresser; Ronald Drez; Walter Driscoll (Mar. 16, 1985; Apr. 1, 1989); Lee Dunlap (Aug. 25, 27, 1988; Sept. 10, 1988; Apr. 8, 1989); Pierce Durham; Edward Feldman; Andrew R. Finlayson; Pat Fitch; Jeanne Forrest; Frank Fowler; John Franklin; Max Friedlander; J. William Fulbright (by Prados Oct. 26, 1990); James Garvey; Richard M. Garwin (by Prados, Oct. 26, 1990); Robert N. Ginsburgh (by Prados, Dec. 6, 1988; Oct. 27, 1989); Ted Golab (Aug. 15, 1985; Apr. 22, 1986); Richard Granet; Alfred M. Gray, Jr.; R. D. Hagewood; Francis X. Harrison; James Hebron (Sept. 24, 1984; Mar. 26, 1987); Larry Henderson; Thomas M. Horne; Kenneth Houghton (Sept. 25, 1988; Apr. 2, 17, 1989; May 7, 1989); Gerald Howland; David Hunt (by Prados, July 14, 1989); Ernest C. Husted, Jr.; Allan B. Imes; Frank Iodice; David C. Isby (by Prados, Mar. 31, 1990); Michael R. James; G. William Jayne (Nov. 10, 1984; Oct. 1, 1988); Bruce Jones; Kenneth D. Jordan; Lawrence Keen (Mar. 12, Dec. 4, 1975; May 31, 1986); Daniel Kelley (Apr. 2, May 23, 1988; by Prados, Feb. 16, 1991); Charles T. Kelly; Jack Kilbright; James Kirk; Lee Klein (July 22, Aug. 5, 1989); Robert Knox; Bill Lanier (Dec. 8, 1968; Jan. 10, 1987); Ronald J. Lauzon; Harray Lavane; Mike Leggett; Frederick Locke (Apr. 22, May 6, 1989); Paul Longrrear; David Lownds; Kevin Macaulay (May 29, June 1, Aug. 22, 1984; May 8, 1985; Sept. 11, 1988); Donald J. Magilligan; Dennis Mannion (June 19, 1984; Aug. 31, 1986; Sept. 25, 1988); Steven McGuirk; John D. and Carolyn Miller (May 27, 28, 1986); Charles Minnicks; Peter Morakon; Tom Nicholson; Ngo Quang Truong (by Prados, Feb. 16, 1991); George W. T. O'Dell; Robert E. Pagano (Oct. 22, Nov. 27, 1988); Gary Parker; James E. Payne (Apr. 24, 1988; Jan. 5, Mar. 18, Apr. 5, 1989); Larry R. Payne; James Perry (May 28, July 6, 1986; May 27, 1989); Edward Prendergast (Mar. 14, June 5, 1986); Tom Quigley; Rick Rasmussen (Mar. 10, 1984; Jan. 7, 1985); James M. Reeder (Apr. 30, May 7, 1989); Sandy Reid; Ronald Ridgway; David Rogers; Michael Rohrlick (June 19, Aug. 6, 1989); Walt W. Rostow (Sept. 9, 1988; by Prados, Sept. 13, 1988; by John Wright, Jan. 31, 1989); Thomas Ryan (Aug. 24, 1986; Sept. 11, 1988); Harve Saal (May 20, June 3, 1989); Hammond Salley; Donald F.

Santner; James Schemelia (June 26, 27, July 31, 1984); John Schlack; Joe Sherman; Timothy Sims (Nov. 26, 1984; July 3, 1985); Bill Smith (May 23, June 14, 1984; Mar. 16, 23, 1985; Apr. 24, 1988; Apr. 2, 1989); Ernest Spencer (Apr. 1, 1989; by Prados, Feb. 16, 1991); Thomas B. Stamper (various, 1969–1970); Jacques Standing; Bill Steptoe; Daniel Sullivan; Robert Sutter; John Tackert; Steven Tatro; John M. Tighe; Rathvon McC. Tompkins (Jan. 7, 1989; USMC oral history, Apr. 13, 1973); Gilbert Wall (Aug. 26, 1988; May 13, 1989); William Waugh (Oct. 30, 1988; Mar. 30, 1989); Edward W. Welchel; William C. Westmoreland (Apr. 23, June 2, 1989; by Ronald Drez, Nov. 4, 1988); James Whitenack; James B. Wilkinson (by John Wright, July 14, 1989); Steven J. Zaloga (by Prados, Mar. 31, 1990).

• *Correspondence and Taped Reminiscences*
The following individuals wrote or taped their recollections, answered questions about which they were knowledgeable, or lent collections of their letters from the time. In some cases (like that of Donald Jacques) families kindly lent these materials.

George B. Anderson; Manuel Babbitt; Elwin E. Bacon; Fred Baker; Johnny Belina; Harper L. Bohr, Jr.; Denny Bowers; Grady Branch; Robert Brewer; Joe Bristol; Phillip Brown; Peter W. Brush; David Buffalo; Thomas W. Bystrom; F. C. Caldwell; John W. Cargile; J. H. Champion; J. Fred Cole; James D. Collins III; Jack Corbett; Richard Cruz; Jeff Culpepper; William H. Dabney; Mike Dagner; Richard Darling; Phillip B. Davidson; Thomas A. Detrick; David Doehrman; Daniel D. Dulude; Lee Dunlap; Thomas Eichler; Joe Falduti; Les Faurebrac; Max Friedlander; Ronald L. Gatewood; Bob Green; H. T. Hagaman; Randy H. Hardy; John Hargesheimer; Robert Harrison; Robert Hatfield; Richard Heath; James Hebron; Dennis Herb; Chuck Hoover; Ernest C. Husted, Jr.; Frank Iodice; Larry E. Jackson; Donald Jacques; G. William Jayne; Steve Johnson; J. Michael Jones; John M. Kaheny; Talis Kaminskis; Daniel Kelley; Gary Kuchera; Martin Kux; Bill Lanier; Michael Lee; David Leverton; Bruce Lewy; Frank Liles; Russell B. Longaway; David Lownds; Albert R. Lumpkin; Kevin Macaulay; Mike McCauley; Jesse J. McNeal; Donald J. Magilligan; Dennis Mannion; Charles S. Martin; Joseph R. Meeks; Bill Messner; Bruce F. Meyers; George A. Miller; John D. and Carolyn Miller; J. G. Miller; Scott Miller; William T. Mitchell III; David D. Moody; Peter Morakon; Bert Mullins; Robert J. Mussari; Ray Nassar; Anthony J. Nazzario; Raymond Nicol; Rick Noyes; Edward H. O'Connor; John J. Padley; Robert E. Pagano; James E. Payne; Larry R. Payne; Kenneth

Pipes; Madeleine Poilane; Tom Quigley; Rick Rasmussen; E. C. Rayburn; C. A. "Gums" Reed; Albert S. Roberts; John R. Roberts; Richard E. Romine; Thomas Ryan; Harve Saal; James Schemelia; Larry J. Seavy-Cioffi; John Seitz; Samuel A. Sharp, Sr., and Family; Timothy Sims; Roger L. Smith; William L. Smith; Ernest Spencer; Thomas Stott; Ray Strischek; George Taylor; Ron Taylor; Gary G. Trowbridge; Don C. Tyler, Sr.; Robert Valentine.

• *Contemporary Diaries*

Ernest C. Husted, Jr.; Martin J. Kux; William T. Mitchell III; Ray William Stubbe.

• *Unpublished Reminiscences or Manuscripts*

Daniel D. Dulude, "Statement," Jan. 5, 1989.

John M. Kaheny, "A Marine Remembers."

Bill Lanier, "Reflections."

Edward H. O'Connor, "Statement," January 1986; "Statement," October 1986.

Edward Prendergast, "Biography," Nov. 8, 1988.

John R. Roberts, Essay, 1972.

John J. Scanlon, "End of Tour Report."

Lawrence J. Seavy-Cioffi, "Our Victory for Alpha One," 1985.

William Stross, "Home from the Woods," 1984.

Ray W. Stubbe, "Khe Sanh Chaplain," 1970; "Khe Sanh," 1971; "Paddles, Parachutes, and Patrols: A History of Specialized Reconnaissance Activities of the United States Marine Corps," 1976.

Carl Torrence, "In Country," 1984.

Edward W. Welchel, "Statement," October 21, 1986.

G. R. Witt, "End of Tour Report."

PUBLISHED SOURCES

• *Official Histories and Documents*

United States Congress. Senate Armed Services Committee. Permanent Investigating Subcommittee. *Hearings: Investigation into Electronic Battlefield Program.* 91st Cong., 2nd Sess. Washington: Government Printing Office, 1971.

• Department of the Army

Vietnam Studies Series

Kelly, Col. Francis J. *U.S. Army Special Forces, 1961–1971.* Washington: Department of the Army, 1973.

Ott, Gen. David E. *Field Artillery, 1954–1973*. Washington: Department of the Army, 1975.

Pearson, Gen. Willard. *The War in the Northern Provinces, 1966–1968*. Washington: Department of the Army, 1975.

Tolson, Gen. John J. *Airmobility, 1961–1971*. Washington: Department of the Army, 1973.

The U.S. Army in Vietnam Series

Bergen, John D. *Military Communications: A Test for Technology*. Washington: Center for Military History, 1986.

Hammond, William. *Public Affairs: The Military and the Media, 1962–1968*. Washington: Center for Military History, 1988.

Occasional Monograph

Albright, John, John A. Cash, and Allan W. Sandstrum. *Seven Firefights in Vietnam*. Washington: Office of the Chief of Military History, 1970.

• Department of the Air Force

The United States Air Force in Southeast Asia Series

Bowers, Ray L. *Tactical Airlift*. Washington: Office of Air Force History, 1983.

Schlight, John. *The War in South Vietnam: The Years of the Offensive, 1965–1968*. Washington: Office of Air Force History, 1988.

Occasional Monographs

Mrozek, Donald J. *Air Power and the Ground War in Vietnam: Ideas and Actions*. Maxwell Air Force Base, Ala.: Air University Press, 1988.

Nalty, Bernard C. *Air Power and the Fight for Khe Sanh*. Washington: Office of Air Force History, 1973.

• United States Marine Corps

U.S. Marines in Vietnam Series

Shulimson, Jack. *An Expanding War, 1966*. Washington: History and Museums Division, Headquarters, USMC, 1982.

Tefler, Maj. Gary L., USMC, LtCol. Lane Rogers, USMC, and V. Keith Fleming, Jr. *Fighting the North Vietnamese, 1967*. Washington: History and Museums Division, Headquarters, USMC, 1984.

Whitlow, Capt. Robert H., USMCR. *The Advisory and Combat Assistance Era, 1954–1964*. Washington: History and Museums Division, Headquarters, USMC, 1977.

Occasional Monograph

Shore, Capt. Moyers S. II, USMC. *The Battle for Khe Sanh*. Washington: Historical Branch, G-3 Division, Headquarters, USMC, 1969.

• Department of State

Foreign Relations of the United States Series

Keefer, Edward C., and David W. Mabon, eds. Vol. 1. *Vietnam, 1958–1960*. Washington: Government Printing Office, 1986.

Landa, Ronald D., and Charles S. Sampson, eds. Vol. 1. *Vietnam, 1961*. Washington: Government Printing Office, 1988.

Baehler, David M., and Charles S. Sampson, eds. Vol. 2. *Vietnam, 1962*. Washington: Government Printing Office, 1990.

• *Other Books*

BDM Corporation. *A Study of Strategic Lessons Learned in Vietnam*. Vol. 6. *Conduct of the War*. McLean, Va., BDM/W-78-128-TR, 1980.

Boettcher, Thomas D. *Vietnam, the Valor and the Sorrow: From the Home Front to the Front Lines in Words and Pictures*. Boston: Little, Brown, 1985.

Braestrup, Peter. *Big Story: How the American Press and Television Reported and Interpreted the Crisis of Tet in Vietnam and Washington*. New Haven: Yale University Press, 1983.

Brandon, Heather. *Casualties: Death in Vietnam, Anguish and Survival in America*. New York: St. Martin's, 1984.

Brennan, Matthew, Jr., ed. *Headhunters: Stories from the 1st Squadron, 9th Cavalry in Vietnam, 1965–1971*. New York: Pocket Books, 1988.

Brewin, Bob, and Sydney Shaw. *Vietnam on Trial: Westmoreland vs. CBS*. New York: Atheneum, 1987.

Broyles, William Jr. *Brothers in Arms: A Journey from War to Peace*. New York: Knopf, 1986.

Burchett, Wilfred G. *Vietnam Will Win!* New York: Monthly Review Press, 1969.

Camp, Richard D., Jr., with Eric Hammel. *Lima-6: A Marine Company Commander in Vietnam, June 1967–January 1968*. New York: Atheneum, 1989.

Chinnery, Philip D., ed. *Life on the Line*. New York: St. Martin's, 1990.

Clifford, Clark, with Richard Holbrooke. *Counsel to the President: A Memoir*. New York: Random House, 1991.

Corson, William R. *The Betrayal*. New York: Norton, 1968.

Davidson, Gen. Phillip B. *Vietnam at War: The History, 1946–1975*. Novato, Calif.: Presidio, 1988.

Dickson, Paul. *The Electronic Battlefield.* Bloomington: Indiana University Press, 1976.

D'Orcival, François, and Jacques-François de Chaunac. *Les Marines à Khe Sanh: Vietnam, 1968.* Paris: Presses de la Cité, 1979.

Drendel, Lou. *Air War over Southeast Asia: A Pictorial Record.* Vol. 2. *1967–1970.* Carrolltown, Tex.: Squadron/Signal Publications, 1983.

Duncan, David D. *War Without Heroes.* New York: Harper & Row, n.d.

Furgurson, Ernest B. *Westmoreland: The Inevitable General.* Boston: Little, Brown, 1968.

Giap, Gen. Vo Nguyen. *Big Victory, Great Task.* New York: Praeger, 1968.

Grant, Zalin. *Survivors: American POWs in Vietnam.* New York: Berkeley, 1985.

Halperin, Morton H., and Arnold Kanter, eds. *Readings in American Foreign Policy: A Bureaucratic Perspective.* Boston: Little, Brown, 1973.

Hammel, Eric. *Khe Sanh: Siege in the Clouds, an Oral History.* New York: Crown, 1989.

Helfley, James C. *By Life or By Death.* Grand Rapids: Zondervan, 1969.

Herr, Michael. *Dispatches.* New York: Knopf, 1977.

Hubbell, John G. *P.O.W.* New York: Reader's Digest Press, 1976.

Johnson, Lyndon Baines. *The Vantage Point: Perspectives on the Presidency.* New York: Holt, Rinehart & Winston, 1971.

Jones, Bruce E. *War Without Windows.* New York: Vanguard, 1988.

Khe Sanh. Hanoi: Giai Publishing House, 1968.

McGarvey, Patrick J. *CIA: The Myth and the Madness.* New York: Saturday Review Press, 1972.

MacLear, Michael. *The Ten Thousand Day War: Vietnam, 1945–1975.* New York: St. Martin's, 1981.

Miller, Carolyn P. *Captured! A Mother's True Story of Her Family's Imprisonment by the Vietcong.* Chappaqua, N.Y.: Christian Herald, 1977.

Mole, Robert L. *Peoples of Tribes of South Vietnam.* Vol. 1. *The Tribes of I Corps.* Saigon: US COMNAVSUPPAC, 1968.

Momyer, Gen. William W. *Air Power in Three Wars.* Washington: Government Printing Office, 1978.

Nguyen Khac Vien, ed. *American Failure.* Vietnamese Studies No. 20. Hanoi: Foreign Languages Publishing House, 1968.

Oberdorfer, Don. *Tet: The Story of a Battle and Its Historic Aftermath.* Garden City, N.Y.: Doubleday, 1971.

Palmer, Gen. David Richard. *Summons of the Trumpet: A History of the Vietnam War from a Military Man's Viewpoint.* New York: Ballantine, 1984.

Patterson, James H. *Provisional Corps Vietnam: Khe Sanh, January–June 1968.* Maxwell Air Force Base, Montgomery, Ala.: Air War College, Research Report no. 3816, 1969.

Pham Van Son and Le Van Duong. *The Viet Cong Tet Offensive.* Saigon: Joint General Staff, 1969.

Pike, Douglas. *PAVN: People's Army of Vietnam.* Novato, Calif.: Presidio, 1986.

Pisor, Robert. *The End of the Line: The Siege of Khe Sanh.* New York: Norton, 1982.

Pittman, Donald D. *Tactical Air Support (Strike) in the Defense of Khe Sanh.* Maxwell Air Force Base, Montgomery, Ala.: Air War College, Research Report no. 3820, 1969.

Prados, John. *The Sky Would Fall: Operation Vulture, the U.S. Bombing Mission in Indochina, 1954.* New York: Dial, 1983.

Prashker, Ivan. *Duty, Honor, Vietnam: Twelve Men of West Point Tell Their Stories.* New York: Warner, 1990.

Rostow, Walt W. *The Diffusion of Powers: An Essay in Recent History, 1957–1972.* New York: Macmillan, 1972.

Santoli, Al. *Everything We Had: An Oral History of the Vietnam War by Thirty-Three American Soldiers Who Fought It.* New York: Random House, 1981.

Schrock, Joann L., et. al. *Minority Groups in the Republic of Vietnam.* Washington: Department of the Army, Pamphlet No. 550-105, 1966.

Sharp, Adm. U.S.G., and Gen. William C. Westmoreland. *Report on the War in Vietnam (As of June 30, 1968).* Washington: Government Printing Office, 1968.

Spencer, Ernest. *Welcome to Vietnam, Macho Man: Reflection of a Khe Sanh Vet.* Corps Press, 1987.

Stanton, Shelby L. *Green Berets at War: U.S. Army Special Forces in Southeast Asia, 1956–1975.* Novato, Calif.: Presidio, 1985.

Stockwell, David B. *Tanks in the Wire: The First Use of Enemy Armor in Vietnam.* New York: Jove, 1990.

Taylor, John M. *General Maxwell Taylor: The Sword and the Pen.* Garden City, N.Y.: Doubleday, 1989.

Taylor, Gen. Maxwell D. *Swords into Plowshares.* New York: Norton, 1972.

Thompson, W. Scott, and Donaldson D. Frizzell, eds. *The Lessons of Vietnam.* New York: Crane, Russak, 1977.

U.S. Naval Construction Battalion Maintenance Unit 301. *Cruisebook 1967–1968.* Privately published.

Vanderbie, Jan. *Prov Rep Vietnam.* Philadelphia: Dorrance, 1970.

Waldron, Miles, and Richard W. Beavers. *The Critical Year, 1968: The XXIV Corps Team.* Historical Study 3-68, *Operation Pegasus.* Headquarters, XXIV Corps, 31st Military History Detachment, 1969.

Walt, Gen. Lewis. *Strange War, Strange Strategy.* New York: Funk, 1970.

Westmoreland, Gen. William C. *A Soldier Reports.* Garden City, N.Y.: Doubleday, 1976.

• *Articles*

"Airpower at Khe Sanh: An Allied Victory." *Commanders' Digest*, vol. 12, no. 3, August 3, 1972.

Althoff, Lt. Col. David L. "Helicopter Operations at Khe Sanh." *Marine Corps Gazette*, May 1969.

Bartlett, Tom. "Robert Mussari: The Human Bomb." *Leatherneck*, May 1987.

Brugioni, Dino A. "The President, Khe Sanh, and the 26th Marines." *Leatherneck*, September 1986.

Carroll, John S. "Report." *Atlantic Monthly*, October 1968.

Dalby, Col. Marion C. "Combat Hotline." *Marine Corps Gazette*, January 1969.

———. "Task Force Hotel's Inland Beachheads." *Marine Corps Gazette*, January 1969.

Deuel, Austin III. "Hill 881-South: San Antonio's Vietnam Memorial." *Fortitudine*, vol. 16, no. 4, Spring 1987.

Early, Capt. John. "Armor in the Wire! MACV Vacillates During Lang Vei Slaughter." *Soldier of Fortune*, November 1979.

Evans, GySgt. Ed. "Khe Sanh Revisited." *Leatherneck*, August 1971.

Galvin, Gen. John R. "The Relief of Khe Sanh." *Military Review*, January 1970.

Graham, Dave. "Ambush! The Horror of Khe Sanh." *Bluebook*, June 1969.

Graves, Jim. "SOG's Secret War." *Soldier of Fortune*, June 1981.

Greenhalgh, William H., Jr. "A-OK: Airpower over Khe Sanh." *Aerospace Historian*, March 1972.

Greenman, Ronald. "Long Night at Lang Vei." *Soldier of Fortune*, February 1985.

Herr, Michael. "Conclusion at Khesanh." *Esquire*, October 1969.

———. "Khesanh." *Esquire*, September 1969.

"History Book Battle: The Red Defeat at Khe Sanh." *U.S. News & World Report*, May 6, 1968.

Husted, Ernie, Jr. "A Christmas SALUTE." *Leatherneck*, December 1979.

———. "The Silent Ambush." *Leatherneck*, August 1980.

———. "Someone's Garden." *Leatherneck*, February 1983.

Kashiwahara, Capt. Ken. "Lifeline to Khe Sanh." *Airman*, July 1968.

McGarry, James III. "Donated Ammo Pouch Helped Save Khe Sanh Vet's Life." *Fortitudine*, vol. 16, no. 4, Spring 1987.

McLaughlin, MajGen. Burl W. "Khe Sanh: Keeping an Outpost Alive." *Air University Review*, November–December 1968.

Martin, Sgt. John. "Khe Sanh." *Leatherneck*, July 1968.

Nalty, Bernard C. "Khe Sanh: No Dien Bien Phu." *Soldier of Fortune*, May 1980.

Nolan, Keith W. "Khe Sanh." *Leatherneck*, December 1981.

Palmer, Laura. "The General at Ease." *MHQ: The Quarterly Journal of Military History*, vol. 1, no. 1, Autumn 1988.

Pipes, Maj. Kenneth W. "Men to Match Their Mountains." *Marine Corps Gazette*, April 1974.

Prados, John. "No Damn Din Bin Phoo! Khe Sanh and the U.S. High Command." *Veteran*, June 1987.

———. "Tet." *Veteran*, February 1988.

———. "The Intelligence at Tet." *Veteran*, February 1989.

Richardson, SSgt. Herb. "Ceremony at Khe Sanh." *Leatherneck*, February 1969.

Scholin, Allen R. "An Airpower Lesson for Giap." *Air Force and Space Digest*, June 1969.

Scipione, Paul A. "The Grunt and the Doc: A True Life Drama from the Vietnam War." *Vietnam Veterans Review*, January 1986.

Strum, Ted R. "Khe Sanh's Deadly Deluge." *Airman*, July 1968.

———. "Countdown to Eternity." *Airman*, May 1970.

Studt, LtCol. John C. "Battalion in the Attack." *Marine Corps Gazette*, July 1970.

Swearengen, Maj. Mark A. "Siege: Forty Days at Khe Sanh." *Marine Corps Gazette*, April 1973.

"TAC: The Difference Between Khe Sanh and Dien Bien Phu." *Armed Forces Journal*, September 1971.

Tolson, Gen. John J. III. "Pegasus." *Army*, December 1971.

Waghelstein, John C. "A Vital Link." In *Infantry in Vietnam*. Fort Benning: Infantry Magazine, 1967.

Walsh, Lt. Peter M. "Filling Trench Lines." *Marine Corps Gazette*, May 1969.

Walt, Gen. Lewis W. "Civil Affairs." *Marine Corps Gazette*, September 1969.

———. "Behind the Battle for Khe Sanh." *Reader's Digest*, May 1970.

Wasson, Col. Glenn. "The Khe Sanh Potato War." *Leatherneck*, May 1988.

Watts, Maj. Claudius E. "Aerial Resupply for Khe Sanh." *Military Review*, December 1972.

Wold, GySgt. John. "Khe Sanh '71." *Leatherneck*, July 1971.

Index